The
Crossword Anagram
Dictionary

Also by R. J. Edwards

The Crossword Phrase Dictionary

The Crossword Completion Dictionary

Devised and Compiled
by R. J. Edwards

The
Crossword Anagram
Dictionary

Stanley Paul
London Melbourne Sydney Auckland Johannesburg

Stanley Paul & Co. Ltd.

An imprint of Century Hutchinson Ltd

62-65 Chandos Place, London WC2N 4NW

Century Hutchinson (Australia) Pty Ltd
16-22 Church Street, Hawthorn, Melbourne, Victoria 3121

Century Hutchinson Ltd (NZ) Ltd
32-34 View Road, Glenfield, Auckland 10

Century Hutchinson (SA) Pty Ltd
PO Box 337, Bergvlei 2012, South Africa

First published 1978 by Barrie & Jenkins Ltd
Reprinted 1982, 1986
© R. J. Edwards 1978

Set by Thorneycroft Photosetters, Birmingham

Printed and bound in Great Britain by
Anchor Brendon Limited, Tiptree, Essex

ISBN 0 09 149660 8

Acknowledgements

The author wishes to thank the staff of the Computer Unit at the University of Warwick, especially Rod Ackland, Mike Hunt and Gerry Sheridan.

How to Use the Dictionary

This book may appear somewhat unusual at first glance, but after a little practice it is very simple and quick to use.

Rearrange the letters of the anagram you wish to solve into alphabetical order, then look up this arrangement of letters in the correct section of the dictionary; you will find the solution on the right.

For example, suppose you wish to solve the anagram 'LID ON MEAL'. First arrange the letters alphabetically; this gives ADEILLMNO. Now look up this transposition in the nine-letter section of the dictionary, where you will find

ADEILLMNO – MEDALLION

In some cases, more than one word will be given for a certain combination of letters, for example:

ACELLOPS – COLLAPSE
– ESCALLOP

In these cases, simply choose whichever solution fits in with the rest of the clue, or with the letters already written in the crossword frame.

Sometimes, the solution may be a word in a form not contained in this dictionary; it may have '—S', '—ES', '—ING', '—D', '—ED', or '—LY' added to it. In these cases, the rest of the clue will usually make it clear what form the solution will take, so you should take out the extra letters, and look up only the basic word in the dictionary. Here are two examples:

'PUTS SIDE AROUND TO CAUSE ARGUMENTS (8)'
'AROUND' here tells you to solve the anagram 'PUTS SIDE'. But the plural 'ARGUMENTS' suggests that the solution is a plural word, so remove a letter 'S', then rearrange the remaining seven letters to find

DEIPSTU – DISPUTE

– so the answer to the clue is 'disputes'.

'GOT SHAPED INTO A BED (8)'
'SHAPED' tells you to solve the anagram 'INTO A BED'. But the past tense 'GOT' suggests that the solution is also in the past tense, so remove the letter 'D', and rearrange the remaining seven letters to find

ABEINOT

This combination of letters is not listed, so assume instead that the solution ends in '—ED', and remove these letters to find

ABINOT – OBTAIN

– so the answer to the clue is 'obtained'.

By intelligent use in this way, the scope of this book can be increased greatly; and after a little practice, you will find that you can solve any anagram within seconds.

Six Letter Words

AAABCL	CABALA	AABIMZ	ZAMBIA	AACINR	ARNICA
AAABIR	ARABIA	AABINN	BANIAN		CARINA
AAABLT	ALBATA	AABLMS	BALSAM	AACIOT	COAITA
AAABNN	BANANA	AABLST	BASALT	AACIRS	AIR-SAC
AAABRZ	BAZAAR	AABLTU	TABULA	AACIRV	CAVIAR
AAACCI	ACACIA	AABMNR	BARMAN	AACISS	CASSIA
AAACDN	CANADA	AABMNT	BANTAM	AACJKL	JACKAL
AAACJN	JACANA		BATMAN	AACKRR	ARRACK
AAACLP	ALPACA	AABNNY	BANYAN	AACKTT	ATTACK
AAADMR	ARMADA	AABORR	ARROBA	AACLMU	MACULA
AAAELZ	AZALEA	AABRTY	BARYTA	AACLNR	CARNAL
AAAGLM	MALAGA	AACCDI	CICADA	AACLNU	LACUNA
AAAGLR	ARGALA	AACCEL	CAECAL	AACLPR	CARPAL
AAAHNV	HAVANA	AACCHM	CHACMA	AACLPT	CAT-LAP
AAAILL	ALALIA	AACCIL	ALCAIC	AACLRS	LASCAR
AAAITX	ATAXIA	AACCKR	CARACK		RASCAL
AAAKLM	KAMALA	AACCLO	CLOACA		SACRAL
AAAKLS	ALASKA	AACCLR	CALCAR	AACLSU	CASUAL
AAAKNR	ANKARA	AACCNN	CANCAN		CAUSAL
AAALMS	SALAAM	AACDEF	FAÇADE	AACLTU	ACTUAL
AAAMNP	PANAMA	AACDER	ARCADE	AACMNR	CARMAN
AAAMRS	SAMARA		CEDARA	AACMNY	CAYMAN
AAANNS	ANANAS	AACDIM	ADAMIC	AACNRY	CANARY
AAARTV	AVATAR	AACDLU	CAUDAL	AACNSV	CANVAS
AABBBO	BAOBAB	AACDMP	MADCAP	AACNTV	VACANT
AABBCY	ABBACY	AACDNR	CANARD	AACPPY	PAPACY
AABCIR	ARABIC	AACEFL	FAECAL	AACRSU	ACARUS
AABCMN	CABMAN	AACEFR	CARAFE	AACRTV	CRAVAT
AABCNT	CANTAB	AACEHP	APACHE	AACSSV	CAVASS
AABCRS	SCARAB	AACELP	PALACE	AADDEL	DAEDAL
AABCSU	ABACUS	AACEMR	CAMERA	AADEGM	DAMAGE
AABDER	ABRADE	AACENT	CATENA	AADEGN	AGENDA
AABDET	ABATED	AACERS	CAESAR	AADEMM	MADAME
AABDEU	AUBADE	AACEST	SEA-CAT	AADEMN	MAENAD
AABDGO	DAGOBA	AACETV	CAVEAT	AADENN	ANDEAN
AABDLL	BALLAD		VACATE	AADENV	NEVADA
AABDOR	ABOARD	AACFIL	FACIAL	AADEPR	PARADE
	ABROAD	AACFIR	AFRICA	AADFIR	AFRAID
AABDRT	TABARD	AACFIS	FASCIA	AADGIO	ADAGIO
AABDRY	BAYARD	AACFLU	FACULA	AADGNU	UGANDA
AABELR	ARABLE	AACFRS	FRACAS	AADGOP	PAGODA
AABELZ	ABLAZE	AACGIM	AGAMIC	AADHIL	DAHLIA
AABEMO	AMOEBA	AACGIR	AGARIC	AADHRZ	HAZARD
AABERZ	ZAREBA	AACHLS	CALASH	AADILR	RADIAL
AABETU	BATEAU	AACHNR	ANARCH	AADKMS	DAMASK
AABFIN	FABIAN	AACHTT	ATTACH	AADLMW	WADMAL
AABGMN	BAGMAN	AACILP	APICAL	AADLMY	MALADY
AABHSW	BASHAW	AACILR	RACIAL	AADLNS	SANDAL
AABILL	LABIAL	AACILS	CALAIS	AADLNU	LANDAU
AABILX	BIAXAL	AACIMN	CAIMAN	AADLNV	VANDAL
AABIMN	BIMANA		MANIAC	AADLOP	APODAL

AADMMN	MADMAN	AAFLOT	AFLOAT	AAKNOR	ANORAK
AADMMR	DAMMAR	AAGGQU	QUAGGA	AAKNSS	KANSAS
AADMOU	AMADOU	AAGGRT	TAG-RAG	AAKNST	ASKANT
AADMRS	MADRAS	AAGHMR	ARMAGH	AAKSSV	KAVASS
AADMRU	MARAUD	AAGHNR	HANGAR	AALLPP	APPALL
AADMRZ	MAZARD	AAGHST	AGHAST	AALLRV	LARVAL
AADMYY	MAY-DAY	AAGILN	AGNAIL		VALLAR
AADPYY	PAY-DAY	AAGILR	ARGALI		
AADRVW	VAWARD	AAGIMN	MAGIAN	AALMMM	MAMMAL
AAEEGT	EATAGE	AAGINN	ANGINA	AALMMS	LAMMAS
AAEELP	PALEAE	AAGINU	IGUANA	AALMNP	NAPALM
AAEERS	SEA-EAR	AAGINV	VAGINA	AALMNU	MANUAL
AAEERT	AERATE	AAGIRS	AIR-GAS	AALMNY	LAYMAN
AAEEYY	AYE-AYE	AAGJRU	JAGUAR	AALMOR	AMORAL
AAEFLM	AFLAME	AAGLNO	ANGOLA	AALMPR	PALMAR
AAEGGR	GARAGE	AAGLXY	GALAXY	AALMPS	PLASMA
AAEGLN	GALENA	AAGMNR	RAGMAN	AALMRU	ALARUM
AAEGLR	ALEGAR	AAGMRY	MAGYAR	AALNNU	ANNUAL
	LAAGER	AAGNOR	ANGORA	AALNPT	PLATAN
AAEGMN	MANAGE	AAGOTU	AGOUTA	AALNST	ASLANT
AAEGNT	AGNATE	AAGRST	GAS-TAR	AALORT	AORTAL
AAEGNU	AUGEAN	AAGRVY	VAGARY	AALOVW	AVOWAL
AAEGRV	RAVAGE	AAHHWW	HAWHAW	AALPPU	PAPULA
AAEGSV	SAVAGE	AAHIIW	HAWAII	AALRST	ASTRAL
AAEHLM	HAEMAL	AAHIPR	PARIAH		TARSAL
AAEHMS	ASHAME	AAHJRR	JARRAH	AALRSY	SALARY
AAEHMT	HAMATE	AAHLLP	PALLAH	AALSSV	VASSAL
AAEHNT	ATHENA	AAHLMT	MALTHA	AALSWY	ALWAYS
AAEHNY	HYAENA	AAHLRS	ASHLAR	AALWYY	WAYLAY
AAEILR	AERIAL	AAHMPY	MAYHAP	AAMMTT	TAM-TAM
AAEIMN	ANEMIA	AAHMST	ASTHMA	AAMNOZ	AMAZON
AAEINT	TAENIA	AAHPPR	PARAPH	AAMNPS	SAMPAN
AAEKNW	AWAKEN	AAHPTY	APATHY	AAMNTU	MANTUA
AAEKRT	KARATE	AAHRSS	HARASS	AAMPPS	PAMPAS
AAELNN	ANNEAL	AAIKLL	ALKALI	AAMQSU	SQUAMA
AAELNT	LANATE	AAILLP	PALLIA	AAMRSW	ASWARM
AAELOR	AREOLA	AAILMN	ANIMAL	AANNTT	NATANT
AAELPP	APPEAL		LAMINA	AANOST	SONATA
AAELPT	PALATE		MANILA	AANPRT	TARPAN
AAELRV	LARVAE	AAILMP	IMPALA		TRAPAN
AAEMMM	MAMMAE	AAILMS	SALAMI	AANPRY	PANARY
AAEMNS	SEAMAN	AAILNR	NARIAL	AANRRT	ARRANT
AAEMNT	AMENTA	AAILNS	SALINA	AANRTT	RATTAN
AAENNZ	ZENANA	AAILNT	ANTLIA		TARTAN
AAENOP	APNOEA	AAILRT	ATRIAL	AANSTV	SAVANT
AAENSU	NAUSEA		LARIAT	AANSTZ	STANZA
AAEPPR	APPEAR	AAILSS	ASSAIL	AANTTV	TAN-VAT
AAEPRT	PATERA	AAILSV	SALIVA	AANTUV	AVAUNT
AAERRR	ARREAR	AAIMMS	MIASMA	AANWYY	ANYWAY
AAERRT	ERRATA	AAIMNR	AIRMAN	AAORRU	AURORA
AAERTU	AURATE	AAIMNS	SAMIAN	AAOTTW	OTTAWA
AAERWX	EAR-WAX	AAINPR	PARIAN	AAPRST	SATRAP
AAERWY	AWEARY	AAINPT	PATINA		SPARTA
AAESWY	SEA-WAY	AAINRT	ANTIAR	AAPWXX	PAX-WAX
AAFFIR	AFFAIR	AAINTT	ATTAIN	AARRTT	TARTAR
	RAFFIA	AAIPRY	APIARY	AARSTT	STRATA
AAFFRY	AFFRAY	AAIPZZ	PIAZZA	AARSTY	ASTRAY
AAFGHN	AFGHAN	AAIRST	TARSIA	AARSWW	WARSAW
AAFINR	FARINA	AAIRVY	AVIARY	ABBBEL	BABBLE
AAFIRS	SAFARI	AAIRWY	AIR-WAY	ABBCRY	CRABBY
AAFKNT	KAFTAN	AAIRZZ	RAZZIA	ABBCSY	SCABBY
AAFLNU	FAUNAL	AAJKNS	SANJAK	ABBDEL	DABBLE
				ABBDER	BARBED

8

	DABBER
ABBDEU	BEDAUB
ABBEGL	GABBLE
ABBEJR	JABBER
ABBELR	BARBEL
	RABBLE
ABBELU	BAUBLE
ABBELW	BAWBLE
	WABBLE
ABBERR	BARBER
ABBERT	BARBET
	RABBET
ABBESS	ABBESS
ABBFLY	FLABBY
ABBHSY	SHABBY
ABBINR	RABBIN
ABBIRT	RABBIT
ABBLSY	SLABBY
ABBMOO	BAMBOO
ABBMOY	BOMBAY
ABBNOO	BABOON
ABBORS	ABSORB
ABCCLU	BUCCAL
ABCDEU	ABDUCE
ABCDIR	BARDIC
ABCDTU	ABDUCT
ABCEEL	BELACE
ABCEEM	BECAME
ABCEGU	CUBAGE
ABCEHL	BLEACH
ABCEHR	BREACH
ABCEJT	ABJECT
ABCEKR	BACKER
ABCELM	BECALM
ABCEMR	CAMBER
ABCEMX	EXCAMB
ABCENO	BEACON
ABCFIR	FABRIC
ABCFNO	CONFAB
ABCGIT	GIB-CAT
ABCHLN	BLANCH
ABCHNR	BRANCH
ABCHOR	BROACH
ABCIIM	IAMBIC
ABCKRU	BUCKRA
ABCLMY	CYMBAL
ABCLOT	COBALT
ABCMOP	MOB-CAP
ABCMOR	CRAMBO
ABCMOT	COMBAT
	TOMBAC
ABCNOR	CARBON
ABCORY	CARBOY
ABDDEE	BEADED
ABDDEL	BLADED
ABDDEN	BANDED
ABDDEY	DAY-BED
ABDDHU	BUDDHA
ABDEEH	BEHEAD
ABDEEK	BEAKED
ABDEEL	BEADLE
ABDEES	DEBASE
ABDEET	DEBATE
ABDEFL	FABLED
ABDEGR	BADGER
ABDEIR	AIR-BED
ABDEIS	BIASED
ABDEKR	DEBARK
ABDELM	BEDLAM
	BELDAM
ABDELO	ALBEDO
ABDENT	TAN-BED
ABDERU	DAUBER
ABDERV	ADVERB
ABDILR	BRIDAL
	RIBALD
ABDINR	RIBAND
ABDINT	BANDIT
ABDIRS	DISBAR
ABDLLY	BALDLY
ABDNOU	ABOUND
ABDNRY	BRANDY
ABDORY	BY-ROAD
ABDRRU	DURBAR
ABDRSU	ABSURD
ABDRWY	BAWDRY
ABEEGL	BEAGLE
ABEEGR	BAREGE
	BARGEE
ABEEHV	BEHAVE
ABEEKR	BEAKER
ABEEKT	BETAKE
ABEELN	BALEEN
	ENABLE
ABEELT	BELATE
ABEERR	BEARER
ABEERT	BEATER
	BERATE
	REBATE
ABEERV	BEAVER
ABEERW	BEWARE
ABEERZ	ZEREBA
ABEFFL	BAFFLE
ABEFHL	BEHALF
ABEFLL	BEFALL
ABEGGR	BEGGAR
ABEGLM	GAMBLE
ABEGLN	BANGLE
ABEGLR	GARBLE
ABEGLT	GABLET
ABEGLU	BELUGA
ABEGOR	BORAGE
ABEHKL	KEBLAH
ABEHLR	HERBAL
ABEHRT	BATHER
	BREATH
ABEIIL	BAILIE
ABEILL	BELIAL
	LIABLE
ABEILS	ISABEL
ABEILT	ALBEIT
	ALBITE
ABEILV	VIABLE
ABEILW	BEWAIL
ABEINT	BINATE
ABEIRS	BRAISE
	RABIES
ABEIRZ	BRAIZE
ABEJOR	JERBOA
ABEJRU	ABJURE
ABEJTU	JUBATE
ABEKMN	EMBANK
ABEKMR	EMBARK
ABEKNR	BANKER
ABEKRY	BAKERY
ABEKST	BASKET
ABELLT	BALLET
ABELMM	EMBALM
ABELMR	AMBLER
	MARBLE
	RAMBLE
ABELNU	NEBULA
	UNABLE
ABELNY	BY-LANE
ABELOR	BOREAL
ABELOT	LOBATE
	OBLATE
ABELRR	BARREL
ABELRT	LABRET
ABELRV	VERBAL
ABELRW	WARBLE
ABELRY	BARELY
	BARLEY
	BLEARY
ABELRZ	BLAZER
ABELST	STABLE
ABELSU	SUABLE
	USABLE
ABELSY	BASELY
ABELTT	BATTLE
	TABLET
ABEMNO	BEMOAN
ABEMNY	BY-NAME
ABENNR	BANNER
ABENRR	BARREN
ABENRT	BANTER
ABENRU	URBANE
ABENRZ	BRAZEN
ABENST	ABSENT
ABENTT	BATTEN
ABENTU	BUTANE
ABENTZ	BEZANT
ABEORT	BORATE
ABEORZ	BEZOAR
ABEPRU	UPBEAR
ABEQRU	BARQUE
ABEQSU	BASQUE
ABERRT	BARTER
ABERST	BREAST
ABERSU	ABUSER
ABERTT	BATTER
	TABRET
ABERTY	BETRAY

ABERUU	BUREAU	ABNOTY	BOTANY	ACDEIV	ADVICE
ABERWY	BEWRAY	ABNRTU	TURBAN	ACDELN	CANDLE
ABESST	BASSET	ABNRUU	AUBURN	ACDELR	CRADLE
ABETTU	BATTUE	ABNRWY	BRAWNY	ACDELS	SCALED
ABETUY	BEAUTY	ABORRU	ARBOUR	ACDELU	CAUDLE
ABFILU	FIBULA	ABORRW	BARROW	ACDELW	CLAWED
ABFOTX	FOX-BAT	ABORSV	BRAVOS	ACDEMP	DECAMP
ABGGIW	BAG-WIG	ABORTU	TABOUR	ACDENO	DEACON
ABGHTU	HAGBUT	ABOSWW	BOW-SAW	ACDENR	DANCER
ABGIKN	BAKING	ABPRTU	ABRUPT	ACDENS	ASCEND
	INK-BAG	ABPSSY	BY-PASS	ACDENT	CADENT
ABGIMR	GAMBIR	ABRRSU	BURSAR		DECANT
ABGIMT	GAMBIT	ABRSSY	BRASSY	ACDEOT	COATED
ABGIMY	BIGAMY	ABSUWY	SUBWAY	ACDEPP	CAPPED
ABGINO	BAGNIO	ACCCIL	CALCIC	ACDERR	CARDER
	GABION	ACCDEE	ACCEDE	ACDERS	SACRED
ABGLMO	GAMBOL	ACCDII	ACIDIC		SCARED
ABGMUY	MAY-BUG	ACCDOR	ACCORD	ACDERT	REDACT
ABHIKL	KIBLAH	ACCEHN	CHANCE	ACDERZ	CRAZED
ABHINS	BANISH	ACCEHT	CACHET	ACDEUX	CAUDEX
ABHMSU	AMBUSH	ACCEIP	ICE-CAP	ACDHMR	DRACHM
ABHNTU	BHUTAN	ACCEIT	ACETIC	ACDIIP	ADIPIC
ABHORR	HARBOR	ACCEKL	CACKLE	ACDIJU	JUDAIC
ABHOST	BATHOS	ACCELN	CANCEL	ACDILP	PLACID
ABHPTY	BY-PATH	ACCELS	CALCES	ACDINR	RANCID
ABIILT	TIBIAL	ACCEMU	CAECUM	ACDIOT	DACOIT
ABIKMO	AKIMBO	ACCENR	CANCER	ACDIOZ	ZODIAC
ABILMU	LABIUM	ACCENT	ACCENT	ACDIST	DICAST
ABILNO	ALBINO	ACCEPT	ACCEPT	ACDLTY	DACTYL
ABILNY	LIBYAN	ACCERS	SCARCE	ACDNOR	CANDOR
ABILRT	TRIBAL	ACCERU	ACCRUE	ACDORW	COWARD
ABILRU	BURIAL	ACCESS	ACCESS	ACEEFF	EFFACE
ABILRZ	BRAZIL	ACCESU	ACCUSE	ACEEFS	FAECES
ABIMRU	BARIUM	ACCGNO	COGNAC	ACEEFT	FACETE
ABIMSU	IAMBUS	ACCHNR	CRANCH	ACEEGN	ENCAGE
ABINOT	OBTAIN	ACCHNY	CHANCY	ACEEHK	HACKEE
ABINRS	BRAINS	ACCHOU	CACHOU	ACEEHN	ACHENE
ABINRY	BINARY	ACCHTY	CATCHY	ACEEIP	APIECE
	BRAINY	ACCILO	CALICO	ACEELN	ENLACE
ABINSU	UNBIAS		CICOLA	ACEELR	CEREAL
ABIORS	ISOBAR			ACEELV	CLEAVE
ABKMOT	TOMBAK	ACCILT	LACTIC	ACEEMN	MENACE
ABKNRS	BRANKS	ACCINY	CYANIC	ACEEMR	AMERCE
ABLLOT	BALLOT	ACCIPR	CAPRIC		RACEME
ABLMOO	ABLOOM	ACCIRT	ARCTIC	ACEEMZ	ECZEMA
ABLMOP	APLOMB	ACCITT	TACTIC	ACEENR	CAREEN
ABLMOW	MOB-LAW	ACCITU	CICUTA	ACEENS	SÉANCE
ABLMRU	BRUMAL	ACCNOO	CACOON		SENECA
	LABRUM	ACCOST	ACCOST	ACEENV	ENCAVE
	LUMBAR	ACCRUY	CURACY	ACEEOT	COATEE
ABLMRY	MARBLY	ACCSTU	CACTUS	ACEEPS	ESCAPE
ABLNOZ	BLAZON	ACCSUU	CAUCUS	ACEERR	CAREER
ABLORU	LABOUR	ACDDEE	DECADE	ACEERS	CREASE
ABLPRU	BURLAP	ACDDEI	CADDIE		SEARCE
ABLPYY	BY-PLAY	ACDDEU	ADDUCE	ACEERT	CERATE
ABLRTU	BRUTAL	ACDDIN	CANDID		CREATE
ABLSTY	STABLY	ACDDIS	CADDIS		ECARTÉ
ABMNOW	BOWMAN	ACDDIT	ADDICT	ACEFFR	CAFFRE
ABMOTW	WOMBAT	ACDEEF	DEFACE	ACEFFT	AFFECT
ABMRUY	BAY-RUM	ACDEGR	CADGER	ACEFHR	CHAFER
ABNORY	BARONY	ACDEHR	ARCHED	ACEFIL	FACILE
		ACDEHT	DETACH		

ACEFIN	FIANCE	ACEKRS	SCREAK		USANCE
ACEFIR	FIACRE	ACEKRT	RACKET	ACENTU	CANUTE
ACEFLU	FECULA	ACEKRU	CAUKER	ACEOPT	CAPOTE
ACEFLY	CALEFY	ACEKRY	CREAKY	ACEORS	COARSE
ACEFNR	FRANCE	ACEKST	CASKET	ACEOSW	SEA-COW
ACEFSS	FASCES	ACELLO	LOCALE	ACEOTV	AVOCET
ACEFSU	FAUCES	ACELLR	CALLER		OCTAVE
ACEFTU	FAUCET		CELLAR	ACEPRS	ESCARP
ACEGHN	CHANGE		RECALL		SCRAPE
ACEGHR	CHARGE	ACELLT	CALLET	ACEPRT	CARPET
ACEGIL	GAELIC	ACELMS	MASCLE	ACEPRU	APERÇU
ACEGIN	INCAGE	ACELMT	CAMLET	ACEPST	ASPECT
ACEGLN	GLANCE	ACELNR	LANCER	ACEPTU	TEA-CUP
ACEGLY	LEGACY	ACELNT	CANTLE	ACEQSU	CASQUE
ACEGNY	AGENCY		CENTAL		SACQUE
ACEGOS	SOCAGE		LANCET	ACERRT	ARRECT
ACEHIS	CHAISE	ACELNU	CUNEAL		CARTER
ACEHKL	HACKLE		UNLACE		CRATER
ACEHLP	CHAPEL	ACELOR	ORACLE		TRACER
	PLEACH	ACELOS	SOLACE	ACERRU	CURARE
ACEHLS	LACHES	ACELOT	LOCATE	ACERRV	CARVER
ACEHLT	CHALET	ACELOV	ALCOVE		CRAVER
	THECAL		COEVAL	ACERSS	CARESS
ACEHMS	SACHEM	ACELPR	CARPEL	ACERST	CASTER
ACEHOR	CHOREA		PARCEL		RECAST
	OCHREA		PLACER	ACERSU	CAUSER
	ORACHE	ACELQU	CALQUE		CESURA
ACEHPR	EPARCH		CLAQUE		SAUCER
	PREACH	ACELRS	SCALER	ACERSY	CREASY
ACEHPY	PEACHY	ACELRT	CARTEL	ACERTU	CURATE
ACEHRR	ARCHER		CLARET	ACESTT	STACTE
ACEHRS	CHASER	ACELRV	CARVEL	ACESUY	CAUSEY
	ESCHAR	ACELST	CASTLE	ACFFHY	CHAFFY
	SEARCH	ACELSU	CLAUSE	ACFGIN	FACING
ACEHRX	EXARCH	ACELSV	CALVES	ACFILS	FISCAL
ACEHST	CHASTE	ACELSX	CALXES	ACFIOS	FIASCO
	SACHET	ACELTT	CATTLE	ACFIPY	PACIFY
	SCATHE	ACELTU	CAUTEL	ACFLNO	FALCON
ACEHSW	CASHEW	ACELYY	CLAYEY	ACFLPU	CAPFUL
ACEILM	MALICE	ACEMNP	ENCAMP	ACFORT	FACTOR
ACEILP	PLAICE	ACEMNR	CARMEN	ACFRTY	CRAFTY
ACEILR	ÉCLAIR	ACEMNU	ACUMEN	ACGGRY	CRAGGY
ACEIMN	ANEMIC	ACEMOP	POMACE	ACGHIN	ACHING
	CINEMA	ACEMOR	AMORCE	ACGHOU	GAUCHO
ACEINN	CANINE	ACEMPR	CAMPER	ACGHTU	CAUGHT
ACEINS	CASEIN	ACEMRS	SCREAM	ACGILL	GALLIC
	INCASE	ACEMRY	CREAMY	ACGILN	LACING
ACEIPS	APICES	ACENNU	NUANCE	ACGILR	GARLIC
ACEIQU	CAIQUE	ACENOR	CORNEA	ACGILS	GLACIS
ACEITV	ACTIVE	ACENPR	PRANCE	ACGINN	CANING
ACEIVV	VIVACE	ACENRS	CASERN	ACGINR	RACING
ACEJKT	JACKET	ACENRT	CANTER	ACGINS	CASING
ACEJLO	CAJOLE		NECTAR	ACGINT	ACTING
ACEKLR	CALKER		RECANT	ACGINV	CAVING
	LACKER		TANREC	ACGIRT	TRAGIC
ACEKLT	TACKLE		TRANCE	ACGNOS	GASCON
ACEKLY	LACKEY	ACENRV	CAVERN	ACGORT	GO-CART
ACEKNR	CANKER		CRAVEN	ACGORU	COUGAR
ACEKPR	PACKER	ACENST	ASCENT	ACGTTU	CATGUT
ACEKPT	PACKET		SECANT	ACHHNU	HAUNCH
ACEKRR	RACKER	ACENSU	UNCASE	ACHHTT	THATCH

ACHIJK	HI-JACK	ACINRY	RIANCY	ACNOTU	TOUCAN
ACHILP	CALIPH	ACINTT	INTACT	ACNSTU	TUSCAN
ACHINR	INARCH	ACINUV	VICUÑA	ACNSTY	SCANTY
ACHINT	CANTHI	ACIORS	SCORIA	ACOOTV	OCTAVO
ACHIRS	RACHIS	ACIORT	AORTIC	ACOPRT	CAPTOR
ACHKLY	CHALKY	ACIOST	SCOTIA	ACORRT	CARROT
ACHKTW	THWACK	ACIOSV	OVISAC		TROCAR
ACHLNU	LAUNCH	ACIOTZ	AZOTIC	ACORSS	ACROSS
	NUCHAL	ACIPRY	PIRACY	ACORST	CASTOR
ACHLOR	CHORAL	ACIPTT	TIP-CAT	ACORTT	COTTAR
	LORCHA	ACIQTU	ACQUIT	ACORTV	CAVORT
ACHLRY	ARCHLY	ACIRRU	CURARI	ACORYZ	CORYZA
ACHMNU	MANCHU	ACIRSS	CRASIS	ACPRSU	CARPUS
ACHMSU	SUMACH	ACIRST	RACIST	ACPSSU	SCAPUS
ACHNOR	ANCHOR	ACIRSY	SYRIAC	ACPSTU	CATSUP
	ARCHON	ACISTT	STATIC		UPCAST
	RANCHO	ACITVY	CAVITY	ACRRSY	SCARRY
ACHNPU	PAUNCH	ACKLTY	TALCKY	ACRRWY	WAR-CRY
ACHNST	SNATCH	ACKNPU	UNPACK	ADDEEH	HEADED
	STANCH	ACKNRY	CRANKY	ADDEEL	LEADED
ACHOPY	POACHY	ACKORY	CROAKY	ADDEEN	DEADEN
ACHOUV	AVOUCH	ACLLMY	CALMLY	ADDEGR	GADDER
ACHPPY	CHAPPY	ACLLOR	COLLAR	ADDEHN	HANDED
ACHPTY	PATCHY	ACLLOW	CALLOW	ADDEIM	DIADEM
ACHRRY	CHARRY	ACLLSU	CALLUS	ADDELN	DANDLE
ACHRST	STARCH	ACLMMY	CLAMMY		LANDED
ACHSTU	CUSHAT	ACLMOR	CLAMOR	ADDELO	LOADED
ACHTTY	CHATTY	ACLMSU	LACMUS	ADDELP	PADDLE
ACIILS	SILICA	ACLMTU	TALCUM	ADDELR	LADDER
ACIILT	ITALIC	ACLNUV	VULCAN		RADDLE
ACIIRT	IATRIC	ACLNUY	LUNACY	ADDELS	SADDLE
ACIKLN	CALKIN	ACLOPU	COPULA	ADDELW	DAWDLE
ACIKNS	INKSAC		CUPOLA		WADDLE
ACIKNT	CATKIN	ACLORR	CORRAL	ADDELY	DEADLY
ACIKPS	ASPICK	ACLORU	OCULAR	ADDEMN	DAMNED
ACIKTT	KIT-CAT	ACLOST	COSTAL		DEMAND
ACILMX	CLIMAX	ACLRRU	CRURAL		MADDEN
ACILNP	CAPLIN	ACLRSW	SCRAWL	ADDEMR	MADDER
ACILNR	CRINAL	ACLRTU	CURTAL	ADDENR	DARNED
ACILNU	UNCIAL	ACLSSY	CLASSY	ADDENS	SADDEN
ACILOR	LORICA	ACMNOR	MACRON	ADDEOR	DEODAR
ACILOS	SOCIAL	ACMOST	MASCOT	ADDEPR	PADDER
ACILOX	OXALIC	ACMOTT	TOM-CAT	ADDGIO	GADOID
ACILRY	RACILY	ACMPSU	CAMPUS	ADDGOO	OGDOAD
ACILSU	CAULIS	ACMRSU	SACRUM	ADDGOY	DOG-DAY
ACILSV	SLAVIC	ACMSTU	MUSCAT	ADDIMR	MADRID
ACIMNO	MANIOC	ACMUUV	VACUUM	ADDIMY	MID-DAY
ACIMOR	ROMAIC	ACNNNO	CANNON	ADDORT	DOTARD
ACIMOS	MOSAIC	ACNNOT	CANNOT	ADEEFL	LEAFED
ACIMOT	ATOMIC		CANTON	ADEEFM	DEFAME
ACIMPS	SCAMPI			ADEEFN	DEAFEN
ACIMPT	IMPACT	ACNNOY	CANYON	ADEEFT	DEFEAT
ACIMRS	RACISM	ACNNRY	CRANNY	ADEEHR	ADHERE
ACIMST	MASTIC	ACNOOP	POONAC		HEADER
ACINNT	TANNIC	ACNOOR	CORONA	ADEEIL	AEDILE
	TIN-CAN		RACOON	ADEEKP	PEAKED
ACINOS	CASINO	ACNOPY	CANOPY	ADEELN	LEADEN
ACINOT	ACTION	ACNORT	CANTOR	ADEELR	DEALER
	ATONIC		CARTON		LEADER
		ACNORY	CRAYON	ADEELT	DELATE
ACINPT	CATNIP	ACNOST	CANTOS		ELATED
ACINRU	URANIC	ACNOTT	OCTANT		

12

ADEELV	LEAVED	ADEIMN	DEMAIN	ADENOT	DONATE
ADEEMN	DEMEAN		MAIDEN	ADENPP	APPEND
ADEEMO	OEDEMA		MEDIAN	ADENPR	PANDER
ADEENP	NEAPED	ADEIMR	ADMIRE		REPAND
ADEENR	ENDEAR	ADEINT	DETAIN	ADENPT	PEDANT
ADEENV	ADVENE	ADEINV	INVADE	ADENPX	EXPAND
ADEEPT	PEDATE	ADEIPR	DIAPER	ADENRR	DARNER
ADEERR	READER		REPAID		ERRAND
ADEERS	SEARED	ADEIRR	ARRIDE	ADENRT	ARDENT
ADEERW	DRAWEE		RAIDER	ADENRU	UNREAD
ADEEST	SEDATE	ADEIRT	TIRADE	ADENRW	WANDER
ADEETT	TEATED	ADEIRV	VARIED		WARDEN
ADEFGN	FAG-END	ADEISU	ADIEUS	ADENRY	DENARY
	FANGED	ADEISV	ADVISE	ADENRZ	ZANDER
ADEFIL	AFIELD	ADEITV	DATIVE	ADENTT	ATTEND
ADEFLO	FEODAL	ADEIUX	ADIEUX	ADENTV	ADVENT
ADEFLR	FARDEL	ADEJRU	ADJURE	ADENWX	WAX-END
	FLARED	ADEKLN	ANKLED	ADEORR	ADORER
ADEFLU	FEUDAL	ADEKLR	DARKLE	ADEPPR	DAPPER
ADEFLY	DEAFLY	ADEKMR	MARKED	ADEPRR	DRAPER
ADEFOR	FEDORA	ADEKMS	MASKED	ADEPRS	SPREAD
ADEFRY	DEFRAY	ADEKNR	DARKEN	ADEPRT	DEPART
ADEGGH	HAGGED	ADEKOS	SOAKED		PETARD
ADEGGJ	JAGGED	ADELLU	ALLUDE	ADEPRW	WARPED
ADEGGL	DAGGLE	ADELMP	PALMED	ADERRT	DARTER
ADEGGR	DAGGER	ADELMR	DERMAL		DARTRE
	RAGGED		MEDLAR		RETARD
ADEGIT	GAITED	ADELMS	DAMSEL		TRADER
ADEGLN	ANGLED	ADELNR	ALDERN	ADERRW	DRAWER
	DANGLE		DARNEL		REDRAW
ADEGNR	DANGER	ADELNS	SENDAL		REWARD
	GANDER	ADELNT	DENTAL		WARDER
	GARDEN	ADELNU	UNLADE	ADERRY	DREARY
ADEGOS	DOSAGE	ADELOR	LOADER	ADERTT	TETRAD
	SEA-DOG		ORDEAL	ADERTV	ADVERT
	SEA-GOD	ADELPP	DAPPLE	ADESTT	STATED
ADEGOT	DOGATE	ADELPR	PEDLAR	ADESTY	STEADY
	DOTAGE	ADELPS	LAPSED	ADFFOR	AFFORD
ADEGRR	REGARD	ADELPW	DEWLAP	ADFFOY	OFF-DAY
ADEHLN	HANDLE	ADELRR	LARDER	ADFFRY	DRAFFY
ADEHLR	HERALD	ADELRY	DEARLY	ADFGIN	FADING
ADEHNR	HARDEN	ADELST	SLATED	ADFGLY	GADFLY
ADEHPT	HEPTAD	ADELVV	VALVED	ADFIRT	ADRIFT
ADEHRS	DASHER	ADELZZ	DAZZLE	ADFIRY	FRIDAY
ADEHRT	DEARTH	ADEMNO	DAEMON	ADFLYY	DAYFLY
	HATRED		NOMADE	ADGILN	LADING
	THREAD	ADEMNP	DAMPEN	ADGINO	GANOID
ADEHSY	HYADES	ADEMNR	REMAND	ADGINR	DARING
ADEHTT	HATTED	ADEMNS	AMENDS	ADGIRV	GRAVID
ADEHYY	HEYDAY		DESMAN	ADGLLY	GLADLY
ADEILL	ALLIED	ADEMNT	TANDEM	ADGLOP	LAPDOG
ADEILM	MEDIAL	ADEMOP	POMADE	ADGNOR	DRAGON
ADEILN	ALDINE	ADEMOW	MEADOW	ADHHOU	HOUDAH
	DELIAN	ADEMPR	DAMPER	ADHHOW	HOWDAH
	DENIAL	ADEMRT	DREAMT	ADHIJS	JADISH
ADEILP	PLEIAD	ADEMRY	DREAMY	ADHINS	DANISH
ADEILS	AISLED	ADEMST	MASTED	ADHIRS	RADISH
	LADIES	ADEMSU	MEDUSA	ADHLRY	HARDLY
ADEILT	DETAIL	ADEMTT	MATTED	ADHMNO	HODMAN
	DILATE	ADEMWY	MAY-DEW	ADHMRU	DURHAM
	TAILED	ADENNU	DUENNA	ADHNNU	UNHAND

13

ADHNSY	SHANDY
ADHOSW	SHADOW
ADHRRU	DHURRA
ADIILN	INLAID
ADIILR	IRIDAL
ADIIMO	DAIMIO
ADIIMR	MID-AIR
ADIINN	INDIAN
ADIJNO	ADJOIN
ADIKMO	MIKADO
ADIKNP	KIDNAP
ADIKOT	DAKOIT
ADILLP	PALLID
ADILMS	DISMAL
ADILNN	INLAND
ADILNS	ISLAND
ADILNY	LYDIAN
ADILOO	OOIDAL
ADILRZ	LIZARD
ADILST	DISTAL
ADIMNO	DOMAIN
ADIMOT	DIATOM
ADIMRS	DISARM
ADIMRU	RADIUM
ADIMRY	MYRIAD
ADIMSS	SADISM
ADIMST	AMIDST
ADIMSY	DISMAY
ADIMWY	MIDWAY
ADINOR	DORIAN
	INROAD
	ORDAIN
ADINOS	ADONIS
ADINPT	PANDIT
ADINPU	UNPAID
ADINRU	DURIAN
ADINRW	DARWIN
	INWARD
ADINSU	UNSAID
ADINTY	DAINTY
ADIORT	ADROIT
ADIPRS	RAPIDS
ADIPSX	SPADIX
ADIRRS	SIRDAR
ADIRSU	RADIUS
ADIRWZ	WIZARD
ADISST	SADIST
ADJSTU	ADJUST
ADKLRY	DARKLY
ADLLOR	DOLLAR
ADLMNO	ALMOND
	DOLMAN
ADLMTU	TALMUD
ADLNOP	POLAND
ADLNOU	UNLOAD
ADLNPU	UPLAND
ADLNRU	LURDAN
ADLORS	DORSAL
ADLOSW	DOWLAS
ADMNOR	RANDOM
ADMNOS	DAMSON
ADMNOY	DYNAMO
	MONDAY
ADMORR	RAMROD
ADMTUY	ADYTUM
ADNOPR	PARDON
ADNORU	AROUND
ADNORW	ONWARD
ADNRST	STRAND
ADNRTU	TUNDRA
ADNSTY	DYNAST
ADNSUY	SUNDAY
ADOPRY	PARODY
ADORRU	ARDOUR
ADORTW	TOWARD
ADPRUW	UPWARD
ADRSWY	SWARDY
ADRTWY	TAWDRY
AEEELS	SEA-EEL
AEEFFR	AFFEER
AEEFLM	FEMALE
AEEFRT	AFREET
AEEGGN	ENGAGE
AEEGGS	SEA-EGG
AEEGLL	ALLEGE
AEEGLP	PELAGE
AEEGLR	REGALE
AEEGLT	EAGLET
	LEGATE
AEEGLU	LEAGUE
AEEGMM	GEMMAE
AEEGMN	MANÈGE
	MÉNAGE
AEEGMR	MEAGRE
AEEGMT	METAGE
AEEGNR	ENRAGE
	GENERA
AEEGNS	SENEGA
AEEGNV	AVENGE
	GENEVA
AEEGOP	APOGEE
AEEGRS	GREASE
AEEGRV	GREAVE
AEEGST	EGESTA
AEEGSW	SEWAGE
AEEHLR	HEALER
AEEHLX	EXHALE
AEEHNV	HEAVEN
AEEHRR	HEARER
	REHEAR
AEEHRS	HEARSE
AEEHRT	HEATER
	HEREAT
AEEHRV	HEAVER
AEEHSV	SHEAVE
AEEKMR	REMAKE
AEEKNW	WEAKEN
AEEKNY	YANKEE
AEEKRT	RETAKE
AEEKRU	EUREKA
AEELLM	MALLEE
AEELMN	ENAMEL
AEELMP	EMPALE
AEELNT	LATEEN
AEELNV	LEAVEN
AEELPR	LEAPER
	REPEAL
AEELPS	ASLEEP
	ELAPSE
	PLEASE
AEELPU	EPAULE
AEELRS	RESALE
	SEALER
AEELRT	ELATER
	RELATE
AEELRV	REVEAL
AEELST	STELAE
	TEASEL
AEELSV	LEAVES
	SLEAVE
AEELSW	WEASEL
AEELWY	LEEWAY
AEEMMM	MAMMEE
AEEMNR	RENAME
AEEMPR	AMPERE
AEEMRS	SEAMER
AEEMSS	SESAME
AEEMSW	SEA-MEW
AEENRR	EARNER
AEENST	SATEEN
	SENATE
AEENUV	AVENUE
AEENWZ	WEAZEN
AEEPPR	RAPPEE
AEEPRR	REAPER
AEEPRS	PARSEE
AEEPRT	REPEAT
AEEPST	PESETA
AEEQTU	EQUATE
AEERRS	ERASER
AEERRT	TEARER
AEERRV	REAVER
AEERRW	WEARER
AEERST	EASTER
	RESEAT
	TEASER
AEERSV	AVERSE
AEERVW	WEAVER
AEESSW	SEE-SAW
AEESTT	ESTATE
	TEA-SET
AEFFGR	GAFFER
AEFFLR	RAFFLE
AEFFLW	WAFFLE
AEFFRZ	ZAFFRE
AEFGLN	FLANGE
AEFGOR	FORAGE
AEFHLL	FELLAH
AEFHRS	AFRESH
AEFHRT	FATHER
AEFHSY	SHEAFY
AEFILL	FAILLE
AEFILN	FINALE

AEFILR	FERIAL	AEGINT	EATING	AEGRTU	RUGATE
AEFIMN	FAMINE	AEGINU	GUINEA	AEGRTY	GYRATE
AEFINN	FENIAN	AEGIRT	GAITER	AEGSTY	STAGEY
AEFIRS	FRAISE	AEGIRV	ARGIVE	AEGTTU	GUTTAE
	SEA-FIR		RIVAGE	AEHHLT	HEALTH
AEFLLN	FALLEN	AEGIRW	EARWIG	AEHHRS	REHASH
AEFLMN	FLAMEN	AEGISV	VISAGE	AEHHRT	HEARTH
AEFLNX	FLAXEN	AEGITU	AUGITE	AEHHST	SHEATH
AEFLOR	LOAFER	AEGITY	GAIETY	AEHHTY	HEATHY
AEFLOT	FOETAL	AEGJLN	JANGLE	AEHIKS	SAKIEH
AEFLRT	FALTER	AEGJST	GAS-JET	AEHILM	HIEMAL
AEFLRU	EARFUL	AEGJTU	JUGATE	AEHILN	INHALE
AEFLRY	FLAYER	AEGKLR	GRAKLE	AEHILW	AWHILE
AEFLST	FESTAL	AEGKST	GASKET	AEHIMT	HAMITE
AEFLSY	SAFELY	AEGLLU	ULLAGE	AEHINR	HERNIA
AEFLTY	FEALTY	AEGLLY	GALLEY	AEHKNR	HANKER
AEFMNO	FOEMAN	AEGLMN	MANGLE		HARKEN
AEFMRR	FARMER	AEGLMY	GLEAMY	AEHKNS	SHAKEN
	FRAMER	AEGLNR	ANGLER	AEHKRS	SHAKER
AEFNNR	FANNER		REGNAL	AEHKRW	HAWKER
AEFNRW	FAWNER	AEGLNT	TANGLE	AEHLLT	LETHAL
AEFNST	FASTEN	AEGLNU	LAGUNE	AEHLMT	HAMLET
AEFNSU	UNSAFE	AEGLOR	GALORE	AEHLNT	LATHEN
AEFNTT	FATTEN		GAOLER	AEHLOT	LOATHE
AEFOSV	FAVOSE	AEGLOT	LEGATO	AEHLRS	LASHER
AEFOSX	SEA-FOX	AEGLPU	PLAGUE	AEHLRT	HALTER
AEFRRT	RAFTER	AEGLRT	TERGAL		LATHER
AEFRRY	RAREFY	AEGLRV	GRAVEL		THALER
AEFRST	FASTER	AEGLRZ	GLAZER	AEHLRU	HAULER
AEFRTW	WAFTER	AEGLSY	SAGELY	AEHLRW	WHALER
AEFSTY	SAFETY	AEGMMR	GAMMER	AEHLSS	HASSLE
AEGGGL	GAGGLE		GRAMME	AEHLTW	WEALTH
AEGGHL	HAGGLE	AEGMNR	GERMAN	AEHLTY	HYETAL
AEGGIN	AGEING		MANGER	AEHMMR	HAMMER
AEGGLR	GARGLE	AEGMNT	MAGNET	AEHMMY	MAYHEM
AEGGLW	WAGGLE	AEGMRU	MAUGRE	AEHMNR	HERMAN
AEGGNR	GANGER	AEGMUZ	ZEUGMA	AEHMNT	ANTHEM
	GRANGE	AEGNNO	NONAGE	AEHMNU	HUMANE
AEGGNU	GANGUE	AEGNNT	GANNET	AEHMOS	HAMOSE
AEGGRS	SAGGER	AEGNOR	ONAGER	AEHMPR	HAMPER
	SEGGAR		ORANGE	AEHMRS	MASHER
AEGGRU	GAUGER	AEGNRR	GARNER	AEHMST	THAMES
AEGGWW	GEW-GAW		RANGER	AEHNPP	HAPPEN
AEGHIR	HEGIRA	AEGNRT	ARGENT	AEHNRT	ANTHER
AEGHIW	AWEIGH		GARNET		TEHRAN
AEGHMO	HOMAGE	AEGNRW	GNAWER	AEHNST	ATHENS
AEGHNR	HANGER	AEGORT	ORGEAT		HASTEN
AEGHRT	GATHER	AEGOTW	TOWAGE	AEHORS	ASHORE
AEGILN	GENIAL	AEGOVY	VOYAGE		HOARSE
AEGILP	PAIGLE	AEGPRT	PARGET	AEHPRR	HARPER
AEGILS	SILAGE	AEGPRU	PRAGUE	AEHPRS	PHRASE
AEGILT	AIGLET	AEGRRT	GARRET		SERAPH
AEGILV	GLAIVE		GARTER		SHAPER
AEGIMN	ENIGMA		GRATER	AEHPRT	TERAPH
AEGIMP	MAGPIE	AEGRRU	ARGUER	AEHPST	SPATHE
AEGIMR	MAIGRE	AEGRRV	GRAVER	AEHRRS	RASHER
	MIRAGE	AEGRRZ	GRAZER		SHARER
AEGINR	EARING	AEGRST	STAGER	AEHRRT	RATHER
	GAINER	AEGRSV	GRAVES	AEHRSS	SHEARS
	REGAIN	AEGRSY	GREASY	AEHRSV	SHAVER
	REGINA	AEGRTT	TARGET		

AEHRSW	HAWSER	AEIPSV	PAVISE	AELMTU	AMULET
	WASHER	AEIRRS	RAISER	AELMTY	TAMELY
AEHRTT	HATTER		SIERRA	AELNNR	LANNER
	THREAT	AEIRRV	ARRIVE	AELNOT	LEAN-TO
AEHRTW	WREATH	AEIRST	SATIRE	AELNPT	PLANET
AEHRTY	EARTHY		STRIAE		PLATEN
	HEARTY	AEIRTT	ATTIRE	AELNRT	ANTLER
AEHSTW	SWATHE		RATITE		RENTAL
AEIJLR	JAILER	AEIRTW	WAITER	AELNRU	NEURAL
AEIKNT	INTAKE	AEISST	SIESTA		UNREAL
AEIKRS	KAISER	AEISSZ	ASSIZE	AELNRV	VERNAL
AEILLN	LINEAL	AEITTV	VITTAE	AELNRY	NEARLY
AEILLS	ALLIES	AEJMST	JETSAM	AELNSU	UNSEAL
AEILMN	MENIAL	AEJNST	SEJANT	AELNTT	LATENT
AEILMP	IMPALE	AEJPRS	JASPER		LATTEN
AEILMS	MESIAL	AEKKNR	KRAKEN		TALENT
AEILNO	EOLIAN	AEKLNR	RANKLE	AELNTU	LUNATE
AEILNP	ALPINE	AEKLNT	ANKLET	AELNTV	LEVANT
	PINEAL	AEKLRT	TALKER	AELNTY	NEATLY
AEILNR	LINEAR	AEKLRW	WALKER	AELOPR	PAROLE
	NAILER	AEKLWY	WEAKLY	AELOPS	ASLOPE
AEILNS	SALINE	AEKMNU	UNMAKE	AELOPT	POT-ALE
AEILNT	ENTAIL	AEKMPU	MAKE-UP	AELORT	LORATE
AEILNV	ALVINE	AEKMRR	MARKER	AELOSV	LOAVES
	VENIAL		REMARK	AELOTZ	ZEALOT
AEILPS	ESPIAL	AEKMRS	MASKER	AELPPR	LAPPER
AEILRR	RAILER	AEKMRT	MARKET	AELPPT	LAPPET
AEILRS	ISRAEL	AEKNSY	SNEAKY	AELPQU	PLAQUE
	SAILER	AEKORS	SOAKER	AELPRT	PALTER
	SERIAL	AEKQRU	QUAKER		PLATER
AEILRT	RETAIL	AEKQSU	SQUEAK	AELPRU	PLEURA
AEILSV	VALISE	AEKRST	SKATER	AELPRY	PARLEY
AEILSY	EASILY		STRAKE		PEARLY
AEIMNR	MARINE		STREAK		PLAYER
	REMAIN		TASKER		REPLAY
AEIMNT	INMATE	AELLMT	MALLET	AELPST	PASTEL
	TAMINE	AELLMY	LAMELY		STAPLE
AEIMRU	UREMIA		MELLAY	AELQSU	SQUEAL
AEIMST	SAMITE	AELLNY	LEANLY	AELRRY	RARELY
AEINNP	PINNAE	AELLPT	PALLET	AELRST	SALTER
AEINNS	INSANE	AELLPY	PALELY		SLATER
	SIENNA	AELLRU	ALLURE	AELRSV	SALVER
AEINNT	INNATE		LAUREL		SERVAL
AEINNV	VIENNA	AELLRW	WALLER		SLAVER
AEINPR	RAPINE	AELLRY	REALLY	AELRSY	SLAYER
AEINRT	RETAIN	AELLTW	WALLET	AELRTT	LATTER
	RETINA	AELLTY	LATELY		RATTLE
AEINRV	RAVINE	AELLVY	VALLEY	AELRTV	TRAVEL
AEINSS	SANIES	AELMNT	LAMENT		VARLET
	SASINE		MANTEL	AELRTY	ELYTRA
AEINSV	SAVINE		MANTLE		LYRATE
AEINTU	AUNTIE		MENTAL		REALTY
AEINTV	NATIVE	AELMNY	MEANLY	AELRUV	VALUER
AEIOPT	OPIATE		NAMELY	AELRWY	LAWYER
AEIOPZ	EPIZOA	AELMOR	MORALE	AELRYY	YEARLY
AEIPRR	RAPIER	AELMPR	PALMER	AELSST	TASSEL
	REPAIR	AELMPS	SAMPLE	AELSTU	SALUTE
AEIPRS	ASPIRE	AELMRT	ARMLET	AELSTV	VESTAL
	PERSIA	AELMRV	MARVEL	AELSUX	SEXUAL
	PRAISE	AELMST	SAMLET	AELSYZ	SLEAZY
AEIPRT	PIRATE	AELMSY	MEASLY	AELTTT	TATTLE

AELTTW	WATTLE
AELTUX	LUXATE
AEMMNR	MERMAN
AEMMRR	RAMMER
AEMNNP	PENMAN
AEMNNR	MANNER
AEMNOY	YEOMAN
AEMNRT	MARTEN
AEMNRU	MANURE
AEMNST	STAMEN
AEMORR	REMORA
	ROAMER
AEMORS	RAMOSE
AEMORT	AMORET
AEMPPR	PAMPER
AEMPRT	TAMPER
AEMPRV	REVAMP
	VAMPER
AEMQRU	MARQUE
AEMQSU	MASQUE
AEMRRW	WARMER
AEMRST	MASTER
	STREAM
AEMRSU	AMUSER
AEMRTT	MATTER
AEMRTU	MATURE
AEMSSU	ASSUME
AEMSTU	MEATUS
AEMSTY	STEAMY
AEMTTU	MUTATE
AENNRT	TANNER
AENNTT	TENANT
AENOPW	WEAPON
AENORS	REASON
	SEÑORA
AENORT	ORNATE
AENOSS	SEASON
AENOTZ	ZONATE
AENPRT	ENTRAP
	PARENT
	TREPAN
AENPRW	ENWRAP
	PAWNER
AENPRY	NAPERY
AENPTT	PATENT
	PATTEN
AENPTU	PEA-NUT
AENRRS	SNARER
AENRRT	ERRANT
	RANTER
AENRRW	WARNER
	WARREN
AENRST	ASTERN
AENRSW	ANSWER
AENRSY	SENARY
AENRTT	RATTEN
AENRTU	NATURE
	TEA-URN
AENRTV	TAVERN
AENRTW	WANTER
AENSST	ASSENT

AENSTU	NASUTE
	UNSEAT
AENSUV	NAEVUS
AENSUY	UNEASY
AENTTU	ATTUNE
AENTTX	EXTANT
AEOPQU	OPAQUE
AEOPTT	APTOTE
	TEA-POT
AEOPTY	TEAPOY
AEORRR	ROARER
AEORSU	AROUSE
AEORSZ	AZORES
AEORTT	ROTATE
AEOSTV	AVOSET
AEOUVZ	ZOUAVE
AEPPRR	RAPPER
AEPPRS	SAPPER
AEPPRU	PAUPER
AEPPRY	PAPERY
	PREPAY
AEPPSY	APEPSY
AEPPTT	TAPPET
AEPRRS	RASPER
AEPRRT	PRATER
AEPRRU	UPREAR
AEPRRW	WARPER
AEPRRY	PRAYER
AEPRSS	PASSER
	REPASS
	SPARSE
AEPRST	REPAST
	TRAPES
AEPRTT	PATTER
AEPSST	STAPES
AEQRSU	SQUARE
AEQRTU	QUARTE
AEQRUV	QUAVER
AEQSUY	QUEASY
AERRST	ARREST
	STARER
AERRSU	RASURE
AERRTT	RATTER
AERRTY	ARTERY
AERSST	ASSERT
AERSSU	ASSURE
AERSTT	TASTER
AERSTV	STARVE
AERSTW	WASTER
AERSTY	ESTRAY
	STAYER
AERSTZ	ERSATZ
AERSWY	SAWYER
AERTTT	TATTER
AERTTY	TREATY
AERTWY	TAWERY
	WATERY
AESSSS	ASSESS
AESSST	ASSETS
AESSTV	STAVES
AESTTT	ATTEST

AESTTU	ASTUTE
	STATUE
AESTWY	SWEATY
AESTXY	EXTASY
AESTYY	YEASTY
AETUXY	EUTAXY
AFFFOR	FAR-OFF
AFFGUW	GUFFAW
AFFIKR	KAFFIR
AFFIMR	AFFIRM
AFFIRT	TARIFF
AFGGLY	FLAGGY
AFGGOT	FAGGOT
AFGISY	GASIFY
AFGLNO	FLAGON
AFGLNU	FUNGAL
AFGLRU	FRUGAL
AFHIMS	FAMISH
AFHIOS	OAFISH
AFHLSY	FLASHY
AFHMOT	FATHOM
AFIILL	FILIAL
AFIILN	FINIAL
AFILMY	FAMILY
AFILNU	INFULA
AFILOR	FOLIAR
AFILRY	FAIRLY
AFILSY	SALIFY
AFIMNR	FIRMAN
AFIMNY	INFAMY
AFIMRY	RAMIFY
AFINNT	INFANT
AFINRU	UNFAIR
AFINRY	FIN-RAY
AFIRTY	RATIFY
AFLLOR	FLORAL
AFLLOW	FALLOW
AFLLTY	FLATLY
AFLLUW	LAWFUL
AFLMNU	MANFUL
AFLMOR	FORMAL
AFLMRU	ARMFUL
	FULMAR
AFLMYY	MAY-FLY
AFLNOT	FONTAL
AFLNTU	FLAUNT
AFLORV	FLAVOR
AFLRTU	ARTFUL
AFLSTY	FASTLY
AFLSWY	SAW-FLY
AFLTUV	VATFUL
AFLTUY	FAULTY
AFMNOT	FANTOM
AFMORT	FORMAT
AFMOSU	FAMOUS
AFORRW	FARROW
AFORUV	FAVOUR
AFRSTU	FRUSTA
AGGHIS	HAGGIS
AGGHSY	SHAGGY
AGGILO	LOGGIA

17

AGGIMN	GAMING	AGLNRY	GNARLY	AHLOPS	PHOLAS
AGGINO	AGOING	AGLNSY	SLANGY	AHLORT	HARLOT
AGGIZZ	ZIGZAG	AGLNTY	TANGLY	AHLOSY	SHOALY
AGGKNY	KNAGGY	AGLNUU	UNGUAL	AHLPSS	SPLASH
AGGLOT	LOGGAT	AGLOTY	OTALGY	AHLPSY	PLASHY
AGGLSY	SLAGGY	AGLRUV	VULGAR	AHLRSY	RASHLY
AGGMOT	MAGGOT	AGLSSY	GLASSY	AHMMSY	SHAMMY
AGGNOW	WAGGON	AGMMNO	GAMMON	AHMNOS	HANSOM
AGGNOX	OXGANG	AGMMNU	MAGNUM	AHMOSY	SHAMOY
AGGNSY	SNAGGY	AGMORS	ORGASM	AHMOTU	MAHOUT
AGGPRY	PYGARG	AGMOYZ	ZYGOMA	AHMRSY	MARSHY
AGGQUY	QUAGGY	AGMPUZ	GAZUMP	AHMRTW	WARMTH
AGHILT	ALIGHT	AGMRTU	TARGUM	AHNNSY	SHANNY
AGHINT	ANIGHT	AGNNRY	GRANNY	AHNOPR	ORPHAN
AGHINV	HAVING	AGNORS	SARONG	AHNOWY	ANYHOW
AGHIRS	GARISH	AGNOTU	NOUGAT	AHNSTY	SHANTY
AGHIRT	ARIGHT	AGNPRS	SPRANG	AHOPRS	PHAROS
	GRAITH	AGORRT	GARROT	AHOPST	PATHOS
AGHLOS	GALOSH	AGORST	GROATS		POTASH
AGHNTU	NAUGHT	AGORSY	ARGOSY	AHOPTT	TOP-HAT
AGIINR	AIRING	AGORTU	RAGOUT	AHOQTU	QUOTHA
AGIJLN	JINGAL	AGOTTU	TAUTOG	AHORRW	HARROW
AGIJSW	JIGSAW	AGRSSY	GRASSY	AHORRY	HORARY
AGIKMN	MAKING	AGRSUY	SUGARY	AHORTT	THROAT
AGIKNR	RAKING	AGRUUY	AUGURY	AHORTU	AUTHOR
AGIKNT	TAKING	AGSTUU	AUGUST	AHORTX	THORAX
AGILLU	LIGULA	AHHKOO	HOOKAH	AHQSSU	SQUASH
AGILMN	LINGAM	AHHLLO	HALLOH	AHRSSU	HUSSAR
	MALIGN	AHHRRU	HURRAH	AHRSTT	STRATH
AGILMP	MAGILP	AHHRST	THRASH	AHRSTW	SWARTH
AGILNP	PALING	AHIILT	LITHIA	AHRSTY	TRASHY
AGILNS	SIGNAL	AHIKRS	RAKISH	AHRTTW	THWART
AGILNU	NILGAU	AHILLS	SHALLI	AIILRY	AIRILY
AGILNY	GAINLY	AHILNR	RHINAL	AIIMMN	MINIMA
AGILOR	GLORIA	AHILNY	LINHAY	AIIMNS	SIMIAN
AGILOS	OIL-GAS	AHILPS	PALISH	AIIMPR	IMPAIR
AGILOT	GALIOT	AHILST	LATISH	AIINNO	IONIAN
AGIMNR	MARGIN	AHILSV	LAVISH	AIINRS	RAISIN
AGIMNY	MAYING	AHILTW	WITHAL	AIIPTW	WAPITI
AGIMST	STIGMA	AHIMOR	MOHAIR	AIJLNU	JULIAN
AGIMWW	WIGWAM	AHIMPS	MISHAP	AIJLOR	JAILOR
AGINNW	AWNING	AHIMRS	MARISH	AIJLOV	JOVIAL
AGINOS	SAIGON	AHINSV	VANISH	AIKLMU	KALIUM
AGINPR	PARING	AHIPRS	PARISH	AIKLNO	KAOLIN
AGINPV	PAVING	AHIPSS	PHASIS	AIKMOO	OOMIAK
AGINRT	RATING	AHIRRS	SIRRAH	AIKMPR	IMPARK
AGINRU	AIR-GUN	AHIRSV	RAVISH	AIKNNN	NANKIN
AGINRV	RAVING	AHIRSW	RAWISH	AIKNNP	NAPKIN
AGINRY	GRAINY	AHIRTW	WRAITH	AILLNW	INWALL
AGINSS	ASSIGN	AHISTU	HIATUS	AILLPR	PILLAR
AGINSV	SAVING	AHKLPU	PULKHA	AILLPU	PILLAU
AGINSY	SAYING	AHKNPU	PUNKAH	AILLUZ	LAZULI
AGIORV	VIRAGO	AHKNST	THANKS	AILLYZ	LAZILY
AGIOTU	AGOUTI	AHLLMO	MOLLAH	AILMNU	ALUMNI
AGIRST	GRATIS	AHLLNU	NULLAH	AILMNY	MAINLY
AGIRTU	GUITAR	AHLLOO	HALLOO	AILMPR	PRIMAL
AGJNOR	JARGON		HOLLOA	AILMRT	MITRAL
AGLLNO	GALLON	AHLLOW	HALLOW	AILMSS	MISSAL
AGLLOP	GALLOP	AHLLRT	THRALL	AILMSY	MISLAY
AGLNOO	LAGOON	AHLLUX	HALLUX	AILMYZ	MAZILY
AGLNOS	SLOGAN	AHLMNY	HYMNAL	AILNOT	TALION

AILNPS	SPINAL		AIOPTU	UTOPIA		ALOPPR	POPLAR
AILNPT	PLAINT		AIPPRR	RIPRAP		ALOPRR	PARLOR
	PLIANT		AIPPRY	PAPYRI		ALOPRT	PATROL
AILNRT	RATLIN		AIPPST	P5AST			PORTAL
	TRINAL		AIPRST	RAPIST		ALOPST	POSTAL
AILNRU	URINAL		AIPRSV	PARVIS		ALORSV	SALVOR
AILNST	STALIN		AIPRSX	PRAXIS		ALORUV	VALOUR
AILNSV	SILVAN		AIPRTT	RAT-PIT		ALOTUW	OUTLAW
AILNTY	LITANY		AIPRTY	PARITY		ALOTUY	OUTLAY
AILNVY	VAINLY		AIPSTW	PIT-SAW		ALPPSU	PALPUS
AILORS	SAILOR			SAW-PIT		ALPRRU	LARRUP
AILORT	RIALTO		AIRRTY	RARITY		ALPRSW	SPRAWL
	TAILOR		AIRSSU	RUSSIA		ALPRTY	PALTRY
AILOSS	ASSOIL		AIRSTT	ARTIST			PARTLY
AILPRS	SPIRAL			STRAIT		ALRSTU	LUSTRA
AILPST	PASTIL		AIRSTU	AURIST		ALRSTY	STYLAR
AILRTU	RITUAL		AIRSTV	TRAVIS		ALRSUW	WALRUS
AILRWY	WARILY		AIRTTY	YTTRIA		ALRTTY	TARTLY
AILSTV	VITALS		AISSST	ASSIST		ALRTUW	TULWAR
AILSUV	VISUAL		AJLOOR	JAROOL		ALRUUV	UVULAR
AILTXY	LAXITY		AJNORT	TROJAN		ALSTVY	VASTLY
AIMMOS	MIMOSA		AJNTUY	JAUNTY		AMMMNO	MAMMON
AIMNNT	TINMAN		AKLLNY	LANKLY		AMMORT	MARMOT
AIMNOT	MANITO		AKLNRY	RANKLY		AMMOSU	OMASUM
AIMNPT	PITMAN		AKLSTY	STALKY		AMMPUW	WAMPUM
AIMNPW	IMPAWN		AKMNSU	UNMASK		AMNNOR	NORMAN
AIMNPY	PAYNIM		AKOORR	KARROO		AMNOOR	MAROON
AIMNRT	ANTRIM		AKQSUW	SQUAWK		AMNOPT	TAMPON
	MARTIN		ALLMOS	SLALOM		AMNORS	RAMSON
AIMNST	MANTIS		ALLMOW	MALLOW			RANSOM
AIMNSU	ANIMUS		ALLNOP	POLLAN		AMNORT	MATRON
AIMOPY	MYOPIA		ALLNOS	LLANOS		AMNOSS	SAMSON
AIMORS	MAORIS		ALLNUU	LUNULA		AMNOTU	AMOUNT
AIMPRT	ARMPIT		ALLOOP	APOLLO		AMNOTY	TOYMAN
	IMPART		ALLOPR	PALLOR		AMNPTY	TYMPAN
AIMPSS	PASSIM		ALLORY	ORALLY		AMNTUU	AUTUMN
AIMRTU	ATRIUM		ALLOSW	SALLOW		AMOORV	MOORVA
AIMRTX	MATRIX		ALLOTW	TALLOW		AMOOTT	TOMATO
AINNNT	TANNIN		ALLOVY	OVALLY		AMORRT	MORTAR
AINNOT	ANOINT		ALLOWW	WALLOW		AMORRU	ARMOUR
	NATION		ALLPRU	PLURAL		AMORRW	MARROW
AINNOW	WANION		ALLQSU	SQUALL		AMORRY	ARMORY
AINNPS	INSPAN		ALLSTY	LASTLY		AMORSS	MORASS
AINOQU	QUINOA			SALTLY		AMORSU	RAMOUS
AINORT	AROINT		ALMNOR	NORMAL		AMPSWY	SWAMPY
	RATION		ALMNOS	SALMON		AMRRTY	MARTYR
AINPRS	SPRAIN		ALMORT	MORTAL		AMRSTU	STRUMA
AINPRW	INWRAP		ALMORU	MORULA		ANNORT	NATRON
AINPSV	SPAVIN		ALMOST	ALMOST		ANNOST	SANTON
AINPTT	TAN-PIT		ALMRWY	WARMLY			SONANT
AINQTU	QUAINT		ALMSUY	ASYLUM		ANNOTW	WANTON
AINRST	STRAIN		ALMTUU	MUTUAL		ANNTTU	NUTANT
AINRSY	SYRIAN			UMLAUT		ANOPRS	PARSON
AINRTU	NUTRIA		ALNNOU	NOUNAL		ANOPRT	PATRON
AINRTY	TYRIAN		ALNOOS	SALOON			TARPON
AINSTT	TANIST		ALNOTV	VOLANT		ANORRW	NARROW
AINSTY	SANITY		ALNRXY	LARYNX		ANORSV	SOVRAN
	SATINY		ALNSTU	SULTAN		ANORTT	ATTORN
AINTVY	VANITY		ALNSVY	SYLVAN		ANORTY	AROYNT
AIOPRV	PAVIOR		ALNTUW	WALNUT			NOTARY
AIOPST	PATOIS		ALOOPS	SALOOP		ANORWY	NORWAY

ANORYZ	ZONARY	BBEGOT	GOBBET	BCIKRY	BRICKY
ANOSSW	SOWANS	BBEHLO	HOBBLE	BCILPU	PUBLIC
ANOSWY	NOWAYS	BBEIIM	IMBIBE	BCIMOR	BROMIC
ANPRTY	PANTRY	BBEIKL	KIBBLE	BCIMSU	CUBISM
ANPRUW	UNWRAP	BBEILN	NIBBLE	BCIRRU	RUBRIC
ANRSTU	SATURN	BBEIRR	BRIBER	BCISTU	CUBIST
ANRSUU	URANUS	BBEJOR	JOBBER	BCMORY	CORYMB
ANRTTU	TRUANT	BBELOW	WOBBLE	BCMRUY	CRUMBY
ANRTTY	TYRANT	BBELPY	PEBBLY	BCNOOR	BRONCO
ANRUWY	UNWARY	BBELRU	LUBBER	BCOOWY	COW-BOY
ANSTXY	SYNTAX		RUBBLE	BDDEIO	BODIED
AOOPTT	POTATO	BBEMNU	BENUMB	BDDEIR	BIDDER
AOORRT	ORATOR	BBEORR	ROBBER	BDDENO	BONDED
AOOTTT	TATTOO	BBERRU	RUBBER	BDDISU	DISBUD
AOPRRT	PARROT	BBGINO	GIBBON	BDEEIL	DEBILE
AOPRRU	UPROAR	BBGIOW	BOB-WIG		EDIBLE
AOPRST	PASTOR	BBHNOO	HOBNOB	BDEEIS	BESIDE
AOPRUV	VAPOUR	BBINOR	RIBBON	BDEEIT	BETIDE
AOQRTU	QUARTO	BBKNOY	KNOBBY	BDEELL	BEDELL
AORRST	ROSTRA	BBLLUU	BULBUL	BDEELT	BELTED
AORRSY	ROSARY	BBLOWY	BY-BLOW	BDEENR	BENDER
AORRTY	ROTARY		WOBBLY	BDEGIR	BEGIRD
AORRWY	ARROWY	BBNNOO	BON-BON		BRIDGE
	YARROW	BBNOSY	SNOBBY	BDEGIU	BUDGIE
AORSST	ASSORT	BBORTU	BURBOT	BDEGTU	BUDGET
AORSTX	STORAX	BBRSUU	SUBURB	BDEHIN	BEHIND
AORSUV	SAVOUR	BBSTUY	STUBBY	BDEHLO	BEHOLD
AORSVY	SAVORY	BCDEEK	BEDECK	BDEHOT	HOT-BED
AORTVY	VOTARY	BCDEIO	BODICE	BDEILL	BILLED
APPPSU	PAPPUS	BCDEMO	COMBED	BDEILM	LIMBED
APRRSY	SPARRY	BCDIOU	CUBOID	BDEILR	BRIDLE
APRSTY	PASTRY	BCEEHR	BREECH	BDEINR	BINDER
AQRRUY	QUARRY	BCEEKR	REBECK		INBRED
AQRTUZ	QUARTZ	BCEEKZ	ZEBECK	BDEIRS	DEBRIS
ARRSTY	STARRY	BCEEMO	BECOME	BDEIRU	BURIED
ARSSST	STRASS	BCEEQU	QUEBEC		RUBIED
ARSSTU	TARSUS	BCEHLN	BLENCH	BDELNO	BLONDE
ARSTUU	TAURUS	BCEHRU	CHERUB	BDELNU	BUNDLE
ARSTUX	SURTAX	BCEIKR	BICKER	BDELOU	DOUBLE
ARSTWY	STRAWY	BCEIOR	CORBIE	BDEMOY	EMBODY
ASSTTU	STATUS	BCEIOX	ICEBOX	BDENNU	UNBEND
BBBEIR	BIBBER	BCEIPS	BICEPS	BDENOR	BONDER
BBBELU	BUBBLE	BCEIRS	SCRIBE	BDENOY	BEYOND
BBBHUU	HUBBUB	BCEIST	BISECT	BDENRU	BURDEN
BBBINO	BOBBIN	BCEJOT	OBJECT	BDEOOT	BOOTED
BBBLUY	BUBBLY	BCEKLU	BUCKLE	BDEOPR	BEDROP
BBCELO	COBBLE	BCEKNO	BECKON	BDEORR	BORDER
BBCEOW	COBWEB	BCEKRU	BUCKER	BDEORT	DEBTOR
BBCHUY	CHUBBY	BCEKTU	BUCKET	BDESTU	BESTUD
BBDEEW	WEBBED	BCELOR	CORBEL	BDESUU	SUBDUE
BBDEIL	DIBBLE	BCEMOR	COMBER	BDFILO	BIFOLD
BBDEIR	DIBBER	BCEMRU	CUMBER	BDFIOR	FORBID
	RIBBED	BCENOU	BOUNCE	BDHIRY	HYBRID
BBDELU	BULBED	BCGORU	COBURG	BDIITT	TIDBIT
BBEELP	PEBBLE	BCHLOT	BLOTCH	BDIKNO	BODKIN
BBEERR	BERBER	BCHNUY	BUNCHY	BDILNU	DUBLIN
BBEEYY	BYE-BYE	BCHOOR	BROOCH	BDILOY	BODILY
BBEFIR	FIBBER	BCHOTY	BOTCHY	BDIMOR	MORBID
BBEGIR	GIBBER	BCIINU	INCUBI	BDIMOY	IMBODY
BBEGIT	GIBBET	BCIIOT	BIOTIC	BDINNU	UNBIND
BBEGLO	GOBBLE	BCIKNO	KINCOB	BDINPU	UPBIND

BDIOTU	OUTBID	BEGLOT	GOBLET	BELSTU	BUSTLE
BDIRTU	TURBID	BEGLRU	BUGLER		SUBLET
BDKLOO	KOBOLD		BURGLE		SUBTLE
BDLLOY	BOLDLY	BEGNOY	BY-GONE	BELTUU	TUBULE
BDLMUY	DUMBLY	BEGORU	BROGUE	BEMNOT	ENTOMB
BDLOOY	BLOODY	BEHILT	BLITHE	BEMNRU	NUMBER
BDLOUY	DOUBLY	BEHIOT	BOTHIE	BEMORS	SOMBRE
BDNOOY	NOBODY	BEHLMU	HUMBLE	BEMORY	EMBRYO
BDOORY	BROODY	BEHLSU	BUSHEL	BEMOSS	EMBOSS
BDORWY	BY-WORD	BEHORT	BOTHER	BEMPRU	BUMPER
BEEEFL	FEEBLE	BEIKOO	BOOKIE	BENNOT	BONNET
BEEELT	BEETLE	BEILLT	BILLET	BENNSU	BUNSEN
BEEEMS	BESEEM	BEILMN	NIMBLE	BENOOR	BORNEO
BEEEPW	BEWEEP	BEILMO	MOBILE	BENORR	REBORN
BEEERZ	BREEZE	BEILMR	LIMBER	BENORT	BRETON
BEEFIL	BELIEF	BEILMW	WIMBLE	BENORU	BOURNE
BEEFLL	BEFELL	BEILNR	BERLIN		UNROBE
BEEFLY	FEEBLY	BEILNU	NUBILE	BENORZ	BRONZE
BEEFOR	BEFORE	BEILOR	BOILER	BENOTY	BETONY
BEEFRT	BEREFT	BEIMRT	TIMBER	BENRRU	BURNER
BEEGNO	BEGONE		TIMBRE	BENRTU	BURNET
BEEGRU	BURGEE	BEIMRU	ERBIUM	BEOOST	BOOTES
	GUEBER		IMBRUE	BEOPST	BESPOT
	GUEBRE	BEINOV	BOVINE	BEORRS	RESORB
BEEHOV	BEHOVE	BEINRU	BRUNEI	BEORSU	BOURSE
BEEHRW	HEBREW		RUBINE	BEORSW	BROWSE
BEEHRY	HEREBY	BEIQSU	BISQUE	BEORTT	BETTOR
BEEHST	BEHEST	BEIRRY	BRIERY	BEORWY	BOWERY
	THEBES	BEIRST	BESTIR		BOWYER
BEEIKL	BELIKE		BISTRE	BEOSSS	OBSESS
BEEILZ	BELIZE	BEIRSU	BRUISE	BEOSTT	OBTEST
BEEIMR	BEMIRE	BEIRTT	BITTER	BEOSTU	OBTUSE
BEEKRS	BREEKS	BEIRTU	BEIRUT	BEOSTW	BESTOW
BEEKRU	REBUKE	BEITUY	UBIETY	BEPRSU	SUPERB
BEELMM	EMBLEM	BEJJUU	JUJUBE	BERTTU	BUTTER
BEELRT	TREBLE	BEJLMU	JUMBLE	BERUZZ	BUZZER
BEEMMR	MEMBER	BEKNOR	BROKEN	BFFIIN	BIFFIN
BEEMRU	EMBRUE	BEKNRU	BUNKER	BFFINO	BOFFIN
BEEMSU	BEMUSE	BEKOOT	BETOOK	BFIILR	FIBRIL
BEENOR	ENROBE	BEKORR	BROKER	BFIINR	FIBRIN
BEEORY	OBEYER	BEKRSU	BUSKER	BFIMOR	BIFORM
BEERRW	BREWER	BELLOU	LOBULE	BFLOTY	BOT-FLY
BEERSU	EREBUS	BELLOW	BELLOW	BFLTUU	TUBFUL
BEERTT	BETTER	BELLTU	BULLET	BGHILT	BLIGHT
BEERTV	BREVET	BELMMU	MUMBLE	BGHIRT	BRIGHT
BEERYZ	BREEZY	BELMRU	LUMBER	BGHMUU	HUMBUG
BEFFRU	BUFFER		RUMBLE	BGHOTU	BOUGHT
	REBUFF	BELMSU	UMBLES	BGIINT	BITING
BEFFTU	BUFFET	BELMTU	TUMBLE	BGILLY	GLIBLY
BEFHOO	BEHOOF	BELNNY	BLENNY	BGILNO	GOBLIN
BEFILO	FOIBLE	BELOOR	BOLERO	BGINOR	BORING
BEFLMU	FUMBLE	BELORT	BOLTER	BGINOX	BOXING
BEFLOO	BEFOOL	BELORU	ROUBLE	BGINTU	TUBING
BEFLOU	BEFOUL	BELORW	BLOWER	BGLNOO	OBLONG
BEFLRY	BELFRY		BOWLER	BGOORU	BURGOO
BEGGLO	BOGGLE	BELOSU	BLOUSE	BHILSU	BLUISH
BEGILO	OBLIGE		OBELUS	BHIOPS	BISHOP
BEGILT	GIBLET	BELOTT	BOTTLE	BHIOSY	BOYISH
BEGINN	BENIGN	BELOWZ	BLOWZE	BHLMUY	HUMBLY
BEGLNO	BELONG		BUTLER	BHRSUY	BRUSHY
BEGLNU	BUNGLE	BELRTY	TREBLY	BIIORV	VIBRIO

21

BIITTT	TITBIT	CCEIPT	PECTIC	CDEEIV	DEVICE
BIJOUX	BIJOUX	CCEKLO	COCKLE	CDEEJT	DEJECT
BIKNSU	BUSKIN	CCEKOP	COPECK	CDEEKN	NECKED
BILLNO	BILLON	CCEKOR	COCKER	CDEEKR	DECKER
BILLOW	BILLOW	CCEKOT	COCKET	CDEELL	CELLED
BILMNY	NIMBLY	CCENOS	SCONCE	CDEELU	CULDEE
BILMUY	BULIMY	CCHHIN	CHINCH	CDEENR	DECERN
BILNOS	LISBON	CCHHRU	CHURCH	CDEENT	DECENT
BILRTY	TRILBY	CCHILN	CLINCH	CDEERS	SCREED
BILSUY	BUSILY	CCHIOR	CHORIC	CDEERU	REDUCE
BIMNSU	NIMBUS	CCHIPU	HICCUP	CDEESU	SEDUCE
BIMSTU	SUBMIT	CCHLTU	CLUTCH	CDEETT	DETECT
BINNOR	INBORN		CULTCH	CDEFII	DEIFIC
BINNOU	BUNION	CCHNRU	CRUNCH	CDEFNU	FECUND
BINOOT	BONITO	CCHORS	SCORCH	CDEFOR	FORCED
BINORT	BRITON	CCHORT	CROTCH	CDEGLU	CUDGEL
BINOSS	BISSON	CCHORU	CROUCH	CDEGOR	CODGER
BIOOST	OBOIST	CCHOST	SCOTCH	CDEHIN	NICHED
BKMNUU	BUNKUM	CCHRTU	CRUTCH	CDEHNR	DRENCH
BLLORY	BROLLY	CCHSTU	SCUTCH	CDEHOU	DOUCHE
BLMOOY	BLOOMY	CCIILN	CLINIC	CDEIKP	PICKED
BLMOSY	SYMBOL	CCIINP	PICNIC	CDEIKR	DICKER
BLNOTU	UNBOLT	CCIIPR	PICRIC	CDEIKW	WICKED
BLOOSU	OBOLUS	CCIIRT	CITRIC	CDEIKY	DICKEY
BLOOTT	BLOTTO		CRITIC	CDEILO	DOCILE
BLOWYZ	BLOWZY	CCIISV	CIVICS	CDEIMR	DERMIC
BLSTUY	SUBTLY	CCILNO	CLONIC	CDEINR	CINDER
BMOORY	BROOMY	CCIMOS	COSMIC	CDEINU	INDUCE
BMOOTT	BOTTOM	CCIMRY	CYMRIC	CDEIOP	EPODIC
BMOOTY	TOMBOY	CCIOPT	COPTIC	CDEIOV	VOICED
BNNORU	UNBORN	CCIPRU	CUPRIC	CDEIPR	PRICED
BNOOST	BOSTON	CCIRSU	CIRCUS	CDEIPT	DEPICT
BNORSU	SUBORN	CCISTY	CYSTIC	CDEIRT	CREDIT
BNORTU	BURTON	CCKOOU	CUCKOO		DIRECT
BNORYY	BRYONY	CCLOTU	OCCULT	CDEKOR	CORKED
BNOSUW	SUN-BOW	CCNOOO	COCOON		DOCKER
BNOTTU	BUTTON	CCNORU	CONCUR	CDEKOT	DOCKET
BNOTUY	BOUNTY	CCOOOR	ROCOCO	CDEKRU	DUCKER
BOOPTY	POT-BOY	CCOPUY	OCCUPY	CDELOW	COWLED
BOORRW	BORROW	CCORSU	CROCUS	CDELRU	CURDLE
BORRUW	BURROW		SUCCOR		CURLED
BORSTU	ROBUST	CCOSTU	STUCCO	CDELTU	DULCET
BORTTU	TURBOT	CCSSUU	CUSCUS	CDEMOO	COMEDO
BSSSUY	BYSSUS	CDDDEO	CODDED	CDEMOY	COMEDY
CCCILY	CYCLIC	CDDEEI	DECIDE	CDENOR	CORNED
CCCOXY	COCCYX	CDDEEO	DECODE	CDENOS	SECOND
CCDEKO	COCKED	CDDEEU	DEDUCE	CDENSU	SECUND
CCDEOT	DECOCT		DEUCED	CDEORR	RECORD
CCEEHR	CRECHE	CDDELO	CODDLE	CDEOSU	ESCUDO
CCEEOR	COERCE	CDDELU	CUDDLE	CDERSU	CURSED
CCEHIL	CLICHÉ	CDDEOR	CORDED	CDERSY	DESCRY
CCEHIM	CHEMIC	CDDETU	DEDUCT	CDERUV	CURVED
CCEHIO	CHOICE	CDDLOY	CLODDY	CDFIOU	FUCOID
CCEHIT	HECTIC	CDEEER	DECREE	CDFIOY	CODIFY
CCEHLN	CLENCH		RECEDE	CDGIIN	DICING
CCEIIL	ICICLE	CDEEES	SECEDE	CDHIOR	ORCHID
CCEILR	CIRCLE	CDEEEX	EXCEED	CDIINT	INDICT
	CLERIC	CDEEFN	FENCED	CDIIOY	IDIOCY
CCEILT	CELTIC	CDEEFT	DEFECT	CDIISV	VISCID
CCEILY	CICELY	CDEEIN	EDENIC	CDILNO	CODLIN
CCEINS	SCENIC	CDEEIT	DECEIT	CDIMTU	DICTUM

CDINOO	CONOID	CEEKPR	PECKER	CEHINT	ETHNIC
CDINSY	SYNDIC	CEEKRY	CREEKY	CEHINV	CHEVIN
CDINTU	INDUCT	CEELOR	CREOLE	CEHIOR	COHEIR
CDISSU	DISCUS	CEELOU	COULEE		HEROIC
CDJNOU	JOCUND	CEELRT	TERCEL	CEHIPR	CERIPH
CDLLOY	COLDLY	CEELRV	CLEVER		CIPHER
CDLOUY	CLOUDY	CEELRW	CREWEL	CEHIRS	RICHES
CDNOOR	CONDOR	CEELRY	CELERY	CEHIRT	CITHER
	CORDON	CEELST	SELECT		THRICE
CDNORU	UNCORD	CEEMNT	CEMENT	CEHIST	ETHICS
CDOORT	DOCTOR	CEEMRR	MERCER	CEHKLU	HUCKLE
CEEEFL	FLEECE	CEENOR	ENCORE	CEHKOR	CHOKER
CEEEGN	EGENCE	CEENPS	SPENCE	CEHKOY	HOCKEY
CEEEGR	GREECE	CEENPT	PECTEN	CEHKST	SKETCH
CEEEHS	CHEESE	CEENRS	CENSER	CEHLOR	CHOLER
CEEENO	EOCENE		SCREEN	CEHLOT	CLOTHE
CEEERS	CREESE		SECERN	CEHMOR	CHROME
CEEFFO	COFFEE	CEENRT	CENTER	CEHNOS	CHOSEN
CEEFFT	EFFECT		CENTRE	CEHNQU	QUENCH
CEEFHL	FLÈCHE		RECENT	CEHNRT	TRENCH
CEEFIR	FIERCE		TENREC	CEHNRW	WRENCH
CEEFLY	FLEECY	CEEORV	CORVEE	CEHNST	STENCH
CEEFNN	FENNEC	CEEPRY	CREEPY	CEHNUU	EUNUCH
CEEFNR·	FENCER	CEEPTX	EXCEPT	CEHOOS	CHOOSE
CEEFSU	FESCUE		EXPECT	CEHORS	COSHER
CEEGIR	CIERGE	CEEPTY	ECTYPE	CEHORT	HECTOR
CEEGNO	CONGEE	CEERSS	RECESS		ROCHET
CEEHKL	HECKLE	CEERST	CERTES		TROCHE
CEEHKY	CHEEKY		RESECT	CEHOSU	CHOUSE
CEEHLN	ELENCH		SECRET	CEHPRY	CYPHER
CEEHLR	LECHER	CEERSU	CEREUS	CEHPSY	PSYCHE
CEEHMS	SCHEME		CERUSE	CEHRRY	CHERRY
CEEHNT	THENCE		RESCUE	CEHRTW	WRETCH
CEEHNW	WHENCE		SECURE	CEHRTY	CHERTY
CEEHOR	CHOREE	CEESSX	EXCESS	CEHSTY	CHESTY
	COHERE	CEESUX	EXCUSE		SCYTHE
	RE-ECHO	CEFFIO	OFFICE	CEHTTY	TETCHY
CEEHOS	ECHOES	CEFFOR	COFFER	CEHTVY	VETCHY
CEEHPS	SPEECH	CEFHIT	FETICH	CEIILT	ELICIT
CEEHQU	CHEQUE	CEFHNR	FRENCH	CEIINS	INCISE
CEEHRT	ETCHER	CEFIKL	FICKLE	CEIINT	INCITE
CEEHRU	EUCHRE	CEFINT	INFECT	CEIJNT	INJECT
CEEHRY	CHEERY	CEFIRR	FERRIC	CEIKKR	KICKER
	REECHY	CEFNOR	CONFER	CEIKLM	MICKLE
CEEHSW	ESCHEW	CEFORR	FORCER	CEIKLN	NICKEL
CEEHSY	CHEESY	CEFORS	FRESCO	CEIKLP	PICKLE
CEEIMT	EMETIC	CEFRUW	CURFEW	CEIKLS	SICKLE
CEEINN	NICENE	CEGGPU	EGG-CUP	CEIKLT	KELTIC
CEEINT	ENTICE	CEGHIO	CHIGOE		TICKLE
CEEINV	EVINCE	CEGHIR	CHIGRE	CEIKNS	SICKEN
CEEIPR	PIECER	CEGINR	CRINGE	CEIKOO	COOKIE
	PIERCE	CEGIST	GESTIC	CEIKPR	PICKER
	RECIPE	CEGLRY	CLERGY	CEIKPT	PICKET
CEEIPS	SPECIE	CEGNOR	CONGER	CEIKRW	WICKER
CEEIRS	CERISE	CEGNOT	COGENT	CEIKRY	CRIKEY
CEEIRT	CERITE	CEGNTY	CYGNET	CEIKTT	TICKET
	RECITE	CEGORR	GROCER	CEIKTW	WICKET
	TIERCE	CEHILN	LICHEN	CEILLO	COLLIE
CEEISX	EXCISE	CEHILS	CHISEL		OCELLI
CEEITX	EXCITE	CEHILT	ELTCHI	CEILNP	PENCIL
CEEJRT	REJECT	CEHINR	ENRICH	CEILNT	CLIENT

CEILNU	NUCLEI	CEKORT	ROCKET		ESCORT
CEILNY	NICELY	CEKOST	SOCKET		SCOTER
CEILOO	COOLIE	CEKPRU	PUCKER		SECTOR
CEILOP	POLICE	CEKRSU	SUCKER	CEORSU	COURSE
CEILOR	RECOIL	CEKRTU	TUCKER		SOURCE
CEILPS	SPLICE	CEKTTU	TUCKET	CEORTT	COTTER
CEILPV	PELVIC	CELLOT	COLLET	CEORTV	COVERT
CEILQU	CLIQUE	CELLRU	CULLER		VECTOR
CEILRS	SLICER	CELLTU	CULLET	CEORTX	CORTEX
CEILRT	RELICT	CELMNU	CULMEN	CEOSST	COSSET
CEILSU	SLUICE	CELMOP	COMPEL	CEPRSU	SPRUCE
CEIMNO	INCOME	CELMOY	COMELY	CERRSU	CURSER
CEIMOX	MEXICO	CELMSU	MUSCLE	CERSSY	CRESSY
CEIMPU	PUMICE	CELMUY	LYCEUM	CERSTU	CRUSET
CEIMRT	METRIC	CELNOR	CORNEL	CERTTU	CUTTER
CEIMRU	CERIUM	CELNOV	CLOVEN	CERTUV	CURVET
CEIMTY	ETYMIC	CELNRU	LUCERN	CESSTU	CESTUS
CEINOR	COINER	CELNTU	LUCENT	CFFHUY	CHUFFY
CEINOS	CO-SINE	CELOOR	COOLER	CFFILY	CLIFFY
CEINOT	NOETIC	CELOOT	OCELOT	CFFINO	COFFIN
	NOTICE	CELOPU	COUPLE	CFFOTU	CUT-OFF
CEINOV	NOVICE	CELORS	CLOSER	CFHILN	FLINCH
CEINPR	PRINCE	CELORT	COLTER	CFHILT	FLITCH
CEINQU	CINQUE	CELORU	COLURE	CFIIST	FISTIC
	QUINCE	CELORV	CLOVER	CFILOR	FROLIC
CEINRT	CRETIN	CELOST	CLOSET	CFIMOR	FORMIC
CEINRW	WINCER	CELOTY	COTYLE	CFIMOT	COMFIT
CEINST	INCEST	CELPTY	YCLEPT	CFISTU	FUSTIC
	INSECT	CELPUU	CUPULE	CFLPUU	CUPFUL
CEINSU	INCUSE	CELRRU	CURLER	CFRSUY	SCURFY
CEINTY	NICETY	CELRTU	CULTER	CGGLOY	CLOGGY
CEINWY	WINCEY		CUTLER	CGHHOU	CHOUGH
CEIOOZ	EOZOIC	CELRUU	CURULE	CGHIOT	GOTHIC
CEIOPR	COPIER	CELRUV	CULVER	CGHLOU	CLOUGH
CEIOPT	POETIC	CELRUW	CURLEW	CGILNY	CLINGY
CEIORR	CORRIE	CELTTU	CUTLET	CGIMNO	COMING
CEIORT	EROTIC		CUTTLE		GNOMIC
CEIOTX	EXOTIC	CEMORR	CREMOR	CGIMNY	GYMNIC
CEIPPT	PEPTIC	CEMOSY	CYMOSE	CGINOP	COPING
CEIPRS	PRÉCIS	CEMRTU	RECTUM	CGINOV	COVING
CEIPSS	PISCES	CENOOR	CEROON	CGINRY	CRYING
CEIPST	SEPTIC	CENOPU	POUNCE	CGNOOU	CONGOU
CEIPTY	ETYPIC	CENORR	CORNER	CHIILL	CHILLI
CEIQRU	CIRQUE	CENORS	CENSOR	CHIILT	LITHIC
CEIRSS	CRISES	CENORT	CORNET	CHIINT	CHITIN
CEIRSU	CRUISE	CENOST	CENTOS	CHIKNY	CHINKY
CEIRUV	CRUIVE	CENOVX	CONVEX	CHILLY	CHILLY
CEISSU	CUISSE	CENOVY	CONVEY	CHILRY	RICHLY
CEJKOY	JOCKEY	CENSSU	CENSUS	CHIMNY	HYMNIC
CEJOOS	JOCOSE	CENSTY	ENCYST	CHIMRS	CHRISM
CEKKSY	KECKSY	CEOOPR	COOPER		SMIRCH
CEKLOR	LOCKER	CEOOTY	COYOTE	CHIMSS	SCHISM
CEKLOT	LOCKET	CEOPPR	COPPER	CHIMTY	MYTHIC
CEKLSU	SUCKLE	CEOPRS	CORPSE	CHINOP	CHOPIN
CEKMOR	MOCKER	CEOPRU	RECOUP		PHONIC
CEKNOR	CONKER	CEOQTU	COQUET	CHINOT	CHITON
	RECKON	CEORRS	SCORER	CHINRU	URCHIN
CEKOOR	COOKER	CEORRT	RECTOR	CHINTZ	CHINTZ
CEKOPT	POCKET	CEORST	CORSET	CHIOPR	ORPHIC
CEKORR	CORKER		CORTES	CHIORS	ORCHIS
	ROCKER		COSTER	CHIPPY	CHIPPY

CHIPRY	CHIRPY	CIOORT	OCTROI	CRSUVY	SCURVY
CHIPSY	PHYSIC	CIOPRT	TROPIC	DDDEEW	WEDDED
CHIPTY	PITCHY	CIOPST	OPTICS	DDDEIL	DIDDLE
CHIQTU	QUITCH	CIORSU	CURIOS		LIDDED
CHIRST	CHRIST	CIORTV	VICTOR	DDDEOP	PODDED
CHIRUZ	ZURICH	CIPPSU	CIPPUS	DDDEOR	DODDER
CHISST	SCHIST	CIPRST	SCRIPT	DDEEER	REEDED
CHISTT	STITCH	CIPRSY	CRISPY	DDEEES	SEEDED
CHISTW	SWITCH	CIRRSU	CIRRUS	DDEEFN	DEFEND
CHITTW	TWITCH	CIRSTT	STRICT	DDEEGR	DREDGE
CHLMOO	MOLOCH	CIRSTU	CITRUS	DDEEIL	MEDDLE
CHLOOS	SCHOOL		RUSTIC	DDEEIN	INDEED
CHLOSU	SLOUCH	CISSTU	CISTUS	DDEEIR	DERIDE
CHLOTT	T-CLOTH	CKLNOU	UNLOCK	DDEELM	MEDDLE
CHMMUY	CHUMMY	CKLOPU	LOCK-UP	DDEELP	PEDDLE
CHMOOR	CHROMO	CKLPUY	PLUCKY	DDEELR	REDDLE
CHMSTU	SMUTCH	CKNORU	UNCORK	DDEELU	DELUDE
CHNOOP	PONCHO	CKOSST	STOCKS	DDEENP	DEPEND
CHNPUY	PUNCHY	CKOSTY	STOCKY	DDEENR	REDDEN
CHOORT	COHORT	CKRSTU	STRUCK	DDEENU	DENUDE
CHOOSY	CHOOSY	CLLOOP	COLLOP	DDEERT	TEDDER
CHOPPY	CHOPPY	CLLOOY	COOLLY	DDEFIL	FIDDLE
CHORSU	CHORUS	CLLORS	SCROLL	DDEFLU	FUDDLE
CHORWY	CHOWRY	CLMNOU	COLUMN	DDEFOR	FODDER
CHOTUY	TOUCHY	CLMOPY	COMPLY	DDEGGO	DOGGED
CIIMSV	CIVISM	CLMPUY	CLUMPY	DDEGOR	DODGER
CIIMTV	VICTIM	CLMSUY	CLUMSY	DDEGRU	DRUDGE
CIINOR	IRONIC	CLNOOY	COLONY	DDEHIN	HIDDEN
CIINRT	NITRIC	CLNOSU	CONSUL	DDEHIS	EDDISH
CIIRSS	CRISIS	CLNRUU	UNCURL	DDEHLU	HUDDLE
CIIRTV	VITRIC	CLOORU	COLOUR	DDEHOO	HOODED
CIKLSY	SICKLY	CLOSTU	LOCUST	DDEIIO	IODIDE
CIKNYZ	ZINCKY	CLOSTY	COSTLY	DDEIIV	DIVIDE
CIKOSY	YOICKS	CLOTTY	CLOTTY	DDEILM	MIDDLE
CIKRTY	TRICKY	CLPRUU	UPCURL	DDEILP	PIDDLE
CIKSTY	STICKY	CLRTUY	CURTLY	DDEILR	RIDDLE
CILLOU	LOCULI	CLSSUU	SULCUS	DDEIMN	MIDDEN
CILLSU	CULLIS	CLSTUU	CULTUS		MINDED
CILMUU	CUMULI	CMMNOO	COMMON	DDEIOV	DEVOID
CILNOU	UNCOIL	CMMRUY	CRUMMY	DDELMU	MUDDLE
CILNTU	INCULT	CMMSUY	SCUMMY	DDELNO	NODDLE
CILOPU	UPCOIL	CMOOSS	COSMOS	DDELOO	DOODLE
CILOPY	POLICY	CMOOSW	MOSCOW	DDELOT	TODDLE
CILORT	LICTOR	CMOSTU	CUSTOM	DDELPU	PUDDLE
CILOSY	COSILY	CMOSUU	MUCOUS	DDELRU	RUDDLE
CILOYZ	COZILY	CMOSUY	CYMOUS	DDEMOO	DOOMED
CILSUY	SLUICY	CMSTUU	SCUTUM	DDENOS	SODDEN
CIMMNU	CUMMIN	CNOOPU	COUPON	DDENRU	DUNDER
CIMMOT	COMMIT	CNOORT	CROTON	DDENSU	SUDDEN
CIMMOX	COMMIX	CNOOTT	COTTON	DDEOOW	WOODED
CIMORU	CORIUM	CNOOVY	CONVOY	DDERRU	RUDDER
CIMOTY	COMITY	CNOTUY	COUNTY	DDHOSY	SHODDY
	MYOTIC	COOPWX	COW-POX	DDINOO	DIODON
CIMPRS	SCRIMP	COPPRY	CROPPY	DDIORS	SORDID
CIMSTY	MYSTIC	COPRSU	CORPUS	DDIOTY	ODDITY
CIMSUV	VISCUM	CORTUY	OUTCRY	DDLPUY	PUDDLY
CINNOU	NUNCIO	COSSTU	CUSTOS	DEEEFR	FEEDER
CINORT	CITRON	CPRSUY	CYPRUS	DEEEGR	DEGREE
CINORZ	ZIRCON	CRRSUY	SCURRY	DEEEJR	JEREED
CINOST	TOCSIN	CRSTUY	CRUSTY	DEEEKL	KEELED
CINOSU	COUSIN		CURTSY	DEEELN	NEEDLE

DEEELT	DELETE		NETTED	DEGLOR	LODGER
DEEEMR	REDEEM		TENTED	DEGLOV	GLOVED
DEEENP	DEEPEN	DEENTX	EXTEND	DEGLSU	SLUDGE
DEEENV	VENDEE	DEENUV	VENDUE	DEGMSU	SMUDGE
DEEERW	WEEDER	DEEOPS	DEPOSE	DEGNRU	GERUND
DEEFGL	FLEDGE	DEEORT	TEREDO	DEGOST	STODGE
DEEFIL	DEFILE	DEEOTV	DEVOTE	DEGRTU	TRUDGE
DEEFIN	DEFINE	DEEOXY	OX-EYED	DEHILS	SHIELD
DEEFIR	DEFIER	DEEPRU	PERDUE	DEHINO	HOIDEN
DEEFNR	FENDER	DEEPSY	SPEEDY	DEHINR	HINDER
DEEGGL	LEGGED	DEEPTU	DEPUTE	DEHIPP	HIPPED
DEEGGP	PEGGED	DEERST	DESERT	DEHIRT	DITHER
DEEGHR	HEDGER	DEERSV	VERSED	DEHKOO	HOOKED
DEEGLN	LEGEND	DEERTX	DEXTER	DEHKSU	HUSKED
DEEGLP	PLEDGE	DEESTT	DETEST	DEHLOR	HOLDER
DEEGLR	LEDGER	DEESTV	DEVEST	DEHLRU	HURDLE
DEEGLS	SLEDGE		VESTED	DEHMOT	METHOD
DEEGLU	DELUGE	DEFFIR	DIFFER	DEHMPU	HUMPED
DEEGNR	GENDER	DEFFLU	DUFFEL	DEHNOR	HORNED
DEEGNU	DENGUE	DEFFNO	OFFEND	DEHNOY	HOYDEN
DEEGRY	GREEDY	DEFFRU	DUFFER	DEHNSU	UNSHED
DEEHLM	HELMED	DEFGIT	FIDGET	DEHORT	DEHORT
DEEHTW	THEWED		GIFTED		RED-HOT
DEEILS	DIESEL	DEFHOO	HOOFED	DEHRSW	SHREWD
DEEILY	EYELID	DEFINN	FINNED	DEIINO	IODINE
DEEIMP	IMPEDE	DEFINR	FINDER	DEIINS	INSIDE
DEEIMS	DEMISE		FRIEND	DEIINT	INDITE
DEEINR	DENIER	DEFIRV	FERVID	DEIINV	DIVINE
	NEREID	DEFKOR	FORKED	DEIIOZ	IODIZE
DEEINV	ENDIVE	DEFLNO	ENFOLD	DEIIRS	IRISED
	VEINED		FONDLE	DEIKLN	KINDLE
DEEIPS	ESPIED	DEFLOR	FOLDER	DEIKLT	KILTED
DEEIRS	DESIRE	DEFLTY	DEFTLY	DEIKNP	PINKED
	RESIDE	DEFMOR	DEFORM	DEIKNY	KIDNEY
DEEIRT	DIETER	DEFNRU	REFUND	DEILLM	MILLED
DEEIRV	DERIVE	DEFOOT	FOOTED	DEILLU	ILLUDE
DEEISV	DEVISE	DEFORT	FORTED	DEILMN	MILDEN
DEEJSS	JESSED	DEFRRU	FURRED	DEILMP	DIMPLE
DEELMY	MEDLEY	DEFTTU	TUFTED	DEILMS	MISLED
DEELNR	LENDER	DEGGIN	EDGING	DEILMW	MILDEW
DEELNY	NEEDLY	DEGGIR	DIGGER	DEILNN	LINDEN
DEELPY	DEEPLY	DEGGIW	WIGGED	DEILNT	DENTIL
DEELRV	DELVER	DEGGOR	DOGGER	DEILOP	DIPLOE
DEELRW	WELDER	DEGGRU	GRUDGE	DEILPP	LIPPED
DEELST	ELDEST		RUGGED	DEILPS	DISPEL
DEEMNO	OMENED	DEGGRY	DREGGY	DEILPX	DIPLEX
DEEMNR	MENDER	DEGILM	MID-LEG	DEILRS	SLIDER
DEEMNT	DEMENT	DEGILN	DINGLE	DEILRV	DRIVEL
DEEMRU	DEMURE	DEGILR	GILDER	DEILRW	WILDER
DEEMRY	REMEDY		GIRDLE	DEILTT	TITLED
DEENOP	DEPONE	DEGINN	ENDING	DEILTU	DILUTE
DEENOT	DENOTE	DEGINR	ENGIRD	DEILWY	WIDELY
DEENPX	EXPEND		RINGED		WIELDY
DEENRR	RENDER	DEGINS	DESIGN	DEIMMR	DIMMER
DEENRS	SENDER	DEGINW	WINGED	DEIMMU	MEDIUM
DEENRT	TENDER	DEGINY	DINGEY	DEIMNO	MONIED
DEENRU	ENDURE	DEGIRR	GIRDER	DEIMNP	IMPEND
DEENRV	NERVED	DEGIST	DIGEST	DEIMNR	MINDER
	VENDER	DEGLNO	GOLDEN		REMIND
DEENSW	SWEDEN	DEGLNU	GULDEN	DEIMRS	DERMIS
DEENTT	DETENT		LUNGED	DEIMTU	TEDIUM

DEINNR	DINNER	DENOPR	PONDER
DEINNT	INDENT	DENORT	RODENT
	INTEND	DENORU	UNDOER
DEINNU	UNDINE	DENORV	VENDOR
DEINOT	DITONE	DENORW	WONDER
DEINPS	SPINED	DENORY	YONDER
DEINPU	UNIPED	DENOTW	WONTED
DEINRT	TINDER	DENRSU	SUNDER
DEINRV	DRIVEN	DENRTY	TRENDY
DEINRW	WINDER	DENSUU	UNUSED
DEINTU	UNITED	DENSUW	SUN-DEW
DEIOOR	OROIDE	DENSYY	SYDNEY
DEIOPR	PERIOD	DEOORT	ROOTED
DEIORT	EDITOR	DEOORV	OVERDO
	TIE-ROD	DEOPRT	DEPORT
DEIORV	DEVOIR	DEOPRW	POWDER
	VOIDER	DEOPST	DESPOT
DEIPPR	DIPPER	DEOPSU	PSEUDO
DEIPRS	SPIDER	DEORRU	ORDURE
	SPIRED	DEORRV	DROVER
DEIPSU	UPSIDE	DEORSW	DROWSE
DEIPTT	PITTED	DEORTU	DETOUR
DEIRRV	DRIVER	DEORUV	DEVOUR
DEIRST	STRIDE	DEOSUX	EXODUS
DEIRSV	DIVERS	DEOTTU	DUETTO
DEIRTV	DIVERT	DEOTUV	DEVOUT
DEISST	DESIST	DEPRUY	DUPERY
DEISSU	DISUSE	DEPTUY	DEPUTY
DEISTV	DIVEST	DERSSU	DURESS
DEITTW	WITTED	DERSSY	DRESSY
DEKNOY	DONKEY	DERSTU	DUSTER
DEKSTU	TUSKED	DFGIIR	FRIGID
DELLOP	POLLED	DFGILU	FULGID
DELLOU	DUELLO	DFIINY	NIDIFY
DELLWY	LEWDLY	DFIIRT	TRIFID
DELMNO	DOLMEN	DFILNO	INFOLD
DELMOR	MOLDER	DFILOR	FLORID
DELMOS	SELDOM	DFIMOY	MODIFY
DELMOU	MODULE	DFIRTY	DRIFTY
DELMOY	MELODY	DFLNOU	UNFOLD
DELMPU	PLUMED	DFLNOY	FONDLY
DELNOO	NOODLE	DFOORX	OXFORD
DELNOR	RONDEL	DGGNOU	DUGONG
DELNOT	DOLENT	DGGOPU	PUG-DOG
DELNOU	NODULE	DGHIIN	HIDING
DELNUY	NUDELY	DGHINY	DINGHY
DELOOP	POODLE	DGHOUY	DOUGHY
DELOPY	DEPLOY	DGIINN	DINING
DELORS	SOLDER	DGIINO	INDIGO
DELOSU	SOULED	DGIINR	RIDING
DELPUX	DUPLEX	DGIINS	SIDING
DELRUY	RUDELY	DGIINV	DIVING
DEMNOR	MODERN	DGINOT	DOTING
DEMORR	DORMER	DGINOU	GUIDON
DEMORW	WORMED	DGINRU	DURING
DEMOST	MODEST		UNGIRD
DEMRRU	MURDER	DGIOTW	GODWIT
DENNOT	TENDON	DGIRTU	TURGID
DENNOU	UNDONE	DGLOOY	GOODLY
DENOOS	NODOSE	DGLSUY	SLUDGY
DENOOW	WOODEN	DGNOOS	GODSON
		DGNORU	GROUND
		DGOSTY	STODGY
		DHIIPS	HISPID
		DHILOS	OLDISH
		DHIMOS	MODISH
		DHINOO	HINDOO
		DHIORR	HORRID
		DHLOPU	UPHOLD
		DHLOSU	SHOULD
		DHNOOU	UNHOOD
		DHNOSU	UNSHOD
		DHORSU	SHROUD
		DHORTU	DROUTH
		DIILMP	LIMPID
		DIILQU	LIQUID
		DIILST	DISTIL
		DIILTY	TIDILY
		DIIMNU	INDIUM
		DIIMOS	IODISM
		DIIMOU	OIDIUM
		DIIMTY	DIMITY
		DIINOP	DIPNOI
		DIKLNY	KINDLY
		DIKNNU	UNKIND
		DILLMY	MILDLY
		DILLWY	WILDLY
		DILMPY	DIMPLY
		DILNNU	DUNLIN
		DILNOO	IDOLON
		DILOSS	DOSSIL
		DILOST	STOLID
		DILOXY	XYLOID
		DIMNOO	DOMINO
		DIMNSU	NUDISM
		DIMOPU	PODIUM
		DIMOSU	SODIUM
		DIMOSW	WISDOM
		DINNUW	UNWIND
		DINOOR	INDOOR
		DINORU	DURION
		DINOSW	DISOWN
		DINOWW	WINDOW
		DINPTU	PUNDIT
		DINPUW	WIND-UP
		DINSTU	NUDIST
		DINTUY	NUDITY
			UNTIDY
		DIOOPS	ISOPOD
		DIOOSU	ODIOUS
		DIOPRT	TORPID
			TRIPOD
		DIORRT	TORRID
		DIOSTU	STUDIO
		DIPRTU	PUTRID
		DIPSTU	STUPID
		DJNNOO	DONJON
		DKOOOO	KOODOO
		DKORSY	DROSKY
		DLLOOP	DOLLOP
		DLLORY	LORDLY
		DLLOUY	LOUDLY

27

DLMOUY	MOULDY	EEFLLO	FELLOE
DLNNOO	LONDON	EEFLLR	FELLER
DLNOSU	UNSOLD	EEFLNN	FENNEL
DLNOTU	UNTOLD	EEFLNS	FLENSE
DLNUUY	UNDULY	EEFLRU	FERULE
DLOORU	DOLOUR	EEFLRX	REFLEX
DMNOOY	MONODY	EEFLRY	FREELY
DMOOSY	SODOMY	EEFLTT	FETTLE
DNORTU	ROTUND	EEFLUY	EYEFUL
	UNTROD	EEFMNO	FOEMEN
DNOSUZ	ZOUNDS	EEFNRU	UNFREE
DNRSUY	SUNDRY	EEFPRR	PREFER
DOOOOV	VOODOO	EEFPTY	TEPEFY
DOPRSY	DROPSY	EEFRRT	FERRET
DORRTY	DRY-ROT	EEFRST	FESTER
DORSSY	DROSSY	EEFRSU	REFUSE
DORSWY	DROWSY	EEFRTT	FETTER
DRSTUY	STURDY	EEFRTU	REFUTE
DRSUYY	DYSURY	EEGGLR	EGGLER
EEEFFT	EFFETE	EEGGOR	GEORGE
EEEFLR	FEELER	EEGGRY	EGGERY
EEEFRR	REEFER	EEGIMR	ÉMIGRÉ
EEEFRZ	FREEZE		RÉGIME
EEEGMR	EMERGE	EEGINN	ENGINE
EEEHST	SEETHE	EEGINS	SEEING
EEEHWZ	WHEEZE	EEGIRV	GRIEVE
EEEJRR	JEERER	EEGLMU	LEGUME
EEEKPR	KEEPER	EEGLNT	GENTLE
EEEKRS	SEEKER	EEGLRT	REGLET
EEELNV	ELEVEN	EEGMNR	GERMEN
EEELPR	PEELER	EEGMRR	MERGER
EEELSS	LESSEE	EEGNOP	PONGEE
EEELSV	SLEEVE	EEGNOR	ENGORE
EEELTY	EYELET	EEGNOX	EXOGEN
EEEMRS	SEEMER	EEGNRT	REGENT
EEEMST	ESTEEM	EEGNRY	ENERGY
EEEMTU	ÉMEUTE		GREENY
EEENRS	SERENE	EEGNST	GENTES
EEENRT	ENTRÉE	EEGRRT	REGRET
EEENRV	VENEER	EEGRRV	VERGER
EEENSS	ESSENE	EEGRSS	EGRESS
EEENSZ	SNEEZE	EEGRSY	GEYSER
EEEOPP	EPOPEE	EEGRTT	GETTER
EEEPPR	PEEPER	EEHINR	HEREIN
EEEPRW	WEEPER		INHERE
EEERRV	REVERE	EEHINT	THEINE
EEERSV	SEVERE	EEHIRT	EITHER
EEERTT	TERETE	EEHITV	THIEVE
EEERVW	WEEVER	EEHKLS	SHEKEL
EEESTT	SETTEE	EEHLMT	HELMET
EEESTV	STEEVE	EEHLPR	HELPER
EEFFOT	TOFFEE	EEHLSV	SHELVE
EEFFSU	EFFUSE	EEHMNP	HEMPEN
EEFGRU	REFUGE	EEHMUX	EXHUME
EEFHIR	HEIFER	EEHNOR	HEREON
EEFHOR	HEREOF	EEHNPW	NEPHEW
EEFILN	FELINE	EEHNRT	NETHER
EEFILR	RELIEF		THRENE
EEFINR	FERINE	EEHNSY	SHEENY
	REFINE	EEHORS	HEROES
EEFIRZ	FRIEZE	EEHORT	HERETO

EEHPRS	HERPES
	SPHERE
EEHRSS	SHEERS
EEHRSY	HERESY
EEHRTT	TETHER
EEHRTW	WETHER
EEHSST	THESES
EEHWYY	WHEYEY
EEHWYZ	WHEEZY
EEIJNN	JINNEE
EEIKLP	KELPIE
EEILLV	VIELLE
EEILNS	ENSILE
	SENILE
EEILRR	RELIER
EEILRS	RESILE
EEILRV	RELIVE
	REVILE
EEILTV	LEVITE
EEILVW	WEEVIL
EEIMNR	ERMINE
EEIMPR	EMPIRE
EEIMSS	MISSEE
EEIMST	SEMITE
EEINPR	REPINE
EEINQU	EQUINE
EEINRS	SEINER
EEINRT	ENTIRE
EEINRV	ENVIER
EEIORS	SOIRÉE
EEIPRX	EXPIRE
EEIPTT	PETITE
EEIPTW	PEEWIT
EEIRRT	RETIRE
EEIRSS	SERIES
EEIRSV	REVISE
EEIRSZ	SEIZER
EEIRVV	REVIVE
EEIRVW	REVIEW
	VIEWER
EEJJNU	JEJUNE
EEJNNT	JENNET
EEJRST	JESTER
EEJRSY	JERSEY
EEJSSW	JEWESS
EEKLMY	MEEKLY
EEKLNN	KENNEL
EEKLNR	KERNEL
EEKLNY	KEENLY
EEKLSY	SLEEKY
EEKLTT	KETTLE
EEKLWY	WEEKLY
EEKMRS	KERMES
EEKORV	REVOKE
EEKPPU	UPKEEP
EEKPRU	PERUKE
EEKRSW	SKEWER
EEKRSY	KERSEY
EELLPT	PELLET
EELLRS	SELLER
EELLRT	TELLER

EELMOT	OMELET	EENRTU	NEUTER	EFHIRS	FISHER
EELMPT	TEMPLE		TENURE	EFHISS	FISHES
EELMRT	MELTER		TUREEN	EFHIST	FETISH
EELMRU	RELUME	EENRTV	VENTER	EFHLSY	FLESHY
EELMRY	MERELY	EENRTX	EXTERN		SHELFY
EELMSY	SEEMLY	EENRVY	VENERY	EFHORT	FOTHER
EELMTT	METTLE	EENTTX	EXTENT	EFIINT	FINITE
EELMTY	MEETLY	EEOPRS	REPOSE	EFILLR	FILLER
EELNNT	LENTEN	EEOPRU	EUROPE		REFILL
EELNPS	SPLEEN	EEOPSX	EXPOSE	EFILLT	FILLET
EELNRT	RELENT	EEOPTU	TOUPEE	EFILNT	INFELT
EELNSS	LENSES	EEORST	STEREO	EFILNY	FINELY
	LESSEN	EEORSV	SOEVER	EFILOS	FILOSE
EELNST	NESTLE	EEOSST	SETOSE	EFILPR	PILFER
EELNTT	NETTLE	EEPPPR	PEPPER	EFILRR	RIFLER
EELNVY	EVENLY	EEPPST	STEPPE	EFILRT	FILTER
EELOPP	PEOPLE	EEPRST	PESTER		LIFTER
EELOVV	EVOLVE	EEPRSU	PERUSE		TRIFLE
EELPRT	PETREL	EEPRSV	VESPER	EFILRU	IREFUL
EELPST	PESTLE	EEPRTU	REPUTE	EFILRY	RIFELY
EELPSY	SLEEPY	EEPRTW	PEWTER	EFILST	ITSELF
EELQSU	SEQUEL	EEPRTX	EXPERT		STIFLE
EELRSS	LESSER	EEPSTT	SEPTET	EFILSU	FUSILE
EELRTT	LETTER	EEPSTY	STEEPY	EFILTU	FUTILE
EELRTW	WELTER	EEPSWY	SWEEPY	EFILWY	WIFELY
EELSSV	SELVES	EERRSV	SERVER	EFILZZ	FIZZLE
	VESSEL	EERRTU	URETER	EFINNR	FINNER
EELSTT	SETTLE	EERRTV	REVERT	EFINRY	FINERY
EELSTY	SLEETY	EERSSV	SÈVRES	EFINST	INFEST
	STEELY	EERSTT	SETTER	EFINSU	INFUSE
EELSYZ	SLEEZY		STREET	EFIPRX	PREFIX
EELTVV	VELVET		TESTER	EFIRST	SIFTER
EELTVW	TWELVE	EERSTU	RETUSE		STRIFE
EEMNOR	MOREEN	EERSTY	YESTER	EFIRTT	FITTER
EEMNOY	YEOMEN	EERSVW	SWERVE	EFIRTY	FERITY
EEMNSS	MENSES	EERTTT	TETTER	EFIRVY	VERIFY
EEMNTU	UNMEET	EERTUY	TUYÈRE	EFLLOW	FELLOW
EEMNYZ	ENZYME	EERTVX	VERTEX	EFLLRU	FULLER
EEMOPT	METOPE	EESSTT	SESTET	EFLMSY	MYSELF
EEMORT	METEOR		TSETSE	EFLNNU	FUNNEL
	REMOTE	EESTTU	SUTTEE	EFLNOY	FELONY
EEMORV	REMOVE	EESTTX	SEXTET	EFLNTU	FLUENT
EEMPRT	TEMPER	EFFGIY	EFFIGY		UNFELT
EEMPRY	EMPERY	EFFGOR	GOFFER	EFLORT	FLORET
EEMPTX	EXEMPT	EFFLMU	MUFFLE	EFLORW	FLOWER
EEMRSU	RESUME	EFFLRU	RUFFLE		FOWLER
EENNPR	PENNER	EFFLUX	EFFLUX	EFLORX	FLEXOR
EENNRT	RENNET	EFFORT	EFFORT	EFLOUW	WOEFUL
EENNSU	UNSEEN	EFFOST	OFFSET	EFLPRU	PURFLE
EENNUV	UNEVEN		SET-OFF	EFLRUU	RUEFUL
EENNUY	ENNUYÉ	EFFPRU	PUFFER	EFLRUX	REFLUX
EENOPR	OPENER	EFFRSU	SUFFER	EFLSUU	USEFUL
	REOPEN	EFGINR	FINGER	EFMNOT	FOMENT
EENOPT	POTEEN		FRINGE	EFMORR	FORMER
EENORW	ERENOW	EFGIRU	FIGURE		REFORM
EENOSV	VENOSE	EFGLNU	ENGULF	EFMTUY	TUMEFY
EENPRT	REPENT	EFGLOR	GOLFER	EFNORZ	FROZEN
EENRRT	RENTER	EFGOOR	FOREGO	EFNOST	SOFTEN
EENRST	RESENT	EFGORR	FORGER	EFNRTU	TURFEN
EENRSU	ENSURE	EFGORT	FORGET	EFNRYZ	FRENZY
EENRTT	TENTER	EFHILS	ELFISH	EFOORR	ROOFER

29

EFOORT	FOOTER	EGILRS	GRILSE		URGENT
EFORRU	FURORE	EGILRU	LIGURE	EGNRTY	GENTRY
EFORRV	FERVOR	EGILST	LEGIST	EGOORV	GROOVE
EFORST	FOREST	EGIMMR	MEGRIM	EGOOST	STOOGE
	FOSTER	EGIMOS	EGOISM	EGOPPT	PEG-TOP
EFOSTU	FOETUS	EGINNS	ENSIGN	EGORRW	GROWER
EFRTTY	FRETTY	EGINOP	PIGEON	EGORSS	OGRESS
EFRTUU	FUTURE	EGINOR	IGNORE	EGORSU	GROUSE
EFSTTU	FUSTET		REGION		RUGOSE
EGGGIL	GIGGLE	EGINOW	WIGEON	EGORSY	GYROSE
EGGGLO	GOGGLE	EGINRR	RINGER	EGPRRU	PURGER
EGGGLU	GUGGLE	EGINRS	RESIGN	EGPRSU	SPURGE
EGGGNO	EGG-NOG		SIGNER	EGRTTU	GUTTER
EGGHIL	HIGGLE		SINGER	EGSSTU	GUSSET
EGGIJL	JIGGLE	EGINSS	GNEISS	EHHIRT	HITHER
EGGIJR	JIGGER	EGINST	INGEST	EHHNPY	HYPHEN
EGGILO	LOGGIE		SIGNET	EHHRST	THRESH
EGGILT	GIGLET	EGINSU	GENIUS	EHIJSW	JEWISH
EGGINR	GINGER	EGINSW	SEWING	EHIKRS	SHRIEK
	NIGGER		SWINGE		SHRIKE
EGGIRR	RIGGER	EGINTW	TWINGE	EHILMO	ELOHIM
EGGJLO	JOGGLE	EGIOPR	PORGIE	EHILRS	RELISH
EGGJLU	JUGGLE	EGIORS	ORGIES	EHILRT	HITLER
EGGJOR	JOGGER	EGIORT	GOITER	EHILSV	ELVISH
EGGLOT	TOGGLE		GOITRE	EHIMMS	IMMESH
EGGLRU	GURGLE	EGIOST	EGOIST	EHIMNR	MENHIR
	LUGGER	EGIPPR	GRIPPE	EHIMNU	INHUME
EGGNTU	NUGGET	EGIRSU	GUISER	EHIMRT	HERMIT
EGGORT	GORGET		REGIUS	EHIMRU	HUMERI
EGGRTU	TUGGER			EHIMST	THEISM
EGHHIR	HIGHER	EGJLNU	JUNGLE	EHINRS	SHINER
EGHHIT	EIGHTH	EGLLTU	GULLET		SHRINE
	HEIGHT	EGLNNU	GUNNEL	EHINRW	WHINER
EGHILS	SLEIGH	EGLNOU	LOUNGE	EHINSW	NEWISH
EGHITW	WEIGHT	EGLNPU	PLUNGE	EHINTW	WHITEN
EGHITY	EIGHTY	EGLNTU	GLUTEN	EHINTZ	ZENITH
EGHLMP	PHLEGM	EGLNTY	GENTLY	EHIOPT	OPHITE
EGHLNT	LENGTH	EGLNUU	UNGLUE	EHIORS	HOSIER
EGHLUY	HUGELY	EGLOPR	PROLEG	EHIORT	HERIOT
EGHMMO	MEGOHM	EGLOPS	GOSPEL	EHIPRS	PERISH
EGHNOU	ENOUGH	EGLORV	GLOVER		RESHIP
EGHNRU	HUNGER		GROVEL		SERIPH
EGHOPR	GOPHER	EGLORW	GLOWER	EHIRSV	SHIVER
EGHOTT	GHETTO	EGLOUY	EULOGY		SHRIVE
EGHRSU	GUSHER	EGLTTU	GUTTLE	EHIRSW	WISHER
EGIILL	GILLIE	EGLUZZ	GUZZLE	EHIRTT	HITTER
EGIIMN	GEMINI	EGMNOR	MONGER		TITHER
EGIINT	IGNITE	EGMNTU	NUTMEG	EHIRTV	THRIVE
EGIITW	TIE-WIG	EGMORU	MORGUE	EHIRTW	WITHER
EGIJLN	JINGLE	EGNNOO	NON-EGO		WRITHE
EGIKNP	PEKING	EGNNRU	GUNNER	EHIRTZ	ZITHER
EGILLR	GRILLE	EGNOOR	OREGON	EHISST	THESIS
EGILLU	LIGULE	EGNOPS	SPONGE	EHISTT	THEIST
EGILMN	MINGLE	EGNORV	GOVERN	EHISTW	WHITES
EGILMP	MEGILP	EGNORY	ERYNGO	EHJOPS	JOSEPH
EGILMT	GIMLET		GROYNE	EHKOOR	HOOKER
EGILNO	LEGION	EGNOTT	GOTTEN	EHLLSY	SHELLY
EGILNR	LINGER	EGNOTU	TONGUE	EHLMOP	PHLOEM
EGILNS	SINGLE	EGNOXY	OXYGEN	EHLMOY	HOMELY
EGILNT	TINGLE	EGNPSU	SPUNGE	EHLMTY	METHYL
EGILPT	PIGLET	EGNPUX	EXPUGN	EHLNOP	HOLPEN
		EGNRTU	GURNET		

EHLOPP	HOPPLE
EHLORW	HOWLER
EHLOST	HOSTEL
EHLOSU	HOUSEL
EHLOSV	SHOVEL
EHLOTW	HOWLET
	THOWEL
EHLRRU	HURLER
EHLRTU	HURTLE
EHLSTU	HUSTLE
EHLSVY	SHELVY
EHMMRU	HUMMER
EHMORT	MOTHER
EHMRRY	RHYMER
EHMRUY	RHEUMY
EHNORR	HORNER
EHNORT	HORNET
	THRONE
EHNOST	HONEST
EHNRTU	HUNTER
EHOOOP	HOOPOE
EHOOPR	HOOPER
EHOORV	HOOVER
EHOOST	SOOTHE
EHOOSV	HOOVES
EHOPPR	HOPPER
EHOPRT	POTHER
	THORPE
EHORSW	SHOWER
EHORTT	TOTHER
EHORTV	THROVE
EHORTX	EXHORT
EHORTY	THEORY
EHPRSY	SPHERY
EHPRYZ	ZEPHYR
EHRRSY	SHERRY
EHRRWY	WHERRY
EHRSSU	RHESUS
	RUSHES
EHRSTY	THYRSE
EIILMS	SIMILE
EIILOT	IOLITE
EIILRV	VIRILE
EIILRX	ELIXIR
EIINSZ	SEIZIN
EIINTV	INVITE
EIIPRT	PITIER
EIIRSS	IRISES
EIIRSV	VISIER
EIIRVZ	VIZIER
EIJKNR	JERKIN
EIJNNO	ENJOIN
EIJNOR	JOINER
	REJOIN
EIJNRU	INJURE
EIJSTU	JESUIT
EIKLLR	KILLER
EIKLLY	LIKELY
EIKLMR	MILKER
EIKLNS	SILKEN
EIKLNT	TINKLE

EIKLNU	UNLIKE
EIKLNW	WELKIN
	WINKLE
EIKLRT	KIRTLE
EIKMOS	ESKIMO
EIKMST	KISMET
EIKNOV	INVOKE
EIKNRS	SINKER
EIKNRT	TINKER
EIKNRW	WINKER
EIKNSV	KNIVES
EIKNTT	KITTEN
EIKPPR	KIPPER
EIKRRS	RISKER
EIKRST	STRIKE
EIKRSV	SKIVER
EILLMR	MILLER
EILLMT	MILLET
EILLMU	ILLUME
EILLNO	LIONEL
	NIELLO
EILLNT	LENTIL
	LINTEL
EILLPU	PILULE
EILLRT	RILLET
	TILLER
EILLTT	LITTLE
EILLVY	LIVELY
	VILELY
EILMNR	LIMNER
	MERLIN
EILMOT	MOTILE
EILMPP	PIMPLE
EILMPS	SIMPLE
EILMPT	LIMPET
EILMPW	WIMPLE
EILMPX	IMPLEX
EILMRS	SMILER
EILMRT	MILTER
EILMTY	TIMELY
EILMZZ	MIZZLE
EILNNT	LINNET
EILNOS	LESION
EILNOT	LIONET
EILNPP	NIPPLE
EILNPS	SPINEL
EILNPT	PINTLE
EILNPU	LUPINE
	UP-LINE
EILNST	ENLIST
	LISTEN
	SILENT
	TINSEL
EILNSV	SNIVEL
EILNTY	LENITY
EILNUV	UNVEIL
EILOOR	ORIOLE
EILOOT	OOLITE
EILOPT	POLITE
EILORT	LOITER
	TOILER

EILORY	OILERY
EILOTT	TOILET
EILOTV	VIOLET
EILPPR	RIPPLE
EILPPT	TIPPLE
EILPRS	LISPER
	PLIERS
EILPRT	TRIPLE
EILPRY	RIPELY
EILPGU	PILEUG
EILPSV	PELVIS
EILRSV	SILVER
	SLIVER
EILRTT	LITTER
	TILTER
EILRTY	TILERY
EILRVY	LIVERY
	VERILY
EILSTU	SUTILE
EILSVW	SWIVEL
EILSWY	WISELY
EILSZZ	SIZZLE
EILTTT	TITTLE
EILTVY	LEVITY
EIMMNU	IMMUNE
EIMMOR	MEMOIR
EIMMRS	SIMMER
EIMMRU	IMMURE
EIMNOR	MERINO
EIMNRT	MINTER
EIMNRV	VERMIN
EIMNTT	MITTEN
EIMNTU	MINUET
	MINUTE
EIMNTY	ENMITY
EIMNZZ	MIZZEN
EIMOPS	IMPOSE
EIMOST	SOMITE
EIMOSV	MOVIES
EIMOTV	MOTIVE
EIMOTY	MOIETY
EIMPRR	PRIMER
EIMPRS	SIMPER
EIMPRT	PERMIT
EIMPRU	IMPURE
	UMPIRE
EIMPTU	IMPUTE
EIMRSS	REMISS
EIMRST	MISTER
	SMITER
EIMRSY	MISERY
EIMSST	TMESIS
EIMSSU	MISUSE
EIMSTY	STYMIE
EINNOT	INTONE
EINNRS	SINNER
EINNRT	INTERN
	TINNER
EINNRW	WINNER
EINNST	SENNIT
	TENNIS

EINNTT	INTENT	EIQRUV	QUIVER	ELMMPU	PUMMEL
EINNTV	INVENT	EIQTUY	EQUITY	ELMNOR	MERLON
EINNTY	NINETY	EIRRTW	WRITER	ELMNOS	SOLEMN
EINORR	IRONER	EIRRVY	RIVERY	ELMNOT	LOMENT
EINORS	SENIOR	EIRSST	RESIST		MOLTEN
EINORT	ORIENT		SISTER	ELMNPU	PLENUM
EINOSS	OSSEIN	EIRSTT	SITTER	ELMOPY	EMPLOY
EINOSW	NOWISE	EIRSTV	STIVER	ELMORS	MORSEL
EINOTT	TONITE		STRIVE	ELMOST	MOLEST
EINPPR	NIPPER	EIRTTT	TITTER	ELMOTT	MOTTLE
EINPPS	PEPSIN	EIRTTV	TRIVET	ELMOTY	MOTLEY
EINPRS	SNIPER	EIRTUV	VIRTUE	ELMOUV	VOLUME
EINPRU	UNRIPE	EIRTVY	VERITY	ELMOXY	OXYMEL
EINPRY	PINERY	EISSTU	TISSUE	ELMPRU	LUMPER
EINPST	INSTEP	EJKNRU	JUNKER		RUMPLE
	SPINET	EJKNTU	JUNKET	ELMRTY	MYRTLE
EINPSU	PUISNE	EJLOST	JOSTLE		TERMLY
	SUPINE	EJLSTU	JUSTLE	ELMSSU	MUSSEL
EINQSU	SEQUIN	EJMPRU	JUMPER	ELMTUY	MUTELY
EINQUU	UNIQUE	EJNOST	JETSON	ELMUZZ	MUZZLE
EINRRS	RINSER	EJORTT	JOTTER	ELNNRU	RUNNEL
EINRRU	RUINER	EKLMMU	KÜMMEL	ELNNTU	TUNNEL
EINRST	INSERT	EKLNOS	KELSON	ELNOOS	LOOSEN
	SINTER	EKLOOR	LOOKER	ELNOPY	OPENLY
EINRSU	INSURE	EKLRRU	LURKER	ELNORT	LENTOR
	URSINE	EKMNOY	MONKEY	ELNOSS	LESSON
EINRTU	TRIUNE	EKMORS	SMOKER	ELNOST	STOLEN
	UNITER	EKMSTU	MUSKET		TELSON
EINRTV	INVERT	EKNNSU	SUNKEN	ELNOSV	SLOVEN
EINRTW	WINTER	EKNOPS	SPOKEN	ELNOUZ	ZONULE
EINRVW	WIVERN	EKNORR	KRONER	ELNOZZ	NOZZLE
EINRVY	VINERY	EKNORW	KNOWER	ELNPTU	PENULT
EINSTV	INVEST	EKNORY	ORKNEY	ELNPTY	PLENTY
EINSUW	UNWISE	EKNOUY	UNYOKE	ELNRTU	RUNLET
EINSUX	UNISEX	EKOPRR	PORKER	ELNSSU	UNLESS
EINSWY	SINEWY	EKORRW	WORKER	ELNUZZ	NUZZLE
	WINSEY	EKORST	STOKER	ELOPPR	LOPPER
EINTTY	ENTITY		STROKE		PROPEL
EIOOST	OTIOSE	EKRRSY	SKERRY	ELOPPT	TOPPLE
EIOPRS	POISER	EKRSTU	TUSKER	ELOPPY	POLYPE
EIOPTT	TIPTOE	EKRTUY	TURKEY	ELOPRT	PETROL
EIORRT	RIOTER	ELLMOW	MELLOW	ELOPRV	PLOVER
EIORST	SORTIE	ELLMTU	MULLET	ELOPTT	POTTLE
EIORSV	VIROSE	ELLMUV	VELLUM	ELORRS	SORREL
EIORSY	OSIERY	ELLNOP	POLLEN	ELORSS	LESSOR
EIOSTV	SOVIET	ELLNOR	ENROLL	ELORST	OSTLER
EIOTUV	OUTVIE	ELLNOY	LONELY	ELORSV	SOLVER
EIOTVV	VOTIVE	ELLNSU	SULLEN	ELORSY	SORELY
EIPPST	SIPPET	ELLNUU	LUNULE	ELORTV	REVOLT
EIPPTT	TIPPET	ELLNUW	UNWELL	ELORTW	TROWEL
EIPQTU	PIQUET	ELLOPX	POLLEX	ELORUV	LOUVRE
EIPRST	ESPRIT	ELLORR	ROLLER		VELOUR
	PRIEST	ELLORT	TOLLER	ELORWY	LOWERY
	SPRITE	ELLOSY	SOLELY		OWLERY
	STRIPE	ELLOVY	LOVELY	ELOSSU	SOLEUS
EIPRSU	UPRISE		VOLLEY	ELOSTU	TOUSLE
EIPRTV	PRIVET	ELLOWY	YELLOW	ELOSTW	LOWEST
EIPRXY	EXPIRY	ELLPTU	PULLET	ELOSVW	WOLVES
EIPSST	STIPES	ELLPUY	PULLEY	ELOTTU	OUTLET
EIPSSW	SWIPES	ELMMOP	POMMEL	ELOTUV	VOLUTE
EIQRSU	SQUIRE	ELMMOS	MOSLEM	ELPPRU	PURPLE

ELPPSU	SUPPLE	ENOTTU	TEUTON	EPPPTU	PUPPET
ELPRTY	PELTRY	ENPRRU	PRUNER	EPPRSU	SUPPER
	PERTLY	ENPRTU	PUNTER	EPRRSU	PURSER
ELPRUY	PURELY	ENPRUY	PENURY	EPRSUU	PURSUE
ELPSUX	PLEXUS	ENPTUW	UNWEPT	EPRTTU	PUTTER
ELPUZZ	PUZZLE	ENRRTU	RETURN	EPRTTY	PRETTY
ELRSTU	LUSTRE		TURNER	EPRUVY	PURVEY
	RESULT	ENRSTU	UNREST	ERRSUU	USURER
	RUSTLE	ENRSTY	SENTRY	ERRSUY	SURREY
	SUTLER	ENRSUU	UNSURE	ERRTTU	TURRET
	ULSTER	ENRTUU	UNTRUE	ERSSST	STRESS
ELRSUY	SURELY	ENRVWY	WYVERN	ERSSTU	RUSSET
ELRTTU	TURTLE	ENSSTU	SUNSET	ERSSTY	TRESSY
ELSSTU	TUSSLE	ENTTWY	TWENTY	ERSSUV	VERSUS
ELSTTY	STYLET	EOOPPS	OPPOSE	ERSTUU	SUTURE
EMMMRU	MUMMER	EOORTT	TOOTER		UTERUS
EMMNOT	MOMENT	EOPPPT	POPPET		
EMMORY	MEMORY	EOPPRR	PROPER	ERSTUV	TURVES
EMMPRU	MUMPER	EOPPRT	TOPPER	ERSTUY	SURETY
EMMRRU	RUMMER	EOPPRY	POPERY	ERSTVY	VESTRY
EMMRSU	SUMMER	EOPRRS	PROSER	ERSUVY	SURVEY
EMMSUU	MUSEUM	EOPRRT	PORTER	ESSSUX	SUSSEX
EMNOPY	EPONYM		REPORT	FFFLUY	FLUFFY
EMNORS	SERMON	EOPRRV	PROVER	FFGINO	OFFING
EMNORT	MENTOR	EOPRRY	ROPERY	FFIINT	TIFFIN
EMNOSY	MONEYS	EOPRST	POSTER	FFILLU	FULFIL
EMNOTY	ETYMON		PRESTO	FFILTU	FITFUL
EMOORS	MOROSE	EOPRSY	OSPREY	FFIMNU	MUFFIN
EMOOSS	OSMOSE	EOPRTT	POTTER	FFINPU	PUFFIN
EMOQSU	MOSQUE	EOPRTU	POUTER	FFIOST	SOFFIT
EMORRT	TREMOR		TROUPE	FFISUX	SUFFIX
EMORSU	MOUSER	EOPRTX	EXPORT	FFLOTY	FLYFOT
EMOTTT	MOTETT	EOPRTY	POETRY	FFNSUY	SNUFFY
EMPPRU	PUMPER	EOPSST	POSSET	FFRRUU	FURFUR
EMPSTU	SEPTUM	EOPSSU	SPOUSE	FFSTUY	STUFFY
EMRRUY	MURREY	EOPTTU	TOUPET	FGGIIZ	FIZGIG
EMRSTU	MUSTER	EOQRTU	QUOTER	FGHILT	FLIGHT
EMRTTU	MUTTER		TORQUE	FGHIRT	FRIGHT
EMSSTY	SYSTEM	EORRRT	TERROR	FGHOTU	FOUGHT
ENNNOP	PENNON	EORRRY	ORRERY	FGIILN	FILING
ENNORW	RENOWN	EORRST	RESORT	FGIINN	FINING
ENNOST	SONNET		ROSTER	FGIINR	FIRING
ENNRRU	RUNNER		SORTER	FGILNU	INGULF
ENNRTU	RUNNET		STORER	FGILNY	FLYING
ENNSTU	UNSENT	EORRSW	WORSER	FGINRY	FRYING
ENNTUU	UNTUNE	EORRSY	ROSERY	FGNSUU	FUNGUS
ENOORS	SEROON	EORRTT	RETORT	FGOORT	FORGOT
ENOOSZ	SNOOZE		ROTTER	FHIINS	FINISH
ENOPRR	PERRON	EORRTV	TROVER	FHILTY	FILTHY
ENOPRS	PERSON	EORSST	TOSSER	FHIRST	SHRIFT
ENOPRV	PROVEN	EORSSU	SEROUS	FHIRTT	THRIFT
ENOPTT	POTENT	EORSTU	OUSTER	FHISSU	HUSSIF
ENORRS	SNORER	EORSTV	STROVE	FHISTY	SHIFTY
ENORST	STONER	EORSTY	OYSTER	FHORTU	FOURTH
	TENSOR		STOREY	FHORTY	FROTHY
ENORSW	WORSEN	EORTTT	TOTTER	FIIKNR	FIRKIN
ENORTT	ROTTEN	EORTTU	TOUTER	FIILLP	FILLIP
ENORTY	TYRONE	EORTTX	EXTORT	FIILVY	VILIFY
ENOSSW	SOWENS	EORTVX	VORTEX	FIIMNR	INFIRM
ENOSTX	SEXTON	EORTWY	TOWERY	FIIMNY	MINIFY
ENOSUV	VENOUS	EOSTTU	OUTSET	FIIMST	MISFIT
				FIINOR	FIORIN

FIITXY	FIXITY	GHNORT	THRONG	GLOOOY	OOLOGY
FIIVVY	VIVIFY	GHNOTU	NOUGHT	GLOPTU	PUTLOG
FIKRSY	FRISKY	GHNRUY	HUNGRY	GLOSSY	GLOSSY
FILLRY	FRILLY	GHORTU	TROUGH	GMNNOO	GNOMON
FILLUW	WILFUL	GHORTW	GROWTH	GMPRUY	GRUMPY
FILMRY	FIRMLY	GIIKLN	LIKING	GMPSUY	GYPSUM
FILMSY	FLIMSY	GIIKNV	VIKING	GNNSUU	UNSUNG
FILNOR	FLORIN	GIILNN	LINING	GNOORT	TROGON
FILNOW	INFLOW	GIILNT	TILING	GNOPPU	OPPUGN
FILNSU	SINFUL	GIILNV	LIVING		POPGUN
FILNTY	FLINTY	GIIMNN	MINING	GNOPSY	SPONGY
FILNUX	INFLUX	GIINNN	INNING	GNORST	STRONG
FILOSS	FOSSIL	GIINOR	ORIGIN	GNPRSU	SPRUNG
FILPTU	UPLIFT	GIINPP	PIPING	GNRSTU	STRUNG
FIMNOR	INFORM	GIINRS	RISING	GOORTT	GROTTO
FINOOS	FOISON	GIINRT	TIRING	GORSUU	RUGOUS
FINOSU	FUSION	GIINRV	VIRGIN	GSYYYZ	SYZYGY
FINOTY	NOTIFY	GIINSZ	SIZING		
FIOPRT	PROFIT	GIKLNY	KINGLY	HHMRTY	RHYTHM
FIOSSY	OSSIFY	GILLUY	UGLILY	HHRSTU	THRUSH
FIOTTU	OUTFIT	GILMNU	LIGNUM	HIIMNS	MINISH
FIPRUY	PURIFY	GILMRY	GRIMLY	HIIMPS	IMPISH
FIPTYY	TYPIFY	GILNOS	LOSING	HIINTW	WITHIN
FIRTUY	FRUITY	GILNOV	LOVING	HIKNRS	SHRINK
FIRYZZ	FRIZZY	GILNOW	LOWING	HIKSWY	WHISKY
FJLOUY	JOYFUL	GILNPU	PULING	HILLOY	HOLILY
FKLNUY	FLUNKY	GILNRU	RULING	HILLPU	UPHILL
FLLOOW	FOLLOW	GILNSY	SINGLY	HILLRS	SHRILL
FLLOUY	FOULLY	GILRSY	GRISLY	HILLRT	THRILL
FLNRUU	UNFURL	GILTUY	GUILTY	HILMOW	WHILOM
FLOPPY	FLOPPY	GIMNOV	MOVING	HILMOY	HOMILY
FLORUY	FLOURY	GIMNOW	MOWING	HILMSU	MULISH
FLOSSY	FLOSSY	GIMNPU	IMPUGN	HILNPT	PLINTH
FLOSTY	SOFTLY	GIMNSU	MUSING	HILNTY	THINLY
FLRRUY	FLURRY	GIMOTU	GOMUTI	HILOPS	POLISH
FNOORU	UNROOF	GINNTU	TUNING	HILOSW	OWLISH
FORRUW	FURROW	GINOOW	WOOING	HILPST	SPILTH
FORSTY	FROSTY	GINORS	SIGNOR	HIMNOY	HOMINY
FORSUU	RUFOUS	GINORT	TRIGON	HIMOPS	MOPISH
FORWYZ	FROWZY	GINOSS	GNOSIS	HIMORS	ROMISH
GGGORY	GROGGY	GINOST	STINGO	HIMPRS	SHRIMP
GGIINP	PIGGIN	GINOTU	OUTING	HIMSTY	SMITHY
GGILOT	GIGLOT	GINPRS	SPRING	HIMSWY	WHIMSY
GGINNO	NOGGIN	GINPRY	PRYING	HINNWY	WHINNY
GGITWY	TWIGGY	GINPTU	PIG-NUT	HINOPS	SIPHON
GGNOOR	GORGON	GINRRU	RUNRIG	HINPSU	PUNISH
GHHILY	HIGHLY	GINRST	STRING		UNSHIP
GHHOTU	THOUGH	GINRTY	TRYING	HINPSX	SPHINX
GHIKNT	KNIGHT	GINSTY	STINGY	HINRSU	INRUSH
GHILPT	PLIGHT	GIOPSS	GOSSIP	HINSTY	SHINTY
GHILST	LIGHTS	GIOPST	SPIGOT	HIOPPS	POPISH
	SLIGHT	GIORRU	RIGOUR	HIOPRT	TROPHI
GHIMNO	HOMING	GIORUV	VIGOUR	HIPPSU	UPPISH
GHIMTY	MIGHTY	GIPSTY	PIG-STY	HIPRST	THRIPS
GHIRTW	WRIGHT	GIRTTY	GRITTY	HIRSTT	THIRST
GHISTT	TIGHTS	GJLNUY	JUNGLY	HIRSTY	THYRSI
GHLOOS	GOLOSH	GLLMUY	GLUMLY	HIRTTY	THIRTY
GHLOPU	PLOUGH	GLMNOO	MONGOL	HISTTY	STITHY
GHLOSU	SLOUGH	GLMOOY	GLOOMY	HJNNOY	JOHNNY
GHLOTU	LOG-HUT	GLMSUY	SMUGLY	HKNOOU	UNHOOK
GHNNUU	UNHUNG	GLNSUY	SNUGLY	HKNSUU	UNHUSK

HLLOOW	HOLLOW	ILLSTY	STILLY	INOPST	PISTON
HLLOWY	WHOLLY	ILMMSU	MUSLIM	INORSY	ROSINY
HLMOTY	THYMOL	ILMNSU	MUSLIN	INORTT	TRITON
HLMPUY	PHYLUM	ILMOSS	LISSOM	INOSUV	VINOUS
HLNOUY	UNHOLY	ILMOSU	LIMOUS	INPRST	SPRINT
HLORUY	HOURLY	ILMOTU	ULTIMO	INPRTU	TURNIP
HLSSUY	SLUSHY	ILMPPY	PIMPLY	INQSTU	SQUINT
HMOOST	SMOOTH	ILMPRY	PRIMLY	INQSUY	QUINSY
HMORUU	HUMOUR	ILMPSY	SIMPLY	INRSXY	SYRINX
HMOSUU	HUMOUS	IIMRTY	TRIMLY	INRTWY	WINTRY
HMSTUY	THYMUS	ILMSTU	LITMUS	IOPPTT	TIPTOP
HNOORU	HONOUR	ILNOOT	LOTION	IOPRRY	PRIORY
HNOPSY	SYPHON	ILNOPP	POPLIN	IOPRST	TRIPOS
HNOPTY	PYTHON	ILNOST	TONSIL	IORRTW	WORRIT
HNORSU	ONRUSH	ILNPST	SPLINT	IORSTU	SUITOR
HNORTW	THROWN	ILNSTU	INSULT	IOSTTU	OUTSIT
HNORTY	THORNY		SUNLIT	IOTTUW	OUTWIT
HNRTUU	UNHURT			IPRSTU	PURIST
HOOPSW	WHOOPS	ILOPPY	POLYPI	IPRTUY	PURITY
HOORRR	HORROR	ILOPRX	PROLIX	IPSTTY	TYPIST
HOOTTY	TOOTHY	ILOPRY	ROPILY	IQRSTU	SQUIRT
HOPPSY	SHOPPY	ILOPST	PISTOL	JLSTUY	JUSTLY
HOPRTY	TROPHY		SPOILT	JNSTUU	UNJUST
HOPSSY	HYSSOP	ILOPTY	POLITY	JOOSUY	JOYOUS
HOPSTU	UPSHOT	ILOQRU	LIQUOR	KMOOSS	KOSMOS
HORTWY	WORTHY	ILPPTU	PULPIT	KMOSUX	MUSK-OX
HPRSUU	UPRUSH	ILPRTY	TRIPLY	KNOTTY	KNOTTY
HPSTUY	TYPHUS	ILRSTY	LYRIST	KRRSUY	SKURRY
HRSTTU	THRUST	ILSTTU	LUTIST	LLNORU	UNROLL
IIIRST	IRITIS	IMMNOS	MONISM	LLOOWY	WOOLLY
IIKNPP	PIPKIN	IMMOOS	SIMOOM	LLORST	STROLL
IIKNSS	SISKIN	IMMOSU	OSMIUM	LLORTY	TROLLY
IILLWY	WILILY	IMMSTU	SUMMIT	LLOSWY	SLOWLY
IILNOV	VIOLIN	IMNNOW	MINNOW	LMOORU	ORMOLU
IILNST	INSTIL	IMNOOR	MORION	LMOSTY	MOSTLY
IILPST	PISTIL	IMNOOT	MOTION	LMPPUY	PLUMPY
IIMMNU	MINIUM	IMNOST	INMOST	LMTTUU	TUMULT
IIMNNO	MINION		MONIST	LNOOPY	POLONY
IIMSTT	TIMIST	IMNOSY	SIMONY	LNOOST	STOLON
IIMTTT	TIMTIT	IMNTUY	MUTINY	LNRUUY	UNRULY
IINNOP	PINION	IMOPRS	PORISM	LOOPRY	POORLY
IINOSV	VISION	IMOPRT	IMPORT	LOPPSY	SLOPPY
IINPPP	PIPPIN	IMOPST	IMPOST	LOPRTY	PORTLY
IINSST	INSIST	IMORRR	MIRROR	LOPTWY	TWO-PLY
IINTTU	INTUIT	IMORRS	MORRIS	LORSUY	SOURLY
IIOSTT	OTITIS	IMOSSY	MYOSIS	LPPSUY	SUPPLY
IIPRST	SPIRIT	IMOSTU	TIMOUS	LRSTUY	SULTRY
IIRSSU	SIRIUS	IMPRSU	PRIMUS	LRUUXY	LUXURY
JNORU	JUNIOR		PURISM	LSSTUY	STYLUS
JNRUY	INJURY	IMQRSU	SQUIRM	MMNOOR	MORMON
JRSTU	JURIST	IMRSTU	TRUISM	MMNOSU	SUMMON
KLNNU	UNLINK	IMSSSU	MISSUS	MMOOTT	TOMTOM
KMNOO	KIMONO	INNOOT	NOTION	MMRRUU	MURMUR
KMSSU	KUMISS	INNORW	INWORN	MNOORU	UNMOOR
KNNSY	SKINNY	INNOSU	UNISON	MNOTTU	MUTTON
KNNTU	UNKNIT	INNOWW	WINNOW	MOORRW	MORROW
KNOPT	INKPOT	INNPSY	SPINNY	MOORTY	MOTORY
KQRUY	QUIRKY	INOOPS	POISON	MOPPRT	PROMPT
LLOPW	PILLOW	INOOPT	OPTION	MOPSTU	UPMOST
LLOWW	WILLOW		POTION	MOQRUU	QUORUM
LLQSU	SQUILL	INOORS	ORISON	MORRUU	RUMOUR
		INOPRS	PRISON		

SIX-LETTER WORDS

MORSTY	STORMY	NOORST	TONSOR	OORRSW	SORROW
MORTUU	TUMOUR	NOORTU	UNROOT	OPRSTU	SPROUT
MOSTTU	UTMOST	NOPSTU	UNSTOP		STUPOR
MPRSTU	TRUMPS	NOPTUW	UPTOWN	OPSSTU	TOSS-UP
MPRSUU	RUMPUS	NORTUU	OUTRUN	OPSTTY	SPOTTY
MPSTUU	SPUTUM	NOSTUY	SNOUTY	OPTTUU	OUTPUT
MPSTUY	STUMPY	NPRTUU	UPTURN	PRSUYY	SYRUPY
MSTTUY	SMUTTY	OOPRRT	TORPOR	RSTTUY	TRUSTY
NNOORY	RONYON	OOPRST	TROOPS	SSTUXY	XYSTUS
NNORUW	UNWORN	OOPRSU	POROUS		
NOOPSY	SPOONY	OOPRTU	UPROOT		

Seven Letter Words

AAAAABLM	ALABAMA	AABCHOR	ABROACH	AABHITT	HABITAT
AAABBCL	CABBALA	AABCIOP	COPAIBA	AABHMNR	BRAHMAN
AAABCTW	CATAWBA	AABCITX	TAXICAB	AABHOST	SABAOTH
AAABDNN	BANDANA	AABCKRR	BARRACK	AABILLR	BARILLA
AAABILX	ABAXIAL	AABCLMU	CALUMBA	AABILMS	BAALISM
AAABINR	ARABIAN	AABCORT	ACROBAT	AABILMY	AMIABLY
AAACCLR	CARACAL	AABDDGH	BAGHDAD	AABILRS	BASILAR
AAACCRS	CARACAS	AABDEGN	BANDAGE	AABINST	ABSTAIN
AAACEHN	ACHAEAN	AABDEIS	DIABASE	AABISTT	ABATTIS
AAACENP	PANACEA	AABDELL	BALLADE	AABLLST	BALLAST
AAACHNT	ACANTHA	AABDENU	BANDEAU	AABLLWY	WALLABY
AAACIJM	JAMAICA	AABDGHN	HANDBAG	AABLMSY	ABYSMAL
AAACIMR	ARAMAIC	AABDGNS	SANDBAG	AABLNSU	BALANUS
AAACLMN	ALMANAC	AABDIMR	BARMAID	AABLNTT	BLATANT
AAACLNT	CATALAN	AABDLRW	BRAD-AWL	AABLPRU	PABULAR
AAACMRS	MASCARA	AABDNNO	ABANDON	AABLRST	ARBLAST
AAACNRV	CARAVAN	AABDNSW	BANDSAW	AABLRTU	TABULAR
AAACNST	CANASTA	AABDORV	BRAVADO	AABLRTY	RATABLY
AAACNTT	CANTATA	AABDRST	BASTARD	AABLSSY	ABYSSAL
AAACRWY	CARAWAY	AABEELT	EATABLE	AABLSTY	BAY-SALT
AAACSSV	CASSAVA	AABEFFL	AFFABLE	AABMNOT	BOATMAN
AAADFRY	FARADAY	AABEGGG	BAGGAGE	AABMORU	MARABOU
AAADMNR	RAMADAN	AABEGGR	GARBAGE	AABNNOZ	BONANZA
AAADMNT	ADAMANT	AABEGLR	ALGEBRA	AABRRUV	BRAVURA
AAAEGNP	APANAGE	AABEGRR	BARRAGE	AACCDES	CASCADE
AAAEIMN	ANAEMIA	AABEGSS	BAGASSE	AACCDIR	CARDIAC
AAAFFLL	ALFALFA	AABEHLT	HATABLE	AACCEET	CETACEA
AAAFIRT	RATAFIA	AABEILM	AMIABLE	AACCHIR	ARCHAIC
AAAFRWY	FARAWAY	AABEILT	BAALITE	AACCHLN	CLACHAN
AAAGGLN	GALANGA		LABIATE	AACCHMP	CHAMPAC
AAAGISS	ASSAGAI	AABELLS	SALABLE	AACCILM	ACCLAIM
AAAGLMM	AMALGAM	AABELMN	NAMABLE	AACCKRR	CARRACK
AAAGMNR	ANAGRAM	AABELMT	TAMABLE	AACCLLO	CLOACAL
AAAHIPS	APHASIA	AABELNO	ABALONE	AACCLLT	CATCALL
AAAHMMT	MAHATMA	AABELPR	PARABLE	AACCLOP	POLACCA
AAAILMR	MALARIA	AABELPY	PAYABLE	AACCNVY	VACANCY
AAAJKRT	JAKARTA	AABELRT	ALBERTA	AACCORU	CURAÇAO
AAAJMPS	PAJAMAS		RATABLE	AACCRSS	CARCASS
AAALLPT	PALATAL	AABELSV	SAVABLE	AACDDEL	DECADAL
AAALMNY	MALAYAN	AABELTU	TABLEAU	AACDDER	ARCADED
AAALMRS	MARSALA		TABULAE	AACDEHM	CHAMADE
AAANNSV	SAVANNA	AABELTX	TAXABLE	AACDEHR	CHARADE
AABBCEG	CABBAGE	AABENRT	ANT-BEAR	AACDEHT	CAT-HEAD
AABBHST	SABBATH	AABERST	ABREAST	AACDELN	DECANAL
AABCCET	BACCATE	AABERTT	TABARET	AACDEMN	CADMEAN
AABCELN	BALANCE	AABFFLY	AFFABLY	AACDEMY	ACADEMY
AABCELP	CAPABLE	AABFILU	FABLIAU	AACDENV	ADVANCE
	PACABLE	AABGIIL	ABIGAIL	AACDENZ	CADENZA
AABCEMR	MACABRE	AABGILM	MAILBAG	AACDETU	CAUDATE
AABCERT	CABARET	AABGINR	BARGAIN	AACDFIR	FARADIC
AABCHMT	AMBATCH	AABHIRT	AIR-BATH	AACDHMR	DRACHMA

37

AACDILR	RADICAL
AACDINT	ANTACID
AACDJKW	JACKDAW
AACDLNS	SCANDAL
AACDLPR	PLACARD
AACDOOV	AVOCADO
AACEEGR	ACREAGE
AACEEHR	EAR-ACHE
AACEETT	ACETATE
AACEFLT	FALCATE
AACEGKP	PACKAGE
AACEGKS	SACKAGE
AACEGNR	CARNAGE
	CRANAGE
AACEGRT	CARTAGE
AACEHNP	PANACHE
AACEHRT	TRACHEA
AACEHTT	ATTACHÉ
AACEHTU	CHÂTEAU
AACEIMN	ANAEMIC
AACEIMR	AMERICA
AACEIMU	CAMAIEU
AACEIPP	CAP-À-PIE
AACEIRV	AVARICE
	CAVIARE
AACEKNP	PANCAKE
AACEKNS	ASKANCE
AACELLN	CANELLA
AACELLT	LACTEAL
AACELMN	MANACLE
AACELMR	CARAMEL
AACELMU	MACULAE
AACELNU	LACUNAE
AACELNV	VALANCE
AACELPT	PLACATE
AACELRV	CARAVEL
AACELTV	CLAVATE
AACEMNV	CAVEMAN
AACENRS	SARACEN
AACENRT	CATERAN
AACERSU	CAESURA
AACERTU	ARCUATE
AACETTU	ACTUATE
AACFINR	AFRICAN
AACFINT	FANATIC
AACFLLY	FALLACY
AACFLTU	FACTUAL
AACGILL	GLACIAL
AACGILM	MAGICAL
AACGLOS	COAL-GAS
AACGNOU	GUANACO
AACHIKR	CHIKARA
AACHIMS	CHIASMA
AACHIRS	ARACHIS
AACHIRT	CITHARA
AACHKSW	HACKSAW
AACHLPS	PASCHAL
AACHMNP	CHAPMAN
AACHNRY	ANARCHY
AACHRRT	CATARRH
AACHRWY	ARCHWAY
AACIINT	ACTINIA

AACIIST	ASIATIC
AACIKNN	CANAKIN
AACILNR	CRANIAL
AACILOX	CO-AXIAL
AACILPS	SPACIAL
AACILPT	CAPITAL
AACINOR	AARONIC
	OCARINA
AACINPT	CAPTAIN
AACINRZ	CZARINA
AACINST	SATANIC
AACINTV	VATICAN
AACIOPT	TAPIOCA
AACIQTU	AQUATIC
AACISTT	ASTATIC
AACJKSS	JACKASS
AACKNRS	RANSACK
AACLMNO	COALMAN
AACLMNT	CLAMANT
AACLMSU	CALAMUS
AACLNNU	CANNULA
AACLNOR	ALCORAN
AACLNRU	LACUNAR
AACLORT	COAL-TAR
AACLOST	COASTAL
AACLPSU	SCAPULA
AACLRVY	CALVARY
	CAVALRY
AACLSUV	VASCULA
AACLTTU	TACTUAL
AACMNRU	ARCANUM
AACMORS	SARCOMA
AACMRSS	SARCASM
AACNPST	CAPSTAN
AACNSSV	CANVASS
AACORTU	AUTO-CAR
AACPSTW	CAT'S-PAW
AACRTTT	ATTRACT
AACRTUY	ACTUARY
AACRTWY	CART-WAY
AACTUWY	CUT-AWAY
AADDEFI	DEAF-AID
AADDENP	DEADPAN
AADDEPY	DEAD-PAY
AADDGNR	GRANDAD
AADDRST	DASTARD
AADEFGR	FARDAGE
AADEGRT	GRADATE
AADEGRY	DRAYAGE
AADEHMS	ASHAMED
AADEHRW	WARHEAD
AADEHWY	HEADWAY
AADEIMR	MADEIRA
AADEIMT	ADAMITE
AADEINR	ARANEID
AADEIRT	RADIATE
	TIARAED
AADEJMR	JEMADAR
AADELLP	PADELLA
AADELMO	ALAMODE
AADELRY	ALREADY
AADELTU	ADULATE

AADEMMN	MAN-MADE
AADEMNT	MANDATE
AADENNP	PANDEAN
AADENNT	ANDANTE
AADENRV	VERANDA
AADENSW	WEASAND
AADENWZ	WEAZAND
AADEPRT	ADAPTER
AADERSW	SEAWARD
AADERTU	AURATED
AADFSTY	FAST-DAY
AADGGHR	HAGGARD
AADGGLR	LAGGARD
AADGIMM	DIGAMMA
AADGIMR	DIAGRAM
AADGLNR	GARLAND
AADGLRU	GRADUAL
AADGMNR	GRANDAM
	GRANDMA
AADGNPR	GRANDPA
AADGNRT	GARDANT
AADGOPR	PODAGRA
AADHLRY	HALYARD
AADHRRV	HARVARD
AADIINN	INDIANA
AADIINR	DIARIAN
AADILMR	ADMIRAL
AADILNP	PALADIN
AADILPS	APSIDAL
AADIMOR	DIORAMA
AADINRT	RADIANT
AADKNRT	TANKARD
AADKRWW	AWKWARD
AADLLMR	MALLARD
AADLLPU	PALUDAL
AADLMNU	LADANUM
AADLNRY	LANYARD
AADLPPU	APPLAUD
AADMNNO	MADONNA
AADMNNS	SANDMAN
AADMNRY	DRAYMAN
AADMNSY	DAYSMAN
AADMORT	MATADOR
AADMRZZ	MAZZARD
AADOPRT	ADAPTOR
AADOPRX	PARADOX
AADORWY	ROADWAY
AADQRTU	QUADRAT
AADRSTY	DAY-STAR
AADRWWY	WAYWARD
AAEEFGL	LEAFAGE
AAEEFLT	TEA-LEAF
AAEEGKL	LEAKAGE
AAEEGLT	GALEATE
AAEEGRV	AVERAGE
AAEEHRT	HETAERA
AAEEMNT	EMANATE
	MANATEE
AAEEPPS	APPEASE
AAEEPRT	PATERAE
AAEFFGR	AGRAFFE
AAEFFNR	FANFARE

AAEFFTT	TAFFETA	AAEKLNT	ALKANET	AAGNOPR	PARAGON
AAEFGTW	WAFTAGE	AAEKMRR	EAR-MARK	AAGNRRY	GRANARY
AAEFRRW	WARFARE	AAEKPRT	PARTAKE	AAGNRTV	VAGRANT
AAEGGNO	ANAGOGE	AAELLLM	LAMELLA	AAHHNPT	NAPHTHA
AAEGHLU	HAULAGE	AAELLPT	PATELLA	AAHHOPR	PHAROAH
AAEGHNT	THANAGE	AAELLRT	LATERAL	AAHILLL	ALL-HAIL
AAEGILR	ALGERIA	AAELMPT	PALMATE	AAHILMT	THALAMI
	REGALIA	AAELNPT	PLATANE	AAHINOP	APHONIA
AAEGINV	VAGINAE	AAELNRS	ARSENAL	AAHLMRS	MARSHAL
AAEGISS	ASSEGAI	AAELNSY	ANALYSE	AAHLNPX	PHALANX
AAEGITT	AGITATE	AAELNYZ	ANALYZE	AAHLNRW	NARWHAL
AAEGJTU	AJUTAGE	AAELORR	AREOLAR	AAHLPST	ASPHALT
AAEGKOS	SOAKAGE	AAELORU	AUREOLA	AAHMOPR	AMPHORA
AAEGLLT	TALLAGE	AAELPPR	APPAREL	AAHNNOS	HOSANNA
AAEGLRR	REALGAR	AAELPPU	PAPULAE	AAHNRTX	ANTHRAX
AAEGLSV	SALVAGE	AAELPRV	PALAVER	AAHPRTW	WARPATH
AAEGMNR	MANAGER	AAELPTU	PLATEAU	AAHPTWY	PATHWAY
AAEGMNT	MAGENTA	AAELRTZ	LAZARET	AAHRSST	SHASTRA
	MAGNATE	AAELSUX	ASEXUAL	AAHRTTW	ATHWART
AAEGMPR	RAMPAGE	AAELTVV	VALVATE	AAIILNT	ITALIAN
AAEGMSS	MASSAGE	AAEMNNT	EMANANT	AAIINNR	IRANIAN
AAEGNNT	TANNAGE	AAEMNPP	PAMPEAN	AAIIRVV	VIVARIA
AAEGNPT	PAGEANT	AAEMNRU	MURAENA	AAIKMNN	MANAKIN
AAEGNRR	ARRANGE	AAEMQSU	SQUAMAE	AAILLLP	PALLIAL
AAEGNRT	TANAGER	AAEMRTU	AMATEUR	AAILLMN	MANILLA
AAEGNTV	VANTAGE	AAENNNT	ANTENNA	AAILLMR	ARMILLA
AAEGPSS	PASSAGE	AAENNST	ANNATES	AAILLMX	MAXILLA
AAEGQUY	QUAYAGE	AAENPST	ANAPEST	AAILLNV	VANILLA
AAEGRRV	RAVAGER		PEASANT	AAILLPP	PAPILLA
AAEGRST	TEAR-GAS	AAENRRT	NARRATE	AAILLRX	AXILLAR
AAEGRTT	REGATTA	AAENRUW	UNAWARE	AAILLXY	AXIALLY
AAEGSSU	ASSUAGE	AAEORRT	AERATOR	AAILMMN	MAILMAN
	SAUSAGE	AAEPPRT	PARAPET	AAILMMS	MIASMAL
AAEGSTW	WASTAGE	AAERSSY	ASSAYER	AAILMMX	MAXIMAL
AAEGTTW	WATTAGE	AAFGORR	FARRAGO	AAILMNR	LAMINAR
AAEGTWY	GATEWAY	AAFILNT	FANTAIL	AAILMNU	ALUMINA
AAEHHPT	APHTHAE	AAFINNT	INFANTA	AAILMNV	MAIL-VAN
AAEHIRT	HETAIRA	AAFLLTY	FATALLY	AAILMRT	MARITAL
AAEHKNT	KHANATE	AAFLWYY	FLYAWAY		MARTIAL
AAEHLPX	HEXAPLA	AAFMNST	FANTASM	AAILNOP	PIANOLA
AAEHNPR	HANAPER	AAFPSUX	FAUX-PAS	AAILNOV	VALONIA
AAEHRSY	HEARSAY	AAGGNWY	GANGWAY	AAILNPT	PLATINA
AAEHSTT	HASTATE	AAGHMNN	HANGMAN	AAILNRY	LANIARY
AAEILMN	LAMINAE	AAGILMY	MYALGIA	AAILNTV	VALIANT
AAEILMS	MALAISE	AAGILNV	VAGINAL	AAILORV	VARIOLA
AAEILNO	AEOLIAN	AAGILOT	OTALGIA	AAILPRT	PARTIAL
AAEILRU	AURELIA	AAGILTW	WAGTAIL		PATRIAL
AAEILRV	VELARIA	AAGIMNS	SIAMANG	AAILPST	SPATIAL
AAEIMNS	AMNESIA	AAGIMNZ	AMAZING	AAILRRV	ARRIVAL
AAEIMNT	AMENTIA	AAGINRR	ARRAIGN	AAILRTV	TRAVAIL
	ANIMATE	AAGINST	AGAINST	AAILRWY	RAILWAY
AAEIMPY	PYAEMIA	AAGINSY	GAINSAY	AAILSSW	WASSAIL
AAEIMRU	URAEMIA	AAGIPRU	PIRAGUA	AAIMMNO	AMMONIA
AAEIMTV	AMATIVE	AAGIRRY	ARGYRIA	AAIMNOS	ANOSMIA
AAEIPPS	APEPSIA	AAGKMSS	GAS-MASK	AAIMNRU	RUMANIA
AAEIPRR	PAREIRA	AAGLLNT	GALLANT	AAIMNST	STAMINA
AAEIPRS	SPIRAEA	AAGLMPS	GAS-LAMP	AAIMRSU	SAMURAI
AAEIPTT	APATITE	AAGLNOY	ANALOGY	AAIMSTV	ATAVISM
AAEIRST	ASTERIA	AAGLNRU	ANGULAR	AAINORV	OVARIAN
AAEIRSX	XERASIA	AAGLRUU	AUGURAL	AAINORZ	ARIZONA
AAEIRTT	ARIETTA	AAGMMRR	GRAMMAR	AAINRST	ARTISAN
AAEISTT	SATIATE	AAGMRRY	GRAMARY	AAINRSU	SAURIAN

AAINRTV	VARIANT	ABBDNOX	BANDBOX
AAINRTZ	TZARINA	ABBEGLR	GABBLER
AAINTTT	ATTAINT	ABBEGRR	GRABBER
AAIORTV	AVIATOR	ABBEGRU	BUGBEAR
AAIQSSU	QUASSIA	ABBELMR	BRAMBLE
AAIRSTU	AUSTRIA	ABBELRS	SLABBER
AAJNRUY	JANUARY	ABBELRU	BARBULE
AAJOPSU	SAPAJOU	ABBERST	STABBER
AAKLNOR	ALKORAN	ABBERSW	SWABBER
AAKLRSU	KURSAAL	ABBHISY	BABYISH
AAKMRUZ	MAZURKA	ABBHRRU	RHUBARB
AALLMPU	AMPULLA	ABBILOT	BOB-TAIL
AALLNSY	NASALLY	ABBLMRY	BRAMBLY
AALLPPY	PAPALLY	ABBMOST	BOMBAST
AALLRVY	VALLARY	ABBMOTU	BUM-BOAT
AALMMNS	ALMS-MAN	ABBQSUY	SQUABBY
AALMMNT	MALTMAN	ABCCCHI	BACCHIC
AALMNOY	ANOMALY	ABCCEIR	BRECCIA
AALMORY	MAYORAL	ABCCEIS	SEBACIC
AALMPRY	PALMARY	ABCCHSU	BACCHUS
AALNNRU	ANNULAR	ABCCILU	CUBICAL
AALNPRT	PLANTAR	ABCCIMR	CAMBRIC
AALNRTU	NATURAL	ABCCIOR	BORACIC
AALNSTT	SALTANT	ABCCKTU	CUTBACK
AALNSTU	SULTANA	ABCCOOT	TOBACCO
AALNSTY	ANALYST	ABCDEEH	BEACHED
AALOPRS	PARASOL	ABCDEEL	DÉBÂCLE
AALORRU	AURORAL	ABCDEHU	DEBAUCH
AALORSU	AROUSAL	ABCDEIR	CARBIDE
AALPPRU	PAPULAR	ABCDELO	COAL-BED
AALPSTU	SPATULA	ABCDEMP	CAMP-BED
AALRSTU	AUSTRAL	ABCDEOR	BROCADE
AALSSTU	ASSAULT	ABCDERU	CUDBEAR
AAMMMRY	MAMMARY	ABCDINS	ABSCIND
AAMNNOT	MONTANA	ABCDIRS	SCABRID
AAMNORS	OARSMAN	ABCDIRT	CATBIRD
AAMNOTY	ANATOMY	ABCDISU	SUBACID
AAMNPRT	RAMPANT	ABCDNOS	ABSCOND
AAMNPTY	TYMPANA	ABCDORR	BROCARD
AAMORSV	SAMOVAR	ABCEEMR	EMBRACE
AAMORTY	AMATORY	ABCEENS	ABSENCE
AAMOSTT	STOMATA	ABCEESU	BECAUSE
AAMPRRT	RAMPART	ABCEGOR	BROCAGE
AAMRSST	MATRASS	ABCEGOS	BOSCAGE
AAMRTWY	TRAMWAY	ABCEHIR	HEBRAIC
AANNOTT	ANNATTO	ABCEHMR	BECHARM
AANPRST	SPARTAN		CHAMBER
AANPSST	PASSANT	ABCEHMT	MACBETH
AANQRTJ	QUARTAN	ABCEILM	ALEMBIC
AANRRTW	WARRANT	ABCEILR	CALIBRE
AANRUWY	RUNAWAY	ABCEILT	CITABLE
AAOPSST	POTASSA	ABCEINR	CARBINE
AAPRSTY	SATRAPY	ABCEINT	CABINET
ABBBELR	BABBLER	ABCEIRS	ASCRIBE
	BLABBER	ABCEISS	SCABIES
	BRABBLE	ABCEKLN	BLACKEN
ABBCDER	CRABBED	ABCEKNR	BRACKEN
ABBCDES	SCABBED	ABCEKRT	BRACKET
ABBDEKR	BARK-BED	ABCEKST	SETBACK
ABBDELR	DABBLER	ABCELLU	BULLACE
ABBDMOR	BOMBARD	ABCELMR	CLAMBER

ABCELOV	VOCABLE
ABCELPU	BLUE-CAP
ABCELRU	CURABLE
ABCELSU	BASCULE
ABCENOW	COW-BANE
ABCENRU	UNBRACE
ABCEOOS	CABOOSE
ABCESSS	ABSCESS
ABCFIKN	FINBACK
ABCGIKN	BACKING
ABCGINR	BRACING
ABCGKLO	BACKLOG
ABCHILS	CHABLIS
ABCHIOT	COHABIT
ABCHKOU	CHABOUK
ABCHKTU	HACKBUT
ABCHNRY	BRANCHY
ABCHSTU	BUSH-CAT
ABCIJNO	JACOBIN
ABCIKSY	SICK-BAY
ABCILOR	CRAB-OIL
ABCILRS	SCRIBAL
ABCILTU	CUBITAL
ABCIMMU	CAMBIUM
ABCIMRU	CUMBRIA
ABCIMST	CAMBIST
ABCINOT	BOTANIC
ABCIOUV	BIVOUAC
ABCIRTY	BARYTIC
ABCJOSU	JACOBUS
ABCKLLY	BLACKLY
ABCKMRU	BUCKRAM
ABCKSTU	SACKBUT
ABCLLOY	CALL-BOY
ABCLLUW	CLUB-LAW
ABCLMOU	COLUMBA
ABCLNOY	BALCONY
ABCORRW	CROWBAR
ABDDEER	BEARDED
ABDDEES	DEBASED
ABDDEIR	BRAIDED
ABDDELR	BLADDER
ABDDENR	BRANDED
ABDDHIS	BADDISH
ABDDINS	DISBAND
ABDEERT	DEBATER
ABDEEST	BESTEAD
ABDEFOR	FORBADE
ABDEGHI	BIGHEAD
ABDEGHR	BEGHARD
ABDEGIR	ABRIDGE
ABDEGNO	BONDAGE
ABDEHLR	HALBERD
ABDEHRT	BREADTH
ABDEILP	PIEBALD
ABDEILS	DISABLE
ABDEILU	AUDIBLE
ABDEINR	BRAINED
ABDELOT	BLOATED
ABDELPU	DUPABLE
ABDELRU	DURABLE

ABDEMNO	ABDOMEN	ABEGGMO	GAMBOGE
ABDENOR	BANDORE	ABEGGRU	BURGAGE
	BROADEN	ABEGGRY	BEGGARY
ABDENRR	BRANDER	ABEGILN	BELGIAN
ABDENSS	BADNESS	ABEGIMN	BEAMING
ABDENSU	SUBDEAN	ABEGIMR	GAMBIER
ABDEORR	BOARDER	ABEGINO	BEGONIA
ABDGIIN	ABIDING	ABEGINR	BEARING
ABDGINR	BRIGAND	ABEGINT	BEATING
ABDHIIT	ADHIBIT	ABEGIPP	BAGPIPE
ABDHNOW	BOW-HAND	ABEGKOR	BROKAGE
ABDHNSU	HUSBAND	ABEGLMR	GAMBLER
ABDILOT	TABLOID		GAMBREL
ABDILRY	RABIDLY	ABEGLNR	BRANGLE
ABDILUY	AUDIBLY	ABEGLOT	GLOBATE
ABDINOR	INBOARD	ABEGLRR	GARBLER
ABDIPRU	UPBRAID	ABEGMOR	EMBARGO
ABDKOOY	DAY-BOOK	ABEGMRU	UMBRAGE
ABDLLOR	BOLLARD	ABEGORX	GEAR-BOX
ABDLMOR	LOMBARD	ABEGOUY	BUOYAGE
ABDLNOR	BANDROL	ABEHIRS	BEARISH
ABDLORY	BROADLY	ABEHISU	BEAUISH
ABDLRUY	DURABLY	ABEHITU	HABITUÉ
ABDLSUU	SUBDUAL	ABEHKRU	HAUBERK
ABDMNNO	BONDMAN	ABEHLMS	SHAMBLE
ABDNOSY	SAND-BOY	ABEHNOS	BONE-ASH
ABDNOYY	ANYBODY	ABEIINR	IBERIAN
ABDNSTY	STAND-BY	ABEIKNR	INBREAK
ABDOORW	BARWOOD	ABEIKNT	BEATNIK
ABDRSTU	BUSTARD	ABEILLO	LOBELIA
ABDRUZZ	BUZZARD	ABEILLP	PLIABLE
ABEEEFT	BEEF-TEA	ABEILLR	BRAILLE
ABEEERV	BEREAVE		LIBERAL
ABEEFFL	EFFABLE	ABEILMX	MIXABLE
ABEEGHR	HERBAGE	ABEILNP	BIPLANE
ABEEGLL	GABELLE	ABEILNS	LESBIAN
ABEEGRW	BREWAGE	ABEILRT	LIBRATE
ABEEHNN	HENBANE		TRIABLE
ABEEHNS	BANSHEE	ABEILST	BESTIAL
ABEEHNT	BENEATH	ABEILSZ	SIZABLE
ABEEHRT	BREATHE	ABEILVV	BIVALVE
ABEEKPS	BESPEAK	ABEIMNT	AMBIENT
ABEEKRR	BREAKER	ABEIOTV	OBVIATE
ABEELLY	EYEBALL	ABEIPST	BAPTISE
ABEELMZ	EMBLAZE	ABEIPTZ	BAPTIZE
ABEELNT	BELTANE	ABEIRRR	BARRIER
	TENABLE	ABEIRRS	BRASIER
ABEELNU	NEBULAE	ABEIRRT	ARBITER
ABEELQU	EQUABLE		RAREBIT
ABEEMRS	BESMEAR	ABEIRRZ	BIZARRE
ABEENRV	VERBENA		BRAZIER
ABEESWX	BEES-WAX	ABEIRTT	BIRETTA
ABEFFLR	BAFFLER	ABEIRTV	VIBRATE
ABEFILN	FINABLE	ABEISUV	ABUSIVE
ABEFILR	FRIABLE	ABEJNOW	JAWBONE
ABEFILX	FIXABLE	ABEKLLY	BLEAKLY
ABEFITY	BEATIFY	ABEKLNT	BLANKET
ABEFLLU	BALEFUL	ABEKPRU	BREAK-UP
ABEFLNU	BANEFUL		UPBREAK
ABEFLST	BELFAST	ABELLMN	BELL-MAN
ABEFORR	FORBEAR	ABELLMT	METBALL
		ABELLOV	LOVABLE
		ABELLRU	RUBELLA
			RULABLE
		ABELLTU	BULLATE
		ABELMNT	LAMBENT
		ABELMNU	ALBUMEN
		ABELMOV	MOVABLE
		ABELMRR	RAMBLER
		ABELMTU	MUTABLE
		ABELNOT	NOTABLE
		ABELNRU	NEBULAR
		ABELNRY	BLARNEY
		ABELNTU	TUNABLE
		ABELOPT	POTABLE
		ABELORT	BLOATER
		ABELORU	RUBEOLA
		ABELOSV	ABSOLVE
		ABELQUY	EQUABLY
		ABELRRW	BRAWLER
			WARBLER
		ABELRST	BLASTER
			STABLER
		ABELRTT	BRATTLE
		ABELRTY	TRYABLE
		ABELRVY	BRAVELY
		ABELSTY	BEASTLY
		ABEMNSU	SUNBEAM
		ABEMORT	BROMATE
		ABEMSSY	EMBASSY
		ABENNRW	BRAN-NEW
		ABENORT	BARONET
		ABENOTY	BAYONET
		ABENQTU	BANQUET
		ABEOOTV	OBOVATE
		ABEOPRT	PROBATE
		ABEOQRU	BAROQUE
		ABEORRT	TABORER
		ABEORST	BOASTER
		ABERRVY	BRAVERY
		ABERSSU	SURBASE
		ABERSTY	BARYTES
		ABERTTY	BATTERY
		ABFFIIL	BAILIFF
		ABFFLOU	BUFFALO
		ABFHLSU	BASHFUL
		ABFIILR	BIFILAR
		ABFLOTY	BOAT-FLY
		ABGGGIN	BAGGING
		ABGHLRU	BURGHAL
		ABGIKNN	BANKING
		ABGILOR	GARBOIL
		ABGKKNO	BANGKOK
		ABGLMOU	LUMBAGO
		ABGLRRU	BURGLAR
		ABGNOOT	TOBOGAN
		ABGNOPR	PROBANG
		ABGOORT	BOTARGO
		ABHIINT	INHABIT
		ABHILNO	HOBNAIL
		ABHILOS	ABOLISH
		ABHILTU	HALIBUT

ABHIORS	BOARISH	ACCEHTU	CATECHU	ACDDEIN	CANDIED
ABHMNSU	BUSHMAN	ACCEHXY	CACHEXY	ACDDEIU	DECIDUA
ABHORRU	HARBOUR	ACCEILN	CALCINE	ACDDEOP	DECAPOD
ABHOTUY	HAUTBOY	ACCEILO	COELIAC	ACDDERU	ADDUCER
ABIILMU	BULIMIA	ACCEILT	CALCITE	ACDDHKO	HADDOCK
ABIILOV	BOLIVIA	ACCEIMR	CERAMIC	ACDDIRS	DISCARD
ABIILRY	BILIARY	ACCEINO	COCAINE	ACDDKOP	PADDOCK
ABIILST	STIBIAL		OCEANIC	ACDEEES	DECEASE
ABIILTY	ABILITY	ACCEINR	CIRCEAN	ACDEEHL	CHALDEE
ABIINRT	BRITAIN	ACCEINV	VACCINE	ACDEELR	DECLARE
ABIKLMN	LAMBKIN	ACCEIPR	CAPRICE	ACDEENV	VENDACE
ABILLMN	BILL-MAN	ACCEIQU	CACIQUE	ACDEERT	CEDRATE
ABILLNP	PINBALL	ACCEIST	ASCETIC	ACDEETU	EDUCATE
ABILLPY	PLIABLY	ACCEKLR	CACKLER	ACDEFIN	FANCIED
ABILMOX	MAILBOX		CLACKER	ACDEFRS	SCARFED
ABILOPR	PARBOIL		CRACKLE	ACDEGGR	CRAGGED
ABILORT	ORBITAL	ACCEKOP	PEACOCK	ACDEGIS	DISCAGE
ABILRRY	LIBRARY	ACCEKRR	CRACKER	ACDEGKO	DOCKAGE
ABIMPST	BAPTISM	ACCELLY	CALYCLE	ACDEGNO	DECAGON
ABINORR	BAR-IRON	ACCELNO	CONCEAL	ACDEGOR	CORDAGE
ABINORW	RAINBOW	ACCELOR	CORACLE	ACDEHIN	ECHIDNA
ABINOST	BASTION	ACCELOT	CACOLET	ACDEHMR	CHARMED
ABINRTV	VIBRANT	ACCELSU	SACCULE	ACDEHMS	CHASMED
ABIPSTT	BAPTIST	ACCENOR	CONACRE	ACDEHOT	CATHODE
ABKLLNY	BLANKLY	ACCENOV	CONCAVE	ACDEHPP	CHAPPED
ABKLRUW	BULWARK	ACCENPT	PECCANT	ACDEILL	CEDILLA
ABKMNOO	BOOKMAN	ACCEPRY	PECCARY	ACDEILM	DECIMAL
ABLLLUY	LULLABY	ACCERSU	ACCURSE		DECLAIM
ABLLNOO	BALLOON		ACCUSER		MEDICAL
ABLLORU	LOBULAR	ACCFIIP	PACIFIC	ACDEILN	ICELAND
ABLMOOT	TOMBOLA	ACCFILY	CALCIFY	ACDEILR	DECRIAL
ABLMOVY	MOVABLY	ACCFLOW	COW-CALF		RADICLE
ABLMPUU	PABULUM	ACCGHIO	CHICAGO	ACDEILT	CITADEL
ABLMTUY	MUTABLY	ACCHIOT	CHAOTIC		DELTAIC
ABLNORW	BARN-OWL	ACCHNRU	CRAUNCH		DIALECT
ABLNOTY	NOTABLY	ACCHPTU	CATCHUP		EDICTAL
ABLNTUY	TUNABLY	ACCHRST	SCRATCH	ACDEINY	CYANIDE
ABLOPYY	PLAYBOY	ACCIINT	ACTINIC	ACDEITT	DICTATE
ABLRTUU	TUBULAR	ACCIIST	SCIATIC	ACDEITY	EDACITY
ABMORTU	TAMBOUR	ACCILMO	COMICAL	ACDELLS	SCALLED
ABNOOSS	BASSOON	ACCILMU	CALCIUM	ACDELNO	CELADON
ABNOTUY	BUOYANT	ACCILNO	CONICAL	ACDELNS	CALENDS
ABOORYZ	BRYOZOA		LACONIC	ACDELST	CASTLED
ABRRSUY	BURSARY	ACCILNY	CYNICAL	ACDELWW	DEW-CLAW
ABRSTUU	ARBUTUS	ACCILOR	CALORIC	ACDEMNU	DECUMAN
ACCDDEI	CADDICE	ACCILOV	VOCALIC	ACDEMOR	COMRADE
ACCDEEN	CADENCE	ACCILRU	CRUCIAL	ACDEMPR	CRAMPED
ACCDEKO	COCKADE	ACCILSS	CLASSIC	ACDENNT	CANDENT
ACCDEKR	CRACKED	ACCISTT	TACTICS	ACDENOR	ACORNED
ACCDESU	ACCUSED	ACCISTU	CAUSTIC	ACDENPT	PANDECT
ACCDFIL	FLACCID	ACCKLMU	CALMUCK	ACDENRU	DURANCE
ACCDILS	SCALDIC	ACCKLOR	CARLOCK	ACDENRY	ARDENCY
ACCEFLU	FELUCCA	ACCKOSS	CASSOCK	ACDENST	DESCANT
ACCEGOS	SOCCAGE		COSSACK	ACDENTU	UNACTED
ACCEHIL	CHALICE	ACCMOPT	ACCOMPT	ACDEOPS	PEASCOD
ACCEHIN	CHICANE		COMPACT	ACDEORS	SARCODE
ACCEHLN	CHANCEL	ACCNOOR	RACCOON	ACDEORT	CORDATE
ACCEHLO	COCHLEA	ACCNOTT	CONTACT		REDCOAT
ACCEHNR	CHANCRE	ACCNOTU	ACCOUNT	ACDEOUV	COUVADE
ACCEHOR	CAROCHE	ACCOPTY	COPY-CAT	ACDEPRS	SCARPED
ACCEHRT	CATCHER	ACDDEHR	CHEDDAR	ACDERSU	CRUSADE

ACDERTT	DETRACT	ACEELNV	ENCLAVE	ACEHHRT	HATCHER
ACDERTU	TRADUCE		VALENCE	ACEHHRU	HACHURE
ACDFIIY	ACIDIFY	ACEELPR	REPLACE	ACEHHTT	HATCHET
ACDGORT	DOG-CART	ACEELRR	CLEARER	ACEHILL	HELICAL
ACDHIIL	CHILIAD	ACEELRT	TREACLE	ACEHILT	ETHICAL
ACDHIRY	DIARCHY	ACEELRV	CLEAVER	ACEHIMN	MACHINE
ACDHOOT	CATHOOD	ACEELVX	EXCLAVE	ACEHIMP	IMPEACH
ACDHOPR	POCHARD	ACEEMRT	CREMATE	ACEHINN	ENCHAIN
ACDHORR	ORCHARD	ACEENNP	PENANCE	ACEHIPR	CHARPIE
ACDIIRT	TRIADIC	ACEENNT	CANTEEN	ACFHIPT	APHETIC
ACDIITY	ACIDITY	ACEENNY	CAYENNE		HEPATIC
ACDILLO	CODILLA	ACEENOT	ACETONE	ACEHIRS	CASHIER
ACDILMO	DOMICAL	ACEENRT	CRENATE	ACEHIRV	ARCHIVE
ACDILOP	PLACOID	ACEENTU	CUNEATE	ACEHKLR	HACKLER
ACDILOR	CORDIAL	ACEEORT	OCREATE	ACEHKLS	SHACKLE
ACDILOT	COTIDAL	ACEEPRR	CAPERER	ACEHKNY	HACKNEY
ACDILTW	WILD-CAT	ACEERRT	CATERER	ACEHLLS	SHELLAC
ACDIMMU	CADMIUM		RETRACE	ACEHLMY	ALCHEMY
ACDIMMO	MONADIC		TERRACE	ACEHLNN	CHANNEL
	NOMADIC	ACEERTX	EXACTER	ACEHLNR	CHARNEL
ACDIMNY	DYNAMIC		EXCRETA	ACEHLOP	EPOCHAL
ACDIOPR	PARODIC	ACEESTY	CAT'S-EYE	ACEHLOR	CHOLERA
	PICADOR	ACEFFHR	CHAFFER		CHORALE
ACDIORS	SARCOID	ACEFHMR	CHAMFER	ACEHLPT	CHAPLET
ACDIORT	CAROTID	ACEFILM	MALEFIC	ACEHLPY	CHEAPLY
ACDIOTY	DACOITY	ACEFINN	FINANCE	ACEHLST	SATCHEL
ACDIRST	DRASTIC	ACEFINR	FANCIER	ACEHLTT	CHATTEL
ACDITUV	VIADUCT	ACEFINS	FASCINE		LATCHET
ACDJNTU	ADJUNCT	ACEFITY	ACETIFY	ACEHMNT	MANCHET
ACDKLOP	PADLOCK	ACEFLRU	CAREFUL	ACEHMRR	CHARMER
ACDLLUY	OUCALLY	ACEFNRU	FURNACE	ACEHNNT	ENCHANT
ACDLNOR	CALDRON	ACEFOTU	OUTFACE	ACEHNRR	RANCHER
ACDMMNO	COMMAND	ACEFRRT	REFRACT	ACEHNRT	CHANTER
ACDMOOW	CAMWOOD	ACEFRRU	FARCEUR	ACEHNST	CHASTEN
ACDNOOR	CARDOON	ACEFRSU	SURFACE	ACEHNTU	UNTEACH
ACDNORU	CANDOUR	ACEFRTU	FURCATE	ACEHOPR	POACHER
ACDORST	COSTARD	ACEGHNR	CHANGER	ACEHPRT	CHAPTER
ACDORSU	CRUSADO	ACEGHOU	GOUACHE		PATCHER
ACDRSTU	CUSTARD	ACEGHOW	COWHAGE	ACEHPRY	EPARCHY
ACEEFIN	FAIENCE	ACEGHRR	CHARGER	ACEHRRT	CHARTER
	FIANCÉE	ACEGILL	ELLAGIC	ACEHRRY	ARCHERY
ACEEFPR	PREFACE	ACEGILN	ANGELIC	ACEHRTT	CHATTER
ACEEGIL	ELEGIAC		GALENIC		RATCHET
ACEEGNT	CENTAGE	ACEGILP	PELAGIC	ACEHRTW	WATCHER
ACEEGSU	ESCUAGE	ACEGILR	GLACIER	ACEHRTY	YACHTER
ACEEHHT	CHEETAH		GRACILE	ACEIILZ	LAICIZE
ACEEHIV	ACHIEVE	ACEGIMR	GRIMACE	ACEIKMR	KERAMIC
ACEEHMT	MACHETE	ACEGINO	COINAGE	ACEIKPR	EAR-PICK
ACEEHNN	ENHANCE	ACEGINR	GRECIAN	ACEIKPX	PICKAXE
ACEEHNP	CHEAPEN	ACEGKLO	LOCKAGE	ACEIKSS	SEASICK
ACEEHNS	ENCHASE	ACEGKLR	GRACKLE	ACEILLR	AIR-CELL
ACEEHRR	REACHER	ACEGLLO	COLLAGE	ACEILLX	LEXICAL
ACEEHRT	CHEATER	ACEGLNO	CONGEAL	ACEILMN	MELANIC
	HECTARE	ACEGNOR	ACROGEN	ACEILMR	MIRACLE
	TEACHER	ACEGNOT	COAGENT		RECLAIM
ACEEHST	ESCHEAT		COGNATE	ACEILMT	CLIMATE
ACEEILP	CALIPEE	ACEGORS	CORSAGE	ACEILMX	EXCLAIM
ACEEKNP	KNEE-CAP	ACEGORU	COURAGE	ACEILMY	MYCELIA
ACEELNR	CLEANER	ACEGOTT	COTTAGE	ACEILNP	PANICLE
ACEELNS	CLEANSE	ACEGSTU	SCUTAGE		PELICAN
	SCALENE	ACEHHLT	HATCHEL	ACEILNR	CARLINE

ACEILNS	SANICLE
ACEILNU	CAULINE
ACEILOR	CARIOLE
ACEILOT	ALOETIC
ACEILPR	REPLICA
ACEILPS	SPECIAL
ACEILPT	PLICATE
ACEILRT	ARTICLE
	RECITAL
ACEILRU	AURICLE
ACEILRV	CALIVER
	CLAVIER
ACEILST	ELASTIC
ACEILSV	VESICAL
ACEILTT	LATTICE
	TACTILE
ACEIMNR	CARMINE
ACEIMPY	PYAEMIC
ACEIMSU	CAESIUM
ACEINNP	PINNACE
ACEINNT	ANCIENT
ACEINOT	ACONITE
ACEINPR	CAPRINE
ACEINPS	PINCASE
ACEINRS	ARSENIC
ACEINRT	CERTAIN
ACEINTT	NICTATE
	TETANIC
ACEINTX	INEXACT
ACEIOPT	ECTOPIA
ACEIORS	SCORIAE
ACEIPPR	EPICARP
ACEIPRS	EPACRIS
ACEIPRT	PARETIC
ACEIPST	SPICATE
ACEIPSU	AUSPICE
ACEIPSZ	CAPSIZE
ACEIPTV	CAPTIVE
ACEIQRU	ACQUIRE
ACEIQUZ	CAZIQUE
ACEIRRR	CARRIER
ACEIRRT	ERRATIC
ACEIRST	STEARIC
ACEIRSV	VARICES
	VISCERA
ACEISST	ASCITES
ACEITTX	EXTATIC
ACEJLOR	CAJOLER
ACEJNOT	JACONET
ACEKKNR	KNACKER
ACEKLNR	CRANKLE
ACEKLNS	SLACKEN
ACEKLPT	PLACKET
ACEKORR	CROAKER
ACEKRRT	TRACKER
ACELLMO	CALOMEL
ACELLNY	CLEANLY
ACELLOT	COLLATE
ACELLPS	SCALPEL
ACELLRY	CLEARLY
ACELMOU	LEUCOMA

ACELMRY	CAMELRY
ACELMTU	CALUMET
ACELNNU	UNCLEAN
ACELNPS	ENCLASP
ACELNPT	CLAP-NET
ACELNRT	CENTRAL
ACELNRU	LUCARNE
	NUCLEAR
	UNCLEAR
ACELNRY	LARCENY
ACELNTT	CANTLET
ACELNTY	LATENCY
ACELNVY	VALENCY
ACELOPT	POLECAT
ACELOQU	COEQUAL
ACELORY	CALOYER
ACELOST	ALE-COST
	LACTOSE
	TALCOSE
ACELOTT	CALOTTE
ACELOTU	OCULATE
ACELOTY	ACOLYTE
ACELOUV	VACUOLE
ACELPPR	CLAPPER
ACELPRS	CLASPER
ACELPRY	PRELACY
ACELPSU	CAPSULE
	SPECULA
ACELPTY	ECTYPAL
ACELQRU	LACQUER
ACELRRW	CRAWLER
ACELRST	SCARLET
ACELRSU	SECULAR
ACELRTT	CLATTER
ACELSTU	SULCATE
ACELTUY	ACUTELY
ACELTXY	EXACTLY
ACEMMRR	CRAMMER
ACEMNOR	CREMONA
	ROMANCE
ACEMOPR	COMPARE
ACEMORU	MORCEAU
ACEMPRS	SCAMPER
ACENNOS	SONANCE
ACENNOT	CONNATE
ACENNOZ	CANZONE
ACENNRY	CANNERY
ACENNST	NASCENT
ACENNTY	TENANCY
ACENORT	ENACTOR
ACENPRR	PRANCER
ACENRTU	CENTAUR
ACENRTY	NECTARY
ACENSTU	NUT-CASE
ACEOOPP	APOCOPE
ACEOOTZ	ECTOZOA
ACEORRT	CREATOR
	REACTOR
ACEORST	COASTER
ACEORSU	ACEROUS
	CAROUSE

ACEORTV	OVERACT
ACEORTX	EXACTOR
ACEOSSU	CASEOUS
ACEOSTT	COSTATE
ACEOSTU	ACETOUS
ACEPRRS	SCRAPER
ACEPRST	SPECTRA
ACEPRTU	CAPTURE
ACEQRTU	RACQUET
ACERRTT	RETRACT
ACERRTY	TRACERY
ACERSST	ACTRESS
ACERSSV	SCARVES
ACERSTT	SCATTER
ACERSTY	SECTARY
ACERTTX	EXTRACT
ACERTUY	CAUTERY
ACESSTY	ECSTASY
ACESTTU	SCUTATE
ACESTTY	TESTACY
ACFFIIT	CAITIFF
ACFFILT	AFFLICT
ACFFIRT	TRAFFIC
ACFFOST	CAST-OFF
ACFGINR	FARCING
ACFHIST	CAT-FISH
ACFHISU	FUCHSIA
ACFIILN	FINICAL
ACFILRY	CLARIFY
ACFIMSS	FASCISM
ACFINNY	INFANCY
ACFINOT	FACTION
ACFINRT	FRANTIC
ACFIRSY	SCARIFY
ACFISST	FASCIST
ACFLRUU	FURCULA
ACFLTTU	TACTFUL
ACFLTUY	FACULTY
ACFORTY	FACTORY
ACGGRSY	SCRAGGY
ACGHIKN	HACKING
ACGHINR	CHAGRIN
ACGHINT	GNATHIC
ACGHIPR	GRAPHIC
ACGIITU	AUGITIC
ACGIKNP	PACKING
ACGIKNS	SACKING
ACGILLN	CALLING
ACGILLO	LOGICAL
ACGILNT	CATLING
ACGILNU	GLUCINA
ACGINNT	CANTING
ACGINOR	ORGANIC
ACGINOT	COATING
ACGINPR	CARPING
ACGINRS	SACRING
ACGINRT	TRACING
ACGINRV	CARVING
	CRAVING
ACGINST	CASTING
ACGIRST	GASTRIC

ACGNNOR	CRANNOG		COAL-PIT	ACKMOTT	MATTOCK
ACGNOOT	OCTAGON		OPTICAL	ACLLLOY	LOCALLY
ACHIIMT	HAMITIC		TOPICAL	ACLLOOR	COROLLA
ACHIJNT	JACINTH	ACILOST	STOICAL	ACLLOPS	SCALLOP
ACHILLP	PHALLIC	ACILOTV	VOLTAIC	ACLLOSU	CALLOUS
ACHILOS	SCHOLIA	ACILOTX	TOXICAL	ACLLOVY	VOCALLY
ACHILRY	CHARILY	ACILPST	PLASTIC	ACLMNUY	CALUMNY
ACHIMOS	CHAMOIS	ACILPSU	SPICULA	ACLMORU	CLAMOUR
ACHIMST	MASTICH	ACILPTY	CLAY-PIT	ACLNOOR	CORONAL
ACHINNU	UNCHAIN		TYPICAL	ACLNOOV	VOLCANO
ACHINPS	SPINACH	ACILRST	CARLIST	ACLNORW	CORN-LAW
ACHINTX	XANTHIC	ACILRTU	CURTAIL	ACLNPSU	UNCLASP
ACHIORT	CHARIOT	ACILRTY	CLARITY	ACLNSTY	SCANTLY
	HARICOT	ACILRYZ	CRAZILY	ACLOPRT	CALTROP
ACHIPPS	SAPPHIC	ACILSUY	SAUCILY	ACLOPSY	CALYPSO
ACHIPST	SPATHIC	ACILTTY	TACITLY	ACLORSU	CAROLUS
ACHIQRU	CHARQUI	ACILTUV	VICTUAL	ACLOSTU	TALCOUS
ACHIRTU	HAIRCUT	ACIMNOP	CAMPION	ACLPRTY	CRYPTAL
ACHIRTY	CHARITY	ACIMNOR	ROMANIC	ACLRSTY	CRYSTAL
ACHISSS	CHASSIS	ACIMNOS	MASONIC	ACLSSTU	CUTLASS
ACHKMMO	HAMMOCK	ACIMNRU	CRANIUM	ACMNOPR	CRAMPON
ACHKOSS	HASSOCK	ACIMNTT	CATMINT	ACMNOPY	COMPANY
ACHLLOO	ALCOHOL	ACIMORR	ARMORIC	ACMNSTU	SANCTUM
ACHLLOR	CHLORAL	ACIMOST	SOMATIC	ACMOPRT	COMPART
ACHLMSY	CHLAMYS	ACIMPRT	PTARMIC	ACMOPSS	COMPASS
ACHLNOY	HALCYON	ACIMPRY	PRIMACY	ACNNNUY	UNCANNY
ACHLNTU	UNLATCH	ACINNOT	CONTAIN	ACNNORY	CANONRY
ACHLORS	SCHOLAR	ACINNST	STANNIC	ACNOORT	CARTOON
ACHMNOO	MANCHOO	ACINOPT	CAPTION	ACNORRU	RANCOUR
ACHMNOR	MONARCH		PACTION	ACNRRTU	CURRANT
	NOMARCH	ACINORR	CARRION	ACNRTUY	TRUANCY
ACHMOPR	CAMPHOR	ACINOSS	CAISSON	ACNSSTU	SANCTUS
ACHMOST	STOMACH		CASSINO	ACOOPSU	OPACOUS
ACHMSUW	CUMSHAW	ACINOTT	TACTION	ACORRTT	TRACTOR
ACHNOVY	ANCHOVY	ACINOTU	AUCTION	ACORRTU	CURATOR
ACHNPSS	SCHNAPS		CAUTION	ACORRTY	CARROTY
ACHNPUY	PAUNCHY	ACINPRY	CYPRIAN	ACORSSU	SARCOUS
ACHNRTY	CHANTRY	ACINRTU	CURTAIN	ACORSTU	SURCOAT
ACHNSTU	CANTHUS	ACIOPRS	PROSAIC	ACORSUU	RAUCOUS
	STAUNCH	ACIOPRT	APRICOT	ACOSTTU	OUTCAST
ACHOPRY	CHARPOY	ACIOPTY	OPACITY	ACOSUUV	VACUOUS
ACHORSU	AUROCHS	ACIORRS	CORSAIR	ACPPRSY	SCRAPPY
ACHRSTY	STARCHY	ACIORSU	CARIOUS	ADDDENO	DEODAND
ACIIKRS	AIRSICK	ACIPRVY	PRIVACY	ADDEEEY	DEAD-EYE
ACIILNS	SALICIN	ACIPSST	SPASTIC	ADDEEGR	DEGRADE
ACIILRY	CILIARY	ACIPTUY	PAUCITY	ADDEEST	DEAD-SET
ACIILSS	LIASSIC	ACIRSST	SACRIST	ADDEFLY	FADEDLY
ACIIMOT	COMITIA	ACIRSSU	CUIRASS	ADDEFRU	DEFRAUD
ACIINPS	PISCINA	ACIRSTT	ASTRICT	ADDEGHO	GODHEAD
ACIINTT	TITANIC	ACIRSTY	SATYRIC	ADDEGJU	ADJUDGE
ACIIPRT	PIRATIC	ACISSTT	STATICS	ADDEGLN	GLADDEN
ACIIRST	SATIRIC	ACISSTU	CASUIST	ADDEGRU	GUARDED
ACILLMS	MISCALL	ACITUVY	VACUITY	ADDEHIR	DIE-HARD
ACILLRY	LYRICAL	ACJKLOW	LOCK-JAW	ADDEHRS	SHARDED
ACILMPS	PLASMIC	ACJKOPT	JACKPOT	ADDEIIS	DAISIED
ACILMSU	MUSICAL	ACJLORU	JOCULAR	ADDEILP	PLAIDED
ACILNOR	CLARION	ACJPTUU	CAJUPUT	ADDEINO	ADENOID
ACILNPY	PLIANCY	ACKKLMU	KALMUCK	ADDEINU	UNAIDED
ACILNTU	LUNATIC	ACKLLOP	POLLACK	ADDEISV	ADVISED
ACILNUV	VINCULA	ACKLLSY	SLACKLY	ADDELPP	DAPPLED
ACILOPT	CAPITOL	ACKLNOU	UNCLOAK	ADDELPR	PADDLER

45

ADDELRS	SADDLER		PERVADE	ADEILSS	AIDLESS
ADDELRW	DAWDLER	ADEERRT	TREADER	ADEILSY	DIALYSE
	WADDLER	ADEERST	ESTRADE	ADEIMMR	MERMAID
ADDELST	STADDLE	ADEERSV	ADVERSE	ADEIMRR	ADMIRER
ADDELSW	SWADDLE	ADEERTW	WATERED		MARRIED
ADDELTW	TWADDLE	ADEFHST	SHAFTED	ADEIMRT	READMIT
ADDENOT	NODATED	ADEFINT	DEFIANT	ADEIMST	MISDATE
ADDENPU	PUDENDA	ADEFLLN	ELF-LAND	ADEIMTY	DAYTIME
ADDENTU	UNDATED	ADEFLLW	DEWFALL	ADEINOR	ANEROID
ADDERSS	ADDRESS	ADEFLTU	DEFAULT	ADEINRR	DRAINER
ADDFHIS	FADDISH	ADEFOOS	SEA-FOOD	ADEINRS	SARDINE
ADDFINY	DANDIFY	ADEFORY	FEODARY	ADEINRT	TRAINED
ADDFIST	FADDIST	ADEFRRT	REDRAFT	ADEINRV	INVADER
ADDGIMN	MADDING	ADEFRUY	FEUDARY	ADEINST	INSTEAD
ADDGINP	PADDING	ADEGGLR	DRAGGLE		SAINTED
ADDGINW	WADDING	ADEGHIN	HEADING	ADEIOPS	ADIPOSE
ADDGOOY	GOOD-DAY	ADEGILN	DEALING	ADEIOTX	OXIDATE
ADDGORW	GODWARD		LEADING	ADEIPPR	PREPAID
ADDHITY	HYDATID	ADEGINR	GRAINED	ADEIPRS	DESPAIR
ADDIINS	DISDAIN		READING	ADEIRST	ASTRIDE
ADDIKTY	KATYDID	ADEGINW	WINDAGE	ADEIRSV	ADVISER
ADDILMN	MIDLAND	ADEGISV	VISAGED	ADEIRTY	DIETARY
ADDIMNO	DIAMOND	ADEGJTU	JUGATED	ADEISWY	WAYSIDE
ADDLLRU	DULLARD	ADEGLNN	ENGLAND	ADEJOPR	JEOPARD
ADDLTWY	TWADDLY	ADEGLNR	DANGLER	ADEKLNY	NAKEDLY
ADEEEPS	DEEP-SEA		GNARLED	ADEKLST	STALKED
ADEEESW	SEAWEED	ADEGNNU	DUNNAGE	ADEKMNR	DENMARK
ADEEFLR	FEDERAL	ADEGNRT	DRAG-NET	ADEKNRR	KNARRED
ADEEGGN	ENGAGED	ADEGORS	DOG'S-EAR	ADEKNSU	UNASKED
ADEEGNR	DERANGE	ADEGORW	DOWAGER	ADELLMU	MEDULLA
	GRANDEE	ADEGOTT	TOGATED	ADELMNR	MANDREL
	GRENADE	ADEGRTY	TRAGEDY	ADELMOR	EARLDOM
ADEEHRR	ADHERER	ADEHILL	DELILAH	ADELNRS	SLANDER
ADEEHRT	HEARTED	ADEHILY	HEADILY	ADELNRU	LURDANE
ADEEILN	DELAINE	ADEHKNS	SHANKED	ADELNST	SLANTED
ADEEIMT	MEDIATE	ADEHLNS	HANDSEL	ADELNTU	LUNATED
ADEEINS	ANISEED	ADEHLSS	SLASHED	ADELNTZ	ZETLAND
ADEEISS	DISEASE	ADEHLTY	DEATHLY	ADELOPR	LEOPARD
	SEASIDE	ADEHNRU	UNHEARD	ADELOPT	TADPOLE
ADEEITV	DEVIATE	ADEHNTU	HAUNTED	ADELORU	ROULADE
ADEEKWY	WEEKDAY	ADEHOPX	HEXAPOD		URODELA
ADEELMR	EMERALD	ADEHORR	HOARDER	ADELPRY	PEDLARY
ADEELMS	MEASLED	ADEHPST	SPATHED	ADELRTX	DEXTRAL
ADEELMT	MEDALET	ADEHRTY	HYDRATE	ADELRTY	LYRATED
ADEELNR	LEARNED		THREADY	ADELRZZ	DAZZLER
ADEELNW	WEALDEN	ADEIILS	SEDILIA	ADELTTW	WATTLED
ADEELPR	PEARLED	ADEIJMR	JEMIDAR	ADELTUV	VAULTED
	PLEADER	ADEILLR	DALLIER	ADEMNNU	MUNDANE
ADEELRT	RELATED	ADEILLY	IDEALLY		UNNAMED
	TREADLE	ADEILMM	DILEMMA	ADEMNRU	DURAMEN
ADEELRW	LEEWARD	ADEILMP	IMPLEAD		MAUNDER
ADEELRY	DELAYER	ADEILMS	MISLEAD		UNARMED
ADEELUV	DEVALUE	ADEILNN	ANNELID	ADEMNSS	MADNESS
ADEEMNR	AMENDER	ADEILNR	IRELAND	ADEMNTU	UNTAMED
	MEANDER	ADEILNU	UNIDEAL	ADEMOWY	MEADOWY
ADEEMRR	DREAMER	ADEILPR	LIP-READ	ADEMRRU	EAR-DRUM
ADEEMSU	MEDUSAE		PREDIAL	ADEMSSU	ASSUMED
ADEENRY	DEANERY	ADEILPS	PLEIADS	ADENNOY	ANODYNE
ADEENTT	DENTATE	ADEILPT	PLAITED	ADENNPT	PENDANT
ADEEPRT	PREDATE	ADEILRT	DILATER	ADENOPR	PANDORE
ADEEPRV	DEPRAVE	ADEILRY	READILY	ADENORU	RONDEAU

46

ADENPUV	UNPAVED	ADHILMO	HALIDOM	ADINOPR	PONIARD
ADENRRY	REYNARD	ADHILNY	HANDILY	ADINRSW	INWARDS
ADENRST	STANDER	ADHILOY	HOLIDAY	ADINSTT	DISTANT
ADENRSU	ASUNDER		HYALOID	ADINTTY	DITTANY
ADENRTV	VERDANT	ADHILRY	HARDILY	ADIOPRT	PAROTID
ADENRUY	UNREADY	ADHILSY	SHADILY	ADIORSU	SAUROID
ADENSSS	SADNESS	ADHIMPS	DAMPISH	ADIORTU	AUDITOR
ADENTUX	UNTAXED	ADHINPU	DAUPHIN	ADIOSVW	DISAVOW
ADEOPRR	EAR-DROP	ADHKORW	DOR-HAWK	ADIPRST	DISPART
ADEORTU	OUTDARE	ADHLLNO	HOLLAND	ADIRSSU	SARDIUS
	READ-OUT	ADHMNOO	MANHOOD	ADIRSUY	DYSURIA
ADEORYZ	ZEDOARY	ADHNNUY	UNHANDY	ADJNORU	ADJOURN
ADEPRRY	DRAPERY	ADHNRSY	SHANDRY	ADKORWY	DAYWORK
ADERRST	STARRED	ADHNRTY	HYDRANT	ADKRSWY	SKYWARD
ADERSSU	ASSURED	ADHNRUY	UNHARDY	ADLLLOR	LOLLARD
ADERSTW	STEWARD	ADHOPST	DASH-POT	ADLLMOW	WADMOLL
ADERSUY	DASYURE	ADHOSWY	SHADOWY	ADLLMOY	MODALLY
ADESTTU	STATUED	ADIIINR	IRIDIAN	ADLLNOW	LOWLAND
ADESTUY	TUESDAY	ADIILNV	INVALID	ADLLOPR	POLLARD
ADFFHNO	OFFHAND	ADIILST	DIALIST	ADLMORU	MODULAR
ADFFIST	DISTAFF	ADIINPR	PRIDIAN	ADLNORU	NODULAR
ADFHLNU	HANDFUL	ADIINST	DISTAIN	ADLNOSY	SYNODAL
ADFHOOS	SHADOOF	ADIINSU	INDUSIA	ADLNRUY	LAUNDRY
ADFILNN	FINLAND	ADIIRST	DIARIST	ADMNOOW	WOODMAN
ADFILOR	FLORIDA	ADIIRTY	ARIDITY	ADMNOQU	QUONDAM
ADFIMNY	DAMNIFY	ADIITVY	AVIDITY	ADMNORT	DORMANT
ADFLORU	FOULARD	ADIJMSU	JUDAISM		MORDANT
ADFOOPT	FOOTPAD	ADIKLOS	ODALISK	ADMNSTU	DUST-MAN
ADFORRW	FORWARD	ADIKMNN	MANKIND	ADMORST	STARDOM
	FROWARD	ADIKMSS	DISMASK	ADMRSTU	DURMAST
ADGGINR	NIGGARD	ADIKOTY	DAKOITY		MUSTARD
ADGHILO	HIDALGO	ADIKPRS	DISPARK	ADNNOOY	NOONDAY
ADGHINS	DASHING	ADILLVY	VALIDLY	ADNOORT	TORNADO
	SHADING	ADILLYY	DAY-LILY	ADNORSW	ONWARDS
ADGHIPR	DIGRAPH	ADILMNR	MANDRIL	ADNORTU	ROTUNDA
ADGHOOR	ROAD-HOG	ADILMNU	MAUDLIN	ADNOSTU	ASTOUND
ADGHRTU	DRAUGHT	ADILMOP	DIPLOMA	ADNRSUW	SUNWARD
ADGIILT	DIGITAL	ADILMOY	AMYLOID	ADNSTYY	DYNASTY
ADGIINO	GONIDIA	ADILMSU	DUALISM	ADOORWY	DOORWAY
ADGILNN	LANDING	ADILNOR	ORDINAL	ADORSTW	TOWARDS
ADGILNO	LOADING	ADILNRU	DIURNAL	ADORSUU	ARDUOUS
ADGILNR	DARLING	ADILNSU	SUNDIAL	ADORTUW	OUTWARD
ADGILNU	LANGUID	ADILOOV	OVOIDAL	ADPRSUW	UPWARDS
ADGILUY	GAUDILY	ADILOPR	DIPOLAR	ADSSTUW	SAWDUST
ADGIMNN	DAMNING	ADILORT	DILATOR	AEEEGLT	LEGATEE
ADGINNW	DAWNING	ADILPRY	RAPIDLY	AEEEGNT	TEENAGE
ADGINOR	GORDIAN	ADILPSY	DISPLAY	AEEEGPR	PEERAGE
ADGINRT	TRADING	ADILPTU	PLAUDIT	AEEELRS	RELEASE
ADGINRW	DRAWING	ADILPVY	VAPIDLY	AEEELTV	ELEVATE
ADGIRZZ	GIZZARD	ADILQSU	SQUALID	AEEFHRT	FEATHER
ADGLLOR	RAG-DOLL	ADILRTY	TARDILY	AEEFILW	ALE-WIFE
ADGLNOO	GONDOLA	ADILSTU	DUALIST	AEEFLLT	LEAFLET
ADGLNOY	DAYLONG	ADILSTY	STAIDLY	AEEFLRW	WELFARE
ADGLNRY	GRANDLY	ADILTUY	DUALITY	AEEFLSU	EASEFUL
ADGMNOR	GORMAND	ADIMOST	MASTOID	AEEFMNR	FREEMAN
ADGNOOR	DRAGOON	ADIMPRY	PYRAMID	AEEFOTV	FOVEATE
ADGNORU	AGROUND	ADIMSST	DISMAST	AEEFRST	FEASTER
ADGNRRU	GURNARD	ADIMSTU	STADIUM	AEEFRTU	FEATURE
ADGORST	DOG-STAR	ADINNOR	ANDIRON	AEEGHNN	GEHENNA
ADHHIRS	HARDISH	ADINNST	STAND-IN	AEEGILL	GALILEE
ADHIKRS	DARKISH	ADINOPP	OPPIDAN	AEEGILM	MILEAGE

AEEGILN	LINEAGE	AEEIMSS	SIAMESE	AEEPPRR	PREPARE
AEEGIPR	PIERAGE	AEEINST	ETESIAN	AEEPRSS	ASPERSE
AEEGLLZ	GAZELLE	AEEINTV	NAÏVETÉ	AEEPRTZ	TRAPEZE
AEEGLMN	GLEEMAN	AEEINVW	INWEAVE	AEERRST	SERRATE
	MÉLANGE	AEEIPTX	EXPIATE	AEERRSU	ERASURE
AEEGLNR	ENLARGE	AEEIRST	SERIATE	AEERRSW	SWEARER
	GENERAL	AEEIRTT	ITERATE	AEERRTT	RETREAT
	GLEANER	AEEISVV	EVASIVE		TREATER
AEEGLNT	ELEGANT	AEEIUVX	EXUVIAE	AEERRVW	WAVERER
AEEGLNV	EVANGEL	AEEKLLT	LAKELET	AEERSST	TESSERA
AEEGLRU	LEAGUER	AEEKNNN	NANKEEN	AEERSSY	ESSAYER
AEEGLRY	EAGERLY	AEEKNRW	WAKENER	AEERSTT	ESTREAT
AEEGLSS	SEA-LEGS	AEEKPRS	SPEAKER	AEERSTU	AUSTERE
AEEGLSV	SELVAGE	AEELMNY	AMYLENE	AEERSTW	SWEATER
AEEGLTV	VEGETAL	AEELMPX	EXAMPLE	AEESTTT	TESTATE
AEEGMMT	GEMMATE	AEELMSS	MEASLES	AEFFGIR	GIRAFFE
AEEGMNR	GERMANE	AEELMST	MALTESE	AEFFKOT	TAKE-OFF
AEEGMSS	MESSAGE	AEELMTU	EMULATE	AEFFLNS	SNAFFLE
AEEGNNV	GENEVAN	AEELNRR	LEARNER	AEFFLRU	FEARFUL
AEEGNOP	PEONAGE	AEELNRT	ETERNAL	AEFFLTU	FATEFUL
AEEGNRT	GRANTEE	AEELNRW	RENEWAL	AEFFQRU	QUAFFER
	REAGENT	AEELNSV	ENSLAVE	AEFFTTY	TAFFETY
AEEGNRV	AVENGER	AEELPRS	PLEASER	AEFGGGO	FOGGAGE
	ENGRAVE		RELAPSE	AEFGILO	FOLIAGE
AEEGNTV	VENTAGE	AEELPRT	PRELATE	AEFGILR	FRAGILE
AEEGPRS	PRESAGE	AEELPRU	PLEURAE	AEFGIRS	GAS-FIRE
AEEGRRT	GREATER	AEELPTT	PALETTE	AEFGIRT	FRIGATE
	REGRATE		PELTATE	AEFGITU	FATIGUE
AEEGRRW	WAGERER	AEELPTU	EPAULET	AEFGLOW	FLOWAGE
AEEGRSV	GREAVES	AEELQSU	SEQUELA	AEFGNRT	ENGRAFT
AEEGTTZ	GAZETTE	AEELRRT	RELATER	AEFGORR	FORAGER
AEEHHNT	HEATHEN	AEELRSS	EARLESS	AEFGORV	FORGAVE
AEEHHRT	HEATHER	AEELRST	STEALER	AEFGRRT	GRAFTER
AEEHKNR	HEARKEN	AEELRSV	SEVERAL	AEFHLTU	HATEFUL
AEEHLNT	LETHEAN	AEELRUV	REVALUE	AEFHRRT	FARTHER
AEEHLOR	EAR-HOLE	AEELTVW	WAVELET	AEFIILT	FILIATE
AEEHLRT	LEATHER	AEEMMPY	EMPYEMA	AEFILMN	INFLAME
AEEHLSY	EYELASH	AEEMMRT	AMMETER	AEFILNT	INFLATE
AEEHLTT	ATHLETE	AEEMNNO	ANEMONE	AEFILNU	INFULAE
AEEHMNT	METHANE	AEEMNNP	PEN-NAME	AEFILOT	FOLIATE
AEEHMRT	THERMAE	AEEMOSW	AWESOME	AEFILRU	FAILURE
AEEHNRT	EARTHEN	AEEMPRT	TEMPERA	AEFIMNR	FIREMAN
	HEARTEN	AEEMQRU	MARQUEE	AEFIMRR	FIREARM
AEEHNTW	WHEATEN	AEEMRST	STEAMER	AEFINNT	INFANTE
AEEHPUV	UPHEAVE	AEEMRSU	MEASURE	AEFINPR	FIRE-PAN
AEEHRRS	SHEARER	AEEMRTY	MÉTAYER	AEFINRR	REFRAIN
AEEHRSW	WHEREAS	AEENNRS	ENSNARE	AEFIRRR	FARRIER
AEEHRTT	THEATER	AEENPST	PENATES	AEFKLNR	FLANKER
	THEATRE	AEENPSX	EXPANSE	AEFKLUW	WAKEFUL
	THEREAT	AEENRST	EARNEST	AEFKORS	FORSAKE
AEEHRTW	WEATHER		EASTERN	AEFLLNN	FLANNEL
	WHEREAT	AEENRTT	ENTREAT	AEFLLSY	FALSELY
	WREATHE		RATTEEN	AEFLNRU	FLÂNEUR
AEEHSSV	SHEAVES		TERNATE		FUNERAL
AEEILNT	LINEATE	AEENRTV	VETERAN	AEFLNTT	FLATTEN
AEEILPT	PILEATE	AEENUVW	UNWEAVE	AEFLORT	FLOATER
AEEILRS	REALISE	AEEOPRT	OPERATE	AEFLPPR	FLAPPER
AEEILRT	ATELIER	AEEORST	ROSEATE	AEFLPRS	FELSPAR
AEEILRZ	REALIZE	AEEORSV	OVERSEA	AEFLPRY	PALFREY
AEEIMNT	MATINÉE	AEEORTV	OVEREAT	AEFLRSU	REFUSAL
AEEIMNX	EXAMINE	AEEORVW	OVERAWE	AEFLRTT	FLATTER

48

SEVEN-LETTER WORDS

AEFLRTU	TEARFUL	AEGINRW	WEARING	AEGORTT	GAROTTE
AEFMNOR	FORAMEN	AEGINST	EASTING	AEGORTU	OUTRAGE
	FOREMAN		INGESTA	AEGORVY	VOYAGER
AEFMORR	FOREARM		TEASING	AEGOSSU	GASEOUS
AEFNOPR	PROFANE	AEGINTV	VINTAGE	AEGOSTW	STOWAGE
AEFNRSS	FARNESS	AEGINVW	WEAVING	AEGOTTV	GAVOTTE
AEFNSST	FATNESS	AEGIRRZ	GRAZIER	AEGPRRS	GRASPER
AEFORRY	FORAYER	AEGIRTV	VIRGATE	AEGPRRY	GRAPERY
AEGGGLU	LUGGAGE	AEGISTY	GASEITY	AEGPSTU	UPSTAGE
AEGGHLR	HAGGLER	AEGLLLY	LEGALLY	AEGTTTU	GUTTATE
AEGGINR	GEARING	AEGLLNO	GALLEON	AEHHJOV	JEHOVAH
AEGGIOR	GEORGIA	AEGLLOR	ALLEGRO	AEHHLTY	HEALTHY
AEGGJRY	JAGGERY	AEGLLOT	TOLLAGE	AEHHSTY	SHEATHY
AEGGRSS	AGGRESS	AEGLLRY	ALLERGY	AEHILNR	HERNIAL
AEGGRST	STAGGER		GALLERY		INHALER
AEGGRSW	SWAGGER		LARGELY	AEHILNY	HYALINE
AEGGRWY	WAGGERY		REGALLY	AEHILPR	HARELIP
AEGHIJR	JAGHIRE	AEGLLTU	GLUTEAL	AEHILTY	HYALITE
AEGHILN	HEALING	AEGLMNR	MANGLER	AEHILVY	HEAVILY
AEGHINR	HEARING	AEGLMPU	PLUMAGE	AEHIMSS	MESSIAH
AEGHINT	HEATING	AEGLNPR	GRAPNEL	AEHIMST	ATHEISM
AEGHINY	HYGEIAN	AEGLNPS	SPANGLE	AEHINRT	HAIRNET
AEGHLRU	LAUGHER	AEGLNRU	GRANULE	AEHINSS	HESSIAN
AEGHNOX	HEXAGON	AEGLNRW	WRANGLE	AEHINSV	EVANISH
AEGHOST	HOSTAGE	AEGLNSU	ANGELUS	AEHIPPT	EPITAPH
AEGIIMN	IMAGINE	AEGLNTT	GANTLET	AEHIPSS	APHESIS
AEGIINR	NIGERIA	AEGLNTW	TWANGLE	AEHIRRR	HARRIER
AEGILLL	ILLEGAL	AEGLNUW	GUNWALE	AEHISTT	ATHEIST
AEGILLP	PILLAGE	AEGLOTV	VOLTAGE	AEHLLYZ	HAZELLY
AEGILLT	TILLAGE	AEGLPPR	GRAPPLE	AEHLMNO	MANHOLE
AEGILLV	VILLAGE	AEGLRRU	REGULAR	AEHLMOR	ARMHOLE
AEGILLY	AGILELY	AEGLRSS	LARGESS	AEHLMRT	THERMAL
AEGILNN	EANLING	AEGLRTU	TEGULAR	AEHLMRU	HUMERAL
AEGILNR	ENGRAIL	AEGLRTY	GREATLY	AEHLNRT	ENTHRAL
AEGILNS	LEASING	AEGLRVY	GRAVELY	AEHLNSU	UNLEASH
	SEALING	AEGLTUV	VULGATE	AEHLORT	LOATHER
AEGILNT	GELATIN	AEGLUVY	VAGUELY		RAT-HOLE
	GENITAL	AEGMMRU	RUMMAGE	AEHLPRS	SPHERAL
AEGILRZ	GLAZIER	AEGMNNO	AGNOMEN	AEHLPSS	HAPLESS
AEGILTY	EGALITY	AEGMNPY	PYGMEAN	AEHLPSY	SHAPELY
AEGIMNN	MEANING	AEGMNRT	GARMENT	AEHLRTY	EARTHLY
AEGIMNT	MINTAGE	AEGMNRY	GERMANY	AEHLSTT	STEALTH
AEGIMPR	EPIGRAM	AEGMNTU	AUGMENT	AEHLTWY	WEALTHY
	PRIMAGE	AEGMOOR	MOORAGE	AEHMMRS	SHAMMER
AEGIMRR	ARMIGER	AEGMOXY	EXOGAMY	AEHMNOS	HOSEMAN
AEGIMRT	MIGRATE	AEGNNOT	TONNAGE	AEHMRSS	SMASHER
	RAG-TIME	AEGNNRT	REGNANT	AEHMRST	HAMSTER
AEGIMRY	IMAGERY	AEGNNTT	TANGENT	AEHNOPR	ORPHEAN
AEGINNR	EARNING	AEGNNTU	TUNNAGE	AEHNOPT	PHAETON
	ENGRAIN	AEGNOPT	PONTAGE	AEHNORT	ANOTHER
	GRANNIE	AEGNORW	WAGONER	AEHNPRS	SHARPEN
AEGINNT	GENTIAN	AEGNOSY	NOSEGAY	AEHNPRT	PANTHER
AEGINNV	ANGEVIN	AEGNPRT	TREPANG	AEHNRSS	HARNESS
AEGINOS	AGONISE	AEGNRRT	GRANTER	AEHNRTU	HAUNTER
AEGINOZ	AGONIZE		REGRANT		UNEARTH
AEGINPP	GENIPAP	AEGNRST	STRANGE	AEHNRTX	NARTHEX
AEGINPS	SPINAGE	AEGNSSY	GAYNESS	AEHORST	EAR-SHOT
AEGINRR	EAR-RING	AEGOPRT	PORTAGE	AEHOSTU	ATHEOUS
AEGINRT	GRANITE	AEGOPST	POSTAGE	AEHPPRS	PERHAPS
	INGRATE	AEGOPTT	POTTAGE	AEHPRRS	SHARPER
AEGINRV	VINEGAR	AEGORST	STORAGE	AEHPRSS	SERAPHS

49

AEHRRTU	URETHRA	AEILOTV	VIOLATE		URINATE
AEHRSST	SHASTER	AEILPRT	PLAITER	AEINRTW	TINWARE
AEHRSTT	SHATTER	AEILPRV	PREVAIL	AEINRVV	VERVAIN
AEHRSTV	HARVEST	AEILPST	TALIPES	AEINSST	ENTASIS
AEHRSVW	WHARVES	AEILQSU	SALIQUE	AEINSTT	INSTATE
AEHRTUU	HAUTEUR	AEILQTU	LIQUATE		SATINET
AEHRTWY	WREATHY	AEILRRT	RETIRAL	AEINSTU	SINUATE
AEHSTUX	EXHAUST		TRAILER	AEINSWY	ANYWISE
AEIIKNT	KAINITE	AEILRSS	AIRLESS	AEINTXY	ANXIETY
AEIILNN	ANILINE	AEILRST	REALIST	AEIOQSU	SEQUOIA
AEIILRS	ISRAELI		SALTIER	AEIORST	OTARIES
AEIIMNT	MINIATE		SALTIRE	AEIOSTZ	AZOTISE
AEIIMTT	IMITATE	AEILRSV	REVISAL	AEIPPRS	APPRISE
AEIINNS	ASININE	AEILRTY	REALITY	AEIPPRT	PERIAPT
AEIINRS	SIRENIA	AEILRVV	REVIVAL	AEIPRRS	PRAISER
AEIINRT	INERTIA	AEILRVY	VIRELAY	AEIPRSS	PARESIS
AEIIPRR	PRAIRIE	AEILRWY	WEARILY	AEIPRST	PIASTER
AEIIRRV	RIVIERA	AEILSTV	ESTIVAL		TRAIPSE
AEIITTV	VITIATE	AEILUVX	EXUVIAL	AEIPRSU	UPRAISE
AEIJLNV	JAVELIN	AEIMMNS	MISNAME	AEIPRSV	PARVISE
AEIJMNS	JASMINE	AEIMNNT	MANNITE	AEIPRTV	PRIVATE
AEIKLMN	MANLIKE	AEIMNOR	MORAINE	AEIPRXY	PYREXIA
AEIKLRW	WARLIKE	AEIMNPR	PERMIAN	AEIPSSV	PASSIVE
AEIKMNP	PIKEMAN	AEIMNRR	MARINER	AEIRRTY	RETIARY
AEIKMST	MISTAKE	AEIMNRS	SIRNAME	AEIRSSZ	ASSIZER
AEILLPS	ILLAPSE	AEIMNRT	MINARET	AEIRSTT	ARTISTE
AEILLRT	LITERAL		RAIMENT		STRIATE
AEILLST	TALLIES	AEIMNTV	VIETNAM	AEIRTTT	TITRATE
AEILLVX	VEXILLA	AEIMNTY	AMENITY	AEIRTUZ	AZURITE
AEILMNP	IMPANEL	AEIMOTZ	ATOMIZE	AEIRTVY	VARIETY
	MANIPLE	AEIMPRT	PRIMATE	AEISSUV	SUASIVE
AEILMNR	MARLINE	AEIMPRV	VAMPIRE	AEISTTU	SITUATE
	MINERAL	AEIMPST	IMPASTE	AEISTTY	SATIETY
AEILMNS	SEMINAL		PASTIME	AEJLOSU	JEALOUS
AEILMNT	AILMENT	AEIMRTU	MURIATE	AEJMSTY	MAJESTY
	ALIMENT	AEIMSSV	MASSIVE	AEJPRSY	JASPERY
AEILMPR	IMPEARL	AEIMSUV	AMUSIVE	AEKLPRS	SPARKLE
AEILMRS	REALISM	AEINNPR	PANNIER	AEKLRST	STALKER
AEILMSS	AIMLESS	AEINNPT	PINNATE	AEKNPRS	SPANKER
	SEISMAL	AEINNRS	INSNARE	AEKNRVY	KNAVERY
AEILNNN	LINNEAN	AEINNRT	ENTRAIN	AEKRSTY	STREAKY
AEILNOP	OPALINE	AEINOPR	OPEN-AIR	AELLMSU	MALLEUS
AEILNOT	ELATION	AEINOPZ	EPIZOAN	AELLNPY	PENALLY
AEILNPS	SPANIEL	AEINORS	ERASION	AELLORV	OVERALL
AEILNPT	PANTILE	AEINOSV	EVASION	AELLPRU	PLEURAL
AEILNPU	PAULINE	AEINPRS	PERSIAN	AELLQUY	EQUALLY
AEILNPX	EXPLAIN	AEINPRT	PAINTER	AELLRST	STELLAR
AEILNRT	ENTRAIL		PERTAIN	AELLSSW	LAWLESS
	LATRINE		REPAINT	AELLTUU	ULULATE
	RELIANT	AEINPST	SAPIENT	AELLUVV	VALVULE
	RETINAL	AEINPTT	PATIENT	AELMMNO	MAMELON
	TRENAIL	AEINPTU	PETUNIA	AELMMRT	TRAMMEL
AEILNRV	RAVELIN	AEINQTU	ANTIQUE	AELMMSY	MALMSEY
AEILNRY	INLAYER	AEINRRT	TERRAIN	AELMNOR	ALMONER
	NAILERY		TRAINER		NEMORAL
AEILNST	SALIENT	AEINRST	STAINER	AELMNOT	OMENTAL
	STANIEL		STEARIN	AELMNRU	NUMERAL
AEILNSY	ELYSIAN	AEINRTT	NITRATE	AELMNTT	MANTLET
AEILNVY	NAÏVELY		TERTIAN	AELMORV	REMOVAL
AEILOPR	PELORIA	AEINRTU	RUINATE	AELMPRS	SAMPLER
AEILOST	ISOLATE		TAURINE	AELMPRT	TEMPLAR

	TRAMPLE	AELSTTY	STATELY	AEORSTT	TOASTER
AELMPRY	LAMPREY	AELSUVY	SUAVELY	AEORTUW	OUTWEAR
AELMRTT	MARTLET	AELTTTW	TWATTLE	AEORTVX	OVERTAX
AELNNPR	PLANNER	AELTTUX	TEXTUAL	AEPPRRT	TRAPPER
AELNNRT	LANTERN	AEMMNOT	MOMENTA	AEPPRRW	WRAPPER
AELNNRU	UNLEARN	AEMMRST	STAMMER	AEPRRRS	SPARRER
AELNNTU	ANNULET	AEMNNRT	REMNANT	AEPRRTU	RAPTURE
AELNOPT	POLENTA	AEMNNSW	NEWSMAN	AEPRSSY	PESSARY
AELNORS	ORLEANS	AEMNORU	ENAMOUR	AEPRSTT	SPATTER
AELNPRT	PANTLER	AEMNPTY	PAYMENT		TAPSTER
	PLANTER	AEMNRST	SMARTEN	AEPRSTU	PASTURE
	REPLANT	AEMNRSU	SURNAME	AEPRSYY	SPRAYEY
AELNPRY	PLENARY	AEMNSTY	AMNESTY	AEPRTXY	APTERYX
AELNPSS	NAPLESS	AEMORST	MAESTRO	AEQRRTU	QUARTER
AELNPTY	PENALTY	AEMPRRT	TRAMPER	AEQRTTU	QUARTET
AELNQUU	UNEQUAL	AEMPRST	STAMPER	AERRSSU	ASSURER
AELNRRS	SNARLER	AEMPTTT	ATTEMPT	AERRSTT	STARTER
AELNRST	SALTERN	AEMRRRY	REMARRY	AERRSTY	STRAYER
	STERNAL	AEMRRTU	ERRATUM	AERSTTU	STATURE
AELNRTT	TRENTAL	AEMRSSU	MASSEUR	AERSTUY	ESTUARY
AELNRTU	NEUTRAL	AEMRSTT	SMATTER	AESTTTU	STATUTE
AELNRTV	VENTRAL	AEMRSTU	STRUMAE	AFFGHIS	FISH-FAG
AELNRUV	UNRAVEL	AEMRSTY	MASTERY	AFFHIRS	RAFFISH
AELNSSU	SENSUAL		STREAMY	AFFILSY	FALSIFY
AELNSSX	LAXNESS	AEMRTTY	MATTERY	AFFIMST	MASTIFF
AELOORS	ROSEOLA	AENNNPT	PENNANT	AFFINRU	FUNFAIR
AELOPRS	REPOSAL	AENNPRS	SPANNER		RUFFIAN
AELOPRT	PROLATE	AENNRTT	ENTRANT	AFFINTY	TIFFANY
AELOPRV	OVERLAP	AENNRTY	TANNERY	AFFNORS	SAFFRON
AELOPST	APOSTLE	AENNSSW	WANNESS	AFFNORT	AFFRONT
AELOPTT	PALETOT	AENOPRS	PERSONA	AFGHIRS	GARFISH
AELORRT	RELATOR	AENOPRT	OPERANT	AFGHRTU	FRAUGHT
AELORTV	LEVATOR		PROTEAN	AFGIILN	FAILING
AELORUU	ROULEAU	AENORST	SENATOR	AFGIINR	FAIRING
AELORVY	OVERLAY		TREASON	AFGILMN	FLAMING
AELOSUZ	ZEALOUS	AENORXY	ANOREXY	AFGILNR	FLARING
AELOSVY	SAVELOY	AENOSTU	SOUTANE	AFGILNT	FATLING
AELPPSU	APPULSE	AENPPRS	SNAPPER	AFGILNU	GAINFUL
AELPRST	PLASTER	AENPRRT	PARTNER	AFGILNY	ANGLIFY
	PSALTER	AENPRST	PASTERN	AFGILRU	FIGURAL
	STAPLER	AENPRSW	SPAWNER	AFGIMNR	FARMING
AELPRSU	PERUSAL	AENPRTT	PATTERN		FRAMING
AELPRSY	PARSLEY	AENPRUV	PARVENU	AFGIMNY	MAGNIFY
	SPARELY	AENPSST	APTNESS	AFGIRTY	GRATIFY
AELPRTT	PARTLET	AENRRTY	TERNARY	AFGOOTT	FAGOTTO
	PLATTER	AENRSSW	RAWNESS	AFHIIRS	FAIRISH
	PRATTLE	AENRSTU	SAUNTER	AFHINOS	FASHION
AELPSSS	SAPLESS	AENRSTV	SERVANT	AFHISSW	SAW-FISH
AELPSTU	PULSATE		VERSANT	AFHLMRU	HARMFUL
AELQRRU	QUARREL	AENRTTU	TAUNTER	AFIILRY	FAIRILY
AELRRSU	SURREAL	AENRTUV	VAUNTER	AFIINRS	FRISIAN
AELRRTW	TRAWLER	AENSTTU	TETANUS	AFILLNY	FINALLY
AELRSST	ARTLESS	AENSTTX	SEXTANT	AFILLPT	PITFALL
AELRSSY	RAYLESS	AEOPPRV	APPROVE	AFILLPU	PAILFUL
AELRSTT	STARTLE	AEOPRRT	PRAETOR	AFILLUV	FLUVIAL
AELRSTU	SALUTER	AEOPRST	ESPARTO	AFILMPY	AMPLIFY
AELRSVY	SLAVERY	AEOPRVY	OVERPAY	AFILNPU	PAINFUL
AELRTTT	TATTLER	AEOQRTU	EQUATOR	AFILNTU	FLUTINA
AELRTTU	TUTELAR	AEOQSUU	AQUEOUS	AFILNTY	FAINTLY
AELRTUV	VAULTER	AEORRSS	RASORES	AFILQUY	QUALIFY
AELRTWZ	WALTZER	AEORRST	ROASTER		

AFILRTY	FRAILTY	AGHORTW	WARTHOG	AGLOOPY	APOLOGY
AFILSSY	SALSIFY	AGIILNR	RAILING	AGMNORU	ORGANUM
AFILSTU	FISTULA	AGIILNS	SAILING	AGMNSTU	MUSTANG
AFILSTY	FALSITY	AGIILNW	WAILING	AGMNSTY	GYMNAST
AFINORS	INSOFAR	AGIILPT	PIGTAIL	AGMOOYZ	ZOOGAMY
AFINSTU	FAUNIST	AGIILTY	AGILITY	AGMOPRR	PROGRAM
	FUSTIAN	AGIINNR	INGRAIN	AGMPRSU	GRAMPUS
AFISSTY	SATISFY	AGIKLNO	OAKLING	AGNNNOO	NONAGON
AFITTUY	FATUITY	AGIKLNT	TALKING	AGNNOOR	ORGANON
AFKLNRY	FRANKLY	AGIKLNW	WALKING	AGNORRT	GRANTOR
AFLLOTU	FALL-OUT	AGIKNOS	SOAKING	AGORRTW	RAGWORT
	OUTFALL	AGILLMU	GALLIUM	AGOSUYZ	AZYGOUS
AFLLPUY	PLAYFUL	AGILLNU	LINGUAL	AGRUUUY	URUGUAY
AFLLUWY	AWFULLY		LINGULA	AHHHISS	HASHISH
AFLMNOU	MOANFUL	AGILLNW	WALLING	AHHLRSY	HARSHLY
AFLMORU	FORMULA	AGILLOR	GORILLA	AHIKMSW	MAWKISH
AFLMORW	WOLFRAM	AGILLOT	GALLIOT	AHIKNSS	SNAKISH
AFLMOST	FLOTSAM	AGILMNT	MALTING	AHIKNSV	KNAVISH
AFLMSUU	FAMULUS	AGILNNT	TANLING	AHILLNT	ANT-HILL
AFLNORT	FRONTAL	AGILNPS	SAPLING	AHILNPS	PLANISH
AFLNTUY	FLAUNTY	AGILNPT	PLATING	AHILPPY	HAPPILY
AFLORUV	FLAVOUR	AGILNPW	LAPWING	AHILPSY	APISHLY
AFMNOOT	FOOTMAN	AGILNRY	ANGRILY	AHILSST	SALTISH
AFMOORS	FORMOSA	AGILNST	LASTING	AHILSSV	SLAVISH
AFMORST	FARMOST		SLATING	AHILSTY	HASTILY
AFMORTU	FOUMART	AGILNTY	GIANTLY	AHIMMRS	RAMMISH
AFOOTWY	FOOTWAY	AGILOPT	GALIPOT	AHIMNNS	MANNISH
AFOSTUU	FATUOUS	AGIMNRT	MIGRANT	AHIMNNU	INHUMAN
AGGHHIS	HAGGISH	AGIMNSU	AMUSING	AHIMNOT	MANIHOT
AGGHIMN	GINGHAM	AGIMNTT	MATTING	AHIMOPR	MORPHIA
AGGHINN	HANGING	AGIMRRT	TRIGRAM	AHIMTUZ	AZIMUTH
AGGHISW	WAGGISH	AGIMRTY	TRIGAMY	AHINNSW	WANNISH
AGGILLN	GALLING	AGINNNT	TANNING	AHINNTX	XANTHIN
AGGILNN	ANGLING	AGINNRW	WARNING	AHINPSS	SPANISH
AGGILNR	GLARING	AGINORR	ROARING	AHINPTY	PYTHIAN
AGGINRS	GAS-RING	AGINORS	SIGNORA	AHINRST	TARNISH
AGGINRT	GRATING	AGINOST	AGONIST	AHINRSV	VARNISH
AGGINRZ	GRAZING	AGINPPT	TAPPING	AHIPRST	HARPIST
AGGINST	STAGING	AGINPRS	SPARING	AHIPRSW	WARSHIP
AGGLOSW	GLASGOW	AGINPRT	PARTING	AHIPSSW	WASPISH
AGGMORR	GROGRAM		PRATING	AHIRSTT	ATHIRST
AGGMOTY	MAGGOTY	AGINPRY	PRAYING		TARTISH
AGHHIWY	HIGHWAY	AGINPSS	PASSING	AHLLOPS	SHALLOP
AGHHTUY	HAUGHTY	AGINRRW	WARRING	AHLLOST	SHALLOT
AGHIKNW	HAWKING	AGINRST	STARING	AHLLOSW	SHALLOW
AGHILNS	LASHING	AGINRSY	SYRINGA	AHLLOTY	LOATHLY
AGHILNT	LATHING	AGINRTY	GIANTRY	AHLLPSU	PHALLUS
AGHILNW	WHALING	AGINSTW	WASTING	AHLLSTU	THALLUS
AGHILOT	GOLIATH	AGINSTY	STYGIAN	AHLMNUY	HUMANLY
AGHILSU	GAULISH	AGINTTT	TATTING	AHLMORU	HUMORAL
AGHINNT	TANGHIN	AGIRTVY	GRAVITY	AHLPRSY	SHARPLY
AGHINRS	GARNISH	AGJLRUU	JUGULAR	AHLPSSY	SPLASHY
AGHINSU	ANGUISH	AGJNOOR	JARGOON	AHMMMOT	MAMMOTH
AGHINSV	SHAVING	AGKNOPT	PAKTONG	AHMNOPS	SHOPMAN
AGHINSW	WASHING	AGLLNOO	GALLOON	AHMNOPT	PHANTOM
AGHIOST	GOATISH	AGLLOSW	GALLOWS	AHMNORY	HARMONY
AGHKOSW	GOSHAWK	AGLLOTT	GLOTTAL	AHMNOSW	SHOWMAN
AGHLMPU	GALUMPH	AGLMORU	GLAMOUR	AHMOOPS	SHAMPOO
AGHLSTY	GHASTLY	AGLNORU	LANGUOR	AHNOOPR	HARPOON
AGHNRUY	HUNGARY	AGLNPSY	SPANGLY	AHNOTTW	WHATNOT
AGHNTUY	NAUGHTY	AGLNTUY	GAUNTLY	AHNPPUY	UNHAPPY

AHNPRXY	PHARYNX	AILQTUY	QUALITY	AIORRRW	WARRIOR
AHOPRTY	ATROPHY	AILRRVY	RIVALRY	AIORRTT	TRAITOR
AHORTTY	THROATY	AILRSTT	STARLIT	AIORSUV	SAVIOUR
AHQSSUY	SQUASHY	AILRTTU	TITULAR		VARIOUS
AHRSTWY	SWARTHY	AILRTUV	VIRTUAL	AIPRTVY	PRAVITY
AIIILMT	MILITIA	AILSTTY	TASTILY	AISSTTT	STATIST
AIIILNT	INITIAL	AILSTUW	LAWSUIT	AISTUVY	SUAVITY
AIIKMNN	MANIKIN	AIMMMUX	MAXIMUM	AJLNORU	JOURNAL
AIILLLP	LAPILLI	AIMMNTU	MANUMIT	AJMNRUY	JURYMAN
AIILLNV	VILLAIN	AIMMOST	ATOMISM	AKKLRSY	SKYLARK
AIILMRS	SIMILAR	AIMMRSX	MARXISM	AKLOPUV	VOLAPUK
AIILMRY	MILIARY	AIMNNOS	MANSION	AKLOTTU	OUTTALK
AIILNOS	LIAISON	AIMNOOR	AMORINO	AKLOTUW	OUTWALK
AIILNPT	PINTAIL	AIMNOPR	RAMPION	AKLRSTY	STARKLY
AIILQSU	SILIQUA	AIMNOPT	TAMPION	AKMNORW	WORKMAN
AIILRTV	TRIVIAL	AIMNORT	TORMINA	AKOOPRT	PARTOOK
AIIMMNS	ANIMISM	AIMNOTU	MANITOU	ALLLOYY	LOYALLY
AIIMNST	ANIMIST	AIMNRRU	MURRAIN	ALLMNOT	TOLL-MAN
AIIMNTT	IMITANT	AIMNRUU	URANIUM	ALLMORY	MORALLY
AIIMNTV	VITAMIN	AIMNSYZ	ZANYISM	ALLNOOW	WALLOON
AIIMRST	SIMITAR	AIMOPST	IMPASTO	ALLNRUU	LUNULAR
AIINNOP	PIANINO	AIMOSTT	ATOMIST	ALLNSTY	SLANTLY
AIINNTY	INANITY	AIMPPRU	AIR-PUMP	ALLOOTX	AXOLOTL
AIINPRS	ASPIRIN	AIMPRRY	PRIMARY	ALLORYY	ROYALLY
AIINPST	PIANIST	AIMQRSU	MARQUIS	ALLOSWW	SWALLOW
AIJNORT	JANITOR	AIMRSTX	MARXIST	ALLOTTY	TOTALLY
AIKLMMN	MILKMAN	AINNOOT	ANTONIO	ALLOTWY	TALLOWY
AIKLMNN	LINKMAN	AINNOOX	OXONIAN	ALLOTYY	LOYALTY
AIKLRTT	TITLARK	AINNQTU	QUINTAN	ALLQSUY	SQUALLY
AIKMNNS	KINSMAN	AINNRTT	INTRANT	ALLRRUY	RURALLY
AILLMPU	PALLIUM	AINNSTT	INSTANT	ALLRSTU	LUSTRAL
AILLMSW	SAWMILL	AINNTUY	ANNUITY	ALLSUUY	USUALLY
AILLNPY	PLAINLY	AINOORT	ONTARIO	ALMNNUY	UNMANLY
AILLNST	INSTALL		ORATION	ALMNOOP	LAMPOON
AILLPRU	PILULAR	AINOOTV	OVATION	ALMNORY	ALMONRY
AILLPUV	PLUVIAL	AINOPPT	APPOINT	ALMNOWY	WOMANLY
AILLTVY	VITALLY	AINOPRS	SOPRANI	ALMNSUU	ALUMNUS
AILMMOR	IMMORAL	AINOPRT	ATROPIN	ALMOPRT	MARPLOT
AILMNNO	NOMINAL	AINOPSS	PASSION	ALMOTTU	MULATTO
AILMNOP	LAMPION	AINOPTU	OPUNTIA	ALMRSTY	SMARTLY
AILMNOS	MALISON		UTOPIAN	ALMRTUU	TUMULAR
	OSMANLI	AINOSSU	SUASION	ALNNSUU	ANNULUS
AILMNOY	ALIMONY	AINOSTT	STATION	ALNOOPT	PLATOON
AILMNPT	IMPLANT	AINOSUX	ANXIOUS	ALNOORT	ORTOLAN
AILMOPT	OPTIMAL	AINOSVY	SYNOVIA	ALNOPPY	PANOPLY
AILNNOT	ANT-LION	AINPPRS	PARSNIP	ALNORUZ	ZONULAR
AILNNPU	PINNULA	AINPQSU	PASQUIN	ALNSUUU	UNUSUAL
AILNPTU	NUPTIAL	AINPQTU	PIQUANT	ALOOPYZ	POLYZOA
AILNQTU	QUINTAL	AINPRST	SPIRANT	ALOORRS	SORORAL
AILNRSU	INSULAR	AINPRTU	PURITAN	ALOPPRU	POPULAR
AILNSTY	NASTILY	AINQRUY	QUINARY	ALOPRRU	PARLOUR
	SAINTLY	AINQSTU	ASQUINT	ALOPSSU	SPOUSAL
AILNTTY	NATTILY	AINRRUY	URINARY	ALOQRRU	RORQUAL
AILOORW	WOORALI	AINRSSU	RUSSIAN	ALOQRSU	SQUALOR
AILOPTT	TALIPOT	AINRSTT	TRANSIT	ALORRST	ROSTRAL
AILOPTV	PIVOTAL	AINRTUY	UNITARY	ALORTYY	ROYALTY
AILOQTU	ALIQUOT	AINSSTU	SUSTAIN	ALOSTTU	OUTLAST
AILORUW	WOURALI	AINTTVY	TANTIVY	ALRSTUU	SUTURAL
AILORUX	UXORIAL	AIOPRTT	PATRIOT	AMMNORY	ROMMANY
AILOSTU	OUTSAIL	AIOPRTY	TOPIARY	AMMNRUY	NUMMARY
AILPQSU	PASQUIL	AIOPRUV	PAVIOUR	AMMOPTU	POMATUM

AMMORWW	MAWWORM	BBEGRRU	GRUBBER	BCELMRU	CRUMBLE
AMMRSUY	SUMMARY	BBEIIMR	IMBIBER	BCELMSU	SCUMBLE
AMNNOSW	SNOWMAN	BBEILNR	NIBBLER	BCENORU	BOUNCER
AMNNOTY	ANTONYM	BBEILQU	QUIBBLE	BCEOORT	OCTOBER
AMNOOTT	OTTOMAN	BBEIRRY	BRIBERY	BCEORSU	OBSCURE
AMNOPRY	PARONYM	BBEJORY	JOBBERY	BCHIIOT	COHIBIT
AMNOPST	POSTMAN	BBEKLOS	BLES-BOK	BCHIKSU	BUCKISH
AMNORST	TRANSOM	BBELORS	SLOBBER	BCHIMOR	RHOMBIC
AMNORSY	MASONRY	BBELRSU	SLUBBER	BCHIOPR	PIBROCH
AMNORTU	ROMAUNT	BBELSTU	STUBBLE	BCHLOTY	BLOTCHY
AMNQTUU	QUANTUM	BBEORRY	ROBBERY	BCIIKLN	NIBLICK
AMNRTTU	TANTRUM	BBGIINR	RIBBING	BCIILOR	COLIBRI
AMOORSU	AMOROUS	BBGINRU	RUBBING	BCIISTU	BISCUIT
AMOPSTT	TOPMAST	BBGINTU	TUBBING	BCILMPU	PLUMBIC
AMORRUY	ARMOURY	BBGIOSU	GIBBOUS	BCINSUU	INCUBUS
AMORRWY	MARROWY	BBHIMOS	MOBBISH	BCIRTUY	BUTYRIC
AMORSSY	MORASSY	BBHIRSU	RUBBISH	BCKLLOU	BULLOCK
AMRSTTU	STRATUM	BBHISTU	TUBBISH	BCKOTTU	BUTTOCK
ANNRTYY	TYRANNY	BBHRSUY	SHRUBBY	BCLMOOU	COULOMB
ANOOPRS	SOPRANO	BBIKTUZ	KIBBUTZ	BCLMRUY	CRUMBLY
ANOORTT	ARNOTTO	BBKLNOY	KNOBBLY	BCOOTTY	BOYCOTT
ANOPRRS	SPORRAN	BBLOSUU	BULBOUS	BDDEGIN	BEDDING
ANOPSTU	OUTSPAN	BBLSTUY	STUBBLY	BDDEILN	BLINDED
ANORSUU	ANUROUS	BCCEILO	ECBOLIC	BDDEINR	BRINDED
ANORWWY	WAYWORN	BCCEILU	CUBICLE	BDDEIRT	DIRT-BED
AOOPPRS	APROPOS	BCCEILY	BICYCLE	BDDENOU	BOUNDED
AOORRTT	ROTATOR	BCCILOU	BUCOLIC	BDDESUU	SUBDUED
AOORRTY	ORATORY	BCCINOO	OBCONIC	BDDGIIN	BIDDING
AOPPRRT	RAPPORT	BCCMOOX	COXCOMB	BDDGINU	BUDDING
AOPRRSW	SPARROW	BCCMSUU	SUCCUMB	BDEEERR	BREEDER
AOPRRTY	PORTRAY	BCDEEIL	DECIBEL	BDEEILL	BELLIED
AOPRSTW	POST-WAR	BCDEHOU	DEBOUCH	BDEEILV	BEDEVIL
AOPRUVY	VAPOURY	BCDEIKS	SICK-BED	BDEEINR	INBREED
AORSSUY	OSSUARY	BCDEIKT	BED-TICK	BDEEINZ	BEDIZEN
AORSUVY	SAVOURY	BCDEIOX	DICE-BOX	BDEEIRR	BERRIED
AOSTTUY	OUTSTAY	BCDELOU	BECLOUD	BDEELNR	BLENDER
APPRRUU	PURPURA	BCDESUU	SUBDUCE	BDEELOV	BELOVED
APPRSUY	PAPYRUS	BCDHOOU	CUBHOOD	BDEELSS	BLESSED
APRSSSU	SURPASS	BCDKORU	BURDOCK	BDEEMSU	BEMUSED
APRSTTU	UPSTART	BCDSTUU	SUBDUCT	BDEENPR	PREBEND
AQRTUYZ	QUARTZY	BCEEEHN	BEECHEN	BDEFLOU	BODEFUL
ARSSTTU	STRATUS	BCEEEHS	BESEECH	BDEGGIR	EGG-BIRD
BBBELRU	BLUBBER	BCEEGIR	ICEBERG	BDEGHIT	BEDIGHT
BBCEILR	CRIBBLE	BCEEHNR	BENCHER	BDEGILO	OBLIGED
BBCELOR	CLOBBER	BCEEKUY	BUCK-EYE	BDEGIOT	BIGOTED
	COBBLER	BCEENOS	OBSCENE	BDEGOOY	GOODBYE
BBCINOU	BUBONIC	BCEHINR	BIRCHEN	BDEHMTU	THUMBED
BBCRSUY	SCRUBBY	BCEHITW	BEWITCH	BDEILNR	BLINDER
BBDEEIT	EBB-TIDE	BCEHLRU	BLUCHER		BRINDLE
BBDEELP	PEBBLED	BCEHORT	BOTCHER		
BBDEENO	BONE-BED	BCEHRTU	BUTCHER	BDEILOP	LOBIPED
BBDEILR	DIBBLER	BCEILMR	CLIMBER	BDEILRT	DRIBLET
	DRIBBLE	BCEILNO	BINOCLE	BDEILRU	BUILDER
		BCEILOR	BRICOLE		REBUILD
BBDEKNO	KNOBBED	BCEIMNO	COMBINE	BDEIMOR	BROMIDE
BBDELOS	BOBSLED	BCEIMOR	MICROBE	BDEINOU	BEDOUIN
BBDESTU	STUBBED	BCEIRSU	SUBERIC	BDEINRY	BINDERY
BBEEERU	BEBEERU	BCEJSTU	SUBJECT	BDEIORR	BROIDER
BBEFILR	FRIBBLE	BCEKLRU	BUCKLER	BDEIORS	DISROBE
BBEGINW	WEBBING	BCEKORT	BROCKET	BDEIORV	OVERBID
BBEGIOS	GIBBOSE	BCEKORU	ROEBUCK	BDEIOSY	DISOBEY
BBEGLOR	GOBBLER			BDEISSU	SUBSIDE

BDEITUY	DUBIETY	BEEKRRU	REBUKER	BEIILSV	VISIBLE
BDELNRU	BLUNDER	BEELLOT	LOBELET	BEIKLNR	BLINKER
BDELORU	BOULDER	BEELMOW	EMBOWEL	BEIKLOS	OBELISK
BDELOTU	DOUBLET	BEELMRT	TREMBLE	BEIKRST	BRISKET
BDELOWZ	BLOWZED	BEELNNO	ENNOBLE	BEILMOR	EMBROIL
BDEMOOR	BEDROOM	BEEMORW	EMBOWER	BEILMRT	TIMBREL
	BOREDOM	BEEMRSU	BURMESE	BEILMSU	SUBLIME
BDENNOU	BOUNDEN	BEEORSV	OBSERVE	BEILNOW	BOWLINE
BDENORU	REBOUND		OBVERSE	BEILOQU	OBLIQUE
BDENORZ	BRONZED		VERBOSE	BEILORR	BROILER
BDENSTU	SUBTEND	BEEORTX	BOX-TREE	BEILRST	BLISTER
BDEOPST	BED-POST	BEEORWY	EYEBROW		BRISTLE
BDEORSU	ROSE-BUD	BEEQSTU	BEQUEST	BEILRTT	BRITTLE
BDEORTU	DOUBTER	BEERRWY	BREWERY	BEILRTY	LIBERTY
	OBTRUDE	BEERSTW	BESTREW	BEILSTU	SUBTILE
	REDOUBT	BEFGIIL	FILIBEG	BEILSTW	BLEWITS
BDERSUU	SUBDUER	BEFILRT	FILBERT	BEIMMRR	BRIMMER
BDFIIOR	FIBROID	BEFILRY	BRIEFLY	BEIMNOR	BROMINE
BDGIINN	BINDING	BEFILSU	FUSIBLE	BEIMNTU	BITUMEN
BDGLLOU	BULL-DOG	BEFINOR	BONFIRE	BEIMORW	IMBOWER
BDHOOOY	BOYHOOD	BEFIORX	FIRE-BOX	BEIMRTU	TERBIUM
BDILLNY	BLINDLY	BEFIRST	FIBSTER	BEINNOS	BENISON
BDINOOR	BRIDOON	BEFLLOT	ELF-BOLT	BEINNOZ	BENZOIN
BDINSTU	DUST-BIN	BEFLMRU	FUMBLER	BEINORW	BROWNIE
BDIOORU	BOUDOIR	BEFOORR	FORBORE	BEINOTT	BOTTINE
BDIOSUU	DUBIOUS	BEFOSUX	FUSE-BOX	BEINRTT	BITTERN
BDIRSTU	DISTURB	BEGGLOR	BOGGLER	BEINRTU	TRIBUNE
BDISSUY	SUBSIDY	BEGHINT	BENIGHT		TURBINE
BDNNOUU	UNBOUND	BEGHRRU	BURGHER	BEINSSY	BYSSINE
BDNOORU	BOURDON	BEGILLY	LEGIBLY	BEIOSTY	OBESITY
BDOOOWX	BOXWOOD	BEGILMU	BELGIUM	BEIRRSU	BRUISER
BEEEGIS	BESIEGE	BEGILNO	IGNOBLE	BEIRSTT	BITTERS
BEEEHIV	BEE-HIVE	BEGILNT	BELTING	BEIRTTU	TRIBUTE
BEEEHNS	SHEBEEN	BEGILNU	BLUEING	BEIRTVY	BREVITY
BEEEILN	BEE-LINE	BEGINOY	BIOGENY	BEITTWX	BETWIXT
BEEEILV	BELIEVE	BEGINRR	BRINGER	BEJKOUX	JUKE-BOX
BEEELPS	PEEBLES	BEGINRW	BREWING	BEKLOOT	BOOKLET
BEEENNZ	BENZENE	BEGINSS	BIGNESS	BELLOSU	SOLUBLE
BEEENTW	BETWEEN	BEGLLOU	GLOBULE	BELLOSW	BELLOWS
BEEFILR	FEBRILE	BEGLMRU	GRUMBLE	BELLOUV	VOLUBLE
BEEFINT	BENEFIT	BEGLNRU	BUNGLER	BELMMRU	MUMBLER
BEEGILL	LEGIBLE	BEGLOOS	GLOBOSE	BELMNOU	NELUMBO
BEEGILO	OBLIGEE	BEGLOSU	GLEBOUS	BELMNSU	NUMBLES
BEEGILU	BEGUILE	BEGNORU	BURGEON	BELMOPR	PROBLEM
BEEGINU	BEGUINE	BEGNOSY	BY-GONES	BELMPRU	PLUMBER
BEEHMOT	BEE-MOTH	BEGNOTU	UNBEGOT	BELMRSU	SLUMBER
BEEHORS	HERBOSE	BEGRSSU	BURGESS	BELMRTU	TUMBLER
BEEHRST	SHERBET	BEHIITX	EXHIBIT		TUMBREL
BEEHRSW	BESHREW	BEHIKNT	BETHINK	BELMSTU	STUMBLE
BEEHRTY	THEREBY	BEHILMS	BLEMISH	BELNSTU	UNBLEST
BEEHRWY	WHEREBY	BEHILMT	THIMBLE	BELORST	BOLSTER
BEEIJLU	JUBILEE	BEHIOTW	HOWBEIT		LOBSTER
BEEIMST	BETIMES	BEHIRRT	REBIRTH	BELORSY	SOBERLY
BEEINOT	EBONITE	BEHLLOP	BELLHOP	BELORTT	BLOTTER
BEEINOZ	EBONIZE	BEHLORT	BROTHEL	BELORTU	TROUBLE
BEEINRZ	ZEBRINE	BEHNRTU	BURTHEN	BELOSTU	BOLETUS
BEEIQUZ	BEZIQUE	BEHOORT	THEORBO	BELRSTU	BLUSTER
BEEIRRV	BREVIER	BEHOPSU	PHOEBUS		BUSTLER
BEEIRTY	EBRIETY	BEHORRT	BROTHER	BEMMOOS	EMBOSOM
BEEKNOT	BETOKEN	BEHORTT	BETROTH	BEMNORW	EMBROWN
BEEKRRS	BERSERK	BEIILRS	RISIBLE	BEMNTTU	BUTMENT

BEMORST	MOBSTER	BILOSSU	SUBSOIL	CCEKNOY	COCKNEY
BEMORSY	EMBRYOS	BILRSTY	BRISTLY	CCEKORT	CROCKET
BEMSSUU	SUBSUME	BIMMOOS	IMBOSOM	CCELLOT	COLLECT
BENNORW	NEWBORN	BIMNORW	IMBROWN	CCELNOY	CYCLONE
BEOPRRV	PROVERB	BIMNOSU	OMNIBUS	CCELNUY	LUCENCY
BEOQTUU	BOUQUET	BIOOSUV	OBVIOUS	CCENNOR	CONCERN
BEPRRTU	PERTURB	BIOPRTY	PROBITY	CCENNOT	CONNECT
BEPRTUY	PUBERTY	BIORSTT	BISTORT	CCENOPT	CONCEPT
BEQRSUU	BRUSQUE	BISSSTU	SUBSIST	CCENORT	CONCERT
BERSTUV	SUBVERT	BLLNTUY	BLUNTLY	CCEORRT	CORRECT
BERTTUY	BUTTERY	BLLOUVY	VOLUBLY	CCESSSU	SUCCESS
BFFNOOU	BUFFOON	BLMOORW	LOBWORM	CCFIRUY	CRUCIFY
BFHIRSU	FURBISH	BLMOOSS	BLOSSOM	CCHIIST	STICHIC
BFILMRU	BRIMFUL	BLOOQUY	OBLOQUY	CCHILOR	CHLORIC
BFIORSU	FIBROUS	BLOOTUW	BLOW-OUT	CCHIMOR	CHROMIC
BFIRTUY	BRUTIFY	BMNOOSU	UNBOSOM	CCHINOR	CHRONIC
BFLLOWY	BLOW-FLY	BMNORUW	MOWBURN	CCHIORY	CHICORY
BGGHIIS	BIGGISH	BNNRTUU	UNBURNT	CCHIOTW	COW-ITCH
BGHINOR	BIG-HORN	BOOPSTY	POSTBOY	CCHIPSY	PSYCHIC
BGHOORU	BOROUGH	CCCNOOT	CONCOCT	CCHNRSU	SCRUNCH
BGHORTU	BROUGHT	CCDEENO	CONCEDE	CCHNRUY	CRUNCHY
BGIILNO	BOILING	CCDEENY	DECENCY	CCIIILS	SILICIC
BGIILNS	SIBLING	CCDEESU	SUCCEED	CCIIRTU	CIRCUIT
BGIKNOR	BROKING	CCDEIIT	DEICTIC	CCIISTY	SICCITY
BGILNOW	BOWLING	CCDEILR	CIRCLED	CCIKLOY	COLICKY
BGILNOY	IGNOBLY	CCDELOU	OCCLUDE	CCIKOPT	COCK-PIT
BGILOOR	OBLIGOR	CCDENOU	CONDUCE	CCILNOU	COUNCIL
BGILOOY	BIOLOGY	CCDIILO	CODICIL	CCILOOP	PICCOLO
BGINNRU	BURNING	CCDIIOR	CRICOID	CCILSTY	CYCLIST
BGINNTU	BUNTING	CCDILOY	CYCLOID	CCINOOT	COCTION
BGIORTY	BIGOTRY	CCDKLOU	CUCKOLD	CCINOTV	CONVICT
BGKLOOO	LOG-BOOK	CCDNOOR	CONCORD	CCIOORS	SIROCCO
BGLOOSU	GLOBOUS	CCDNOTU	CONDUCT	CCIOPTU	OCCIPUT
BGLOSSU	BUGLOSS	CCEEHKR	CHECKER	CCIPRTY	CRYPTIC
BHIIINT	INHIBIT	CCEEHOU	COUCHEE	CCLOPSY	CYCLOPS
BHIINRS	BRINISH	CCEEHRS	SCREECH	CCMOOOR	MOROCCO
BHIIRST	BRITISH	CCEEILN	LICENCE	CCNOOTU	COCO-NUT
BHIKOOS	BOOKISH	CCEEINS	SCIENCE	CCNOSSU	CONCUSS
BHILOTU	HOLIBUT	CCEEIRV	CREVICE	CCORSUU	SUCCOUR
BHILPSU	PUBLISH	CCEELRY	RECYCLE	CCORSUY	SUCCORY
BHIMSTU	BISMUTH	CCEENRY	RECENCY	CDDDEEI	DECIDED
BHINRSU	BURNISH	CCEERSY	SECRECY	CDDEEII	DEICIDE
BHIOORS	BOORISH	CCEFNOT	CONFECT	CDDEEIR	DECIDER
BHiOSWZ	SHOWBIZ	CCEGNOY	COGENCY	CDDEENS	DESCEND
BHIRSTU	BRUTISH	CCEHIKN	CHICKEN	CDDEEUW	CUDWEED
BHLRSUU	BULRUSH	CCEHINT	TECHNIC	CDDELOU	CLOUDED
BHMORSU	RHOMBUS	CCEHKLU	CHUCKLE	CDDEORW	CROWDED
BHOOSTW	BOWSHOT	CCEHORT	CROCHET	CDDERSU	SCUDDER
BIILLNO	BILLION	CCEIKLR	CLICKER	CDDIIOS	DISCOID
BIILLOU	BOUILLI	CCEIKRT	CRICKET	CDDIIRU	DRUIDIC
BIILLTW	TWIBILL	CCEILOT	COCTILE	CDDIKOP	PIDDOCK
BIILOSU	BILIOUS	CCEILRR	CIRCLER	CDDIORS	DISCORD
BIILSVY	VISIBLY	CCEILRT	CIRCLET	CDDKORU	RUDDOCK
BIIMNOU	NIOBIUM	CCEILTU	CUTICLE	CDEEEFL	FLEECED
BIJNOSU	SUBJOIN	CCEIMNO	MECONIC	CDEEEFN	DEFENCE
BIKLRSY	BRISKLY	CCEINOR	CORNICE	CDEEEIV	DECEIVE
BIKMNPU	BUMPKIN	CCEINOS	CONCISE	CDEEEPR	PRECEDE
BILLNOU	BULLION	CCEINOT	CONCEIT	CDEEERS	SECEDER
BILLOPX	PILL-BOX	CCEINRT	CENTRIC	CDEEERT	DECREET
BILLOWY	BILLOWY	CCEIOPP	COPPICE	CDEEFII	EDIFICE
BILMRTU	TUMBRIL	CCEIPST	SCEPTIC	CDEEFLT	DEFLECT

CDEEFOR	DEFORCE	CDELLOU	COLLUDE	CEEERRT	ERECTER
CDEEHIS	DEHISCE	CDELMSU	MUSCLED	CEEERST	SECRETE
CDEEHST	CHESTED	CDELNOO	CONDOLE	CEEERTX	EXCRETE
CDEEILN	DECLINE	CDELNOY	CONDYLE	CEEETUX	EXECUTE
CDEEILP	PEDICEL	CDELORS	SCOLDER	CEEFFNO	OFFENCE
CDEEIMN	ENDEMIC	CDELOTU	CLOUTED	CEEFKLR	FRECKLE
CDEEIOS	DIOCESE	CDELRUY	CRUDELY	CEEFLRT	REFLECT
CDEEIRR	DECRIER	CDEMMNO	COMMEND	CEEFNOR	ENFORCE
CDEELPU	DECUPLE	CDEMMOO	COMMODE	CEEFPRT	PERFECT
CDEELPY	YCLEPED	CDEMNNO	CONDEMN		PREFECT
CDEELRU	ULCERED	CDEMNOP	COMPEND	CEEGINR	ENERGIC
CDEELSU	SECLUDE	CDEMORU	DECORUM		GENERIC
CDEELUX	EXCLUDE	CDENNOO	CONDONE	CEEGINT	GENETIC
CDEENRT	CREDENT	CDENNOT	CONTEND	CEEGINU	EUGENIC
CDEENST	DESCENT	CDENOPU	POUNCED	CEEGLLO	COLLEGE
CDEEOPR	PROCEED	CDENORS	CORSNED	CEEGLNT	NEGLECT
CDEERRU	REDUCER	CDENORW	CROWNED	CEEGLOU	ECLOGUE
CDEERST	CRESTED	CDENPUY	PUDENCY	CEEGNRY	REGENCY
CDEERSU	SEDUCER	CDENRUY	DUNCERY	CEEGORT	CORTÈGE
CDEFIIT	DEFICIT	CDEOORR	CORRODE	CEEHILS	HELICES
CDEFINO	CONFIDE	CDEOOTV	DOVE-COT	CEEHILV	VEHICLE
CDEFKOR	FROCKED	CDEOPRU	PRODUCE	CEEHIMR	CHIMERE
CDEFNTU	DEFUNCT	CDEORSS	CROSSED	CEEHIMS	CHEMISE
CDEHILP	DELPHIC	CDEORUU	DOUCEUR	CEEHINS	CHINESE
CDEHINN	CHINNED	CDFILUY	DULCIFY	CEEHIRT	HERETIC
CDEHINO	HEDONIC	CDGIKOS	DOG-SICK	CEEHKLR	HECKLER
CDEHIOW	COWHIDE	CDGILNO	CODLING	CEEHLNO	ECHELON
CDEHIRT	DITCHER	CDGINNO	CONDIGN	CEEHLOW	COW-HEEL
CDEHOPU	POUCHED	CDHIIST	DISTICH	CEEHLRY	CHEERLY
CDEHORW	COWHERD	CDHILOS	COLDISH		LECHERY
CDEHSSU	DUCHESS	CDHIOOR	CHOROID	CEEHLSS	CHESSEL
CDEHSTY	SCYTHED	CDHIPTY	DIPTYCH	CEEHMRS	SCHEMER
CDEIINS	INDICES	CDIIIOT	IDIOTIC	CEEHNRW	WENCHER
CDEIINT	IDENTIC	CDIILLY	IDYLLIC	CEEHORT	TROCHEE
CDEIIST	DEISTIC	CDIINOR	CRINOID	CEEHPPR	PERCHER
CDEIISU	SUICIDE	CDIINOT	DICTION	CEEHQRU	CHEQUER
CDEIKLP	PICKLED	CDIINOZ	ZINCOID	CEEIJOR	REJOICE
CDEIKNS	DICKENS	CDIIOSS	CISSOID	CEEIKNT	NECKTIE
CDEIKRR	DERRICK	CDIIOTY	IDIOTCY	CEEILNR	RECLINE
CDEILLO	COLLIDE	CDILLOO	COLLOID	CEEILNS	LICENSE
CDEILMO	MELODIC	CDILLUY	LUCIDLY		SELENIC
CDEILNU	INCLUDE	CDIMMOU	MODICUM		SILENCE
CDEILTU	DUCTILE	CDIMNOO	MONODIC	CEEILPS	ECLIPSE
CDEIMNO	DEMONIC	CDIMOSU	MUSCOID	CEEILRT	TIERCEL
CDEIMOT	DEMOTIC	CDINOSY	SYNODIC	CEEILST	SECTILE
CDEINOT	CTENOID	CDINOTU	CONDUIT	CEEILSV	VESICLE
CDEINOZ	ZINCODE	CDIOTUV	OVIDUCT	CEEIMNO	MIOCENE
CDEINRS	DISCERN	CDIRSUY	DYSURIC	CEEIMNT	CENTIME
	RESCIND	CDIRTUY	CRUDITY	CEEIMRS	MERCIES
CDEINRU	INDUCER	CDISSSU	DISCUSS	CEEINNS	INCENSE
CDEINRY	CINDERY	CDLOOPY	LYCOPOD	CEEINRS	SINCERE
CDEINSX	EXSCIND	CDOOOPT	OCTOPOD	CEEINRT	ENTERIC
CDEIORT	CORDITE	CDOPRTU	PRODUCT		ENTICER
CDEIORV	DIVORCE	CDOSTUY	CUSTODY	CEEINRV	CERVINE
CDEIOST	CESTOID	CEEEFLR	FLEECER	CEEIOPT	PICOTEE
CDEIPRT	PREDICT	CEEEHRR	CHEERER	CEEIORT	COTERIE
CDEIRTV	VERDICT	CEEEINP	EPICENE	CEEIPRR	PIERCER
CDEISST	DISSECT	CEEEIRV	RECEIVE	CEEIPRS	PRECISE
CDEISSY	ECDYSIS	CEEENRS	RECENSE	CEEIPRT	RECEIPT
CDEKLOW	WEDLOCK	CEEENSS	ESSENCE	CEEIPRU	EPICURE
CDEKOOR	CROOKED	CEEEPRR	CREEPER	CEEIPSS	SPECIES

CEEIRRT	RECITER	CEFIIOR	ORIFICE	CEHKLMO	HEMLOCK
CEEIRSV	SERVICE	CEFIITV	FICTIVE	CEHKPTU	KETCHUP
CEEIRTX	EXCITER	CEFIKLR	FLICKER	CEHKSTY	SKETCHY
CEEITTZ	ZETETIC	CEFILNT	INFLECT	CEHLORT	CHORTLE
CEEJORT	EJECTOR	CEFILNU	FUNICLE	CEHLOST	CLOTHES
CEEKLNT	NECKLET	CEFILRU	LUCIFER	CEHLQSU	SQUELCH
CEEKLPS	SPECKLE	CEFINNO	CONFINE	CEHLRRU	LURCHER
CEEKRRW	WRECKER	CEFINOR	CONIFER	CEHMNRU	MUNCHER
CEELLLU	CELLULE	CEFIOOT	ICEFOOT	CEHNOOR	COEHORN
CEELMNT	CLEMENT	CEFIPSY	SPECIFY	CEHNORV	CHEVRON
CEELMOW	WELCOME	CEFIRTY	CERTIFY	CEHNPRU	PUNCHER
CEELNOS	ENCLOSE		RECTIFY	CEHNTUY	CHUTNEY
CEELNRT	LECTERN	CEFKLOT	FETLOCK	CEHOORS	CHOOSER
CEELNRU	LUCERNE	CEFKLRY	FRECKLY	CEHOORT	CHEROOT
CEELORT	ELECTOR	CEFLNOU	FLOUNCE	CEHOPPR	CHOPPER
	ELECTRO	CEFLNUY	FLUENCY	CEHORSZ	SCHERZO
CEELPRT	PRELECT	CEFMORY	COMFREY	CEHORTU	RETOUCH
CEELRSU	RECLUSE	CEFNORU	FROUNCE		TOUCHER
CEELRTU	LECTURE	CEFNOSS	CONFESS	CEHORUV	VOUCHER
CEELRTY	ERECTLY	CEFNOST	CONFEST	CEHRRSU	CRUSHER
CEELTTU	LETTUCE	CEFNOSU	CONFUSE	CEHRSTT	STRETCH
CEEMNRU	CERUMEN	CEFNOTU	CONFUTE	CEIIKNT	KINETIC
CEEMOPR	COMPEER	CEFOPRS	FORCEPS	CEIILLS	SILICLE
	COMPERE	CEFORRT	CROFTER	CEIILNN	INCLINE
CEEMOPT	COMPETE	CEGGIOR	GEORGIC	CEIILTV	LEVITIC
CEEMRRY	MERCERY	CEGHINT	ETCHING	CEIIMMT	MIMETIC
CEENNOU	ENOUNCE	CEGHORU	COUGHER	CEIIMNS	MENISCI
CEENNOV	CONVENE	CEGIILN	CIELING	CEIIMPR	EMPIRIC
CEENNRT	CENTNER	CEGILNR	CRINGLE	CEIIMSS	SEISMIC
CEENORZ	COZENER	CEGINRR	CRINGER	CEIIMST	SEMITIC
CEENPRS	SPENCER	CEGKLOR	CORK-LEG	CEIIMTT	TITMICE
CEENRSU	CENSURE	CEGLOSU	GLUCOSE	CEIINOV	INVOICE
CEENRSY	SCENERY	CEGNOST	CONGEST	CEIINPS	PISCINE
CEEOPST	PECTOSE	CEGNRUY	URGENCY	CEIINRT	CITRINE
CEEORRT	ERECTOR	CEGORRY	GROCERY		CRINITE
CEEORRV	RECOVER	CEGORSU	SCOURGE	CEIINSS	ICINESS
CEEORSU	CEREOUS	CEHHIRS	CHERISH	CEIINSU	CUISINE
CEEORTW	COW-TREE	CEHIINR	HIRCINE	CEIINTZ	CITIZEN
CEEPPRT	PRECEPT	CEHIKNT	KITCHEN	CEIIRST	ERISTIC
CEEPPRU	PREPUCE		THICKEN	CEIIRSU	CRUISIE
CEEPRST	RESPECT	CEHIKPS	PECKISH	CEIJSTU	JUSTICE
	SCEPTER	CEHIKTT	THICKET	CEIKLNR	CLINKER
	SCEPTRE	CEHILMN	MECHLIN		CRINKLE
	SPECTER	CEHILRV	CHERVIL	CEIKLPR	PRICKLE
	SPECTRE	CEHIMNY	CHIMNEY	CEIKLRT	TICKLER
CEEPRTX	EXCERPT	CEHIMOR	HOMERIC		TRICKLE
CEERRSU	RESCUER	CEHIMRT	THERMIC	CEIKLST	STICKLE
	SECURER	CEHIMST	CHEMIST	CEIKNQU	QUICKEN
CEERRSW	SCREWER	CEHINOP	CHOPINE	CEIKPRR	PRICKER
CEERRUV	RECURVE	CEHINOT	HENOTIC	CEIKPRT	PRICKET
CEERSST	CRESSET	CEHINPR	PHRENIC	CEIKPST	SKEPTIC
CEFFIOR	OFFICER		PINCHER	CEIKRRT	TRICKER
CEFFISU	SUFFICE	CEHINRT	CITHERN	CEIKRST	RICKETS
CEFFLSU	SCUFFLE	CEHINST	STHENIC		STICKER
CEFFORS	SCOFFER	CEHINSU	ECHINUS	CEIKRTY	RICKETY
CEFGINN	FENCING	CEHIOPS	HOSPICE	CEILLOR	COLLIER
CEFHILR	FILCHER	CEHIOTV	CHEVIOT	CEILMOP	COMPILE
CEFHILY	CHIEFLY	CEHIPPR	CHIPPER		POLEMIC
CEFHITT	FITCHET	CEHIPRR	CHIRPER	CEILMPR	CRIMPLE
CEFHITW	FITCHEW	CEHIPRS	SPHERIC	CEILNOS	INCLOSE
CEFIILT	FICTILE	CEHIPRT	PITCHER	CEILNOT	LECTION

CEILNOX	LEXICON	CEKNORS	CONKERS	CENORTU	COUNTER
CEILNPS	SPLENIC	CEKNRWY	WRYNECK		RECOUNT
CEILNST	STENCIL	CEKOORY	COOKERY		TROUNCE
CEILOPR	PELORIC	CEKORRY	ROCKERY	CENORTV	CONVERT
CEILOSS	OSSICLE	CEKPRUY	PUCKERY	CENORUV	UNCOVER
CEILPPR	CLIPPER	CEKRRTU	TRUCKER	CENOSSY	COYNESS
	CRIPPLE	CELLNOO	COLONEL	CENOSTT	CONTEST
CEILPSU	SPICULE	CELLOSU	OCELLUS	CENOSTU	CONTUSE
CEILRSV	CLIVERS	CELLOSY	CLOSELY	CENOTTX	CONTEXT
CEILRSY	CLERISY	CELLRCU	SCULLER	CENRRTU	CURRENT
CEILRTU	UTRICLE	CELLRUY	CRUELLY	CENRSTU	ENCRUST
CEILSSS	SCISSEL	CELMNOO	MONOCLE	CENRSUW	UNSCREW
CEIMNOT	ENTOMIC	CELMOPX	COMPLEX	CENRTUY	CENTURY
CEIMOQU	COMIQUE	CELMPRU	CRUMPLE	CEOOPRS	SCOOPER
CEIMORR	MORRICE	CELNOOS	CONSOLE	CEOOPRY	COOPERY
CEIMORT	MORTICE	CELNOSU	COUNSEL	CEOORST	SCOOTER
CEIMOTT	TOTEMIC		UNCLOSE	CEOPPRR	CROPPER
CEIMPRR	CRIMPER	CELNSUU	NUCLEUS	CEOPPRY	COPPERY
CEIMRSU	MURICES	CELOPRU	COUPLER	CEOPRRU	PROCURE
CEINNOV	CONNIVE	CELOPSU	CLOSE-UP	CEOPRSS	PROCESS
CEINOPR	PORCINE		OPUSCLE	CEOPRTT	PROTECT
CEINORV	CORVINE	CELOPTU	COUPLET	CEOPRUU	COUPURE
CEINOSS	CESSION		OCTUPLE	CEOQRTU	CROQUET
CEINOST	SECTION	CELORST	COSTREL	CEORRSU	COURSER
CEINPRS	PINCERS	CELORSU	CLOSURE		SCOURER
CEINPST	INSPECT	CELORTU	COULTER	CEORRSY	SORCERY
CEINRST	CISTERN	CELORVY	CLOVERY	CEORRTY	RECTORY
CEINRUV	INCURVE	CELPRSU	SCRUPLE	CEORSSU	SUCROSE
CEINTTX	EXTINCT	CELRSTU	CLUSTER	CEPPRRU	CRUPPER
CEIOPSU	PICEOUS	CELRSTY	CLYSTER	CEPPRSU	SCUPPER
CEIORRS	CIRROSE	CELRTTU	CLUTTER	CEPRSSU	PERCUSS
	CROSIER	CELRTUU	CULTURE	CEPRSSY	CYPRESS
CEIORRU	COURIER	CELRTUV	CULVERT	CEPSSTU	SUSPECT
CEIORRZ	CROZIER	CELRTUY	CRUELTY	CERSTUY	CURTSEY
CEIORTT	COTTIER		CUTLERY	CFFHINO	CHIFFON
CEIORTV	EVICTOR	CELSTTU	SCUTTLE	CFFIKKO	KICK-OFF
CEIORVY	VICEROY	CEMMNOT	COMMENT	CFFRSUY	SCRUFFY
CEIOSTV	COSTIVE	CEMMNOU	COMMUNE	CFGINOR	FORCING
CEIOSTX	COEXIST	CEMMOOV	COMMOVE	CFHIMYY	CHYMIFY
CEIOSTY	SOCIETY	CEMMOTU	COMMUTE	CFIIIMR	MIRIFIC
CEIPPST	PEPTICS	CEMMRSU	SCUMMER	CFIIIVV	VIVIFIC
CEIPQTU	PICQUET	CEMNNOT	CONTEMN	CFIIKNY	FINICKY
CEIPRRS	CRISPER	CEMNOOY	ECONOMY	CFIILNT	INFLICT
CEIPRSY	SPICERY	CEMNOSU	CONSUME	CFIINOT	FICTION
CEIPRTU	CUPRITE	CEMOOPS	COMPOSE	CFIIOSS	OSSIFIC
	PICTURE	CEMOOTU	OUTCOME	CFIKOSS	FOSSICK
CEIPRTY	PYRETIC	CEMOPTU	COMPUTE	CFILORU	FLUORIC
CEIRRRU	CURRIER	CEMOSTU	COSTUME	CFIMNOR	CONFIRM
CEIRRSU	CRUISER	CEMPRTU	CRUMPET	CFIORSY	SCORIFY
CEIRRTU	RECRUIT	CEMRRUY	MERCURY	CFKNORU	UNFROCK
CEIRSTT	TRISECT	CENNOOT	CONNOTE	CFLMRUU	FULCRUM
CEIRSUV	CURSIVE	CENNOST	CONSENT	CFLNOUX	CONFLUX
CEJNORU	CONJURE	CENNOTT	CONTENT	CFMNOOR	CONFORM
CEJOPRT	PROJECT	CENNOTV	CONVENT	CFMOORT	COMFORT
CEKKLNU	KNUCKLE	CENOORR	CORONER	CFOSSUU	FUSCOUS
CEKKNOR	KNOCKER		CROONER	CGHILPY	GLYPHIC
CEKLLRY	CLERKLY	CENOORT	CORONET	CGHINNO	CHIGNON
CEKLPRU	PLUCKER	CENOPSY	SYNCOPE	CGIIKMM	GIMMICK
CEKLRTU	TRUCKLE	CENOPTY	POTENCY	CGIIKNP	PICKING
CEKMORY	MOCKERY	CENOQRU	CONQUER	CGIIKNT	TICKING
CEKNOOV	CONVOKE	CENORRS	SCORNER	CGIIMNN	MINCING

CGIKNSU	SUCKING	CIIPRTY	PYRITIC	CMOOPST	COMPOST
CGILNOS	CLOSING	CIJNNOO	CONJOIN	CMORSTU	SCROTUM
CGILNOY	CLOYING	CIKLLOR	ROLLICK	CNNORTU	NOCTURN
CGILNRU	CURLING	CIKLLUY	LUCKILY	CNNORUW	UNCROWN
CGILOSS	GLOSSIC	CIKLPRY	PRICKLY	CNOOPPR	POPCORN
CGILOTT	GLOTTIC	CIKLQUY	QUICKLY	CNOORST	CONSORT
CGILPTY	GLYPTIC	CIKRSTY	TRICKSY	CNOORTT	CONTORT
CGINNNO	CONNING	CILLNNO	LINCOLN	CNOORTU	CONTOUR
CGINNNU	CUNNING	CILLNOU	CULLION	CNOOTTY	COTTONY
CGINNOS	CONSIGN	CILMOPY	OLYMPIC	CNORTUY	COUNTRY
CGINOST	GNOSTIC	CILNPSU	SCULPIN	COOPRRT	PROCTOR
CGINPPU	CUPPING	CILOOPT	CO-PILOT	COOPRTU	OUTCROP
CGINRSU	CURSING	CILOPRY	PYLORIC	COOPSTU	OCTOPUS
CGINTTU	CUTTING	CILOPSW	COWSLIP	COOSTTY	OTOCYST
CHHINTU	UNHITCH	CILOSTU	OCULIST	COPRRTU	CORRUPT
CHIIKSS	SICKISH	CILPRSY	CRISPLY	COPRSUU	CUPROUS
CHIIMSU	ISCHIUM	CILPRTU	CULPRIT	CORRSUY	CURSORY
CHIKLLO	HILLOCK	CIMMOSS	COSMISM	DDDESTU	STUDDED
CHIKLTY	THICKLY	CIMNOOR	MORONIC	DDEEFIL	DEFILED
CHIKORY	HICKORY	CIMNORS	CRIMSON	DDEEFIN	DEFINED
CHILOOS	COOLISH	CIMOORS	MORISCO	DDEEFLU	DEEDFUL
CHILOST	COLTISH	CIMOOST	OSMOTIC	DDEEGRR	DREDGER
CHIMMOR	MICROHM	CIMOTYZ	ZYMOTIC	DDEEHRS	SHEDDER
CHIMORS	CHRISOM	CINNORU	UNICORN	DDEEIMS	MISDEED
CHIMRRY	MYRRHIC	CINNOTU	UNCTION	DDEEIRR	DERIDER
CHINOOR	CHORION	CINOSST	CONSIST	DDEELMR	MEDDLER
CHINOPS	PHONICS	CINOSTU	SUCTION	DDEELPR	PEDDLER
CHINORS	CORNISH	CINOSUZ	ZINCOUS	DDEELRT	TREDDLE
CHINOSU	CUSHION	CINRSTU	INCRUST	DDEELRU	DELUDER
CHINQSU	SQUINCH	CIOOPRS	SCORPIO	DDEEOTV	DEVOTED
CHIORST	CHORIST	CIOOPRT	PORTICO	DDEERTU	DETRUDE
	OSTRICH	CIOOPSU	COPIOUS	DDEFLRU	FUDDLER
CHIPRRU	CHIRRUP	CIOPSTY	COPYIST	DDEGILR	GRIDDLE
CHIPRRY	PYRRHIC	CIORSUU	CURIOUS	DDEGIMO	DEMI-GOD
CHIPSSY	PHYSICS	CIORTVY	VICTORY	DDEGINW	WEDDING
CHIRRSU	CURRISH	CIOSSSY	SYCOSIS	DDEGNOS	GODSEND
CHKMMOU	HUMMOCK	CIOSSUV	VISCOUS	DDEGNOU	DUDGEON
CHLOPST	SPLOTCH	CIPSTTY	STYPTIC	DDEGNWY	GWYNEDD
CHMOSUY	CHYMOUS	CIRTUVY	CURVITY	DDEGOSS	GODDESS
CHNORTU	COTHURN	CJNORUY	CONJURY	DDEHIRS	REDDISH
CHNOTUU	UNCOUTH	CKLLOOR	ROLLOCK	DDEHIRY	HYDRIDE
CHNPPUU	PUNCH-UP	CKLNUUY	UNLUCKY	DDEHNRU	HUNDRED
CIIILLT	ILLICIT	CKLOORW	ROWLOCK	DDEHRSU	SHUDDER
CIIIMRS	IRICISM	CKLOOTU	LOCK-OUT	DDEHRSY	SHREDDY
CIIKMMM	MIMMICK	CKLOPTU	POT-LUCK	DDEIIOX	DIOXIDE
CIILLTY	LICITLY	CKNSTUU	UNSTUCK	DDEIIRV	DIVIDER
CIILLVY	CIVILLY	CKOPTTU	PUTTOCK	DDEIKNR	KINDRED
CIILNOP	CIPOLIN	CKOSSTU	TUSSOCK	DDEILMP	DIMPLED
CIILNOS	SILICON	CLLMOSU	MOLLUSC	DDEILNW	DWINDLE
CIILNOT	NILOTIC	CLLOOPS	SCOLLOP	DDEILOT	DELTOID
CIILNUV	UNCIVIL	CLMOOPT	COMPLOT	DDEILTW	TWIDDLE
CIILOOT	OOLITIC	CLMOSUU	OSCULUM	DDEIMNU	MUEDDIN
CIILOPT	POLITIC	CLMSUUU	CUMULUS	DDEINST	DISTEND
CIILOST	SOLICIT	CLNOORT	CONTROL	DDEISTU	STUDIED
CIILPSY	SPICILY	CLNOOSS	CONSOLS	DDEKMOU	DUKEDOM
CIILSSS	SCISSIL	CLNOSTU	CONSULT	DDELOPR	PLODDER
CIIMMRY	MIMICRY	CLOORUY	COLOURY	DDELORT	TODDLER
CIINOOT	COITION	CLORSSY	CROSSLY	DDELPRU	PUDDLER
CIINORS	INCISOR	CLORTUY	COURTLY	DDEMNOT	ODDMENT
CIINPRS	CRISPIN	CMMNOOS	COMMONS	DDENOPS	DESPOND
CIIOSUV	VICIOUS	CMOOPRT	COMPORT	DDENORT	TRODDEN

DDENORU	REDOUND	DEEINRX	INDEXER	DEERRSS	DRESSER
	UNDERDO	DEEINST	DESTINE		REDRESS
DDENOSS	ODDNESS	DEEINSW	ENDWISE	DEERRUV	VERDURE
DDEOORW	REDWOOD		SINEWED	DEERSST	DESSERT
DDEOOWY	DYE-WOOD	DEEINSX	INDEXES		TRESSED
DDEOPRW	DEWDROP	DEEINTT	DINETTE	DEERTUX	EXTRUDE
DDGIILY	GIDDILY	DEEINTV	EVIDENT	DEFFISU	DIFFUSE
DDGINNO	NODDING	DEEINWZ	WIZENED	DEFFLMU	MUFFLED
DDGINPU	PUDDING	DEEIOPS	EPISODE	DEFFLRU	RUFFLED
DDGOOOW	DOGWOOD	DEEIOPT	EPIDOTE	DEFFNOR	FORFEND
DDHIISY	YIDDISH	DEEIORS	OSIERED	DEFGGOR	FROGGED
DDHORSY	DRY-SHOD	DEEIPRS	PRESIDE	DEFGINR	FRINGED
DDILMUY	MUDDILY	DEEIPRV	DEPRIVE	DEFGIOR	FIRE-DOG
DDILRUY	RUDDILY	DEEIPSS	DESPISE	DEFGIRU	FIGURED
DDIPRRY	DRIP-DRY	DEEIPST	DESPITE	DEFGITY	FIDGETY
DDMNOOR	DROMOND	DEEIRRS	DESIRER	DEFIILN	INFIDEL
DEEEGLP	PLEDGEE		SERRIED	DEFIIMW	MIDWIFE
DEEEGRT	DETERGE	DEEIRRT	RETIRED	DEFILRU	DIREFUL
DEEEHLW	WHEEDLE	DEEIRSU	RESIDUE	DEFILXY	FIXEDLY
	WHEELED	DEEIRSV	DEVISER	DEFIPRY	PERFIDY
DEEEISV	DEVISEE		DIVERSE	DEFIRRT	DRIFTER
DEEEKNW	WEEK-END	DEEIRTU	ERUDITE	DEFLLOU	DOLEFUL
DEEELPT	DEPLETE	DEEIRTV	RIVETED	DEFLNOP	PENFOLD
DEEELSV	SLEEVED	DEEITTV	VIDETTE	DEFLNOT	TENFOLD
DEEEMNS	DEMESNE	DEELLRW	DWELLER	DEFMORS	SERFDOM
DEEEOTV	DEVOTEE	DEELLRY	ELDERLY	DEFNORT	FRONTED
DEEERSV	DESERVE	DEELMOR	REMODEL	DEFNORU	FOUNDER
DEEETTV	VEDETTE	DEELMPU	DEPLUME		REFOUND
DEEFFIN	EFFENDI	DEELMTT	METTLED	DEFORST	DEFROST
DEEFGIN	FEEDING	DEELNRS	SLENDER	DEGGHIN	HEDGING
	FEIGNED	DEELNSS	ENDLESS	DEGGILN	GELDING
DEEFHLS	FLESHED	DEELNSY	DENSELY	DEGGNOU	GUDGEON
DEEFHLU	HEEDFUL	DEELOPR	DEPLORE	DEGGRTU	DRUGGET
DEEFILR	DEFILER	DEELOPV	DEVELOP	DEGHILT	DELIGHT
	FIELDER	DEELOPX	EXPLODE	DEGHIST	SIGHTED
DEEFINR	REFINED	DEELORU	URODELE	DEGHLOO	DOG-HOLE
DEEFIRZ	FRIEZED	DEELOTV	DOVELET	DEGIKLO	GODLIKE
DEEFLNU	NEEDFUL	DEELOVV	DEVOLVE	DEGILLY	GELIDLY
DEEFMOR	FREEDOM	DEELPRU	PRELUDE	DEGILNU	INDULGE
DEEFRTT	FRETTED	DEELSTT	SETTLED	DEGILRU	GUILDER
DEEGIRV	DIVERGE	DEEMNOY	MONEYED	DEGILRW	WERGILD
DEEGLPR	PLEDGER	DEEMORS	EMERODS	DEGILUV	DIVULGE
DEEGLPT	PLEDGET	DEEMORV	REMOVED	DEGINNP	PENDING
DEEGNNO	ENDOGEN	DEENNPT	PENDENT	DEGINOP	PIDGEON
DEEGOSY	GEODESY	DEENOPS	SPONDEE	DEGINOR	GROINED
DEEHIKV	KHEDIVE	DEENORS	ENDORSE		NEGROID
DEEHLLS	SHELLED	DEENORT	ERODENT	DEGINOW	WIDGEON
DEEILNS	LINSEED	DEENORW	ENDOWER	DEGINRR	GRINDER
DEEILNY	NEEDILY	DEENPPR	PERPEND	DEGIORT	GOITRED
DEEILRV	DELIVER	DEENPRS	SPENDER	DEGIRSS	DIGRESS
	LIVERED	DEENPRT	PRETEND	DEGLNNO	ENDLONG
DEEILRW	WIELDER	DEENRSS	REDNESS	DEGLOSS	GODLESS
DEEILRY	YIELDER	DEENRST	STERNED	DEGNNOU	DUNGEON
DEEILSY	SEEDILY	DEENRTU	DENTURE	DEGNOPR	PRONGED
DEEIMMS	MISDEEM	DEEOPSX	EXPOSED	DEGNORU	GUERDON
DEEIMNR	ERMINED	DEEORRR	ORDERER		UNDERGO
DEEIMPR	DEMIREP	DEEORRS	REREDOS	DEGNOTU	TONGUED
DEEIMRT	DEMERIT	DEEORTW	TOWERED	DEGOORS	DOG-ROSE
	DIMETER	DEEORUV	OVERDUE	DEHIMOR	HEIRDOM
DEEINNT	DENTINE	DEEPRRU	PERDURE	DEHIMOT	ETHMOID
DEEINNZ	DENIZEN	DEEPRSS	DEPRESS	DEHIOSU	HIDEOUS

DEHIRRU	HURRIED	DEINRTU	INTRUDE	DENORRU	ROUNDER
DEHIRSV	DERVISH		UNTRIED	DENORSU	RESOUND
DEHISSW	SWEDISH	DEINRTY	TINDERY	DENORUW	WOUNDER
DEHLORW	WHORLED	DEINSST	DISSENT	DENOSTU	SNOUTED
DEHMOTU	MOUTHED	DEINSTT	DENTIST	DENPRTU	PRUDENT
DEHNOOW	HOEDOWN	DEINSTY	DENSITY	DENPSSU	SUSPEND
DEHNOPU	UNHOPED		DESTINY	DENRSSU	UNDRESS
DEHNRTU	THUNDER	DEINSUZ	UNSIZED	DENRSSY	DRYNESS
DEHOOTT	TOOTHED	DEIOPPP	POPPIED	DENSTTU	STUDENT
DEIIKLS	DISLIKE	DEIOPRT	PROTEID		STUNTED
DEIILMT	LIMITED	DEIOPRV	PROVIDE	DEOOPPS	OPPOSED
DEIILOS	IDOLISE	DEIOPSS	DISPOSE	DEOOPRT	TORPEDO
DEIIMNO	DOMINIE	DEIOPST	DEPOSIT	DEOPPRR	DROPPER
DEIINOT	EDITION	DEIOPTV	PIVOTED	DEOPRWY	POWDERY
	TENIOID	DEIORST	STORIED	DEOPSTT	SPOTTED
DEIINRS	INSIDER	DEIORSV	DEVISOR	DEORSTW	WORSTED
DEIINRT	INDITER		VISORED	DEORSTY	DESTROY
DEIINRV	DIVINER	DEIORTT	DETROIT	DEOSSYY	ODYSSEY
	DRIVE-IN	DEIORTU	OUTRIDE	DEOSTUU	DUTEOUS
DEIIORT	DIORITE	DEIORWW	WIDOWER	DEPRRSU	SPURRED
DEIIOSX	OXIDISE	DEIOSTU	OUTSIDE	DEPRRUY	PRUDERY
DEIIOXZ	OXIDIZE		TEDIOUS	DERSSTU	TRUSSED
DEIISTT	DIETIST	DEIOSUV	DEVIOUS	DERSTUU	SUTURED
DEIJNOT	JOINTED	DEIPRST	STRIPED	DFFIIMR	MIDRIFF
DEIKLLS	SKILLED	DEIPRTY	DIRT-PYE	DFFIMOR	DIFFORM
DEIKLRT	KIRTLED	DEIPSTU	DISPUTE	DFGHIOS	DOGFISH
DEIKNOS	DOESKIN	DEIRSTU	STUDIER	DFGIINN	FINDING
DEIKNRR	DRINKER	DEISSTU	STUDIES	DFGIINY	DIGNIFY
DEIKNRS	REDSKIN	DEKNNRU	DRUNKEN	DFGILNO	FOLDING
DEIKOSY	DISYOKE	DEKNOTT	KNOTTED	DFGINOU	FUNGOID
DEILLNW	INDWELL	DEKNRTU	TRUNKED	DFILMNU	MINDFUL
DEILLQU	QUILLED	DEKORWY	DYE-WORK	DFILNOP	PINFOLD
DEILLSS	LIDLESS	DELLOPR	REDPOLL	DFILOSX	SIXFOLD
DEILMNT	MIDLENT	DELMORS	SMOLDER	DFILTUU	DUTIFUL
DEILMOP	IMPLODE	DELMORU	MOULDER	DFNORUY	FOUNDRY
DEILMOY	MYELOID		REMOULD	DGGGIIN	DIGGING
DEILMPP	PIMPLED	DELMOTT	MOTTLED	DGGHIOS	DOGGISH
DEILMXY	MIXEDLY	DELMOUV	VOLUMED	DGGIILN	GILDING
DEILNOT	LENTOID	DELNORU	ROUNDEL		GLIDING
DEILNPS	SPINDLE	DELNOSS	OLDNESS	DGGILNO	LODGING
DEILNRT	TENDRIL	DELNPRU	PLUNDER	DGHIILN	HILDING ~~
DEILNSW	SWINDLE	DELNRTU	RUNDLET	DGHIINS	DISHING
DEILNTU	DILUENT		TRUNDLE	DGHILNO	HOLDING
DEILOPS	DESPOIL	DELNSSU	DULNESS	DGHIOPS	GODSHIP
	SOLIPED	DELOPRT	DROPLET	DGHORTU	DROUGHT
DEILORS	SOLDIER	DELORRY	ORDERLY	DGHOTUY	DOUGHTY
DEILRVY	DEVILRY	DELOTUV	VOLUTED	DGIILNS	SLIDING
DEILRZZ	DRIZZLE	DEMMRRU	DRUMMER	DGIILNW	WILDING
DEILSTT	STILTED	DEMNOTU	MOUNTED	DGIILRY	RIGIDLY
DEIMNNU	MINUEND	DEMNOUV	UNMOVED	DGIIMOS	SIGMOID
DEIMNSS	DIMNESS	DEMOOPP	POPEDOM	DGIINNW	WINDING
DEIMNUX	UNMIXED	DEMOOPR	PREDOOM	DGIINST	TIDINGS
DEIMOOR	MOIDORE	DEMOSTY	MODESTY	DGIINTY	DIGNITY
DEIMORS	MISDOER	DENNOTU	UNNOTED	DGIKMNO	KINGDOM
DEIMOST	MODISTE	DENNOUW	UNOWNED	DGIKNOS	DOGSKIN
DEINNTW	TWINNED	DENOOUW	UNWOOED	DGILLOY	GODLILY
DEINOPS	DISPONE	DENOPRS	RESPOND	DGILNYY	DYINGLY
DEINOPT	POINTED	DENOPRT	PORTEND	DGILRUY	GUILDRY
DEINORS	INDORSE		PROTEND	DGINNOU	UNDOING
DEINPST	STIPEND	DENOPRU	POUNDER	DGINNUY	UNDYING
DEINRTT	TRIDENT	DENOPUX	EXPOUND	DGINORW	WORDING

DGIOPRY	PRODIGY	DLLORWY	WORLDLY
DGISSTU	DISGUST	DLMNOOY	MYLODON
DGLNOUY	UNGODLY	DLMOSUU	MODULUS
DGLOOOW	LOGWOOD	DLNORUY	ROUNDLY
DGLOSYY	DYSLOGY	DLNOSUY	SOUNDLY
DGOORTT	DOG-TROT	DLOOPWY	PLYWOOD
DHIILOT	LITHOID	DLOPRUY	PROUDLY
DHIILSW	WILDISH	DNNOOSW	SNOWDON
DHIIMMS	DIMMISH	DNNOSUU	UNSOUND
DHIIMPS	MIDSHIP	DNNOSUW	SUNDOWN
DHIIOPX	XIPHOID	DNOORTU	OROTUND
DHIIORZ	RHIZOID	DOOORSU	ODOROUS
DHIKSSU	DUSKISH	DOOORTU	OUTDOOR
DHILLSU	DULLISH	DOOPRSY	PROSODY
DHILMUY	HUMIDLY	EEEEFRR	REFEREE
DHILNOP	DOLPHIN	EEEEGTX	EXEGETE
DHILOST	DOLTISH	EEEFFFO	FEOFFEE
DHILPSY	SYLPHID	EEEFGRU	REFUGEE
DHILRTY	THIRDLY	EEEFLRR	FLEERER
DHIMORU	RHODIUM	EEEFORS	FORESEE
DHIMPSU	DUMPISH	EEEFRRZ	FREEZER
DHINNOS	DONNISH	EEEGILS	ELEGISE
DHINNSU	DUNNISH	EEEGINP	EPIGENE
DHINORS	DRONISH	EEEGIPR	PERIGEE
DHIOPTY	TYPHOID	EEEGLNT	GENTEEL
DHIORTY	THYROID	EEEGNPR	EPERGNE
DHIPRSU	PRUDISH	EEEGNRV	REVENGE
DHLMOOU	HOODLUM	EEEGNTT	GENETTE
DHMMRUU	HUMDRUM	EEEGRRT	REGREET
DHMNOYY	HYMNODY	EEEGRUX	EXERGUE
DHORSUY	HYDROUS	EEEHLRW	WHEELER
DHORTUY	DROUTHY	EEEHNRW	WHENE'ER
DIIIMRU	IRIDIUM	EEEHRRW	WHERE'ER
DIIINPS	INSIPID	EEEHSTT	ESTHETE
DIIJNOS	DISJOIN	EEEILRV	RELIEVE
DIIKLNS	DISLINK	EEEIMRT	EREMITE
DIILLST	DISTILL	EEEIRRV	REVERIE
DIILMTY	TIMIDLY	EEEIRSZ	RESEIZE
DIILRTY	DIRTILY	EEEKLLU	UKELELE
DIILVVY	VIVIDLY	EEEKLNR	KNEELER
DIILYZZ	DIZZILY	EEELMNT	ELEMENT
DIIMSSS	DISMISS	EEELPRS	SLEEPER
DIIMSUV	VIDIMUS	EEELPRT	REPLETE
DIIORSV	DIVISOR	EEELPST	STEEPLE
DIITUVY	VIDUITY	EEELRTV	LEVERET
DIKLSUY	DUSKILY	EEELSSY	EYELESS
DILLOSY	SOLIDLY	EEEMMSS	MESEEMS
DILMTUY	TUMIDLY	EEEMRTX	EXTREME
DILORWY	WORDILY	EEENNTT	ENTENTE
DILOSTY	STYLOID	EEENPST	STEEPEN
DILRYZZ	DRIZZLY	EEENPSX	EXPENSE
DIMMOST	MIDMOST	EEENRRS	SNEERER
DIMNNOO	MIDNOON	EEENRRT	TERRENE
DIMNOPU	IMPOUND	EEENRRW	RENEWER
DIMRUUV	DUUMVIR	EEENRUV	REVENUE
DINOORS	INDOORS	EEENSTW	SWEETEN
DINORWW	WINDROW	EEEORSV	OVERSEE
DIOORST	DISROOT	EEEORSY	EYESORE
DIOPRST	DISPORT	EEEPRSS	PEERESS
DIORSTT	DISTORT	EEEPRST	STEEPER
DIPRSTU	DISRUPT	EEEPRSW	SWEEPER

EEEQSUZ	SQUEEZE
EEERRRV	REVERER
EEERRST	STEERER
EEERRSV	RESERVE
	REVERSE
EEERSTV	EVEREST
EEFFFNO	ENFEOFF
EEFFFOR	FEOFFER
EEFFGLU	EFFULGE
EEFFINT	FIFTEEN
EEFFNOS	OFFENSE
EEFFORR	OFFERER
EEFGILN	FEELING
EEFGLLU	GLEEFUL
EEFGLOR	FORELEG
EEFHLRS	FLESHER
	HERSELF
EEFHNRS	FRESHEN
EEFHORT	THEREOF
EEFHORW	WHEREOF
EEFHRRS	FRESHER
	REFRESH
EEFHRST	FRESHET
EEFILLX	FLEXILE
EEFILRT	FERTILE
EEFILST	FELSITE
EEFINRR	REFINER
EEFINRW	FIRE-NEW
EEFINSS	FINESSE
EEFISTV	FESTIVE
EEFLLTY	FLEETLY
EEFLNOS	ONESELF
EEFLRRU	FERRULE
EEFLRTU	FLEURET
EEFLRUX	FLEXURE
EEFMNRT	FERMENT
EEFMPRU	PERFUME
EEFMTTU	FUMETTE
EEFNRRW	RENFREW
EEFNRRY	FERNERY
EEFNRTV	FERVENT
EEFNSSW	FEWNESS
EEFORRV	FOREVER
EEFRRSU	REFUSER
EEFRRTU	REFUTER
EEGGHTU	THUGGEE
EEGGILN	NEGLIGÉ
EEGGNOR	ENGORGE
EEGGNOY	GEOGENY
EEGGORR	REGORGE
EEGHINY	HYGIENE
EEGHIRW	WEIGHER
EEGHNRT	GREENTH
EEGIKNP	KEEPING
EEGILNT	GENTILE
EEGILST	ELEGIST
EEGIMMR	IMMERGE
EEGIMNR	REGIMEN
EEGIMNS	SEEMING
EEGIMNT	MEETING
	TEEMING

EEGINNU	GENUINE	EEILOTZ	ZEOLITE	EEIRRSV	REVISER
EEGINNV	EVENING	EEILPRR	REPLIER	EEIRRTV	RIVETER
EEGINPW	WEEPING	EEILPRT	REPTILE	EEIRRTW	REWRITE
EEGINRT	INTEGER	EEILPRU	PUERILE	EEIRRVV	REVIVER
EEGINRV	VEERING	EEILPSS	PELISSE	EEIRSSU	REISSUE
EEGINSS	GENESIS	EEILPST	EPISTLE	EEIRSTV	RESTIVE
EEGINTX	EXIGENT	EEILRRV	REVILER	EEIRSUZ	SEIZURE
EEGISTV	VESTIGE	EEILRST	LEISTER	EEJLRWY	JEWELRY
EEGLLSS	LEGLESS		STERILE	EEJNORY	ENJOYER
EEGLMMU	GEMMULE	EEILRSU	LEISURE	EEJPRRU	PERJURE
EEGLNOR	ERELONG	EEILRSV	SERVILE	EEKLLSY	SLEEKLY
EEGLNOZ	LOZENGE	EEILRVZ	ELZEVIR	EEKLNOS	KEELSON
EEGLNRY	GREENLY	EEILSSS	SESSILE	EEKLRST	KESTREL
EEGMNST	SEGMENT	EEILSUV	ELUSIVE	EELLMOS	MOSELLE
EEGNORS	NEGROES	EEILTTX	TEXTILE	EELLMRS	SMELLER
EEGNPUX	EXPUNGE	EEILVWY	WEEVILY	EELLPRS	RESPELL
EEGNRSS	NEGRESS	EEIMMNS	IMMENSE		SPELLER
EEGOPRT	PROTÉGÉ	EEIMMRS	IMMERSE	EELLQRU	QUELLER
EEGRRSS	REGRESS	EEIMNNO	NOMINEE	EELMPTT	TEMPLET
EEGRRUY	GRUYÈRE	EEIMNNT	EMINENT	EELMRST	SMELTER
EEGRSSU	GUESSER	EEIMNSS	NEMESIS	EELNOPV	ENVELOP
EEGRSTU	GESTURE	EEIMOPT	EPITOME	EELNPSY	SPLEENY
EEHHRTW	WHETHER	EEIMPRR	PREMIER	EELNQUY	QUEENLY
EEHINOR	HEROINE	EEIMPRS	EMPRISE	EELNSTY	TENSELY
EEHINRR	ERRHINE		PREMISE	EELNTTU	LUNETTE
EEHINRT	NEITHER	EEIMPRT	EMPTIER	EELOPRS	LEPROSE
	THEREIN	EEIMQRU	REQUIEM	EELOPRX	EXPLORE
EEHINRW	WHEREIN	EEIMRRT	TRIREME	EELOPTU	EEL-POUT
EEHIORZ	HEROIZE	EEIMRTT	TERMITE	EELORSV	RESOLVE
EEHIPRT	PRITHEE	EEINNPS	PENNIES	EELORVV	REVOLVE
EEHIPSV	PEEVISH	EEINNRV	INNERVE	EELOSST	OSSELET
EEHIPTT	EPITHET	EEINNST	INTENSE	EELPPRX	PERPLEX
EEHIRSS	HEIRESS	EEINNTW	ENTWINE	EELPRST	SPELTER
EEHISTV	THIEVES	EEINOPR	PIONEER	EELPRSU	REPULSE
EEHKLOY	KEYHOLE	EEINPRR	REPINER	EELPRVY	REPLEVY
EEHLRST	SHELTER	EEINPRT	PETRINE	EELPSTY	STEEPLY
EEHLSSU	HUELESS	EEINPSV	PENSIVE	EELQRUY	QUEERLY
EEHLSSV	SHELVES	EEINQRU	ENQUIRE	EELRRVY	REVELRY
EEHMORT	THEOREM	EEINQTU	QUIETEN	EELRSST	TRESSEL
EEHNNRY	HENNERY	EEINRRT	REINTER	EELRSTT	SETTLER
EEHNORT	THEREON		RENTIER		STERLET
EEHNORW	NOWHERE	EEINRRV	VERNIER		TRESTLE
	WHEREON	EEINRSV	INVERSE	EELRSTW	SWELTER
EEHNSTV	SEVENTH	EEINRTU	RETINUE		WRESTLE
EEHORTT	THERETO		REUNITE	EELRSTY	TERSELY
EEHORTW	WHERETO		UTERINE	EELSSSU	USELESS
EEHORVW	HOWEVER	EEINSTX	SIXTEEN	EELSTWY	SWEETLY
	WHOEVER	EEINSTY	SYENITE	EELTVVY	VELVETY
EEHOSTY	EYESHOT	EEIOPST	POETISE	EEMMNOT	MEMENTO
EEHRTTW	WHETTER	EEIOPTZ	POETIZE	EEMNNOV	ENVENOM
EEILLPS	ELLIPSE	EEIORSV	EROSIVE	EEMNOOS	SOMEONE
EEILMRV	VERMEIL	EEIPPTT	PIPETTE	EEMNORY	MONEYER
EEILNNO	LEONINE	EEIPRRS	REPRISE	EEMOPRR	EMPEROR
EEILNNT	LENIENT		RESPIRE	EEMOPRW	EMPOWER
EEILNNV	ENLIVEN	EEIPRST	RESPITE	EEMORRS	REMORSE
EEILNPS	PENSILE	EEIPRSV	PREVISE	EEMORRV	REMOVER
EEILNST	TENSILE	EEIPRVW	PREVIEW	EEMPRSS	EMPRESS
EEILNTT	ENTITLE	EEIQRRU	REQUIRE	EEMPRSU	PRESUME
EEILOPT	PETIOLE	EEIQRSU	ESQUIRE		SUPREME
EEILORV	OVERLIE	EEIQRTU	REQUITE	EEMPRTT	TEMPTER
	RELIEVO	EEIRRRT	TERRIER	EEMPRTU	PERMUTE

EEMPSTT	TEMPEST	EFGGILP	EGG-FLIP	EFLNORW	FERN-OWL
EENNOSS	ONENESS	EFGHIRT	FIGHTER	EFLNSSU	FULNESS
EENNPTU	NEPTUNE		FREIGHT	EFLNTUU	TUNEFUL
EENNRUV	UNNERVE	EFGILMN	FLEMING	EFLOORR	FLOORER
EENNSSW	NEWNESS	EFGILNT	FELTING	EFLOORY	FOOLERY
EENPRST	PRESENT	EFGIMNT	FIGMENT	EFLORSU	OURSELF
	SERPENT	EFGINOR	FOREIGN	EFLORTT	FORTLET
EENPRTV	PREVENT	EFGINRU	GUNFIRE	EFLORVY	FLYOVER
EENQSTU	SEQUENT	EFGIORV	FORGIVE	EFLORWW	WERWOLF
EENRRUV	NERVURE	EFGLNTU	FULGENT	EFLORWY	FLOWERY
EENRSTW	WESTERN	EFGNOOR	FORGONE	EFLRSTU	FLUSTER
EENRTUV	VENTURE	EFGORRU	FERRUGO		RESTFUL
EENSSTW	WETNESS	EFGORRY	FORGERY	EFLRTTU	FLUTTER
EENSTVY	SEVENTY	EFHILMS	FLEMISH	EFMOPRR	PERFORM
EEOOPRS	OPEROSE		HIMSELF	EFNOOST	FESTOON
EEOPRRV	REPROVE	EFHILSS	SELFISH	EFNORRU	FORERUN
EEOPRSX	EXPOSER	EFHIRST	SHIFTER	EFNORTU	FORTUNE
EEOPRTT	TREETOP	EFHIRSY	FISHERY	EFOOPRR	REPROOF
EEOPSST	POETESS	EFHISUW	HUSWIFE	EFOOPRT	FORETOP
EEOPSSU	ESPOUSE	EFHLLPU	HELPFUL	EFOPPRY	FOPPERY
EEORRST	RESTORE	EFHLLSY	FLESHLY	EFOPRSS	PROFESS
EEORSTT	ROSETTE	EFHLOOX	FOXHOLE	EFOPRSU	PROFUSE
EEORSTV	OVERSET	EFHLOPU	HOPEFUL	EFORRSU	FERROUS
EEORSTX	XEROTES	EFHLRSY	FRESHLY	EFORRTY	TORREFY
EEPPPRY	PEPPERY	EFHLSTY	THYSELF	EFORRUV	FERVOUR
EEPPRST	STEPPER	EFHLTTW	TWELFTH	EFPRTUY	PUTREFY
EEPPSUY	EUPEPSY	EFHRRTU	FURTHER	EFPSTUY	STUPEFY
EEPRRSS	REPRESS	EFIILRY	FIERILY	EGGGILN	LEGGING
EEPRRSU	PERUSER	EFIILSS	FISSILE	EGGGILR	GIGGLER
EEPRRTV	PERVERT	EFIKRST	FRISKET	EGGHILR	HIGGLER
EEPRSSX	EXPRESS	EFILLOO	FOLIOLE	EGGILRW	WRIGGLE
EEPRSTU	PERTUSE	EFILLUW	WILEFUL	EGGINNS	GINSENG
EEPRTTX	PRETEXT	EFILMNU	FULMINE	EGGINRS	SNIGGER
EEQRRUY	EQUERRY	EFILMOT	FILEMOT	EGGIPRY	PIGGERY
EEQRSTU	QUESTER	EFILNOX	FLEXION	EGGIRRT	TRIGGER
	REQUEST	EFILNSS	FINLESS	EGGIRWY	WIGGERY
EERRSTW	WRESTER	EFILOPR	PROFILE	EGGJLRU	JUGGLER
EERRTTU	UTTERER	EFILORT	TREFOIL	EGGLMSU	SMUGGLE
EERSTTU	TRUSTEE	EFILPPR	FLIPPER	EGGLNSU	SNUGGLE
EERSTUV	VESTURE	EFILQUY	LIQUEFY	EGGLOOY	GEOLOGY
EERTTUX	TEXTURE	EFILRRT	TRIFLER	EGGLPRU	PLUGGER
EFFFOOR	FEOFFOR	EFILRTT	FLITTER	EGGNOOY	GEOGONY
EFFHILW	WHIFFLE	EFILRZZ	FRIZZLE	EGGSSTU	SUGGEST
EFFHIRS	SHERIFF	EFIMNTT	FITMENT	EGHIINV	INVEIGH
EFFHLSU	SHUFFLE	EFINSST	FITNESS	EGHIKNR	GHERKIN
EFFIIST	FIFTIES	EFIOPRR	PORIFER	EGHILNP	HELPING
EFFIKLS	SKIFFLE	EFIOPRT	FIRE-POT	EGHILNS	ENGLISH
EFFILRY	FIREFLY	EFIORRT	ROTIFER		SHINGLE
EFFINST	STIFFEN	EFIORST	FORTIES	EGHILNT	LIGHTEN
EFFIORT	FORFEIT	EFIPRTY	PETRIFY	EGHILRT	LIGHTER
EFFLMRU	MUFFLER	EFIRRRU	FURRIER		RELIGHT
EFFLNSU	SNUFFLE	EFIRRTT	FRITTER	EGHILST	SLEIGHT
EFFLOSU	SOUFFLÉ	EFIRRTY	TERRIFY	EGHINNU	UNHINGE
EFFLRRU	RUFFLER	EFIRSSU	FISSURE	EGHINRR	HERRING
EFFLRTU	FRETFUL	EFIRSTU	SURFEIT	EGHINTT	TIGHTEN
	TRUFFLE	EFIRSVY	VERSIFY	EGHIORS	OGREISH
EFFNRSU	SNUFFER	EFIRTUV	FURTIVE	EGHIRRT	RIGHTER
EFFOPRR	PROFFER	EFIRTUX	FIXTURE	EGHITWY	WEIGHTY
EFFPRUY	PUFFERY	EFISTTY	TESTIFY	EGHLNOR	LEGHORN
EFFRSTU	STUFFER	EFKLNUY	FLUNKEY	EGHLNTY	LENGTHY
EFFSSUU	SUFFUSE	EFLMOSU	FULSOME	EGHNORU	ROUGHEN

EGHNOTU	TOUGHEN	EGMNOYZ	ZYMOGEN	EHISSTU	HUSSITE
EGHRTUY	THEURGY	EGMORTU	GOURMET	EHISTTW	WETTISH
EGIILMT	LEGITIM	EGNNPTU	PUNGENT	EHLMNOT	MENTHOL
EGIILNT	LIGNITE	EGNNRUY	GUNNERY	EHLNORT	HORNLET
EGIIMNP	IMPINGE	EGNNTUU	UNGUENT	EHLNTTY	TENTHLY
EGIIMSV	MISGIVE	EGNOOYZ	ZOOGENY	EHLOOPT	POTHOLE
EGIINNV	VEINING	EGNOPRS	SPONGER	EHLORST	HOLSTER
EGIINRT	TIGRINE	EGNOPRY	PROGENY		HOSTLER
EGIIPRW	PERIWIG	EGNORRW	WRONGER	EHLORTY	HELOTRY
EGIIPSS	GIPSIES	EGNORSS	ENGROSS	EHLRSTU	HUSTLER
EGIKLNT	KINGLET	EGNORSU	SURGEON	EHLSTTU	SHUTTLE
EGILLNT	TELLING	EGNRRTU	GRUNTER	EHMOOST	SMOOTHE
EGILLNY	YELLING	EGNRTTU	TURGENT	EHMOOSW	SOMEHOW
EGILMMN	LEMMING	EGOORSY	GOOSERY	EHMORST	SMOTHER
EGILMMR	GLIMMER	EGOPRRU	REGROUP	EHMORTU	MOUTHER
EGILMNT	MELTING	EGORRUY	ROGUERY	EHMORTY	MOTHERY
EGILMOU	ELOGIUM	EGRRSUY	SURGERY	EHMPRTU	THUMPER
EGILMPS	GLIMPSE	EHHILLS	HELLISH	EHMRRTU	MURTHER
EGILNOT	LENTIGO	EHHINRS	RHENISH	EHMRSUU	HUMERUS
EGILNRS	SLINGER	EHHIRTT	THITHER	EHNOPUY	EUPHONY
EGILNRT	RINGLET	EHHIRTW	WHITHER	EHNORRT	HORRENT
	TRINGLE	EHIINRT	INHERIT	EHNORRY	HERONRY
EGILNST	GLISTEN	EHIKNRT	RETHINK	EHNORST	SHORTEN
EGILNSW	SWINGLE		THINKER	EHNORSU	UNHORSE
EGILNTW	WINGLET	EHIKRRS	SHIRKER	EHNOSST	HOTNESS
EGILRST	GLISTER	EHIKRSW	WHISKER	EHNOSTT	SHOTTEN
	GRISTLE	EHIKSWY	WHISKEY	EHNOSTY	HONESTY
EGILRTT	GLITTER	EHILLRT	THILLER	EHNOSUU	UNHOUSE
EGILRZZ	GRIZZLE	EHILNOP	PINHOLE	EHNSSSY	SHYNESS
EGILSSW	WIGLESS	EHILNPS	PLENISH	EHOORST	SHOOTER
EGIMNPT	PIGMENT	EHILOPT	HOPLITE		SOOTHER
EGIMOST	EGOTISM	EHILOST	ELOHIST	EHOPPRS	SHOPPER
EGINNOP	OPENING		HOSTILE	EHOPPRT	PROPHET
EGINNPU	PENGUIN	EHILPRT	PHILTER	EHOPPRW	WHOPPER
EGINNRT	RINGENT		PHILTRE	EHOPRST	STROPHE
EGINNTT	NETTING	EHILRRW	WHIRLER	EHORRTW	THROWER
EGINORT	GENITOR	EHILRST	SLITHER	EHORSTU	SHOUTER
EGINOSU	IGNEOUS	EHILRSV	SHRIVEL	EHORSWY	SHOWERY
EGINPRS	SPRINGE	EHILSTT	THISTLE	EHOSSST	HOSTESS
EGINPTT	PETTING	EHILSTW	WHISTLE	EHRSTTU	SHUTTER
EGINRRW	WRINGER	EHILTTW	WHITTLE	EIIKLMS	MISLIKE
EGINRSS	INGRESS	EHIMORS	HEROISM	EIILLNV	VILLEIN
EGINRSW	SWINGER	EHIMORZ	RHIZOME	EIILMPR	IMPERIL
EGINRSY	SYRINGE	EHIMPRW	WHIMPER	EIILMRS	MILREIS
EGINRTT	GITTERN	EHIMSWY	WHIMSEY	EIILMRT	LIMITER
EGINSTT	SETTING	EHINNRT	THINNER	EIILMSS	MISSILE
EGINSTW	WESTING	EHINOPX	PHOENIX	EIILMST	ELITISM
EGIOPRS	SERPIGO	EHINORS	INSHORE	EIILNOS	ELISION
EGIORTV	VERTIGO	EHINOSU	HEINOUS		LIONISE
EGIOSTT	EGOTIST	EHINRTZ	ZITHERN	EIILNOV	OLIVINE
EGIPPRR	GRIPPER	EHINSSS	SHINESS	EIILNOZ	LIONIZE
EGIPRUU	GUIPURE	EHIORSY	HOSIERY	EIILORV	RILIEVO
EGIRSST	TIGRESS	EHIPPRS	SHIPPER	EIILQSU	SILIQUE
EGLMNOR	MONGREL	EHIPPRW	WHIPPER	EIILSTT	ELITIST
EGLNOOY	NEOLOGY	EHIPRST	HIPSTER	EIILSTU	UTILISE
EGLNORU	LOUNGER	EHIPRSW	WHISPER	EIILTUZ	UTILIZE
EGLNOUV	UNGLOVE	EHIPSTT	PETTISH	EIIMMST	MISTIME
EGLNPRU	PLUNGER	EHIRRTV	THRIVER	EIIMNRT	INTERIM
EGLORRW	GROWLER	EHIRSTU	HIRSUTE		TERMINI
EGLORSS	GLOSSER	EHIRSTW	WITHERS	EIIMNRV	MINIVER
EGLRSUU	REGULUS	EHIRSVY	SHIVERY	EIIMOSS	MEIOSIS

EIIMPRS	PISMIRE	EILNRTY	INERTLY	EINNORV	ENVIRON
EIIMPST	PIETISM	EILNSSS	SINLESS	EINNOST	TENSION
EIIMPTY	IMPIETY	EILNSTU	UTENSIL	EINNOSV	VENISON
EIIMSSV	MISSIVE	EILNVXY	VIXENLY	EINNOTT	TONTINE
EIINNQU	QUININE	EILOOST	OSTIOLE	EINNPRS	SPINNER
EIINNTW	INTWINE	EILOOTZ	ZOOLITE	EINNPSY	SPINNEY
EIINPRS	INSPIRE	EILOPRS	SPOILER	EINNRTV	VINTNER
EIINQRU	INQUIRE	EILOPRT	POITREL	EINNTUW	UNTWINE
EIINRTV	INVITER	EILOPST	PISTOLE	EINOOPZ	EPIZOON
EIINTUV	UNITIVE	EILOPTX	EXPLOIT	EINOORS	EROSION
EIIPSTT	PIETIST	EILORSS	RISSOLE	EINOOZZ	OZONIZE
EIIRSTV	REVISIT	EILORTT	TORTILE	EINOPRT	POINTER
	VISITER		TRIOLET		PROTEIN
EIISSTX	SIXTIES	EILORTU	OUTLIER	EINOPSS	SPINOSE
EIJNORY	JOINERY	EILOSTT	LITOTES	EINOQUX	EQUINOX
EIJNPRU	JUNIPER	EILOTUV	OUTLIVE	EINORSV	VERSION
EIJNRRU	INJURER	EILPPRS	SLIPPER	EINORTU	ROUTINE
EIJPRTU	JUPITER	EILPPRT	TIPPLER	EINOSSS	SESSION
EIJSSUV	JUSSIVE	EILPPST	STIPPLE	EINOSUV	ENVIOUS
EIKKLRS	SELKIRK	EILPRTT	TRIPLET		NIVEOUS
EIKLLNW	INKWELL	EILPRUU	PURLIEU	EINPPRS	NIPPERS
EIKLLST	SKILLET	EILPSTT	SPITTLE		SNIPPER
EIKLNRW	WRINKLE	EILPSTU	STIPULE	EINPPST	SNIPPET
EIKLNSS	KINLESS	EILPTTY	PETTILY	EINPRRT	PRINTER
EIKLNTW	TWINKLE	EILQRUU	LIQUEUR		REPRINT
EIKLSTT	SKITTLE	EILQTUY	QUIETLY	EINQRUY	ENQUIRY
EIKMMRS	SKIMMER	EILRSTT	SLITTER	EINQSTU	INQUEST
EIKMORS	IRKSOME	EILRSVY	SILVERY	EINQTTU	QUINTET
EIKNNRS	SKINNER	EILRTTY	TRITELY	EINQTUU	UNQUIET
EIKNRST	STINKER	EILRTUV	RIVULET	EINRRSU	INSURER
EIKNRTT	KNITTER	EILSSTW	WITLESS	EINRSSU	SUNRISE
	TRINKET	EILSTTY	STYLITE	EINRSTT	STINTER
EIKPPRS	SKIPPER		TESTILY	EINRTTW	WRITTEN
EIKRRST	SKIRRET	EIMMPRU	PREMIUM	EINRTWY	WINTERY
	STRIKER	EIMMRRT	TRIMMER	EINSSTW	WITNESS
EILLMNU	MULLEIN	EIMMRSW	SWIMMER	EINSTTW	ENTWIST
EILLMOT	MELILOT	EIMNNOT	MENTION	EINSTTY	TENSITY
EILLNSS	ILLNESS	EIMNOOS	NOISOME	EINTTUY	TENUITY
EILLOSV	VILLOSE	EIMNOOT	EMOTION	EIOPRRT	PIERROT
EILLPRS	SPILLER	EIMNOPS	PEONISM	EIOPRST	REPOSIT
EILLRST	STILLER	EIMNOPT	PIMENTO		RIPOSTE
	TRELLIS	EIMNORS	MERSION	EIOPSTU	PITEOUS
EILLRSW	SWILLER	EIMNOST	MOISTEN	EIORRRW	WORRIER
EILLRSY	SILLERY	EIMNOSW	WINSOME	EIORRST	ROISTER
EILMOPR	IMPLORE	EIMNPTU	PINETUM	EIORSSU	SERIOUS
EILMOSS	LISSOME	EIMNRST	MINSTER	EIORTTV	TORTIVE
EILMPRY	PRIMELY	EIMNSTT	SMITTEN	EIPPPSU	PUPPIES
EILMPSU	IMPULSE	EIMNUZZ	MUEZZIN	EIPPRRT	TRIPPER
EILMRRY	MERRILY	EIMOPRS	PROMISE	EIPRRTY	TRIPERY
EILMRSU	MISRULE	EIMOPRV	IMPROVE	EIPRSST	PERSIST
EILMRSY	MISERLY	EIMORST	MORTISE	EIPRSTT	SPITTER
EILMSUY	ELYSIUM	EIMOSTU	TIMEOUS	EIPRSTY	PYRITES
EILNNPU	PINNULE	EIMOSTZ	MESTIZO	EIPRUVW	PURVIEW
EILNOSS	LIONESS	EIMPRSS	IMPRESS	EIQRSTU	QUERIST
EILNOSU	ELUSION		PREMISS	EIQSTUU	QUIETUS
EILNOTU	OUTLINE	EIMPRTU	IMPUTER	EIRRRST	STIRRER
EILNOTV	VIOLENT	EIMPSTU	IMPETUS	EIRRSTV	STRIVER
EILNOVV	INVOLVE	EIMRSSU	SURMISE	EIRSTTW	TWISTER
EILNPTY	INEPTLY	EIMRTUX	MIXTURE	EIRSTWZ	SWITZER
EILNPUV	VULPINE	EINNOPS	PENSION	EIRSUVV	SURVIVE
EILNRSV	SILVERN	EINNORU	REUNION	EIRTTTW	TWITTER

EJJMNUU	JEJUNUM	EMMNOTU	OMENTUM	EOPSSSS	POSSESS
EJLOSSY	JOYLESS	EMNOORT	MONTERO	EOPSTTU	OUTSTEP
EJNORUY	JOURNEY	EMNORRU	MOURNER	EOQRSTU	QUESTOR
EJOORVY	OVERJOY	EMNORST	MONSTER	EORRTTT	TROTTER
EJPRRUY	PERJURY	EMNORTT	TORMENT	EORRTTU	TORTURE
EKKLRSU	SKULKER	EMNORTU	REMOUNT	EORSSTU	OESTRUS
EKMNPTU	UNKEMPT	EMNORTV	VERMONT	EORTTTY	TOTTERY
EKNOORS	SNOOKER	EMNRSTU	STERNUM	EPRRSUU	PURSUER
EKNORUY	YOUNKER	EMOOPRT	PROMOTE		USURPER
EKNRTUY	TURNKEY	EMOOSTT	MOTTOES	EPRRTUU	RUPTURE
EKOOPRV	PROVOKE	EMOOSTW	TWOSOME	EPRSTTU	SPUTTER
EKOORRY	ROOKERY	EMPRSTU	STUMPER	ERRSTTU	TRUSTER
EKORRST	STROKER		SUMPTER	ERSTTTU	STUTTER
ELLMPUU	PLUMULE	EMPRTTU	TRUMPET	FFFILOT	LIFT-OFF
ELLNOOW	WOOLLEN	EMRSTYY	MYSTERY	FFGIINR	GRIFFIN
ELLNOSW	SWOLLEN	ENNNRUY	NUNNERY	FFGINOR	GRIFFON
ELLOOSY	LOOSLEY	ENNORTU	NEUTRON	FFGLRUY	GRUFFLY
ELLOPTU	POLLUTE	ENNPSTU	UNSPENT	FFHHISU	HUFFISH
ELLORRT	TROLLER	ENNRSTU	STUNNER	FFHILTY	FIFTHLY
ELLORTY	TROLLEY	ENOOPSY	SPOONEY	FFHOOSW	SHOW-OFF
ELLOSTU	SELL-OUT	ENOORSU	ONEROUS	FFILSTY	STIFFLY
ELMMPTU	PLUMMET	ENOOTXY	OXYTONE	FFINOPT	PONTIFF
ELMOORT	TREMOLO	ENOPRST	POSTERN	FFIORTY	FORTIFY
ELMOPSU	PLUMOSE	ENOPRTT	PORTENT	FFKLOSU	SUFFOLK
ELMOSUU	EMULOUS	ENOPSST	STEPSON	FGGILNO	GOLFING
ELMPPRU	PLUMPER	ENORRST	SNORTER	FGGILOY	FOGGILY
ELMPRUY	PLUMERY	ENORRTT	TORRENT	FGGINOR	FORGING
ELMRTUU	MULTURE	ENORRUV	OVERRUN	FGHIINS	FISHING
ELMRTUY	ELYTRUM	ENORSSY	SENSORY	FGHILTY	FLIGHTY
ELMSSSU	SUMLESS	ENORSTU	TONSURE	FGHNOOR	FOG-HORN
ELNOOSU	UNLOOSE	ENORSUV	NERVOUS	FGIILLN	FILLING
ELNOPRY	PRONELY	ENORTUY	TOURNEY	FGIILNS	FILINGS
ELNOPTU	OPULENT	ENOSTUU	TENUOUS	FGIILNY	LIGNIFY
ELNORTY	ELYTRON	ENPRRSU	SPURNER	FGIINSY	SIGNIFY
ELNOSSS	SONLESS	ENPRSTU	PUNSTER	FGIINTT	FITTING
ELNOSSW	LOWNESS	ENPSTUW	UNSWEPT	FGILNOP	FOPLING
ELNOSTV	SOLVENT	ENRRSUY	NURSERY	FGILNOW	FLOWING
ELNOTUZ	ZONULET	ENRRTUU	NURTURE	FGILNTU	FLUTING
ELNOTVY	NOVELTY	ENRRTUY	TURNERY	FGILORY	GLORIFY
ELNRSTY	STERNLY	ENRSSWY	WRYNESS	FGIMOSY	FOGYSIM
ELNSSSU	SUNLESS	ENRSTTU	ENTRUST	FGINOOR	ROOFING
ELNSSSY	SLYNESS	EOOPPRS	OPPOSER	FGINOOT	FOOTING
ELOORTT	ROOTLET		PROPOSE	FGINRRU	FURRING
ELOPPST	STOPPLE	EOOPRRT	TROOPER	FGISTUU	FUGUIST
ELOPRRW	PROWLER	EOOPRTV	OVERTOP	FGLNORU	FURLONG
ELOPRSU	LEPROUS	EOORRST	ROOSTER	FGNOORU	FOURGON
	SPORULE	EOOSSSU	OSSEOUS	FGNOSUU	FUNGOUS
ELOPRSY	LEPROSY	EOOTTUV	OUTVOTE	FHIINNS	FINNISH
ELOPRTT	PLOTTER	EOPPRRS	PROSPER	FHILOOS	FOOLISH
ELOPSST	TOPLESS	EOPPRSS	OPPRESS	FHILOSW	WOLFISH
ELORSUY	ELUSORY	EOPPRST	STOPPER	FHILSUW	WISHFUL
ELORTTY	LOTTERY	EOPPRSU	PURPOSE	FHINRSU	FURNISH
ELORTVY	OVERTLY	EOPPSSU	SUPPOSE	FHINSSU	SUNFISH
ELOSSTY	SYSTOLE	EOPRSSW	PROWESS	FHIOPPS	FOPPISH
ELPRUZZ	PUZZLER	EOPRSTT	PROTEST	FHIORRY	HORRIFY
ELPSTUU	PUSTULE	EOPRSTU	PETROUS	FHIOSST	SOFTISH
ELRSTWY	SWELTRY		POSTURE	FHIRTTY	THRIFTY
ELRTTUY	UTTERLY		SPOUTER	FHLRTUU	HURTFUL
ELRTUUV	VULTURE	EOPRSUU	UPROUSE		RUTHFUL
ELSSSUY	ULYSSES	EOPRTTY	POTTERY	FHNOTUX	FOX-HUNT
EMMMRUY	MUMMERY	EOPRTVY	POVERTY	FIIIKNN	FINIKIN

FIILLMO	MILFOIL	GHHORTU	THROUGH	GIJNOTT	JOTTING
FIILPTU	PITIFUL	GHHOTTU	THOUGHT	GIKMNOS	SMOKING
FIINOSS	FISSION	GHIILRS	GIRLISH	GIKNNOW	KNOWING
FIINRTY	NITRIFY	GHIINNS	SHINING	GIKNORW	WORKING
FIIRTVY	VITRIFY	GHIINST	INSIGHT	GILLNOR	ROLLING
FIJSTUY	JUSTIFY	GHIINTT	TITHING	GILLNYY	LYINGLY
FIKLLSU	SKILFUL	GHIINTW	WHITING	GILMNPU	LUMPING
FIKLNOW	WOLFKIN	GHIIRST	TIGRISH	GILNNSU	UNSLING
FIKLNSU	SKINFUL	GHIKLNU	HULKING	GILNOOT	TOOLING
FILLMOY	MOLLIFY	GHILLTY	LIGHTLY	GILNOPP	LOPPING
FILLNUY	NULLIFY	GHILNOS	LONGISH	GILORTY	TRILOGY
FILLOTU	TOILFUL	GHILNOW	HOWLING	GILOSTT	GLOTTIS
FILLOTY	LOFTILY	GHILNSY	SHINGLY	GILRSTY	GRISTLY
FILNNUY	FUNNILY	GHILNTY	NIGHTLY	GILRTUY	LITURGY
FILNOUX	FLUXION	GHILRTY	RIGHTLY	GILRYZZ	GRIZZLY
FILNTUY	UNFITLY	GHILSTY	SIGHTLY	GIMNNOR	MORNING
FILORST	FLORIST	GHILTTY	TIGHTLY	GIMNOOR	MOORING
FILRSTY	FIRSTLY	GHINNOT	NOTHING	GIMNOSU	MOUSING
FILRYZZ	FRIZZLY	GHINNTU	HUNTING	GIMNOWY	WYOMING
FILSSUY	FUSSILY	GHINOSU	HOUSING	GINNNOO	NOONING
FILSTTU	FLUTIST	GHINOSW	SHOWING	GINNNPU	PUNNING
FILSTUW	WISTFUL	GHINOTT	TONIGHT	GINNNRU	RUNNING
FILSTWY	SWIFTLY	GHINPSU	PUSHING	GINNRTU	TURNING
FIMMMUY	MUMMIFY	GHIORSU	ROGUISH	GINOPPT	TOPPING
FIMNORU	UNIFORM	GHIPRST	SPRIGHT	GINOPST	POSTING
FIMOORV	OVIFORM	GHIPRTU	UPRIGHT	GINORSU	ROUSING
FIMORRT	TRIFORM	GHLORUY	ROUGHLY	GINORTT	ROTTING
FIMORTY	MORTIFY	GHLOSTY	GHOSTLY	GINOTWW	WIGTOWN
FIMRTUY	FURMITY	GHLOSUY	SLOUGHY	GINPRSY	SPRINGY
FIMSTYY	MYSTIFY	GHLOTUY	TOUGHLY	GINRSTY	STRINGY
FIOORSU	FURIOSO	GHMORSU	SORGHUM	GIOOPRR	PORRIGO
FIOPSTX	POSTFIX	GHNOSTU	GUNSHOT	GIOPRRU	PRURIGO
FIORSUU	FURIOUS		SHOTGUN	GIOPSSY	GOSSIPY
FKLNOOR	NORFOLK	GHORTUW	WROUGHT	GLMOOYY	MYOLOGY
FLLOSUU	SOULFUL	GHORTUY	YOGHURT	GLMORUW	LUGWORM
FLLOUWY	WOFULLY	GIIJNNO	JOINING	GLNNOOR	LORGNON
FLLSTUU	LUSTFUL	GIIKLLN	KILLING	GLNOOOY	NOOLOGY
FLMNOOU	MOUFLON	GIIKLNN	INKLING	GLNOOPR	PROLONG
FLMOOOT	TOMFOOL	GIIKNNP	KINGPIN	GLNOOPY	POLYGON
FLMOORU	ROOMFUL	GIIKNNS	SINKING	GLNORWY	WRONGLY
FLNOORR	FORLORN	GIIKNPS	PIGSKIN	GLNOTTU	GLUTTON
FLOOTUW	OUTFLOW	GIIKNRS	GRISKIN	GLNOUYY	YOUNGLY
FLOSUUV	FULVOUS	GIILLMN	MILLING	GLOOORY	OROLOGY
FMRSTUU	FRUSTUM	GIILLNW	WILLING	GLOOOTY	OTOLOGY
FOORTTX	FOXTROT	GIILMNS	SMILING	GLOOOYZ	ZOOLOGY
FORRUWY	FURROWY	GIILMPR	PILGRIM	GLORSSY	GROSSLY
GGGIINR	RIGGING	GIILMRY	GRIMILY	GMMOSUU	GUMMOUS
GGGIINW	WIGGING	GIILNTT	TITLING	GMORSUU	GRUMOUS
GGHHIOS	HOGGISH	GIILNTW	WITLING	GMORTUW	MUGWORT
GGHIIPS	PIGGISH	GIILRST	STRIGIL	GMRUYYZ	ZYMURGY
GGHIMSU	MUGGISH	GIIMNPR	PRIMING	GNNRUUW	UNWRUNG
GGHINSU	GUSHING	GIIMNSS	MISSING	GNOOOYZ	ZOOGONY
GGIINNO	INGOING	GIINNNT	TINNING	GNOOPPS	POP-SONG
GGIINPR	GRIPING	GIINNNW	WINNING	GOORTUW	OUTGROW
GGILNNO	LONGING	GIINNOR	IRONING	HHIIPPS	HIPPISH
GGILNOS	GOSLING	GIINNTT	TINTING	HHIISTW	WHITISH
GGILNOW	GLOWING	GIINNTW	TWINING	HHIORSW	WHORISH
GGIMMNU	GUMMING	GIINOPR	PIG-IRON	HIILMTU	LITHIUM
GGINNOO	ONGOING	GIINORS	SIGNIOR	HIILPTY	PITHILY
GGINPRU	PURGING	GIINRTW	WRITING	HIILRTT	TRILITH
GGIPRSY	SPRIGGY	GIINSTT	SITTING	HIINSSW	SWINISH

HIKLSUY	HUSKILY	IILMOSS	LIMOSIS	ILOORTY	OLITORY
HIKMNOS	MONKISH	IILMSTU	STIMULI	ILOOSST	SOLOIST
HIKNNOR	INKHORN	IILMSTY	MISTILY	ILOPSUY	PIOUSLY
HIKRSTU	TURKISH	IILNORS	SIRLOIN	ILORRSY	SORRILY
HILLOPT	HILLTOP	IILNOSY	NOISILY	ILRSSUU	SILURUS
HILLRSY	SHRILLY	IILOPRT	TRIPOLI	ILRSTUY	RUSTILY
HILMPSU	LUMPISH	IILORTV	VITRIOL	ILSSTTY	STYLIST
HILNNTY	NINTHLY	IILOSTV	VIOLIST	IMNOOPP	POMPION
HILOOTT	OTOLITH	IILPRVY	PRIVILY	IMNOOPT	TOMPION
HILOSTU	LOUTISH	IILPSTY	TIPSILY	IMNOORT	MONITOR
HILOSWY	SHOWILY	IILTTUY	UTILITY	IMNOOSU	OMINOUS
HILOTWW	WHITLOW	IILTTWY	WITTILY	IMNOOSY	ISONOMY
HILSSTY	STYLISH	IIMMMNU	MINIMUM	IMNOPPU	PUMPION
HILSTTY	THISTLY	IIMNOSS	MISSION	IMOOPRX	PROXIMO
HILSTXY	SIXTHLY	IIMNOSZ	ZIONISM	IMORSTU	TOURISM
HIMMNTU	THUMMIN	IIMNPRT	IMPRINT	IMORSTY	TORYISM
HIMMPSU	MUMPISH	IIMOPSU	IMPIOUS	IMOSSYZ	ZYMOSIS
HIMNOOS	MOONISH	IIMOSSU	SIMIOUS	IMRSSTU	SISTRUM
HIMOORS	MOORISH	IINNOOP	OPINION		TRISMUS
HIMOPRS	ROMPISH	IINORTT	INTROIT	IMRTTUY	YTTRIUM
HIMOPSS	SOPHISM	IINOSTZ	ZIONIST	INNOSTU	NONSUIT
HIMORTU	THORIUM	IINOTTU	TUITION	INOOPRT	PORTION
HIMPRTU	TRIUMPH	IINQRUY	INQUIRY	INOORST	TORSION
HIMSSTU	ISTHMUS	IINRTTY	TRINITY	INOOSUX	NOXIOUS
HINNNSU	NUNNISH	IINSTTW	INTWIST	INOPSSU	SPINOUS
HINOORZ	HORIZON	IIORSTV	VISITOR	INORSTU	NITROUS
HINOPPS	SHIPPON	IIOSSTT	OSTITIS	INORSUU	RUINOUS
HINOPSS	SONSHIP	IIPRTVY	PRIVITY	INOSSUU	SINUOUS
HINORSU	NOURISH	IJKLLOY	KILLJOY	INSTTUW	UNTWIST
HINOSSW	SNOWISH	IJLLLOY	JOLLILY	IOOPRSV	PROVISO
HINSTUW	WHITSUN	IJLLOTY	JOLLITY	IOORSSS	SOROSIS
HIOPRSW	WORSHIP	IJLNOQU	JONQUIL	IOORSTT	RISOTTO
HIOPSST	SOPHIST	IJLNOTY	JOINTLY	IOORSTU	RIOTOUS
HIORSSU	SOURISH	IKLLSUY	SULKILY	IOPRSTT	TROPIST
HIORSTY	HISTORY	IKLMOPS	MILKSOP	IORSTTU	TOURIST
HIOSSTT	SOTTISH	IKLMOSY	SMOKILY	IPRRSTU	STIRRUP
HIOTTUW	WITHOUT	IKLMRUY	MURKILY	IPRSTUU	PURSUIT
HIRSTTU	RUTTISH	IKLNPSU	SKULPIN	JNOORSU	SOJOURN
HIRSTTY	THIRSTY	IKLNRWY	WRINKLY	KLLMOSU	MOLLUSK
HKNOOWW	KNOWHOW	IKMNPPU	PUMPKIN	KLOOOTU	LOOKOUT
HLMNOTY	MONTHLY	IKMOSSU	KOUMISS		OUTLOOK
HLORSTY	SHORTLY	IKNORSS	KINROSS	KNNNOUW	UNKNOWN
HLPRSUU	SULPHUR	IKNPSTU	SPUTNIK	KOORTUW	OUTWORK
HMMNOOY	HOMONYM	ILLMNOU	MULLION	LLMPPUY	PLUMPLY
HMMRTUY	THRUMMY	ILLNPUU	LUPULIN	LLOOPRT	TROLLOP
HNNORSU	UNSHORN	ILLNTUY	NULLITY	LMOPSUU	PLUMOUS
HNOOPTY	TYPHOON	ILLOPRY	PILLORY	LMRSTUU	LUSTRUM
HNRTTUU	UNTRUTH	ILLOPWY	PILLOWY	LMSTUUU	TUMULUS
HOOPSTY	TOYSHOP	ILLOSUV	VILLOUS	LNNOPSU	NONPLUS
HOPRSTU	HOTSPUR	ILLOWWY	WILLOWY	LNRTUUY	UNTRULY
HOPRTUW	UPTHROW	ILLRSUY	SURLILY	LOPPSUY	POLYPUS
HOPSTUY	TYPHOUS	ILLSTUY	LUSTILY	LOPRSUY	PYLORUS
HORSTUU	OUTRUSH	ILMNOOT	MOONLIT	LOPRTUY	POULTRY
HRSSTUY	THYRSUS	ILMOORY	ROOMILY	LOSTTUY	STOUTLY
IIIKMNN	MINIKIN	ILMORTU	TURMOIL	LPRSSUU	SURPLUS
IIISTTW	WISTITI	ILNOPRU	PURLOIN	MMNOSSU	SUMMONS
IILLLSY	SILLILY	ILNORST	NOSTRIL	MNNOOOS	MONSOON
IILLMNO	MILLION	ILNORSU	SURLOIN	MNNOSYY	SYNONYM
IILLNOP	PILLION	ILNOSTT	STILTON	MNOOOYZ	ZOONOMY
IILLNST	INSTILL	ILNOSTY	STONILY	MNORSTU	NOSTRUM
IILMNOS	LIONISM	ILOOORS	ROSOLIO	MOOOTYZ	ZOOTOMY

MOOPPSU	POMPOUS	NNORSUW	UNSWORN	OOPRTUU	OUTPOUR
MOOPSSU	OPOSSUM	NOOORTT	TORONTO	OOPSSTT	TOSSPOT
MOOPSTT	TOPMOST	NOOPRSS	SPONSOR	OOPSTTU	OUTPOST
MOOSTTU	OUTMOST	NOORTUW	WORN-OUT	OPPRRTU	PURPORT
MORRSTU	ROSTRUM	NOPSSTU	SUNSPOT	OPPRSTU	SUPPORT
NNOGOPT	PONTOON	NORTTUU	TURN-OUT	ORSTTUU	SURTOUT
NNOOPRU	PRONOUN	OOORTTU	OUTROOT		
NNOOPST	NON-STOP	OOPRSTV	PROVOST		

Eight Letter Words

AAAACCRR	CARACARA	AAAHIMNR	MAHARANI	AABCELNR	BALANCER
AAAACNRS	ANASARCA	AAAHMNRT	AMARANTH		BARNACLE
AAAADMTV	AMADAVAT	AAAHNNSV	SAVANNAH	AABCELOR	ALBACORE
AAAAGGRR	AGAR-AGAR	AAAILLMR	MALARIAL	AABCENRR	CANBERRA
AAABBILT	ABBATIAL	AAAILLPT	PALATIAL	AABCEORT	BOAT-RACE
AAABCCRT	BACCARAT	AAAILMMM	MAMMALIA	AABCGKLO	CLOAK-BAG
AAABCHLS	CALABASH	AAAILMNR	MALARIAN	AABCHILR	BRACHIAL
AAABCNRU	CARNAUBA	AAAILNST	ALSATIAN	AABCHKLS	BACKLASH
AAABCPRY	CAPYBARA	AAAIMMST	MIASMATA	AABCHKRS	SHABRACK
AAABDNRS	SARABAND	AAAINOPR	PARANOIA	AABCIILS	BASILICA
AAABDNRT	ABRADANT	AAAIPSSV	PIASSAVA	AABCILLR	BACILLAR
AAABEHRT	BARATHEA	AAAKNRSS	ARKANSAS	AABCILMS	BALSAMIC
AAABGRTU	RUTABAGA	AAALLPRX	PARALLAX	AABCILMY	AMICABLY
AAABINSS	ANABASIS	AAALNNTU	ANNULATA	AABCILNN	CANNIBAL
AAABINTV	BATAVIAN	AAALNRTT	TARLATAN	AABCILST	BASALTIC
AAABLOPR	PARABOLA	AAAMNOPR	PANORAMA	AABCIMNR	CAMBRIAN
AAACCEPR	CARAPACE	AAAPQRTU	PARAQUAT	AABCINNO	BACONIAN
AAACCIMM	CAIMACAM	AABBCDRS	SCABBARD	AABCINNR	CINNABAR
AAACCRTT	CATARACT	AABBCINR	BARBICAN	AABCINNS	CANNABIS
AAACDINN	CANADIAN	AABBCIRR	BARBARIC	AABCISSS	ABSCISSA
AAACDINR	ACARIDAN	AABBCIST	SABBATIC	AABCRSTT	ABSTRACT
	ARCADIAN	AABBCTTY	TABBY-CAT	AABDDEET	DEAD-BEAT
AAACDNNO	ANACONDA	AABBEELR	BEARABLE	AABDEELR	READABLE
AAACEHNR	ARCHAEAN	AABBEILL	BAILABLE	AABDEERY	BAYADÈRE
AAACILMN	MANIACAL	AABBELLM	BLAMABLE	AABDEGIN	BADINAGE
AAACILSY	CALISAYA	AABBELLS	BASE-BALL	AABDEHHI	DAHABIEH
AAACINTV	CAVATINA	AABBELRY	BEARABLY	AABDEKRY	DAYBREAK
AAACKMRT	TAMARACK	AABBLLMY	BLAMABLY	AABDELLU	LAUDABLE
AAACLMRY	CALAMARY	AABCCELS	CASCABEL	AABDELMN	DAMNABLE
AAACNOSV	CASANOVA	AABCCHNT	BACCHANT	AABDELOR	ADORABLE
AAACSTWY	CASTAWAY	AABCCKLP	BLACK-CAP	AABDELRW	DRAWABLE
AAADEFWY	FADE-AWAY	AABCCKLW	CLAWBACK	AABDELRY	READABLY
AAADKRRV	AARDVARK	AABCCMOT	CATACOMB	AABDEMNS	BEADS-MAN
AAADMNTU	TAMANDUA	AABCDEIT	ABDICATE	AABDENTU	UNABATED
AAAEGLRT	ALTARAGE	AABCDHKN	BACKHAND	AABDENVW	WAVEBAND
AAAEGNPP	APPANAGE	AABCDHKR	HARDBACK	AABDEORS	SEA-BOARD
AAAEHMNT	ANATHEMA	AABCDINT	ABDICANT	AABDERRW	BEARWARD
AAAENNRZ	NAZAREAN	AABCDKRW	BACKWARD	AABDGNOV	VAGABOND
AAAERTWY	TEARAWAY		DRAWBACK	AABDGOTU	GADABOUT
AAAFGINR	GRAAFIAN	AABCEENY	ABEYANCE	AABDHNST	SAND-BATH
AAAFINST	FANTASIA	AABCEERT	ACERBATE	AABDINNR	RAINBAND
AAAFINUV	AVIFAUNA	AABCEERV	CAVE-BEAR	AABDKNNS	SAND-BANK
AAAGGLLN	GALANGAL	AABCEILM	AMICABLE	AABDLLUY	LAUDABLY
AAAGHIPR	AGRAPHIA	AABCEINR	CARABINE	AABDLMNY	DAMNABLY
AAAGHNTY	YATAGHAN	AABCEIRT	BACTERIA	AABDLORR	LABRADOR
AAAGINRR	AGRARIAN	AABCEJNO	JACOBEAN		LARBOARD
AAAGLRST	ASTRAGAL	AABCEKLM	CLAMBAKE	AABDLORY	ADORABLY
AAAGMPRR	PARAGRAM	AABCELLP	PLACABLE	AABDNNTU	ABUNDANT
AAAGNPRS	PARASANG	AABCELLR	CABALLER	AABDNRRY	BARN-YARD
AAAGPRUY	PARAGUAY	AABCELLS	SCALABLE	AABDRSTY	BASTARDY

AABEEGKR	BREAKAGE	AABILRVY	VARIABLY	AACDEJNT	ADJACENT
AABEEGNT	ABNEGATE	AABIMORS	AMBROSIA	AACDELNR	CALENDAR
AABEEHLL	HEALABLE	AABINORS	ABRASION	AACDENRW	WAR-DANCE
AABEEKRT	TEA-BREAK	AABINRTZ	BARTIZAN	AACDEOTV	ADVOCATE
AABEELLS	SALEABLE	AABIORTT	ABATTOIR	AACDEQUY	ADEQUACY
AABEELMN	AMENABLE	AABLLNST	TAN-BALLS	AACDERST	CADASTRE
	NAMEABLE	AABLLPPY	PALPABLY	AACDGINR	CARDIGAN
AABEELMT	TAMEABLE	AABLLPRT	TRAP-BALL	AACDHINP	HANDICAP
AABEELRW	WEARABLE	AABLLSTU	BLASTULA	AACDIIMT	ADAMITIC
AABEFLMR	FARMABLE	AABLMNOR	ABNORMAL	AACDIINS	ASCIDIAN
AABEFLMU	FLAMBEAU	AABLMNTU	AMBULANT	AACDIJLU	JUDAICAL
AABEGLLM	BALL-GAME	AABLOTUY	LAYABOUT	AACDILMT	DALMATIC
AABEGLRU	ARGUABLE	AABLPSSY	PASSABLY	AACDILNO	DIACONAL
AABEGMNR	BARGEMAN	AABMORTU	MARABOUT	AACDILNR	CARDINAL
AABEGNOR	BARONAGE	AABMOSSU	ABOMASUS	AACDILNV	VANDALIC
AABEGORT	ABROGATE	AABNNOST	ABSONANT	AACDILOZ	ZODIACAL
AABEGOST	SABOTAGE	AABORRRT	BARRATOR	AACDIMRT	DRAMATIC
AABEHIRR	HERBARIA	AABRRRTY	BARRATRY	AACDINOR	ORCADIAN
AABEHLPS	SHAPABLE	AACCCHHU	CACHUCHA	AACDIRTY	CARYATID
AABEHLPT	ALPHABET	AACCCRUY	ACCURACY	AACDITUY	AUDACITY
AABEHLSW	WASHABLE	AACCDEIM	ACADEMIC	AACDKLNU	AUCKLAND
AABEIKRR	AIR-BRAKE	AACCDELO	ACCOLADE	AACDLORT	CART-LOAD
AABEILLS	ISABELLA	AACCDENU	CADUCEAN	AACDMMOR	CARDAMOM
AABEILRS	RAISABLE	AACCDERS	CARD-CASE	AACEEFIT	FACETIAE
AABEILRV	VARIABLE	AACCDHIL	CHALDAIC	AACEEGIR	ACIERAGE
AABEILST	SATIABLE	AACCDOVY	ADVOCACY	AACEEGKU	AGUE-CAKE
AABEILTV	ABLATIVE	AACCEEFH	FACE-ACHE	AACEEGLV	CLEAVAGE
AABEINST	BASANITE	AACCEENT	CETACEAN	AACEEIMT	EMACIATE
AABEKNRS	NEBRASKA	AACCELOR	CARACOLE	AACEEKPR	RAPE-CAKE
AABEKNRV	BRAKE-VAN	AACCENRT	CARCANET	AACEELRT	LACERATE
AABELLNO	LOANABLE	AACCERTU	ACCURATE	AACEELST	ESCALATE
AABELLPP	PALPABLE		CARUCATE	AACEELTU	ACULEATE
AABELLPS	LAPSABLE	AACCFILR	FARCICAL	AACEEMRT	MACERATE
AABELLSV	SALVABLE	AACCGILT	GALACTIC	AACEEMST	CASEMATE
AABELLSY	SALEABLY	AACCHINR	ANARCHIC	AACEENRS	CESAREAN
AABELLUV	VALUABLE	AACCHLOR	CHARCOAL	AACEEPSS	SEA-SCAPE
AABELMNY	AMENABLY	AACCHLOT	CACHALOT	AACEERTV	ACERVATE
AABELNNT	TANNABLE	AACCHMNO	COACHMAN	AACEETUV	EVACUATE
AABELOVW	AVOWABLE	AACCIIST	SCIATICA	AACEETVX	EXCAVATE
AABELPRS	SPARABLE	AACCILRU	ACICULAR	AACEFFIN	AFFIANCE
AABELPSS	PASSABLE	AACCILTT	TACTICAL	AACEGHNT	CHANTAGE
AABELRTY	BETRAYAL	AACCIORU	CARIACOU	AACEGILN	ANGELICA
AABELSTT	TASTABLE	AACCIPTY	CAPACITY	AACEGILT	GLACIATE
AABELTTU	TABULATE	AACCJORU	CARCAJOU	AACEGIRR	CARRIAGE
AABELTUX	TABLEAUX	AACCLLRU	CALCULAR	AACEGIRV	VICARAGE
AABENRRT	ABERRANT	AACCLMNY	CLAMANCY	AACEGKRT	TRACKAGE
AABENRST	RATSBANE	AACCLPRS	CALC-SPAR	AACEHILL	HELIACAL
AABGGRRT	BRAGGART	AACCLRSU	SACCULAR	AACEHIMR	CHIMAERA
AABGILRU	BULGARIA	AACCLTTU	CALCUTTA	AACEHIMT	HAEMATIC
AABGLMNU	GALBANUM	AACCOSTT	STACCATO	AACEHLRT	TRACHEAL
AABHIIMP	AMPHIBIA	AACDDETY	TEA-CADDY	AACEILLM	CAMELLIA
AABHILTU	HABITUAL	AACDEEHH	HEADACHE	AACEILLN	ALLIANCE
AABHINTT	HABITANT	AACDEELS	ESCALADE		CANAILLE
AABIILRS	BRASILIA	AACDEEPS	ESCAPADE	AACEILMN	CALAMINE
AABILLLY	LABIALLY	AACDEFLT	FALCATED	AACEILMT	CALAMITE
AABILLST	BALLISTA	AACDEGMR	DECAGRAM	AACEILNS	CANALISE
AABILNOR	BARONIAL	AACDEHHY	HEADACHY	AACEILNZ	CANALIZE
AABILNOT	ABLATION	AACDEHIN	HACIENDA	AACEILOP	ALOPECIA
AABILNTY	BANALITY	AACDEHRT	CATHEDRA	AACEILRT	TAIL-RACE
AABILOST	SAIL-BOAT	AACDEIMS	CAMISADE	AACEILRV	CAVALIER
AABILRST	ARBALIST	AACDEINR	RADIANCE	AACEIMNR	AMERICAN

AACEINRT	CARINATE	AACILMNT	CALAMINT	AADDRSTY	DASTARDY
AACEINRV	VARIANCE		CLAIMANT	AADEEGLT	GALEATED
AACEIPTT	CAPITATE	AACILMTY	CALAMITY	AADEEGMN	ENDAMAGE
AACEITTV	ACTIVATE	AACILNRV	CARNIVAL	AADEELRW	DELAWARE
AACEKRSW	SEA-WRACK	AACILNTT	ATLANTIC	AADEENTT	ANTEDATE
AACEKRTT	ATTACKER	AACILNTU	NAUTICAL		EDENTATA
AACELLOT	ALLOCATE	AACILNTY	ANALYTIC	AADEEQTU	ADEQUATE
AACELMNP	PLACEMAN	AACILOPR	CARAP-OIL	AADEFLNS	SAND-FLEA
AACELMTU	MACULATE	AACILPRU	PIACULAR	AADEFLRY	DEFRAYAL
AACELNPR	PARLANCE	AACILPSZ	CAPSIZAI	AADEFOTU	AUTO-DA-FÉ
AACELNPT	PLACENTA	AACILRTY	ALACRITY	AADEGILL	DIALLAGE
AACELRSU	CAESURAL	AACILRUU	AURICULA	AADEGILT	GLADIATE
AACEMNPS	SPACEMAN	AACILSTT	CAT'S-TAIL	AADEGINR	DRAINAGE
AACEMRSS	MASSACRE		STATICAL		GARDENIA
AACENORS	SEA-ACORN	AACIMMNO	AMMONIAC	AADEGINT	INDAGATE
AACENPRS	PANCREAS	AACIMNOR	MACARONI	AADEGITT	AGITATED
AACENPSU	SAUCE-PAN	AACIMORT	AROMATIC	AADEGLMN	MAGDALEN
AACENRST	CANASTER	AACINNOT	CATONIAN	AADEGRTU	GRADUATE
AACENRTY	CATENARY	AACINOTV	VACATION	AADEHIWY	HIDEAWAY
AACENRVZ	CZAREVNA	AACINQTU	ACQUAINT	AADEHLMP	HEADLAMP
AACENTUV	EVACUANT	AACINSTZ	STANZAIC	AADEHMNS	HEADSMAN
AACEOSST	SEA-COAST	AACIPRTY	RAPACITY	AADEHNRV	VERANDAH
AACERSTT	CASTRATE	AACIRRTT	TARTARIC	AADEHRRW	HARDWARE
AACERTTT	TRACTATE	AACKKNPS	KNAPSACK	AADEILPS	PALISADE
AACESUWY	CAUSEWAY	AACKMNST	TACKSMAN	AADEILPT	LAPIDATE
AACFILLY	FACIALLY	AACLLMRY	CLAY-MARL	AADEILRS	SALARIED
AACFIRRT	AIRCRAFT		LACRYMAL	AADEILTV	VALIDATE
AACFIRTT	ARTIFACT	AACLLNRY	CARNALLY	AADEIMNR	MARINADE
AACGHIRR	CHIRAGRA	AACLLRSY	RASCALLY	AADEIMNT	ANIMATED
AACGIIMN	MAGICIAN	AACLLSUY	CASUALLY	AADEIMRV	MARAVEDI
AACGILLN	GALLICAN		CAUSALLY	AADEIMST	DIASTEMA
AACGILNN	ANGLICAN	AACLLTUY	ACTUALLY	AADEIPRS	PARADISE
AACGILNV	GALVANIC	AACLMNNS	CLANSMAN	AADEIPTV	ADAPTIVE
AACGILRT	TRAGICAL	AACLMRRU	MACRURAL	AADEISST	DIASTASE
AACGIMNN	MANGANIC	AACLNNOT	CANTONAL	AADEKMNR	MANDRAKE
AACGIMNP	CAMPAIGN	AACLORRU	ORACULAR	AADELLWY	WELLADAY
AACGIMUU	GUAIACUM	AACLORSU	CAROUSAL	AADELMNR	ALDERMAN
AACGISTY	SAGACITY	AACLPPRT	CLAPTRAP	AADELMNS	DALESMAN
AACGLMOU	GLAUCOMA	AACLPRSU	CAPSULAR	AADELMPT	DATE-PALM
AACGNRVY	VAGRANCY		SCAPULAR		PALMATED
AACHHTWY	HATCHWAY	AACLPRTY	CALYPTRA	AADELMYZ	AMAZEDLY
AACHILNP	CHAPLAIN	AACLPTTU	CATAPULT	AADEMRRU	MARAUDER
AACHILPS	CALIPASH	AACLRSUV	VASCULAR	AADEQRTU	QUADRATE
AACHIMNN	CHINAMAN	AACLRTUX	CURTAL-AX	AADERRRW	REARWARD
AACHIMNR	CHAIRMAN	AACLSTUY	CASUALTY	AADERSTW	EASTWARD
AACHIMNS	SHAMANIC	AACMNOOR	MACAROON	AADFGNNO	FANDANGO
AACHIMRR	ARMCHAIR	AACMNPRY	RAMPANCY	AADFHMNR	FARMHAND
AACHIMRS	ARCHAISM	AACNRSTT	TRANSACT	AADFLLLN	LANDFALL
	CHARISMA	AACOPRSU	ACARPOUS	AADFLORW	AARDWOLF
AACHINNO	NOACHIAN	AACORTTU	AUTOCRAT	AADFLOTX	TOAD-FLAX
AACHINSW	CHAINSAW	AADDDEEH	DEAD-HEAD	AADFMRRY	FARMYARD
AACHLMNO	MONACHAL	AADDDGNR	GRAND-DAD	AADGILLR	GALLIARD
AACHLMOS	CHLOASMA	AADDEEHT	DEAD-HEAT	AADGILMR	MADRIGAL
AACHMNTW	WATCHMAN	AADDEEMT	DEAD-MEAT	AADGILNO	DIAGONAL
AACHMNUY	NAUMACHY	AADDEFLL	DEAD-FALL	AADGIMPR	PARADIGM
AACHMPRY	PHARMACY	AADDEHLN	HEADLAND	AADGINRU	GUARDIAN
AACHNSTU	ACANTHUS	AADDEMRY	DAY-DREAM	AADGIQRU	QUADRIGA
AACHOPPR	APPROACH	AADDHIMN	HANDMAID	AADGLOPR	PODAGRAL
AACIILRT	IATRICAL	AADDLLNY	LANDLADY	AADGMNOR	DRAGOMAN
AACIILRV	VICARIAL	AADDLNRW	LANDWARD	AADGNRUV	VANGUARD
AACIJLMO	MAJOLICA	AADDNRST	STANDARD	AADHHIPS	PADISHAH

AADHILLR	HALLIARD	AAEELRTU	LAUREATE	AAEIKLLS	ALKALISE
AADHILNR	HANDRAIL	AAEELTUV	EVALUATE	AAEIKLLZ	ALKALIZE
AADHILNT	THAILAND	AAEENNRZ	NAZARENE	AAEILLMX	MAXILLAE
AADHILRV	HAVILDAR	AAEENRTT	ANT-EATER	AAEILLPP	PAPILLAE
AADHINRR	HARRIDAN	AAEENSTU	NAUSEATE	AAEILLPT	PALLIATE
AADHLPSS	SLAP-DASH	AAEEPPRR	REAPPEAR	AAEILLRY	AERIALLY
AADIIMNN	INDIAMAN	AAEEPRST	SEPARATE	AAEILMNT	LAMINATE
AADIINRR	AIR-DRAIN	AAEERSTW	SEA-WATER	AAEILMRT	MATERIAL
AADIKLLO	ALKALOID	AAEFGHRW	WHARFAGE	AAEILNNN	LINNAEAN
AADILLLO	ALLODIAL	AAEFGLLL	FLAGELLA	AAEILNPT	PALATINE
AADILLOS	SALAD-OIL	AAEFGLOT	FLOATAGE	AAEILNRV	VALERIAN
AADILLRY	RADIALLY	AAEFMRSW	SAW-FRAME	AAEILNSZ	NASALIZE
AADILMNN	MAINLAND	AAEFNRRT	TARA-FERN	AAEILPPZ	PAPALIZE
AADILMNO	DOMAINAL	AAEFRRWY	WAYFARER	AAEILPRT	PARIETAL
AADILNPR	PRANDIAL	AAEGGIOT	AGIOTAGE	AAEILRRT	ARTERIAL
AADILORR	RAILROAD	AAEGGLNU	LANGUAGE	AAEILRTV	VARIETAL
AADILPRY	LAPIDARY	AAEGGNOW	WAGONAGE	AAEILSTV	AESTIVAL
AADIMNNR	MANDARIN	AAEGGOPR	PARAGOGE		SALIVATE
AADIMNRT	TAMARIND	AAEGHLNP	PHALANGE		
AADIMNRY	DAIRYMAN	AAEGHNRU	HARANGUE	AAEILSTX	SAXATILE
AADIMNRZ	ZAMINDAR	AAEGILNP	PELAGIAN	AAEILTVX	LAXATIVE
AADIMNSS	DAMASSIN	AAEGILNR	ALGERIAN	AAEIMNNR	ARMENIAN
AADIMNTU	ADIANTUM	AAEGILRS	GASALIER	AAEIMNPT	IMPANATE
AADIMNUV	VANADIUM	AAEGIMNS	MAGNESIA	AAEIMNRZ	MAZARINE
AADINOPR	PARANOID	AAEGIMNZ	MAGAZINE	AAEINORT	AERATION
AADINOPS	DIAPASON	AAEGIMRR	MARRIAGE	AAEINRST	ARTESIAN
AADINPRS	SPANIARD	AAEGINPS	PAGANISE		ERASTIAN
AADIORRT	RADIATOR	AAEGINPT	PAGINATE	AAEINRSU	EURASIAN
AADIRRSY	DISARRAY	AAEGINPZ	PAGANIZE	AAEINRTZ	NAZARITE
AADJNTTU	ADJUTANT	AAEGINTV	NAVIGATE	AAEINSTV	SANATIVE
AADKLMNR	LANDMARK		VAGINATE	AAEIPPRS	APPRAISE
AADKORWY	WORKADAY	AAEGIPRU	PERIAGUA	AAEIPRST	ASPIRATE
AADLMNNS	LANDSMAN	AAEGIVWY	GIVEAWAY		PARASITE
AADLMNRY	MARYLAND	AAEGLLMS	SMALLAGE		
AADLMNUU	LAUDANUM	AAEGLLPR	PELLAGRA	AAEIPRTZ	TRAPEZIA
AADLMPVY	DAVY-LAMP	AAEGLLST	STALLAGE	AAEJNNPR	JAPANNER
AADLORST	LOADSTAR	AAEGLNOU	ANALOGUE	AAEKPRRT	PARTAKER
AADLORTU	ADULATOR	AAEGLSVY	SAVAGELY	AAELLLMR	LAMELLAR
AADMMNSU	MANDAMUS	AAEGMNRV	GRAVAMEN	AAELLLPR	PARALLEL
AADMORRT	TRAM-ROAD	AAEGMORS	SAGAMORE	AAELLORV	ALVEOLAR
AADNNPSU	PANDANUS	AAEGMRRV	MARGRAVE	AAELLPST	STAPELLA
AADNOSWY	NOWADAYS	AAEGNRRR	ARRANGER	AAELMNRT	MATERNAL
AADNQRTU	QUADRANT	AAEGNRTU	RUNAGATE	AAELMNSS	SALESMAN
AADNQRUY	QUANDARY	AAEGNSTT	STAGNATE	AAELMPRT	MALAPERT
AADOPSUY	PADUASOY	AAEGORRT	ARROGATE	AAELMPTY	PLAYMATE
AADORSVY	SAVOYARD	AAEGPPRW	WRAPPAGE	AAELMRSY	LAMASERY
AADRSTUY	SATURDAY	AAEGRSSS	SEA-GRASS	AAELMRTT	MALTREAT
AAEEEGLS	SEA-EAGLE	AAEGRSTW	WATER-GAS	AAELNNTU	ANNULATE
AAEEFRRS	SEAFARER	AAEGRSVY	SAVAGERY	AAELNOSS	SEASONAL
AAEEGILN	ALIENAGE	AAEHILPR	PARHELIA	AAELNPRT	PARENTAL
AAEEGLLN	ENALLAGE	AAEHIMNT	HAEMATIN		PATERNAL
AAEEGNRS	SANGAREE	AAEHINNT	ATHENIAN	AAELNPST	PLEASANT
AAEEHRTW	AWEATHER	AAEHINST	ASTHENIA	AAELNRTT	ALTERANT
	WHEATEAR	AAEHKMRY	HAYMAKER	AAELNSTT	ATLANTES
AAEEILNT	ALIENATE	AAEHLNTX	EXHALANT	AAELORTY	ALEATORY
AAEEKMNS	NAMESAKE	AAEHLPRS	PEARLASH	AAELPPSU	APPLAUSE
AAEEKNSS	SEA-SNAKE	AAEHLPUV	UPHEAVAL	AAELPRST	PALESTRA
AAEEKPRT	PARAKEET	AAEHMORT	ATHEROMA	AAELPRSY	PARALYSE
AAEELLLM	LAMELLAE	AAEHNPST	PHEASANT	AAELPRYZ	PARALYZE
AAEELNPS	SPELAEAN	AAEIKKMZ	KAMIKAZE	AAELPSTV	PALSTAVE
AAEELPRY	LEAP-YEAR	AAEIKLLN	ALKALINE	AAELPTUX	PLATEAUX
				AAEMMNRT	ARMAMENT

AAEMNPRS	PARMESAN
	SPEARMAN
AAEMNRST	SARMENTA
AAEMNRTW	WATERMAN
AAEMOTTU	AUTOMATE
AAEMPTTU	AMPUTATE
AAEMQSTU	SQUAMATE
AAEMRRTU	ARMATURE
AAEMRRTW	WATER-RAM
AAENNOTT	ANNOTATE
AAENORTU	AERONAUT
AAENPPRT	APPARENT
	TRAPPEAN
AAENPSTT	ANTEPAST
AAENRSUW	UNAWARES
AAEOPSTT	APOSTATE
AAEORSTT	AEROSTAT
AAEPRTTY	TEA-PARTY
AAERRTTT	TARTRATE
AAERRTTW	WATER-RAT
AAERSTTU	SATURATE
AAFFINPR	PARAFFIN
AAFFLPST	PALSTAFF
AAFFLSTU	AFFLATUS
AAFFNNOR	FANFARON
AAFGLNRT	FLAGRANT
AAFGNRRT	FRAGRANT
AAFHIRST	AIR-SHAFT
AAFHLMST	HALF-MAST
AAFIILMR	FAMILIAR
AAFIKLLY	ALKALIFY
AAFILLNR	RAINFALL
AAFILMST	FATALISM
AAFILSTT	FATALIST
AAFILTTY	FATALITY
AAFIMNOR	FORAMINA
AAFINNOV	FAVONIAN
AAFLLPRT	FALL-TRAP
AAGHILNN	HANGNAIL
AAGHINPS	PAGANISH
AAGHKMNY	GYMKHANA
AAGHLNPY	ANAGLYPH
AAGHMNOY	MAHOGANY
AAGILLUZ	ALGUAZIL
AAGILMNO	MAGNOLIA
AAGILMNR	ALARMING
	MARGINAL
AAGILPRY	PLAGIARY
AAGILRUU	AUGURIAL
AAGIMNPS	PAGANISM
AAGIMNSY	GYMNASIA
AAGIMPTU	PATAGIUM
AAGINOST	SANTIAGO
AAGINSSY	ASSAYING
AAGIORTT	AGITATOR
AAGKNOOR	KANGAROO
AAGLLOWY	GALLOWAY
AAGLNRRU	GRANULAR
AAGLRSTU	GASTRULA
AAGMNORT	MARTAGON
AAGNNSTT	STAGNANT

AAGNOPRT	TRAGOPAN
AAGNORRT	ARROGANT
AAGNORTU	ARGONAUT
AAGNSTUU	AUGUSTAN
AAGORSSS	SARGASSO
AAHILNNT	INHALANT
AAHILPSY	PHYSALIA
AAHINORT	HORATIAN
AAHINPRT	PARTHIAN
AAHIPSXY	ASPHYXIA
AAHKLLMR	HALLMARK
AAHKLMOO	OKLAHOMA
AAHKMOTW	TOMAHAWK
AAHLLOPT	ALLOPATH
AAHLMSTU	THALAMUS
AAHMNORT	MARATHON
AAHMNOTX	XANTHOMA
AAHMNPST	PHANTASM
AAHNORRY	HONARARY
AAHNPSTY	PHANTASY
AAHOPRTU	AUTOHARP
AAIILNUX	UNIAXIAL
AAIILPRR	RIPARIAL
AAIIMNNR	ARMINIAN
AAIIMNNT	MAINTAIN
AAIIMNRS	ARIANISM
AAIINNTT	TITANIAN
AAIINOTV	AVIATION
AAIINPRS	PARISIAN
AAIIPRST	APIARIST
AAIJNRYZ	JANIZARY
AAIKMNST	ANTIMASK
AAIKMRST	TAMARISK
AAIKNPST	PAKISTAN
AAIKSSTW	SWASTIKA
AAILLLUV	ALLUVIAL
AAILLMMM	MAMMILLA
AAILLMNT	MANTILLA
AAILMNOR	MANORIAL
AAILMNRU	MANURIAL
AAILMNRY	LAMINARY
AAILMNST	STAMINAL
	TALISMAN
AAILMORR	ARMORIAL
AAILMRST	ALARMIST
AAILNNOT	NATIONAL
AAILNNPT	PLANTAIN
AAILNNST	ANNALIST
AAILNORT	NOTARIAL
	RATIONAL
AAILNPRT	AIR-PLANT
AAILNSSY	ANALYSIS
AAILNTTY	NATALITY
AAILORRS	RASORIAL
AAILORRV	VARIOLAR
AAILPPRU	PUPARIAL
AAILPPST	PAPALIST
AAILRSVY	SALIVARY
AAIMNORV	MORAVIAN
AAIMNPRZ	MARZIPAN
AAIMNSST	SATANISM

AAIMNSTY	MAINSTAY
AAIMQRUU	AQUARIUM
AAINNOTT	NATATION
AAINNRTU	TURANIAN
AAINORRS	ROSARIAN
AAINOTTX	TAXATION
AAINPRST	ASPIRANT
	PARTISAN
AAINPRTW	WAR-PAINT
AAINPRTZ	PARTIZAN
AAINQRTU	QUATRAIN
AAINQTTU	AQUATINT
AAINRSSY	ASSYRIAN
AAINRSTU	AUSTRIAN
AAINRSTY	SANITARY
AAINSSSS	ASSASSIN
AAINSSTT	SATANIST
AAIOPSTU	AUTOPSIA
AAIQRSUU	AQUARIUS
AAIRSTWY	STAIRWAY
AAJMMORR	MARJORAM
AAKMMNRS	MARKSMAN
AALLLLMP	PALLMALL
AALLMNTY	TALLYMAN
AALLMNUY	MANUALLY
AALLNNUY	ANNUALLY
AALLRUVV	VALVULAR
AALMNORT	MATRONAL
AALMNTTU	TANTALUM
AALMNTUU	AUTUMNAL
AALOPPRV	APPROVAL
AALOPRST	PASTORAL
AALORTUV	VALUATOR
AALORTVY	LAVATORY
AALRSSVY	VASSALRY
AALRSTTW	STALWART
AALRSTUY	SALUTARY
AAMMRSSU	MARASMUS
AAMOPRRU	PARAMOUR
AANNOSST	ASSONANT
AANNRSTY	STANNARY
AANOOPPX	OPOPANAX
AANORRRT	NARRATOR
AANORSTY	SANATORY
AANORTTY	NATATORY
AANRRTWY	WARRANTY
AAOPSSTY	APOSTASY
AAOSTWWY	STOWAWAY
AARSTTUY	STATUARY
ABBBDEEL	BEDABBLE
ABBCEERU	BARBECUE
ABBCEGIR	CRIBBAGE
ABBCEIKT	BACKBITE
ABBCEKNO	BACKBONE
ABBCELRS	SCRABBLE
ABBCELRU	CURBABLE
ABBCIILL	BIBLICAL
ABBCIINR	RABBINIC
ABBCIKRT	BRICKBAT
ABBCINOY	CABIN-BOY
ABBDDEIL	BIDDABLE

77

Code	Word	Code	Word	Code	Word
ABBDHOOY	BABYHOOD	ABCEGKLL	BLACK-LEG	ABDDEEHT	DEATH-BED
ABBEERTT	BARBETTE	ABCEGKLO	BLOCKAGE	ABDDEENR	REED-BAND
ABBEILOT	BILOBATE	ABCEHLOR	BACHELOR	ABDDEEST	BEDSTEAD
ABBEINTT	TABBINET	ABCEHLSU	CHASUBLE	ABDDEINR	BRANDIED
ABBELOPR	PROBABLE	ABCEHMOT	HECATOMB	ABDDELRY	BLADDERY
ABBELORU	BELABOUR	ABCEHORR	BROACHER	ABDDENOR	DEAD-BORN
ABBELQSU	SQUABBLE	ABCEHORU	BAROUCHE	ABDDILRY	LADYBIRD
ABBENORS	BASE-BORN	ABCEIJOT	JACOBITE	ABDDIMNO	BONDMAID
ABBEORRS	RE-ABSORB	ABCEIKRT	BRICK-TEA	ABDEEENR	ABERDEEN
ABBEORTW	BROWBEAT	ABCEILNN	BINNACLE	ABDEEERV	BEAVERED
ABBERRRY	BARBERRY	ABCEILOR	CABRIOLE	ABDEEGLR	BELGRADE
ABBERRYY	BAYBERRY	ABCEILOS	SOCIABLE	ABDEEILN	DENIABLE
ABBHILSY	SHABBILY	ABCEILTT	BITTACLE	ABDEEIST	DIABETES
ABBILLOT	BOAT-BILL	ABCEILTU	BACULITE	ABDEELLW	WELDABLE
ABBILLSU	SILLABUB	ABCEINTU	INCUBATE	ABDEEMNS	BEAM-ENDS
ABBIRSUU	SUBURBIA	ABCEIORT	BORACITE		BEDESMAN
ABBLOPRY	PROBABLY	ABCEIRRT	CRIBRATE	ABDEENNR	BANNERED
ABBNRSUU	SUBURBAN	ABCEIRTT	BRATTICE	ABDEEPRS	BESPREAD
ABCCDHIK	DABCHICK	ABCEIRTY	ACERBITY	ABDEERST	BREASTED
ABCCEEHN	BECHANCE	ABCEJLTY	ABJECTLY	ABDEFLNU	FUNDABLE
ABCCEELP	PECCABLE	ABCEKOOS	BOOKCASE	ABDEFLOR	FORDABLE
ABCCEILY	CELIBACY		CASEBOOK	ABDEGGIL	DIGGABLE
ABCCEKMO	COMEBACK	ABCELLPU	CULPABLE	ABDEGILN	BLINDAGE
ABCCHOOX	COACH-BOX	ABCELMRS	SCRAMBLE	ABDEGILU	GUIDABLE
ABCCILOR	CARBOLIC	ABCELOOT	BOOT-LACE	ABDEGINO	GABIONED
ABCCILOT	COBALTIC	ABCELORT	BROCATEL	ABDEGINS	DEBASING
ABCCINOR	CARBONIC	ABCELOST	OBSTACLE	ABDEGLOT	GLOBATED
ABCCKLLO	BALL-COCK	ABCEOSUX	SAUCE-BOX	ABDEGNOS	DOG'S-BANE
ABCCKOOT	COCK-BOAT	ABCERRTU	CARBURET	ABDEHITU	HABITUDE
ABCDDEOR	BROCADED	ABCERTUU	CUBATURE	ABDEHKLU	BULK-HEAD
ABCDEEFK	FEED-BACK	ABCESTUU	SUBACUTE	ABDEHLLU	BULL-HEAD
ABCDEELU	EDUCABLE	ABCFILOS	BIFOCALS	ABDEHLOT	BOLT-HEAD
ABCDEGIR	BIRDCAGE	ABCFLLLU	BULL-CALF	ABDEIIRT	DIATRIBE
ABCDEHNR	BRANCHED	ABCGIKLN	BLACKING	ABDEILMN	MANDIBLE
ABCDEIIT	DIABETIC	ABCHIKLS	BLACKISH	ABDEILNR	BILANDER
ABCDEIKS	BACKSIDE	ABCHIKRS	BRACKISH	ABDEILNT	BIDENTAL
ABCDEKLO	BLOCKADE	ABCHINOR	BRONCHIA	ABDEILOV	VOIDABLE
ABCDENTU	ABDUCENT	ABCHIOOR	BORACHIO	ABDEILTU	DUTIABLE
ABCDFRUY	FARCY-BUD	ABCHIRRT	TRIBRACH	ABDEINOR	DEBONAIR
ABCDIILO	DIABOLIC	ABCHKMPU	HUMPBACK	ABDEINSU	UNBIASED
ABCDIKLR	BALDRICK	ABCHKOOP	CHAP-BOOK	ABDEISSU	DISABUSE
ABCDILLR	BIRD-CALL	ABCHKOOS	CASH-BOOK	ABDEITTU	DUBITATE
	CALL-BIRD	ABCHMOTX	MATCHBOX	ABDEKLSW	SKEW-BALD
ABCDIRSU	SUBACRID	ABCIISTY	BASICITY	ABDEKORY	KEYBOARD
ABCDKOOR	BACK-DOOR	ABCILLSU	BACILLUS	ABDELLOR	BEAD-ROLL
ABCDOORW	CRAB-WOOD	ABCILLSY	SYLLABIC	ABDELNOZ	BLAZONED
ABCDOPRU	CUPBOARD	ABCILMOU	COLUMBIA	ABDELNSS	BALDNESS
ABCDORTU	ABDUCTOR	ABCILNPU	PUBLICAN	ABDELORU	LABOURED
ABCDORUY	OBDURACY	ABCILOSY	SOCIABLY	ABDEMOOR	ROOD-BEAM
ABCEEHLM	BÉCHAMEL	ABCILRRU	RUBRICAL	ABDENNRW	BRAND-NEW
ABCEEHLR	BLEACHER	ABCIOSSU	SCABIOUS	ABDENRTU	BREAD-NUT
ABCEEILT	CELIBATE	ABCJKOOT	BOOT-JACK		TURBANED
ABCEEIMN	AMBIENCE		JACKBOOT	ABDENTTU	DÉBUTANT
ABCEELNO	BONE-LACE	ABCKLOTU	BLACKOUT	ABDEORRU	ARBOURED
ABCEELRR	CEREBRAL	ABCKMOST	BACKMOST	ABDEORRW	WARDROBE
ABCEELRT	BRACELET	ABCLLPUY	CULPABLY	ABDEORSW	SOW-BREAD
ABCEERRT	CRAB-TREE	ABCLSSSU	SUBCLASS	ABDEORTU	OBDURATE
ABCEFIIT	BEATIFIC	ABCNORTY	CORYBANT	ABDEPSTU	BUDAPEST
ABCEFIKR	BACKFIRE	ABCNOUYY	BUOYANCY	ABDERSTW	BEDSTRAW
ABCEFINO	BONIFACE	ABCORSSU	SCABROUS	ABDFHINS	BAND-FISH
ABCEFLSS	BASS-CLEF	ABCRSTTU	SUBTRACT	ABDGIINR	BRAIDING

ABDGILNR	BARDLING	ABEENNRT	BANNERET	ABEINNOZ	BEZONIAN
ABDGINOR	BOARDING	ABEENNRU	EBURNEAN	ABEINNPR	BRINE-PAN
ABDHILLN	HANDBILL	ABEENRRT	BANTERER	ABEINORR	AIR-BORNE
ABDHILNS	BLANDISH	ABEENRSS	BARENESS	ABEINORT	BARITONE
ABDHINRS	BRANDISH	ABEENSSS	BASENESS		OBTAINER
ABDHIRTY	BIRTHDAY	ABEEORRV	OVERBEAR	ABEINOST	BOTANISE
ABDHKNOO	HANDBOOK	ABEERRRT	BARTERER	ABEINOTZ	BOTANIZE
ABDIIJLR	JAILBIRD	ABEERRTV	VERTEBRA	ABEINRST	BANISTER
ABDIINOS	OBSIDIAN	ABEERRTY	BETRAYER	ABEINSST	BASSINET
ABDIKLNR	BLINKARD	ABEESTWY	SWEET-BAY	ABEIORTV	ABORTIVE
ABDILORW	WILD-BOAR	ABEFILLL	FALLIBLE	ABEIPRRS	SPARERIB
ABDILRRY	RIBALDRY	ABEFILLR	FIREBALL	ABEIRRVY	BREVIARY
ABDILRZZ	BLIZZARD	ABEFILSY	FEASIBLY	ABEIRSTY	BESTIARY
ABDKOOOR	ROAD-BOOK	ABEFITUY	BEAUTIFY		SYBARITE
ABDLLSTU	DUST-BALL	ABEFLLMU	BLAMEFUL	ABEJMOOR	JEROBOAM
ABDLRSUY	ABSURDLY	ABEFOORT	BAREFOOT	ABEKLNOW	KNOWABLE
ABDNORUY	BOUNDARY	ABEFRRUY	FEBRUARY	ABEKLORW	WORKABLE
ABEEEGRV	BEVERAGE	ABEGGLRY	BEGGARLY	ABEKNNOT	BANK-NOTE
ABEEEHTT	HEBETATE	ABEGHILP	PHILABEG	ABEKOORY	YEAR-BOOK
ABEEEENST	ABSENTEE	ABEGIKNN	BEAN-KING	ABEKORTU	OUTBREAK
ABEEFILR	BALE-FIRE	ABEGILNT	TANGIBLE	ABELLLOT	TOLLABLE
ABEEFILS	FEASIBLE	ABEGILOT	OBLIGATE	ABELLLSY	SYLLABLE
ABEEFILT	FLEABITE	ABEGIPPS	BAGPIPES	ABELLMRU	UMBRELLA
ABEEGIRV	VERBIAGE	ABEGKORS	GROSBEAK	ABELLOSV	SOLVABLE
ABEEGRST	ABSTERGE	ABEGMORT	BERGAMOT	ABELLRVY	VERBALLY
ABEEHIRZ	HEBRAIZE	ABEGNRTU	BURGANET	ABELMNNO	NOBLEMAN
ABEEHLLL	HEELBALL	ABEGRRUV	BURGRAVE	ABELMNOZ	EMBLAZON
ABEEHLLR	HAREBELL	ABEHILNR	HIBERNAL	ABELMOOT	MOOTABLE
ABEEHQTU	BEQUEATH	ABEHILTT	TITHABLE	ABELMSSY	ASSEMBLY
ABEEHRRT	BREATHER	ABEHIMNO	BOHEMIAN	ABELNORZ	BLAZONER
ABEEIKLL	LIKEABLE	ABEHINST	ABSINTHE	ABELNRYZ	BRAZENLY
ABEEIILR	RELIABLE	ABEHIRST	HEBRAIST	ABELNSTU	UNSTABLE
ABEEIILV	LEVIABLE	ABEHLMSS	SHAMBLES	ABELNSTY	ABSENTLY
ABEEILNP	PLEBEIAN	ABEHMNOR	HORNBEAM	ABELOPRT	PORTABLE
ABEEILNS	BASE-LINE	ABEHNSTU	SUNBATHE	ABELOPRV	PROVABLE
ABEEILNV	ENVIABLE	ABEHORRR	ABHORRER	ABELOQTU	QUOTABLE
ABEEILPX	EXPIABLE	ABEHORST	BAT-HORSE	ABELORRU	LABOURER
ABEEILRT	LIBERATE	ABEIILMT	IMITABLE	ABELORST	SORTABLE
ABEEILSZ	SEIZABLE	ABEIILNN	BIENNIAL	ABELORSV	ABSOLVER
	SIZEABLE	ABEIILPT	PITIABLE	ABELOSTU	ABSOLUTE
ABEEIPRS	BEPRAISE	ABEIILRS	BISERIAL	ABELOSTW	BESTOWAL
ABEEIRTV	BREVIATE	ABEIILST	SIBILATE	ABELRSTU	BALUSTER
ABEEJMOR	JAMBOREE	ABEIJLTU	JUBILATE	ABELRTTU	BURLETTA
ABEELLLT	TELLABLE	ABEIJMNN	BENJAMIN		REBUTTAL
ABEELMMR	EMBALMER	ABEIKLLM	LAMBLIKE	ABELSTUU	SUBULATE
ABEELMPR	PREAMBLE	ABEIKNRS	BEARSKIN	ABEMMNOO	MOONBEAM
ABEELMSS	ASSEMBLE	ABEILLLT	TILLABLE	ABEMNOTU	UMBONATE
	BEAMLESS	ABEILLMT	TIME-BALL	ABEMNPRU	PENUMBRA
ABEELMTT	EMBATTLE	ABEILLOV	VIOLABLE	ABEMNTTU	ABUTMENT
ABEELNOP	BEANPOLE	ABEILLRY	RELIABLY	ABEMORRS	EMBRASOR
ABEELNRT	RENTABLE	ABEILMNT	BAILMENT	ABENOPSU	SUBPOENA
ABEELORX	EXORABLE	ABEILMOR	BROMELIA	ABENORSS	BARONESS
ABEELRRY	ALE-BERRY	ABEILNRU	RUINABLE	ABENORTY	BARYTONE
ABEELRSV	BESLAVER	ABEILNVY	ENVIABLY	ABENRRTU	BURNT-EAR
ABEELSSS	BASELESS	ABEILPRT	PARTIBLE	ABEOPPRY	PAPER-BOY
ABEELSSU	SUB-LEASE	ABEILPSS	PASSIBLE	ABEORSTU	SABOTEUR
ABEELSTT	TESTABLE	ABEILSSU	ISSUABLE	ABEORTTU	OBTURATE
ABEEMMNR	MEMBRANE	ABEILSTU	SUITABLE		TABOURET
ABEEMNOR	BEMOANER	ABEILSUX	BISEXUAL	ABEORTUV	OUTBRAVE
ABEEMNST	BASEMENT	ABEIMRTV	VERBATIM	ABEOSSST	ASBESTOS
ABEEMNTT	ABETMENT	ABEIMSSU	IAMBUSES	ABEOSTUV	SUBOVATE

ABEQRSUU	ARQUEBUS	ABIMNOSU	BIMANOUS
ABERSSTU	ABSTRUSE	ABIMORSU	BIRAMOUS
ABFFLLPU	PUFF-BALL	ABINOORT	ABORTION
ABFIILLR	FIBRILLA	ABINOSTT	BOTANIST
ABFILLLY	FALLIBLY	ABINRTUY	URBANITY
ABFILSTU	FABULIST	ABIOPRSU	BIPAROUS
ABFLLOOT	FOOTBALL	ABIORRST	ARBORIST
ABFLOSTU	BOASTFUL	ABIORRTV	VIBRATOR
ABFLOSUU	FABULOUS	ABIORTUY	OBITUARY
ABGGNOOT	TOBOGGAN	ABKKMOOR	BOOKMARK
ABGHMORU	BROUGHAM	ABKLLNOR	BANKROLL
ABGIIMST	BIGAMIST	ABKNPRTU	BANKRUPT
ABGIINNO	BIGNONIA	ABLLMOOR	BALL-ROOM
ABGILLMN	LAMBLING	ABLLNOSW	SNOW-BALL
ABGILMNR	MARBLING	ABLLRTUY	BRUTALLY
	RAMBLING	ABLLSSUY	SYLLABUS
ABGILNNT	BANTLING	ABLMNRUU	ALBURNUM
ABGILNOT	OBLIGANT		LABURNUM
ABGILNRW	BRAWLING	ABLNORYZ	BLAZONRY
ABGILNST	STABLING	ABLNRSUU	SUBLUNAR
ABGILNTY	TANGIBLY	ABLOOSTT	BOOT-LAST
ABGILOOT	OBLIGATO	ABLOPRVY	PROVABLY
ABGINNRX	BANXRING	ABLOSSUU	SABULOUS
ABGINOST	BOSTANGI	ABLPRTUY	ABRUPTLY
ABGLLORU	GLOBULAR	ABNOORRT	ROBORANT
ABGLMOPU	PLUMBAGO	ABNORTUU	RUNABOUT
ABGLNOUW	BUNGALOW	ACCCENPY	PECCANCY
ABGLORSU	GLABROUS	ACCCILLY	CYCLICAL
ABGLRRUY	BURGLARY	ACCDDIIT	DIDACTIC
ABGNORSU	OSNABURG	ACCDEILU	CAUDICLE
ABHIINRS	BRAINISH	ACCDEILY	DELICACY
ABHILSST	STABLISH	ACCDEINT	ACCIDENT
ABHISTTZ	SITZ-BATH	ACCDEIRT	ACCREDIT
ABHKOOOT	BOAT-HOOK	ACCDELSU	CUL-DE-SAC
	BOOK-OATH	ACCDERSU	ACCURSED
ABHLLOOY	BALLYHOO	ACCDESUU	CADUCEUS
ABHLSSTU	SALT-BUSH	ACCDGHOO	COACH-DOG
ABHMNSUU	SUBHUMAN	ACCDILOY	CALYCOID
ABHMOORT	BATHROOM	ACCDILTY	DACTYLIC
ABHOORST	TARBOOSH	ACCDINOR	CANCROID
ABIIKLSS	BASILISK		DRACONIC
ABIILMNO	BINOMIAL	ACCDIOOR	CORACOID
ABIILMNS	ALBINISM	ACCDLLOY	CLAY-COLD
ABIILNOT	LIBATION	ACCDOSUU	CADUCOUS
ABIILNST	SIBILANT	ACCEEIMR	ICECREAM
ABIILPTY	PITIABLY	ACCEEKLN	NECKLACE
ABIILRTU	AIR-BUILT	ACCEELNR	CLARENCE
ABIIMNOT	AMBITION	ACCEELOS	COALESCE
ABIJLNTU	JUBILANT	ACCEENST	ACESCENT
ABIKLMNS	LAMBSKIN	ACCEEPRT	ACCEPTER
ABIKNORR	IRONBARK	ACCEFFIY	EFFICACY
ABIKRSTZ	BRITZSKA	ACCEFILS	FASCICLE
ABILLLPY	PLAYBILL	ACCEGKOS	SAGE-COCK
ABILMNOU	OLIBANUM	ACCEGNOY	COAGENCY
ABILMOPS	BIOPLASM	ACCEHIKP	CHICK-PEA
ABILNOOT	OBLATION	ACCEHILM	ALCHEMIC
ABILNOTU	ABLUTION		CHEMICAL
ABILNRTU	TRIBUNAL	ACCEHILP	CEPHALIC
ABILORTY	LIBATORY	ACCEHIMN	MECHANIC
ABILOSSV	BASS-VIOL	ACCEHINR	CHICANER
ABILSTUY	SUITABLY	ACCEHNNY	CYNANCHE

ACCEHNOR	ENCROACH		
ACCEHNRY	CHANCERY		
ACCEILLN	CANCELLI		
ACCEILLR	CLERICAL		
ACCEILLU	CAULICLE		
ACCEILLV	CLAVICLE		
ACCEILNS	SCENICAL		
ACCEILNT	CANTICLE		
ACCEILNV	CLAVECIN		
ACCEILNY	CALYCINE		
ACCEILRV	CERVICAL		
ACCEINRT	NEARCTIC		
ACCEINRY	CYRENAIC		
ACCEIOTV	COACTIVE		
ACCEIPRT	PRACTICE		
ACCEISTT	ECSTATIC		
ACCEKLNR	CRACKNEL		
ACCEKRRS	CRACKERS		
ACCELMNY	CYCLAMEN		
ACCELNOV	CONCLAVE		
ACCELNRU	CARUNCLE		
ACCELRSY	SCARCELY		
ACCENNSY	NASCENCY		
ACCENORT	ACCENTOR		
ACCENOST	CO-SECANT		
ACCEORTU	ACCOUTRE		
ACCFFLTU	CALC-TUFF		
ACCFHLTY	CATCHFLY		
ACCGHINT	CATCHING		
ACCGIKMR	GIMCRACK		
ACCGINSU	ACCUSING		
ACCGLOOY	CACOLOGY		
ACCHHITT	CHIT-CHAT		
ACCHIIRT	RACHITIC		
ACCHILMY	CHYMICAL		
ACCHILOR	ORICHALC		
ACCHILOT	CATHOLIC		
ACCHINNO	CINCHONA		
ACCHINPU	CAPUCHIN		
ACCHIORT	THORACIC		
	TROCHAIC		
ACCHKLOR	CHARLOCK		
ACCHNOOR	CORONACH		
ACCHNOTU	COUCHANT		
ACCHORTU	CARTOUCH		
ACCIILLN	CLINICAL		
ACCIILMT	CLIMATIC		
ACCIILRT	CRITICAL		
ACCIINOT	ACONITIC		
ACCIIRTX	CICATRIX		
ACCIKLOT	COCKTAIL		
ACCILNOV	VOLCANIC		
ACCILORT	CORTICAL		
ACCILRRU	CIRCULAR		
ACCIMNOS	MOCCASIN		
ACCIMPSU	CAPSICUM		
ACCINOOS	OCCASION		
ACCINORT	NARCOTIC		
ACCINORV	CAVICORN		
ACCIORST	ACROSTIC		
	SOCRATIC		

ACCIOSTU	ACOUSTIC	ACDEIJNU	JAUNDICE	ACDIIRST	CARDITIS
ACCIRSTY	SCARCITY	ACDEILLM	MEDALLIC	ACDIIRTY	ACRIDITY
ACCKOOOT	COCKATOO	ACDEILLN	DECLINAL	ACDIISST	SADISTIC
ACCLLSUU	CALCULUS	ACDEILNP	PANICLED	ACDILLPY	PLACIDLY
ACCMOSTU	ACCUSTOM	ACDEILNV	VINE-CLAD	ACDILMTU	TALMUDIC
ACCNOPRU	ACORN-CUP	ACDEILPT	PLICATED	ACDIMNSY	DYNAMICS
ACCNOPTU	OCCUPANT	ACDEIMNO	COMEDIAN	ACDIMOSY	DOCIMASY
ACCNORTT	CONTRACT		DEMONIAC	ACDINOPS	SPONDAIC
ACDDEEES	DECEASED	ACDEIMNP	PANDEMIC	ACDINORS	SARDONIC
ACDDEEHT	DETACHED	ACDEIMRT	DERMATIC	ACDINORW	CORDWAIN
ACDDEEIT	DEDICATE	ACDEINNR	CRANNIED	ACDINSTY	DYNASTIC
ACDDEELR	DECLARED	ACDEINOP	CANOPIED	ACDIOPRS	SPORADIC
ACDDEENT	DECADENT	ACDEINOS	DIOCESAN	ACDIORTT	DICTATOR
ACDDEESU	SADDUCEE	ACDEINOV	VOIDANCE	ACDIPRST	ADSCRIPT
ACDDEHKN	DECK-HAND	ACDEINPT	PEDANTIC	ACDIRSTT	DISTRACT
ACDDEINR	RIDDANCE	ACDEINST	DISTANCE	ACDLNORU	CAULDRON
ACDDEKLO	DEAD-LOCK	ACDEIORS	IDOCRASE	ACDLNOST	SCOTLAND
	DECK-LOAD	ACDEIOSU	EDACIOUS	ACDLOOOR	COLORADO
ACDDENTU	ADDUCENT	ACDEKNPU	UNPACKED	ACDLOOOW	WOOD-COAL
ACDDHKOS	SHADDOCK	ACDEKOST	STOCKADE	ACDLOORT	DOCTORAL
ACDDILNY	CANDIDLY	ACDELLNU	UNCALLED	ACDLORWY	COWARDLY
ACDDINNU	UNCANDID	ACDELLOS	SO-CALLED	ACDLOSTU	COAL-DUST
ACDDKORY	DOCKYARD	ACDELMSU	MUSCADEL	ACDMMNOO	COMMANDO
ACDDORTU	ADDUCTOR	ACDELNOR	COLANDER	ACDMNORY	DORMANCY
ACDEEEFT	DEFECATE	ACDELNPU	UNPLACED	ACDNOORV	CORDOVAN
ACDEEEKS	SEED-CAKE	ACDELNRY	DRY-CLEAN	ACDNOOTU	DUCATOON
ACDEEEMR	REED-MACE	ACDELOTU	OCULATED	ACDNOSTW	DOWNCAST
ACDEEERS	DECREASE	ACDELRSY	SACREDLY	ACDNOSUU	ADUNCOUS
ACDEEFFT	AFFECTED	ACDELSTU	SULCATED	ACDOPRST	POST-CARD
ACDEEFIN	DEFIANCE	ACDEMORT	DEMOCRAT	ACDORTUY	COURT-DAY
ACDEEILT	DELICATE	ACDENNOR	ORDNANCE	ACDRSTTU	DUST-CART
ACDEEIMT	DECIMATE	ACDENNST	SCANDENT	ACEEEGLN	ELEGANCE
	MEDICATE	ACDENOPR	ENDOCARP	ACEEENSV	EVANESCE
ACDEEINU	AUDIENCE	ACDENRVY	VERDANCY	ACEEERRT	RECREATE
ACDEEIPS	DISPEACE	ACDEORRT	REDACTOR	ACEEERTT	ETCETERA
ACDEEJKT	JACKETED	ACDEORTU	EDUCATOR	ACEEERTX	EXECRATE
ACDEELNR	CALENDER	ACDEQTUU	AQUEDUCT	ACEEFFIN	CAFFEINE
ACDEELRR	DECLARER	ACDERRSU	CRUSADER	ACEEFHWY	WHEY-FACE
ACDEELRT	DECRETAL	ACDERRTU	TRADUCER	ACEEFLPU	PEACEFUL
ACDEENNT	TENDANCE	ACDFFHNU	HANDCUFF	ACEEGHNX	EXCHANGE
ACDEENOT	ANECDOTE	ACDFFIRT	DIFFRACT	ACEEGHRR	RECHARGE
ACDEENRT	DECANTER	ACDFFLOS	SCAFFOLD	ACEEGKRW	WRECKAGE
	NECTARED	ACDFIILU	FIDUCIAL	ACEEGLNY	ELEGANCY
ACDEENRV	CAVERNED	ACDGHOTW	DOG-WATCH	ACEEGNOZ	COZENAGE
ACDEEOPS	PEASECOD		WATCH-DOG	ACEEGNSV	SCAVENGE
ACDEEORT	DECORATE	ACDGIMOT	DOGMATIC	ACEEHIMN	MANICHEE
ACDEFOTW	TWO-FACED	ACDGIOPR	PODAGRIC	ACEEHINT	ECHINATE
ACDEFRTU	FURCATED	ACDHILPR	PILCHARD	ACEEHLOS	SHOE-LACE
ACDEGGRS	SCRAGGED	ACDHINSW	SANDWICH	ACEEHMRS	CASHMERE
ACDEGHIL	GADHELIC	ACDHIOPS	SCAPHOID	ACEEHPRR	PREACHER
ACDEGHOP	DOG-CHEAP	ACDHIPST	DISPATCH	ACEEHRRS	RESEARCH
ACDEGINU	GUIDANCE	ACDHLNOR	CHALDRON		SEARCHER
ACDEGIRS	DISGRACE	ACDIIJLU	JUDICIAL	ACEEHRTT	CATHETER
ACDEHILR	HERALDIC	ACDIILMS	DISCLAIM	ACEEHRTY	CHEATERY
ACDEHIMS	SCHIEDAM	ACDIILSU	SUICIDAL	ACEEHSTT	TEA-CHEST
ACDEHKRU	ARCHDUKE	ACDIIMOR	DIORAMIC	ACEEILMN	CAMELINE
ACDEHLNR	CHANDLER	ACDIIMOT	DIATOMIC	ACEEILNP	CAPELINE
ACDEHPST	DESPATCH	ACDIIMSU	ASCIDIUM	ACEEILNR	RELIANCE
ACDEHRST	STARCHED	ACDIINNT	INDICANT	ACEEILNS	SALIENCE
ACDEIILT	CILIATED	ACDIINOT	DIATONIC	ACEEILPS	ESPECIAL
ACDEIINT	INDICATE	ACDIINPR	PINDARIC	ACEEINPS	SAPIENCE

ACEEINPT	PATIENCE
ACEEINRS	INCREASE
ACEEINRT	ITERANCE
ACEEINTV	ENACTIVE
ACEEIRSW	WISEACRE
ACEEIRTV	CREATIVE
	REACTIVE
ACEEISTV	VESICATE
ACEEKLMR	MACKEREL
ACEELLNT	LANCELET
ACEELLOT	OCELLATE
ACEELLRR	CELLARER
ACEELLRT	CELLARET
ACEELMNO	CAMELEON
ACEELNPT	PENTACLE
ACEELNRR	LARCENER
ACEELNRS	CLEANSER
ACEELNRU	CERULEAN
ACEELNTT	TENTACLE
ACEELNTU	NUCLEATE
ACEELPTU	PECULATE
ACEELPTY	CLYPEATE
ACEELRSS	CARELESS
ACEELRSV	CLEAVERS
ACEELRTU	ULCERATE
ACEEMNST	CASEMENT
ACEEMORS	RACEMOSE
ACEEMRRS	SCREAMER
ACEEMRRY	CREAMERY
ACEENNRT	ENTRANCE
ACEENPRR	PARCENER
ACEENRRT	RECANTER
	RECREANT
ACEENRST	SARCENET
ACEENRTT	ENTRACTE
ACEEORST	CERATOSE
	CREASOTE
ACEEOSTT	ECOSTATE
ACEERRTU	CREATURE
ACEERSST	CATERESS
	CERASTES
ACEERSSU	SURCEASE
ACEERSSV	CREVASSE
ACEERTTU	ERUCTATE
ACEESSTT	CASSETTE
ACEFFHRU	CHAUFFER
ACEFGLRU	GRACEFUL
ACEFHIKS	FISHCAKE
ACEFIIPR	PACIFIER
ACEFIIRT	ARTIFICE
ACEFILOZ	FOCALIZE
ACEFILRY	FIRE-CLAY
ACEFIMPR	CAMP-FIRE
ACEFIORR	AIR-FORCE
ACEFIRTY	FERACITY
ACEFLLOV	CALF-LOVE
ACEFLMNO	FLAMENCO
ACEFLNOR	FALCONER
ACEFLNOT	CONFLATE
	FALCONET
ACEFLNRY	CRANE-FLY

ACEFLRTU	FULCRATE
ACEFNORV	CONFERVA
ACEFORST	FORECAST
ACEFRRTU	FRACTURE
ACEGGILN	CAGELING
ACEGHINT	CHEATING
	TEACHING
ACEGIINV	VICINAGE
ACEGILLR	ALLERGIC
ACEGILMU	MUCILAGE
ACEGILNR	CLEARING
ACEGILPS	PELASGIC
ACEGIMNR	GERMANIC
ACEGIMNT	MAGNETIC
ACEGINRT	CATERING
ACEGINSW	WING-CASE
ACEGINTX	EXACTING
ACEGIOTT	COGITATE
ACEGIRST	AGRESTIC
ACEGKRTU	TRUCKAGE
ACEGMNOY	GEOMANCY
ACEGMNRS	CRAGSMEN
ACEGNNOY	CYANOGEN
ACEGNNTY	TANGENCY
ACEGORTT	COTTAGER
ACEGORTY	CATEGORY
ACEHHIRR	HIERARCH
ACEHHMNN	HENCHMAN
ACEHHRTT	THATCHER
ACEHHRTY	THEARCHY
ACEHIIRT	HIERATIC
ACEHIJPT	JAPHETIC
ACEHILNT	ETHNICAL
ACEHILPR	PARHELIC
ACEHILTT	ATHLETIC
ACEHIMPT	EMPHATIC
ACEHIMTT	THEMATIC
ACEHINOT	INCHOATE
ACEHINST	ASTHENIC
ACEHIPRS	SERAPHIC
ACEHIPRT	CHAPITER
ACEHIPST	PASTICHE
ACEHIPTT	PATHETIC
ACEHIRSW	ARCHWISE
ACEHIRTT	THEATRIC
ACEHISST	CHASTISE
ACEHLLOR	ORCHELLA
ACEHLNPT	PLANCHET
ACEHLOST	ESCHALOT
ACEHLPRT	CHAPTREL
ACEHLSTY	CHASTELY
ACEHMNRT	MERCHANT
ACEHMNSS	CHESS-MAN
ACEHMORT	CHROMATE
ACEHMSTU	MUSTACHE
ACEHNNPT	PENCHANT
ACEHNOPR	CHAPERON
ACEHNOPT	CENOTAPH
ACEHNORR	RANCHERO
ACEHNORT	ANCHORET
ACEHNRSS	ARCHNESS

ACEHNRST	SNATCHER
	STANCHER
ACEHNSTU	UNCHASTE
ACEHOPRR	REPROACH
ACEHORRV	OVERARCH
ACEHORTT	THEOCRAT
ACEHORTU	OUTREACH
ACEHOSST	CASE-SHOT
ACEHPRSU	PURCHASE
ACEHPRTY	PATCHERY
ACEHRRST	STARCHER
ACEHRRTT	TETRARCH
ACEHRSSU	CHASSEUR
ACEHRTTY	TRACHYTE
ACEIILST	SILICATE
ACEIIMTU	MAIEUTIC
ACEIINTV	INACTIVE
ACEIIRRT	CRITERIA
ACEIJMST	MAJESTIC
ACEIKMNN	NICKNAME
ACEIKMRV	MAVERICK
ACEILLMN	CANE-MILL
ACEILLMT	METALLIC
ACEILLNT	CLIENTAL
ACEILLOS	LOCALISE
ACEILLOZ	LOCALIZE
ACEILLPS	ALLSPICE
ACEILLRV	CAVILLER
ACEILMMO	CAMOMILE
ACEILMNO	COAL-MINE
ACEILMNP	MANCIPLE
ACEILMOS	CAMISOLE
ACEILMPS	MISPLACE
ACEILMRT	METRICAL
ACEILMST	CLEMATIS
ACEILNNP	PINNACLE
ACEILNNR	ENCRINAL
ACEILNOR	CAROLINE
ACEILNPT	PECTINAL
ACEILNRT	CLARINET
ACEILOPR	CAPRIOLE
ACEILOPT	POETICAL
ACEILORR	CARRIOLE
ACEILORT	LORICATE
ACEILOSV	VOCALISE
ACEILOTV	LOCATIVE
ACEILOVZ	VOCALIZE
ACEILPRS	CALIPERS
ACEILPRT	PRELATIC
ACEILPRU	PECULIAR
ACEILPTY	ETYPICAL
ACEILPXY	EPICALYX
ACEILRSV	VISCERAL
ACEILRTV	VERTICAL
ACEILTVY	ACTIVELY
ACEIMMNP	PEMMICAN
ACEIMNRU	MANICURE
ACEIMNSY	SYCAMINE
ACEIMPSS	ESCAPISM
ACEIMRST	MATRICES
ACEIMRTU	MURICATE

ACEINNOS	CANONISE	ACELPTUY	EUCALYPT	ACGGIIOS	ISAGOGIC
ACEINNOZ	CANONIZE	ACELQRUU	CLAQUEUR	ACGHIIMN	MICHIGAN
ACEINNST	INSTANCE	ACELRRSW	SCRAWLER	ACGHILOR	OLIGARCH
ACEINNSU	NUISANCE	ACELRTTU	CULTRATE	ACGHIMNR	CHARMING
ACEINNTU	UNCINATE	ACELSSTT	TACTLESS	ACGHINST	SCATHING
ACEINORS	SCENARIO	ACEMNORR	ROMANCER	ACGHINTY	YACHTING
ACEINORT	CREATION	ACEMNRUY	NUMERACY	ACGHIPRS	GRAPHICS
	REACTION	ACEMOOST	COMATOSE	ACGHORSU	CHORAGUS
ACEINORV	VERONICA	ACEMORRT	CREMATOR	ACGIILNO	LOGICIAN
ACEINOST	CANOEIST	ACEMORSW	CASE-WORM	ACGIIMST	SIGMATIC
ACEINOTV	INVOCATE	ACEMORSY	SYCAMORE	ACGIINRT	GRANITIC
ACEINOTX	EXACTION	ACEMORTY	COMETARY	ACGIKLNT	TACKLING
ACEINPTT	PITTANCE	ACEMORUX	MORCEAUX	ACGIKLRY	GARLICKY
ACEINRRY	CINERARY	ACENNNOU	ANNOUNCE	ACGIKMNS	SMACKING
ACEINRSS	RACINESS	ACENNOSS	CANONESS	ACGIKNOR	CROAKING
ACEINRST	CANISTER	ACENNOTT	CO-TENANT	ACGILRSU	SURGICAL
ACEINRTT	INTERACT	ACENNOTV	COVENANT	ACGINNRU	UNCARING
ACEINRVY	VICENARY	ACENNOTZ	CANZONET	ACGINOST	AGNOSTIC
ACEINSTV	VESICANT	ACENOPTW	CAPETOWN		COASTING
ACEINTTU	TUNICATE	ACENOQTU	COTQUEAN	ACGINPRS	SCRAPING
ACEINTTX	EXCITANT	ACENORRW	CARE-WORN	ACGIORSU	GRACIOUS
ACEINTTY	TENACITY	ACENORST	ANCESTOR	ACGIORUW	GUICOWAR
ACEIOPRT	OPERATIC	ACENORSU	CARNEOUS	ACGJLNOU	CONJUGAL
ACEIORSV	VARICOSE		NACREOUS	ACGLMOUU	COAGULUM
ACEIOTVV	VOCATIVE	ACENORTU	OUTRANCE	ACGLNORU	CLANGOUR
ACEIPPRR	PERICARP	ACENPTTU	PUNCTATE	ACGLOSUU	GLAUCOUS
ACEIPRST	CRISPATE	ACENRSTU	ETRUSCAN	ACGNNOOT	CONTANGO
	PRACTISE		RECUSANT	ACHHINTW	WHIN-CHAT
ACEIPRTY	APYRETIC	ACENRSTY	ANCESTRY	ACHHINTY	HYACINTH
ACEIPSST	ESCAPIST	ACENRTTU	TRUNCATE	ACHHLPRY	PHYLARCH
ACEIRSTT	CRISTATE	ACEOORTV	OVERCOAT	ACHHRSTU	CRUSH-HAT
ACEIRTTU	URTICATE	ACEOPPRS	COPPERAS	ACHIILMS	CHILIASM
ACEIRTTV	TRACTIVE	ACEORRSU	CAROUSER	ACHIINRT	TRICHINA
ACEIRTUV	CURATIVE	ACEORRTT	RETROACT	ACHIIRST	RACHITIS
ACEIRTVY	VERACITY	ACEORSTV	OVERCAST	ACHIIRSU	ISCHURIA
ACEJLORY	CAJOLERY	ACEPSTTY	TYPECAST	ACHIKKSW	KICKSHAW
ACEKNRRT	RACK-RENT	ACERTTUW	CUTWATER	ACHILMOP	OMPHALIC
ACELLLRU	CELLULAR	ACFFIILO	OFFICIAL	ACHILMRS	CHRISMAL
ACELLNOT	CALL-NOTE	ACFFILNU	FANCIFUL	ACHILMTY	MYTHICAL
ACELLOPS	COLLAPSE	ACFGIIMN	MAGNIFIC	ACHILNNS	CLANNISH
	ESCALLOP	ACFGITUY	FUGACITY	ACHILNPS	CLANSHIP
ACELLSTU	SCUTELLA	ACFGKNOP	PACKFONG	ACHILORT	ACROLITH
ACELMNSS	CALMNESS	ACFGLNOR	CORN-FLAG	ACHILPSY	PHYSICAL
ACELMORS	SCLEROMA	ACFHILNO	FALCHION	ACHILRUY	CHYLURIA
ACELMORY	CLAYMORE	ACFHILOS	COAL-FISH	ACHILRVY	CHIVALRY
ACELMSTU	MUSCATEL	ACFHIRSW	CRAWFISH	ACHIMNOP	CHAMPION
ACELMTUU	CUMULATE	ACFHIRSY	CRAYFISH	ACHIMNOR	HARMONIC
ACELNNRS	SCRANNEL	ACFHLTUW	WATCHFUL	ACHIMNSU	INASMUCH
ACELNORV	NOVERCAL	ACFIILTY	FACILITY	ACHIMPSS	SCAMPISH
ACELNOVY	CONVEYAL	ACFIIMPS	PACIFISM	ACHIMRST	CHARTISM
ACELOPPU	POPULACE	ACFIIPST	PACIFIST	ACHINSTY	SCYTHIAN
ACELOPRT	PECTORAL	ACFILRTY	CRAFTILY	ACHIRRTY	TRIARCHY
ACELOPTU	COPULATE	ACFILSSY	CLASSIFY	ACHIRSTT	CHARTIST
ACELOPTY	CALOTYPE	ACFINORT	FRACTION	ACHISTTY	CHASTITY
ACELORSS	LACROSSE	ACFINSTY	SANCTIFY	ACHKMORS	SHAMROCK
ACELORST	SECTORAL	ACFIOSTU	FACTIOUS	ACHLLORY	CHORALLY
ACELORSU	CAROUSEL	ACFLNORY	FALCONRY	ACHLNSTY	STANCHLY
ACELORSY	COARSLEY	ACFLOOPS	FOOLSCAP	ACHLOTWX	WAX-CLOTH
ACELOSTU	OSCULATE	ACFLORSU	SCROFULA	ACHMNORY	MONARCHY
ACELPRST	SPECTRAL	ACFMOTTU	FACTOTUM		NOMARCHY
ACELPRSU	SPECULAR	ACGGIINT	GIGANTIC	ACHMORTU	OUTMARCH

83

ACHNPPSS	SCHNAPPS	ACIMMOSS	ACOSMISM
ACHOTTUW	OUTWATCH	ACIMNNNO	CINNAMON
ACHPRSTU	SHARP-CUT	ACIMNOOR	ACROMION
ACIIILMN	INIMICAL	ACIMNORT	ROMANTIC
ACIIILNV	CIVILIAN	ACIMNORY	ACRIMONY
ACIIINST	SINAITIC	ACIMNOST	MONASTIC
ACIIKNNN	CANNIKIN	ACIMNPTY	TYMPANIC
ACIILLSU	SILICULA	ACIMORST	ACROTISM
ACIILMNR	CRIMINAL	ACIMOSST	MASSICOT
ACIILMPT	PALMITIC	ACIMOSTT	MASTICOT
ACIILNOR	IRONICAL		STOMATIC
ACIIMNOS	SIMONIAC	ACIMRRSY	MISCARRY
ACIIMNST	ACTINISM	ACINNOSS	SCANSION
ACIIMNSU	MUSICIAN	ACINNOST	CANONIST
ACIIMNTY	IMITANCY		SANCTION
	INTIMACY	ACINNRTY	TYRANNIC
ACIIMRST	SCIMITAR	ACINOOPR	PICAROON
ACIIMRTU	MURIATIC	ACINOOTV	VOCATION
ACIIMSTT	ATTICISM	ACINORSS	NARCOSIS
ACIIMTUV	VIATICUM	ACINORST	CAST-IRON
ACIINNOS	SOCINIAN	ACINORTT	TRACTION
ACIINNOT	INACTION	ACINOSSY	CYANOSIS
	NICOTIAN	ACINOSTT	OSCITANT
ACIINOPT	OPTICIAN	ACINOSTW	WAINSCOT
ACIINOTT	CITATION	ACINOSWX	COXSWAIN
ACIIORTV	VICTORIA	ACINOTTX	TOXICANT
ACIIPPST	PAPISTIC	ACINPQUY	PIQUANCY
ACIIRSST	TRIASSIC	ACINRSST	SANSCRIT
ACIIRSTT	ARTISTIC	ACINRTTU	TACITURN
ACIISTTV	ACTIVIST	ACINSTTY	SANCTITY
ACIITTVY	ACTIVITY	ACIOPRST	PISCATOR
ACIITVVY	VIVACITY	ACIOPSST	POTASSIC
ACIJKKPS	SKIP-JACK	ACIOPSSU	SPACIOUS
ACIJRSSU	JURASSIC	ACIOPSTU	CAPTIOUS
ACIKLLST	SALT-LICK	ACIORTTY	ATROCITY
ACIKLMST	MALSTICK		CITATORY
ACIKLNRY	CRANKILY	ACIORTVY	VORACITY
ACILLLMY	CLAY-MILL	ACIOSTUU	CAUTIOUS
ACILLLPS	CLAP-SILL	ACIRRTUX	CURATRIX
ACILLMOS	LOCALISM	ACIRSSTY	SACRISTY
ACILLNOO	COLONIAL	ACISTTUY	ASTUCITY
ACILLNOR	CARILLON	ACKLOOPW	WOOLPACK
ACILLNOS	SCALLION	ACKLOOSW	WOOLSACK
ACILLOSY	SOCIALLY	ACKLORST	ROCK-SALT
ACILLOTY	LOCALITY	ACLLLLOR	ROLL-CALL
ACILMNOP	COMPLAIN	ACLLNORW	CORNWALL
ACILMNOS	LACONISM	ACLLOORT	COLLATOR
ACILMOPR	PROCLAIM	ACLLOOSS	COLOSSAL
ACILMSTY	MYSTICAL	ACLLORUY	OCULARLY
ACILNOOT	LOCATION	ACLLRTUU	CULTURAL
ACILNOPT	PLATONIC	ACLMMNOU	COMMUNAL
ACILNOSU	UNSOCIAL	ACLMNORU	COLUMNAR
ACILNOSV	SLAVONIC	ACLMRSUU	MUSCULAR
ACILNOUV	UNIVOCAL	ACLMSUUV	VASCULUM
ACILNRUY	CULINARY	ACLNORSU	CONSULAR
ACILNSTU	SULTANIC	ACLNORSW	CORN-LAWS
ACILNSTY	SCANTILY	ACLNOSTU	OSCULANT
ACILOPRT	TROPICAL	ACLNPTUU	PUNCTUAL
ACILOSTV	VOCALIST	ACLOOPRR	CORPORAL
ACILOTVY	VOCALITY	ACLOPRXY	XYLOCARP
ACILPRSU	SPICULAR	ACLOSSTU	OUTCLASS

ACMMNOSY	SCAMMONY
ACMNOORT	MONOCRAT
ACMNOSST	SCOTSMAN
ACMOORRT	MOTOR-CAR
ACMORRTY	CROMARTY
ACMORSTW	WORM-CAST
ACMORSTY	COSTMARY
ACNNOSTT	CONSTANT
ACNOORRY	CORONARY
ACNOORSU	CANOROUS
ACNORRTY	CONTRARY
ACNORSTT	CONTRAST
ACNORSWW	CROWN-SAW
ACNORTTU	TURN-COAT
ACOPRRTT	PROTRACT
ACORSSWY	CROSSWAY
ACRRSTUU	ARCTURUS
ADDDEEGR	DEGRADED
ADDDEEIM	DIADEMED
ADDDEMNU	ADDENDUM
ADDEEFIL	DEFILADE
ADDEEGNR	DERANGED
ADDEEGOR	DOG-EARED
ADDEEHLY	ALDEHYDE
ADDEEHNR	HARDENED
ADDEEILN	DEADLINE
ADDEEILP	DEEP-LAID
ADDEEILT	DETAILED
ADDEEISS	DISEASED
ADDEELMS	ALMS-DEED
ADDEEMNR	DEMANDER
ADDEEMTU	DEAD-MUTE
ADDEENSS	DEADNESS
ADDEEPRT	DEPARTED
ADDEEPRV	DEPRAVED
ADDEFILY	FIELD-DAY
ADDEFLRU	DREADFUL
ADDEHILR	DIHEDRAL
ADDEHMRU	DRUMHEAD
ADDEIITV	ADDITIVE
ADDEIORS	ROADSIDE
ADDEIPPR	DIDAPPER
ADDEISSU	DISSUADE
ADDEKORW	DEAD-WORK
ADDELNSU	UNSADDLE
ADDELOOR	ELDORADO
ADDELRST	STRADDLE
ADDELRSY	SADDLERY
ADDELRTW	TWADDLER
ADDENNSU	SAND-DUNE
ADDEPRSU	SUPERADD
ADDFFILO	DAFFODIL
ADDFFNRU	DANDRUFF
ADDGORSW	GODWARDS
ADDHINSY	DANDYISH
ADDHLOOY	LADYHOOD
ADDIILUV	DIVIDUAL
ADDIINOT	ADDITION
ADDIINRT	TRINIDAD
ADDIMNSY	DANDYISM
ADDINNOR	ORDINAND

ADDINRWW	WINDWARD	ADEEIMRT	DIAMETER	ADEFLLUY	FEUDALLY
ADDKNRRU	DRUNKARD	ADEEIMTT	MEDITATE	ADEFLNOR	FORELAND
ADDLLNOR	LANDLORD	ADEEINRT	DETAINER	ADEFLPRS	FELDSPAR
ADDLNOOW	WOODLAND	ADEEISTV	SEDATIVE	ADEFORRW	FOREWARD
ADDMOOSY	DOOMSDAY	ADEEITVW	TIDE-WAVE	ADEFORUV	FAVOURED
ADDNORWW	DOWNWARD	ADEEKLNR	KALENDER	ADEFSSTT	STEDFAST
ADEEEFRT	FEDERATE	ADEELLLP	LAPELLED	ADEGGLRY	RAGGEDLY
ADEEEGLT	DELEGATE	ADEELLMT	METALLED	ADEGGOPY	PEDAGOGY
ADEEEGNR	RENEGADE	ADEELLRW	WELL-READ	ADEGGRTY	GADGETRY
ADEEENRS	SERENADE	ADEELLSS	LEADLESS	ADEGHHOS	HOGSHEAD
ADEEENTT	EDENTATE	ADEELLTY	ELATEDLY	ADEGHITY	EIGHT-DAY
ADEEERTT	DATE-TREE	ADEELLWY	WALL-EYED	ADEGHLNO	HEADLONG
ADEEFHNR	FREEHAND	ADEELMNO	LEMONADE	ADEGHNNU	UNHANGED
ADEEFHOR	FOREHEAD	ADEELNOR	OLEANDER	ADEGHORT	GOATHERD
ADEEFILN	ENFILADE	ADEELNRT	ANTLERED	ADEGHRTU	DAUGHTER
ADEEFIRR	RAREFIED	ADEELNRV	LAVENDER	ADEGIITT	DIGITATE
ADEEFLMS	SELF-MADE	ADEELNSU	UNSEALED	ADEGILLR	GRILLADE
ADEEFLSS	FADELESS	ADEELOST	DESOLATE	ADEGILNP	PLEADING
ADEEFMNR	FREEDMAN	ADEELPPT	LAPPETED	ADEGILOU	DIALOGUE
ADEEFNOT	TONE-DEAF	ADEELPST	PEDESTAL	ADEGILSS	GLISSADE
ADEEFNSS	DEAFNESS	ADEELRTV	TRAVELED	ADEGIMNR	MARGINED
ADEEFORT	FOREDATE	ADEELSST	DATELESS	ADEGIMOR	IDEOGRAM
ADEEFRTU	FEATURED	ADEELSTY	SEDATELY	ADEGINOS	DIAGNOSE
ADEEGIRS	DISAGREE	ADEEMNNR	MANNERED	ADEGINRT	GRADIENT
ADEEGITT	TIDE-GATE	ADEEMNOT	NEMATODE	ADEGISSU	DISUSAGE
ADEEGLNR	ENLARGED	ADEEMNSS	SEEDSMAN	ADEGLLNU	GLANDULE
ADEEGMNR	GENDARME	ADEEMNST	STAMENED	ADEGLMOS	GLADSOME
ADEEGMOP	MEGAPODE	ADEEMNTW	METEWAND	ADEGLNPS	SPANGLED
ADEEGNNR	ENDANGER	ADEEMORT	MODERATE	ADEGLNRS	GLANDERS
ADEEGNRR	GARDENER	ADEEMPST	STAMPEDE	ADEGLNSS	GLADNESS
ADEEGNRU	UNDER-AGE	ADEEMRSU	MEASURED	ADEGLNUZ	UNGLAZED
ADEEGORT	DEROGATE	ADEEMRTY	METEYARD	ADEGMNOY	ENDOGAMY
ADEEGRRR	REGARDER	ADEENNRU	UNEARNED	ADEGNOPU	POUNDAGE
ADEEGRRU	REDARGUE	ADEENOPW	WEAPONED	ADEGNORT	DRAGONET
ADEEGRSS	DRESSAGE	ADEENOSS	SEASONED	ADEGNRRU	GRANDEUR
ADEEGRTT	TARGETED	ADEENOTT	DETONATE	ADEGORTW	WATER-DOG
ADEEGSWY	EDGEWAYS	ADEENRRW	WANDERER	ADEGRRST	DRAGSTER
ADEEHHST	SHEATHED	ADEENRSS	DEARNESS	ADEHHIPS	HEADSHIP
ADEEHILN	HEADLINE	ADEENRTT	ATTENDER	ADEHIKNS	SKINHEAD
ADEEHIRR	DEER-HAIR	ADEENSSU	DANSEUSE	ADEHILNN	HANDLINE
ADEEHISV	ADHESIVE	ADEENTTV	VENDETTA	ADEHILNP	DELPHIAN
ADEEHLSS	HEADLESS	ADEEPRSU	PERSUADE	ADEHINOS	ADHESION
ADEEHMMO	HOME-MADE	ADEEPRTU	DEPURATE	ADEHINPS	DEANSHIP
ADEEHMNN	MENHADEN	ADEEPSWY	SPEEDWAY	ADEHIORS	RHODESIA
ADEEHNRT	ADHERENT	ADEERRRT	RETARDER	ADEHJLOT	JOLTHEAD
	NEATHERD	ADEERRRW	REREWARD	ADEHKNRS	REDSHANK
ADEEHORV	OVERHEAD		REWARDER	ADEHKNSU	SKEAN-DHU
ADEEIILS	IDEALISE	ADEERRST	SERRATED	ADEHLNRW	LANDWEHR
ADEEIILZ	IDEALIZE	ADEERTTT	TATTERED	ADEHLOPS	ASPHODEL
ADEEIJMR	JEREMIAD	ADEERVYY	EVERYDAY		PHOLADES
ADEEILMR	REMEDIAL	ADEFGIRS	GAS-FIRED	ADEHLRRY	HERALDRY
ADEEILMV	MEDIEVAL	ADEFHILS	DEAL-FISH	ADEHMNOS	HANDSOME
ADEEILNT	DATE-LINE	ADEFHLNT	LEFT-HAND	ADEHMNOT	THANEDOM
	LINEATED	ADEFHLTU	DEATHFUL	ADEHMNRS	HERDSMAN
ADEEILPS	PLEIADES	ADEFHNOR	FOREHAND	ADEHMNRU	UNHARMED
ADEEILPT	DEPILATE	ADEFIILR	AIRFIELD	ADEHMOOR	HEADROOM
	PILEATED	ADEFILNT	INFLATED	ADEHMORW	HOMEWARD
ADEEILRS	SIDEREAL	ADEFILOT	FOLIATED	ADEHMOST	HEADMOST
ADEEILSS	IDEALESS	ADEFIMPR	FIRE-DAMP	ADEHMOSU	MADHOUSE
ADEEILSV	SEA-DEVIL	ADEFINRW	FINEDRAW	ADEHNORV	OVERHAND
ADEEIMNT	DEMENTIA	ADEFIORS	FORESAID	ADEHNPTU	UNPATHED

ADEHNRSS	HARDNESS	ADEINOTT	ANTIDOTE	ADENPRUW	UNWARPED
ADEHNRTU	UNTHREAD	ADEINOTV	DONATIVE	ADENQRSU	SQUANDER
ADEHNSSU	SUN-SHADE	ADEINPPX	APPENDIX	ADENRRWY	WARDENRY
ADEHNSUW	UNWASHED	ADEINPRU	UNREPAID	ADENRSTU	TRANSUDE
ADEHNTTX	TEXT-HAND	ADEINPSV	SPAVINED	ADENSTTU	UNTASTED
ADEHOPRS	RHAPSODE	ADEINRST	STRAINED	ADENSTUY	UNSTEADY
ADEIILMS	IDEALISM	ADEINRSU	DENARIUS	ADEOORRT	TOREADOR
ADEIILRS	DISRAELI	ADEINRSV	SANDIVER	ADEOPRRT	PREDATOR
ADEIILST	IDEALIST	ADEINRTU	DATURINE		TEAR-DROP
ADEIILTV	DILATIVE		INDURATE	ADEOPRTT	TETRAPOD
ADEIILTY	IDEALITY	ADEINRUV	UNVARIED	ADEOPSTT	POST-DATE
ADEIIMNR	MERIDIAN	ADEINRVY	VINEYARD	ADEORRST	ROADSTER
ADEIINOT	IDEATION	ADEIOPST	DIOPTASE	ADEORRVW	OVERDRAW
	TAENIOID	ADEIOPTV	ADOPTIVE	ADEORSST	ASSORTED
ADEIINST	ADENITIS	ADEIORST	ASTEROID	ADEORSTX	EXTRADOS
ADEIIRST	IRISATED	ADEIPTTU	APTITUDE	ADEPRRTU	RAPTURED
ADEIKLLY	LADYLIKE	ADEIQSUY	QUAYSIDE	ADERRSTT	REDSTART
ADEIKLSW	SIDE-WALK	ADEIRRWW	WIRE-DRAW	ADERSTWW	WESTWARD
ADEILLNU	UNALLIED	ADEIRSST	DISASTER	ADFFLRUU	FRAUDFUL
ADEILMNY	MAIDENLY	ADEIRSTT	STRIATED	ADFGINNU	UNFADING
ADEILMPP	PALMIPED	ADEISSTT	DISTASTE	ADFHIOST	TOAD-FISH
ADEILMRY	DREAMILY	ADEISSWY	SIDEWAYS	ADFHIRSW	DWARFISH
ADEILMST	MEDALIST	ADEISTTU	SITUATED	ADFHLOST	HOLDFAST
ADEILNNR	INLANDER	ADEITTTU	ATTITUDE	ADFIILPY	LAPIDIFY
ADEILNOP	PALINODE	ADEJOPRY	JEOPARDY	ADFIIRST	FIRST-AID
ADEILNOT	DELATION	ADEJRSTU	ADJUSTER	ADFILLNW	WINDFALL
ADEILNPU	PALUDINE		READJUST	ADFILMNO	MANIFOLD
ADEILNRS	ISLANDER	ADEKLMRY	MARKEDLY	ADFLLNOW	DOWNFALL
ADEILOPS	SEPALOID	ADEKLNSU	UNSLAKED	ADFLMOPR	FRAMPOLD
ADEILOPT	PETALOID	ADEKMORS	DARKSOME	ADFORRSW	FORWARDS
ADEILORT	IDOLATER	ADEKNRSS	DARKNESS	ADGGLRSU	SLUGGARD
ADEILORX	EXORDIAL	ADELLMRU	MEDULLAR	ADGGORSS	DOG-GRASS
ADEILOST	DIASTOLE	ADELLNSS	LANDLESS	ADGHHILN	HIGHLAND
ADEILOTV	DOVETAIL	ADELLRWW	DRAW-WELL	ADGHHIOR	HIGHROAD
ADEILPRT	DIPTERAL	ADELMNOS	SAND-MOLE	ADGHILNN	HANDLING
ADEILPRV	DEPRIVAL	ADELMOTU	MODULATE	ADGHILPY	DIAGLYPH
ADEILRRY	DREARILY	ADELMPTU	DATE-PLUM	ADGHILTY	DAYLIGHT
ADEILRSU	RESIDUAL	ADELNORV	OVERLAND	ADGHINOR	HOARDING
ADEILRSY	DIALYSER	ADELNPRS	SPANDREL	ADGHINPR	HANDGRIP
ADEILRTT	DETRITAL	ADELNPRU	PENDULAR	ADGHLNNO	LONGHAND
ADEILSTY	STEADILY		UPLANDER	ADGHRTUY	DRAUGHTY
ADEILTTU	ALTITUDE	ADELNRTY	ARDENTLY	ADGIILLN	DIALLING
	LATITUDE	ADELNRUY	UNDERLAY	ADGIILLO	GLADIOLI
ADEIMNOT	DOMINATE	ADELNTUU	UNDULATE	ADGIILTY	ALGIDITY
	NEMATOID	ADELNUUV	UNVALUED	ADGIINNY	DIGYNIAN
ADEIMNRZ	ZEMINDAR	ADELOORV	OVERLOAD	ADGIINRY	DAIRYING
ADEIMNSS	SIDESMAN	ADELOPSU	PALUDOSE	ADGIKLNR	DARKLING
ADEIMNTY	DYNAMITE	ADELORST	LODESTAR	ADGILLNW	WINDGALL
ADEIMORT	MEDIATOR	ADELOVWY	AVOWEDLY	ADGILMOR	MARIGOLD
ADEIMOSS	SESAMOID	ADELRTUY	ADULTERY	ADGILNOT	DOG-LATIN
ADEIMRSS	SIDE-ARMS	ADELSTTY	STATEDLY	ADGILNRY	DARINGLY
ADEINNOV	DEVONIAN	ADEMNOPR	POMANDER	ADGILNZZ	DAZZLING
ADEINNPT	PINNATED	ADEMNPSS	DAMPNESS	ADGILOPR	PRODIGAL
ADEINNSX	DISANNEX	ADEMNRRU	UNDERARM	ADGILORY	GYROIDAL
ADEINNTU	INUNDATE	ADENNOTU	UNATONED	ADGINNST	STANDING
ADEINOPT	ANTIPODE	ADENNTUW	UNWANTED	ADGINOOR	RIGADOON
ADEINORR	ORDAINER	ADENOORW	WANDEROO	ADGMNORU	GOURMAND
	REORDAIN	ADENOPRR	PARDONER	ADGNNORS	GRANDSON
ADEINORT	ORDINATE	ADENOPSY	DYSPNOEA	ADHHINPW	WHIP-HAND
	RODENTIA	ADENOUVW	UNAVOWED	ADHHIPRS	HARDSHIP
ADEINOST	SEDATION	ADENPRTY	PEDANTRY	ADHIINOP	OPHIDIAN

ADHILLNS	SAND-HILL	ADINOPRR	RAINDROP	AEEEMNST	EASEMENT
ADHILPSY	LADYSHIP	ADINORRY	ORDINARY	AEEEMPRT	PERMEATE
ADHIMNOS	ADMONISH	ADINORSU	DINOSAUR	AEEENPTT	PATENTEE
ADHIMOPP	AMPHIPOD	ADINORTU	DURATION	AEEENRTV	ENERVATE
ADHINSST	STANDISH	ADIOOPSS	APODOSIS		VENERATE
ADHIPRSW	WARDSHIP	ADIOPPST	POST-PAID	AEEEPRRT	REPARTEE
ADHIPRSY	SHIP-YARD	ADIOPRST	PARODIST		REPEATER
ADHIRTWW	WITHDRAW	ADIOPSTT	TOAD-SPIT	AEEEPSTW	SWEET-PEA
ADHLLNOS	HOLLANDS	ADIORRST	STAIR-ROD	AEEERSST	TESSERAE
ADHLMORT	THRALDOM	ADIORSVY	ADVISORY	AEEERTWY	EYE-WATER
ADHMOPRS	DRAM-SHOP	ADIORTUY	AUDITORY	AEEFFLRI	TAFFEREL
ADHNOSTU	THOUSAND	ADIRRWYZ	WIZARDRY	AEEFFNRT	AFFERENT
ADHOORYZ	HYDROZOA	ADKLOORW	WOOD-LARK	AEEFGIRR	FERRIAGE
ADHOPRSY	RHAPSODY	ADKMOORR	DARK-ROOM	AEEFHRTY	FEATHERY
ADHRSTUY	THURSDAY	ADLLLORY	LOLLARDY	AEEFKOPR	FOREPEAK
ADIIKLMM	MILKMAID	ADLLNORU	ALL-ROUND	AEEFLLRW	FAREWELL
ADIILLMR	MILLIARD	ADLMNOOR	MOORLAND	AEEFLLSS	LEAFLESS
ADIILLUV	DILUVIAL	ADLMOORU	MALODOUR	AEEFLMSS	FAMELESS
ADIILNOT	DILATION	ADLMOPSY	PSALMODY		SELF-SAME
ADIILNSU	INDUSIAL	ADLNOPRU	PAULDRON	AEEFLNRU	FUNEREAL
ADIILNSW	WIND-SAIL	ADLOORWW	WOOLWARD	AEEFLRSS	FEARLESS
ADIILNTY	DAINTILY	ADLORTWY	TOWARDLY	AEEFMNOR	FORENAME
ADIILNUV	DILUVIAN	ADMMNOOS	DOOMSMAN	AEEFMORS	FEARSOME
ADIILOPP	DIPLOPIA	ADMNNORY	MONANDRY	AEEFNRST	FASTENER
ADIILSSY	DIALYSIS	ADMNOOST	MASTODON	AEEFNRTT	FATTENER
ADIILTVY	VALIDITY	ADMOORRW	WARD-ROOM	AEEFNSSS	SAFENESS
ADIINOTU	AUDITION	ADMORRSW	SWORD-ARM	AEEGGIRV	AGGRIEVE
ADIINRST	DISTRAIN	ADNOOQRU	QUADROON	AEEGGLPP	EGG-APPLE
ADIIPRTY	RAPIDITY	ADNOOSVW	ADVOWSON	AEEGGNNR	GANGRENE
ADIIPSTY	SAPIDITY	ADNOQRSU	SQUADRON	AEEGGNOS	GASOGENE
ADIIRSTT	DISTRAIT	ADNORSXY	SARDONYX	AEEGGNOZ	GAZOGENE
ADIKNNST	INKSTAND	ADNORTUW	UNTOWARD	AEEGHILN	HEGELIAN
ADILLMNR	MANDRILL	ADOOPRRT	TRAP-DOOR	AEEGHIRT	HERITAGE
ADILLMOU	ALLODIUM	ADOPRSSW	PASSWORD	AEEGHNRS	SHAGREEN
ADILLMSY	DISMALLY	ADORSTUW	OUTWARDS	AEEGHRRT	GATHERER
ADILLNPS	LANDSLIP	ADORSTUY	SUDATORY		REGATHER
ADILLOSW	DISALLOW	AEEEGGNR	RE-ENGAGE	AEEGILLS	LEGALISE
ADILLOSY	DISLOYAL	AEEEGLRT	RELEGATE	AEEGILLZ	LEGALIZE
ADILLSTY	DISTALLY	AEEEGLRV	LEVERAGE	AEEGILMN	LIEGEMAN
ADILMNNO	MANDOLIN	AEEEGNRS	SEA-GREEN	AEEGILNS	ENSILAGE
ADILMOPT	DIPLOMAT	AEEEGNRT	GENERATE	AEEGILNT	GELATINE
ADILMOPY	OLYMPIAD		TEENAGER		LEGATINE
ADILMOTY	MODALITY	AEEEGRST	STEERAGE	AEEGILRS	GASELIER
ADILMPSU	PALUDISM	AEEEGRSW	SEWERAGE	AEEGILST	ELEGIAST
ADILNNSU	DISANNUL	AEEEGTTV	VEGETATE	AEEGILTV	LEVIGATE
ADILNOOR	DOOR-NAIL	AEEEHLRT	ETHEREAL	AEEGIMNT	GEMINATE
ADILNRWY	INWARDLY	AEEEHLTW	WHEAT-EEL	AEEGIMRT	EMIGRATE
ADILNSSW	WINDLASS	AEEEHMPR	EPHEMERA	AEEGINPR	PERIGEAN
ADILOPSS	DISPOSAL	AEEEHRRS	REHEARSE	AEEGINSS	ASSIGNEE
ADILORTY	ADROITLY	AEEEHSTT	AESTHETE	AEEGINSV	ENVISAGE
	DILATORY	AEEEIMNX	EXAMINEE	AEEGINTV	NEGATIVE
	IDOLATRY	AEEEKKPS	KEEPSAKE	AEEGIPQU	EQUIPAGE
ADILRTWY	TAWDRILY	AEEELLSV	SEA-LEVEL	AEEGLLOW	EAGLE-OWL
ADIMMNSY	DYNAMISM	AEEELNRV	VENEREAL	AEEGLMRT	TELEGRAM
ADIMNNOT	DOMINANT	AEEELPRR	REPEALER	AEEGLMRY	MEAGRELY
ADIMOPRY	MYRIAPOD	AEEELPRS	EEL-SPEAR	AEEGLNNT	ENTANGLE
ADIMOSTY	TOADYISM	AEEELQSU	SEQUELAE	AEEGLNOS	GASOLENE
ADINNOOT	DONATION	AEEELRRS	RELEASER	AEEGLNOT	ELONGATE
ADINNORT	ORDINANT	AEEELRRV	REVEALER	AEEGLNRR	ENLARGER
ADINOOPT	ADOPTION	AEEELRST	TEASELER	AEEGLNSY	ANGLESEY
ADINOOTT	DOTATION	AEEEMMRT	METAMERE	AEEGLRTU	REGULATE

AEEGLSSY	EYE-GLASS	AEEILRRT	RETAILER	AEELNRTX	EXTERNAL
AEEGLTTU	TUTELAGE	AEEILRTT	LITERATE	AEELNSST	LATENESS
AEEGMMOS	GAMESOME	AEEILRTV	LEVIRATE	AEELNSWY	WESLEYAN
AEEGMNSS	GAMENESS		RELATIVE	AEELNTUV	EVENTUAL
AEEGMRST	GAMESTER	AEEILRVW	REVIEWAL	AEELOPRV	OVERLEAP
AEEGMSSU	MESSUAGE	AEEILTTV	LEVITATE	AEELORTT	TOLERATE
AEEGNNNO	ENNEAGON	AEEIMMNT	MEANTIME	AEELORTV	ELEVATOR
AEEGNNRT	GENERANT	AEEIMNRX	EXAMINER	AEELOTTT	TEETOTAL
AEEGNPRS	SAP-GREEN	AEEIMSTT	ESTIMATE	AEELPRRT	PALTERER
AEEGNRRV	ENGRAVER	AEEINNRS	ANSERINE	AEELPRSU	PLEASURE
AEEGNRST	ESTRANGE	AEEINNTV	VENETIAN	AEELRRSV	REVERSAL
	SERGEANT	AEEINPRT	APERIENT		SLAVERER
AEEGNSSS	SAGENESS	AEEINPTT	PIANETTE	AEELRRTV	TRAVELER
AEEGRRRT	REGRATER	AEEINRRT	RETAINER	AEELRSST	TEARLESS
AEEHIMTT	HEMATITE	AEEINRST	STEARINE	AEELRSTY	EASTERLY
AEEHINPS	EPHESIAN	AEEINSSS	EASINESS	AEELSSVW	WAVELESS
AEEHIPRS	PHARISEE	AEEINSTT	ANISETTE	AEEMMSST	MESSMATE
AEEHIPTT	HEPATITE	AEEIPPST	APPETISE	AEEMNNRT	REMANENT
AEEHIPTZ	HEPATIZE	AEEIPPSU	EUPEPSIA	AEEMNNSS	MEANNESS
AEEHISTT	HESITATE	AEEIPPTT	APPETITE	AEEMNPRY	EMPYREAN
AEEHKLLR	RAKEHELL	AEEIPPTZ	APPETIZE	AEEMNPTV	PAVEMENT
AEEHKLLU	KEELHAUL	AEEIPRRR	REPAIRER	AEEMNRTU	NUMERATE
AEEHLLRS	EAR-SHELL	AEEIRSTT	TREATISE	AEEMNRTV	AVERMENT
AEEHLMNW	WHEELMAN	AEEISTTT	STEATITE	AEEMNSSS	SAMENESS
AEEHLMNY	HYMENEAL	AEEITUVX	EXUVIATE	AEEMNSST	TAMENESS
AEEHLMPT	HELPMATE	AEEJLNPT	JET-PLANE	AEEMNSTU	MANSUETE
AEEHLNPT	ELEPHANT	AEEJNRST	SERJEANT	AEEMPPRR	PAMPERER
AEEHLNRT	LEATHERN	AEEKLLST	SKELETAL	AEEMPRRT	TAMPERER
AEEHLNSS	HALENESS	AEEKMOTY	YOKE-MATE	AEEMPRTT	ATTEMPER
AEEHLNVY	HEAVENLY	AEEKMRRR	REMARKER	AEEMQRRU	REMARQUÉ
AEEHLOSU	ALE-HOUSE	AEEKMRRT	MARKETER	AEEMRRST	STREAMER
AEEHLRTY	LEATHERY	AEEKNSSW	WEAKNESS	AEEMRSST	MASSETER
AEEHMNNY	HYMENEAN	AEEKNSTT	STAKE-NET	AEEMRSSU	REASSUME
AEEHMRTY	ERYTHEMA	AEEKORST	KREASOTE	AEEMRSTT	TEAMSTER
AEEHNOPR	EARPHONE	AEEKORTV	OVERTAKE	AEEMSSSU	MASSEUSE
AEEHNRST	HASTENER		TAKE-OVER	AEENNRSS	NEARNESS
AEEHNRTT	THREATEN	AEEKQRSU	SQUEAKER	AEENNSSS	SANENESS
AEEHNRTW	WATER-HEN	AEELLLTT	TELL-TALE	AEENNSST	NEATNESS
AEEHNRWY	ANYWHERE	AEELLRTW	WALL-TREE	AEENOPRU	EUROPEAN
AEEHORRV	OVERHEAR	AEELLSTT	STELLATE	AEENORRS	REASONER
AEEHORSS	SEA-HORSE	AEELMNOS	SEA-LEMON	AEENORSS	SEASONER
	SEA-SHORE	AEELMNPS	ENSAMPLE	AEENORTV	RENOVATE
AEEHORTV	OVERHEAT	AEELMNSS	LAMENESS	AEENPPTT	APPETENT
AEEHRTVW	WHATEVER		MANELESS	AEENRRRW	WARRENER
AEEILMMT	MEAL-TIME		NAMELESS	AEENRRSS	RARENESS
AEEILMNT	MELANITE	AEELMNTT	MANTELET	AEENRRSW	ANSWERER
AEEILNPR	PERINEAL	AEELMPRT	PALM-TREE	AEENRRTV	TAVERNER
AEEILNPS	PENALISE	AEELMPRX	EXEMPLAR	AEENRSST	ASSENTER
AEEILNPT	PETALINE	AEELMPRY	EMPYREAL		SARSENET
	TAPE-LINE	AEELMPTT	PALMETTE	AEENRTTY	ENTREATY
AEEILNRT	ENTAILER	AEELMSSS	SEAMLESS	AEEOPRRT	PERORATE
	TREENAIL	AEELMSST	MATELESS	AEEOPRTT	OPERETTA
AEEILNSV	VASELINE		TAMELESS	AEEORRSV	SEA-ROVER
AEEILORT	AEROLITE	AEELNNSS	LEANNESS	AEEORRTV	OVERRATE
AEEILOTT	ETIOLATE	AEELNOPR	PERONEAL	AEEORSSV	OVERSEAS
AEEILPPP	APPLE-PIE	AEELNOPT	ANTELOPE	AEEPPRRR	PREPARER
AEEILPRS	ESPALIER	AEELNPPS	SPALPEEN	AEEPRRRT	PARTERRE
AEEILQSU	EQUALISE	AEELNPSS	PALENESS	AEEPRRTU	APERTURE
AEEILQUX	EXEQUIAL	AEELNRSS	REALNESS	AEEPRSSS	PASSERES
AEEILQUZ	EQUALIZE	AEELNRSV	ENSLAVER	AEERRRST	ARRESTER
AEEILRRS	REALISER	AEELNRTV	RELEVANT	AEERRSST	REASSERT

AEERRSSU	REASSURE	AEFLSTUW	WASTEFUL
AEERRSTU	TREASURE	AEFMNRRY	FERRYMAN
AEERRSTV	TRAVERSE	AEFMORST	FOREMAST
AEERSTTT	ATTESTER	AEFNNSTU	UNFASTEN
AEERSTWZ	TWEAZERS	AEFNOPRR	PROFANER
AEFFGRSU	SUFFRAGE	AEFNORRW	FOREWARN
AEFFHILL	HALF-LIFE	AEFNRRST	TRANSFER
AEFFIMRR	AFFIRMER	AEFNSSST	FASTNESS
	REAFFIRM	AEFOORTW	FOOTWEAR
AEFFLNTU	AFFLUENT	AEFOPRRT	FOREPART
AEFFORST	AFFOREST	AEFORRSW	FORSWEAR
AEFGHIST	SEAFIGHT	AEFORRUV	FAVOURER
AEFGIMTU	FUMIGATE	AEGGGLSS	EGG-GLASS
AEFGIRTU	FIGURATE	AEGGINOR	GEORGIAN
	FRUITAGE	AEGGINOS	SEA-GOING
AEFGLLOP	FLAGPOLE	AEGGIOPR	ARPEGGIO
AEFGLMNU	FUGLEMAN	AEGGLNPT	EGG-PLANT
AEFGLRTU	GRATEFUL	AEGGLORY	GARGOYLE
AEFGMNRT	FRAGMENT	AEGGMORT	MORTGAGE
AEFGNORT	FRONTAGE	AEGGNRST	GANGSTER
AEFGOORT	FOOTGEAR	AEGHHORT	EARTH-HOG
AEFHIKRS	FREAKISH	AEGHILNR	NARGHILE
AEFHILMT	HALF-TIME		NARGILEH
AEFHLMSU	SHAMEFUL	AEGHILNS	SHEALING
AEFHLRTY	FATHERLY	AEGHILNT	ATHELING
AEFHLTWY	WHEAT-FLY	AEGHILRT	LITHARGE
AEFHMNRS	FRESHMAN	AEGHINRS	SHEARING
AEFHRSTT	FARTHEST	AEGHIPPR	EPIGRAPH
AEFIILNS	FINALISE	AEGHIPRT	GRAPHITE
AEFIIPRT	APERITIF	AEGHLRTU	LAUGHTER
AEFIITVX	FIXATIVE	AEGHLRTY	LETHARGY
AEFILMNR	RIFLEMAN	AEGHMNOP	PHENOGAM
AEFILMNT	FILAMENT	AEGHMOPT	APOTHEGM
AEFILNNR	INFERNAL	AEGHNOPT	HEPTAGON
AEFILORS	FORESAIL	AEGHNORV	HANGOVER
AEFILRTT	FILTRATE		OVERHANG
AEFILRTU	FILATURE	AEGHORST	SHORTAGE
AEFILSTV	FESTIVAL	AEGIILLU	AIGUILLE
AEFILSTW	FLATWISE	AEGIILTT	LITIGATE
AEFILTUU	FAUTEUIL	AEGIIMNR	MIGRAINE
AEFIMMMR	MAMMIFER	AEGIIMTT	MITIGATE
AEFIMNST	MANIFEST	AEGIIRRT	IRRIGATE
AEFIMORR	AERIFORM	AEGIKLNW	WEAKLING
AEFINOPR	PINAFORE	AEGIKNNS	SNEAKING
AEFINRSS	FAIRNESS	AEGIKNNW	WAKENING
AEFIRRRY	FARRIERY	AEGIKNPS	SPEAKING
AEFKLLOT	FOLK-TALE	AEGILLMS	LEGALISM
AEFLLSSW	FLAWLESS	AEGILLNY	GENIALLY
AEFLLSTY	FESTALLY	AEGILLPR	PILLAGER
AEFLMORU	FORMULAE	AEGILLRU	GUERILLA
	FUMAROLE	AEGILLRV	VILLAGER
AEFLNNOT	FONTANEL	AEGILLTU	LIGULATE
AEFLNRTU	FLAUNTER	AEGILLTY	LEGALITY
AEFLNSST	FLATNESS	AEGILMNR	GERMINAL
AEFLNSUY	UNSAFELY		MALINGER
AEFLORRW	ELF-ARROW	AEGILMNT	LIGAMENT
AEFLORST	FORESTAL	AEGILNNR	LEARNING
AEFLORSU	FUSAROLE	AEGILNNW	WEANLING
AEFLOSTT	FALSETTO	AEGILNNY	YEANLING
AEFLRTTY	FLATTERY	AEGILNOR	REGIONAL
AEFLSTTU	TASTEFUL	AEGILNOS	GASOLINE

AEGILNOT	LEGATION
AEGILNPS	PLEASING
AEGILNRT	INTEGRAL
	TRIANGLE
AEGILNRY	YEARLING
AEGILNSS	GAINLESS
AEGILNST	GENITALS
	STEALING
AEGILNSV	LEAVINGS
	EVENGALI
AEGILOPT	PILOTAGE
AEGILORS	GIRASOLE
	SERAGLIO
AEGILPPU	PUPILAGE
AEGILRSY	GREASILY
AEGILRTU	LIGATURE
AEGILRTY	REGALITY
AEGILRVW	LAWGIVER
AEGIMNRT	EMIGRANT
AEGIMNRU	GERANIUM
AEGIMPRU	UMPIRAGE
AEGIMQRU	QUAGMIRE
AEGINNOT	NEGATION
AEGINNRS	EARNINGS
AEGINNRY	YEARNING
AEGINNSU	SANGUINE
AEGINORS	ORGANISE
AEGINORZ	ORGANIZE
AEGINRSS	REASSIGN
AEGINRST	GANISTER
AEGINRSW	SWEARING
AEGINRTT	TREATING
AEGINRTV	VINTAGER
AEGINRTW	WATERING
AEGINSST	GIANTESS
AEGLLOPR	GALLOPER
AEGLLORY	ALLEGORY
AEGLLOTT	TOLL-GATE
AEGLLRVY	GRAVELLY
AEGLMNNO	MANGONEL
AEGLNNPT	PLANGENT
AEGLNNSY	LANGSYNE
AEGLNOPT	GANTLOPE
AEGLNRRW	WRANGLER
AEGLNRST	STRANGLE
AEGLNRSY	LARYNGES
AEGLNTTU	GAUNTLET
AEGLNTUU	UNGULATE
AEGLOOPU	APOLOGUE
AEGLOORY	AEROLOGY
AEGLOPRY	PLAYGOER
AEGLORSU	GLAREOUS
AEGLORTY	GEOLATRY
AEGLRSTU	GESTURAL
AEGLRTTU	GUTTERAL
AEGMMRRU	RUMMAGER
AEGMNORV	MANGROVE
AEGMNOXY	XENOGAMY
AEGMNRTU	ARGUMENT
AEGMORSS	GOSSAMER
AEGMSTTU	STEAM-TUG

AEGNNOPT	PENTAGON	AEHMNORS	HORSEMAN
AEGNNPRT	PREGNANT	AEHMOPRT	METAPHOR
AEGNOPRR	PARERGON	AEHMOSTW	SOMEWHAT
AEGNORRY	ORANGERY	AEHMPRST	HAMPSTER
AEGNORST	RAG-STONE	AEHMSTTY	AMETHYST
AEGNORTT	TETRAGON	AEHNNOPT	PANTHEON
AEGNORTY	NEGATORY	AEHNNPSU	UNSHAPEN
AEGNRRST	STRANGER	AEHNNSUV	UNSHAVEN
AEGNRSSY	GRAYNESS	AEHNOPST	STANHOPE
AEGOPPST	STOPPAGE	AEHNORST	SHERATON
AEGORRTT	GAROTTER	AEHNRSSS	RASHNESS
	GARROTTE	AEHNRTTU	EARTH-NUT
AEGORTTU	TUTORAGE	AEHNSTUW	UNSWATHE
AEGORUVY	VOYAGEUR	AEHOPSST	SPATHOSE
AEGOSSTV	GAS-STOVE	AEHOPSTU	TAP-HOUSE
AEGPRRSU	SPUR-GEAR	AEHOPTVY	TOP-HEAVY
AEGRRSSY	RYE-GRASS	AEHORRSW	WAR-HORSE
AEGRSTTY	STRATEGY	AEHORSTT	RHEOSTAT
AEHHNRSW	HERNSHAW	AEHORSTU	SHARE-OUT
AEHHRRST	THRASHER	AEHPRSST	SHARP-SET
AEHIILNR	HAIR-LINE	AEHPRSUX	HARUSPEX
AEHIIOPT	ETHIOPIA	AEHPRSUY	EUPHRASY
AEHILLNT	THALLINE	AEHRRTTW	THWARTER
AEHILNNT	INHALENT	AEHRSTTY	SHATTERY
AEHILNOP	APHELION	AEIIINTT	INITIATE
AEHILNTZ	ZENITHAL	AEIILLTV	ILLATIVE
AEHILRSS	HAIRLESS	AEIILMNN	MAINLINE
AEHILRTY	HEARTILY	AEIILMNS	ALIENISM
AEHIMNSU	HUMANISE		MILESIAN
AEHIMNUZ	HUMANIZE	AEIILMPR	IMPERIAL
AEHIMPRS	SAMPHIRE	AEIILMST	ISLAMITE
	SERAPHIM	AEIILMTT	MILITATE
AEHIMPSS	EMPHASIS	AEIILNQU	AQUILINE
	MISSHAPE	AEIILNST	ALIENIST
AEHIMPST	SHIPMATE		LATINISE
AEHINPPY	EPIPHANY	AEIILNTZ	LATINIZE
AEHINPRT	PERIANTH	AEIILPRT	REPTILIA
AEHINPST	THESPIAN	AEIILRTT	LITERATI
AEHINSSZ	HAZINESS	AEIIMMRT	MARITIME
AEHINSTT	HESITANT	AEIIMMSX	MAXIMISE
AEHIPPRS	SAPPHIRE	AEIIMMXZ	MAXIMIZE
AEHIRRSV	RAVISHER	AEIIMNTT	INTIMATE
AEHIRSTY	HYSTERIA	AEIIMNTU	MINUTIAE
AEHISSTU	HIATUSES	AEIIMRST	SERIATIM
AEHKNNSU	UNSHAKEN	AEIINNRS	SIRENIAN
AEHLLNRT	ENTHRALL	AEIINRSS	AIRINESS
AEHLMMNS	HELMSMAN	AEIINSVV	INVASIVE
AEHLMNOT	METHANOL	AEIIPRSW	PAIRWISE
AEHLMNUY	HUMANELY	AEIIRRTT	IRRITATE
AEHLMPPT	PAMPHLET	AEIIRSST	SATIRISE
AEHLMRSS	HARMLESS	AEIIRSTW	WISTERIA
AEHLNPRS	SHRAPNEL	AEIIRSTZ	SATIRIZE
AEHLNRTU	LUTHERAN	AEIITTTV	TITIVATE
AEHLOPRT	PLETHORA	AEIJLOSU	JALOUSIE
AEHLORSY	HOARSELY	AEIKLNSS	SEAL-SKIN
AEHLORUV	OVERHAUL	AEIKLRST	STARLIKE
AEHLPSST	PATHLESS	AEIKMNST	MISTAKEN
AEHLPSTU	SULPHATE	AEIKMPSS	MISSPEAK
AEHLRRTU	URETHRAL	AEIKNRTW	KNITWEAR
AEHLSTTY	STEALTHY	AEIKRSST	ASTERISK
AEHMNNPY	NYMPHEAN	AEILLLNY	LINEALLY

AEILLNNO	LANOLINE
AEILLNRY	LINEARLY
AEILLNVY	VENIALLY
AEILLOTV	VOLATILE
AEILLPST	PASTILLE
AEILLRRY	RAILLERY
AEILLRSY	SERIALLY
AEILLRTT	ILL-TREAT
AEILLSSS	SAILLESS
AEILLSST	TAILLESS
AEILLSUV	ALLUSIVE
AEILMMNS	MELANISM
AEILMMNU	IMMANUEL
AEILMMOR	MEMORIAL
AEILMMOT	IMMOLATE
AEILMNOS	SEMOLINA
AEILMNRT	TERMINAL
AEILMNST	SALT-MINE
AEILMOPR	PROEMIAL
AEILMORS	MORALISE
AEILMORZ	MORALIZE
AEILMPRV	PRIMEVAL
AEILMPTY	PLAYTIME
AEILMRTT	REMITTAL
AEILMRUV	VELARIUM
AEILMSTU	SIMULATE
AEILMTTU	MUTILATE
	ULTIMATE
AEILNNRT	INTERNAL
AEILNNSY	INSANELY
AEILNNTY	INNATELY
AEILNORT	ORIENTAL
	RELATION
AEILNOST	INSOLATE
AEILNPSS	PAINLESS
AEILNPTT	TINPLATE
AEILNRSS	RAINLESS
AEILNRTT	TRAIL-NET
AEILNRTV	INTERVAL
AEILNSSZ	LAZINESS
AEILNSTU	INSULATE
AEILNSUY	UNEASILY
AEILNTVY	NATIVELY
	VENALITY
AEILNUVV	UNIVALVE
AEILOPRS	POLARISE
AEILOPRT	PETIOLAR
AEILOPRZ	POLARIZE
AEILOPST	SPOLIATE
AEILORTT	LITERATO
AEILPRRS	REPRISAL
AEILPRST	PILASTER
AEILPSUV	PLAUSIVE
AEILQRTU	REQUITAL
AEILQSUY	QUEASILY
AEILQTUY	EQUALITY
AEILRRSU	RURALISE
AEILRRTY	LITERARY
AEILRTVV	TRIVALVE
AEIMMNNT	IMMANENT
AEIMMNOT	AMMONITE

AEIMMRTU	IMMATURE	AEIPTTUV	PUTATIVE	AELOPPTU	POPULATE
AEIMNNOT	NOMINATE	AEIQRRRU	QUARRIER	AELOPPXY	APOPLEXY
AEIMNOPT	PTOMAINE	AEIRRTTY	TERTIARY	AELOPQUY	OPAQUELY
AEIMNORS	ROMANISE	AEIRSSTW	WAITRESS	AELOPRRV	REPROVAL
AEIMNORT	MARONITE	AEISSSTY	ESSAYIST	AELOPRST	PETROSAL
AEIMNORZ	ROMANIZE	AEJLOSUY	JEALOUSY	AELOPSSU	ESPOUSAL
AEIMNOSW	WOMANISE	AEKKMNOO	KAKEMONO		SEPALOUS
AEIMNRSU	ANEURISM	AEKLMRUW	LUKEWARM	AELORTYZ	ZEALOTRY
AEIMNRSY	SEMINARY	AEKLNNSS	LANKNESS	AELOTUUV	OUTVALUE
AEIMNRTT	MARTINET	AEKLNOSY	ANKYLOSE	AFIPRRTT	PRATTLER
AEIMNRTU	RUMINATE	AEKLOPRW	ROPE-WALK	AELPRSSY	SPARSELY
AEIMNSSZ	MAZINESS	AEKLORVW	WALK-OVER	AELPRSTY	PLASTERY
AEIMORST	AMORTISE	AEKMORTW	TEAM-WORK		PSALTERY
	ATOMISER		WORK-MATE	AELQRSUY	SQUARELY
AEIMORTT	AMORETTI	AEKNNRSS	RANKNESS	AELRRTVY	VARLETRY
AEIMORTZ	AMORTIZE	AEKOPSTU	OUTSPEAK	AELRSSST	STARLESS
	ATOMIZER	AEKORSTV	OVERTASK	AELRSTTU	LUSTRATE
AEIMOTTV	MOTIVATE	AELLLRTU	TELLURAL	AELRTTUY	TUTELARY
AEIMQRSU	MARQUISE	AELLMNTY	MENTALLY	AELSTTUY	ASTUTELY
AEIMQSUU	ESQUIMAU	AELLNPRU	PRUNELLA	AEMMORST	MARMOSET
AEIMRSST	ASTERISM	AELLNPSS	PLANLESS	AEMNNORS	NORSEMAN
AEIMRSSY	EMISSARY	AELLNPTT	PLANTLET	AEMNNORT	ORNAMENT
AEIMSSTT	MISSTATE	AELLNSST	TALLNESS	AEMNOORT	ANTEROOM
AEINNOOS	SEA-ONION	AELLNTTY	LATENTLY	AEMNOPRW	MANPOWER
AEINNOPV	PAVONINE	AELLNTUU	LUNULATE	AEMNORRS	RANSOMER
AEINNORS	RAISONNÉ	AELLORSV	OVERALLS	AEMNORSV	OVERSMAN
AEINNOTT	INTONATE	AELLORWW	WALLOWER	AEMNORTY	MONETARY
AEINNOTV	INNOVATE	AELLOSUV	ALVEOLUS	AEMNORYY	YEOMANRY
	VENATION	AELLRTTY	LATTERLY	AEMNPRSS	PRESSMAN
AEINNSSV	VAINNESS	AELLSSST	SALTLESS	AEMNPRSU	SUPERMAN
AEINOPPT	ANTIPOPE	AELLSUXY	SEXUALLY	AEMNRRUY	NUMERARY
AEINOQTU	EQUATION	AELMNNRY	MANNERLY	AEMNRSSW	WARMNESS
AEINORRT	ANTERIOR	AELMNOPS	PLEONASM	AEMNRSTU	MENSTRUA
AEINORRW	IRONWARE	AELMNOST	SALMONET	AEMOOSST	MAESTOSO
AEINORST	SEÑORITA	AELMNOYY	YEOMANLY	AEMOOSTT	TOMATOES
AEINORSV	AVERSION	AELMOOPT	OMOPLATE	AEMOPRTW	TAPE-WORM
AEINOTVX	VEXATION	AELMOPRR	PREMOLAR	AEMORRRU	ARMOURER
AEINPRRT	TERRAPIN	AELMOPRT	TEMPORAL	AEMORRST	REARMOST
AEINPRST	PINASTER	AELMOPTT	PALMETTO	AEMORRSY	ROSEMARY
AEINPRUV	PERUVIAN	AELMORTU	EMULATOR	AEMORSSY	MAYORESS
AEINPSTY	EPINASTY	AELMOSSS	MOLASSES	AEMQRSSU	MARQUESS
AEINPTTY	ANTITYPE	AELMPRRT	TRAMPLER	AEMRSSTT	MATTRESS
AEINQTTU	EQUITANT	AELMRSTT	MALTSTER	AENNORST	RESONANT
AEINRRST	RESTRAIN	AELMRSTY	MASTERLY	AENNORSU	UNREASON
	STRAINER	AELMRTUY	MATURELY	AENNOSTW	TENON-SAW
AEINRRTV	VERATRIN	AELMSSST	MASTLESS	AENNRSWY	SWANNERY
AEINRSSW	WARINESS	AELNNOOP	NAPOLEON	AENNRTTY	TENANTRY
AEINRSTT	STRAITEN	AELNNOSU	ANNULOSE	AENOOPST	TEASPOON
AEINRSUZ	SUZERAIN	AELNOOTZ	ENTOZOAL	AENORSUV	RAVENOUS
AEINSSWX	WAXINESS	AELNOPRS	PERSONAL	AENORTTY	ATTORNEY
AEINSUVV	VESUVIAN	AELNORTT	TOLERANT	AENOSSUU	NAUSEOUS
AEIOPPST	APPOSITE	AELNORTY	ORNATELY	AENPRSTT	TRANSEPT
AEIOPRRT	PRETORIA	AELNPRSU	PURSLANE	AENQRRTU	QUARTERN
	PRIORATE	AELNPTTU	PETULANT	AENRRRTY	ERRANTRY
AEIOPRSV	VAPORISE	AELNRSTT	SLATTERN	AENRSSTT	TARTNESS
AEIOPRTX	EXPIATOR	AELNRSXY	LARYNXES	AENSSSTV	VASTNESS
AEIOPRVZ	VAPORIZE	AELNRTTW	TRAWL-NET	AEOOPRRT	OPERATOR
AEIOPTTV	OPTATIVE	AELNSSST	SALTNESS	AEOOPSTT	POTATOES
AEIORTTV	ROTATIVE	AELNTTUX	EXULTANT	AEOPPRRV	APPROVER
AEIPRSTY	ASPERITY	AELOPPRS	PROLAPSE	AEOPRRST	RAPTORES
AEIPRSVY	VESPIARY	AELOPPSU	PAPULOSE	AEOPRRUV	VAPOURER

AEOPRSSV	OVERPASS	AFIINOTX	FIXATION	AGHMNPSU	SPHAGNUM
	PASSOVER	AFIKLNNR	FRANKLIN	AGIIINNS	INSIGNIA
AEOPRSTT	PROSTATE	AFILLLOT	FLOTILLA	AGIIINRV	VIRGINIA
AEOPRSTU	APTEROUS	AFILLOST	SAIL-LOFT	AGIILNNU	INGUINAL
AEOPRTTW	WATER-POT	AFILLTUY	FAULTILY	AGIILNNY	INLAYING
AEOPRTWX	WATER-POX	AFILMNOR	FORMALIN	AGIILNOR	ORIGINAL
AEOPTTUY	AUTOTYPE		INFORMAL	AGIILNOT	INTAGLIO
AEOQRSTU	QUAESTOR	AFILNPPT	FLIPPANT		LIGATION
AEORRSST	ASSERTOR	AFILNRUY	UNFAIRLY	AGIILNOX	GLOXINIA
AEORRSTT	ROSTRATE	AFILNSTU	INFLATUS	AGIILNRV	VIRGINAL
AEORSSSS	ASSESSOR	AFILORTY	FILATORY	AGIILNTT	LITIGANT
AEORSSTV	VOTARESS	AFILRSTU	FISTULAR	AGIILNTV	VIGILANT
AEORSTTT	TESTATOR	AFILSTTU	FLAUTIST	AGIIMNTT	MITIGANT
AEORSTTU	OUTSTARE	AFIMMNOR	MANIFORM	AGIINNPT	PAINTING
AEORSTUW	OUTSWEAR	AFIMNOPR	NAPIFORM	AGIINNRT	TRAINING
AEORSTVY	OVERSTAY	AFIMNOSU	INFAMOUS	AGIINPRS	ASPIRING
AEPPRRST	STRAPPER	AFIMORRU	AURIFORM	AGIKLMOR	KILOGRAM
AEPRSSST	TRESPASS	AFIMORRV	VARIFORM	AGIKLNST	STALKING
AEPRSTTU	STUPRATE	AFIMORSV	VASIFORM	AGIKLNTY	TAKINGLY
AEPRSTTY	TAPESTRY	AFINNOTU	FOUNTAIN	AGIKNNPS	SPANKING
AEQRSTTU	SQUATTER	AFINNRTY	INFANTRY	AGIKNOST	GOATSKIN
AERRSTUY	TREASURY	AFINOPSY	SAPONIFY	AGILLMNY	MALIGNLY
AERSTTVY	TRAVESTY	AFINQTUY	QUANTIFY	AGILLNRU	ALLURING
AFFFFIRR	RIFFRAFF	AFINRSTX	TRANSFIX	AGILLNSY	SIGNALLY
AFFGHIRT	AFFRIGHT	AFIRSTTY	STRATIFY	AGILLOPT	GALLIPOT
AFFGIIRT	GRAFFITI	AFKLNOTU	OUTFLANK	AGILLPUY	PLAGUILY
AFFGIORT	GRAFFITO	AFKMOORT	FOOTMARK	AGILLSSY	GLASSILY
AFFGLNRU	FAR-FLUNG	AFLLLORY	FLORALLY	AGILMOPR	LIPOGRAM
AFFHILTU	FAITHFUL	AFLLLUWY	LAWFULLY	AGILNNOP	PANGOLIN
AFFIINTY	AFFINITY	AFLLMNUY	MANFULLY	AGILNNRS	SNARLING
AFFINOSU	AFFUSION	AFLLMORY	FORMALLY	AGILNNUY	UNGAINLY
AFFIPSTT	TIP-STAFF	AFLLNUUW	UNLAWFUL	AGILNORT	TRIGONAL
AFFLLOOT	FOOTFALL	AFLLORSU	ALL-FOURS	AGILNOTY	ANTILOGY
AFGGGILN	FLAGGING	AFLLRTUY	ARTFULLY	AGILNPTT	PLATTING
AFGHILNT	FAN-LIGHT	AFLMOPRT	PLATFORM	AGILNRST	STARLING
AFGHINRT	FARTHING	AFLMOSUY	FAMOUSLY	AGILNRSU	SINGULAR
AFGHINST	SHAFTING	AFNOOPRS	SPAN-ROOF	AGILNRTW	TRAWLING
AFGHLNSU	FLASH-GUN	AGGGIYZZ	ZIGZAGGY	AGILNRVY	RAVINGLY
AFGILMNO	FLAMINGO	AGGHILST	GAS-LIGHT	AGILNSVY	SAVINGLY
AFGILNOT	FLOATING	AGGHLOOT	GOLGOTHA	AGILNTTT	TATTLING
AFGILNTT	FLATTING	AGGIINNR	GRAINING	AGILNTTW	WATTLING
AFGINRTU	FIGURANT	AGGILMNO	GLOAMING	AGILNTUV	VAULTING
AFGLLNOT	FLATLONG	AGGILNNO	GANGLION	AGIMMOSY	MISOGAMY
AFGLLRUY	FRUGALLY	AGGILNNT	GNATLING	AGIMNORS	ORGANISM
AFGLLSSU	GLASSFUL	AGGILNRY	GRAYLING	AGIMNORY	AGRIMONY
AFGLNNOO	GONFALON	AGGINPRS	GRASPING	AGIMNPST	STAMPING
AFGNNNOO	GONFANON	AGGLMOOR	LOGOGRAM	AGIMNRRY	MARRYING
AFHIKNRS	FRANKISH	AGHHLOTU	ALTHOUGH	AGIMNSSU	ASSUMING
AFHILLSY	FLASHILY	AGHIIRTT	AIR-TIGHT	AGINNOPT	POIGNANT
AFHIOSSU	FASHIOUS	AGHILMTY	ALMIGHTY	AGINNORT	IGNORANT
AFHIRSST	STARFISH	AGHILNOT	LOATHING	AGINNTTU	TAUNTING
AFHKLNTU	THANKFUL	AGHILNSS	SLASHING	AGINORRS	GARRISON
AFHLLOTU	LOATHFUL	AGHILNSU	LANGUISH	AGINORST	ORGANIST
AFHLRTUW	WRATHFUL	AGHILRSY	GARISHLY	AGINORTY	GYRATION
AFHOOPTT	FOOTPATH	AGHILTWX	WAX-LIGHT	AGINPPRT	TRAPPING
AFIILLLY	FILIALLY	AGHINNTY	ANYTHING	AGINPPRW	WRAPPING
AFIILLNU	UNFILIAL	AGHINPRS	PHRASING	AGINRRST	STARRING
AFIILNRU	UNIFILAR	AGHINSSW	SWASHING	AGINRSTY	STING-RAY
AFIILNST	FINALIST	AGHIPRRT	TRIGRAPH	AGIOORSU	ORAGIOUS
AFIILNTY	FINALITY	AGHIRSTT	STRAIGHT	AGIRTTUY	GRATUITY
AFIINNOS	SAINFOIN	AGHLMOOR	HOLOGRAM	AGKLLSUU	SKUA-GULL

92

AGKORSSW	GAS-WORKS	AIILMNST	LATINISM
AGLLPRSU	SPURGALL	AIILMNTT	MILITANT
AGLLRUVY	VULGARLY	AIILMRTY	LIMITARY
AGLMOOTY	ATMOLOGY		MILITARY
AGLMOPYY	POLYGAMY	AIILMSTV	VITALISM
AGLNOSWY	LONGWAYS	AIILNOPV	PAVILION
AGLOOPST	GOAL-POST	AIILNORT	TRAIN-OIL
AGLOPRTU	PORTUGAL	AIILNOSV	VISIONAL
AGLORSSY	GLOSSARY	AIILNRSU	SILURIAN
AGLPSSSY	SPY-GLASS	AIILNSTT	LATINIST
AGLSTUUY	AUGUSTLY	AIILNTTY	LATINITY
AGMMNOOR	MONOGRAM	AIILSTTV	VITALIST
AGMMNOOY	MONOGAMY	AIILTTVY	VITALITY
AGMNNOSW	GOWNSMAN	AIIMMSTX	MAXIMIST
AGMNOORY	AGRONOMY	AIIMNNOS	INSOMNIA
AGNORTUY	NUGATORY	AIIMNPSS	SINAPISM
AGORRTYY	GYRATORY	AIIMNTTU	TITANIUM
AGORSTTY	GYROSTAT	AIIMORTT	IMITATOR
AHHILPSW	WHIP-LASH	AIIMPRTY	IMPARITY
AHHNORTW	HAWTHORN	AIIMRUVV	VIVARIUM
AHIILRTY	HILARITY	AIIMSSTT	MASTITIS
AHIKLRSY	RAKISHLY	AIINNOSV	INVASION
AHIKNPRS	PRANKISH	AIINNSTY	INSANITY
AHIKPRSS	SPARKISH	AIINRRTT	IRRITANT
AHILLMSS	SMALLISH	AIINSTTV	VISITANT
AHILLMTU	THALLIUM	AIINTTVY	NATIVITY
AHILLSVY	LAVISHLY	AIIORTTV	VITIATOR
AHILMQSU	QUALMISH	AIIRSSTT	SATIRIST
AHILNOPS	SIPHONAL	AIJKKNOU	KINKAJOU
AHILOORT	LOTHARIO	AIJLLOVY	JOVIALLY
AHILOPST	HOSPITAL	AIJLNTUY	JAUNTILY
AHILRSTY	TRASHILY	AIJMORTY	MAJORITY
AHIMMNSU	HUMANISM	AIJNOPPY	POPINJAY
AHIMNOSW	WOMANISH	AIKLOTTW	KILOWATT
AHIMNSTU	HUMANIST	AIKNNOOS	NAINSOOK
AHIMNTUY	HUMANITY	AIKNNSSW	SWANSKIN
AHIMOPRS	APHORISM	AIKNRSST	SANSKRIT
AHINNOPT	ANTIPHON	AILLMUUV	ALLUVIUM
AHINOSST	ASTONISH	AILLNOST	STALLION
AHINPPSS	SNAPPISH	AILLNOSU	ALLUSION
AHINPRST	TRANSHIP	AILLNOUV	ALLUVION
AHINQSUV	VANQUISH	AILLNPTY	PLIANTLY
AHKMORTU	KHARTOUM	AILLORTT	LITTORAL
AHLLNOOS	SHALLOON	AILLOSTY	LOYALIST
AHLLNOTW	TOWN-HALL	AILLPRSY	SPIRALLY
AHLNNORT	LANTHORN	AILLRTUY	RITUALLY
AHLORRTY	HARLOTRY	AILLSUVY	VISUALLY
AHLRTTWY	THWARTLY	AILMMNUU	ALUMINUM
AHMNNSTU	HUNTSMAN	AILMMORT	IMMORTAL
AHMPSTYY	SYMPATHY	AILMNOOR	MONORAIL
AHMQSSUU	MUSQUASH	AILMNOPY	OLYMPIAN
AHNOPPSW	PAWNSHOP	AILMNPTU	PLATINUM
AHNOPSST	SNAP-SHOT	AILMNRUY	LUMINARY
AHNOSTUX	XANTHOUS	AILMOORT	MOTORIAL
AHOOPRWW	WAR-WHOOP	AILMOPRX	PROXIMAL
AHOPSTUW	SOUTHPAW	AILMORST	MORALIST
AIIILLVX	LIXIVIAL	AILMORSU	SOLARIUM
AIIKNNNP	PANNIKIN	AILMORSY	ROYALISM
AIILLNOT	ILLATION	AILMORTY	MORALITY
AIILLNVY	VILLAINY	AILMOSTU	SOLATIUM
AIILLPRS	SPIRILLA	AILMOSTV	VOLTAISM
AILMPPSY	MISAPPLY		
AILMPSST	PSALMIST		
AILMPSTY	PTYALISM		
AILMRRSU	RURALISM		
AILMRSTU	ALTRUISM		
	ULTRAISM		
AILNNOOT	NOTIONAL		
AILNNOSW	SON-IN-LAW		
AILNNOTU	LUNATION		
AILNOOPT	OPTIONAL		
AILNOPRU	UNIPOLAR		
AILNOSUV	AVULSION		
AILNOSVY	SYNOVIAL		
AILNOTTY	TONALITY		
AILNOTUX	LUXATION		
AILNQRTU	TRANQUIL		
AILNQTUY	QUAINTLY		
AILNRUWY	UNWARILY		
AILNSTTU	LUTANIST		
AILNSTUU	NAUTILUS		
AILOOPRT	TROOPIAL		
AILOORTV	VIOLATOR		
AILOPRTY	POLARITY		
AILORSTY	ROYALIST		
	SOLITARY		
AILORTTU	TUTORIAL		
AILOTTTY	TOTALITY		
AILPPRUY	PUPILARY		
AILPRSTU	STIPULAR		
AILRSTTU	ALTRUIST		
	ULTRAIST		
AILRSTTY	STRAITLY		
AILRSUVV	SURVIVAL		
AIMMMNOU	AMMONIUM		
AIMMNORS	ROMANISM		
AIMMNORT	MORTMAIN		
AIMNNOTU	MOUNTAIN		
AIMNNOTY	ANTIMONY		
AIMNNRTU	RUMINANT		
AIMNORST	ROMANIST		
AIMNORTY	MINATORY		
AIMNOSSX	SAXONISM		
AIMNOTTU	MUTATION		
AIMNRSTT	TRANSMIT		
AIMNRSTU	NATURISM		
AIMOPSSY	SYMPOSIA		
AIMORRUV	VARIORUM		
AIMOSSTT	SOMATIST		
AIMRTTUY	MATURITY		
AINNOOTT	NOTATION		
AINNOTTU	NUTATION		
AINOOPTT	POTATION		
AINOORTT	ROTATION		
AINORSST	ARSONIST		
AINORSTT	STRONTIA		
AINOSSTX	SAXONIST		
AINPRSSU	PRUSSIAN		
AINPSSTU	PUISSANT		
AINQTTUY	QUANTITY		
AINRSTTU	NATURIST		
AINRSTTY	TANISTRY		

AIOPRRTT	PORTRAIT	BBDELLMU	DUMB-BELL	BCEILNRU	RUNCIBLE
AIOPRSST	PROTASIS	BBDELSTU	STUBBLED	BCEILPRU	REPUBLIC
AIORSTTV	VOTARIST	BBDGINRU	DRUBBING	BCEINOVX	BICONVEX
AIPPRSTT	TRAPPIST	BBDILORT	BIRD-BOLT	BCEJOORT	OBJECTOR
AIPPRSTY	PAPISTRY	BBDOSUYY	BUSY-BODY	BCEKLNUU	UNBUCKLE
AIPRSSTU	UPSTAIRS	BBEELLLU	BLUEBELL	BCENORRY	BY-CORNER
AJKLNSTU	SALT-JUNK	BBEFILRR	FRIBBLER	BCEORRSU	OBSCURER
AKKORSTW	TASK-WORK	BBEILQRU	QUIBBLER	BCEORRWY	COW-BERRY
AKLNNOPT	PLANKTON	BBEILRRY	BILBERRY	BCFIIMOR	MORBIFIC
AKLNOTTW	TOWN-TALK	BBEIMMOT	TIME-BOMB	BCFILORY	FORCIBLY
AKLORSTW	SALT-WORK	BBELLRUY	LUBBERLY	BCFIMORU	CUBIFORM
AKLPRRSU	LARKSPUR	BBELORSY	SLOBBERY	BCFLOOTU	CLUB-FOOT
AKMOPRST	POST-MARK	BBENORSY	SNOBBERY	BCFOORRU	CURB-ROOF
ALLLPRUY	PLURALLY	BBHINOSS	SNOBBISH	BCGIILMN	CLIMBING
ALLMNORY	NORMALLY	BBHIOOSY	BOOBYISH	BCGIILOO	BIOLOGIC
ALLMOPSX	SMALLPOX	BBIKLNOO	BOBOLINK	BCGIKLOW	WIG-BLOCK
ALLMORTY	MORTALLY	BBILLOYY	BILLY-BOY	BCGINNOU	BOUNCING
ALLMTUUY	MUTUALLY	BBILOSUU	BIBULOUS	BCHIKLOS	BLOCKISH
ALMMNRUU	NUMMULAR	BBIMNOSS	SNOBBISM	BCHIOORY	CHOIRBOY
ALMMORTW	MALTWORM	BBNORSTU	STUBBORN	BCHKOSTU	BUCK-SHOT
ALMNORTY	MATRONLY	BCCEHIRU	CHERUBIC	BCHNORSU	BRONCHUS
ALMOORTU	ALUM-ROOT	BCCEILRU	CRUCIBLE	BCIIMORU	CIBORIUM
ALMOPPST	LAMPPOST	BCCEMRUU	CUCUMBER	BCIKKNSU	BUCKSKIN
ALNNOTWY	WANTONLY	BCCIIMOR	MICROBIC	BCIKLNOT	BLOCK-TIN
ALNOPRST	PLASTRON	BCCILOOR	BROCCOLI	BCILLPUY	PUBLICLY
ALNORRWY	NARROWLY	BCCIRTUU	CUCURBIT	BCILMOSY	SYMBOLIC
ALNPPSTU	SUPPLANT	BCDDEHIL	CHILDBED	BCINOSSU	SUBSONIC
ALOOPPRS	PROPOSAL	BCDEEEHR	BREECHED	BCINOSTU	SUB-TONIC
ALOORSUV	VALOROUS	BCDEEEMR	DECEMBER	BCKOOOPY	COPY-BOOK
ALOORTYZ	ZOOLATRY	BCDEEHNR	BEDRENCH	BCLMOORU	CLUB-ROOM
ALOPPRYY	POLYPARY	BCDEEIKN	BENEDICK	BCLMOSSU	CLUB-MOSS
ALOPPSUU	PAPULOUS	BCDEEILR	CREDIBLE	BCMORSUU	CUMBROUS
ALOPSTUU	PATULOUS	BCDEEILU	EDUCIBLE	BCOORSSW	CROSSBOW
ALORSTTW	SALTWORT	BCDEEIRS	DESCRIBE	BCORSTTU	OBSTRUCT
ALORTUWY	OUTLAWRY	BCDEILRY	CREDIBLY	BDDEEINT	INDEBTED
ALPPSTUY	PLATYPUS	BCDEIMNO	COMBINED	BDDEEINW	BIND-WEED
ALPRSTUU	PUSTULAR	BCDIIPSU	BICUSPID	BDDEILNR	BRINDLED
AMMNPTUY	TYMPANUM	BCDIKLLU	DUCK-BILL	BDDEINNU	UNBIDDEN
AMNNOSTW	TOWNSMAN	BCDILMOY	MOLYBDIC	BDDELOOR	BLOOD-RED
AMNNSTTU	STUNTMAN	BCDINRUU	RUBICUND	BDDGOOSY	DOG'S-BODY
AMNOOTUY	AUTONOMY	BCEEEFIN	BENEFICE	BDDHIMSU	BUDDHISM
AMNOOTXY	TAXONOMY	BCEEEHRS	BREECHES	BDDHISTU	BUDDHIST
AMNOPRYY	PARONYMY	BCEEFILN	FENCIBLE	BDEEEGNO	EDGE-BONE
AMOORTWY	MOTORWAY	BCEEFNOR	CORN-BEEF	BDEEEHTU	HEBETUDE
AMOPRSXY	PAROXYSM	BCEEIILM	IMBECILE	BDEEEMMR	MEMBERED
AMOQSSUU	SQUAMOUS	BCEEINOT	CENOBITE	BDEEFINR	BEFRIEND
AMORRTUY	MORTUARY	BCEEIRTT	BRETTICE	BDEEFOOR	FOREBODE
ANPRSTUU	PURSUANT	BCEELOOR	BORECOLE	BDEEFOOW	BEEF-WOOD
AOOOPRTZ	PROTOZOA	BCEELRTU	TUBERCLE	BDEEGGRU	BEGRUDGE
AOOPRSUV	VAPOROUS	BCEEMNRU	ENCUMBER	BDEEGILN	BLEEDING
AOORRTTY	ROTATORY	BCEEMRRU	CEREBRUM	BDEEGINR	BREEDING
AOPPRSST	PASSPORT	BCEERRSU	CERBERUS	BDEEHLNO	BEHOLDEN
BBBCEOWY	COBWEBBY	BCEFILOR	FORCIBLE	BDEEHLOR	BEHOLDER
BBBEINOT	BOBBINET	BCEGIMNO	BECOMING	BDEEIILN	INEDIBLE
BBCEILRS	SCRIBBLE	BCEGLNOO	CONGLOBE	BDEEILLU	ELUDIBLE
BBCEMNOU	BUNCOMBE	BCEHORRU	BROCHURE	BDEEILNV	VENDIBLE
BBCERRSU	SCRUBBER	BCEHORTY	BOTCHERY	BDEEILRW	BEWILDER
BBCILSTU	CLUBBIST	BCEHRTUY	BUTCHERY	BDEEIMRT	TIMBERED
BBDEILRU	BLUE-BIRD	BCEIILMS	MISCIBLE	BDEEINOT	OBEDIENT
BBDEINRU	UNBERBID	BCEIILNV	VINCIBLE	BDEEIRST	BESTRIDE
BBDEKOOT	BOOK-DEBT	BCEIINRS	INSCRIBE	BDEEIRSY	BIRD'S-EYE

BDEELLRW	WELL-BRED	BEEELMNS	ENSEMBLE	BEGHLNOU	BUNG-HOLE
BDEELMNO	EMBOLDEN	BEEELMRS	RESEMBLE	BEGIILLY	ELIGIBLY
BDEELORU	REDOUBLE	BEEELMZZ	EMBEZZLE	BEGILLLU	GULLIBLE
BDEEMNOT	BODEMENT	BEEEMMRR	REMEMBER	BEGILNNY	BENIGNLY
BDEEMOSS	EMBOSSED	BEEFILLX	FLEXIBLE	BEGILNSS	BLESSING
BDEENNOT	BONNETED	BEEFILNU	UNBELIEF		GLIBNESS
BDEEORRR	BORDERER	BEEFNORR	FREEBORN	BEGINNOR	RING-BONE
BDEEOSTT	BESOTTED	BEEGHLMR	BERGMEHL	BEGLLOTU	GLOBULET
BDEERRTU	TRUEBRED	BEEGIILL	ELIGIBLE	BEGLMRRU	GRUMBLER
BDEERRWY	DEW-BERRY	BEEGIILX	EXIGIBLE	BEGNOORU	BOURGEON
BDEGLLOY	BELLY-GOD	DCCGILNT	BEETLING	BEGNSSUU	SUB-GENUS
BDEGLNOU	BLUDGEON	BEEGILRU	BEGUILER	BEHILLTY	BLITHELY
BDEIILMR	BIRD-LIME	BEEGINNR	BEGINNER	BEHILMRW	WHIMBREL
BDEIILTY	DEBILITY	BEEGINSW	BEESWING	BEHILORR	HORRIBLE
BDEIKNSU	BUSKINED	BEEGMRSU	SUBMERGE	BEHILRTU	THURIBLE
BDEILLMU	BDELLIUM	BEEHHMOT	BEHEMOTH	BEHIMNOO	BONHOMIE
BDEILNVY	VENDIBLY	BEEHILMN	BLENHEIM	BEHINNOS	SHIN-BONE
BDEILOSS	BODILESS	BEEHNRRT	BRETHREN	BEHINOSW	WISH-BONE
BDEILRST	BRISTLED	BEEIKLWY	BIWEEKLY	BEHIOTWY	WHITEBOY
BDEIMORR	IMBORDER	BEEILLLR	LIBELLER	BEHLLOOW	BLOW-HOLE
BDEINOOW	WOODBINE	BEEILLTT	BELITTLE	BEHMNOOR	HOMEBORN
BDEINRUU	UNBURIED	BEEILNSS	SENSIBLE	BEHOOOST	BOOT-HOSE
BDEIORRY	BROIDERY	BEEILRRT	TERRIBLE	BEIILLMT	TIME-BILL
BDEIRSSU	DISBURSE	BEEIMRTT	EMBITTER	BEIILMMO	IMMOBILE
BDELLOOR	DOOR-BELL	BEEKNOST	STEENBOK	BEIILMOS	MOBILISE
BDELNOSS	BOLDNESS	BEELLOPR	BELL-ROPE	BEIILMOZ	MOBILIZE
BDELNOTU	UNBOLTED	BEELLSUY	BULL'S-EYE	BEIIMRTT	IMBITTER
BDELOORV	OVERBOLD	BEELLTUW	TUBEWELL	BEIINPRT	BRINE-PIT
BDELORTU	TROUBLED	BEELMRRT	TREMBLER	BEIINSTT	STIBNITE
BDEMNSSU	DUMBNESS	BEELMRRU	LUMBERER	BEILLMNO	BONE-MILL
BDEMOOSY	SOMEBODY	BEELNOSS	NOBLESSE	BEILLNTU	BULLETIN
BDEMOOTT	BOTTOMED	BEELNSSU	BLUENESS	BEILMMOS	EMBOLISM
BDENNRUU	UNBURDEN	BEELNTTU	BETEL-NUT	BEILMRSS	BRIMLESS
	UNBURNED	BEELOOST	OBSOLETE	BEILNNTU	BUNTLINE
BDENOSTU	BONE-DUST	BEELRTUU	TRUEBLUE	BEILNSSY	SENSIBLY
BDENRUUY	UNDERBUY	BEEMNORV	NOVEMBER	BEILOPPW	BLOWPIPE
BDEORRSU	SUBORDER	BEEMNRRU	NUMBERER	BEILOPSS	POSSIBLE
BDEORRTU	OBTRUDER	BEEMRSSU	SUBMERSE	BEILORST	STROBILE
BDFLOTUU	DOUBTFUL	BEENPRST	BESPRENT	BEILORTT	LIBRETTO
BDGIILNN	BLINDING	BEENRTTU	BRUNETTE	BEILRRTY	TERRIBLY
BDGIILNU	BUILDING	BEEOORTT	BEET-ROOT	BEILRSTY	BLISTERY
BDGILNOU	DOUBLING		BOOT-TREE	BEILRTTY	BITTERLY
BDGINORS	SONG-BIRD	BEEORRSV	OBSERVER	BEILSTTU	SUBTITLE
BDGNRUUY	BURGUNDY	BEEORSSU	SUBEROSE	BEIMORTY	BIOMETRY
BDHIMOOR	RHOMBOID	BEEORSTU	TUBEROSE	BEINORTZ	BRONZITE
BDIIMRUU	RUBIDIUM	BEEORSTW	BESTOWER	BEINSSSU	BUSINESS
BDILLOOY	BLOODILY	BEERRSTW	BREWSTER	BEIORRTU	ROBURITE
BDILMORY	MORBIDLY	BEERRTTU	REBUTTER	BEIORSTY	SOBRIETY
BDILNPRU	PURBLIND	BEERSSUV	SUBSERVE	BEKLNORY	BROKENLY
BDIMNORU	MORIBUND	BEERSTTY	BY-STREET	BEKLOORT	BROOKLET
BDIMOSTU	MISDOUBT	BEESTTTU	TEST-TUBE	BEKMOOSX	SMOKE-BOX
BDINORSW	SNOW-BIRD	BEFGIILL	FILLIBEG	BEKNNORU	UNBROKEN
BDIOORTY	BOTRYOID	BEFGIINR	BRIEFING	BEKNOOOT	NOTEBOOK
BDKNOOOR	DOOR-KNOB	BEFILLXY	FLEXIBLY	BEKOOTTX	TEXT-BOOK
BDKOOORW	WORD-BOOK	BEFINOTU	BUFONITE	BELLLLPU	BELL-PULL
BDKOOSTU	STUD-BOOK	BEFLLLUY	BELLYFUL	BELLNORW	WELL-BORN
BDLNOOOU	DOUBLOON	BEFLORUW	FURBELOW	BELMOORY	BLOOMERY
BEEEEFLN	ENFEEBLE	BEFNOORR	FORBORNE	BELMORSY	SOMBRELY
BEEEGIRS	BESIEGER	BEGHIILP	PHILIBEG	BELMOSST	TOMBLESS
BEEEGRTT	BEGETTER	BEGHINOR	NEIGHBOR	BELMPRUY	PLUMBERY
BEEEILRV	BELIEVER	BEGHINRT	BRIGHTEN	BELMRRUY	MULBERRY

BELMRSTU	STUMBLER	BIILNOTY	NOBILITY	CCEIIKLN	NICKELIC
BELNOSUU	NEBULOUS	BIIQTUUY	UBIQUITY	CCEIILNT	ENCLITIC
BELOOPRT	BOLT-ROPE	BILOPSSY	POSSIBLY	CCEIILOR	LICORICE
BELOOSST	BOOTLESS	BINNORTW	TWIN-BORN	CCEIILPT	ECLIPTIC
BELOOTUV	OBVOLUTE	BIOOPSTT	POST-OBIT	CCEIILST	SCILICET
BELORRTU	TROUBLER	BIOPRSTW	BOWSPRIT	CCEIINNR	ENCRINIC
BELOSTUY	OBTUSELY	BIORSTUY	BISTOURY	CCEILMOP	COMPLICE
BELPRSUY	SUPERBLY	BKMOOORW	BOOKWORM	CCEILNUY	UNICYCLE
BELRSSSU	BRUSSELS	BKOOOPST	BOOK-POST	CCEILRRU	CURRICLE
BELRSTUY	BLUSTERY	BLMOOOTY	LOBOTOMY	CCEILRTY	TRICYCLE
BELSTTUY	SUBTLETY	BLMOOSSY	BLOSSOMY	CCEIMNOO	ECONOMIC
BEMNNSSU	NUMBNESS	BLOSTUUU	TUBULOUS	CCEIMOST	COSMETIC
BEMNOORT	TROMBONE	BMOORSSU	SOMBROUS	CCEIMRRU	MERCURIC
BEMOORRS	SOMBRERO	BNNOTTUU	UNBUTTON	CCEINNOV	CONVINCE
BENNOSSU	SNUB-NOSE	BNNRSTUU	SUN-BURNT	CCEINOOR	COERCION
BENORRSU	SUBORNER	BNOOOSTW	SNOW-BOOT	CCEINOTT	TECTONIC
BENORRTU	TRUEBORN	BORSTTUU	OUTBURST	CCEINPRT	PRECINCT
BEOORRRW	BORROWER	CCCEEILT	ECLECTIC	CCEINRTU	CINCTURE
BEORRRUW	BURROWER	CCCEILNY	ENCYCLIC	CCEIOPRU	OCCUPIER
BEORSSUU	SUBEROUS	CCCIINSU	SUCCINIC	CCEIOSTT	SCOTTICE
BEORSTUU	TUBEROUS	CCCILNOY	CYCLONIC	CCEIPRTU	CUT-PRICE
BERSSTTU	BUTTRESS	CCCILOPY	CYCLOPIC	CCEKORRY	CROCKERY
BFFNOSUX	SNUFF-BOX	CCCINSTU	SUCCINCT	CCEKORSU	COCKSURE
BFGLLORU	BULL-FROG	CCCKOORW	COCK-CROW	CCELMOPT	COMPLECT
BFIIORSS	FIBROSIS	CCCLOSUU	COCCULUS	CCELOPSY	CYCLOPES
BFILLSSU	BLISSFUL	CCDEEENR	CREDENCE	CCENOORT	CONCERTO
BGGGILNO	BOGGLING	CCDEEENOR	CONCEDER	CCENORTY	CORNETCY
BGGIILNO	OBLIGING	CCDEHORT	CROTCHED	CCENRRUY	CURRENCY
BGGIILNY	GIBINGLY	CCDEHRTU	CRUTCHED	CCEOPRUY	REOCCUPY
BGGILNNU	BUNGLING	CCDEIINO	COINCIDE	CCFIIRUX	CRUCIFIX
BGHILMNU	HUMBLING	CCDEINOT	OCCIDENT	CCFILNOT	CONFLICT
BGHILNSU	BLUSHING	CCDELNOU	CONCLUDE	CCFKLOOT	COCK-LOFT
BGHILRTY	BRIGHTLY	CCDHIIOR	DICHROIC	CCGHHIOU	HICCOUGH
BGHNOTUU	UNBOUGHT	CCDHINOO	CONCHOID	CCHHNRUU	UNCHURCH
BGHORRUX	ROXBURGH	CCDKOOOW	WOODCOCK	CCHHOOWW	CHOW-CHOW
BGIIMMNR	BRIMMING	CCEEHRSY	SCREECHY	CCIILLRY	CYRILLIC
BGILLNOU	GLOBULIN	CCEEILNR	ENCIRCLE	CCIIMNSY	CYNICISM
BGILMMNU	MUMBLING	CCEEILPY	EPICYCLE	CCIKKLOP	PICKLOCK
BGILMNOO	BLOOMING	CCEEILRT	ELECTRIC	CCIKOPRS	CROP-SICK
BGILMNPU	PLUMBING	CCEEIMNU	ECUMENIC	CCILORUU	CURCULIO
BGILMNTU	TUMBLING	CCEEINOR	CICERONE	CCJNNOTU	CONJUNCT
BGILNORT	RING-BOLT	CCEEINOV	CONCEIVE	CCKKOORR	ROCK-CORK
BGINNORW	BROWNING	CCEEIORV	COERCIVE	CCKNORTU	TURN-COCK
BGLOORYY	BRYOLOGY	CCEEKLOR	COCKEREL	CCKOOPST	STOP-COCK
BHHIKSSU	BUKSHISH	CCEELMNY	CLEMENCY	CCLLOTUY	OCCULTLY
BHIIOPRT	PROHIBIT	CCEEMMNO	COMMENCE	CCORSSTU	CROSSCUT
BHIKLLOO	BILL-HOOK	CCEEMMOR	COMMERCE	CDDEEEJT	DEJECTED
BHILLNOR	HORNBILL	CCEENNOS	ENSCONCE	CDDEEKNU	UNDECKED
BHILLSTU	BULLSHIT	CCEENORT	CONCRETE	CDDEEKUW	DUCK-WEED
BHILNSTU	BLUNTISH	CCEENRST	CRESCENT	CDDEELSU	SECLUDED
BHILORRY	HORRIBLY	CCEFIIPS	SPECIFIC	CDDEELUY	DEUCEDLY
BHILOSYY	BOYISHLY	CCEFIRRU	CRUCIFER	CDDGHILO	GODCHILD
BHINORSW	BROWNISH	CCEFLOOS	FLOCCOSE	CDDHILOS	CLODDISH
BHIORRST	SHORT-RIB	CCEHILNR	CLINCHER	CDDKNOPU	DUCK-POND
BHKOOOOT	BOOT-HOOK	CCEHILOR	CHOLERIC	CDEEEINV	EVIDENCE
BHLOOOTT	TOLBOOTH	CCEHILOY	CHOICELY	CDEEEIRV	DECEIVER
BHLRSUUY	BULRUSHY	CCEHINOR	ENCHORIC	CDEEELOS	COLE-SEED
BHMORSTU	THROMBUS	CCEHIORT	RICOCHET	CDEEEPTX	EXPECTED
BHMRRSUU	RUM-SHRUB	CCEHLMOR	CROMLECH	CDEEERSS	RECESSED
BIILMOTY	MOBILITY	CCEHORTT	CROTCHET	CDEEFFOR	COFFERED
BIILNOOV	OBLIVION	CCEHRSTU	SCUTCHER	CDEEFIIT	FETICIDE

CDEEFKLR	FRECKLED	CDEIIMST	DIMESTIC
CDEEFORS	FRESCOED	CDEIINNT	INCIDENT
CDEEFORT	DEFECTOR	CDEIINOS	DECISION
CDEEGIIR	REGICIDE	CDEIINRT	INDIRECT
CDEEGIOS	GEODESIC	CDEIIOPR	PERIODIC
CDEEGIOT	GEODETIC	CDEIIOPS	EPISODIC
CDEEHILN	LICHENED	CDEIIRTU	DIURETIC
CDEEHIPR	DECIPHER	CDEIKLWY	WICKEDLY
CDEEHLSU	SCHEDULE	CDEILLPU	PELLUCID
CDEEHRTW	WRETCHED	CDEILMOS	MELODICS
CDEEIIMN	MEDICINE	CDEILMRU	DULCIMER
CDEEIIMP	EPIDEMIC	CDEILNRY	CYLINDER
CDEEIISV	DECISIVE	CDEILORV	COVERLID
CDEEIITT	DIETETIC	CDEILOSS	DISCLOSE
CDEEIKRW	WICKERED	CDEILRTY	DIRECTLY
CDEEILNS	LICENSED	CDEINORS	CONSIDER
CDEEILNT	DENTICLE	CDEINORT	DOCTRINE
CDEEILRT	DERELICT	CDEINORU	DECURION
CDEEIMNR	ENDERMIC	CDEINOUV	UNVOICED
CDEEIMOR	MEDIOCRE	CDEINPRS	PRESCIND
CDEEIMRV	DECEMVIR	CDEIOPST	DESPOTIC
CDEEINNT	INDECENT	CDEIORRT	CREDITOR
CDEEIORV	DIVORCEE		DIRECTOR
CDEEIPRT	DECREPIT	CDEIORRV	DIVORCER
CDEEIPRU	PEDICURE	CDEIORSV	DISCOVER
CDEEIRST	DISCREET	CDEKNOOU	UNCOOKED
	DISCRETE	CDELLORS	SCROLLED
CDEEKLPS	SPECKLED	CDELLOTU	CLOUDLET
CDEELNPU	PEDUNCLE	CDELMNOU	COLUMNED
CDEELNTY	DECENTLY	CDELMPRU	CRUMPLED
CDEELORV	CLOVERED	CDELNOSS	COLDNESS
CDEELPRU	PRECLUDE	CDELNOSY	SECONDLY
CDEENNOS	CONDENSE	CDELOORU	COLOURED
CDEENNOU	DENOUNCE		DECOLOUR
CDEENNPY	PENDENCY	CDELRSUY	CURSEDLY
CDEENNTY	TENDENCY	CDELRTUU	CULTURED
CDEENORR	CORNERED	CDEMNOOW	DOWN-COME
CDEENORS	SECONDER	CDEMNOTU	DOCUMENT
	SEED-CORN	CDEMOOPS	COMPOSED
CDEENOTX	COEXTEND	CDEMOSTU	COSTUMED
CDEENPRU	PRUDENCE	CDENORTU	CORNUTED
CDEEOPRS	PROCEEDS	CDEOOPST	POSTCODE
CDEEORRR	RECORDER	CDEOORSU	DECOROUS
CDEEORTT	DETECTOR	CDEOPRRU	PRODUCER
CDEFHIMO	CHIEFDOM	CDFNNOOU	CONFOUND
CDEFIIOR	CODIFIER	CDGHIILN	CHILDING
CDEFINNU	INFECUND	CDGIKLNU	DUCKLING
CDEFLORY	FORCEDLY	CDGILNOS	SCOLDING
CDEFNOSU	CONFUSED	CDHHIILS	CHILDISH
CDEHIILO	HELICOID	CDHIOORT	TROCHOID
CDEHIIMO	HOMICIDE	CDHIOPRW	WHIP-CORD
CDEHILNR	CHILDREN	CDHIOPRY	HYDROPIC
CDEHILOR	CHLORIDE	CDHIORRT	TRICHORD
CDEHIMOT	METHODIC	CDHLOOPY	COPYHOLD
CDEHIOTY	THEODICY	CDIILOTY	DOCILITY
CDEIIKNR	CIDERKIN	CDIILTUY	LUCIDITY
CDEIILMO	DOMICILE	CDIINSTT	DISTINCT
CDEIILNN	INCLINED	CDIIOPRT	DIOPTRIC
CDEIILNO	INDOCILE	CDIIPTUY	CUPIDITY
CDEIILPS	DISCIPLE	CDIIRSTT	DISTRICT
CDEIILRU	RIDICULE	CDIJNSTU	DISJUNCT

CDIKKOPR	DROP-KICK
CDIKLOPS	SLIP-DOCK
CDIKNOSW	WIND-SOCK
CDILLOUY	CLOUDILY
CDILOORS	DISCOLOR
CDILOOTY	COTYLOID
CDINNQUU	QUIDNUNC
CDINOOOR	CORONOID
CDINORSW	DISCROWN
CDINOSTU	DISCOUNT
CDIOOPRS	PROSODIC
CDIOORRR	CORRIDOR
CDIOPRSU	CUSPIDOR
CDJLNOUY	JOCUNDLY
CDKOOORW	ROCK-WOOD
CDLLLOOP	CLODPOLL
CDMNOOPU	COMPOUND
CDMNORUU	CORUNDUM
CDOORRUY	CORDUROY
CEEEEIPY	EYE-PIECE
CEEEFFRT	EFFECTER
CEEEFNOR	CONFEREE
CEEEGINX	EXIGENCE
CEEEGITX	EXEGETIC
CEEEILNN	LENIENCE
CEEEILNS	LICENSEE
CEEEILRT	ERECTILE
CEEEILTV	ELECTIVE
CEEEIMNN	EMINENCE
CEEEINNT	ENCEINTE
CEEEIPRV	PERCEIVE
CEEEIRRV	RECEIVER
CEEEIRSX	EXERCISE
CEEEIRTV	ERECTIVE
CEEEJRRT	REJECTER
CEEEMRTY	CEMETERY
CEEENNST	SENTENCE
CEEENPRS	PRESENCE
CEEENPRT	PRETENCE
CEEENQSU	SEQUENCE
CEEEPRTX	EXPECTER
CEEERSST	SESTERCE
CEEFFORT	EFFECTOR
CEEFHIKR	KERCHIEF
CEEFHIRY	CHIEFERY
CEEFHISS	CHIEFESS
CEEFHLRU	CHEERFUL
CEEFILRY	FIERCELY
CEEFINRT	FRENETIC
CEEFLNTU	FECULENT
CEEFNORR	CONFRÈRE
CEEFNRVY	FERVENCY
CEEFOPRR	PERFORCE
CEEFORSS	FRESCOES
CEEFORST	COST-FREE
	SCOT-FREE
CEEGGILS	EGG-SLICE
CEEGHINR	CHEERING
CEEGHLOW	COG-WHEEL
CEEGINSU	EUGENICS
CEEGINXY	EXIGENCY

CEEGNNOR	CONGENER	CEEKLRSS	RECKLESS
CEEGNORT	COREGENT	CEEKNORR	RECKONER
CEEGNORV	CONGREVE	CEELLMOU	MOLECULE
	CONVERGE	CEELLRVY	CLEVERLY
CEEHILLN	CHENILLE	CEELLSSU	CLUELESS
	HELLENIC	CEELMOPT	COMPLETE
CEEHILRY	CHEERILY	CEELMORW	WELCOMER
CEEHILTV	HELVETIC	CEELNOPU	OPULENCE
CEEHIMRT	HERMETIC	CEELNORT	ELECTRON
CEEHINOR	CO-INHERE	CEELNPTU	CENTUPLE
CEEHIOSV	COHESIVE	CEELNRTY	RECENTLY
CEEHIPRT	HERPETIC	CEELNSTU	ESCULENT
CEEHISTT	ESTHETIC	CEELORSS	CORELESS
CEEHKRST	SKETCHER	CEELORST	CORSELET
CEEHLNSU	ELENCHUS		SELECTOR
CEEHLRSU	HERCULES	CEELORTV	COVERLET
CEEHNNRT	ENTRENCH	CEELRRTU	LECTURER
CEEHNORT	COHERENT	CEELRSSU	CURELESS
CEEHNQRU	QUENCHER	CEELRSTY	SECRETLY
CEEHNRRT	RETRENCH	CEELRSUY	SECURELY
	TRENCHER	CEEMNORY	CEREMONY
CEEHOPRY	CORYPHEE	CEEMOORV	OVERCOME
CEEIIMRT	EREMITIC	CEENNORT	CRETONNE
CEEIJNOT	EJECTION	CEENNORU	RENOUNCE
CEEIJORR	REJOICER	CEENNORV	CONVENER
CEEIJRUV	VERJUICE	CEENOPTW	TWOPENCE
CEEIKLPR	PICKEREL	CEENORSV	CONSERVE
CEEILLLP	PELLICLE		CONVERSE
CEEILNNY	LENIENCY	CEENORVY	CONVEYER
CEEILNOP	PLIOCENE		RECONVEY
CEEILNOT	ELECTION	CEEOORST	CREOSOTE
CEEILNOV	VIOLENCE	CEEOQTTU	COQUETTE
CEEILNRS	SILENCER	CEEORRRS	SORCERER
CEEILNRU	CERULEIN	CEEORRSU	RECOURSE
CEEILOSS	SOLECISE		RESOURCE
CEEILOSZ	SOLECIZE	CEEORRVY	RECOVERY
CEEILRSU	CISELURE	CEEORTTV	CORVETTE
CEEILRSV	VERSICLE	CEEORTUX	EXECUTOR
CEEILRTU	RETICULE	CEERRTUZ	CREUTZER
CEEILRTY	CELERITY	CEFFIORU	COIFFURE
CEEILSTT	TESTICLE	CEFFLORU	FORCEFUL
CEEIMMRS	MESMERIC	CEFFLRSU	SCUFFLER
CEEIMNPS	SPECIMEN	CEFGHINT	FETCHING
CEEIMORT	METEORIC	CEFGLNUY	FULGENCY
CEEINNSS	NICENESS	CEFHIIMS	MISCHIEF
CEEINORT	ERECTION	CEFIILTY	FELICITY
	NEOTERIC	CEFIIPRT	PETRIFIC
CEEINORV	OVERNICE	CEFIIRRT	TERRIFIC
CEEINPRT	PRENTICE	CEFIKLOR	FIRELOCK
CEEINPSX	SIXPENCE	CEFILLLO	FOLLICLE
CEEINRSU	INSECURE	CEFILMRU	CRIMEFUL
	SINECURE		MERCIFUL
CEEINRTT	RETICENT	CEFILNOT	FLECTION
CEEIORST	ESOTERIC	CEFILOUV	VOICEFUL
CEEIORSX	EXORCISE	CEFINORS	FORENSIC
CEEIORTT	EROTETIC	CEFIORTY	FEROCITY
CEEIORTX	EXOTERIC	CEFKLOOR	FORELOCK
CEEIORXZ	EXORCIZE	CEFLLOSU	FLOSCULE
CEEIPPTU	EUPEPTIC	CEFLNSTU	SCENTFUL
CEEIRSTU	CERUSITE	CEFLOORS	FORCLOSE
CEEIRSTV	VERTICES	CEFORSTU	FRUCTOSE

CEGHIINY	HYGIENIC		
CEGHIMNS	SCHEMING		
CEGHIRTU	THEURGIC		
CEGHNORS	GROSCHEN		
CEGIILOP	EPILOGIC		
CEGIINNT	ENTICING		
CEGIINPR	PIERCING		
CEGIINTX	EXCITING		
CEGIIOST	EGOISTIC		
CEGILNOO	NEOLOGIC		
CEGILNRY	GLYCERIN		
CEGINOOP	GEOPONIC		
CEGINOPY	PYOGENIC		
CEGINORV	COVERING		
CEGLNOTY	COGENTLY		
CEGLOOTY	CETOLOGY		
CEGMNNOO	COGNOMEN		
CEGNNPUY	PUNGENCY		
CEGNORSS	CONGRESS		
CEGORRSU	SCOURGER		
CEHIIMOS	ISOCHEIM		
CEHIIMPT	MEPHITIC		
CEHIIOPT	ETHIOPIC		
CEHIISTT	ETHICIST		
	THEISTIC		
CEHIKLSU	SUCHLIKE		
CEHIKSTT	THICKSET		
CEHILMTW	WITCH-ELM		
CEHILMTY	METHYLIC		
CEHILNOR	CHLORINE		
CEHILNSS	CHINLESS		
CEHILORT	CHLORITE		
	CLOTHIER		
CEHILPTY	PHYLETIC		
CEHIMNOW	CHOW-MEIN		
CEHIMORT	CHROMITE		
CEHINOOS	COHESION		
CEHINOPT	PHONETIC		
CEHINOPU	EUPHONIC		
CEHINRSS	RICHNESS		
CEHINRST	CHRISTEN		
CEHIORRT	RHETORIC		
CEHIPRSS	SPHERICS		
CEHIRSTY	HYSTERIC		
CEHIRTTW	TWITCHER		
CEHIRTWY	WITCHERY		
CEHISSUW	SUCHWISE		
CEHKRSTU	HUCKSTER		
CEHLNNOU	LUNCHEON		
CEHLNOTU	UNCLOTHE		
CEHMNSSU	MUCHNESS		
CEHMORUV	OVERMUCH		
CEHNNOPU	PUNCHEON		
CEHNNOSU	NONESUCH		
CEHNOORS	SCHOONER		
CEHNSTTU	CHESTNUT		
CEHOORSU	OCHREOUS		
CEHOPPRY	PROPHECY		
CEHOPSUY	CHOP-SUEY		
CEIIILSV	CIVILISE		
CEIIILVZ	CIVILIZE		

CEIIINSV	INCISIVE	CEIMSSTY	SYSTEMIC	CEMNOORR	CROMORNE
CEIIJSTU	JESUITIC	CEINNNOT	INNOCENT	CEMNOPTT	CONTEMPT
CEIIKLMR	LIMERICK	CEINNORV	CONNIVER	CEMNORSU	CONSUMER
CEIIKMMR	MIMICKER	CEINNOTU	CONTINUE	CEMOOPRS	COMPOSER
CEIIKNST	KINETICS	CEINOOTZ	ENTOZOIC	CEMOPRSS	COMPRESS
CEIILLPT	ELLIPTIC		ENZOOTIC	CEMOPRTU	COMPUTER
CEIILLSU	SILICULE	CEINOPPR	CORN-PIPE	CEMORSTU	CUSTOMER
CEIILMOT	CIMOLITE	CEINOPRS	CONSPIRE	CEMPRSTU	SPECTRUM
CEIILOPP	EPIPLOIC	CEINOPRT	INCEPTOR	CENNORRT	CORN-RENT
CEIILOTZ	ZEOLITIC	CEINOPRV	PROVINCE	CENNORTU	NOCTURNE
CEIILPTX	EXPLICIT	CEINOPTU	UNPOETIC	CENOOPST	CCOOP-NET
CEIIMORS	ISOMERIC	CEINORSS	NECROSIS	CENOORSU	CORNEOUS
CEIINNOT	NICOTINE	CEINORTT	CONTRITE	CENOORVY	CONVEYOR
CEIINOSX	EXCISION	CEINORTU	NEUROTIC	CENOQSTU	CONQUEST
CEIINOTV	EVICTION	CEINORTV	CONTRIVE	CENORSTU	CONSTRUE
CEIINRSU	INCISURE	CEINOSTT	CENTOIST	CENORSUY	CYNOSURE
	SCIURINE	CEINOTTU	TEUTONIC	CENOSSTU	COUNTESS
CEIIOPRS	IRISCOPE	CEINPRSS	PRINCESS	CENPRTUU	PUNCTURE
CEIIQRTU	CRITIQUE	CEINRTTU	TINCTURE	CENRSSTU	CURTNESS
CEIJNORT	INJECTOR	CEIOPRRU	CROUPIER	CEOOOPST	OTOSCOPE
CEIKKNRS	KNICKERS	CEIOPRSU	PRECIOUS	CEOOSTUV	COVETOUS
CEIKLRST	STICKLER	CEIOPSSU	SPECIOUS	CEOPPRST	PROSPECT
	STRICKLE	CEIORRTU	COURTIER	CEOPRSUU	CUPREOUS
CEIKNRST	STRICKEN	CEIORSTV	VORTICES	CEOQRTUY	COQUETRY
CEIKNSSS	SICKNESS	CEIORSTX	EXORCIST	CEORRSSU	CURSORES
CEIKQSTU	QUICKSET	CEIORTTU	TOREUTIC	CEORSTUY	COURTESY
CEIKRRTY	TRICKERY	CEIPRRST	RESCRIPT	CEPRSTUU	CUTPURSE
CEILLNOU	NUCLEOLI	CEIRRSTT	RESTRICT	CERSSUUX	EXCURSUS
CEILLORY	COLLIERY	CEIRSSTV	VICTRESS	CFFIRTUY	FRUCTIFY
CEILLRTU	TELLURIC	CEIRSTUY	SECURITY	CFHIIORR	HORRIFIC
CEILMMUY	MYCELIUM	CEJLOOSY	JOCOSELY	CFIIILSY	SILICIFY
CEILMNOP	COMPLINE	CEJNORRU	CONJURER	CFIILMNU	FULMINIC
CEILMNOT	MONTICLE	CEJNRTUU	JUNCTURE	CFIILOPR	PROLIFIC
CEILMOPR	COMPILER	CEKKNTUY	KENTUCKY	CFIIMNOS	SOMNIFIC
	COMPLIER	CEKLLSSU	LUCKLESS	CFIINORT	FRICTION
CEILMOSS	SOLECISM	CEKLRRTU	TRUCKLER	CFIMNOOR	CONIFORM
CEILNOOS	COLONISE	CEKNOPST	PENSTOCK	CFIMNORU	UNCIFORM
CEILNOOZ	COLONIZE	CEKOORRS	ROCK-ROSE	CFINNOTU	FUNCTION
CEILNPRY	PRINCELY	CELLNTUU	LUCULENT	CFLNORSU	SCORNFUL
CEILNRTU	LINCTURE	CELLRSUY	SCULLERY	CFNNOORT	CONFRONT
CEILNRUV	CULVERIN	CELMNOUY	UNCOMELY	CFOOORTW	CROW-FOOT
CEILOPTU	EPULOTIC	CELMPRTU	PLECTRUM	CFRSTUUU	USUFRUCT
	POULTICE	CELMPSUU	SPECULUM	CGHIILLN	CHILLING
CEILORST	CLOISTER	CELNOORS	CONSOLER	CGHIINPP	CHIPPING
CEILORTY	CRYOLITE	CELNOOSS	COOLNESS	CGHIINTW	WITCHING
CEILOSST	SOLECIST	CELNOOVV	CONVOLVE	CGHIKNOS	SHOCKING
	SOLSTICE	CELNOPUU	UNCOUPLE	CGHILNOT	CLOTHING
CEILOSSU	COULISSE	CELNORTW	CROWNLET	CGHIMPSY	SPHYGMIC
CEILOTVY	VELOCITY	CELNOSUV	CONVULSE	CGHINNOT	NOTCHING
CEILPRSU	SURPLICE	CELNOSVY	SOLVENCY	CGHINOPP	CHOPPING
CEILRRSU	SCURRILE	CELNOVXY	CONVEXLY	CGHINOTU	TOUCHING
CEIMMNNO	MNEMONIC	CELOOPSS	CESSPOOL	CGHINRSU	CRUSHING
CEIMMNOU	ENCOMIUM	CELOORTW	COLEWORT	CGHNOOSU	SOUCHONG
CEIMMORT	RECOMMIT	CELOPSUU	OPUSCULE	CGIIILNT	LIGNITIC
CEIMNORT	INTERCOM	CELORSST	CROSSLET	CGIIKLNT	TICKLING
CEIMNNSU	MENISCUS	CELORSUU	ULCEROUS	CGIIKNPR	PRICKING
CEIMOOSZ	MESOZOIC	CELORTVY	COVERTLY	CGIIKNRT	TRICKING
CEIMOPRS	COMPRISE	CELPRRSU	SCRUPLER	CGIILNPP	CLIPPING
CEIMORSX	EXORCISM	CELPRSUY	SPRUCELY	CGIILOST	LOGISTIC
CEIMORSY	ISOCRYME	CEMMNOOR	COMMONER	CGIILRTU	LITURGIC
CEIMRRTU	TURMERIC	CEMMORTU	COMMUTER	CGIIMNNO	INCOMING

CGIINOOS	ISOGONIC	CIILORST	CLITORIS	COOPRRRU	PROCUROR
CGIKLNSU	SUCKLING	CIILOSST	SCIOLIST	COOPRSUY	UROSCOPY
CGILMNUU	GLUCINUM	CIIMNOST	MONISTIC	DDDDEEOR	DODDERED
CGILNOOR	COLORING	CIIMOSST	STOICISM	DDDEIINV	DIVIDEND
CGILNOPU	COUPLING	CIINNSTT	INSTINCT	DDDEINOR	DENDROID
CGILNOSW	SCOWLING	CIINOSSS	SCISSION	DDEEEFNR	DEFENDER
CGILPSTY	GLYPTICS	CIINOTTY	TONICITY	DDEEEHNU	UNHEEDED
CGIMNNOO	GNOMONIC	CIINPSTU	SINCIPUT	DDEEELSS	DEEDLESS
	ONCOMING	CIIOPRST	PORISTIC	DDEEEMNT	DEMENTED
CGINNORW	CROWNING	CIIOQTUX	QUIXOTIC	DDEEFMOR	DEFORMED
CGINORSS	CROSSING	CIISSTTY	CYSTITIS	DDEEGOTW	TWO-EDGED
CGINORSU	COURSING	CIJNNOOT	CONJOINT	DDEEIINT	INEDITED
CGINOSTU	SCOUTING	CIJNNOTU	JUNCTION	DDEEINNT	INDENTED
CGINSTTU	TUNGSTIC	CIJOOSTY	JOCOSITY		INTENDED
CGLMOOYY	MYCOLOGY	CIKLLPUY	PLUCKILY	DDEEINRT	DENDRITE
CHHIIKST	THICKISH	CIKLNOST	LINSTOCK	DDEEIPRV	DEPRIVED
CHHIIPST	PHTHISIC	CIKMOORS	SICK-ROOM	DDEEOPRW	POWDERED
CHHILRSU	CHURLISH	CIKOSSTT	STOCKIST	DDEERRUV	VERDURED
CHHIMRTY	RHYTHMIC	CILLMNOR	CORN-MILL	DDEFNNUU	UNFUNDED
CHHNORSU	RHONCHUS	CILLMSUY	CLUMSILY	DDEGGLOY	DOGGEDLY
CHHOOPTT	HOTCHPOT	CILLNOSU	SCULLION	DDEGILMN	MEDDLING
CHIIKLST	TICKLISH	CILMNOPU	PULMONIC	DDEGILOS	DISLODGE
CHIIKRST	TRICKISH	CILMNUUV	VINCULUM	DDEGNORU	UNDERDOG
CHIILQSU	CLIQUISH	CILMOPSY	OLYMPICS	DDEGRRUY	DRUDGERY
CHIINOPS	SIPHONIC	CILNOOST	COLONIST	DDEHIISS	SIDE-DISH
CHIINORT	ORNITHIC	CILNOOTU	LOCUTION	DDEHILNY	HIDDENLY
CHIIORST	HISTORIC	CILNOPTU	PLUTONIC	DDEHINOR	DIHEDRON
CHIKMNPU	CHIPMUNK	CILNOSUY	COUSINLY	DDEHORSU	SHROUDED
CHIKMNTU	MUTCHKIN	CILOORRT	TRICOLOR	DDEIINSW	SIDE-WIND
CHILMOSU	SCHOLIUM	CILOOSSU	SCIOLOUS	DDEIIOPS	DIOPSIDE
CHILNOSW	CLOWNISH	CILOSSTY	SYSTOLIC	DDEILNPS	SPLENDID
CHILOTUY	TOUCHILY	CILOSSUU	LUSCIOUS	DDEILNRU	UNRIDDLE
CHIMMORU	CHROMIUM	CILRSTTY	STRICTLY	DDEILOPS	LOP-SIDED
CHIMNOSU	INSOMUCH	CILRSTUY	CRUSTILY	DDEINOSW	DISENDOW
CHINOPTY	HYPNOTIC	CILRSUVY	SCURVILY	DDEINOWW	WINDOWED
	PYTHONIC	CIMNOSTU	MISCOUNT	DDEIOPRS	DROPSIED
CHINOSUY	CUSHIONY	CIMOOOTZ	ZOOTOMIC	DDEIOPRV	PROVIDED
CHIOORSU	ICHOROUS	CIMOSTUY	MUCOSITY	DDEIORRS	DISORDER
CHIOPRST	STROPHIC	CINNQUUX	QUINCUNX	DDELNSUY	SUDDENLY
CHIORSTT	THROSTIC	CINOOPRS	SCORPION	DDELOOWY	WOOL-DYED
CHIOSSTT	SCOTTISH	CINOOSUV	COVINOUS	DDEMNOUU	DUODENUM
CHIPRTTY	TRIPTYCH	CINOPSTY	SYNOPTIC	DDGGINNO	DINGDONG
CHIPSSTY	PSYCHIST	CINOSTUV	VISCOUNT	DDGIILMN	MIDDLING
CHIRRSSU	SCIRRHUS	CINRSTTU	INSTRUCT	DDGILNOP	PLODDING
CHLNOOOP	COLOPHON	CINRSTUY	SCRUTINY	DDGILNPU	PUDDLING
CHLOPSTY	SPLOTCHY	CIORSSSS	SCISSORS	DDIIIIVV	DIVI-DIVI
CHLORTUY	CHOULTRY	CJNOORRU	CONJUROR	DDIIMMUY	DIDYMIUM
CIIILMPT	IMPLICIT	CKKNOPRU	PUNK-ROCK	DDIIMRSU	DRUIDISM
CIIILMSU	SILICIUM	CKKOORRW	ROCK-WORK	DDIIQTUY	QUIDDITY
CIIILSTV	CIVILIST	CKOOPSTT	STOCK-POT	DDILOOWW	WILD-WOOD
CIIILTVY	CIVILITY	CLLOOQUY	COLLOQUY	DDILORSY	SORDIDLY
CIIINNOS	INCISION	CLMMNOOY	COMMONLY	DDIMOSUY	DIDYMOUS
CIIINTVY	VICINITY	CLNOOOWY	CONY-WOOL	DDINOOOT	ODONTOID
CIIJRSTU	JURISTIC	CLOOOPRT	PROTOCOL	DDLMORSU	DOLDRUM
CIIKLPST	LIPSTICK	CLOOSSSU	COLOSSUS	DDMNOOTY	TOM-NODDY
CIIKLSST	SICK-LIST	CLOPRSTU	SCULPTOR	DEEEEMRR	REDEEMER
CIIKNPPR	PIN-PRICK	CMMNNOOU	UNCOMMON	DEEEFINR	NEEDFIRE
CIILMOPY	IMPOLICY	CMNOPSTU	CONSUMPT	DEEEFIPP	FEED-PIPE
CIILMOSS	SCIOLISM	CNOOOORT	OCTOROON	DEEEFLRX	REFLEXED
CIILMQSU	CLIQUISM	CNOSTUUU	UNCTUOUS	DEEEFNRS	FERN-SEED
CIILOPST	POLITICS	COOOPRRT	ROOT-CROP	DEEEFNRT	DEFERENT

DEEEFRRR	DEFERRER	DEEGOTUW	GOUTWEED
DEEEGIPR	PEDIGREE	DEEHHPRS	SHEPHERD
DEEEGISW	EDGEWISE	DEEHILSV	DISHEVEL
DEEEGLSS	EDGELESS	DEEHINRR	HINDERER
DEEEGLSV	SELVEDGE	DEEHIRTY	HEREDITY
DEEEGNNR	ENGENDER	DEEHNORT	DETHRONE
DEEEHLMT	HELMETED	DEEHOSUY	DYE-HOUSE
DEEEHLRW	WHEEDLER	DEEIILRV	LIVERIED
DEEEHLSS	HEEDLESS	DEEIIPRU	PRIE-DIEU
DEEEILVW	WEEVILED	DEEIIRSS	DIERESIS
DEEEINNN	NEINDEEN	DEEIINGT	GIDENITE
DEEEINTV	EVENTIDE	DEEIIRSV	DERISIVE
DEEEIPPR	REED-PIPE	DEEIISSW	SIDEWISE
DEEEIPTX	EXPEDITE	DEEIKLNN	ENKINDLE
DEEELNSS	NEEDLESS	DEEIKLNR	REKINDLE
DEEELPST	STEEPLED	DEEIKNPS	SKIN-DEEP
DEEELRTT	LETTERED	DEEILLMP	MILLEPED
DEEEMPRT	TEMPERED	DEEILMNU	DEMI-LUNE
DEEEMRST	DEEMSTER	DEEILMOS	MELODISE
DEEEENPRT	REPETEND	DEEILMOZ	MELODIZE
DEEENPSS	DEEPNESS	DEEILNOT	DELETION
DEEENRRR	RENDERER	DEEILNRU	UNDERLIE
DEEENRRV	REVEREND	DEEILNSS	!DLENESS
DEEENRTX	EXTENDER	DEEILOPT	PETIOLED
DEEERRRV	VERDERER	DEEILORT	DOLERITE
DEEERRST	DESERTER	DEEILORV	EVILDOER
DEEERRSV	RESERVED	DEEILPSY	SPEEDILY
DEEERSTX	EXSERTED	DEEILRSU	LEISURED
DEEFFNOR	OFFENDER	DEEILRVY	DELIVERY
DEEFGINR	FINGERED	DEEILSST	TIDELESS
DEEFHLOR	FREEHOLD	DEEILSUV	DELUSIVE
DEEFIINT	DEFINITE	DEEILTUY	YULE-TIDE
DEEFIIRS	FIRESIDE	DEEIMMOS	SEMI-DOME
DEEFILNX	INFLEXED	DEEIMNOR	DOMINEER
DEEFINRZ	FRENZIED	DEEIMNOS	DEMONISE
DEEFIORS	FORESIDE	DEEIMNOZ	DEMONIZE
DEEFLNTU	DEFLUENT	DEEIMNPT	PEDIMENT
DEEFLORW	DEFLOWER	DEEIMNRR	REMINDER
	FLOWERED	DEEIMNST	SEDIMENT
DEEFMORR	DEFORMER	DEEIMPRR	PERIDERM
	REFORMED	DEEINNUV	UNENVIED
DEEFMPPU	FEED-PUMP	DEEINORT	ORIENTED
DEEFNRRU	REFUNDER	DEEINOTZ	DETONIZE
DEEFNSST	DEFTNESS	DEEINPSS	DISPENSE
DEEFRTUY	DUTY-FREE	DEEINRST	INSERTED
DEEGGHHO	HEDGEHOG		RESIDENT
DEEGGLOR	DOGGEREL	DEEINRTV	INVERTED
DEEGGNOR	ENGORGED	DEEINRTX	DEXTRINE
DEEGHOPS	SHEEP-DOG	DEEINSSW	DEWINESS
DEEGHORW	HEDGEROW		WIDENESS
DEEGIINN	INDIGENE	DEEIOPRX	PEROXIDE
DEEGILNS	SEEDLING	DEEIORRV	OVERRIDE
DEEGILRY	GREEDILY	DEEIPRSS	DESPISER
DEEGIMRU	DEMIURGE		DISPERSE
DEEGINPS	SPEEDING	DEEIQRUV	QUIVERED
DEEGINRS	DESIGNER	DEEIQTUU	QUIETUDE
	RESIGNED	DEEIRRTV	VERDITER
DEEGINST	SIGNETED	DEEIRSST	EDITRESS
DEEGIRST	DIGESTER	DEEIRSSV	DISSEVER
DEEGJPRU	PREJUDGE	DEELLMOR	MODELLER
DEEGLOPS	DOG-SLEEP	DEELLOVW	VOWELLED
DEELMNOO	MELODEON
DEELMRUY	DEMURELY
DEELNORT	REDOLENT
DEELNRTY	TENDERLY
DEELNSSW	LEWDNESS
DEELORRS	SOLDERER
DEELORSV	RESOLVED
DEELORTT	DOTTEREL
DEEMOORT	ODOMETER
DEEMORTU	UDOMETER
DEEMNRRU	DEMURRER
	MURDERER
DEENNOPT	DEPONENT
DEENNOPU	UNOPENED
DEENNORW	RENOWNED
DEENNSSU	NUDENESS
DEENORRS	ENDORSER
DEENORRW	WONDERER
DEENRSSU	RUDENESS
DEENRSTU	SEDERUNT
DEENRSUV	UNVERSED
DEEOORSV	OVERDOSE
DEEORSTX	DEXTROSE
DEEPRSTU	PERTUSED
DEERRTTU	TURRETED
DEERSTUV	VESTURED
DEFFILOV	FIVEFOLD
DEFFIRSU	DIFFUSER
DEFFLRTU	TRUFFLED
DEFFSTUY	DYE-STUFF
DEFGIINY	EDIFYING
DEFHIINS	FIENDISH
DEFHIOOW	WIFEHOOD
DEFIILRW	WILDFIRE
DEFIILTY	FIDELITY
DEFIIMOR	MODIFIER
DEFIINTU	FINITUDE
DEFIINTY	IDENTIFY
DEFILMOW	DEMI-WOLF
DEFILNRY	FRIENDLY
DEFILORU	FLUORIDE
DEFILPRU	PRIDEFUL
DEFILRVY	FERVIDLY
DEFINRTT	DRIFT-NET
DEFINSTU	UNSIFTED
DEFIOORW	FIREWOOD
DEFLNORU	FLOUNDER
DEFLOOSS	FOODLESS
DEFMNORU	UNFORMED
DEFMOOOR	FOREDOOM
DEFNNOSS	FONDNESS
DEFOORRW	FOREWORD
DEGGIORS	DISGORGE
DEGGIPRS	SPRIGGED
DEGGLRUY	RUGGEDLY
DEGHILNS	SHINGLED
DEGHNORY	HYDROGEN
DEGIILNT	DILIGENT
DEGIILNY	YIELDING
DEGIILTY	GELIDITY
DEGIIMSU	MISGUIDE

DEGIINNT	INDIGENT	
DEGIISSU	DISGUISE	
DEGIJMSU	MISJUDGE	
DEGILLNU	DUELLING	
DEGILLNW	DWELLING	
DEGILMNO	GOLDMINE	
DEGILNOS	SIDELONG	
DEGILOOY	IDEOLOGY	
DEGILRZZ	GRIZZLED	
DEGINNNU	UNENDING	
DEGINNRU	ENDURING	
DEGINNTU	UNTINGED	
DEGINORV	RING-DOVE	
DEGINRSS	DRESSING	
DEGINRST	STRINGED	
DEGIOPRR	PORRIDGE	
DEGJMNTU	JUDGMENT	
DEGLMNOT	LODGMENT	
DEGLOOUU	DUOLOGUE	
DEGNOOSS	GOODNESS	
DEHIILSV	DEVILISH	
DEHIIMST	DITHEISM	
DEHIISTT	DITHEIST	
DEHIJMNO	DEMIJOHN	
DEHILMOS	DEMOLISH	
DEHILOPS	POLISHED	
DEHIMNOS	HEDONISM	
DEHINOPS	SPHENOID	
DEHINOST	HEDONIST	
DEHIOPRS	SPHEROID	
DEHIOPRT	TROPHIED	
DEHIORSS	DISHORSE	
DEHLMORY	HYDROMEL	
DEHLOPRU	UPHOLDER	
DEHLORSU	SHOULDER	
DEHLRSWY	SHREWDLY	
DEHMOORW	WHOREDOM	
DEHNORTY	THRENODY	
DEHNRTUY	THUNDERY	
DEHOPRST	POTSHERD	
DEIIISVV	DIVISIVE	
DEIILLMP	MILLIPED	
DEIILLMT	TIDE-MILL	
DEIILMRU	DELIRIUM	
DEIILNPV	VILIPEND	
DEIILNVY	DIVINELY	
DEIILORZ	IDOLIZER	
DEIINNPP	PINNIPED	
DEIINORS	DERISION	
	IRONSIDE	
DEIINOST	SEDITION	
DEIINPPW	WINDPIPE	
DEIINPRS	INSPIRED	
DEIINPRT	INTREPID	
DEIINPTU	UNPITIED	
DEIINRST	DISINTER	
DEIINSST	TIDINESS	
DEIINSTU	DISUNITE	
DEIINTTY	IDENTITY	
DEIIORXZ	OXIDIZER	
DEIIPRST	SPIRITED	
DEIIQSTU	DISQUIET	
DEIKLNRW	WRINKLED	
DEIKNNSS	KINDNESS	
DEILLOPW	PILLOWED	
DEILLSTU	DUELLIST	
DEILMNSS	MILDNESS	
	MINDLESS	
DEILMOOT	DOLOMITE	
DEILMOST	MELODIST	
DEILMOTV	DEMI-VOLT	
DEILMPPU	PLUMIPED	
DEILMPTU	MULTIPED	
DEILNNOT	INDOLENT	
DEILNNOW	DOWN-LINE	
DEILNOSU	DELUSION	
	UNSOILED	
DEILNRSW	SWINDLER	
DEILNSSW	WILDNESS	
	WINDLESS	
DEILNTTU	UNTITLED	
DEILNTUY	UNITEDLY	
DEILNUWY	UNWIELDY	
DEILORSY	SOLDIERY	
DEILOSSV	DISSOLVE	
DEILOSTU	SOLITUDE	
DEILSTUY	SEDULITY	
DEIMMNOS	DEMONISM	
DEIMMOST	IMMODEST	
DEIMNOOS	DOMINOES	
DEIMNOST	DEMONIST	
DEIMNPSS	MISSPEND	
DEIMNPTU	IMPUDENT	
DEIMNRTU	RUDIMENT	
DEIMOOST	SODOMITE	
DEIMORSU	DIMEROUS	
DEIMORUX	EXORDIUM	
DEIMRSUU	RESIDUUM	
DEINNNOU	INNUENDO	
DEINNOOT	NOONTIDE	
DEINNPRU	UNDERPIN	
DEINOOTV	DEVOTION	
DEINOPTW	DEW-POINT	
DEINORSW	WINDROSE	
DEINORVW	OVERWIND	
DEINOSSV	VOIDNESS	
DEINRRTU	INTRUDER	
DEINRSTT	STRIDENT	
DEINSTUU	UNSUITED	
DEIOPRRV	PROVIDER	
DEIOPRSV	DISPROVE	
DEIORRTU	OUTRIDER	
DEIORSSU	DESIROUS	
DEIORSTU	OUTSIDER	
DEIRSSST	DISTRESS	
DEIRSTTU	DETRITUS	
DELLNSSU	DULLNESS	
DELLOOTW	WELL-TO-DO	
DELLORRY	DROLLERY	
DELMNPUU	PENDULUM	
DELMORSU	SMOULDER	
DELMOSTY	MODESTLY	
DELNOOWY	WOODENLY	
DELNOPRS	SPLENDOR	
DELNOSSU	LOUDNESS	
DELOORRV	OVERLORD	
DELOORTY	ROOTEDLY	
DELORSSW	WORDLESS	
DELORSUY	DELUSORY	
DELOSSUU	SEDULOUS	
DELOTUVY	DEVOUTLY	
DEMOORSU	DORMOUSE	
DENOORTX	NEXT-DOOR	
DENOPRUV	UNPROVED	
DENORSTU	TONSURED	
DENORSUU	UNSOURED	
DENRRSUY	DRY-NURSE	
DEOOORSW	ROSEWOOD	
DEOOPPRT	PTEROPOD	
DEOOPRST	DOOR-STEP	
DEOPRRTU	PROTRUDE	
DEOPRSST	TOP-DRESS	
DEORSTUX	DEXTROUS	
DFFLOORU	FOURFOLD	
DFFOORUW	WOODRUFF	
DFGHILOS	GOLDFISH	
DFGIILRY	FRIGIDLY	
DFGILNNO	FONDLING	
DFGILNOO	FLOODING	
DFGKNORU	DUNG-FORK	
DFHINOPS	FISHPOND	
DFHLOOOT	FOOTHOLD	
DFIILMTU	MULTIFID	
DFIILOSY	SOLIDIFY	
DFIILTUY	FLUIDITY	
DFILLORY	FLORIDLY	
DFILLOWW	WILD-FOWL	
DFIMOOOR	IODOFORM	
DFIOOPRS	DISPROOF	
DFLOOORT	ROOD-LOFT	
DFNOOPRU	PROFOUND	
DGGGINRU	GRUDGING	
DGGIINNR	GRINDING	
DGGIRSTU	DRUGGIST	
DGHIIMNT	MIDNIGHT	
DGHILLNU	DUNGHILL	
DGHILOOR	GIRLHOOD	
DGHLORSU	GOLD-RUSH	
DGHNOTUU	DOUGH-NUT	
DGHOOOTT	DOG-TOOTH	
DGHORTUY	DROUGHTY	
DGIIIRTY	RIGIDITY	
DGIIKLNN	KINDLING	
DGIILLNR	DRILLING	
DGIILRTY	TIRGIDLY	
DGIIMNOU	GONIDIUM	
DGIINORR	GRIDIRON	
DGIINPPR	DRIPPING	
DGILLNOR	LORDLING	
DGILLOOW	GOODWILL	
DGILMNOU	MOULDING	
DGILMNPU	DUMPLING	
DGINNOSU	SOUNDING	

DGINOPPR	DROPPING	DMOOORWW	WORMWOOD	EEELMOPY	EMPLOYEE
DGINOSUY	DIGYNOUS	DNNOOTWW	DOWN-TOWN	EEELMOTT	OMELETTE
DGLOOOXY	DOXOLOGY	DNNORTUW	DOWN-TURN	EEELMRTU	MULETEER
DHHILOIW	WITHHOLD	DNOOPPRU	PROPOUND	EEELNOPV	ENVELOPE
DHIIIMNS	DIMINISH	DNOOPRSW	SNOW-DROP	EEELNRSW	NEWSREEL
DHIIMNSU	HINDUISM	DNOOPRUW	DOWNPOUR	EEELNRSY	SERENELY
DHIIMTUY	HUMIDITY	DNOORSUW	WONDROUS	EEELOPPR	REPEOPLE
DHIKNOOW	HOODWINK	DNORRSUU	SURROUND	EEELPRSS	PEERLESS
DHILLNOW	DOWNHILL	DOOOPRST	DOOR-POST	EEELRSST	TREELESS
DHILLOPY	PHYLLOID	DOOORSTU	OUTDOORS	EEELRSVY	SEVERELY
DIIILMO3Y	MODI3HLY	DOOPRRTW	DROPWORT	EEEMNNTT	TENEMENT
DHILOPRS	LORDSHIP	DOORRSUU	ORDUROUS	EEEMNORZ	MEZEREON
DHILOPSS	SLIP-SHOD	EEEEGMRR	RE-EMERGE	EEEMNSST	MEETNESS
DHILORRY	HORRIDLY	EEEEGNSV	GENEVESE	EEEMORRV	EVERMORE
DHIMNOST	HINDMOST	EEEEFFNRT	EFFERENT	EEEMRSST	SEMESTER
DHIMOOOY	OMOHYOID	EEEEFFRVW	FEVERFEW	EEENNSSV	EVENNESS
DHIOOPRZ	RHIZOPOD	EEEEFNRSS	FREENESS	EEENORVW	OVERWEEN
DHMNOOOT	HOMODONT	EEEEFRRRT	FERRETER	EEENORVY	EVERYONE
DHNOOSWW	SHOW-DOWN	EEEEGHINT	EIGHTEEN	EEENPPRS	PREPENSE
DHNORSUU	UNSHROUD	EEEEGILNV	ENVEIGLE	EEENPRRT	REPENTER
DHOOORTX	ORTHODOX	EEEEGINNR	ENGINEER	EEENPRST	PRETENSE
DIIILTVY	LIVIDITY	EEEEGINRS	ENERGISE	EEENRRST	RESENTER
DIIIMOST	IDIOTISM	EEEEGINRZ	ENERGIZE	EEENRRTV	REVERENT
DIIIMTTY	TIMIDITY	EEEEGISSX	EXEGESIS	EEEORRST	ROSE-TREE
DIIINOSV	DIVISION	EEEEGLMOS	GLEESOME	EEEORRSV	OVERSEER
DIIINTVY	DIVINITY	EEEEGMNRT	EMERGENT	EEEPPRST	PESTERER
DIIIRTVY	VIRIDITY	EEEEGMORT	GEOMETER	EEEPPRSU	REPERUSE
DIIJNOST	DISJOINT	EEEEGNRRV	REVENGER	EEEPPRSV	PERVERSE
DIILLMNW	WINDMILL	EEEEGNRRY	GREENERY		PRESERVE
DIILLQUY	LIQUIDLY	EEEHIRTZ	ETHERIZE	EEEPPRTW	PEWTERER
DIILMUUV	DILUVIUM	EEEEHLNTV	ELEVENTH	EEEPSTTT	SEPTETTE
DIILNOTU	DILUTION	EEEEHLNTY	ETHYLENE	EEEQRSUZ	SQUEEZER
DIILNOUV	DILUVION	EEEEHMNTV	VEHEMENT	EEERRSTT	RESETTER
DIILNTUY	UNTIDILY	EEEEHNNPT	NEPENTHE	EEERSTVX	VERTEXES
DIILOSTY	SOLIDITY	EEEEHNNQU	HENEQUEN	EEERSTWZ	TWEEZERS
DIIMNNOO	DOMINION	EEEEHNRVW	WHENEVER	EEESSTTT	SESTETTE
DIIMNSUU	INDUSIUM	EEEEHRRVW	WHEREVER	EEFFISUV	EFFUSIVE
DIIMOPRS	PRISMOID	EEEILLRV	REVEILLE	EEFFLNTU	EFFLUENT
DIIMPUXY	PYXIDIUM	EEEEILNPR	PELERINE	EEFFRRSU	SUFFERER
DIIMTTUY	TUMIDITY	EEEEILNST	SELENITE	EEFGIILR	FILIGREE
DIINNORS	DINORNIS	EEEEILRRV	RELIEVER	EEFGILNT	FLEETING
DIINNOSU	DISUNION	EEEILSTV	TELEVISE	EEFGINRZ	FREEZING
DIIOPRTY	PITYROID	EEEEILTVZ	TELEVIZE	EEFGLNRY	GREENFLY
DIKLNNUY	UNKINDLY	EEEEIMRTT	REMITTEE	EEFGLNUV	VENGEFUL
DILOOSUY	ODIOUSLY	EEEEINNNT	NINETEEN	EEFGNOOR	FOREGONE
DILORSWY	DROWSILY	EEEEINNSV	VIENNESE	EEFGOORR	FOREGOER
DILPSTUY	STUPIDLY	EEEEINPRT	PINE-TREE	EEFHILLR	HELL-FIRE
DILRSTUY	STURDILY	EEEEINRSS	EERINESS	EEFHIRSV	FEVERISH
DIMMNORY	MYRMIDON	EEEEINRST	ETERNISE	EEFHLLPS	SELF-HELP
DIMNOOST	MONODIST	EEEEINRTZ	ETERNIZE	EEFHLMOT	HOMEFELT
DIMNOSTU	DISMOUNT	EEEEIPRRV	REPRIEVE	EEFHORRT	THEREFOR
DIMNOSUW	UNWISDOM	EEEEIQSUX	EXEQUIES	EEFHORSW	FORESHEW
DIMORSWY	ROWDYISM	EEEEIRRTV	RETRIEVE	EEFIIKLL	LIFELIKE
DINOOSTY	NODOSITY	EEEEIRRTV	REVIEWER	EEFIIKLW	WIFELIKE
DINOPRTY	DRY-POINT	EEEJLLRW	JEWELLER	EEFIILMT	LIFETIME
DINRSTUY	INDUSTRY	EEEEKMNSS	MEEKNESS	EEFIIMNN	FEMININE
DIOSSTUU	STUDIOUS	EEEEKNNSS	KEENNESS	EEFIIMNS	FEMINISE
DIRSSTTU	DISTRUST	EEEEKNORS	KEROSENE	EEFIIMNZ	FEMINIZE
DKOOORWW	WOOD-WORK	EEELLLRV	LEVELLER	EEFIIRRV	VERIFIER
DLOOORSU	DOLOROUS	EEELLPRR	REPELLER	EEFIKNNP	PENKNIFE
DLOOPPYY	POLYPODY	EEELLRRV	REVELLER	EEFILLSS	LIFELESS

EEFILPRR	PILFERER	EEGINOST	EGESTION	EEIILLOP	EOLIPILE
EEFILRSU	FUSILEER	EEGINPSW	SWEEPING	EEIILLRV	LIVELIER
EEFIMSTU	TIME-FUSE	EEGINRRS	RESIGNER	EEIILMNT	MELINITE
EEFINNSS	FINENESS	EEGINRST	STEERING	EEIILNPP	PIPELINE
EEFINRRY	REFINERY	EEGINSSU	GENIUSES	EEIILNTV	LENITIVE
EEFINRSS	RIFENESS	EEGINSTW	SWEETING	EEIIMSSV	EMISSIVE
EEFIRRSU	SURE-FIRE	EEGINTTV	VIGNETTE	EEIINNST	NINETIES
EEFLLNSS	FELLNESS	EEGIOPSU	EPIGEOUS	EEIINPRV	VIPERINE
EEFLLORT	FORETELL	EEGIPRST	PRESTIGE	EEIINRRV	RIVERINE
EEFLLOSV	SELF-LOVE	EEGIRRST	REGISTER	EEIJLNNU	JULIENNE
EEFLLRXY	REFLEXLY	EEGIRSTT	GRISETTE	EEIJLNUV	JUVENILE
EEFLLSSS	SELFLESS	EEGLMNTU	EMULGENT	EEIKLNSS	LIKENESS
EEFLMSSU	FUMELESS	EEGLNNTU	UNGENTLE	EEIKLORT	LORIKEET
EEFLNOST	FELSTONE	EEGMMOSU	GEMMEOUS	EEIKLPST	SPIKELET
EEFLNRTU	REFLUENT	EEGMNTTU	TEGUMENT	EEIKOQUV	EQUIVOKE
EEFLNTUV	EVENTFUL	EEGMORSU	GRUESOME	EEILLPSY	SLEEPILY
EEFLORTV	LEFTOVER	EEGMORTY	GEOMETRY	EEILLSSV	VEILLESS
EEFLORTW	FLOWERET	EEGNNOSV	EVENSONG	EEILLTVY	VELLEITY
EEFLORWW	WEREWOLF	EEGNORSU	GENEROUS	EEILMNSU	SELENIUM
EEFLOSUX	FLEXUOSE	EEGNRSSY	GREYNESS	EEILMSST	TIMELESS
EEFMNORT	FOMENTER	EEGNRSUY	GUERNSEY	EEILMSUV	EMULSIVE
EEFMORRR	REFORMER	EEHHIPSS	SHEEPISH	EEILNNST	SENTINEL
EEFMPRRU	PERFUMER	EEHHIRTW	HEREWITH	EEILNOPR	LEPORINE
EEFNORST	ENFOREST	EEHILNPW	PINWHEEL	EEILNPRV	REPLEVIN
	SOFTENER	EEHILORT	HOTELIER	EEILNRSS	REINLESS
EEFNORTU	FOURTEEN	EEHIMRST	ERETHISM	EEILNRST	LISTENER
EEFNQRTU	FREQUENT		ETHERISM		RE-ENLIST
EEFNRTTU	UNFETTER	EEHINNRS	ENSHRINE	EEILNRTY	ENTIRELY
EEFOOHRT	ROOF-TREE	EEHINNRT	INHERENT		LIENTERY
EEFOPRST	POST-FREE	EEHINPRT	NEPHRITE	EEILNSSV	EVILNESS
EEFORRST	FORESTER		TREPHINE		VILENESS
	FOSTERER	EEHINRTT	THIRTEEN	EEILORRT	LOITERER
EEFORRSU	FERREOUS	EEHINRTW	WHITENER	EEILORVV	OVERLIVE
EEFORRTY	FERETORY	EEHIOPPS	HOSEPIPE	EEILPPSY	EPILEPSY
EEGGHLLS	EGG-SHELL	EEHIORST	THEORISE	EEILPRST	EPISTLER
EEGGINNR	GREENING	EEHIORTZ	THEORIZE	EEILRSST	TIRELESS
EEGGINRT	GREETING	EEHIPPTY	EPIPHYTE	EEILSSVW	VIEWLESS
EEGGORTT	GO-GETTER	EEHIPRRS	PERISHER	EEIMMORS	MEMORISE
EEGHHINT	HEIGHTEN	EEHIQRSU	QUEERISH	EEIMMORZ	MEMORIZE
EEGHIIST	EIGHTIES	EEHIRRSW	WHERRIES	EEIMMOST	SOMETIME
EEGHILTW	WHITE-LEG	EEHIRSTT	TEE-SHIRT	EEIMMSTU	SEMI-MUTE
EEGHINRS	GREENISH	EEHIRTVY	THIEVERY	EEIMNORS	EMERSION
EEGHINST	SHEETING	EEHISSTW	SWEETISH	EEIMNOST	SEMITONE
EEGHINTT	TEETHING	EEHLLPSS	HELPLESS	EEIMNOTZ	MONETIZE
EEGHISTY	EYESIGHT	EEHLMOSS	HOMELESS	EEIMNPRU	PERINEUM
EEGHLNNT	LENGTHEN	EEHLOPSS	HOPELESS	EEIMNRTU	MUTINEER
EEGHMNOY	HEGEMONY	EEHLOSSS	SHOELESS	EEIMOPRS	REIMPOSE
EEGHNSSU	HUGENESS	EEHLPRSU	SPHERULE	EEIMORST	TIRESOME
EEGHORTT	TOGETHER	EEHMNOOS	MOONSHEE	EEIMORTV	OVERTIME
EEGIILNV	INVEIGLE	EEHMOORT	RHEOTOME	EEIMPPRS	EPISPERM
EEGIINTV	GENITIVE	EEHNNORT	ENTHRONE	EEIMPRRS	SIMPERER
EEGILNPS	SLEEPING	EEHNOPRU	HEREUPON	EEIMQSTU	MESQUITE
EEGILNRR	LINGERER	EEHNOPTY	NEOPHYTE	EEIMRRTT	REMITTER
EEGILNST	STEELING	EEHNORTU	HEREUNTO		TRIMETER
EEGILOPU	EPILOGUE	EEHNPRSU	SHEEP-RUN	EEIMRSTU	EMERITUS
EEGILOSU	EULOGISE	EEHOORSV	OVERSHOE	EEIMRTTY	TEMERITY
EEGILOUZ	EULOGIZE	EEHOOTTY	EYE-TOOTH	EEINNPTT	PENITENT
EEGIMNNS	MENINGES	EEHOPPSW	PEEP-SHOW	EEINNSTT	SENTIENT
EEGIMNRT	REGIMENT	EEHORRTX	EXHORTER	EEINOPPR	PEPERINO
EEGIMNRU	MERINGUE	EEHORTTU	THEREOUT	EEINORSV	EVERSION
EEGINNSZ	SNEEZING	EEIIKLSW	LIKEWISE	EEINORTX	EXERTION

EEINPRSS	RIPENESS		TONELESS	EEORRSTX	EXTRORSE
EEINPRSU	RESUPINE	EELNSSTU	TUNELESS	EEORRTTT	TOTTERER
EEINPRTX	INEXPERT	EELNSTTU	UNSETTLE	EEORRTUV	OVERTURE
EEINRRST	REINSERT	EELOPPST	ESTOPPEL		TROUVÈRE
EEINRRSU	REINSURE	EELOPRRX	EXPLORER	EEPQRRUU	PERRUQUE
EEINRSSU	ENURESIS	EELORRSV	RESOLVER	EEPRRSSU	PRESSURE
EEINRSTT	INTEREST	EELORRTV	REVOLTER	EFFGINOR	OFFERING
EEINRSTU	ESURIENT	EELORRUV	OVERRULE	EFFHIILS	FILE-FISH
EEINRSTV	REINVEST	EELORRVV	REVOLVER	EFFHIISW	FISHWIFE
	SERVIENT	EELORSTU	RESOLUTE	EFFHIITT	FIFTIETH
EEINRSTY	SERENITY	EELORSTY	TYROLESE	EFFHILRW	WHIFFLER
EEINRSUV	UNIVERSE	EELORTTU	ROULETTE	EFFHLRSU	SHUFFLER
EEINRTTY	ENTIRETY	EELORTUV	REVOLUTE	EFFINOSU	EFFUSION
	ETERNITY		TRUELOVE	EFFIORTW	WRITE-OFF
EEINSSSW	WISENESS	EELPRTXY	EXPERTLY	EFFLMNUU	UNMUFFLE
EEINSSSX	SEXINESS	EELPSTUX	SEXTUPLE	EFFLNRSU	SNUFFLER
EEINSTTW	TWENTIES	EELRRSTW	WRESTLER	EFGHINRT	FRIGHTEN
EEINSTTX	EXISTENT	EELRSSST	RESTLESS	EFGIILNU	FIGULINE
EEIOPRRV	OVERRIPE	EELRSTWY	WESTERLY	EFGIINNR	INFRINGE
EEIOPRRW	WIRE-ROPE	EEMMNOTV	MOVEMENT	EFGIINRU	FIGURINE
EEIORRTX	EXTERIOR	EEMMOORS	MEROSOME	EFGIITUV	FUGITIVE
EEIORSVW	OVERWISE	EEMNSSTU	MUTENESS	EFGILLNO	LIFELONG
EEIORVWW	WIRE-WOVE		TENESMUS	EFGILLUU	GUILEFUL
EEIPPRRS	PERSPIRE	EEMNSTTV	VESTMENT	EFGILNTW	LEFT-WING
EEIPRSTX	PRE-EXIST	EEMOORRV	MOREOVER	EFGILPRU	FIRE-PLUG
EEIPRTUV	ERUPTIVE	EEMOOSSX	EXOSMOSE	EFGIOPTT	PETTIFOG
EEIQRRTU	REQUITER	EEMOPRRS	PREMORSE	EFGLOOVX	FOXGLOVE
EEIRRSST	RESISTER	EEMOQRSU	MORESQUE	EFGNSSUU	FUNGUSES
EEIRSTVY	SEVERITY	EEMORSST	SOMERSET	EFHIINRS	FINISHER
EEJJLNUY	JEJUNELY	EEMOTTTU	TEE-TOTUM	EFHIIPRS	FIRE-SHIP
EEJPRRRU	PERJURER	EEMRRTTU	MUTTERER	EFHIORTT	FORTIETH
EEKLLNRY	KERNELLY	EENNNOSS	NONSENSE	EFHIRRTU	THURIFER
EEKLNNNU	UNKENNEL	EENNOPSS	OPENNESS	EFHLOPST	FLESHPOT
EEKLNOST	SKELETON	EENNOPTX	EXPONENT	EFHOORSW	FORESHOW
EEKNOSTY	KEYSTONE	EENOORTV	OVERTONE	EFHRSTTU	FURTHEST
EEKOORST	KREOSOTE	EENOPPRS	PROPENSE	EFIIILRV	VILIFIER
EEKRRTUZ	KREUTZER	EENOPRSS	RESPONSE	EFIIINNT	INFINITE
EELLMPTU	PLUMELET	EENOPRTT	ENTREPOT	EFIIKRRS	FIRE-RISK
EELLNORR	ENROLLER	EENOPRXY	PYROXENE	EFIILNRT	INFILTER
EELLNSTU	ENTELLUS	EENORSSS	SORENESS	EFIILNTY	FINITELY
EELLOSSV	LOVELESS	EENORSTX	EXTENSOR	EFIIMMNS	FEMINISM
EELLRSSU	RULELESS	EENPRSST	PERTNESS	EFIIMNST	FEMINIST
EELMNOOS	LONESOME	EENPRSSU	PURENESS	EFIINORR	INFERIOR
EELMNSUY	UNSEEMLY	EENPRSTU	PURSENET	EFIINPSX	SPINIFEX
EELMNTTU	TEMULENT	EENPSSSU	SUSPENSE	EFIINSUV	INFUSIVE
EELMNTUY	UNMEETLY	EENRRTUV	VENTURER	EFIIPRRU	PURIFIER
EELMOPRY	EMPLOYER	EENRSSTU	TRUENESS	EFIIPRST	SPITFIRE
EELMORTY	REMOTELY	EENRSTUW	WET-NURSE	EFIIPRTY	TYPIFIER
EELMOSSV	MOVELESS	EEOOPRTZ	ZOETROPE	EFIIRVVY	REVIVIFY
EELMPPRU	EMPURPLE	EEOPRRRT	REPORTER	EFIKNORS	FORESKIN
EELMRSST	TERMLESS	EEOPRRRV	REPROVER	EFILLLSW	SELF-WILL
EELMRSTY	SMELTERY	EEOPRRTX	EXPORTER	EFILLRUY	IREFULLY
EELMSSST	STEMLESS		RE-EXPORT	EFILLTUY	FUTILELY
EELNNUVY	UNEVENLY	EEOPRSSU	ESPOUSER	EFILMSUY	EMULSIFY
EELNOPPU	UNPEOPLE		REPOUSSÉ	EFILNNTU	INFLUENT
EELNOPRT	PETRONEL	EEOPRSTV	OVERSTEP	EFILNORU	FLUORINE
EELNOQTU	ELOQUENT	EEOPRSUX	EXPOSURE	EFILORTU	FLUORITE
EELNORST	ENTRESOL	EEOPSSTW	SWEET-SOP	EFILPSTU	SPITEFUL
EELNOSSS	NOSELESS	EEORRRST	RESORTER	EFIMNORR	INFORMER
	SOLENESS		RESTORER		RENIFORM
EELNOSST	NOTELESS		RETRORSE	EFIMNORS	ENSIFORM

EFIMNRSS	FIRMNESS	EGHILNSV	SHELVING
EFIMORRT	RETIFORM	EGHILPRT	PLIGHTER
EFINNPSU	FINESPUN	EGHIOTUW	OUTWEIGH
EFINORRT	FRONTIER	EGHLOOOR	HOROLOGE
EFIOPRRT	PORT-FIRE	EGHLOOTY	ETHOLOGY
EFIPPRRY	FRIPPERY		THEOLOGY
EFIRRRUY	FURRIERY	EGHLOPRU	PLOUGHER
EFIRRTUY	FRUITERY	EGHNOOTY	THEOGONY
EFKLLOOR	FOLK-LORE	EGHNORUV	OVERHUNG
EFKNOORW	FOREKNOW	EGHNOTUU	HUGUENOT
EFKORRTW	FRETWORK	EGHNRSTT	STRENGTH
EFLLNSSU	FULLNESS	EGHORRTW	REGROWTH
EFLLNTUY	FLUENTLY	EGHORSTU	ROUGHEST
EFLLOORW	FOLLOWER	EGIIKKLN	KINGLIKE
EFLLOUWY	WOEFULLY	EGIILMMN	IMMINGLE
EFLLRUUY	RUEFULLY	EGIILNOR	RELIGION
EFLLSUUY	USEFULLY	EGIIMOPT	IMPETIGO
EFLMMRUY	FLUMMERY	EGIINORS	SEIGNIOR
EFLMORRY	FORMERLY	EGIINRRT	RETIRING
EFLMORSS	FORMLESS	EGIINRTU	INTRIGUE
EFLNORTT	FRONTLET	EGIINRTV	RIVETING
EFLNOSSU	FOULNESS	EGIITUXY	EXIGUITY
EFLOORSS	ROOFLESS	EGILLMNS	SMELLING
EFLOORVW	OVERFLOW	EGILLNOV	LIVELONG
EFLOPRUW	POWERFUL	EGILLNPS	SPELLING
EFLORSUY	YOURSELF	EGILLNSW	SWELLING
EFLOSUUX	FLEXUOUS	EGILLOOR	GLORIOLE
EFLPRSUU	PURSEFUL	EGILMOUU	EULOGIUM
EFLRSTUU	FRUSTULE	EGILNNST	NESTLING
EFMNRTUY	FRUMENTY	EGILNORW	LOWERING
	FURMENTY	EGILNOSU	LIGNEOUS
EFMOORST	FOREMOST	EGILNOSW	LONGWISE
EFMOORSU	FOURSOME	EGILNRST	STERLING
EFNNOOOR	FORENOON	EGILNSSU	UGLINESS
EFNQOOTT	FOOTNOTE	EGILNSSW	WINGLESS
EFNOSSST	SOFTNESS	EGILNSTT	SETTLING
EFOOORST	FOOTSORE	EGILOSTU	EULOGIST
EFOOPSTT	FOOTSTEP	EGIMNOSU	GEMINOUS
EFOORSTT	FOOT-REST	EGIMNPRU	IMPUGNER
EFORRSST	FORTRESS	EGIMNPTT	TEMPTING
EFORRSTY	FORESTRY	EGIMNRSS	GRIMNESS
EGGHIRWY	WHIGGERY	EGIMORST	ERGOTISM
EGGHRTUY	THUGGERY	EGINNORT	NITROGEN
EGGILNRY	GINGERLY	EGINNORV	VIGNERON
EGGILRRW	WRIGGLER	EGINNRRU	UNERRING
EGGJLRUY	JUGGLERY	EGINOPRY	PIGEONRY
EGGLMRSU	SMUGGLER	EGINORSY	SEIGNORY
EGGLORUY	GURGOYLE	EGINORTW	TOWERING
EGGLRSTU	STRUGGLE	EGINPRRS	SPRINGER
EGGNOOPS	EGG-SPOON	EGINPRSS	PRESSING
EGGNOOSY	GEOGNOSY	EGINRRST	STRINGER
EGGNRSUY	SNUGGERY	EGIORSUV	GRIEVOUS
EGGOORSU	GORGEOUS	EGIOSUUX	EXIGUOUS
EGHHILTY	EIGHTHLY	EGIRRSTY	REGISTRY
EGHHINSS	HIGHNESS	EGISSYYZ	SYZYGIES
EGHIILNR	HIRELING	EGLMNOOS	LONGSOME
EGHIILNS	SHEILING	EGLMNOOY	MENOLOGY
EGHIINTV	THIEVING	EGLMNSSU	GLUMNESS
EGHIIPTT	TITHE-PIG	EGLNNTUY	UNGENTLY
EGHIIRST	TIGERISH	EGLNOOOY	OENOLOGY
EGHILNSS	SHINGLES	EGLNOOPY	PENOLOGY

EGLNOSSS	SONGLESS
EGLNRTUY	URGENTLY
EGLOOPRU	PROLOGUE
EGLOOPTY	LOGOTYPE
EGMNOOOS	MONGOOSE
EGMNOOSU	MUNGOOSE
EGMNSSSU	SMUGNESS
EGNNOOTY	ONTOGENY
EGNNSSSU	SNUGNESS
EGNNSTTU	TUNGSTEN
EGNOORRV	GOVERNOR
EGNORSST	SONGSTER
EGNORSTU	STURGEON
EGOOPRRU	PROROGUE
EGOORRVW	OVERGROW
EGOPRRSS	PROGRESS
EGOPSSUY	GYPSEOUS
EHHIIPRS	HEIRSHIP
EHHIISTV	THIEVISH
EHHIOPRS	HEROSHIP
EHHIORTT	HITHERTO
EHHIOTTW	WHITE-HOT
EHHIRSSW	SHREWISH
EHHNOORS	SHOE-HORN
EHIIKLNS	HELSINKI
EHIIMPST	MEPHITIS
EHIINNOS	INHESION
EHIINSVX	VIXENISH
EHIIPRSV	VIPERISH
EHIIRSTT	THIRTIES
EHIISTTX	SIXTIETH
EHIJLSWY	JEWISHLY
EHIJOSTV	JEHOVIST
EHIKMNST	METHINKS
EHILLMOP	PHILOMEL
EHILMOOR	HEIRLOOM
EHILMOST	HELOTISM
EHILNOPT	THOLE-PIN
EHILNOSS	HOLINESS
EHILOOPZ	ZOOPHILE
EHILOPRS	POLISHER
EHILPSST	PITHLESS
EHILPSTU	SULPHITE
EHILRSTW	WHISTLER
EHIMMNUY	HYMENIUM
EHIMNOPR	MORPHINE
EHIMNPST	SHIPMENT
EHIMNRRU	MURRHINE
EHIMORST	ISOTHERM
EHIMPRRS	SHRIMPER
EHIMPSUU	EUPHUISM
EHIMRSTY	SMITHERY
EHINNSST	THINNESS
EHINNSSU	SUNSHINE
EHINOPPR	HORNPIPE
EHINOSTU	OUTSHINE
EHINPRSU	PUNISHER
EHIORSTT	THEORIST
EHIORTWZ	HOWITZER
EHIPQSUY	PHYSIQUE
EHIPRSTW	WHIPSTER

EHIRRSTT	THIRSTER
EHKMOORW	HOMEWORK
EHKNNRSU	SHRUNKEN
EHLLOOOP	LOOPHOLE
EHLMORTY	MOTHERLY
EHLNOSTY	HONESTLY
EHLOOPRT	PORT-HOLE
EHLORSTY	HOSTELRY
EHLORTTT	THROTTLE
EHLRSSTU	HURTLESS
EHLRSSTU	RUTHLESS
EHMMRRTU	THRUMMER
EHMNOOST	SMOOTHEN
EHMNOPSU	HOMESPUN
EHMOOPTY	HOMOTYPE
EHMORSTY	SMOTHERY
EHNNORRT	NORTHERN
EHNOORRU	HONOURER
EHNOORSW	WHORESON
EHNOOSSW	SNOW-SHOE
EHNORSTU	SOUTHERN
EHNRSSTU	HUNTRESS
EHOOPRTY	ORTHOEPY
EHOOPSTU	POT-HOUSE
EHOOPTYZ	ZOOPHYTE
EHOPPRSY	PROPHESY
EHOPRSUV	PUSH-OVER
EIIIMMNZ	MINIMIZE
EIIKLOPS	SPIKE-OIL
EIIKNNSS	INKINESS
EIIILLVY	LIVELILY
EIIILMNR	MILLINER
EIIILMNU	ILLUMINE
EIIILPSS	ELLIPSIS
EIIILSUV	ILLUSIVE
EIILMNNT	LINIMENT
EIILMNOT	LIMONITE
EIILMOPT	IMPOLITE
EIILMPST	SLIME-PIT
EIILMSTT	MISTITLE
EIILMSTY	MYELITIS
EIILNOSS	OILINESS
EIILNSSW	WILINESS
EIILNSTY	SENILITY
EIILNTUV	VITULINE
EIILOPPS	SOIL-PIPE
EIILOPST	PISOLITE
EIILOTVV	VOLITIVE
EIILPSST	PITILESS
EIIMMNNT	IMMINENT
EIIMMNSU	IMMUNISE
EIIMNORT	MINORITE
EIIMNOSS	EMISSION
EIIMNRSS	MIRINESS
EIIMNRST	MINISTER
EIIMNRTT	INTERMIT
EIIMNRTX	INTERMIX
EIIMOPST	OPTIMISE
EIIMOPTZ	OPTIMIZE
EIIMOSSV	OMISSIVE
EIIMPRSS	MISPRISE
EIIMPRSZ	MISPRIZE
EIIMQSTU	QUIETISM
EIINNNPS	NINEPINS
EIINOPTT	PETITION
EIINORRT	INTERIOR
EIINORSV	REVISION
EIINPRRS	INSPIRER
EIINPRST	PRISTINE
EIINPTUV	PUNITIVE
EIINQRRU	INQUIRER
EIINQTUY	INEQUITY
EIINRSST	SINISTER
EIINRSSW	WIRINESS
EIINRSTU	NEURITIS
EIIOPSTV	POSITIVE
EIIOQSTU	QUIETIST
EIJNORTU	JOINTURE
EIJNOSTT	JETTISON
EIJRSTUY	JESUITRY
EIKLLNTW	WELL-KNIT
EIKLLNUY	UNLIKELY
EIKLLORV	OVERKILL
EIKLLSSS	SKILLESS
EIKLMNOS	MOLESKIN
EIKLNPRS	SPRINKLE
EIKLNSSS	SKINLESS
EIKLSSTT	SKITTLES
EIKNOPRS	ROSE-PINK
EIKNPRTU	TURNPIKE
EILLMNOU	LINOLEUM
EILLMPSS	MISSPELL
EILLMPTU	MULTIPLE
EILLMUVX	VEXILLUM
EILLNPST	ILL-SPENT
EILLNPUU	LUPULINE
EILLNSTY	SILENTLY
EILLNSVY	SNIVELLY
EILLOPTY	POLITELY
EILLOSST	TOILLESS
EILLRSVY	SILVERLY
EILLSSST	LISTLESS
EILLSTUV	VITELLUS
EILMNOSU	EMULSION
EILMNRST	MINSTREL
EILMNSSS	SLIMNESS
EILMNSTU	MUSLINET
EILMNTUY	MINUTELY
EILMOOST	TOILSOME
EILMOPRS	SPERM-OIL
EILMPPRU	IMPURPLE
EILMPRUY	IMPURELY
EILMRSSY	REMISSLY
EILNNOST	INSOLENT
EILNNOSW	SNOW-LINE
EILNNTTY	INTENTLY
EILNOOPP	EPIPLOON
EILNOPTU	UNPOLITE
EILNOSSW	LEWISSON
EILNOSTV	NOVELIST
EILNOSUV	EVULSION
EILNOTUV	INVOLUTE
EILNPRST	SPLINTER
EILNPSUY	SUPINELY
EILNQUUY	UNIQUELY
EILNRSUU	URSULINE
EILNRTUV	VIRULENT
EILNRTWY	WINTERLY
EILNSSTT	TINTLESS
EILNSTTU	LUTENIST
EILNSUWY	UNWISELY
EILOPPTY	POLYPITE
EILOPRSU	PERILOUS
EILOPRTW	PILEWORT
EILORRTU	ULTERIOR
EILORTTY	TOILETRY
EILOSTTT	STILETTO
EILPPRSU	PERIPLUS
	SUPPLIER
EILPPRSY	SLIPPERY
EILPRSTT	SPLITTER
EILPRSTY	PRIESTLY
EILPRSUY	PLEURISY
EILPRTTY	PRETTILY
EILQRRSU	SQUIRREL
EILRSSST	STIRLESS
EILRSSTY	SISTERLY
EILRSTTW	WRISTLET
EIMMNNTU	MUNIMENT
EIMMNORS	MISNOMER
EIMMOPRU	EMPORIUM
EIMMOSTT	TOTEMISM
EIMNNOTT	OINTMENT
EIMNOOPS	EMPOISON
EIMNOPRT	ORPIMENT
EIMNOPST	NEPOTISM
EIMNOPTT	IMPOTENT
EIMNORSU	MONSIEUR
EIMNORTW	TIME-WORN
EIMNORTY	ENORMITY
EIMNPRSS	PRIMNESS
EIMNPSST	MISSPENT
EIMNRSST	TRIMNESS
EIMNRSTU	TERMINUS
EIMOORST	MOTORISE
EIMOPPRR	IMPROPER
EIMOPRRS	PRIMROSE
	PROMISER
EIMOPRRT	IMPORTER
	REIMPORT
EIMOPRRV	IMPROVER
EIMOPRST	IMPOSTER
EIMOQSTU	MISQUOTE
EIMORRWW	WIRE-WORM
EIMORSTU	MOISTURE
EIMOSSTZ	MESTIZOS
EIMOSTTU	TITMOUSE
EIMRRSSU	SURMISER
EIMRSSST	MISTRESS
EINNORSV	ENVIRONS
EINNORTV	INVENTOR
EINNORWW	WINNOWER

EINNPSSU	PUNINESS	ELMNUUZZ	UNMUZZLE	FFHILOSW	WOLF-FISH
EINNPSXY	SIXPENNY	ELMOORSY	MOROSELY	FFHOOOST	OFFSHOOT
EINNRTTU	NUTRIENT	ELNOPTTY	POTENTLY	FFIILMOR	FILIFORM
EINOOPRS	POISONER	ELNORSTU	TURNSOLE	FFILLTUY	FITFULLY
EINOPRRS	PRISONER	ELNORTTY	ROTTENLY	FFILRTUU	FRUITFUL
EINOPRSS	ROPINESS	ELNOSSSW	SLOWNESS	FFIMORSU	FUSIFORM
EINOPRSY	EPYORNIS	ELNPRTUU	PURULENT	FFLMNOOU	MOUFFLON
EINOPRTU	ERUPTION	ELOOPSSS	SESS-POOL	FGGGILNO	FLOGGING
EINOPRTW	PORT-WINE	ELOPPRRY	PROPERLY	FGGHIINT	FIGHTING
EINOPSTT	NEPOTIST	ELOPRSTY	PROSTYLE	FGGHINTU	GUNFIGHT
EINOQSTU	QUESTION	ELOPRSUV	OVERPLUS	FGHILRTU	RIGHTFUL
EINOQTTU	QUOTIENT	ELOPSSST	SPOTLESS	FGHLORUU	FURLOUGH
EINORRST	INTRORSE	ELORTTTU	TROUTLET	FGIILLNR	FRILLING
EINORSSS	ROSINESS	ELPRSTTU	SPLUTTER	FGIILNRT	TRIFLING
EINORSSU	NEUROSIS	ELRSTTUY	SLUTTERY	FGILNOOR	FLOORING
	RESINOUS	EMMMNOTU	MOMENTUM	FGILNOOT	FOOTLING
EINORSTV	INVESTOR	EMMNNOTU	MONUMENT	FGINORST	FROSTING
EINORSUV	SOUVENIR	EMMNORSU	SUMMONER	FGKLNOOS	FOLK-SONG
EINOSTVY	VENOSITY	EMMNOTTU	TOMENTUM	FGLNORUW	WRONGFUL
EINPRRST	SPRINTER	EMMNOTYY	METONYMY	FGNOORTU	UNFORGOT
EINPRRTU	PRURIENT	EMMRRRUU	MURMURER	FHHIKOOS	FISH-HOOK
EINPRSST	SPINSTER	EMMRSTYY	SYMMETRY	FHIILLTY	FILTHILY
EINQRTTU	QUIT-RENT	EMNNOOOT	MONOTONE	FHILLOOT	FOOT-HILL
EIOOPPRS	PORPOISE	EMNOORSU	ENORMOUS	FHILMPSU	LUMPFISH
EIOOPPST	OPPOSITE	EMNOOSUV	VENOMOUS	FHILMRTU	MIRTHFUL
EIOORSTT	TORTOISE	EMNORSTT	SORTMENT	FHILORSU	FLOURISH
EIOPRRSS	PRIORESS	EMNORSUU	NUMEROUS	FHILORTY	FROTHILY
EIOPRRSU	SUPERIOR	EMOOPRRT	PROMOTER	FHIMPRSU	FRUMPISH
EIOPRSTV	SPORTIVE	EMOOPRSZ	ZOOSPERM	FHINRTTU	UNTHRIFT
EIOPRSUV	PERVIOUS	EMOPPRRT	PROMPTER	FHLLOSTU	SLOTHFUL
	PREVIOUS	EMORSSTU	STRUMOSE	FHLMOTUU	MOUTHFUL
	VIPEROUS	EMOSSTTW	WESTMOST	FHLOOTTU	TOOTHFUL
EIOPRTTT	TRIPTOTE	EMPRRTUY	TRUMPERY	FHLORTUY	FOURTHLY
EIOPRTTY	PETITORY	EMPRSTTU	STRUMPET	FHLOTUUY	YOUTHFUL
EIORRRST	ERRORIST	ENNOOOTZ	ENTOZOON	FHLRTTUU	TRUTHFUL
EIORRSST	RESISTOR	ENNOOPPT	OPPONENT	FHOOOORST	FORSOOTH
EIORRSTV	SERVITOR	ENNOPTWY	TWOPENNY	FIIILNOP	FILIPINO
EIORSSTY	SEROSITY	ENNPRRUU	RUNNER-UP	FIIINNTY	INFINITY
EIORSTUV	VITREOUS	ENOOPPST	POSTPONE	FIIKLRSY	FRISKILY
EIPPRRST	STRIPPER	ENOOPRSS	POORNESS	FIILLMSY	FLIMSILY
EIPRRSSU	SURPRISE	ENOORRVW	OVERWORN	FIILMNRY	INFIRMLY
EJNSSSTU	JUSTNESS	ENORRTUU	TOURNURE	FIILMOPR	PILIFORM
EKLNOOOR	ONLOOKER	ENORRTUV	OVERTURN	FIILMPSY	SIMPLIFY
EKLNOSST	KNOTLESS		TURNOVER	FIILTTUY	FUTILITY
EKLOOORV	OVERLOOK	ENORSSSU	SOURNESS	FIIMOPRS	PISIFORM
EKMRSTUY	MUSKETRY	ENOSSSUU	SENSUOUS	FIINNOSU	INFUSION
EKNNOPSU	UNSPOKEN	EOOOPRSZ	ZOOSPORE	FIINORTU	FRUITION
EKOORRVW	OVERWORK	EOOPPRRS	PROPOSER	FIKKLNOS	KINSFOLK
EKOPRSTU	UP-STROKE	EOPPRRTY	PROPERTY	FILLLUWY	WILFULLY
ELLLNSUY	SULLENLY	EOPPRSSU	SUPPOSER	FILLNUUW	UNWILFUL
ELLMNOSY	SOLEMNLY	EOPRRSST	PORTRESS	FILORSTY	FROSTILY
ELLMOORW	WELL-ROOM	EOPRRSTU	POSTURER	FILSTTUY	STULTIFY
ELLNORWW	WELL-WORN	EOPRRUVY	PURVEYOR	FIMMNOOR	OMNIFORM
ELLNOSVY	SLOVENLY	EORRRTTU	TORTURER	FIMMORRU	MURIFORM
ELLNOUVY	UNLOVELY	EORRSSTU	TROUSERS	FIMOPRRY	PYRIFORM
ELLOPRTU	POLLUTER	EORRSUVY	SURVEYOR	FIMORTUY	FUMITORY
ELLOPRUV	PULLOVER	EORSSTTU	TUTORESS	FINORSUY	INFUSORY
ELLOSSSU	SOULLESS	EPPRSSSU	SUPPRESS	FIORTTUY	FORTUITY
ELMMNOTU	LOMENTUM	ERRSTTTU	STRUTTER	FIRTTUUY	FUTURITY
ELMMNOTY	MOMENTLY	FFGILNRU	RUFFLING	FJLLOUYY	JOYFULLY
ELMNOOSS	MOONLESS	FFGINSTU	STUFFING	FLMNORUU	MOURNFUL

FLMORSTU	STORMFUL	
FLNOOPSU	SPOONFUL	
FLOPRSTU	SPORTFUL	
FLRSTTUU	TRUSTFUL	
GGGGIILN	GIGGLING	
GGHHIISW	WHIGGISH	
GGHIILNT	LIGHTING	
GGHIIPRS	PRIGGISH	
GGHILSSU	SLUGGISH	
GGIIKLNN	KINGLING	
GGIILLNR	GRILLING	
GGIINNOR	GROINING	
GGIINNST	STINGING	
GGIINNSW	SWINGING	
GGILNORW	GROWLING	
GGINNOSS	SING-SONG	
GGINNRTU	GRUNTING	
GGINOOTU	OUTGOING	
GGINOPRU	GROUPING	
GGLLOOWY	GOLLYWOG	
GHHIOSTU	TOUGHISH	
GHHOORTU	THOROUGH	
GHIIKNNT	THINKING	
GHIIKNPS	KINGSHIP	
GHIILLNS	SHILLING	
GHIILMTY	MIGHTILY	
GHIILTTW	TWILIGHT	
GHIINPPS	SHIPPING	
GHIINPPW	WHIPPING	
GHIINRRW	WHIRRING	
GHIINRST	SHIRTING	
GHIINRTV	THRIVING	
GHIIOSTV	VISIGOTH	
GHIKLNTY	KNIGHTLY	
GHIKLSTY	SKY-LIGHT	
GHILLSTY	SLIGHTLY	
GHILNRUY	HUNGRILY	
GHILNSTU	SUNLIGHT	
GHILPRTY	TRIGLYPH	
GHIMNPTU	THUMPING	
GHIMNSTU	GUNSMITH	
GHINOOST	SHOOTING	
	SOOTHING	
GHINOSTU	SOUTHING	
GHINOSUY	YOUNGISH	
GHINSSTU	HUSTINGS	
GHIORTTU	OUTRIGHT	
GHLMOOOY	HOMOLOGY	
GHLOOORY	HOROLOGY	
GHNOSTUU	UNSOUGHT	
GHOORTUY	YOGHOURT	
GHOPRTUW	UPGROWTH	
GIIINNOT	IGNITION	
GIIINNTV	INVITING	
GIIINSTV	VISITING	
GIIJMNOS	JINGOISM	
GIIJNOST	JINGOIST	
GIIKLNNT	TINKLING	
GIIKMMNS	SKIMMING	
GIIKNNTT	KNITTING	
GIIKNPPS	SKIPPING	
GIIKNRST	STRIKING	
GIILLNQU	QUILLING	
GIILLTUY	GUILTILY	
GIILMMNS	SLIMMING	
GIILMPSU	PUGILISM	
GIILNNTW	TWINLING	
GIILNPPR	RIPPLING	
GIILNQTU	QUILTING	
GIILNRST	STIRLING	
GIILNSTU	LINGUIST	
GIILNSTY	STINGILY	
GIILPSTU	PUGILIST	
GIIMMNRT	TRIMMING	
GIIMMNSW	SWIMMING	
GIIMNNOY	IGNOMINY	
GIIMNOPS	IMPOSING	
GIIMNOTV	VOMITING	
GIINNPRT	PRINTING	
GIINNRTU	UNTIRING	
GIINPPRT	TRIPPING	
GIINPRSU	UPRISING	
GIINRRST	STIRRING	
GIJKLNOY	JOKINGLY	
GIKNNOST	KINGSTON	
GILLMOOY	GLOOMILY	
GILLNORT	TROLLING	
GILLNOVY	LOVINGLY	
GILLNPUY	PULINGLY	
GILLOSSY	GLOSSILY	
GILMNOVY	MOVINGLY	
GILMNSUY	MUSINGLY	
GILMPRUY	GRUMPILY	
GILNNRSU	NURSLING	
GILNOOSY	SINOLOGY	
GILNOTUY	OUTLYING	
GILNRSTU	LUSTRING	
GILOOORS	ROSOGLIO	
GILOOOST	OOLOGIST	
GILOORSU	GLORIOUS	
GILOOSTY	SITOLOGY	
GIMNNORU	MOURNING	
GIMNNOTU	MOUNTING	
GIMNOPTU	GUMPTION	
GIMNORRW	RINGWORM	
GINNNSTU	STUNNING	
GINNRSTU	UNSTRING	
GINOOPST	STOOPING	
GINOPPST	STOPPING	
GINOPRST	SPORTING	
GINOPSST	SIGN-POST	
GINORRWY	WORRYING	
GINPPRSU	UPSPRING	
GINRSSTU	TRUSSING	
GIOORRSU	RIGOROUS	
GIOORSTU	GOITROUS	
GIOORSUV	VIGOROUS	
GIOPRSSY	GOSSIPRY	
GIORSTUY	RUGOSITY	
GLLOOPTY	POLYGLOT	
GLMNOOOY	NOMOLOGY	
GLMOOOPY	POMOLOGY	

GLMOORWW	GLOWWORM
GLMOOYYZ	ZYMOLOGY
GLNOOOSY	NOSOLOGY
GLNOOOTY	ONTOLOGY
GLNOPYYY	POLYGYNY
GLNORSTY	STRONGLY
GLNORTUW	LUNGWORT
GLNOTTUY	GLUTTONY
GLOOPTYY	TYPOLOGY
GNNRSTUU	UNSTRUNG
GNOORJUW	WRONGOUS
GOOPPPRU	POP-GROUP
GOORTTUW	GOUTWORT
HHIINNST	THINNISH
HHIIPSST	PHTHISIS
HHOOPPRS	PHOSPHOR
HIIILMNS	NIHILISM
HIIILNST	NIHILIST
HIIILNTY	NIHILITY
HIIIMRSS	IRISHISM
HIIKMRSS	SKIRMISH
HIIKQRSU	QUIRKISH
HIIKSSTT	SKITTISH
HIILMOST	HOMILIST
HIILMTUY	HUMILITY
HIILPSSY	SYPHILIS
HIIMNSTT	TINSMITH
HIKOOPSS	SPOOKISH
HILLMSUY	MULISHLY
HILLNOUY	UNHOLILY
HILMNOOT	MONOLITH
HILOOPYZ	ZOOPHILY
HILOPPSY	POPISHLY
HILORTWY	WORTHILY
HILPPRSU	PURPLISH
HILSSTTU	SLUTTISH
HIMMOPRU	PHORMIUM
HIMNOPRX	PHORMINX
HIMNORTU	THORINUM
HIMOPRSW	SHIP-WORM
HIMORSTU	HUMORIST
HINNSSUY	SUNSHINY
HINOPSSY	HYPNOSIS
HINOPSTW	TOWNSHIP
HIPPPSUY	PUPPYISH
HKNOORRW	HORNWORK
HKOOPRSW	WORKSHOP
HLLLOOWY	HOLLOWLY
HLMOOSTY	SMOOTHLY
HLOOPPSS	SLOP-SHOP
HLPRSUUY	SULPHURY
HMMNOOYY	HOMONYMY
HMMOORSU	MUSHROOM
HMNOPSYY	SYMPHONY
HMOOORSW	SHOW-ROOM
HMOORSUU	HUMOROUS
HNOOPRST	POST-HORN
HNORTUWY	UNWORTHY
HOPPRRYY	PORPHYRY
IIILLNOS	ILLINOIS
IIILMUVX	LIXIVIUM

IIILRTVY	VIRILITY	IKLNOOSW	SKIN-WOOL
IIIMMPRS	IMPRIMIS	IKNOPSTT	STINK-POT
IIINORRS	IRRISION	IKORSTTU	OUTSKIRT
IIINPRST	INSPIRIT	ILLLMOOW	WOOL-MILL
IIINQTUY	INIQUITY	ILLLMOPS	PLIMSOLL
IIIOSTTU	OUISTITI	ILLLOOPP	LOLLIPOP
IIKLLLMS	SILK-MILL	ILLMOPRW	PILLWORM
IILLNORT	TRILLION	ILLMPTUY	MULTIPLY
IILLNOSU	ILLUSION	ILLOPPSS	SLIPSLOP
IILMOTTY	MOTILITY	ILLORSUY	ILLUSORY
IILNOOTV	VOLITION	ILMNOSUU	LUMINOUS
IIMMNTUY	IMMUNITY	ILMSSTUU	STIMULUS
IIMMOPST	OPTIMISM	ILMSTTUY	SMUTTILY
IIMMSTTU	MITTIMUS	ILNOORTW	TOIL-WORN
IIMNNOOT	MONITION	ILNOOSTU	SOLUTION
IIMNNOSU	UNIONISM	ILNOPSSW	SNOW-SLIP
IIMNNOTU	MUNITION	ILNOPSTU	UNSPOILT
IIMNOOSS	OMISSION	ILOOPPRS	PROPOLIS
IIMNOPRS	IMPRISON	ILOPPSTU	POPULIST
IIMNORTT	INTROMIT	ILOPSUUV	PLUVIOUS
IIMNORTY	MINORITY	ILRSTTUY	TRUSTILY
IIMNPRST	MISPRINT	IMNOORTY	MONITORY
IIMNPTUY	IMPUNITY	IMNOSTUU	MUTINOUS
IIMNRSTY	MINISTRY	IMOOPRST	IMPOSTOR
IIMOPSTT	OPTIMIST	IMOOQSTU	MOSQUITO
IIMORSSU	MISSOURI	IMOORSTT	MOTORIST
IIMOTTVY	MOTIVITY	IMOORSTU	TIMOROUS
IIMPRTUY	IMPURITY	IMOORTVY	VOMITORY
IIMRRTUV	TRIUMVIR	IMPPPSUY	PUPPYISM
IIMSSTUW	SWIMSUIT	IMRSSTTU	MISTRUST
IINNOPPT	PINPOINT	INNNORTU	TRUNNION
IINNOSTU	UNIONIST	INNOOPSS	SPONSION
IINOOPST	POSITION	INOOPSTT	SPITTOON
IINOSTVY	VINOSITY	INOORSTY	SONORITY
IIOOSTTY	OTIOSITY	INOPRTTU	PRINT-OUT
IIOPRRTY	PRIORITY	INOPRTUY	PUNITORY
IKLMORSW	SILK-WORM	INOPSSSY	SYNOPSIS
INPRSTTU	TURNSPIT		
IOOPRSTY	POROSITY		
IOORSSUV	VOUSSOIR		
IOORSTTU	TORTIOUS		
IOORSTUV	VIRTUOSO		
IOORSUUX	UXORIOUS		
IOPRSSUU	SPURIOUS		
IOPRSTTU	OUTSTRIP		
IORRSUVV	SURVIVOR		
IORSSUUU	USURIOUS		
IORSTUUV	VIRTUOUS		
JLNSTUUY	UNJUSTLY		
JLOOSUYY	JOYOUSLY		
KLLMNSUU	NUMSKULL		
KMOOORRW	WORKROOM		
LLOOPRYY	ROLY-POLY		
LMNOOOPY	MONOPOLY		
LMOORSWW	SLOW-WORM		
LMOOSSSU	MOLOSSUS		
LMOPPRTY	PROMPTLY		
LNOOOPRT	POLTROON		
LNOOOPYZ	POLYZOON		
LNOOPPRY	PROPYLON		
LOOPPSUU	POPULOUS		
LOOPPSUY	POLYPOUS		
LORSSTUU	LUSTROUS		
MMOOPPRU	PUMPROOM		
MNNOOOTY	MONOTONY		
MNOOOPTY	TOPONOMY		
MNOOORXY	OXYMORON		
MNORSTUU	SURMOUNT		
MOOORRTW	TOMORROW		
MORSSTUU	STRUMOUS		
NNOOOPST	SPONTOON		
NOOORSSU	SONOROUS		
NOOPSTTW	POST-TOWN		
OORSTTUU	TORTUOUS		

Nine Letter Words

AAAACCHMT	TACAMAHAC	AAADELMMR	MARMALADE	AABBORRSU	BARBAROUS
AAAACDKLY	ALACK-A-DAY	AAADHHPRZ	HAPHAZARD	AABCCEHNT	BACCHANTE
AAAACIRRU	ARAUCARIA	AAADIOPPR	PARAPODIA	AABCCELSU	ACCUSABLE
AAAACMNRT	CATAMARAN	AAADMNRTY	MANDATARY	AABCCHKKU	HUCKABACK
AAAAHHJMR	MAHARAJAH	AAAEEHMNR	MAHARANEE	AABCCHNOW	CHAW-BACON
AAAAMPRTT	PARAMATTA	AAAEGGRTV	AGGRAVATE	AABCCIKKP	PICKABACK
AAABBINRR	BARBARIAN	AAAEGILNS	ANALGESIA	AABCCIORT	ACROBATIC
AAABCCHLN	BACCHANAL	AAAEGLLLT	TALEGALLA	AABCCJKKL	BLACK-JACK
AAABCCHNR	CHARABANC	AAAEGLNNS	SALANGANE	AABCCKLLO	COAL-BLACK
AAABCHIRT	BATRACHIA	AAAEGLSSV	VASSALAGE	AABCDDEFL	BALD-FACED
AAABCLMOR	CARAMBOLA	AAAELNNTT	ANTENATAL	AABCDDORR	CARDBOARD
AAABCLMRU	AMBULACHA	AAAELPRST	PALAESTRA	AABCDEEFR	BAREFACED
AAABDELPT	ADAPTABLE	AAAENRRTT	TARTAREAN	AABCDEILL	CEBADILLA
AAABDILLS	SABADILLA	AAAFLORST	SOLFATARA	AABCDEIRR	BARRICADE
AAABEILLV	AVAILABLE	AAAFRSSSS	SASSAFRAS	AABCDEKLL	BLACK-LEAD
AAABEKRWY	BREAKAWAY	AAAGHPPRR	PARAGRAPH	AABCDEKLP	BACK-PEDAL
AAABELLPT	PALATABLE	AAAGPRSSU	ASPARAGUS	AABCDEMSU	AMBUSCADE
AAABELRST	ALABASTER	AAAHIMNRU	MARIHUANA	AABCDENNU	ABUNDANCE
AAABIPRSS	PARABASIS	AAAHKNRST	ASTRAKHAN	AABCDHILN	BALDACHIN
AAABLLPTY	PALATABLY	AAAIJMNRU	MARIJUANA	AABCDKRSW	BACKWARDS
AAACCDELV	CAVALCADE	AAAILMMMN	MAMMALIAN	AABCDLOPR	CLAPBOARD
AAACCEHIM	CACHAEMIA	AAAILMNPR	PALMARIAN	AABCDNOOR	CARBONADO
AAACCINSU	CAUCASIAN	AAAILNPPT	ANTIPAPAL	AABCDORST	BROADCAST
AAACCLMNO	CALAMANCO	AAAILNSST	ASSAILANT	AABCEEELP	PEACEABLE
AAACDHINR	ARACHNIDA	AAAILPPRS	APPRAISAL	AABCEEHLR	REACHABLE
AAACDHNRS	SANDARACH	AAAILRSTU	AUSTRALIA	AABCEEHLT	TEACHABLE
AAACDLMRU	DULCAMARA	AAAIMNNOZ	AMAZONIAN	AABCEEKNR	CANE-BRAKE
AAACDLRST	CADASTRAL	AAAIMNNST	TASMANIAN	AABCEELLR	LACERABLE
AAACEENRS	CAESAREAN	AAAIMNORT	INAMORATA	AABCEELLV	CLEAVABLE
AAACEHLNV	AVALANCHE	AAAIMNRST	SAMARITAN	AABCEELPS	ESCAPABLE
AAACEIMNT	CATAMENIA	AAAIPRSTX	PARATAXIS	AABCEELPY	PEACEABLY
AAACFILNT	FANATICAL	AAALNPSTY	ANAPLASTY	AABCEELRT	CREATABLE
AAACHLNRT	CHARLATAN	AAALNRTTU	TARANTULA		TRACEABLE
AAACHLRRT	CATARRHAL	AAAPPRSTU	APPARATUS	AABCEENRR	ABERRANCE
AAACILLMR	CAMARILLA	AABBCCIRR	BRIC-À-BRAC	AABCEERTT	BRACTEATE
AAACILNPT	APLANATIC	AABBCDKLN	BLACK-BAND	AABCEFIRT	FABRICATE
AAACILNRU	LACUNARIA	AABBCDKOR	BACKBOARD	AABCEFOSU	FABACEOUS
AAACILNST	CASTALIAN	AABBCILMS	CABBALISM	AABCEFOTU	ABOUT-FACE
	SATANICAL	AABBCILST	CABBALIST	AABCEGILR	ALGEBRAIC
AAACILRTU	ACTUARIAL	AABBCKLLL	BLACK-BALL	AABCEGKLM	BLACK-GAME
AAACINRSU	CASUARINA	AABBDEELT	DEBATABLE	AABCEGLMR	CABLEGRAM
AAACINSTT	ANASTATIC	AABBDNRSS	BRASS-BAND	AABCEGPRT	CARPET-BAG
AAACLLRSU	CLAUSALAR	AABBEEKLR	BREAKABLE	AABCEHILR	HEBRAICAL
AAACLMNPU	CAMPANULA	AABBEHILT	HABITABLE	AABCEHINR	BRANCHIAE
AAACLMPST	CATAPLASM	AABBEIILT	BILABIATE	AABCEHLMT	MATCHABLE
AAACMRTUX	TARAXACUM	AABBEIRRS	BARBARISE	AABCEILLM	CLAIMABLE
AAADDHMRY	HAMADRYAD	AABBEIRRZ	BARBARIZE	AABCEILLN	CABALLINE
AAADEFGMR	MEGAFARAD	AABBIMRRS	BARBARISM	AABCEILMR	BICAMERAL
AAADEFIST	ASAFETIDA	AABBIRRTY	BARBARITY	AABCEILNP	INCAPABLE
AAADEGNTV	ADVANTAGE	AABBIRSSU	BABIRUSSA	AABCEILRT	CALIBRATE

AABCEKPPR	PAPERBACK	AABEELLLM	MALLEABLE	AABLLLOWY	ALLOWABLY
AABCEKRTW	BACKWATER	AABEELLRT	ALTERABLE	AABLLRTUY	TABULARLY
AABCELLSS	CLASSABLE	AABEELNTU	UNEATABLE	AABLMNORY	MYROBALAN
AABCELMNU	AMBULANCE	AABEELORT	ELABORATE	AABLMORTT	ALTAR-TOMB
AABCELMOR	CARAMBOLE	AABEELPRR	REPARABLE	AABLORSST	ALBATROSS
AABCELPPR	CRAB-APPLE	AABEELPRS	SEPARABLE	AACCCHIRS	SACCHARIC
AABCELRTT	TRACTABLE	AABEELPRY	REPAYABLE	AACCDHLRU	ARCHDUCAL
AABCELRTU	TRABECULA	AABEELTTX	BATTLE-AXE	AACCDNORT	ACCORDANT
AABCELRTY	TRACEABLY	AABEEMNTT	ABATEMENT	AACCEEKMR	CREAM-CAKE
AABCENORT	CARBONATE	AABEEQRSU	ARABESQUE	AACCEELNR	CLEARANCE
AABCFHKLS	FLASH-BACK	AABEFKRST	BREAKFAST	AACCEHINR	CANE-CHAIR
AABCFLLNY	FANCY-BALL	AABEFLLMM	FLAMMABLE	AACCEHRRT	CHARACTER
AABCHHIRT	BATH-CHAIR	AABEGGINO	GABIONAGE	AACCEILMT	ACCLIMATE
AABCHILNR	BRANCHIAL	AABEGHLLU	LAUGHABLE	AACCEILNT	ANALECTIC
AABCHIMNR	BRAHMANIC	AABEGILNV	NAVIGABLE	AACCEINRR	CERCARIAN
AABCHRRUY	BRACHYURA	AABEGINRR	BARGAINER	AACCEINTV	VACCINATE
AABCIKLLM	BLACK-MAIL	AABEGIRRT	ARBITRAGE	AACCELLTU	CALCULATE
AABCILLSY	BASICALLY	AABEGKMRS	BERGAMASK	AACCELMNU	CALCANEUM
AABCILNOT	BOTANICAL	AABEGKNNT	BANK-AGENT	AACCELNTU	ACCENTUAL
AABCILOPR	PARABOLIC	AABEGLNRT	GRANTABLE	AACCERSSY	ACCESSARY
AABCILRUV	VIBRACULA	AABEGLPRS	GRASPABLE	AACCERSTU	CRUSTACEA
AABCLORSS	COAL-BRASS	AABEGNORT	ABNEGATOR	AACCHILNY	CHINA-CLAY
AABCMNOTT	COMBATANT	AABEHITTU	HABITUATE	AACCHINRS	SACCHARIN
AABDDENNO	ABANDONED	AABEHMNST	ABASHMENT	AACCHIRTT	CATHARTIC
AABDDHORS	DASH-BOARD	AABEIILLZ	LABIALIZE	AACCIILST	SCIATICAL
AABDDORRT	DART-BOARD	AABEILLNR	BALLERINA	AACCIINTT	TACTICIAN
AABDEEGLL	BALD-EAGLE	AABEILLRT	BILATERAL	AACCILLNO	LACONICAL
AABDEEILU	BEAU-IDEAL	AABEILMNU	UNAMIABLE	AACCILLSS	CLASSICAL
AABDEELMN	AMENDABLE	AABEILNRT	TRAINABLE	AACCILNNO	CANONICAL
AABDEGINR	GABARDINE	AABEILRSU	SUBAERIAL	AACCILPRT	PRACTICAL
AABDEGLRU	GUARDABLE	AABEIMNOT	ABOMINATE	AACCILSTT	STALACTIC
AABDEHNSU	UNABASHED	AABEINRST	ABSTAINER	AACCIMNOR	CARCINOMA
AABDEILLT	DILATABLE	AABEIRRTT	ARBITRATE		MACARONIC
AABDEILMR	ADMIRABLE	AABEKLNST	BEANSTALK	AACCINPTY	CAPTAINCY
AABDEILNR	DRAINABLE	AABELLLMR	ALARM-BELL	AACCINRTT	ANTARCTIC
AABDEILOV	AVOIDABLE	AABELLLOW	ALLOWABLE	AACCIOPRT	CAPACITOR
AABDEILRV	ADVERBIAL	AABELLPPR	PALPEBRAL	AACCIOPSU	CAPACIOUS
AABDEILSV	ADVISABLE	AABELMNST	STABLE-MAN	AACCIRSST	SARCASTIC
AABDELPPY	DAPPLE-BAY	AABELMNTU	UNTAMABLE	AACCLLRUY	CALCULARY
AABDEMORT	DREAMBOAT	AABELOPRV	VAPORABLE	AACCLMSTY	CATACLYSM
AABDEMRTU	ADUMBRATE	AABELORST	ASTROLABE	AACCMNOPY	ACCOMPANY
AABDGNNOW	BANDWAGON	AABELPRRY	REPARABLY	AACCOPRRS	SARCOCARP
AABDIJNOR	JABORANDI	AABELPRSY	SEPARABLY	AACCORTUY	AUTOCRACY
AABDILLST	BALLADIST	AABELRSSU	ASSURABLE	AACDDEHMR	DEAD-MARCH
AABDILMNO	ABDOMINAL	AABELRSTU	SATURABLE	AACDDEINT	CANDIDATE
AABDILMRY	ADMIRABLY	AABEMRRSS	EMBARRASS	AACDDELOP	DECAPODAL
AABDILSVY	ADVISABLY	AABEOPPRT	APPROBATE	AACDDENSU	SADDUCEAN
AABDINOST	BASTINADO	AABGHLLUY	LAUGHABLY	AACDEEFLT	DEFALCATE
AABDINSTW	WAISTBAND	AABGHOPRR	BAROGRAPH	AACDEEIMT	EMACIATED
AABDLORUY	DAY-LABOUR	AABGILNRU	BULGARIAN	AACDEEIRT	ERADICATE
AABDORRST	STARBOARD	AABGILRRT	GIBRALTAR	AACDEELRT	LACERATED
AABEEEGLR	AGREEABLE	AABHIIMNP	AMPHIBIAN	AACDEEMNS	DAMASCENE
AABEEFNST	BEAN-FEAST	AABHINRSW	BRAINWASH	AACDEEMRT	CAMERATED
AABEEGGLU	GAUGEABLE	AABIILNRR	LIBRARIAN		DEMARCATE
AABEEGLLT	BAGATELLE	AABILMOPY	AMBLYOPIA	AACDEEMST	CASEMATED
AABEEGLRY	AGREEABLY	AABILMORS	AMBROSIAL	AACDEFFIN	AFFIANCED
AABEEHLLX	EXHALABLE	AABILMPST	BAPTISMAL	AACDEFIST	FASCIATED
AABEEHLPS	SHAPEABLE	AABILNOTT	BATTALION	AACDEGLNO	DECAGONAL
AABEEHRST	TABASHEER	AABINOSTW	BOATSWAIN	AACDEGNOS	GASCONADE
AABEEILLN	ALIENABLE	AABIRRRTY	ARBITRARY	AACDEHLLN	DANCE-HALL
AABEEKLPS	SPEAKABLE	AABKLOTUW	WALKABOUT	AACDEHLRT	CATHEDRAL

AACDEILLN	DALLIANCE	AACEGNRSU	CANE-SUGAR	AACENRSSU	ASSURANCE
AACDEILLT	DIALECTAL		SUGAR-CANE	AACENRSSV	CANVASSER
AACDEILLV	CEVADILLA	AACEGORTT	GREATCOAT	AACEOOPPT	APOCOPATE
AACDEILMR	CREAM-LAID	AACEHILMO	CHOLAEMIA	AACEORTVX	EXCAVATOR
AACDEILTU	ACIDULATE	AACEHILMT	MALACHITE	AACERRTTT	ATTRACTER
AACDEINOT	DIACONATE	AACEHILNS	SELACHIAN	AACFFINRY	FANCY-FAIR
AACDEINOV	AVOIDANCE	AACEHILPT	CALIPHATE	AACFGLNRY	FLAGRANCY
AACDELMNS	CANDLEMAS		HEPATICAL	AACFGNRRY	FRAGRANCY
AACDELNOT	ANECDOTAL	AACEHIMNN	MANICHEAN	AACFIILNN	FINANCIAL
AACDELNPS	LANDSCAPE	AACEHIMNT	MACHINATE	AACFIILRT	TRIFACIAL
AACDEMNTU	MANDUCATE	AACEHINRR	RANCHERIA	AACFILNOT	FACTIONAL
AACDENNNO	CANNONADE	AACEHINRW	CHINAWARE		FALCATION
AACDENNST	ASCENDANT	AACEHIOPT	APOTHECIA	AACFILORT	FACTORIAL
AACDENORR	CARRONADE	AACEHIPTT	APATHETIC	AACFINSTT	FANTASTIC
AACDENOSS	CASSONADE	AACEHIRSY	EASY-CHAIR	AACFMNRST	CRAFTSMAN
AACDENOTU	COADUNATE	AACEHKRSV	HAVERSACK	AACGGHINN	CHAIN-GANG
AACDHINOR	ARACHNOID	AACEHMNPR	MARCHPANE	AACGHILPR	GRAPHICAL
AACDHLNRS	CRASH-LAND	AACEHNSSS	SASSENACH	AACGHIMNP	CHAMPAIGN
AACDILLRY	RADICALLY	AACEHPRTU	PARACHUTE	AACGILLMY	MAGICALLY
AACDILMNO	MONADICAL	AACEHRRTY	TRACHEARY	AACGILLOS	SCAGLIOLA
AACDILMNY	DYNAMICAL	AACEIILNT	LACINIATE	AACGILNOR	ORGANICAL
AACDILOPR	PARODICAL	AACEIINRR	CINERARIA	AACGIMMRT	GRAMMATIC
AACDIMRST	DRAMATICS	AACEIIRTV	VICARIATE	AACGIMPRT	PRAGMATIC
AACDIOSUU	AUDACIOUS	AACEIJKRT	AIR-JACKET	AACGIOSSU	SAGACIOUS
AACDIQRTU	QUADRATIC	AACEILLRV	VARICELLA	AACGLNOOT	OCTAGONAL
AACDIRSSY	DYSCRASIA	AACEILLTV	VACILLATE	AACGLNOTU	COAGULANT
AACDJNTUY	ADJUTANCY	AACEILMNP	CAMPANILE	AACGNNSTY	STAGNANCY
AACDLMORS	RASCALDOM	AACEILMPS	ECLAMPSIA	AACHIIPRS	PHARISAIC
AACDOORTV	ADVOCATOR	AACEILMTV	CALMATIVE	AACHIIRRV	CHARIVARI
AACEEEGNR	CAREENAGE	AACEILNNR	CARNELIAN	AACHILOPR	PAROCHIAL
AACEEFIRT	CAFETERIA	AACEILNPP	APPLIANCE	AACHILOPT	CHIPOLATA
AACEEGLLR	CELLARAGE	AACEILNRS	ARSENICAL	AACHILPST	ASPHALTIC
AACEEGNRR	CARRAGEEN	AACEILNRZ	CARNALIZE	AACHIMNOR	HARMONICA
AACEEHHRT	HEARTACHE	AACEIMNTU	ACUMINATE	AACHIMNRS	ANARCHISM
AACEEHLPT	CEPHALATE	AACEIMRSS	CAESARISM	AACHIMRRT	MATRIARCH
AACEEHRTX	EXARCHATE	AACEIMRST	MARCASITE	AACHIMSTT	ASTHMATIC
AACEEJLTU	EJACULATE	AACEIMSTT	MASTICATE	AACHINRST	ANARCHIST
AACEEKMPR	PACEMAKER	AACEINNRT	INCARNATE	AACHIPRRT	PATRIARCH
AACEEKRRT	CARE-TAKER	AACEINRST	ASCERTAIN	AACHIRSTT	CATHARIST
AACEELNPS	PLEASANCE		CARTESIAN	AACHLLMRY	LACHRYMAL
AACEELNRT	NECTAREAL		SECTARIAN	AACHLMNOR	MONARCHAL
AACEELPRT	PARACLETE	AACEIOSST	ASSOCIATE	AACHLMOST	STOMACHAL
AACEELRTT	ALTERCATE	AACEIPTTV	CAPTIVATE	AACHMNORW	CHAR-WOMAN
AACEENNRT	NECTAREAN	AACEIRSST	STAIRCASE	AACHMNSTY	YACHTSMAN
AACEEOPRS	AEROSPACE	AACEISTUV	CAUSATIVE	AACHNOTTY	CHATOYANT
AACEEPRSS	CASSAREEP	AACELLMNR	CELLARMAN	AACHOPPRY	APOCRYPHA
AACEFGNRR	FRAGRANCE	AACELLNOW	ALLOWANCE	AACIILMRS	RACIALISM
AACEFGORT	FACTORAGE	AACELLNPT	PLACENTAL	AACIILNST	CASTILIAN
AACEFINST	FASCINATE	AACELLSTY	CLAY-SLATE	AACIILPRT	PIRATICAL
AACEGHLNR	ARCHANGEL	AACELMSST	CLASS-MATE	AACIILRST	RACIALIST
AACEGHMNP	CHAMPAGNE	AACELNNTU	ANTELUCAN		SATIRICAL
AACEGHNOR	ANCHORAGE	AACELNRST	ANCESTRAL	AACIIMMST	MIASMATIC
AACEGHRST	GATECRASH	AACELORST	ESCALATOR	AACIIMOTX	AXIOMATIC
AACEGILLN	GALENICAL	AACELPSTU	CAPSULATE	AACIINPRT	PATRICIAN
AACEGILRT	CARTILAGE	AACELPSTY	CATALEPSY	AACIIRRTU	URTICARIA
AACEGIMNO	EGOMANIAC	AACELRTUW	CATERWAUL	AACIISTTV	ATAVISTIC
AACEGISTT	CASTIGATE	AACEMNOPR	CAMPANERO	AACILLNRY	ANCILLARY
AACEGKRWY	GRAYWACKE	AACEMNRST	SACRAMENT	AACILLPRY	CAPILLARY
AACEGLOTU	CATALOGUE	AACENNNOY	ANNOYANCE	AACILLPTY	CAPITALLY
	COAGULATE	AACENNOSS	ASSONANCE	AACILMPST	PLASMATIC
AACEGNORR	ARROGANCE	AACENORST	OSTRACEAN	AACILMRSS	RASCALISM

AACILMSSU	CASUALISM	AADEESTTV	DEVASTATE
AACILNNUV	VULCANIAN	AADEFGRSU	SAFEGUARD
AACILNOPT	PLACATION	AADEFHNOR	AFOREHAND
AACILNOTT	LACTATION	AADEFIORS	AFORESAID
AACILNPPT	APPLICANT	AADEFMPRT	AFTER-DAMP
AACILNRST	CARNALIST	AADEFMRST	FARMSTEAD
AACILNRTY	CARNALITY	AADEFRRTW	AFTERWARD
AACILOSSU	SALACIOUS	AADEFSSTT	STEADFAST
AACILPRTU	CAPITULAR	AADEGHNRY	HYDRANGEA
AACILPRTY	PARALYTIC	AADEGINRT	TRAGEDIAN
AACILQTTU	ACQUITTAL	AADEGINTV	VAGINATED
AACILRRTU	ARTICULAR	AADEGIPRS	DISPARAGE
AACILRRUU	AURICULAR	AADEGLLOP	GALLOPADE
AACILRSTY	RASCALITY	AADEGLNTU	ANGULATED
AACILSSTY	CATALYSIS	AADEGMSUU	GAUDEAMUS
AACILSTTU	ACTUALIST	AADEGNRRT	REGARDANT
AACILSTUY	CAUSALITY	AADEGRRVY	GRAVEYARD
AACILTTUY	ACTUALITY	AADEGRSTU	DATE-SUGAR
AACIMNOPR	PANORAMIC	AADEHHKNS	HANDSHAKE
AACIMNORS	MACARONIS	AADEHIMOT	HAEMATOID
AACIMORTU	AMAUROTIC	AADEHIORR	DIARRHOEA
AACIMOTTU	AUTOMATIC	AADEHIPRT	APARTHEID
AACIMRTTU	TRAUMATIC	AADEHLMNN	MANHANDLE
AACINNORT	CARNATION	AADEHLMPS	LAMPSHADE
AACINOOTV	AVOCATION	AADEHLMSY	ASHAMEDLY
AACINOPRS	CAPARISON	AADEHMMNO	MAHOMEDAN
AACINORRV	CARNIVORA	AADEHMNST	DEATHSMAN
AACINORTU	ARCUATION	AADEHMNSU	UNASHAMED
AACINOSST	CASSATION	AADEHRRTW	EARTHWARD
AACINOSTU	CAUSATION	AADEIINRT	DIETARIAN
AACINRSST	SACRISTAN	AADEIIRRT	IRRADIATE
AACIOPRSU	RAPACIOUS	AADEILLPT	DIAL-PLATE
AACIOSTTW	WAISTCOAT	AADEILMNN	ALMANDINE
AACLLNOPT	COAL-PLANT	AADEILMNT	LAMINATED
AACLLRSTU	CLAUSTRAL	AADEILMRT	DIAMETRAL
AACLNRUUV	AVUNCULAR	AADEILNNR	ADRENALIN
AACLPRSUY	SCAPULARY	AADEILNSV	VANDALISE
AACLRRTUY	CARTULARY	AADEILRTY	RADIATELY
AACMMOORS	COSMORAMA	AADEIMRST	DRAMATISE
AACMNOTTU	CATAMOUNT	AADEIMRTZ	DRAMATIZE
AACNRSTUY	SANCTUARY	AADEINRTT	ANTI-TRADE
AACORSSWY	CASSOWARY		ATTAINDER
AADDELLNS	SANDALLED	AADEIPPRS	DISAPPEAR
AADDELMNR	DREAMLAND	AADEIPRST	DISPARATE
AADDELRST	ASTRADDLE	AADEIPRTY	PAEDIATRY
AADDEMNNT	DEMANDANT	AADEKMRRT	TRADEMARK
AADDEORST	ROADSTEAD	AADELMMOR	MELODRAMA
AADDIIMRY	DAIRY-MAID	AADELMNOR	EALDORMAN
AADDIINRV	DRAVIDIAN	AADEMMNOR	MEMORANDA
AADDINPRT	DANDIPRAT	AADEMMRST	AMSTERDAM
AADDLRSTY	DASTARDLY	AADEMNPRS	AMPERSAND
AADEEFLPR	FLAP-EARED	AADEMNRST	TRADESMAN
AADEEGLMN	MAGDALENE	AADEMOQRU	AQUADROME
AADEEGNOR	ORANGEADE	AADENNPPT	APPENDANT
AADEEGNPP	APPENDAGE	AADENNTTT	ATTENDANT
AADEEHRTT	DEATH-RATE	AADENPPRS	SANDPAPER
AADEEILMV	MEDIAEVAL	AADENPRTU	PANDURATE
AADEEKMNS	DAMASKEEN	AADERRSVY	ADVERSARY
AADEELNPS	ESPLANADE	AADERSSTW	EASTWARDS
AADEEMRSU	ADMEASURE	AADFFIITV	AFFIDAVIT
AADEEPPRT	PARAPETED	AADFILNRY	FAIRY-LAND

AADFIMRRY	DAIRY-FARM
AADFMNRST	DRAFTSMAN
AADGGHLRY	HAGGARDLY
AADGHIMPR	DIAPHRAGM
AADGILORT	GLADIATOR
AADGIMORR	RADIOGRAM
AADGINORT	GRADATION
AADGLLNRU	GLANDULAR
AADGLLRUY	GRADUALLY
AADGMNRSU	GUARDSMAN
AADGORRTU	GRADUATOR
AADHINOTT	THANATOID
AADHORSUZ	HAZARDOUS
AADIIMNRY	DIMYARIAN
AADIINNRW	DARWINIAN
AADIINORT	RADIATION
AADIINRRT	IRRADIANT
AADILLMOR	ARMADILLO
AADILLMPU	PALLADIUM
AADILLOPS	SAPODILLA
AADILMNOT	DALMATION
AADILMNSV	VANDALISM
AADILMORT	MALADROIT
AADILMPRY	PYRAMIDAL
AADILMRTY	ADMIRALTY
AADILNOPT	ANTIPODAL
AADILNOTT	ANTIDOTAL
AADILNOTU	ADULATION
AADILNRTY	RADIANTLY
AADILOSVW	DISAVOWAL
AADIMNNOT	DAMNATION
AADIMRSTT	DRAMATIST
AADINOORT	ADORATION
AADINPRRT	DRAIN-TRAP
AADKLRWWY	AWKWARDLY
AADLORTUY	LAUDATORY
AADLRWWYY	WAYWARDLY
AADMMNOOR	MONODRAMA
AADMNORTY	DAMNATORY
	MANDATORY
AAEEFLOTV	FAVEOLATE
AAEEGGGRT	AGGREGATE
AAEEGHRST	GAS-HEATER
AAEEGINTV	EVAGINATE
AAEEGIRTV	VARIEGATE
AAEEGMNNS	MANGANESE
AAEEGNPRT	PARENTAGE
AAEEGNRRR	REARRANGE
AAEEGNRTU	GUARANTEE
AAEEHLRRS	REHEARSAL
AAEEHMNTU	ATHENAEUM
AAEEHMNTX	EXANTHEMA
AAEEHRTWY	THEREAWAY
AAEEIKLMU	LEUKAEMIA
AAEEILLTV	ALLEVIATE
AAEEILRTT	RETALIATE
AAEEIMNRT	REANIMATE
AAEEKLNNP	PALANKEEN
AAEEKNPTW	WAPENTAKE
AAEEKPRRT	PARRAKEET
AAEELLPPT	APPELLATE

114

AAEELMSTT	STALEMATE	
AAEELNOPR	AEROPLANE	
AAEELNRTT	ALTERNATE	
AAEELPPSX	SEX-APPEAL	
AAEEMMNTZ	AMAZEMENT	
AAEEMPRRT	PARAMETER	
AAEENRSSW	AWARENESS	
AAEENTTTU	ATTENUATE	
AAEEOPRTV	EVAPORATE	
AAEEPRRTY	RATEPAYER	
AAEFFIILT	AFFILIATE	
AAEFGHMNR	FERMANAGH	
AAEFGINRS	SEAFARING	
AAEFGIRSX	SAXIFRAGE	
AAEFHLRTX	EARTH-FLAX	
AAEFHMRTT	AFTERMATH	
AAEFILMRR	FIRE-ALARM	
AAEFILRTY	FAIRY-TALE	
AAEFINTTU	INFATUATE	
AAEFLLRTW	WATERFALL	
AAEFLNRRT	FRATERNAL	
AAEGGILLN	GALINGALE	
AAEGHLLPY	HYPALLAGE	
AAEGHLNOX	HEXAGONAL	
AAEGHLNPR	PHALANGER	
AAEGHLNPS	PHALANGES	
AAEGHMNOP	PHAENOGAM	
AAEGHNOPR	ORPHANAGE	
AAEGHNRRU	HARANGUER	
AAEGIKNNW	AWAKENING	
AAEGILNNT	GALANTINE	
AAEGILNOS	ANALOGISE	
AAEGILNOZ	ANALOGIZE	
AAEGILNPS	PELASGIAN	
AAEGILNRU	NEURALGIA	
AAEGILNSV	GALVANISE	
AAEGILNVZ	GALVANIZE	
AAEGIMMNS	MISMANAGE	
AAEGIMNNS	MAGNESIAN	
AAEGIMNNT	MANGANITE	
AAEGIMNRR	MARGARINE	
AAEGINNRT	ARGENTINA	
AAEGINRRR	ARRAIGNER	
AAEGINRSY	GAINSAYER	
AAEGIRTTV	GRAVITATE	
AAEGISTTT	SAGITTATE	
AAEGLLNRY	LARYNGEAL	
AAEGLNRTU	GRANULATE	
AAEGLPRSV	PALSGRAVE	
AAEGLRTTU	GRATULATE	
AAEGMNNOR	ORANGEMAN	
AAEGMNORT	MATRONAGE	
AAEGMNPRT	PENTAGRAM	
AAEGMNRTT	TERMAGANT	
AAEGMRSTT	STRATAGEM	
AAEGNOPRS	PARSONAGE	
AAEGNOPRT	PATRONAGE	
AAEGNPRTY	PAGEANTRY	
AAEGOPPRT	PROPAGATE	
AAEGOPRSU	AREOPAGUS	
AAEGPRSTU	PASTURAGE	

AAEHILLLU	ALLELUIAH	
AAEHILNTV	LEVIATHAN	
AAEHLNPSX	PHALANXES	
AAEHLOPPR	PHALAROPE	
AAEHMMMNR	HAMMERMAN	
AAEHMMNOT	MAHOMETAN	
AAEHNPSWW	WAPENSHAW	
AAEIILMNS	ANIMALISE	
AAEIILMNZ	ANIMALIZE	
AAEIILNRZ	ALIZARINE	
AAEIIMNNT	INANIMATE	
AAEIINSTT	INSATIATE	
AAEIKLTTV	TALKATIVE	
AAEILLMNT	ALIMENTAL	
AAEILLPPT	PAPILLATE	
AAEILLPSS	PAILLASSE	
AAEILMPRV	PRIMAEVAL	
AAEILNORT	ALIENATOR	
	RATIONALE	
AAEILNSTT	TANTALISE	
AAEILNTTZ	TANTALIZE	
AAEILPPTT	PALPITATE	
AAEILRSSW	WASSAILER	
AAEIMNNOT	EMANATION	
AAEIMNNTX	EXAMINANT	
AAEIMNOTZ	ANATOMIZE	
AAEIMNSTT	STAMINATE	
AAEIMORTZ	AROMATIZE	
AAEINPPRT	APPERTAIN	
AAEINRRTV	NARRATIVE	
AAEINRSTU	ESTUARIAN	
AAEIPPRRS	APPRAISER	
AAEIRRTTZ	TARTARIZE	
AAEISSSUV	ASSUASIVE	
AAEJKLRWY	JAYWALKER	
AAEKMRRTW	WATERMARK	
AAEKMRSTY	STAYMAKER	
AAELLLRTY	LATERALLY	
AAELLMNTY	ALLAYMENT	
AAELLMPTY	PALMATELY	
AAELLNPPT	APPELLANT	
AAELLPPRW	WALLPAPER	
AAELMMORR	MARMOREAL	
AAELMNOSU	MAUSOLEAN	
AAELNPRTY	PLANETARY	
AAELNPSTT	PANTALETS	
AAELNRSTT	TRANSLATE	
AAELNSTTU	SULTANATE	
AAELOPSTU	APETALOUS	
AAELORTTZ	LAZARETTO	
AAELPSTTU	SPATULATE	
AAELRSSTU	SALERATUS	
AAEMMNSST	AMASSMENT	
AAEMNPRTT	APARTMENT	
AAEMNSSTT	STATESMAN	
AAEMPRSTY	PAYMASTER	
AAENNTTTU	ATTENUANT	
AAENPRSTY	PEASANTRY	
AAENRRRTW	WARRANTER	
AAEOPRRST	SEPARATOR	
AAEOPRSTT	PASTORATE	

AAFFGNRSU	SUFFRAGAN	
AAFFIMNRT	AFFIRMANT	
AAFGILMNS	FALANGISM	
AAFGINRWY	WAYFARING	
AAFILLNOP	FALLOPIAN	
AAGGIMRRS	GARGARISM	
AAGGLMNOR	GLAMORGAN	
AAGHIKMNY	HAYMAKING	
AAGHILNRS	SHANGRI-LA	
AAGHINNRU	HUNGARIAN	
AAGIILLOPR	ALLOGRAPH	
AAGHOPRTU	AUTOGRAPH	
AAGIIMNNT	ANIMATING	
AAGIIMNRY	IMAGINARY	
AAGIINOTT	AGITATION	
AAGILLNPP	APPALLING	
AAGILLNTV	GALLIVANT	
AAGILLORT	ALLIGATOR	
AAGILMMNU	MAGNALIUM	
AAGILMNNT	MALIGNANT	
AAGILMNSV	GALVANISM	
AAGILMNSY	GYMNASIAL	
AAGILMNYZ	AMAZINGLY	
AAGILNOST	ANALOGIST	
	NOSTALGIA	
AAGILNRUU	INAUGURAL	
AAGILNRUV	VULGARIAN	
AAGILNSTV	GALVANIST	
AAGIMNPRT	PTARMIGAN	
AAGIMSSST	MASSAGIST	
AAGINOPRS	SPORANGIA	
AAGINORTV	NAVIGATOR	
AAGLLLNTY	GALLANTLY	
AAGLLNNTU	UNGALLANT	
AAGLLNRTY	GALLANTRY	
AAGLMMMOY	MAMMALOGY	
AAGLNOOSU	ANALOGOUS	
AAGNNNOTY	NANNY-GOAT	
AAGNNORTU	ORANG-UTAN	
AAGNORRTU	GUARANTOR	
AAHHIJPRS	RAJAHSHIP	
AAHILMTUZ	AZIMUTHAL	
AAHILORTU	AUTHORIAL	
AAHIMMNSS	SHAMANISM	
AAHIMNSTU	AMIANTHUS	
AAHIINPTTY	ANTIPATHY	
AAHLLMOSW	HALLOWMAS	
AAHLLOPTY	ALLOPATHY	
AAHLMPSTU	ASPHALTUM	
AAHMNPPRY	PARANYMPH	
AAHORTVWY	THROW-AWAY	
AAIIILMRT	MILITARIA	
AAIILMMNS	ANIMALISM	
AAIILMNTY	ANIMALITY	
AAIILMPRT	IMPARTIAL	
	PRIMATIAL	
AAIILNOSU	LOUISIANA	
AAIILRUXY	AUXILIARY	
AAIIMNNOT	ANIMATION	
AAIINNRTU	UNITARIAN	
AAIINOPRT	TOPIARIAN	

AAIINORTV	VARIATION	
AAIINOSTT	SATIATION	
AAILLMRRY	ARMILLARY	
AAILLMRSY	AMARYLLIS	
AAILLMRTY	MARTIALLY	
AAILLMRXY	MAXILLARY	
AAILLNOST	ALLANTOIS	
AAILLNTVY	VALIANTLY	
AAILLPPRY	PAPILLARY	
AAILLPRTY	PARTIALLY	
AAILLPSTY	SPATIALLY	
AAILMNPRU	MANIPULAR	
AAILMNTTU	MATUTINAL	
AAILMORSU	MALARIOUS	
AAILMPRSU	MARSUPIAL	
AAILNNOSV	SLAVONIAN	
AAILNOPPT	PALPATION	
AAILNOPSS	PASSIONAL	
AAILNOSTT	SALTATION	
	STATIONAL	
AAILNOSTV	SALVATION	
AAILNOTUV	VALUATION	
AAILNPRTU	TARPAULIN	
AAILOPRRT	RAPTORIAL	
AAILORRST	SARTORIAL	
AAILPRSSY	PARALYSIS	
AAIMMNNOO	MONOMANIA	
AAIMMNRST	MARTINMAS	
AAIMMORRY	MYRIORAMA	
AAIMNOORT	INAMORATO	
AAIMNOSTT	ANATOMIST	
AAIMNRSTT	TARANTISM	
AAIMORSSU	AMAUROSIS	
AAINNNTTU	ANNUITANT	
AAINNORRT	NARRATION	
AAINNRSTU	SATURNIAN	
AAINQRTUY	ANTIQUARY	
AAINSSSTT	ASSISTANT	
AAIOPPRRT	APPARITOR	
AALLNRTUY	NATURALLY	
AALLPRSTU	PALUSTRAL	
AALMNOOSU	ANOMALOUS	
AALMNPRTY	RAMPANTLY	
AALMORTYY	MAYORALTY	
AALNNOOPT	PANTALOON	
AALNNRTUU	UNNATURAL	
AALNOPUZZ	PUZZOLANA	
AALOPRRTY	PORTRAYAL	
AALORSTTY	SALTATORY	
AAMNOOTTU	AUTOMATON	
AAMNOPRTU	PARAMOUNT	
AAMNQRRUY	QUARRYMAN	
AANNOORTT	ANNOTATOR	
AANORRRTW	WARRANTOR	
AANORSTTU	ASTRONAUT	
AAORRSTTU	TARTAROUS	
ABBBCELLU	CLUBBABLE	
ABBCDELRY	CRABBEDLY	
ABBCDIKLR	BLACKBIRD	
ABBCEIKRT	BACKBITER	
ABBCEILLM	CLIMBABLE	

ABBCEKLNO	BONE-BLACK	
ABBCHIKRT	BATH-BRICK	
ABBCIIOSU	BIBACIOUS	
ABBCIMOST	BOMBASTIC	
ABBDEELNO	BLADE-BONE	
ABBDELLNY	BELLY-BAND	
ABBDELOTU	DOUBTABLE	
ABBDELSUU	SUBDUABLE	
ABBDHLOOT	BLOOD-BATH	
ABBDILLOR	BILLBOARD	
ABBDIMORR	BROAD-BRIM	
ABBDMNOOR	BOMBARDON	
ABBEELRRY	BLAEBERRY	
ABBEERRRY	BEAR-BERRY	
ABBEIMNOZ	BOMBAZINE	
ABBELMOOZ	BAMBOOZLE	
ABBELOSTY	STABLE-BOY	
ABBENORST	ABSORBENT	
ABBGILMNR	BRAMBLING	
ABBGILOOT	OBBLIGATO	
ABBHIOPST	ABBOTSHIP	
ABBIMNNOR	RIBBONMAN	
ABBLLOOTX	BALLOT-BOX	
ABBOOPRTY	BOOBY-TRAP	
ABCCCEFIO	BECCAFICO	
ABCCCKKLO	BLACKCOCK	
ABCCDEFHU	CHUB-FACED	
ABCCEENRU	BUCCANEER	
ABCCEINOV	BICONCAVE	
ABCCELNRU	CARBUNCLE	
ABCCEMNRU	CUMBRANCE	
ABCCFIMOR	BACCIFORM	
ABCCHHKNU	HUNCHBACK	
ABCCIIJNO	JACOBINIC	
ABCCIIJOT	JACOBITIC	
ABCCIKLRY	BRICK-CLAY	
ABCCIKRST	CRAB-STICK	
ABCCILLUY	CUBICALLY	
ABCCIRSTU	SUBARCTIC	
ABCCMOORY	MOBOCRACY	
ABCDDEEHU	DEBAUCHED	
ABCDDEEIL	DECIDABLE	
ABCDDEFLO	BOLD-FACED	
ABCDDEILU	ADDUCIBLE	
ABCDEEEHU	DEBAUCHEE	
ABCDEEHMR	CHAMBERED	
ABCDEEHRU	DEBAUCHER	
ABCDEEIKR	BRIDE-CAKE	
ABCDEEILM	MEDICABLE	
ABCDEEILR	CALIBERED	
ABCDEGIMR	CAMBRIDGE	
ABCDEHKLO	BLOCKHEAD	
ABCDEIKLS	BACKSLIDE	
ABCDEILNO	BALCONIED	
ABCDELLNO	BLOND-LACE	
ABCDENORR	BREAD-CORN	
ABCDENORS	ABSCONDER	
ABCDENOSU	SUBDEACON	
ABCDEOORT	OBCORDATE	
ABCDHIOPR	CHIPBOARD	
ABCDINOOT	BANDICOOT	

ABCDINOTU	ABDUCTION	
ABCDKOOSW	BACKWOODS	
ABCDKORSW	BACKSWORD	
ABCEEELRT	CELEBRATE	
ABCEEELRX	EXECRABLE	
ABCEEENRR	CERBEREAN	
ABCEEFIRS	BRIEFCASE	
ABCEEGKNR	GREENBACK	
ABCEEHLLY	BELLYACHE	
ABCEEHLRY	BLEACHERY	
ABCEEHMRR	CHAMBERER	
ABCEEHMST	BEECH-MAST	
ABCEEILSX	EXCISABLE	
ABCEEILTX	EXCITABLE	
ABCEEINOS	OBEISANCE	
ABCEEKKNR	BREAK-NECK	
ABCEELMNS	SEMBLANCE	
ABCEELNRT	CELEBRANT	
ABCEELNST	ALBESCENT	
ABCEELORV	REVOCABLE	
ABCEELOTV	COVETABLE	
ABCEELRSU	RESCUABLE	
	SECURABLE	
ABCEELRXY	EXECRABLY	
ABCEELSUX	EXCUSABLE	
ABCEEMORR	EMBRACEOR	
ABCEEMORT	EMBROCATE	
ABCEEMRRY	EMBRACERY	
ABCEEOSSU	SEBACEOUS	
ABCEEPRRU	CUP-BEARER	
ABCEFILRU	FEBRICULA	
ABCEFIRTU	BIFURCATE	
ABCEFOSTU	OBFUSCATE	
ABCEGILOT	COGITABLE	
ABCEHILTY	CHALYBITE	
ABCEHINOT	AITCHBONE	
ABCEHKLOS	SHOEBLACK	
ABCEHKMNR	BENCH-MARK	
ABCEHKORS	HORSEBACK	
ABCEHKRRY	HACKBERRY	
ABCEHKTUW	BUCKWHEAT	
ABCEHLNRT	BRANCHLET	
ABCEHLOTU	TOUCHABLE	
ABCEHRSTU	BUCHAREST	
ABCEIILNS	SIBILANCE	
ABCEIILRS	IRASCIBLE	
ABCEIIMRT	IMBRICATE	
ABCEIJNOT	ABJECTION	
ABCEILMOT	METABOLIC	
ABCEILORT	CABRIOLET	
ABCEILRTU	LUBRICATE	
ABCEILSTU	BISULCATE	
ABCEIMOTV	COMBATIVE	
ABCEIMRTU	BACTERIUM	
ABCEINORS	CARBONISE	
ABCEINORZ	CARBONIZE	
ABCEJNSTU	SUBJACENT	
ABCEKLNSS	BLACKNESS	
ABCEKLPRU	PARBUCKLE	
ABCELMOOR	ROCAMBOLE	
ABCELMRRS	SCRAMBLE	

ABCELNOST	CONSTABLE	ABDEEILNS	DISENABLE	ABDINRSTW	WRISTBAND
ABCELNOTU	COUNTABLE	ABDEEILRS	DESIRABLE	ABDIRSTUY	ABSURDITY
ABCELOSTT	ECTOBLAST	ABDEEILRV	DERIVABLE	ABEEEEFRT	BEEF-EATER
ABCELRSTU	SCRUTABLE	ABDEEILSV	DEVISABLE	ABEEEFKST	BEEFSTEAK
ABCELRTUU	LUCUBRATE	ABDEEITTU	BEATITUDE	ABEEEFLRR	REFERABLE
ABCELSUXY	EXCUSABLY	ABDEELLRR	BARRELLED	ABEEEFLRZ	FREEZABLE
ABCENORTY	BARONETCY	ABDEELMTT	EMBATTLED	ABEEEGLNR	GENERABLE
ABCENRRRY	CRANBERRY	ABDEELNOR	BANDEROLE	ABEEEGLRU	BELEAGUER
ABCENRTUU	BUCENTAUR		BANDOLEER	ABEEEGLRV	BEVEL-GEAR
ABCEN3OTU	SUBSTANCE	ABDEELNOT	DENOTABLE	ABEEEGLTV	VEGETABLE
ABCEOOPRS	BAROSCOPE	ABDEELNPR	PREBENDAL	ABEEEKLST	FEL-BASKET
ABCFHIKLS	BLACK-FISH	ABDEELNRU	ENDURABLE	ABEEELMPR	PERMEABLE
ABCHHIKSS	BACKSHISH	ABDEELOPS	DEPOSABLE	ABEEELNRV	VENERABLE
ABCHIILLN	CHILBLAIN	ABDEELRSS	BEARDLESS	ABEEELNRW	RENEWABLE
ABCHILNOR	BRONCHIAL	ABDEEMNRT	DEBARMENT	ABEEELRSV	SEVERABLE
ABCHKMTTU	THUMB-TACK	ABDEEMRSY	EMBER-DAYS	ABEEERRTV	VERTEBRAE
ABCIIIKLW	BAILIWICK	ABDEENRRT	BARTENDER	ABEEFFILN	INEFFABLE
ABCIIILPT	BICIPITAL	ABDEENTTU	DEBUTANTE	ABEEFILNR	INFERABLE
ABCIIKNRS	BRAIN-SICK	ABDEERRST	REDBREAST	ABEEFILRS	BAS-RELIEF
ABCIILLMU	UMBILICAL	ABDEFILNY	DEFINABLY	ABEEFLRSU	REFUSABLE
ABCIILLST	BALLISTIC	ABDEFINRR	FIRE-BRAND	ABEEFLRTU	REFUTABLE
ABCIILMOR	MICROBIAL	ABDEGIIRR	BRIGADIER	ABEEFLSSU	SELF-ABUSE
ABCIILNOS	BASILICON	ABDEHIINR	HEBRIDIAN	ABEEGHILW	WEIGHABLE
ABCIILNSY	SIBILANCY	ABDEHILNO	HOBNAILED	ABEEGHNOR	HABERGEON
ABCIILRSY	IRASCIBLY	ABDEHLOOT	BLOOD-HEAT	ABEEGILLV	LEVIGABLE
ABCIIMNOR	MICROBIAN	ABDEHLOTW	DEATH-BLOW	ABEEGKORR	BROKERAGE
ABCIINNRT	BRITANNIC	ABDEIILNU	INAUDIBLE	ABEEGLNPR	PREGNABLE
ABCIIRSTY	SYBARITIC	ABDEIKLNR	DRINKABLE	ABEEGLNPS	BESPANGLE
ABCIKLLST	BLACK-LIST	ABDEIKMRS	DISEMBARK	ABEEGLOPR	PORBEAGLE
ABCILLORU	BILOCULAR	ABDEILNNO	BANDOLINE	ABEEGNORZ	BRONZE-AGE
ABCILMSTY	CYMBALIST	ABDEILRSY	DESIRABLY	ABEEGRSTU	SUGAR-BEET
ABCILNNOU	CONNUBIAL	ABDEILRVY	DERIVABLY	ABEEHILRT	HERITABLE
ABCILNORU	BINOCULAR	ABDEIMNRS	BRIDESMAN	ABEEHIMSV	MISBEHAVE
ABCILNRTU	LUBRICANT	ABDEINOST	BASTIONED	ABEEHINRT	HIBERNATE
ABCILNRUY	INCURABLY	ABDEINRSS	RABIDNESS		INBREATHE
ABCILORRU	ORBICULAR	ABDEINSSU	UNBIASSED	ABEEHKORS	BRAKE-SHOE
ABCILORTU	TUBICOLAR	ABDEINSSW	BAWDINESS	ABEEHKOSU	BAKEHOUSE
ABCIMRSTY	CAMBISTRY	ABDEKNORW	BREAK-DOWN	ABEEHLMPS	BLASPHEME
ABCINORTU	INCUBATOR	ABDELLMOU	MOULDABLE	ABEEHLNOW	WHALEBONE
ABCINOSTY	OBSTINACY	ABDELNNSS	BLANDNESS	ABEEHNORT	BONE-EARTH
ABCKKNOST	BANK-STOCK	ABDELNOSV	BOND-SLAVE	ABEEHORTU	HEREABOUT
ABCLMORUY	COLUMBARY	ABDELNOUW	WOUNDABLE	ABEEIINRT	INEBRIATE
ABCLOSSTU	SUBCOSTAL	ABDELNRUY	ENDURABLY	ABEEILMNO	MELIBOEAN
ABCNORSTU	OBSCURANT	ABDELORUV	BOULEVARD	ABEEILMRS	MISERABLE
ABDDDEELR	BLADDERED	ABDELTTUU	TUBULATED	ABEEILMST	ESTIMABLE
ABDDEEGHI	BIG-HEADED	ABDENORRY	ERRAND-BOY	ABEEILNQU	INEQUABLE
ABDDEELLU	DELUDABLE	ABDENORSS	BROADNESS	ABEEILPRX	EXPIRABLE
ABDDEIILV	DIVIDABLE	ABDENRSTY	BY-STANDER	ABEEILQTU	EQUITABLE
ABDDEIORS	BROADSIDE	ABDEOORRV	OVERBOARD	ABEEILRSV	VERBALISE
	SIDEBOARD	ABDFOOORT	FOOT-BOARD	ABEEILRTV	AVERTIBLE
ABDDGORUY	BODY-GUARD	ABDGIILNY	ABIDINGLY		VERITABLE
ABDDNRSTU	DUST-BRAND	ABDGILNNR	BRANDLING	ABEEILRVV	REVIVABLE
ABDEEELRY	BLEAR-EYED	ABDGINOXY	BOXING-DAY	ABEEILRVZ	VERBALIZE
ABDEEFILN	DEFINABLE	ABDHIMRTY	DITHYRAMB	ABEEINRTV	BINERVATE
ABDEEGGLR	BEDRAGGLE	ABDHIOPRS	SHIPBOARD	ABEEINSST	ASBESTINE
ABDEEHLLT	DEATH-BELL	ABDHLNSUY	HUSBANDLY	ABEEIPRTZ	REBAPTIZE
ABDEEIILR	DIABLERIE	ABDHNRSUY	HUSBANDRY	ABEEIRRSS	BRASSIÈRE
ABDEEILLW	WIELDABLE	ABDIILLRS	BILLIARDS	ABEEJLNOY	ENJOYABLE
ABDEEILMS	DEMISABLE	ABDIMNNOT	BADMINTON	ABEEKLNSS	BLEAKNESS
ABDEEILMT	BEDLAMITE	ABDINNORR	BRAND-IRON	ABEELLLMT	BELL-METAL
ABDEEILNR	BREADLINE	ABDINOWWY	BAY-WINDOW		

ABEELLMSS	BLAMELESS	ABEHLMSTU	BUSH-METAL	ABEKMOORT	BOOT-MAKER
ABEELLMTU	UMBELLATE	ABEHLNOOR	HONORABLE	ABELLORTY	TOLERABLY
ABEELLORT	TOLERABLE	ABEHLORPY	HYPERBOLA	ABELMNORY	EMBRYONAL
ABEELMMOR	MEMORABLE	ABEHLORTT	BETROTHAL	ABELNNTUU	UNTUNABLE
ABEELMNRU	NUMERABLE	ABEHNORRT	ABHORRENT	ABELNRSTU	SUBALTERN
ABEELMORV	REMOVABLE		EARTH-BORN	ABELNRTTU	TURNTABLE
ABEELMPRY	PERMEABLY	ABEHNRRTU	HEARTBURN	ABELOOPPS	OPPOSABLE
ABEELMPTT	TEMPTABLE	ABEHOOSTU	BOATHOUSE	ABELOSTTY	STYLOBATE
ABEELMRSU	RESUMABLE		HOUSEBOAT	ABEMOOPRR	BROOM-RAPE
ABEELNNTU	UNTENABLE	ABEHORRRU	HARBOURER	ABEMORRTU	ARBORETUM
ABEELNQUU	UNEQUABLE	ABEIILLLR	ILLIBERAL	ABENNSTTU	SUBTENANT
ABEELNRVY	VENERABLY	ABEIILLMT	LIMITABLE	ABENORSTV	OBSERVANT
ABEELPRSU	SUPERABLE	ABEIILLRT	BILITERAL	ABEOORRSU	ARBOREOUS
ABEELPRTU	REPUTABLE	ABEIILRRT	IRRITABLE	ABEPRRRSY	RASPBERRY
ABEELRRTV	VERTEBRAL	ABEIILRTV	VIBRATILE	ABFHLLSUY	BASHFULLY
ABEELRTTU	UTTERABLE	ABEIILSST	STABILISE	ABFIIORSU	BIFARIOUS
ABEEMMNTY	EMBAYMENT	ABEIILSTZ	STABILIZE	ABFILMSUY	SUBFAMILY
ABEEMORRT	BAROMETER	ABEIINNRT	INEBRIANT	ABGHILMNS	SHAMBLING
ABEEMRRSU	EMBRASURE	ABEIIPRTT	BIPARTITE	ABGHINORR	ABHORRING
ABEENQRTU	BANQUETER	ABEIIRSSV	VIBRISSAE	ABGHIOPRY	BIOGRAPHY
ABEENQTTU	BANQUETTE	ABEIKNRRV	RIVER-BANK	ABGIILLNU	BILINGUAL
ABEENRRSY	NASEBERRY	ABEILLLRY	LIBERALLY	ABGIIMTUY	AMBIGUITY
ABEENRTUX	EXUBERANT	ABEILLPSU	PLAUSIBLE	ABGILNORU	LABOURING
ABEEOPRRT	REPROBATE	ABEILMMOV	IMMOVABLE	ABGIMOSUU	AMBIGUOUS
ABEEOSTUU	BEAUTEOUS	ABEILMMTU	IMMUTABLE	ABHIINORT	INHABITOR
ABEEPRSTT	BESPATTER	ABEILMOPS	IMPOSABLE	ABHIKMRRT	BIRTH-MARK
ABEFFILNY	INEFFABLY	ABEILMPTU	IMPUTABLE	ABHILNRTY	LABYRINTH
ABEFGILNR	FRANGIBLE	ABEILMRSV	VERBALISM	ABIIILLTY	LIABILITY
ABEFGILRU	FIGURABLE	ABEILMRSY	MISERABLY	ABIIILNTY	INABILITY
ABEFIILOT	BIFOLIATE	ABEILMSTU	SUBLIMATE	ABIIILTVY	VIABILITY
ABEFIIMRT	FIMBRIATE	ABEILMSTY	ESTIMABLY	ABIILLNRT	BRILLIANT
ABEFILTUU	BEAUTIFUL	ABEILNORS	SAILBORNE	ABIILMNNO	BINOMINAL
ABEFLLLMU	FLABELLUM	ABEILNPRT	PRINTABLE	ABIILMRST	TRIBALISM
ABEFLLLUY	BALEFULLY	ABEILNPSU	SUBALPINE	ABIILNOOT	ABOLITION
ABEFLLNUY	BANEFULLY	ABEILNRSS	BRAINLESS	ABIILNORT	LIBRATION
ABEFORRTY	FERRY-BOAT	ABEILNRSU	INSURABLE	ABIILRRTY	IRRITABLY
ABEGHINRT	BREATHING	ABEILORRT	LIBERATOR	ABIILSTTY	STABILITY
ABEGHMRRU	HAMBURGER	ABEILORTT	TRILOBATE	ABIILSTUY	SUABILITY
ABEGIILLT	LITIGABLE	ABEILPPST	BLAST-PIPE	ABIIMOSTU	AMBITIOUS
ABEGIILNT	IGNITABLE	ABEILQTUY	EQUITABLY	ABIINORTV	VIBRATION
ABEGIINOR	ABORIGINE	ABEILRSTU	BRUTALISE	ABILLNOPT	BALL-POINT
ABEGIMRRS	AMBERGRIS	ABEILRSTV	VERBALIST	ABILLPSUY	PLAUSIBLY
ABEGINNNT	BENIGNANT	ABEILRTUZ	BRUTALIZE	ABILMMOVY	IMMOVABLY
ABEGJORTU	OBJURGATE	ABEILRTVY	VERITABLY	ABILMMTUY	IMMUTABLY
ABEGJSTUU	SUBJUGATE	ABEILSUVY	ABUSIVELY	ABILNRTUZ	BRAZIL-NUT
ABEGLLLSS	BELL-GLASS	ABEILTTTT	TITTLEBAT	ABILOORSU	LABORIOUS
ABEGLRSSU	BLUE-GRASS	ABEIMNRST	TRIBESMAN	ABILORRTY	LIBRATORY
ABEGMNOOR	BOOMERANG	ABEIMNRSU	SUBMARINE	ABILRSSUY	SALISBURY
ABEHIINNR	HIBERNIAN	ABEIMPRST	REBAPTISM	ABILRSTUY	SALUBRITY
ABEHIINRT	INHABITER	ABEINNSTT	ABSTINENT	ABILRTTUY	BRUTALITY
ABEHIKLNT	THINKABLE	ABEINNTYZ	BYZANTINE	ABINOOPRT	PROBATION
ABEHILMOP	AMPHIBOLE	ABEINOSTT	OBSTINATE	ABIORRTVY	VIBRATORY
ABEHILRST	HERBALIST	ABEINPRST	BREAST-PIN	ABIRRTTUY	TRIBUTARY
ABEHILRTY	HERITABLY	ABEINRTTU	TRIBUNATE	ABKLLOOST	BOOK-STALL
ABEHILSST	ESTABLISH		TURBINATE	ABLMNORSU	SUBNORMAL
ABEHIMRRU	HERBARIUM	ABEIOPRTV	PROBATIVE	ABLNORSUU	ALBURNOUS
ABEHINRRY	ANHYBRITE	ABEIRRRST	BARRISTER	ABLNRSUUY	SUBLUNARY
ABEHIOPRU	EUPHORBIA	ABEIRTTTU	ATTRIBUTE	ABNORTTUU	ABOUT-TURN
ABEHIORUV	BEHAVIOUR	ABEKKMOOR	BOOK-MAKER	ABOOPRRTY	PROBATORY
ABEHIRRTT	BIRTHRATE	ABEKLNNSS	BLANKNESS	ACCCDEEIN	ACCIDENCE
ABEHLMPSY	BLASPHEMY	ABEKLOOPT	BOOK-PLATE	ACCCEEENS	ACESCENCE

Code	Word	Code	Word	Code	Word
ACCCEGLOY	COCCYGEAL	ACCEHKLOT	COCKLE-HAT	ACCIISSTU	CASUISTIC
ACCCHKOOR	COCKROACH	ACCEHLOOT	CHOCOLATE	ACCIKNOSW	COCKSWAIN
ACCCIIOPR	CAPRICCIO	ACCEHMNTT	CATCHMENT	ACCILLMOY	COMICALLY
ACCCNOPUY	OCCUPANCY	ACCEHORTY	THEOCRACY	ACCILLNOY	CONICALLY
ACCDDEEEN	DECADENCE	ACCEHRRST	SCRATCHER	ACCILLNYY	CYNICALLY
ACCDDEHOR	DECACHORD	ACCEIIMNT	CINEMATIC	ACCILNORV	CLAVICORN
ACCDDIIST	DIDACTICS	ACCEIINRT	CIRCINATE	ACCILOSUV	ACCLIVOUS
ACCDEEIST	DESICCATE	ACCEIIRTZ	CICATRIZE	ACCINOPRR	CAPRICORN
ACCDEFILS	FASCICLED	ACCEIISTV	SICCATIVE	ACCINOSTY	OSCITANCY
ACCDEFILY	DECALCIFY	ACCEILNTU	INCULCATE	ACCINOTVY	CONCAVITY
ACCDEGKOR	DECK-CARGO	ACCEILPST	SCEPTICAL	ACCINSTTY	SYNTACTIC
ACCDEGLNO	CLOG-DANCE	ACCEILRTU	CIRCULATE	ACCIOPRTT	CATOPTRIC
ACCDEHIKR	DECK-CHAIR	ACCEIMOSU	MICACEOUS	ACCIOSSTU	ACOUSTICS
ACCDEIILN	ICELANDIC	ACCEINORT	ACCRETION	ACCLLOSUU	CALCULOUS
ACCDEIILT	DIALECTIC	ACCEINOSS	ACCESSION	ACCLMOPTY	COMPACTLY
ACCDEINST	DESICCANT	ACCEINSTU	ENCAUSTIC	ACCLRSSUU	SUCCURSAL
ACCDEIORW	COWARDICE	ACCEINSTX	EXSICCANT	ACCMMOORS	MACROCOSM
ACCDEKOSS	CASSOCKED	ACCEIORTT	CORTICATE	ACCMNOTUY	CONTUMACY
ACCDELMOR	COLD-CREAM	ACCEKNORR	CORN-CRAKE	ACCNNOSTY	CONSTANCY
ACCDELNOY	CALCEDONY	ACCELLOOT	COLLOCATE	ACCNORSTU	CORUSCANT
ACCDEMORY	DEMOCRACY	ACCELLTUU	CUCULLATE	ACCOPRRUY	PROCURACY
ACCDFILLY	FLACCIDLY	ACCELNOPY	CYCLOPEAN	ACDDEEEIT	DEDICATEE
ACCDGINOR	ACCORDING	ACCELNOVY	CONCAVELY	ACDDEEITU	DECIDUATE
ACCDHHRUY	ARCHDUCHY	ACCELNPTY	PECCANTLY	ACDDEEORT	DECORATED
ACCDHIKLS	CLACK-DISH	ACCELPRTU	CLARET-CUP	ACDDEGNOO	DODECAGON
ACCDHORTW	CATCH-WORD	ACCENOOTV	CONVOCATE	ACDDEIORT	DEDICATOR
ACCDIIIRT	DIACRITIC	ACCENORSU	CANCEROUS	ACDDHHNSU	DACHSHUND
ACCDILLOY	CYCLOIDAL	ACCEORRSW	SCARECROW	ACDDIILOS	DISCOIDAL
ACCDINOOR	ACCORDION	ACCEORSSY	ACCESSORY	ACDDIILRU	DRUIDICAL
ACCDNOORT	CONCORDAT	ACCEORSTU	CORUSCATE	ACDDIINOT	ADDICTION
ACCEEHIST	CATECHISE	ACCFFHHIN	CHAFFINCH	ACDDINOTU	ADDUCTION
ACCEEHITZ	CATECHIZE	ACCFIILOR	CALORIFIC	ACDEEEHNR	ADHERENCE
ACCEEHKMT	CHECKMATE	ACCFIMORS	SACCIFORM	ACDEEEMRT	DECAMETRE
ACCEEHLOT	COCHLEATE	ACCFINNOU	CONFUCIAN	ACDEEEPRT	DEPRECATE
ACCEEHNPR	PERCHANCE	ACCGHLNOO	CACHOLONG	ACDEEERST	DESECRATE
ACCEEHOST	CACOETHES	ACCGIKLNR	CRACKLING	ACDEEFNTU	FECUNDATE
ACCEEIQSU	ACQUIESCE	ACCHHIILR	CHILIARCH	ACDEEGLOU	DECALOGUE
ACCEEIRTV	ACCRETIVE	ACCHHMNRU	CHURCHMAN	ACDEEGNNO	ENDECAGON
ACCEEISTX	EXSICCATE	ACCHIILRV	CHIVALRIC	ACDEEHINT	ECHINATED
ACCEEKLOR	EAR-COCKLE	ACCHIINNP	CHINCAPIN	ACDEEHKNY	HACKNEYED
ACCEELPST	SPECTACLE	ACCHILLOO	ALCOHOLIC	ACDEEHNNT	ENCHANTED
ACCEENNST	CANESCENT	ACCHILPSY	PSYCHICAL	ACDEEHRRT	CHARTERED
ACCEENORT	CONCREATE	ACCHIMNOR	MONARCHIC	ACDEEIJTV	ADJECTIVE
ACCEENRRY	RECREANCY	ACCHIMOPR	CAMPHORIC	ACDEEILMN	DEMI-LANCE
ACCEENRSU	RECUSANCE	ACCHIMORT	CHROMATIC		ENDEMICAL
ACCEEORSU	CERACEOUS	ACCHIMOST	STOMACHIC	ACDEEILMR	DECLAIMER
ACCEEOSTU	CETACEOUS	ACCHIRTTY	TRACHYTIC	ACDEEILNN	CELANDINE
ACCEFHLNU	CHANCEFUL	ACCHKLMOT	MATCHLOCK	ACDEEILNR	ICELANDER
ACCEFIIRS	SACRIFICE	ACCHKLOST	SACKCLOTH	ACDEEILNT	DECLINATE
ACCEFILSU	FASCICULE	ACCHKOOOP	COCK-A-HOOP	ACDEEILRT	DECALITRE
ACCEHHIOR	COACH-HIRE	ACCHLLOPT	CATCH-POLL	ACDEEILTU	ELUCIDATE
ACCEHILNO	COCHINEAL	ACCHLOORT	COLCOTHAR	ACDEEIMNP	IMPEDANCE
ACCEHILNT	TECHNICAL	ACCHMNOST	SCOTCHMAN	ACDEEIOPR	ADIPOCERE
ACCEHILOR	CHOLERAIC	ACCHNOOPY	CACOPHONY	ACDEEIPRT	PREDICATE
ACCEHIMNS	MECHANICS	ACCIILLSY	SALICYLIC	ACDEEISST	ECSTASIED
	MISCHANCE	ACCIILNOR	CONCILIAR	ACDEEITUV	EDUCATIVE
ACCEHIMST	CATECHISM	ACCIILOPT	OCCIPITAL	ACDEELLNV	CLEVELAND
	SCHEMATIC	ACCIILTVY	ACCLIVITY	ACDEELLOT	DECOLLATE
ACCEHINRY	CHICANERY	ACCIINOOZ	CAINOZOIC		OCELLATED
ACCEHIRTT	ARCHITECT	ACCIINRTY	INTRICACY	ACDEELNRR	CALENDRER
ACCEHISTT	CATECHIST	ACCIIOPST	PASTICCIO	ACDEELNRS	ESCLANDRE

ACDEELNTT	TENTACLED
ACDEELSTY	DECASTYLE
ACDEENNRU	ENDURANCE
ACDEENOSS	DEACONESS
ACDEEOPRR	CROP-EARED
ACDEERSTT	SCATTERED
ACDEESSTU	DECUSSATE
ACDEFFIST	DISAFFECT
ACDEFFMOR	COFFER-DAM
ACDEFIIIL	EDIFICIAL
ACDEFIILT	FETICIDAL
ACDEFILLO	COAL-FIELD
ACDEFKLNO	FOLK-DANCE
ACDEGGIMO	DEMAGOGIC
ACDEGGIOP	PEDAGOGIC
ACDEGHIRS	DISCHARGE
ACDEGIILR	REGICIDAL
ACDEGIRRS	DISGRACER
ACDEGIRRT	CARTRIDGE
ACDEHHIKT	THICKHEAD
ACDEHHORX	HEXACHORD
ACDEHIITT	DIATHETIC
ACDEHINNR	HINDRANCE
ACDEHINRT	THEANDRIC
ACDEHIPRT	DIRT-CHEAP
ACDEHIPST	CADETSHIP
ACDEHKMOP	CHOKE-DAMP
ACDEHLNOT	DECATHLON
ACDEHLNRY	CHANDLERY
ACDEHMNTU	UNMATCHED
ACDEHMPRY	PACHYDERM
ACDEHNSTU	UNSCATHED
ACDEHNTUW	UNWATCHED
ACDEHORSS	CROSS-HEAD
ACDEIIINT	DIETICIAN
ACDEIILMN	ADMINICLE
	MEDICINAL
ACDEIILNT	IDENTICAL
ACDEIILNX	INDEXICAL
ACDEIILRV	VERIDICAL
ACDEIIMMY	IMMEDIACY
ACDEIIMRT	DIAMETRIC
	MATRICIDE
ACDEIINOT	DIANOETIC
ACDEIINTV	VINDICATE
ACDEIIPRR	PARRICIDE
ACDEIIPRT	PATRICIDE
ACDEILLMY	DECIMALLY
	MEDICALLY
ACDEILOST	DISLOCATE
ACDEILPRU	PEDICULAR
ACDEILPTU	DUPLICATE
ACDEIMNNO	DOMINANCE
ACDEIMNNT	MENDICANT
ACDEIMNSU	MUSCADINE
ACDEIMNTY	MENDACITY
ACDEIMORT	DECIMATOR
ACDEIMRTU	MURICATED
ACDEINNOR	ORDINANCE
ACDEINORR	CORIANDER
ACDEINORS	DINOCERAS

ACDEINORT	REDACTION
ACDEINOTU	EDUCATION
ACDEINPRT	PREDICANT
ACDEINSTY	ASYNDETIC
	SYNDICATE
ACDEINTTU	TUNICATED
ACDEIPRST	PRACTISED
ACDEIPSTU	CUSPIDATE
ACDEIRSTY	DICASTERY
ACDEIRTTU	DICTATURE
ACDEKNRTU	UNTRACKED
ACDELLOPS	SCALLOPED
ACDELNNOO	COLONNADE
ACDELNNTU	CANDLE-NUT
ACDELPRSY	CLEPSYDRA
ACDEMMMNO	COMMENDAM
ACDEMMNOR	COMMANDER
ACDEMOORT	MOTORCADE
ACDENNRST	TRANSCEND
ACDENOOTT	COTTONADE
ACDENORSY	SECONDARY
ACDENRRTU	TRUNCATED
ACDEOORRT	DECORATOR
ACDEOORTT	DOCTORATE
ACDEOPRRT	CARPET-ROD
ACDEORRTT	DETRACTOR
ACDEORSST	DRESS-COAT
ACDEORSTU	CERATODUS
ACDFIIRUY	FIDUCIARY
ACDFINNOT	CONFIDANT
ACDFNTTUY	CANDYTUFT
ACDFOORTW	WOODCRAFT
ACDGHIMOY	DICHOGAMY
ACDGIMOST	DOGMATICS
ACDGLLOOR	DOG-COLLAR
ACDHIILMO	HOMICIDAL
ACDHILMUY	DIACHYLUM
ACDHILNOY	DIACHYLON
ACDHILRSY	CHRYSALID
ACDHILRUY	HYDRAULIC
ACDHIOPRS	RHAPSODIC
ACDHIOSUV	DISAVOUCH
ACDHLOOSY	DAY-SCHOOL
ACDHLORTY	CLOTH-YARD
ACDHNORTU	COURTHAND
ACDHORTWW	WATCHWORD
ACDIIILOT	IDIOTICAL
ACDIIIMOT	IDIOMATIC
ACDIIJLRU	JURIDICAL
ACDIIJRUY	JUDICIARY
ACDIILMNO	DOMINICAL
ACDIILOST	DIASTOLIC
ACDIILPTY	PLACIDITY
ACDIILSTU	DUALISTIC
ACDIIMNNO	DOMINICAN
ACDIIMPRY	PYRAMIDIC
ACDIINORT	INDICATOR
ACDIINOSY	DIONYSIAC
ACDIINOTT	DICTATION
ACDIINRTY	RANCIDITY
ACDIIRTTX	DICTATRIX

ACDIKNQSU	QUICKSAND
ACDILLLOO	COLLOIDAL
ACDILLOOR	CORALLOID
ACDILLORY	CORDIALLY
ACDILMOPS	PSALMODIC
ACDILMOPY	DIPLOMACY
ACDILNORT	DOCTRINAL
ACDILNOSY	SYNODICAL
ACDILOPRS	DROPSICAL
ACDILOSTU	CUSTODIAL
ACDILOSUU	ACIDULOUS
ACDIMOPSS	SPASMODIC
ACDIMORTY	MORDACITY
ACDINOSTU	CUSTODIAN
ACDIORTTY	DICTATORY
ACDJOORTU	COADJUTOR
ACDMOOSUV	MUSCOVADO
ACDOORRSS	CROSS-ROAD
ACDORRTUY	COURT-YARD
ACEEEFIRS	CEASE-FIRE
ACEEEFLNR	FREE-LANCE
ACEEEGNNV	VENGEANCE
ACEEEHIPT	PETECHIAE
ACEEEILMP	PIECEMEAL
ACEEEKRRT	RACKETEER
ACEEELNRV	RELEVANCE
ACEEELNTU	ENUCLEATE
ACEEELNTY	ACETYLENE
ACEEELSSS	CEASELESS
ACEEENPPT	APPETENCE
ACEEENRSV	SEVERANCE
ACEEFFHRR	CHAFFERER
ACEEFFHRU	RÉCHAUFFÉ
ACEEFFLNU	AFFLUENCE
ACEEFFLTU	EFFECTUAL
ACEEFFNRY	FANCY-FREE
ACEEFHLNP	HALFPENCE
ACEEFIKNS	CASE-KNIFE
ACEEFILPR	FIREPLACE
ACEEFINRT	INTERFACE
ACEEFIRSS	FRICASSEE
ACEEFLORR	CORAL-REEF
ACEEFMORT	FORCEMEAT
ACEEGHIRU	GAUCHERIE
ACEEGHLLN	CHALLENGE
ACEEGHNRX	EXCHANGER
ACEEGILNR	ENERGICAL
	GENERICAL
ACEEGILNS	CINGALESE
ACEEGILNT	CLIENTAGE
	GENETICAL
ACEEGILNV	EVANGELIC
ACEEGILRS	SACRILEGE
ACEEGINOT	NEGOCIATE
ACEEGINRV	GRIEVANCE
ACEEGIRTT	CIGARETTE
ACEEGLLOU	COLLEAGUE
ACEEGLNRT	RECTANGLE
ACEEGLRSS	GRACELESS
ACEEGMNOR	GEOMANCE
ACEEGNORU	ENCOURAGE

ACEEGNRSV	SCAVENGER		TOLERANCE	ACEFIKRTU	FRUIT-CAKE
ACEEGNRSY	SERGEANCY	ACEELNPTU	PETULANCE	ACEFILNNO	FALCONINE
ACEEGOOPR	COOPERAGE	ACEELNRSS	CLEARNESS	ACEFILNSS	FANCILESS
ACEEHHTUX	HEXATEUCH	ACEELNRTU	CALENTURE	ACEFILOSU	FILACEOUS
ACEEHILPT	PETECHIAL	ACEELNRVY	RELEVANCY	ACEFINORT	FORNICATE
ACEEHILRT	HERETICAL	ACEELOPRT	PERCOLATE	ACEFIORST	FACTORISE
ACEEHILRV	CHEVALIER	ACEELORRT	CORAL-TREE	ACEFIORSU	FERACIOUS
ACEEHIMNS	MECHANISE		CORRELATE	ACEFIOSTU	FACETIOUS
ACEEHIMNZ	MECHANIZE	ACEELORSS	CASSEROLE	ACEFJLNOR	JERFALCON
ACEEHIMPR	IMPEACHER	ACEELORTU	URCEOLATE	ACEFLLLSU	FULL-SCALE
ACEEHISTT	AESTHETIC	ACEELPSTU	SPECULATE	ACEFLLRUY	CAREFULLY
ACEEHKPST	PACKSHEET	ACEELPTUX	EXCULPATE	ACEFLRSST	CRAFTLESS
ACEEHLMNO	CHAMELEON	ACEELRTUY	ELECTUARY	ACEFLTTUU	FLUCTUATE
ACEEHLNRU	HERCULEAN	ACEELSSSU	CAUSELESS	ACEFNRRTU	RUNECRAFT
ACEEHLNSS	SENESCHAL	ACEELSSTT	CAST-STEEL	ACEFOPRRT	AFTER-CROP
ACEEHLRSS	REACHLESS	ACEEMNNTT	ENACTMENT	ACEFORRRT	REFRACTOR
ACEEHLRTW	CARTWHEEL	ACEEMNPST	SCAPEMENT	ACEFOSTUU	TUFACEOUS
ACEEHMTTU	HUMECTATE	ACEEMNRRY	MERCENARY	ACEGHILRT	LETHARGIC
ACEEHNNRT	ENCHANTER	ACEEMORVW	CREAM-WOVE	ACEGHINPR	PREACHING
ACEEHNOPR	CHAPERONE	ACEENNNOR	CANNONEER	ACEGHINRS	SEARCHING
ACEEHNPSS	CHEAPNESS	ACEENNRST	RENASCENT	ACEGHOPRR	CEROGRAPH
ACEEHNRST	CHASTENER	ACEENNRTY	CENTENARY	ACEGHRRSU	SURCHARGE
ACEEHNRTY	CYTHEREAN	ACEENPRRT	CARPENTER	ACEGIILNS	ANGLICISE
ACEEHORRS	RACEHORSE	ACEENPTTX	EXPECTANT	ACEGIILNV	VIGILANCE
ACEEHORRV	OVERREACH	ACEENRRTU	CRENATURE	ACEGIILNZ	ANGLICIZE
ACEEHORST	ESCHEATOR	ACEENRSSY	NECESSARY	ACEGIIMNT	ENIGMATIC
ACEEHPRTY	ARCHETYPE	ACEENRTTU	UTTERANCE	ACEGIIRRT	GERIATRIC
ACEEHRRRT	CHARTERER	ACEENSSTU	ACUTENESS	ACEGILLLO	COLLEGIAL
ACEEHRRTT	CHATTERER	ACEENSSTX	EXACTNESS	ACEGILLNO	COLLEGIAN
ACEEHRRTY	TREACHERY	ACEENTTUX	EXECUTANT	ACEGILLOR	ALLEGORIC
ACEEILLST	CELESTIAL	ACEEOOPRT	CO-OPERATE	ACEGILLOT	COLLIGATE
ACEEILLTV	VELLICATE	ACEEOPRRT	PROCREATE	ACEGILNNO	CONGENIAL
ACEEILMRT	CARMELITE	ACEEOSSTU	SETACEOUS	ACEGILNRU	NEURALGIC
ACEEILNRT	INTERLACE	ACEEPRRTU	RECAPTURE	ACEGIMMRS	SCRIMMAGE
	LACERTINE	ACEERRSST	CREATRESS	ACEGIMNOT	GEOMANTIC
	RECLINATE	ACEERRSTT	SCATTERER	ACEGIMNRS	SCREAMING
ACEEILPTX	EXPLICATE	ACEERRSTY	SECRETARY	ACEGIMTUZ	ZEUGMATIC
ACEEIMMNN	IMMANENCE	ACEERRTUV	RECURVATE	ACEGINNOR	IGNORANCE
ACEEIMMNT	MINCEMEAT	ACEERSSTU	SECATEURS	ACEGINNSU	UNCEASING
ACEEIMNRT	INCREMATE	ACEFFGINT	AFFECTING	ACEGINPRT	CARPETING
ACEEIMNSX	EXCISEMAN	ACEFFHRUU	CHAUFFEUR	ACEGINPRY	PANEGYRIC
ACEEIMPRT	IMPRECATE	ACEFFIIOT	OFFICIATE	ACEGIOPRR	PAREGORIC
ACEEIMRSS	CASSIMERE	ACEFFINOT	AFFECTION	ACEGIRSTT	STRATEGIC
ACEEIMRTT	METRICATE	ACEFFOSTU	SUFFOCATE	ACEGJLRTU	CLARET-JUG
ACEEINNRT	NECTARINE	ACEFGHLNU	CHANGEFUL	ACEGJNOTU	CONJUGATE
ACEEINNTU	ENUNCIATE	ACEFGLNOR	GERFALCON	ACEGKOORS	GAS-COOKER
ACEEINOPR	CAPONIERE	ACEFHIINT	CHIEFTAIN	ACEGLMNRY	CLERGYMAN
ACEEINPRU	EPICUREAN	ACEFHINRS	FRANCHISE	ACEGMMNOO	COMMONAGE
ACEEINPTT	PECTINATE	ACEFHIPRY	PREACHIFY	ACEGMMRSU	SCRUMMAGE
ACEEIORTX	EXCORIATE	ACEFHIRTU	FAITH-CURE	ACEGNNOTT	CO-TANGENT
ACEEIPRTT	CREPITATE	ACEFHLSTU	SCATHEFUL	ACEGNNPRY	PREGNANCY
ACEEIPSTX	EXPISCATE	ACEFHMNNR	FRENCHMAN	ACEGORRTU	CORRUGATE
ACEEIRSTV	VISCERATE	ACEFHOSUV	VOUCHSAFE	ACEHHIRRY	HIERARCHY
ACEEIRTTX	EXTRICATE	ACEFIILMS	FACSIMILE	ACEHHMNTT	HATCHMENT
ACEEIRTUZ	CAUTERIZE	ACEFIILRR	CLARIFIER	ACEHHMOTY	THEOMACHY
ACEELLORT	ELECTORAL	ACEFIINNR	FINANCIER	ACEHHOOTT	TOOTHACHE
ACEELLPSS	PLACELESS	ACEFIIRRS	SCARIFIER	ACEHHPRTY	HEPTARCHY
ACEELNNOR	ALE-CONNER	ACEFIIRRT	ARTIFICER	ACEHIINNP	PHENICIAN
ACEELNNRU	CANNELURE	ACEFIIRTV	FRICATIVE	ACEHIINPR	CHAIN-PIER
ACEELNNSS	CLEANNESS	ACEFIITTV	FACTITIVE	ACEHIIPPT	EPITAPHIC
ACEELNORT	COETERNAL	ACEFIJKKN	JACK-KNIFE	ACEHIISTT	ATHEISTIC

ACEHIKORT	ARTICHOKE	ACEIILSTV	CALVITIES	ACEIMPRST	SPERMATIC
ACEHILLTY	ETHICALLY	ACEIIMMNR	CIMMERIAN	ACEIMRTTU	MICTURATE
ACEHILMMO	CHAMOMILE	ACEIIMNRT	CRIMINATE	ACEINNORT	CONTAINER
ACEHILMST	ALCHEMIST	ACEIIMNSS	MESSIANIC		CRENATION
ACEHILNNO	CHELONIAN	ACEIIMRST	ARMISTICE	ACEINNOSS	ASCENSION
ACEHILNOR	ENCHORIAL	ACEIINRTT	INTRICATE	ACEINNRSU	INSURANCE
ACEHILNTU	UNETHICAL	ACEIINTTT	NICTITATE	ACEINNRTU	RUNCINATE
ACEHILNTY	THYLACINE	ACEIIRSTT	CERATITIS		UNCERTAIN
ACEHILPRS	SPHERICAL	ACEIKLMNS	SICKLEMAN	ACEINNSST	INCESSANT
ACEHILRUV	VEHICULAR	ACEILLLXY	LEXICALLY	ACEINOOTV	EVOCATION
ACEHILSTT	ATHLETICS	ACEILLMOP	POLEMICAL	ACEINORRV	CARNIVORE
ACEHIMMNS	MECHANISM	ACEILLMOT	COLLIMATE	ACEINORTU	CAUTIONER
ACEHIMNRY	MACHINERY	ACEILLNOR	COLLINEAR	ACEINORTZ	NARCOTIZE
ACEHIMNST	MECHANIST		CORALLINE	ACEINOSST	CESSATION
ACEHIMORY	CHERIMOYA	ACEILLORT	CORALLITE	ACEINOSTU	TENACIOUS
ACEHIMRTU	RHEUMATIC	ACEILLOST	OSCILLATE	ACEINOSUV	VINACEOUS
ACEHINNOT	OENANTHIC	ACEILLOTV	COLLATIVE	ACEINPRSS	SCARPINES
ACEHINORT	ANCHORITE	ACEILLPRS	CALLIPERS	ACEINPRTT	CREPITANT
ACEHINRRU	HURRICANE	ACEILLPSY	SPECIALLY	ACEINPRUY	PECUNIARY
ACEHINRSS	CHARINESS	ACEILMNOP	POLICEMAN	ACEINPSSU	PUISSANCE
ACEHINSST	CAITHNESS	ACEILMNOR	COAL-MINER	ACEINQTTU	QUITTANCE
ACEHINSTY	HESITANCY	ACEILMNRU	NUMERICAL	ACEINRSSZ	CRAZINESS
ACEHINTTU	AUTHENTIC	ACEILMNSU	MASCULINE	ACEINRTTY	CERTAINTY
ACEHIPPSS	SPACESHIP	ACEILMNTU	CULMINATE	ACEINRTUV	INCURVATE
ACEHIRSTU	EUCHARIST	ACEILMOPT	PTOLEMAIC	ACEINSSSU	SAUCINESS
ACEHKLNSU	UNSHACKLE	ACEILMORS	LACRIMOSE	ACEINSTTY	INTESTACY
ACEHLMSST	MATCHLESS	ACEILMOSU	LIMACEOUS	ACEIOPRRS	ACROSPIRE
ACEHLNOSY	ANCHYLOSE	ACEILMRRU	MERCURIAL	ACEIOPTTT	PETTICOAT
ACEHLORRT	TROCHLEAR	ACEILNNOR	CORNELIAN	ACEIORSST	OSTRACISE
ACEHLPSSU	SPHACELUS	ACEILNNOT	OCTENNIAL	ACEIORSTZ	OSTRACIZE
ACEHMNOPY	CYMOPHANE	ACEILNNTY	ANCIENTLY	ACEIORSUV	VERACIOUS
ACEHMNOTY	THEOMANCY	ACEILNOPR	PORCELAIN	ACEIOSSTW	COASTWISE
ACEHMNPRT	PARCHMENT	ACEILNORS	CENSORIAL	ACEIPRRST	PRACTISER
ACEHMNSTY	SCYTHEMAN	ACEILNORT	CLARIONET	ACEIRSTTU	RUSTICATE
ACEHMORST	STOMACHER	ACEILNOST	COAST-LINE	ACEJLMSUU	MAJUSCULE
ACEHMORTV	OVERMATCH		SECTIONAL	ACEKLNSSS	SLACKNESS
ACEHMOSTU	MOUSTACHE	ACEILNOTU	INOCULATE	ACEKLRSST	TRACKLESS
ACEHNNRTT	TRENCHANT	ACEILNPTU	INCULPATE	ACEKNNRSS	CRANKNESS
ACEHNPRTY	PENTARCHY	ACEILNRTU	CENTURIAL	ACEKNORSU	CANKEROUS
ACEHORRST	CART-HORSE	ACEILNRTY	CERTAINLY	ACEKRSTUW	AWE-STRUCK
	ORCHESTRA	ACEILNSSS	SCALINESS	ACELLLMOU	COLUMELLA
ACEHORSTY	THEOCRASY	ACEILNSUV	VULCANISE	ACELLMORU	MOLECULAR
ACEHPRRSU	PURCHASER	ACEILNTUV	VULCANITE	ACELLNNUY	UNCLEANLY
ACEHRRTTY	TETRARCHY	ACEILNUVZ	VULCANIZE	ACELLNRTY	CENTRALLY
ACEIIILST	ITALICISE	ACEILOPPS	EPISCOPAL	ACELLOQUY	COEQUALLY
ACEIIKMNT	KINEMATIC	ACEILOPST	SCAPOLITE	ACELLRSUY	SECULARLY
ACEIILLTV	LEVITICAL	ACEILOQUV	EQUIVOCAL	ACELMMNOS	COMMENSAL
ACEIILMMT	MIMETICAL	ACEILORRT	RECTORIAL	ACELMOPST	ECTOPLASM
ACEIILMPR	EMPIRICAL	ACEILORST	SECTORIAL	ACELMORRU	CLAMOURER
ACEIILMPT	IMPLICATE	ACEILPRTU	PLICATURE	ACELMORSY	LACRYMOSE
ACEIILMST	CLIMATISE	ACEILPSTU	SPICULATE	ACELNNOOR	OLECRANON
ACEIILMTZ	CLIMATIZE	ACEILPSTY	SPECIALTY	ACELNOOSV	VOLCANOES
ACEIILNNV	VICENNIAL	ACEILRSTV	CAT-SILVER	ACELNOPRV	PROVENÇAL
ACEIILNPS	CISALPINE	ACEILRSUV	VESICULAR	ACELNOSSV	VOCALNESS
ACEIILNST	INELASTIC	ACEILRTUV	LUCRATIVE	ACELNOSTU	CONSULATE
	SCIENTIAL	ACEILTTUV	CULTIVATE	ACELNPRTU	CRAPULENT
ACEIILOSS	SOCIALISE	ACEIMMNNY	IMMANENCY	ACELNPTUY	PETULANCY
ACEIILOST	SOCIALITE	ACEIMNORT	CREMATION	ACELNRTTU	RELUCTANT
ACEIILOSZ	SOCIALIZE	ACEIMNOST	ENCOMIAST	ACELOOPRR	CORPOREAL
ACEIILRST	ERISTICAL	ACEIMNPTU	PNEUMATIC	ACELOPRRU	OPERCULAR
	REALISTIC	ACEIMNRST	MISCREANT	ACELOPRTU	PECULATOR

ACELOSTUU	CAUTELOUS	ACGHLMOOY	LOGOMACHY	ACHLLORSY	SCHOLARLY
ACEMNOPSS	ENCOMPASS	ACGIILLLO	ILLOGICAL	ACHLMNOOS	SCHOOLMAN
ACEMNORTU	MUCRONATE	ACGIILLMS	GALLICISM	ACHLOOSTU	HOLOCAUST
ACEMOOPSU	POMACEOUS	ACGIILMNS	ANGLICISM	ACHLOPRYY	POLYARCHY
ACEMORRTY	CREMATORY	ACGIILRTY	GRACILITY	ACHLOPTUY	PATCHOULY
ACEMOSTVY	VASECTOMY	ACGIIMSTT	STIGMATIC	ACHNOPSTY	SYCOPHANT
ACEMPRSUY	SUPREMACY	ACGIINNOR	INORGANIC	ACHOPSTUY	HYPOCAUST
ACENNNORU	ANNOUNCER	ACGIINNOT	INCOGNITA	ACHORTTTU	CUT-THROAT
ACENNOOPR	CORNOPEAN	ACGIINOST	AGONISTIC	ACIIIMNST	ANIMISTIC
ACENNOOTT	CONNOTATE	ACGIIORST	ORGIASTIC	ACIIINPPR	PRINCIPIA
ACENNORTU	CONNATURE	ACGILLLOY	LOGICALLY	ACIIKNOOZ	KAINOZOIC
ACENNSSST	SCANTNESS	ACGILNNST	SCANTLING	ACIILLNOS	ISOCLINAL
ACENOOPRT	CO-OPERANT	ACGILNOST	NOSTALGIC	ACIILLNST	SCINTILLA
ACENOPRRT	COPARTNER	ACGILNOXY	COAXINGLY	ACIILLOPT	POLITICAL
	PROCREANT	ACGILNPRY	CARPINGLY	ACIILMNPU	MUNICIPAL
ACENOPSTY	SYNCOPATE	ACGIMNORR	CAIRNGORM	ACIILMNSV	CALVINISM
ACENORRTU	RACONTEUR	ACGIMNOTU	CONTAGIUM	ACIILMNTY	MILITANCY
ACENORSSS	SCANSORES	ACGIMNSTY	GYMNASTIC	ACIILMOSS	SOCIALISM
ACENORSTU	COURTESAN	ACGIMOPRT	PICTOGRAM	ACIILMOSU	MALICIOUS
	NECTAROUS	ACGIMOTYZ	ZYGOMATIC	ACIILMQTU	QUITCLAIM
ACENORSUV	CAVERNOUS	ACGINNOOT	COGNATION	ACIILNOOT	COALITION
ACENORUVV	VANCOUVER		CONTAGION	ACIILNOPT	PLICATION
ACENOSTUU	CUTANEOUS	ACGINNOPY	POIGNANCY	ACIILNOVV	CONVIVIAL
ACENPRRTY	CARPENTRY	ACGINNOST	COGNISANT	ACIILNPPR	PRINCIPAL
ACENPRSUU	PURSUANCE	ACGINNOTZ	COGNIZANT	ACIILNSTV	CALVINIST
ACENPTTUU	PUNCTUATE	ACGINPTUY	PUGNACITY	ACIILOPRT	PICTORIAL
ACENRSSSS	CRASSNESS	ACGMOPRTY	CRYPTOGAM	ACIILOSST	SOCIALIST
ACEOOPRRT	CORPORATE	ACHHIIRST	RHACHITIS	ACIILOSTY	SOCIALITY
ACEOORSSU	ROSACEOUS	ACHHINNOT	CHTHONIAN	ACIILPRTY	PYRITICAL
ACEOPRSTT	SPECTATOR	ACHHINOPS	CHINA-SHOP	ACIILQUZZ	QUIZZICAL
ACEORRRTT	RETRACTOR	ACHHINOST	CHAIN-SHOT	ACIIMNNOS	INSOMNIAC
ACEORRTTX	EXTRACTOR	ACHHLLLOT	CLOTH-HALL	ACIIMNORT	MORTICIAN
ACERRTUUV	CURVATURE	ACHIIKNNP	CHINKAPIN	ACIIMORTT	TRIATOMIC
ACFFIILNO	OFFICINAL	ACHIILMSW	WHIMSICAL	ACIIMOSST	MOSAICIST
ACFGIKNRT	KINGCRAFT	ACHIIMNST	MACHINIST	ACIIMPRST	PRISMATIC
ACFGIOSUU	FUGACIOUS	ACHIINPSY	PHYSICIAN	ACIINNOTU	INCAUTION
ACFGLNORY	GYRFALCON	ACHIINRST	CHRISTIAN	ACIINORTV	VICTORIAN
ACFHLNORW	HALF-CROWN	ACHIIOPST	PISTACHIO	ACIINPRTU	PURITANIC
ACFHMORSU	FORASMUCH	ACHIIPRSV	VICARSHIP	ACIIOPRTT	PATRIOTIC
ACFIIILMR	MIRIFICAL	ACHIIRRTT	ARTHRITIC	ACIIOPTZZ	PIZZICATO
ACFIILLNY	FINICALLY	ACHIIRSTV	ARCHIVIST	ACIIORSUV	VICARIOUS
ACFIILNOT	FICTIONAL	ACHIKKNPT	PICKTHANK	ACIIOSUVV	VIVACIOUS
ACFIIMNOR	ACINIFORM	ACHILLMSU	MUSIC-HALL	ACIIPRSTT	PATRISTIC
ACFIIOPRV	VAPORIFIC	ACHILMPTY	LYMPHATIC	ACIIPTTVY	CAPTIVITY
ACFILNNOR	FRANCOLIN	ACHILNORT	ANTICHLOR	ACIISSTTT	STATISTIC
ACFILNPPY	FLIPPANCY	ACHILOPTU	PATCHOULI	ACIKKNNOT	ANTIKNOCK
ACFILNRUU	FUNICULAR	ACHILOSST	SCHOLIAST	ACIKLPSST	SLAPSTICK
ACFIMOPRR	CAPRIFORM	ACHILRSSY	CHRYSALIS	ACILLMSUY	MUSICALLY
ACFIMORRY	FORMICARY	ACHILRSTY	STARCHILY	ACILLNNSY	SYNCLINAL
ACFINORTU	FURCATION	ACHIMMNOS	MONACHISM	ACILLNOOT	COLLATION
ACFIORSTU	FRACTIOUS	ACHIMMOSS	MASOCHISM	ACILLOPTY	OPTICALLY
ACFKNORWY	FANCY-WORK	ACHIMNORS	HARMONICS		TOPICALLY
ACFLLORSU	FLOSCULAR	ACHIMNOST	MACINTOSH	ACILLORST	CLOISTRAL
ACFLITTUY	TACTFULLY	ACHIMNPPU	CHAIN-PUMP	ACILLOSTY	CALLOSITY
ACFLNTTUU	FLUCTUANT	ACHIMOSST	MASOCHIST		STOICALLY
ACFLOORTY	OLFACTORY	ACHIMRSST	CHRISTMAS	ACILLPTYY	TYPICALLY
ACGGILRSY	SCRAGGILY	ACHINNOST	STANCHION	ACILMMOTT	COMMITTAL
ACGHHILSS	HIGH-CLASS	ACHINOPRT	ANTHROPIC	ACILMNOPT	COMPLAINT
ACGHHINTT	THATCHING	ACHINRSTY	STRYCHNIA		COMPLIANT
ACGHILORY	OLIGARCHY	ACHIOPPRS	HIPPOCRAS	ACILMNOSV	VOLCANISM
ACGHINNOT	GNATHONIC	ACHKOPRTW	PATCHWORK	ACILMNSUU	UNMUSICAL

ACILMNSUV	VULCANISM	
ACILMPTUU	CAPITULUM	
ACILNNOTU	CONTINUAL	
ACILNOSTU	SULCATION	
ACILNOSTV	VOLCANIST	
ACILOOPRS	ACROPOLIS	
ACILOOPST	APOSTOLIC	
ACILOORST	CASTOR-OIL	
ACILOQTUY	LOQUACITY	
ACILORRSU	CURSORIAL	
ACILORSTU	SUCTORIAL	
ACILRRTUU	UTRICULAR	
ACIMMNOOT	MONATOMIC	
ACIMNNOOP	COMPANION	
ACIMNOOTX	TAXONOMIC	
ACIMNOPRR	CRAMP-IRON	
ACIMNORST	NARCOTISM	
ACIMOPSSY	SYMPOSIAC	
ACIMORSST	OSTRACISM	
ACINNORST	CONSTRAIN	
ACINOORST	OSTRACION	
ACINRSSSU	NARCISSUS	
ACIOORSTU	ATROCIOUS	
ACIOORSUV	VORACIOUS	
ACIOSSTUU	ASTUCIOUS	
ACIRSSTUY	CASUISTRY	
ACJKOPRST	JOCKSTRAP	
ACJLLORUY	JOCULARLY	
ACKLMOOOR	CLOAK-ROOM	
ACLLLOSUY	CALLOUSLY	
ACLLOORRY	COROLLARY	
ACLMNOORU	COLOURMAN	
ACLMOOPST	CAMP-STOOL	
ACLMOORSS	CLASSROOM	
ACLMOORSU	CLAMOROUS	
ACLNNORTU	NOCTURNAL	
ACLNOORTT	CONTRALTO	
ACLOPRSUU	CRAPULOUS	
ACLOPRTTU	PLUTOCRAT	
ACLOPRTUY	CULPATORY	
ACMNOORRT	CORMORANT	
ACMNOOSTU	COSMONAUT	
ACMORRSUU	MACRUROUS	
ACMORSTUY	CUSTOMARY	
ACNNNOOST	CONSONANT	
ACNOOPRST	CORPOSANT	
ACNOORRSU	RANCOROUS	
ADDDEERSS	ADDRESSED	
ADDDEIMNO	DIAMONDED	
ADDDEKNRU	DEAD-DRUNK	
ADDEEEPRT	DEPREDATE	
ADDEEERSS	ADDRESSEE	
ADDEEFNNT	DEFENDANT	
ADDEEGHIP	PIGHEADED	
ADDEEGLNR	GLANDERED	
ADDEEHOSU	DEAD-HOUSE	
ADDEEHRTY	DEHYDRATE	
ADDEEILRV	DARE-DEVIL	
ADDEEIOTX	DEOXIDATE	
ADDEEIPPR	DRAPERIED	
ADDEELPPW	DEWLAPPED	
ADDEELRSS	DREADLESS	
ADDEEMNRU	UNDREAMED	
ADDEENNPT	DEPENDANT	
ADDEENSWY	WEDNESDAY	
ADDEEOPRS	DESPERADO	
ADDEERRSS	ADDRESSER	
	READDRESS	
ADDEGGINR	DEGRADING	
ADDEGIITT	DIGITATED	
ADDEGIMNN	MADDENING	
ADDEGIRRS	DISREGARD	
ADDEGLRUY	GUARDEDLY	
ADDEGNRUU	UNGUARDED	
ADDEHIILP	DIDELPHIA	
ADDEHINSY	HENDIADYS	
ADDEHNNRU	UNDERHAND	
ADDEHNORU	ROUNDHEAD	
ADDEIIIMT	DIMIDIATE	
ADDEILLNS	LANDSLIDE	
ADDEILMMN	MIDDLEMAN	
ADDEILNNO	DANDELION	
ADDEILSVY	ADVISEDLY	
ADDEIMORT	DERMATOID	
ADDEINSUV	UNADVISED	
ADDELNTUU	UNDULATED	
ADDEMORRY	DROMEDARY	
ADDENNORU	UNADORNED	
ADDENNRTU	REDUNDANT	
ADDENNTUU	UNDAUNTED	
ADDENOORT	DEODORANT	
ADDENORUY	DUODENARY	
ADDEPQRUU	QUADRUPED	
ADDFIIQRU	QUADRIFID	
ADDHHIOOR	HARDIHOOD	
ADDHLOOTU	ADULTHOOD	
ADDINORSU	DIANDROUS	
ADDNORSWW	DOWNWARDS	
ADEEEEGLY	EAGLE-EYED	
ADEEEFHRT	FEATHERED	
ADEEEHRTW	WEATHERED	
ADEEEILNT	DELINEATE	
ADEEENRRS	SERENADER	
ADEEEPRST	DESPERATE	
ADEEFFILR	FIELDFARE	
ADEEFGINN	DEAFENING	
ADEEFHIRT	DEATH-FIRE	
ADEEFILOT	DEFOLIATE	
ADEEFILSU	FEUDALISE	
ADEEFILUZ	FEUDALIZE	
ADEEFIMST	DEFEATISM	
ADEEFISTT	DEFEATIST	
ADEEFLORT	DEFLORATE	
	FLOREATED	
ADEEFLPRY	PALFREYED	
ADEEFLRTU	DEFAULTER	
ADEEFMNOR	FORENAMED	
ADEEFNOST	STONE-DEAF	
ADEEGGINS	DISENGAGE	
ADEEGGMOU	DEMAGOGUE	
ADEEGGNNU	UNENGAGED	
ADEEGGOPU	PEDAGOGUE	
ADEEGINNR	ENDEARING	
	ENGRAINED	
	GRENADINE	
ADEEGINRR	GRENADIER	
ADEEGINRT	DENIGRATE	
ADEEGINST	DESIGNATE	
ADEEGLNNR	GREENLAND	
ADEEGLNRY	LEGENDARY	
ADEEGLOOW	EAGLE-WOOD	
ADEEGLTTU	TEGULATED	
ADEEGMNRR	GERMANDER	
ADEEGMNRT	GARMENTED	
ADEEGMRRU	DEMURRAGE	
ADEEGNNUV	UNAVENGED	
ADEEHHLSW	DASH-WHEEL	
ADEEHHNOP	HEADPHONE	
ADEEHIKLT	DEATHLIKE	
ADEEHINSS	HEADINESS	
ADEEHKLRS	SHELDRAKE	
ADEEHLLOS	LEASEHOLD	
ADEEHLSST	DEATHLESS	
ADEEHMOST	HOMESTEAD	
ADEEHNPPR	APPREHEND	
ADEEHOSWY	EYESHADOW	
ADEEHRSTW	WATERSHED	
ADEEHSTUX	EXHAUSTED	
ADEEIILRZ	IDEALIZER	
ADEEIIMMT	IMMEDIATE	
ADEEIIMTV	MEDIATIVE	
ADEEIIMTZ	MEDIATIZE	
ADEEIIRSS	DIAERESIS	
ADEEILMPR	EPIDERMAL	
	IMPLEADER	
ADEEILMTY	MEDIATELY	
ADEEILPSS	DISPLEASE	
ADEEIMMNS	MISDEMEAN	
ADEEIMNRR	REMAINDER	
ADEEINRSS	READINESS	
ADEEINRUW	UNWEARIED	
ADEEINSTT	DESTINATE	
ADEEIOPTV	VIDEOTAPE	
ADEEIPRRS	DESREPAIR	
ADEEIPRTU	REPUDIATE	
ADEEIRSTV	ADVERTISE	
ADEEIRTTX	EXTRADITE	
ADEEKNNSS	NAKEDNESS	
ADEEKNRTU	UNDERTAKE	
ADEELLLRU	LAURELLED	
ADEELLNRY	LEARNEDLY	
ADEELLRTV	TRAVELLED	
ADEELLSST	TASSELLED	
ADEELLSTT	STELLATED	
ADEELMMOR	MELODRAME	
ADEELMNOP	PADEMELON	
ADEELMRSS	DREAMLESS	
ADEELNNRU	UNLEARNED	
ADEELNPTU	PENDULATE	
ADEELNRRS	SLANDERER	
ADEELNRTU	UNRELATED	
ADEELNSSW	WALDENSES	
ADEELORST	DESOLATER	

124

ADEELRRTU	ADULTERER	ADEGINORS	GRANDIOSE	ADEIMNPRS	PANDERISM
ADEELRSTY	STEELYARD		ORGANISED	ADEIMNRSU	NURSEMAID
ADEELRSVY	ADVERSELY	ADEGINORZ	ORGANIZED	ADEIMNRTY	DYNAMITER
ADEEMMNNT	AMENDMENT	ADEGINRRS	GRANDSIRE	ADEIMNRYZ	ZEMINDARY
ADEEMNOPR	PROMENADE	ADEGINRRW	REWARDING	ADEIMORTT	TREMATOID
ADEEMNORT	EMENDATOR	ADEGINSSU	GAUDINESS	ADEIMRTUX	ADMIXTURE
ADEEMNORU	DEMEANOUR	ADEGIPRRT	PARTRIDGE	ADEIMRTXY	TAXIDERMY
	ENAMOURED	ADEGIRTTU	GRATITUDE	ADEINNNTT	INTENDANT
ADEEMNRRU	MAUNDERER	ADEGLLNOO	GALLOONED	ADEINNRTU	UNTRAINED
ADEEMOORR	AERODROME	ADEGLNOST	GLADSTONE	ADEINNSSS	SANDINESS
ADEEMOPRR	MADREPORE	ADEGNNNGO	CHANDNLLE	ALGINNSIII	HNSIGINED
ADEEMORRZ	ZERODERMA	ADEGNOORS	GOOSANDER	ADEINNTTU	UNTAINTED
ADEEMORTT	TREMATODE	ADEGNORSU	DANGEROUS	ADEINOPPT	APPOINTED
ADEENORUV	ENDEAVOUR	ADEHHNOOT	THANEHOOD	ADEINOPRR	PREORDAIN
ADEENPRSS	PANDERESS	ADEHIISST	DIATHESIS	ADEINOPST	ANTIPODES
ADEENRRTU	UNDERRATE	ADEHIKNPS	HANDSPIKE	ADEINOTUX	EXUDATION
ADEENRRUW	UNDERWEAR	ADEHILMOT	ETHMOIDAL	ADEINPPRS	SANDPIPER
ADEENRSTY	SEDENTARY	ADEHILNOR	HODIERNAL	ADEINPRSS	RAPIDNESS
ADEENRTTV	ADVERTENT	ADEHILRRT	TRIHEDRAL	ADEINPSSV	VAPIDNESS
ADEENRTUV	ADVENTURE	ADEHIMOSU	HOUSEMAID	ADEINRSST	TARDINESS
ADEENRTUW	UNWATERED	ADEHINNSS	HANDINESS	ADEINSSST	STAIDNESS
ADEEOPRSV	EAVESDROP	ADEHINOPU	AUDIPHONE	ADEIOPRSU	DEIPAROUS
ADEEORRTV	OVERTRADE	ADEHINRRS	HARDINESS	ADEIOPRTZ	TRAPEZOID
ADEEPRRSU	PERSUADER	ADEHINSSS	SHADINESS	ADEIPPRSU	DISPAUPER
ADEEPRRTU	DEPARTURE	ADEHIOPRT	APHRODITE	ADEIPPSSY	DYSPEPSIA
ADEEPRSTU	DEPASTURE	ADEHIRRTT	THIRD-RATE	ADEIPRTVY	DEPRAVITY
ADEERSTYY	YESTERDAY	ADEHKNNTU	UNTHANKED	ADEIRRSUY	RESIDUARY
ADEFGHORT	GODFATHER	ADEHMORSW	HOMEWARDS	ADEISTTUV	VASTITUDE
ADEFGIRRU	FIRE-GUARD	ADEHORRSY	DRAY-HORSE	ADEKOPRSW	SPADEWORK
ADEFGLOOT	FLOOD-GATE	ADEIILNRT	DRAIN-TILE	ADELLMRUY	MEDULLARY
ADEFGLRRU	REGARDFUL	ADEIILNST	DISENTAIL	ADELLNORW	LOWLANDER
ADEFHIMST	HAMFISTED	ADEIILOPS	EPISODIAL	ADELLNOUY	UNALLOYED
ADEFHLNOZ	HALF-DOZEN	ADEIILORT	EDITORIAL	ADELLNTUU	LUNULATED
ADEFHLOOS	FALSEHOOD	ADEIILQTU	LIQUIDATE	ADELMNNUY	MUNDANELY
ADEFIILQU	QUALIFIED	ADEIIMNOT	MEDIATION	ADELMNOPS	ENDOPLASM
ADEFILLSU	FUSILLADE	ADEIIMOTT	DIATOMITE	ADELNNORW	LANDOWNER
ADEFILMSU	FEUDALISM	ADEIINOTV	DEVIATION	ADELNOOST	LOADSTONE
ADEFILNOT	DEFLATION	ADEIINPPR	DRAINPIPE	ADELNORUY	ROUNDELAY
ADEFILNTY	DEFIANTLY	ADEIIPRSS	DISPRAISE	ADELNRSSU	LAUNDRESS
ADEFILSTU	FEUDALIST	ADEIIPSST	DISSIPATE	ADELNRTVY	VERDANTLY
ADEFILTUY	FEUDALITY	ADEIIRTTV	TRADITIVE	ADELNSSTU	DAUNTLESS
ADEFINNRW	FINEDRAWN	ADEIKNPPR	KIDNAPPER	ADELOOOSW	ALOES-WOOD
ADEFMNNTU	FUNDAMENT	ADEIKNPRS	SPIKENARD	ADELOOPRT	DOOR-PLATE
ADEFORTUY	FEUDATORY	ADEILLMNO	MEDALLION	ADELOORST	DESOLATOR
ADEGGIITZ	DZIGGETAI	ADEILLMOT	METALLOID	ADELPQRUU	QUADRUPLE
ADEGGINNR	GARDENING	ADEILLMRT	TREADMILL	ADELRRSTY	DRYSALTER
ADEGGINRR	REGARDING	ADEILLMST	MEDALLIST	ADELRSSUY	ASSUREDLY
ADEGHHILT	HEADLIGHT	ADEILLQRU	QUADRILLE	ADEMNNORT	ADORNMENT
ADEGHIOPR	EIDOGRAPH	ADEILMNNO	MANDOLINE	ADEMNPSTU	UNSTAMPED
	IDEOGRAPH	ADEILMNST	DISMANTLE	ADEMOORRT	MODERATOR
ADEGHLORS	GASHOLDER	ADEILMORR	MAIL-ORDER	ADENNOSST	SANDSTONE
ADEGIILOZ	DIALOGIZE	ADEILMPTU	AMPLITUDE	ADENNOSTY	ASYNDETON
ADEGIINNR	INGRAINED	ADEILNOPP	PANOPLIED	ADENOORST	TORNADOES
ADEGIKLNV	GAVELKIND	ADEILNOPT	PLANETOID	ADENOORTT	DETONATOR
ADEGILNOR	GIRANDOLE	ADEILNRRT	INTERLARD	ADENRSSUU	UNASSURED
ADEGILNOS	ALONGSIDE	ADEILOQSU	ODALISQUE	ADEOPRRTU	DEPURATOR
ADEGILNRU	GERUNDIAL	ADEILPRSS	DISPERSAL	ADEOPRRTY	PREDATORY
ADEGIMNTU	MAGNITUDE	ADEILPRSY	DISPLAYER	ADEOPRSTU	OUTSPREAD
ADEGIMOST	DOGMATISE	ADEILPTTU	PLATITUDE	ADEOQRTTU	TORQUATED
ADEGIMOTZ	DOGMATIZE	ADEILSSTU	LASSITUDE	ADEORRSTT	ROSTRATED
ADEGINNRW	WANDERING	ADEIMNPRR	REPRIMAND	ADERSSTWW	WESTWARDS

ADFFIIMRS	DISAFFIRM	ADILLNRUY	DIURNALLY	AEEFINSTT	FESTINATE
ADFGLNORY	DRAGON-FLY	ADILLQSUY	SQUALIDLY	AEEFLNRST	FENESTRAL
ADFHINRST	FIRST-HAND	ADILMNOOS	SALMONOID	AEEFLNSSS	FALSENESS
ADFHLOORY	FOOLHARDY	ADILMSTTU	TALMUDIST	AEEFLRRTT	FLATTERER
ADFIORSUV	DISFAVOUR	ADILNSTTY	DISTANTLY	AEEFMNORS	FREEMASON
ADFKLMOOR	FLOOD-MARK	ADILOOPRS	PROSODIAL	AEEFOPRRT	PERFORATE
ADFLLOOST	FALDSTOOL	ADILOPRSV	DISPROVAL	AEEFORSTT	FORETASTE
ADFLORRWY	FROWARDLY	ADIMNOORT	ADMONITOR	AEEGGINNS	GAS-ENGINE
ADFNOORSZ	SFORZANDO	ADINNORTW	DOWN-TRAIN	AEEGGLNOY	GENEALOGY
ADGGILNRY	NIGGARDLY	ADINNOSST	DISSONANT	AEEGGMORT	MORTGAGEE
ADGHHILNS	HIGHLANDS	ADINOOPRS	PROSODIAN	AEEGGRRSW	SWAGGERER
ADGHHINRT	RIGHT-HAND	ADINPSTTU	DISPUTANT	AEEGHIMRT	HERMITAGE
ADGHIIOPR	IDIOGRAPH	ADIOSSSUU	ASSIDUOUS	AEEGHLPRT	TELEGRAPH
ADGHILLLU	GUILDHALL	ADJMMORRU	DRUM-MAJOR	AEEGIINNR	AIR-ENGINE
ADGHINRTW	NIGHTWARD	ADLMOORTU	MODULATOR	AEEGILLST	LEGISLATE
ADGHNORUY	GRAYHOUND	ADLNOPRYY	POLYANDRY	AEEGILNNT	EGLANTINE
ADGIIILNT	DIGITALIN	ADLOOOSTT	TOADSTOOL		INELEGANT
ADGIIILST	DIGITALIS	ADLOPRSWY	SWORDPLAY	AEEGILNRV	REVEALING
ADGIIJNNO	ADJOINING	ADLORSUUY	ARDUOUSLY	AEEGIMNNN	ENGINEMAN
ADGIILMOS	SIGMOIDAL	ADLORTUWY	OUTWARDLY	AEEGIMNRT	GERMINATE
ADGIILOST	DIALOGIST	ADMMORRTY	MARTYRDOM	AEEGIMNST	MAGNETISE
ADGIINNNT	INDIGNANT	ADMNORSSW	SWORDSMAN	AEEGIMNTZ	MAGNETIZE
ADGIINORT	GRANITOID	ADNNOSSWW	SWANSDOWN	AEEGIMRRT	REMIGRATE
ADGIINOSS	DIAGNOSIS	AEEEFHRRT	HEREAFTER	AEEGINNRR	ENGRAINER
ADGIINRTY	DIGNITARY	AEEEFIRRT	FIRE-EATER	AEEGINNRT	ARGENTINE
ADGILLOSU	GLADIOLUS	AEEEFSTTT	ESTAFETTE	AEEGINOPS	ESPIONAGE
ADGILNORY	ADORINGLY	AEEEGGRST	SEGREGATE	AEEGINOTT	NEGOTIATE
ADGIMMOST	DOGMATISM	AEEEGIMNR	MENAGERIE	AEEGINPRT	REPEATING
ADGIMOSTT	DOGMATIST	AEEEGLRRV	GEAR-LEVER	AEEGINPRV	GRAPEVINE
ADGINNOOU	IGUANODON	AEEEGMNRT	AGREEMENT	AEEGINRTT	INTEGRATE
ADGINPRSY	DAYSPRING	AEEEGNRSS	EAGERNESS	AEEGIOPSU	EPIGAEOUS
ADGLNOOTY	ODONTALGY	AEEEGRRRT	GARRETEER	AEEGLLNRY	GENERALLY
ADGOOPRST	GASTROPOD	AEEEGRRTT	TARGETEER	AEEGLLNTY	ELEGANTLY
ADHHNOORU	HOARHOUND	AEEEGRTTZ	GAZETTEER	AEEGLMNNT	GENTLEMAN
ADHHNORST	SHORTHAND	AEEEHLMPR	EPHEMERAL	AEEGLMNST	SEGMENTAL
ADHIILLOT	LITHOIDAL	AEEEHMRTX	HEXAMETER	AEEGLMORT	GLOMERATE
ADHIIMPSS	AMIDSHIPS	AEEEHRRRS	REHEARSER	AEEGLNNPT	PENTANGLE
ADHIIOPTY	IDIOPATHY	AEEEIRRTT	REITERATE	AEEGLNRSS	LARGENESS
ADHIKNORW	HANDIWORK	AEEEKLTTT	TEA-KETTLE	AEEGLRSSV	GRAVELESS
ADHILNNUY	UNHANDILY	AEEELLMNT	ELEMENTAL	AEEGMNRRS	MERGANSER
ADHINOOST	SAINTHOOD	AEEELNUVZ	VENEZUELA	AEEGMNRTU	AUGMENTER
ADHINSTTW	WITHSTAND	AEEELPTTU	EPAULETTE	AEEGMORST	GASOMETER
ADHMNOOOW	WOMANHOOD	AEEEMNRST	ERASEMENT	AEEGNOPRS	PERSONAGE
ADHMOORSY	HYDROSOMA	AEEEMNRTU	ENUMERATE	AEEGNORRT	GENERATOR
ADHNORRTW	NORTHWARD	AEEEMORRT	AEROMETER	AEEGNORTU	ENTOURAGE
ADHNORSUY	ANHYDROUS		AREOMETER	AEEGNOTTW	WAGONETTE
ADHORSTUW	SOUTHWARD	AEEEMPRTT	TEMPERATE	AEEGNOTXY	OXYGENATE
ADIILMSSS	DISMISSAL	AEEEMSTTW	SWEETMEAT	AEEGNPRSS	PASSENGER
ADIILNOPT	PLATINOID	AEEENORTX	EXONERATE	AEEGNRSST	GREATNESS
ADIILOORV	VARIOLOID	AEEENPRTT	PENETRATE	AEEGNRSSV	GRAVENESS
ADIIMNOSS	ADMISSION	AEEENRRST	EASTERNER	AEEGNSSUV	VAGUENESS
ADIIMNRSW	DARWINISM	AEEENTTUV	EVENTUATE	AEEGOPRRT	PORTERAGE
ADIINNOSY	DIONYSIAN	AEEENTTUX	EXTENUATE		REPORTAGE
ADIINOOTX	OXIDATION	AEEFFILRT	AFTER-LIFE	AEEGPRTUX	EXPURGATE
ADIINOQTU	QUOTIDIAN	AEEFGILPR	PILFERAGE	AEEHHNRTY	HEATHENRY
ADIINORTT	TRADITION	AEEFGLLOT	FLAGEOLET	AEEHHNSTU	UNSHEATHE
ADIINRSTT	DISTRAINT	AEEFHLMST	FLESH-MEAT	AEEHILMNW	MEANWHILE
ADIIPRSTY	DISPARITY	AEEFHLRTT	HEARTFELT	AEEHIMPSS	EMPHASISE
ADIISSTUY	ASSIDUITY	AEEFILNSS	LEAFINESS	AEEHIMPSZ	EMPHASIZE
ADIKMNNOW	WOMANKIND	AEEFILOTX	EXFOLIATE	AEEHINPRS	HESPERIAN
ADILLMNOO	ALMOND-OIL	AEEFIMORT	AFORETIME	AEEHINRTW	INWREATHE

AEEHINSSV	HEAVINESS	AEEILRSTV	VERSATILE	AEELPRSTT	SALTPETRE
AEEHIPRSS	APHERESIS	AEEILRTTU	ELUTRIATE	AEELPRSTU	PULSE-RATE
AEEHKMORS	SHOEMAKER	AEEILSSUX	SEXUALISE	AEELRSSTW	WATERLESS
AEEHLLNOW	HALLOWE'EN	AEEILSUXZ	SEXUALIZE	AEELRSTUY	AUSTERELY
AEEHLLOSW	WHOLESALE	AEEILSVVY	EVASIVELY	AEELRSTVY	SEVERALTY
AEEHLMPRY	MELAPHYRE	AEEIMNNZZ	MEZZANINE	AEELSSSTT	TASTELESS
AEEHLMSSS	SHAMELESS	AEEIMNRTT	TERMINATE	AEEMMNORT	MANOMETER
AEEHLPSSS	SHAPELESS	AEEIMNRTV	VERMINATE	AEEMMNSTU	AMUSEMENT
AEEHLPTTY	TELEPATHY	AEEIMNSST	MEATINESS	AEEMMORTT	ATMOMETER
AEEHLRSST	HEARTLESS	AEEIMNSTT	ESTAMINET	AEEMMPRUY	EMPYREUMA
AEEHLRTWY	WEATHERLY	AEEIMORSW	WEARISOME	AEEMMRRST	STAMMERER
AEEHLSTXY	HEXASTYLE	AEEIMPRSS	PARSEEISM	AEEMNNOTT	ATONEMENT
AEEHMMPSY	EMPHYSEMA	AEEIMPRTT	IMPETRATE	AEEMNNPRT	PERMANENT
AEEHMNNOP	PHENOMENA	AEEIMRSTT	TASIMETER	AEEMNOPSU	MENOPAUSE
AEEHMOPRS	SEMAPHORE	AEEINNRTT	ENTERTAIN	AEEMNORUV	MANOEUVRE
AEEHMORST	HEARTSOME	AEEINNRTV	INNERVATE	AEEMNPRTY	REPAYMENT
	HORSEMEAT	AEEINNSST	INSENSATE	AEEMNRSST	STEERSMAN
AEEHNRTUW	UNWREATHE	AEEINORTT	ORIENTATE	AEEMNRTTT	TREATMENT
AEEHOPRTY	AEROPHYTE	AEEINPRSS	PARENESIS	AEEMNSTTT	STATEMENT
AEEHORRSW	RAREESHOW	AEEINPSVX	EXPANSIVE		TESTAMENT
AEEHORSUW	WAREHOUSE	AEEINRRTV	VERATRINE	AEEMORRTY	AEROMETRY
AEEHPRSTU	SUPERHEAT	AEEINRSSW	WEARINESS	AEEMORRTU	AMOURETTE
AEEHRRSTV	HARVESTER	AEEINRSTT	REINSTATE	AEEMPRRTU	PREMATURE
AEEIILMNT	ELIMINATE	AEEINRSTU	ESTUARINE	AEEMPRTTU	PERMUTATE
AEEIILRSS	SERIALISE	AEEINSTTT	INTESTATE	AEEMRRSTT	SMATTERER
AEEIILRST	ISRAELITE	AEEINTTTV	ATTENTIVE	AEENNPRTT	PENETRANT
AEEIINRTT	ITINERATE		TENTATIVE		REPENTANT
AEEIIPPRT	PERIPETIA	AEEIOPRTV	OPERATIVE	AEENOPRST	ESPERANTO
AEEIIPRTV	APERITIVE	AEEIPPRST	APPETISER		PERSONATE
AEEIIRSTV	VARIETIES	AEEIPPRTZ	APPETIZER	AEENOPTTT	POTENTATE
AEEIIRTTV	ITERATIVE	AEEIPPRUZ	PAUPERIZE	AEENORRTV	VENERATOR
AEEIIRTVZ	VIZIERATE	AEEIPRRST	SPARTERIE	AEENPPRSW	NEWSPAPER
AEEIJMNSS	JESSAMINE	AEEIPRRTV	PRIVATEER	AEENPRRTU	ENRAPTURE
AEEIKLNSS	LEAKINESS	AEEIPRSSV	ASPERSIVE	AEENPRSSS	SPARENESS
AEEIKMNSY	YANKEEISM	AEEIPRSVV	PERVASIVE	AEENPRSTY	SEPTENARY
AEEIKRRSS	SERASKIER	AEEIPRTTX	EXTIRPATE	AEENRRSTU	SAUNTERER
AEEILLMNT	METALLINE	AEEIRSSTV	ASSERTIVE	AEENSSSTW	WASTENESS
AEEILLMST	METALLISE	AEEJLMRSU	JERUSALEM	AEEOPRSTT	POETASTER
AEEILLMTZ	METALLIZE	AEEJMORTT	MAJORETTE	AEEORSTTV	OVERSTATE
AEEILLNOT	LINEOLATE	AEEKQRSSU	QUAKERESS	AEEORSTTW	TWO-SEATER
AEEILLSTT	SATELLITE	AEELLNRTY	ETERNALLY	AEEQRTTTU	QUARTETTE
AEEILMNNT	LINEAMENT	AEELLRRTV	TRAVELLER	AEEQRTUUX	EXEQUATUR
AEEILMNSS	MEALINESS	AEELLRSST	TESSELLAR	AEERRRSTU	SERRATURE
AEEILMORT	MELIORATE	AEELLRSVY	SEVERALLY		TREASURER
AEEILMRTU	ELATERIUM	AEELLSSUV	VALUELESS	AEERRRSTV	TRAVERSER
AEEILMTUV	EMULATIVE	AEELMNPSS	AMPLENESS	AEESTTTTU	STATUETTE
AEEILNNPR	PERENNIAL	AEELMPRXY	EXEMPLARY	AEFFIILRS	FALSIFIER
AEEILNNSX	SEXENNIAL	AEELMRSTT	STREAMLET	AEFFIJMOR	FIFE-MAJOR
AEEILNNTV	LEVANTINE	AEELNPRTV	PREVALENT	AEFFIKPST	PIKESTAFF
	VALENTINE	AEELNQSSU	EQUALNESS	AEFFILLUV	EFFLUVIAL
AEEILNOTV	ELEVATION	AEELNRSST	ALERTNESS	AEFFLLRUY	FEARFULLY
AEEILNPPP	PINEAPPLE	AEELNRSTY	EARNESTLY	AEFFLLTUY	FATEFULLY
AEEILNPRX	EXPLAINER	AEELNSSST	STALENESS	AEFFLORSW	SAFFLOWER
AEEILNPSX	EXPANSILE	AEELORTVY	ELEVATORY	AEFGHORRT	FORGATHER
AEEILNRSS	EARLINESS	AEELORUVV	OVERVALUE	AEFGIIMNR	MAGNIFIER
AEEILNSST	ESSENTIAL	AEELPPRRU	PUERPERAL	AEFGIIRRT	GRATIFIER
AEEILNTTV	VENTILATE	AEELPPRTU	PERPETUAL	AEFGILNRT	FALTERING
AEEILOPTT	PETIOLATE	AEELPQTTU	PLAQUETTE	AEFGINNST	FASTENING
EEILQRSU	EQUALISER	AEELPRRST	PLASTERER	AEFGINRTU	FIGURANTE
EEILQUVV	EQUIVALVE	AEELPRRSU	REPERUSAL	AEFGIORSS	OSSIFRAGE
EEILRRTV	RETRIEVAL	AEELPRRTU	PRELATURE	AEFGISTTU	FUSTIGATE

127

AEFGLLLMU	FLAGELLUM	AEGGLNNOR	LONG-RANGE	AEGIMMNSU	MAGNESIUM
AEFGLORTW	AFTER-GLOW	AEGGLRRST	STRAGGLER	AEGIMNNNU	UNMEANING
AEFGNOPRT	FRONT-PAGE	AEGGMORRT	MORTGAGER	AEGIMNNRT	GERMINANT
AEFHHLLTU	HEALTHFUL	AEGGNOSUY	SYNAGOGUE	AEGIMNORS	ORANGEISM
AEFHIKMST	MAKESHIFT	AEGGORRSS	AGGRESSOR	AEGINNORS	REASONING
AEFHILPST	FISH-PLATE	AEGHHINST	SHEATHING	AEGINNORW	NORWEGIAN
AEFHILSST	FAITHLESS	AEGHIKNRS	SHRINKAGE	AEGINNORZ	ORGANZINE
AEFHIMNRS	FISHERMAN	AEGHILNRS	SHEARLING	AEGINNOSS	SEASONING
AEFHINORS	FASHIONER	AEGHILNRT	EARTHLING	AEGINNRST	GANNISTER
AEFHIPRSS	FISH-SPEAR	AEGHILNSV	SHAVELING	AEGINNRTT	INTEGRANT
AEFHLLTUY	HATEFULLY	AEGHILRTY	LIGHT-YEAR	AEGINOPRS	SINGAPORE
AEFHLNNPY	HALFPENNY	AEGHIMNRT	NIGHTMARE	AEGINORRS	ORGANISER
AEFHLNSSW	NEWSFLASH	AEGHIMORR	HIEROGRAM	AEGINORRZ	ORGANIZER
AEFHLORTW	EARTH-WOLF	AEGHIMPPR	EPIPHRAGM	AEGINOSTT	GESTATION
AEFHMORSU	FARMHOUSE	AEGHINNPP	HAPPENING	AEGINRRTU	GARNITURE
AEFIILMPR	AMPLIFIER	AEGHINOPS	SIPHONAGE	AEGINRSTU	SIGNATURE
AEFIILNNT	INFANTILE	AEGHINRRS	GARNISHER	AEGIPRTUV	PURGATIVE
AEFIIMNNS	FENIANISM	AEGHIPPRY	EPIGRAPHY	AEGIRRRST	REGISTRAR
AEFIINNNT	INFANTINE	AEGHIPSTT	SPAGHETTI	AEGLLOSSW	GALLOWSES
AEFIINRTU	INFURIATE	AEGHLOOPR	OLEOGRAPH	AEGLLRRUY	REGULARLY
AEFIKLNSS	FLAKINESS	AEGHLOPTT	HEPTAGLOT	AEGLNORSU	GRANULOSE
AEFILMMOR	ORIFLAMME	AEGHLORTT	LARGHETTO	AEGLNRSST	STRANGLES
AEFILMNTU	FULMINATE	AEGHLRSTU	SLAUGHTER	AEGLNRSTY	STRANGELY
AEFILMORS	FORMALISE	AEGHNOOPY	HYPOGAEON	AEGLORRTU	REGULATOR
AEFILNNUZ	INFLUENZA	AEGIILLRS	GRISAILLE	AEGLORTTY	TETRALOGY
AEFILNORT	REFLATION	AEGIILMNR	REGIMINAL	AEGMMOPRR	PROGRAMM
AEFIMMNRT	FIRMAMENT	AEGIILMSV	VIGESIMAL	AEGMOOSUX	EXOGAMOU
AEFIMNOST	MANIFESTO	AEGIILNSZ	SIGNALIZE	AEGMORSSY	GOSSAMER
AEFIMORTV	FORMATIVE	AEGIILNTV	GENITIVAL	AEGMORSTY	GASOMETRY
AEFINNSST	FAINTNESS		VIGILANTE	AEGNNPRTU	REPUGNANT
AEFINORSU	NEFARIOUS	AEGIILNTY	GENIALITY	AEGOOPRRT	PROROGATE
AEFINPSTY	SAFETY-PIN	AEGIILSTV	VESTIGIAL	AEGORRRTT	GARROTTER
AEFINSSTT	FATTINESS	AEGIIMMRT	IMMIGRATE	AEGORRSTU	SURROGATE
AEFIORTUV	FAVOURITE	AEGIIMNNX	EXAMINING	AEHHILLLS	SHILLELAH
AEFIRRSTT	FIRST-RATE	AEGIIINNRT	RETAINING	AEHHILLTY	HEALTHILY
AEFKLLUWY	WAKEFULLY	AEGIINORT	ORIGINATE	AEHHINPST	THANESHIP
AEFKLNOSW	SNOWFLAKE	AEGIINSTT	INSTIGATE	AEHHISTWW	WHITEWAS
AEFKMORRW	FRAMEWORK	AEGIKMNRT	MARKETING	AEHHLNTUY	UNHEALTHY
AEFKNNRSS	FRANKNESS	AEGILLLLY	ILLEGALLY	AEHHLOPTY	HALOPHYTE
AEFLLMNOW	FELLOW-MAN	AEGILLLNU	GALLINULE	AEHHMOOPT	HOMEOPAT
AEFLLNTTU	FLATULENT	AEGILLNNP	PANELLING	AEHHNOPTY	THEOPHAN
AEFLLORST	FORESTALL	AEGILLNTU	LINGULATE	AEHHNORSW	HERONSHA
AEFLLSSTU	FAULTLESS	AEGILLRRU	GUERRILLA	AEHHNRSSS	HARSHNES
AEFLMORTU	FORMULATE	AEGILMNNT	ALIGNMENT	AEHHOPPST	PHOSPHATE
AEFLMRSTU	MASTERFUL	AEGILMNNY	MEANINGLY	AEHIILMTU	HUMILIATE
AEFLNOPRY	PROFANELY	AEGILMNPT	PIGMENTAL	AEHIIMRST	HETAIRISM
AEFLNSSUW	AWFULNESS	AEGILMORR	RIGMAROLE	AEHIINOPT	ETHIOPIAN
AEFLPRRUY	PRAYERFUL	AEGILMORS	GLAMORISE	AEHIINRSS	HAIRINESS
AEFMNOORW	FOREWOMAN	AEGILNNOO	NEOLOGIAN	AEHIIPSTT	HEPATITIS
AEFMORSTT	AFTERMOST	AEGILNORY	LEGIONARY	AEHIKNSSS	SHAKINESS
AEFNNOORT	AFTERNOON	AEGILNRTU	GRANULITE	AEHIKQRSU	QUAKERISH
AEFNORTTU	FORTUNATE	AEGILNSSW	WINE-GLASS	AEHILLMOP	PHILOMELA
AEFNRSSTU	TRANSFUSE	AEGILOOPS	APOLOGISE	AEHILLPTY	PHILATELY
AEFOPRRTY	PREFATORY	AEGILOOPZ	APOLOGIZE	AEHILLTWY	WEALTHILY
AEFRRSTTU	FRUSTRATE	AEGILOOTY	AETIOLOGY	AEHILMNPS	NEPHALISM
AEGGHIKNT	KNIGHTAGE	AEGILRRRU	IRREGULAR	AEHILNNOT	ANTHELION
AEGGHINRT	GATHERING	AEGILRSUV	VULGARISE	AEHILNOPR	PARHELION
AEGGHOPRY	GEOGRAPHY	AEGILRUVZ	VULGARIZE	AEHILNORT	LIONHEART
AEGGINNRV	ENGRAVING	AEGIMMNOT	GEMMATION	AEHILNOST	HAILSTONE
AEGGINORR	GREGORIAN	AEGIMMNRU	GERMANIUM	AEHILNPST	NEPHALIST
AEGGINPRT	PARGETING	AEGIMMNST	MAGNETISM	AEHILNQRU	HARLEQUI

AEHILOSTT	HELIOSTAT	AEIILNRTY	LINEARITY
AEHILPPTY	EPIPHYTAL	AEIILNSTW	WAISTLINE
AEHIMNNOT	ANTHEMION	AEIILNTVY	VENIALITY
AEHIMNORS	HARMONISE	AEIILORST	SOLITAIRE
AEHIMNORZ	HARMONIZE	AEIILRSTY	SERIALITY
AEHIMNPSS	MISSHAPEN	AEIILSSUV	VISUALISE
AEHIMNPST	PANTHEISM	AEIILSUVZ	VISUALIZE
AEHIMPSST	STEAMSHIP	AEIIMNPTT	IMPATIENT
AEHIMQSSU	SQUEAMISH	AEIIMNRTU	MINIATURE
AEHINORSS	HOARINESS	AEIIMPSSV	IMPASSIVE
AEHINPPSS	HAPPINESS	AEIINNRSS	RAININESS
AEHINPSSS	APISHNESS	AEIINNRTT	ITINERANT
AEHINPSTT	PANTHEIST	AEIINNSTU	INSINUATE
AEHINRRST	TARNISHER	AEIINOPTX	EXPIATION
AEHINRRSV	VARNISHER	AEIINORTT	ITERATION
AEHINSSST	HASTINESS	AEIINOTTV	NOVITIATE
AEHINSSSW	WASHINESS	AEIINRRTY	ITINERARY
AEHIORSTT	HESITATOR	AEIIPRTTV	PARTITIVE
AEHIORSTU	AUTHORISE	AEIIPRTVV	PRIVATIVE
AEHIORTTV	HORTATIVE	AEIIPSTTT	STIPITATE
AEHIORTUZ	AUTHORIZE	AEIJMNNSS	JANSENISM
AEHJLNOPP	APPLE-JOHN	AEIJNNSST	JANSENIST
AEHKLNSST	THANKLESS	AEIKLMNOW	WOMANLIKE
AEHKORRTW	EARTHWORK	AEIKLNRUW	UNWARLIKE
AEHLLMRTY	THERMALLY	AEIKMQRSU	QUAKERISM
AEHLMOOST	LOATHSOME	AEIKNNPRS	SPINNAKER
AEHLMOSSU	ALMS-HOUSE	AEILLLRTY	LITERALLY
AEHLNNOPR	ALPENHORN	AEILLMNRY	MILLENARY
AEHLNPSUY	UNSHAPELY	AEILLMSSY	AIMLESSLY
AEHLNRTUY	UNEARTHLY	AEILLMSTT	METALLIST
AEHLOPRSY	HORSEPLAY	AEILLNOPT	POLLINATE
AEHLOPSUY	PLAYHOUSE	AEILLNPRY	PLENARILY
AEHMMOORT	HARMOTOME	AEILLNRST	REINSTALL
AEHMNNSSU	HUMANNESS	AEILLNRTU	TELLURIAN
AEHMNRRWY	WHERRYMAN	AEILLNSTY	SALIENTLY
AEHMORRTW	EARTHWORM	AEILLOPPS	PAPILLOSE
AEHNNRSSU	UNHARNESS	AEILLOPPT	POPLITEAL
AEHNOOPRR	HARPOONER	AEILLPRSU	PLURALISE
AEHNOOPSX	SAXOPHONE	AEILLPRUZ	PLURALIZE
AEHNORSTT	NORTH-EAST	AEILLPSTU	PULSATILE
AEHNPRSSS	SHARPNESS	AEILLRRTY	ARTILLERY
AEHOOORRT	OTORRHOEA	AEILLRVXY	VEXILLARY
AEHOOPSTT	OSTEOPATH	AEILMNNSS	MANLINESS
AEHOOSSTU	OASTHOUSE	AEILMNOOT	EMOTIONAL
AEHORSSTU	AUTHORESS	AEILMNORS	NORMALISE
AEHORSTWY	SEAWORTHY	AEILMNORZ	NORMALIZE
AEHOSSTTU	SOUTH-EAST	AEILMNOSS	MELANOSIS
AEHRSSTUU	THESAURUS	AEILMNOTU	EMULATION
AEIIILRVZ	VIZIERIAL	AEILMNPSU	ASPLENIUM
AEIIILTVX	LIXIVIATE	AEILMNPTU	PENULTIMA
AEIIIMTTV	IMITATIVE	AEILMNRVY	LIVERYMAN
AEIIKKTTW	KITTIWAKE	AEILMNTTY	MENTALITY
AEIIKRSTT	KERATITIS	AEILMORRS	MORALISER
AEIILLTTT	TITILLATE	AEILMORRZ	MORALIZER
AEIILNNRT	TRIENNIAL	AEILMSSVY	MASSIVELY
AEIILNOTV	INVIOLATE	AEILMSTTU	STIMULATE
AEIILNPRT	REPTILIAN	AEILNNOPR	NONPAREIL
AEIILNPTV	PLAINTIVE	AEILNNPSU	PENINSULA
EIILNPTZ	PLATINIZE	AEILNNPTY	PINNATELY
EIILNRRT	TRILINEAR	AEILNNTUV	UNIVALENT
AEIILNRSU	UNISERIAL	AEILNOOPS	POLONAISE
AEIINNPSS	RANITIPOLE(?)		

AEILNOPRT	RANTIPOLE
AEILNOPTT	POTENTIAL
AEILNORSS	SENSORIAL
AEILNORTT	NATROLITE
AEILNOSSS	SESSIONAL
AEILNPRTY	INTERPLAY
AEILNPSTY	SAPIENTLY
AEILNPTTY	PATIENTLY
AEILNPTUV	PULVINATE
AEILNRSUV	UNIVERSAL
AEILNRTUY	UNREALITY
AEILNSSST	SLATINESS
AEILNSSST	STAINLESS
AEILNSSTT	TAINTLESS
AEILNSSTW	SLANTWISE
AEILNSUUX	UNISEXUAL
AEILOOSTT	OSTIOLATE
AEILOPRRS	POLARISER
AEILOPRRZ	POLARIZER
AEILORSST	TAILORESS
AEILORTTX	TEXTORIAL
AEILPPRTU	PREPUTIAL
AEILPRSTT	PRELATIST
AEILPRTVY	PRIVATELY
AEILPSSVY	PASSIVELY
AEILPSTTU	STIPULATE
AEILPSTUV	PULSATIVE
AEILQRRUY	RELIQUARY
AEILRTUUX	LUXURIATE
AEILSSUVY	SUASIVELY
AEILSTUXY	SEXUALITY
AEIMMMNOT	MAMMONITE
AEIMMNNRS	MANNERISM
AEIMMNOPT	PANTOMIME
AEIMMRSSU	SUMMARISE
AEIMMRSUZ	SUMMARIZE
AEIMNNOPU	PNEUMONIA
AEIMNNOST	MINNESOTA
AEIMNNOTT	MENTATION
AEIMNNRST	MANNERIST
AEIMNORRZ	ROMANIZER
AEIMNORTZ	MATRONIZE
AEIMNPRST	SPEARMINT
AEIMNRTTY	MATERNITY
AEIMNSSSS	MASSINESS
AEIMOPRTX	PROXIMATE
AEIMOPSTT	OPTIMATES
AEIMPPRSU	PAUPERISM
AEIMPRRTT	PART-TIMER
AEIMPRTUZ	TRAPEZIUM
AEIMRRTTY	TERMITARY
AEIMRRTYZ	MARTYRIZE
AEINNNOTW	NEWTONIAN
AEINNNPTU	NEPTUNIAN
AEINNOPSX	EXPANSION
AEINNORST	NESTORIAN
AEINNORTV	NERVATION
	VERNATION
AEINNOSST	SENSATION
AEINNOTTT	ATTENTION
AEINNPPSS	NAPPINESS

AEINNRSTT	TRANSIENT	
AEINNRSTU	SATURNINE	
AEINNRSTY	TYRANNISE	
AEINNRTYZ	TYRANNIZE	
AEINNSSST	NASTINESS	
AEINNSSTT	NATTINESS	
AEINNSSTW	TAWNINESS	
AEINOOPRT	OPERATION	
AEINOPPRT	REAPPOINT	
AEINOPRSS	ASPERSION	
AEINOPRST	PATRONISE	
AEINOPRSY	AEPYORNIS	
AEINOPRTZ	PATRONIZE	
AEINORRST	SERRATION	
AEINORSST	ASSERTION	
AEINORSSU	ARSENIOUS	
AEINORSTT	STATIONER	
AEINPPSSS	SAPPINESS	
AEINPRRST	TRANSPIRE	
AEINPRTTY	PATERNITY	
AEINRRSTT	RESTRAINT	
AEINRRTTV	TRAVERTIN	
AEINRSSTT	RESISTANT	
AEINRSSTU	SUSTAINER	
AEIOPRTXY	EXPIATORY	
AEIOSTUVX	VEXATIOUS	
AEIQRTTUZ	QUARTZITE	
AEIRRSSTT	TRAITRESS	
AEIRRTTTU	TRITURATE	
AEIRSTTTX	TESTATRIX	
AEIRSTTUY	AUSTERITY	
AEJLLOSUY	JEALOUSLY	
AEJOPSTUX	JUXTAPOSE	
AEKLLSSST	STALKLESS	
AEKMNOPSS	SPOKESMAN	
AELLLMOSU	MALLEOLUS	
AELLLRSTU	STELLULAR	
AELLLSSWY	LAWLESSLY	
AELLMNOTT	ALLOTMENT	
AELLMNRUY	NUMERALLY	
AELLMNSSS	SMALLNESS	
AELLNOTTT	ATTOLLENT	
AELLNPSST	PLANTLESS	
AELLNQUUY	UNEQUALLY	
AELLNRTUY	NEUTRALLY	
AELLNSSUY	SENSUALLY	
AELLORSWW	SWALLOWER	
AELLOSUYZ	ZEALOUSLY	
AELLRSSTY	ARTLESSLY	
AELLTTUXY	TEXTUALLY	
AELMMOSUU	MAUSOLEUM	
AELMNNNTU	ANNULMENT	
AELMNNOOP	MONOPLANE	
AELMNORWW	LAWNMOWER	
AELMNRSTU	MENSTRUAL	
AELNRRUVY	VULNERARY	
AELNRSTTU	RESULTANT	
AELNSSSTU	SULTANESS	
AELOORRTT	TOLERATOR	
AELOPRRTY	PROLETARY	
	PYROLATER	

AELOPSTTU	POSTULATE	
AELPPRRUU	PURPUREAL	
AELPSTTUU	PUSTULATE	
AELQRRTUY	QUARTERLY	
AEMMNORTY	MOMENTARY	
AEMMNRSTU	SARMENTUM	
AEMMRSTYY	ASYMMETRY	
AEMNORRTU	NUMERATOR	
AEMNORSTY	MONASTERY	
AEMNRSSST	SMARTNESS	
AEMNRSTTU	TRANSMUTE	
AEMOPRRTY	TEMPORARY	
AEMOPSTTY	ASYMPTOTE	
AEMQRRTUY	MARQUETRY	
AENOORRST	RESONATOR	
AENOORRTV	RENOVATOR	
AENOPRSST	PATRONESS	
	TRANSPOSE	
AEOPRRRTY	PORTRAYER	
AEOPRRSTT	PROSTRATE	
AEOQRRSSU	SQUARROSE	
AEOQRSTUZ	QUARTZOSE	
AEORSSTUU	TROUSSEAU	
AEPPRSTUU	SUPPURATE	
AEPQRRTUY	PARQUETRY	
AERRSTTWY	STEWARTRY	
AFFIILNPT	PLAINTIFF	
AFFILLNTY	FLAYFLINT	
AFFILNRUY	RUFFIANLY	
AFGGILNOS	FOG-SIGNAL	
AFGHILLNT	NIGHTFALL	
AFGHORSTU	FAR-SOUGHT	
AFGIILRTY	FRAGILITY	
AFGILNNTU	FLAUNTING	
AFGILNORV	FLAVORING	
AFGILRTUY	FRUGALITY	
AFGINNPRY	FRYING-PAN	
AFHIMNOSW	FISHWOMAN	
AFHLLMRUY	HARMFULLY	
AFIIILNOT	FILIATION	
AFIILNNOT	INFLATION	
AFIILNOOT	FOLIATION	
AFIIMNRRY	INFIRMARY	
AFIINNOST	SAINTFOIN	
AFIINORSU	INFUSORIA	
AFILLNOUX	FLUXIONAL	
AFILLNPUY	PAINFULLY	
AFILLOOPR	APRIL-FOOL	
AFILLORRT	TRIFLORAL	
AFILMMORS	FORMALISM	
AFILMORRV	LARVIFORM	
AFILMORST	FORMALIST	
AFILMORTY	FORMALITY	
AFILNOOTT	FLOTATION	
AFIMNNORT	INFORMANT	
AFIMNOORT	FORMATION	
AFIMORRTU	TAURIFORM	
AFINOPRTY	PROFANITY	
AFKLOOSTT	FOOT-STALK	
AFLLLPUYY	PLAYFULLY	
AFLMORRUY	FORMULARY	

AFLOORSUV	FLAVOROUS	
AFLOPRRSU	FLUOR-SPAR	
AFMNORRST	TRANSFORM	
AGGHILOOY	HAGIOLOGY	
AGGHILSWY	WAGGISHLY	
AGGIILNVW	LAWGIVING	
AGGILNNOS	GANGLIONS	
AGGILNPSY	GASPINGLY	
AGHHILTUY	HAUGHTILY	
AGHHINRST	THRASHING	
AGHHLOOPR	HOLOGRAPH	
AGHHMOOPR	HOMOGRAPH	
AGHIINPST	GIANTSHIP	
AGHIINRSV	RAVISHING	
AGHILLMPT	LAMPLIGHT	
AGHILMORT	LOGARITHM	
AGHILNPTY	PLAYTHING	
AGHILNTUY	NAUGHTILY	
AGHILOOPT	LOTOPHAGI	
AGHILRSTT	STARLIGHT	
AGHIMNRST	HAMSTRING	
AGHIMOPRY	AMPHIGORY	
AGHIMORST	HISTOGRAM	
AGHIPRSUU	AUGURSHIP	
AGHLMNOPU	PLOUGHMAN	
AGHLNOOTY	ANTHOLOGY	
AGHLNOSTU	ONSLAUGHT	
AGHLOOPTY	PATHOLOGY	
AGHLOPPRY	POLYGRAPH	
AGHLOPRXY	XYLOGRAPH	
AGHMNOOPR	MONOGRAPH	
	PHONOGRAM	
AGHMOPRYY	MYOGRAPHY	
AGHOOPRRY	OROGRAPHY	
AGHOOPRYZ	ZOOGRAPHY	
AGIIILNRV	VIRGILIAN	
AGIIKLMNR	GRIMALKIN	
AGIIILLNRY	RAILINGLY	
AGIILLNWY	WAILINGLY	
AGIILMNTY	MALIGNITY	
AGIILNORT	TAILORING	
AGIILNSSS	ISINGLASS	
AGIIMMNRT	IMMIGRANT	
AGIIMNORT	MIGRATION	
AGIIMRSTT	TRIGAMIST	
AGIINNORS	SIGNORINA	
AGIINNRTY	TRIGYNIAN	
AGIINRSTY	SIGNITARY	
AGIIRSSTT	GASTRITIS	
AGIIRSTTU	GUITARIST	
AGIKLNPRS	SPARKLING	
AGILLNSTY	LASTINGLY	
AGILMNNOO	MONGOLIAN	
AGILMNOPY	PYGMALION	
AGILMNSUY	AMUSINGLY	
AGILMRSUV	VULGARISM	
AGILNNRWY	WARNINGLY	
AGILNORVY	VAINGLORY	
AGILNPRSY	SPARINGLY	
AGILNRSTT	STARTLING	
AGILNRSTY	STARINGLY	

AGILOOPST	APOLOGIST	AIIIMNOTT	IMITATION
AGILRRTUY	GARRULITY	AIIINNNOT	INANITION
AGILRTUVY	VULGARITY	AIIINORTT	INITIATOR
AGIMMNSUY	GYMNASIUM	AIIINOTTV	VITIATION
AGIMNORSU	IGNORAMUS	AIIJLOTVY	JOVIALITY
AGIMORRTY	MIGRATORY	AIILLMRSY	SIMILARLY
AGINNPRSU	UNSPARING	AIILLRTVY	TRIVIALLY
AGINNRUVY	UNVARYING	AIILMMNUU	ALUMINIUM
AGINOPRTU	PURGATION	AIILMNORT	TRINOMIAL
AGINORSTY	SIGNATORY	AIILMPRRY	PRIMARILY
AGINPPRST	STRAPPING	AIILMRSTU	RITUALISM
	TRAPPINGS	AIILNOOST	ISOLATION
AGLLNOOPY	POLYGONAL	AIILNOOTV	VIOLATION
AGLMOORSU	GLAMOROUS	AIILNOQTU	LIQUATION
AGLNORSUU	GRANULOUS	AIILNRSST	SINISTRAL
AGLOORSTY	ASTROLOGY	AIILPRSTU	SPIRITUAL
AGLOOTTUY	TAUTOLOGY	AIILRSTTU	RITUALIST
AGLORRSUU	GARRULOUS	AIILSTUVY	VISUALITY
AGLORSSTW	GLASSWORT	AIIMMPRSV	VAMPIRISM
AGMMNOORS	GROOMSMAN	AIIMNNTUY	UNANIMITY
AGMNSSTUY	NYSTAGMUS	AIIMNOPSS	IMPASSION
AGNNOPPTU	OPPUGNANT	AIIMNOSTY	ANIMOSITY
AGNNRRSTUY	STRANGURY	AIIINNORTU	RUINATION
AGOPRRTUY	PURGATORY		URINATION
AGORSTTUY	GUSTATORY	AIINNOSTU	SINUATION
AHHILMOPT	PHILOMATH	AIINOPRTT	PARTITION
AHIILORSU	HILARIOUS	AIINOPRTV	PRIVATION
AHIILOSST	HALITOSIS	AIINORSTT	STRIATION
AHIILPRSV	RIVALSHIP	AIINORSVY	VISIONARY
AHIINORST	HISTORIAN	AIINORTTT	ATTRITION
AHIINPSST	SAINTSHIP		TITRATION
AHIIPPRTY	HIPPIATRY	AIINOSTTU	SITUATION
AHIIPRSSZ	SIZARSHIP	AIINQTTUY	ANTIQUITY
AHIIRRSTT	ARTHRITIS	AIINRTUVV	VITRUVIAN
AHIJMOPRS	MAJORSHIP	AIIOPRSSS	PSORIASIS
AHIKLMSWY	MAWKISHLY	AIIOPRSTT	PAROTITIS
AHIKLNSVY	KNAVISHLY	AIIPRTTUY	PITUITARY
AHILLSSVY	SLAVISHLY	AIIPSSTVY	PASSIVITY
AHILMNNUY	INHUMANLY	AIKLNOSSY	ANKYLOSIS
AHILMPRTU	TRIUMPHAL	AIKMNNOSW	KINSWOMAN
AHILNOPTY	NOTAPHILY	AILLMMORY	IMMORALLY
AHILNPPUY	UNHAPPILY	AILLMNNOY	NOMINALLY
AHILPSSWY	WASPISHLY	AILLMPRSU	PLURALISM
AHIMMNORU	HARMONIUM	AILLNORST	TONSILLAR
AHIMNORST	HARMONIST	AILLNRSUY	INSULARLY
AHIMOPSUX	AMPHIOXUS	AILLPRSTU	PLURALIST
AHINNOOPT	PHONATION	AILLPRTUY	PLURALITY
AHINNOPTY	ANTIPHONY	AILLRTTUY	TITULARLY
AHINOORTT	HORTATION	AILLRTUVY	VIRTUALLY
AHIOPPRRY	PORPHYRIA	AILMMOORT	IMMOLATOR
AHIOPPSSY	APOPHYSIS	AILMMRSUY	SUMMARILY
AHIOPRSUV	VAPOURISH	AILMMTTUU	ULTIMATUM
AHIORTTUY	AUTHORITY	AILMNOPST	PLATONISM
AHLLLOSWY	SHALLOWLY	AILMNORTU	TOURMALIN
AHLLOPSUY	APHYLLOUS	AILMNOSUU	ALUMINOUS
AHLORSTTW	STALWORTH	AILMNSTTU	STIMULANT
AHMOOPRSU	AMORPHOUS	AILMORSTU	SIMULATOR
AHNOPSTYY	HYPONASTY	AILMORTTU	MUTILATOR
AHOOPRRTX	PROTHORAX	AILMORTTY	MORTALITY
AHOORRTTY	HORTATORY	AILMOSSTY	ATMOLYSIS
AIILLNTY	INITIALLY	AILMPRSTY	PALMISTRY

AILNNOPTU	PLUTONIAN
AILNNSTTY	INSTANTLY
AILNOORST	TONSORIAL
	TORSIONAL
AILNOOTUV	OVULATION
AILNOPSTT	PLATONIST
AILNOPSTU	PLATINOUS
	PULSATION
AILNORSTU	INSULATOR
AILNOSUXY	ANXIOUSLY
AILNPPSTU	SUPPLIANT
AILNPQTUY	PIQUANTLY
AILNRTUUX	LUXURIANT
AILOOPRST	SPOLIATOR
AILOORSUV	VARIOLOUS
AILORSUVY	SAVOURILY
	VARIOUSLY
AILPRRSSU	SURPRISAL
AIMMMMNOS	MAMMONISM
AIMMMNOST	MAMMONIST
AIMMNORTY	MATRIMONY
AIMMNOSTU	SUMMATION
AIMMPRSUU	MARSUPIUM
AIMMRSSTU	SUMMARIST
AIMNNOORT	NOMINATOR
AIMNNOPST	POINTSMAN
AIMNNOSUU	UNANIMOUS
AIMNNOTYY	ANONYMITY
AIMNOPRSY	PARSIMONY
AIMNOPRTT	IMPORTANT
AIMNOPRTY	PATRIMONY
AIMNORRTU	RUMINATOR
AIMOPSSTU	POTASSIUM
AINNNOSTU	UNISONANT
AINNOOPRT	PRONATION
AINNOORTV	INNOVATOR
AINOOPPRT	APPORTION
AINOOQTTU	QUOTATION
AINOPRSST	SOPRANIST
AINOPRSSU	UNIPAROUS
AIOOPRSUV	OVIPAROUS
AIORRSSTU	SARTORIUS
AKLMNORWY	WORKMANLY
AKMNOORWW	WORKWOMAN
ALLNOOPYZ	POLYZONAL
ALLNOPTTU	POLLUTANT
ALLNSUUUY	UNUSUALLY
ALLOOPRTY	ALLOTROPY
ALLOPPRUY	POPULARLY
ALMMNRUUY	NUMMULARY
ALMMNSSUU	MUSSULMAN
ALMNNOUWY	UNWOMANLY
ALMNOPRUY	PULMONARY
ALMOORSUY	AMOROUSLY
ALNOPPRUU	UNPOPULAR
ALNOPSTTU	POSTULANT
ALNORTUVY	VOLUNTARY
ALOPRSTUY	PULSATORY
AMNNOOSUY	ANONYMOUS
AMNOORSTY	ASTRONOMY
AMNOPRSST	SPORTSMAN

131

AMOOORSTV	VASOMOTOR	BCEEIPRRS	PRESCRIBE	BDDENNOUU	UNBOUNDED
AMPRSTUUY	SUMPTUARY	BCEELNOSY	OBSCENELY	BDDENOTUU	UNDOUBTED
ANNORSTUY	TYRANNOUS	BCEEMNRTU	RECUMBENT	BDDENSUUU	UNSUBDUED
ANOPRRSTT	TRANSPORT	BCEENPSTU	PUBESCENT	BDDFILLNO	BLINDFOLD
ANORSUUVY	UNSAVOURY	BCEFFIOOX	BOX-OFFICE	BDDFMNOUU	DUMBFOUND
AOOORRRTW	ARROWROOT	BCEFIIKRR	FIRE-BRICK	BDEEEELRV	BELVEDERE
AOPRRSTUU	RAPTUROUS	BCEFIJOTY	OBJECTIFY	BDEEENRTU	DEBENTURE
AORSTTTUY	STATUTORY	BCEFKLTUU	BUCKETFUL	BDEEFIILS	DISBELIEF
BBBEEELMU	BUMBLE-BEE	BCEHIOQUU	CHIBOUQUE	BDEEFLORW	FLOWER-BED
BBBEGLMUU	BUBBLE-GUM	BCEHLLNPU	BELL-PUNCH	BDEEGGLOW	BOW-LEGGED
BBCCHKLOU	CHUBB-LOCK	BCEHLOSUU	CLUB-HOUSE	BDEEIILLN	INDELIBLE
BBCEHKMOT	BOMB-KETCH	BCEHMNOOY	HONEYCOMB	BDEEILLRW	BRIDEWELL
BBCEILRRS	SCRIBBLER	BCEIILPSU	PUBLICISE	BDEEILMSS	DISSEMBLE
BBCEIRSSU	SUBSCRIBE	BCEIILPUZ	PUBLICIZE	BDEEIMMRS	DISMEMBER
BBCIIILST	BIBLICIST	BCEIINOST	BISECTION	BDEEIMORR	EMBROIDER
BBDEIORRW	BOWER-BIRD	BCEIJNOOT	OBJECTION	BDEEIORRR	BROIDERER
BBDELMMOU	BUMBLEDOM	BCEILMNOU	COLUMBINE	BDEEIRSTT	BED-SITTER
BBEEEEINRR	BERBERINE	BCEILMOTU	COLUMBITE	BDEELLSSY	BLESSEDLY
BBEGHIIRS	GIBBERISH	BCEILNORU	COLUBRINE	BDEELNRRU	BLUNDERER
BBEGHILOS	BOBSLEIGH	BCEIMNNTU	INCUMBENT	BDEELNSSU	UNBLESSED
BBEGORTTU	BOG-BUTTER	BCEIMNORY	EMBRYONIC	BDEEMRSSU	SUBMERSED
BBEHLLMOS	BOMB-SHELL	BCEIMORTY	EMBRYOTIC	BDEEORVYY	EVERYBODY
BBEHRRSUY	SHRUBBERY	BCEINOSTY	OBSCENITY	BDEFILLOO	LIFE-BLOOD
BBEMNORUX	BOX-NUMBER	BCEINSSUU	INCUBUSES	BDEFINORY	BOYFRIEND
BBEERRTTU	BUTTER-BUR	BCEIOPRRS	PROSCRIBE	BDEFLOSTU	SELF-DOUBT
BBFMOOOPR	BOMB-PROOF	BCEIORSTT	OBSTETRIC	BDEGHINRU	EDINBURGH
BBGHILNOO	HOBGOBLIN	BCELORSUY	OBSCURELY	BDEGIIILR	DIRIGIBLE
BBGIIOSTY	GIBBOSITY	BCEMOORSY	CORYMBOSE	BDEGIILOS	DISOBLIGE
BBGILOSUY	GIBBOUSLY	BCENORSTU	CURB-STONE	BDEGINNNU	UNBENDING
BBIIMNORS	RIBBONISM	BCEORRRWY	CROW-BERRY	BDEHIIINT	INHIBITED
BCCCKMOOS	COCKSCOMB	BCEPRTTUU	BUTTERCUP	BDEHIIRYZ	HYBRIDIZE
BCCEEEILOR	COERCIBLE	BCFFIKSTU	BUFF-STICK	BDEIIILSV	DIVISIBLE
BCCEHIKNP	PINCHBECK	BCGILMNSU	SCUMBLING	BDEIIILTY	EDIBILITY
BCCEINNOU	CONCUBINE	BCHHIKSSU	BUCKSHISH	BDEIILLNY	INDELIBLY
BCCIILSTY	BICYCLIST	BCHIIOPRS	BISHOPRIC	BDEIILSTV	DEVIL'S-BIT
BCCIORSTU	SCORBUTIC	BCHKNORTU	BUCKTHORN	BDEIISSSU	SUBSIDISE
BCCMOORXY	COXCOMBRY	BCHKOOTTU	BUCK-TOOTH	BDEIISSUZ	SUBSIDIZE
BCCMORRUY	CURRY-COMB	BCHLOOOSY	SCHOOL-BOY	BDEILNNSS	BLINDNESS
BCDDEEILU	DEDUCIBLE	BCHMOOOTT	TOOTHCOMB	BDEILORUV	OVERBUILD
BCDDIIKRY	DICKY-BIRD	BCIIKKLNR	BRICK-KILN	BDEIMMNST	DISENTOMB
BCDEEEFIN	BENEFICED	BCIILMSUU	UMBILICUS	BDEINRSST	BIRD'S-NEST
BCDEEEINO	OBEDIENCE	BCIILPSTU	PUBLICIST	BDEIRRSTU	DISTURBER
BCDEEILRU	REDUCIBLE	BCIILPTUY	PUBLICITY	BDELLOOSS	BLOODLESS
BCDEEIRRS	DESCRIBER	BCIIMOSTY	SYMBIOTIC	BDELLORUZ	BULLDOZER
BCDEELRTU	TUBERCLED	BCIKKORRW	BRICKWORK	BDELMNPUU	UNPLUMBED
BCDEEMNTU	DECUMBENT	BCILLORSS	CROSSBILL	BDELNOSSU	BOUNDLESS
BCDEIILNU	INDUCIBLE	BCILLORSW	CROW'S-BILL	BDELOOSTT	BLOOD-TEST
BCDEORRSS	CROSS-BRED	BCILMMOUU	COLUMBIUM	BDELOSSTU	DOUBTLESS
BCDHKNOUU	BUCK-HOUND	BCIOOPRSS	PROBOSCIS	BDFIOORST	BIRD'S-FOOT
BCDOPRTUY	BY-PRODUCT	BCIORSTUY	OBSCURITY	BDHIIMRSY	HYBRIDISM
BCEEEEHRS	BESEECHER	BCIPRSSTU	SUBSCRIPT	BDHIIRTYY	HYBRIDITY
BCEEEHKNO	CHEEK-BONE	BCMNOOORR	BROOM-CORN	BDHLOOOST	BLOOD-SHOT
BCEEEKLPS	BESPECKLE	BCDDDEEINR	BEDRIDDEN	BDHOORSUW	BRUSHWOOD
BCEEFFGOU	COFFEE-BUG	BDDEEORTU	REDOUBTED	BDIIIILSVY	DIVISIBLY
BCEEGHINR	BREECHING	BDDEFINOR	FORBIDDEN	BDIIMORTY	MORBIDITY
BCEEHKOOR	CHOKE-BORE	BDDEHLOOS	BLOODSHED	BDIIRTTUY	TURBIDITY
BCEEIJOTV	OBJECTIVE	BDDEIISUV	SUBDIVIDE	BDILMNORW	BLIND-WORM
BCEEILLOS	BELLICOSE	BDDEIILNRU	UNBRIDLED	BDILOSUUY	DUBIOUSLY
BCEEILRTY	CELEBRITY	BDDEIMOSY	DISEMBODY	BDINOOWWW	BOW-WINDOW
BCEEINOOT	COENOBITE	BDDEINRSU	DISBURDEN	BEEEEHNRS	SHEBEENER
BCEEINRTT	CENTRE-BIT			BEEEEKMRW	EMBER-WEEK

BEEEGIMNS	BESEEMING	BEGHINORU	NEIGHBOUR	BFIINORSU	FIBRINOUS
BEEEGNOOW	WOEBEGONE	BEGHLNORU	BUGLE-HORN	BFILNOTUU	BOUNTIFUL
BEEEHLLOR	HELLEBORE	BEGIILLLY	ILLEGIBLY	BFIMORRSU	BURSIFORM
BEEEHORSU	BEER-HOUSE	BEGIIMNRT	TIMBERING	BFINORRST	FIRST-BORN
BEEEILMNT	BELEMNITE	BEGIINNTY	BENIGNITY	BGHLOOPUY	PLOUGHBOY
BEEEIMRSV	SEMIBREVE	BEGIINSST	BIESTINGS	BGIILMOOR	IMBROGLIO
BEEEKOPRX	BOX-KEEPER	BEGILMNRT	TREMBLING	BGIILOOST	BIOLOGIST
BEEEKRRRS	BERSERKER	BEGINORSU	SUBREGION	BGIKNOPRS	SPRINGBOK
BEEELMRZZ	EMBEZZLER	BEGINORSV	OBSERVING	BGILOOSTY	GLOBOSITY
BEEELSSSU	SUBLESSEE	BEGIOORSU	BOURGEOIS	BGINNORTU	BINTURONG
BEEEMNORY	BEER-MONEY	BEHIILPST	PHLEBITIS	BGINORSTW	BOW-STRING
BEEEMPRST	SEPTEMBER	BEHIIORTX	EXHIBITOR	BGLLOOSUU	GLOBULOUS
BEEENOSSS	OBESENESS	BEHIIRSTT	BITTERISH	BGLMOOSYY	SYMBOLOGY
BEEFFGIRU	FEBRIFUGE	BEHIKLOSV	BOLSHEVIK	BHIIINORT	INHIBITOR
BEEFFHLUW	BUFF-WHEEL	BEHILPRSU	PUBLISHER	BHILMNOTY	BIMONTHLY
BEEFIILMS	MISBELIEF		REPUBLISH	BHILOORSY	BOORISHLY
BEEFILRSS	BRIEFLESS	BEHINRRSU	BURNISHER	BHILRSTEY	BRUTISHLY
BEEFKLRUU	REBUKEFUL	BEHINSSSU	BUSHINESS	BHLLOOOTT	TOLLBOOTH
BEEGHIRTY	EYE-BRIGHT	BEHLMSSTU	THUMBLESS	BIIILNSVY	INVISIBLY
BEEGIILLL	ILLEGIBLE	BEHLORRTY	BROTHERLY	BIILMSTUY	SUBLIMITY
BEEGIILNV	BELIEVING	BEHLORSST	THROBLESS	BIILOOSUV	OBLIVIOUS
BEEGILLNW	WELLBEING	BEHNNRTUU	UNBURTHEN	BIILOQTUY	OBLIQUITY
BEEGINSST	BEESTINGS	BEHNORSTU	BUHRSTONE	BIIMOPRTY	IMPROBITY
BEEGINSTT	BESETTING	BEIIILNSV	INVISIBLE	BIIMOSSSY	SYMBIOSIS
BEEHIIRTX	EXHIBITER	BEIILLNSY	SIBYLLINE	BILLNORST	STILL-BORN
BEEHILLMS	EMBELLISH	BEIILMOSS	OMISSIBLE	BILMMOSSY	SYMBOLISM
BEEHINRTT	TEREBINTH	BEIILORTT	TRILOBITE	BILMOSSTY	SYMBOLIST
BEEHIORRV	HERBIVORE	BEIILSTUZ	SUBTILIZE	BILOOSUVY	OBVIOUSLY
BEEHLOPRY	HYPERBOLE	BEIKLNSSU	BULKINESS	BILORSSTU	STROBILUS
BEEIINRTY	INEBRIETY	BEIKNRSSS	BRISKNESS	BIMOPSTUU	BUMPTIOUS
BEEILLNOR	REBELLION	BEILLLOSU	LIBELLOUS	BINOOOSUX	OBNOXIOUS
BEEILLNTU	EBULLIENT	BEILLMSUY	SUBLIMELY	BINOORSTU	OBTRUSION
BEEILOTTU	OUBLIETTE	BEILLNOSU	INSOLUBLE	BKMOORUUZ	ZUMBOORUK
BEEILSTUV	VESTIBULE	BEILLOQUY	OBLIQUELY	BKOOORSTY	STORY-BOOK
BEEIMRRSU	REIMBURSE	BEILLSTUY	SUBTILELY	BLLORTTUU	BULL-TROUT
BEEINRTTU	BUTTERINE	BEILMOSSY	SYMBOLISE	BLMORSSUU	SLUMBROUS
BEEIQRTTU	BRIQUETTE	BEILMOSYZ	SYMBOLIZE	BLOORSTUU	TROUBLOUS
BEELLORTW	BELL-TOWER	BEILNPRTU	BLUE-PRINT	BLSSSTUUU	SUBSULTUS
BEELMNORU	MELBOURNE	BEILNRSSU	BURLINESS	CCCEEINRT	ECCENTRIC
BEELMRRSU	SLUMBERER	BEIMNORST	BRIMSTONE	CCCEILOOT	COCCOLITE
BEELNNOSS	NOBLENESS	BEIMRTTUY	YTTERBIUM	CCCENOORT	CONCOCTER
BEELNOSTU	BLUE-STONE	BEINOOSSS	OBSESSION	CCCHIINNO	CINCHONIC
BEELORSVY	VERBOSELY	BEIOORRRT	BRIER-ROOT	CCCHILMOU	COLCHICUM
BEELQRSUU	BURLESQUE	BEIOQRSTU	SOBRIQUET	CCCHILOOT	COCCOLITH
BEENORSSS	SOBERNESS	BEIORSTUV	OBTRUSIVE	CCDDEKOUY	DECOY-DUCK
BEENORSTU	TENEBROUS	BEIORSTVY	VERBOSITY	CCDEEEHKR	CHECKERED
BEEORSTTU	SOUBRETTE	BEKLOOOSU	BOOK-LOUSE	CCDEEERSU	SUCCEEDER
BEEPRRRTU	PERTURBER	BELMOOORW	ELBOW-ROOM	CCDEEHIKW	CHICKWEED
BEEPRRSTY	PRESBYTER	BELMOPSUU	PLUMBEOUS	CCDEEIINN	INCIDENCE
BEERRSTUV	SUBVERTER	BELNNSSTU	BLUNTNESS	CCDEEINNY	INDECENCY
BEFFLNSSU	BLUFFNESS	BELNOORVW	OVERBLOWN	CCDEEINOT	CONCEITED
BEFGIINTT	BEFITTING	BELNRTTUU	TURBULENT	CCDEENNOR	CONCERNED
BEFHIRRSU	FURBISHER	BELQRSUUY	BRUSQUELY	CCDEENORS	CRESCENDO
	REFURBISH	BEMNOOSTT	TOMBSTONE	CCDEENORT	CONCERTED
BEFHKLOOS	BOOKSHELF	BEMNORTUU	OUTNUMBER	CCDEILOOR	CROCODILE
BEFIILNSU	INFUSIBLE	BENNORSSW	BROWNNESS	CCDEINOOT	DECOCTION
BEFILNTTY	FLYBITTEN	BENOOSTUU	BOUNTEOUS	CCDEINOUV	CONDUCIVE
BEFIORSTT	FROSTBITE	BENORSTTU	OBSTRUENT	CCDEINRTU	CINCTURED
BEFLRTTUY	BUTTERFLY	BENRTTTUU	BUTTER-NUT	CCDHHIRSU	DISCHURCH
BEGGIINNN	BEGINNING	BFFIIMORR	FIBRIFORM	CCDIILNRY	CYLINDRIC
BEGGILNNO	BELONGING	BFGHILLTU	BULL-FIGHT	CCDKLLOUY	CUCKOLDLY

CCDKLMOOU	CUCKOLDOM	CCHILOORT	CHLOROTIC
CCDKLORUY	CUCKOLDRY	CCHIOPSTY	PSYCHOTIC
CCDNOORTU	CONDUCTOR	CCHLNOOTY	COLOCYNTH
CCEEEFLNU	FECULENCE	CCIIILNOS	ISOCLINIC
CCEEEEHHRR	RECHERCHÉ	CCIIILNRT	TRICLINIC
CCEEEHNOR	COHERENCE	CCIIIMRST	CRITICISM
CCEEEINNS	NESCIENCE	CCIILOPRT	PROCLITIC
CCEEEINRT	RETICENCE	CCIINNOOS	CONCISION
CCEEFFOPU	COFFEE-CUP	CCIIRRTUY	CIRCUITRY
CCEEHLORT	CERECLOTH	CCILMOSTU	OCCULTISM
CCEEIIPPR	PRECIPICE	CCILNOORU	COUNCILOR
CCEEIKRRT	CRICKETER	CCILNOOSU	OCCLUSION
CCEEILNOR	RECONCILE	CCIMMOORS	MICROCOSM
CCEEINNNO	INNOCENCE	CCINOOSSU	CONSCIOUS
CCEEINRTX	EXCENTRIC	CCINOPRST	CONSCRIPT
CCEELLORT	RECOLLECT	CCINORSTT	CONSTRICT
CCEENNORT	CONCENTRE	CCKKLOORW	CLOCK-WORK
CCEFIIRRU	CRUCIFIER	CCKOOPPPY	POPPYCOCK
CCEFKNOYY	COCKNEYFY	CCNORSTTU	CONSTRUCT
CCEGIINTY	CYNEGITIC	CDDDEEILY	DECIDEDLY
CCEHILNOR	CHRONICLE	CDDDEEINU	UNDECIDED
CCEHKLNOT	NECKCLOTH	CDDEEEFLT	DEFLECTED
CCEHNOSTU	SCUTCHEON	CDDEEIKRU	EIDER-DUCK
CCEHORTTY	CROTCHETY	CDDEEITUV	DEDUCTIVE
CCEIIIRST	CRITICISE	CDDEEMNRU	CREDENDUM
CCEIIIRTZ	CRITICIZE	CDDEHIILP	DIDELPHIC
CCEIILMST	CELTICISM	CDDEIINRT	DENDRITIC
CCEIKLOSW	CLOCKWISE	CDDEIIRST	DISCREDIT
CCEILNOSY	CONCISELY	CDDEIMOOU	DUODECIMO
CCEILORST	SCLEROTIC	CDDEINOTU	DEDUCTION
CCEIMNOOS	ECONOMICS	CDDEIOSUU	DECIDUOUS
CCEIMORTY	MICROCYTE	CDDELNOUU	UNCLOUDED
CCEINNNOY	INNOCENCY	CDDELOOOP	OPODELDOC
CCEINNOTT	CONTICENT	CDDHHILOO	CHILDHOOD
CCEINORRT	INCORRECT	CDEEEEFNR	DEFERENCE
CCEINOSTT	TECTONICS	CDEEEEFITV	DEFECTIVE
CCEIOPRTY	PRECOCITY	CDEEEFORW	COWFEEDER
CCEKORRSW	CORKSCREW	CDEEEGINX	EXCEEDING
CCELLNOOY	COLONELCY	CDEEEHQRU	CHEQUERED
CCELLOORT	COLLECTOR	CDEEEIMRT	DECIMETRE
CCELNSTUU	SUCCULENT	CDEEEINPT	CENTIPEDE
CCELOPRSU	CORPUSCLE	CDEEEINRS	RESIDENCE
CCELORRTY	CORRECTLY	CDEEEINRT	INTERCEDE
CCENNNORU	UNCONCERN	CDEEEINUV	UNDECEIVE
CCENNOORT	CONNECTOR	CDEEEIPTV	DECEPTIVE
CCENOOORY	COCOONERY	CDEEEIRTV	DECRETIVE
CCENOORSU	CONCOURSE	CDEEEITTV	DETECTIVE
CCEOOORRT	CORRECTOR	CDEEELNOR	REDOLENCE
CCEOPPRUY	PREOCCUPY	CDEEELORT	ELECTRODE
CCEORRSUU	SUCCOURER	CDEEEMNRT	DECREMENT
CCEORSSSU	SUCCESSOR	CDEEENPRT	PRECEDENT
CCFGHIKOT	COCK-FIGHT	CDEEEOORT	RETROCEDE
CCFHKLLOU	CHOCK-FULL	CDEEFIINT	DEFICIENT
CCFIILOOR	COLORIFIC	CDEEFIIOT	FOETICIDE
CCFIMORRU	CRUCIFORM	CDEEFIIRT	CERTIFIED
CCGHHINOU	CHINCOUGH	CDEEFILTU	DECEITFUL
CCGHHINRU	CHURCHING	CDEEFINOT	DEFECTION
CCGHIIKLN	CHICKLING	CDEEFKLOT	FETLOCKED
CCGHINORS	SCORCHING	CDEEFLORT	DEFLECTOR
CCHHILLRU	CHURCHILL	CDEEFNOSS	CONFESSED
CCHHIMRSU	CHURCHISM	CDEEGIILN	DILIGENCE
CCEEIINRT		CDEEGIIMR	GERMICIDE
		CDEEGIINN	INDIGENCE
		CDEEGLLRU	CUDGELLER
		CDEEGNOST	CONGESTED
		CDEEHILLS	CHISELLED
		CDEEHINST	DEHISCENT
		CDEEHNORV	CHEVRONED
		CDEEIILRT	DECILITRE
		CDEEIILTV	VIDELICET
		CDEEIIMPR	EPIDERMIC
		CDEEIIMRV	VERMICIDE
		CDEEIIPST	PESTICIDE
		CDEEIIRTV	DIRECTIVE
		CDEEIISTT	DIETETICS
		CDEEIJNOT	DEJECTION
		CDEEIJPRU	PREJUDICE
		CDEEILLNP	PENCILLED
		CDEEILNNO	INDOLENCE
		CDEEILORR	CORDELIER
		CDEEIMNPU	IMPUDENCE
		CDEEINNSU	SECUNDINE
		CDEEINOPT	DECEPTION
		CDEEINORT	RECONDITE
		CDEEINOTT	DETECTION
		CDEEINNRS	DISCERNER
		CDEEINRSY	RESIDENCY
		CDEEIORRS	CROSIERED
		CDEEIPRTU	DEPICTURE
		CDEEIRSTT	DECRETIST
		CDEEIRTTU	CERTITUDE
			RECTITUDE
		CDEEISTUV	SEDUCTIVE
		CDEEKNRWY	WRYNECKE[?]
		CDEELLNRU	CULLENDER
		CDEELMNTU	DEMULCEN[?]
		CDEELMOPX	DECOMPLE[?]
		CDEELNORY	REDOLENCY
		CDEEMMNOR	RECOMMEN[?]
		CDEEMOOPS	DECOMPOS[?]
		CDEENNORS	CONDENSE[?]
		CDEENNORT	CONTENDE[?]
		CDEENNORU	DENOUNCE[?]
		CDEENNOTT	CONTENTE[?]
		CDEENOORT	CORONETE[?]
		CDEENOPRS	DROP-SCE[?]
		CDEENRRTU	DECURREN[?]
		CDEENRSSU	CRUDENES[?]
		CDEEOPRRU	PROCEDUR[?]
			REPRODUC[?]
		CDEEOORRTY	DECRETOR[?]
		CDEFGIINU	FUNGICIDE
		CDEFIINST	DISINFECT
		CDEFILNOR	CORNFIEL[?]
		CDEFIMNOR	CONFIRME[?]
		CDEFINNOT	CONFIDEN[?]
		CDEFINTUY	FECUNDIT[?]
		CDEGIIMRU	DEMIURGI[?]
		CDEHIIKLL	CHILDLIKE
		CDEHIIOPT	PITHECOID
		CDEHILLSS	CHILDLESS
		CDEHILPST	STEPCHILD

134

CDEHINOSU	CUSHIONED	
CDEHNOTUU	UNTOUCHED	
CDEIIILSV	CIVILISED	
CDEIIILVZ	CIVILIZED	
CDEIILLNO	DECILLION	
CDEIILNTU	INDUCTILE	
CDEIILOSU	DELICIOUS	
CDEIILPUV	VULPICIDE	
CDEIILTVY	DECLIVITY	
CDEIIMNOS	MENISCOID	
CDEIIMNTY	MENDICITY	
CDFIIIMNOT	MISDIRECT	
CDEIINORT	DIRECTION	
CDEIINRTT	INTERDICT	
CDEIINTUV	INDUCTIVE	
CDEIIOOSU	DIOECIOUS	
CDEIIORVV	DIVORCIVE	
CDEIIRRTX	DIRECTRIX	
CDEILLLOU	CELLULOID	
CDEILNSSU	LUCIDNESS	
CDEILOSUV	DECLIVOUS	
CDEILPRSU	SURPLICED	
CDEILRTUY	CREDULITY	
CDEIMMNOO	INCOMMODE	
CDEIMNNOT	CONDIMENT	
CDEIMNOPR	PRINCEDOM	
CDEIMNORU	INDECORUM	
CDEINNOTU	CONTINUED	
	UNNOTICED	
CDEINORTU	INTRODUCE	
	REDUCTION	
CDEINOSTU	SEDUCTION	
CDEINRSSU	CURDINESS	
CDEIOOPRT	PORTICOED	
CDEIOPRRT	PREDICTOR	
CDEIORRTY	DIRECTORY	
CDEIORSST	DISSECTOR	
CDEIORSSU	DISCOURSE	
CDEIORSTU	CUSTODIER	
CDEIORSVY	DISCOVERY	
CDEIPPSTY	DYSPEPTIC	
CDEKLOORY	CROOKEDLY	
CDEKOOSTV	STOCKDOVE	
CDELLOSSU	CLOUDLESS	
CDELNOOST	STONE-COLD	
CDELNOOTY	COTYLEDON	
CDELNORSU	SCOUNDREL	
CDELOORUV	OVERCLOUD	
CDELORSUU	CREDULOUS	
CDEMMOOOR	COMMODORE	
CDENNORUW	UNCROWNED	
CDENOORRT	CORRODENT	
CDENOORTT	CONTORTED	
CDENORSSU	UNCROSSED	
CDEOOOPSW	COPSE-WOOD	
CDEOORRVW	OVERCROWD	
CDEOORSST	DOCTORESS	
CDFFILTUU	DIFFUCULT	
CDFGHILNO	GOLDFINCH	
CDFGIINNO	CONFIDING	
CDFHINORY	CHONDRIFY	

CDFIIMOST	DISCOMFIT	
CDFIIORSU	SUDORIFIC	
CDFIMOORR	CORDIFORM	
CDHHIIOTY	ICHTHYOID	
CDHHILOST	DISH-CLOTH	
CDHIIMORS	DICHROISM	
CDHILOSTU	DISH-CLOUT	
CDHIMOOTY	DICHOTOMY	
CDHIOOPRY	CHIROPODY	
CDHMNOOOR	MONOCHORD	
CDHOOOTUW	TOUCHWOOD	
CDIIINNOT	INDICTION	
CDIIISTVY	VISCIDITY	
CDIIJOSUU	JUDICIOUS	
CDIILPTUY	DUPLICITY	
CDIILTTUY	DUCTILITY	
CDIINNOOT	CONDITION	
CDIINNOTU	INDUCTION	
CDIIOOPRS	SCORPIOID	
CDIIOPRST	DIOPTRICS	
CDIIPRSTU	TRICUSPID	
CDIJNOTUY	JOCUNDITY	
CDIKMRSTU	DRUM-STICK	
CDILLNOOO	COLLODION	
CDILOORSU	DISCOLOUR	
CDILORSUU	LUDICROUS	
CDIMMNOOS	DISCOMMON	
CDIMMOOTY	COMMODITY	
CDMNNORUU	CONUNDRUM	
CDNNOOTUW	COUNT-DOWN	
CDOOORRSSW	CROSSWORD	
CEEEEFNRR	REFERENCE	
CEEEEGMNR	EMERGENCE	
CEEEEHMNV	VEHEMENCE	
CEEEENRRV	REVERENCE	
CEEEFFITV	EFFECTIVE	
CEEEFFLNU	EFFLUENCE	
CEEEFINNR	INFERENCE	
CEEEFPRRT	PERFECTER	
CEEEGINRT	ENERGETIC	
CEEEGISTX	EXEGETICS	
CEEEGMNRY	EMERGENCY	
CEEEHINNR	INHERENCE	
CEEEHLNTY	ENTELECHY	
CEEEHLOPR	CREEPHOLE	
CEEEHLRSS	CHEERLESS	
CEEEHLRUV	CHEVELURE	
CEEEHMNVY	VEHEMENCY	
CEEEHQRUX	EXCHEQUER	
CEEEIIMPT	TIMEPIECE	
CEEEILLNT	CLIENTÈLE	
CEEEILLNT	CELESTINE	
CEEEILRTT	TIERCELET	
CEEEILSTV	SELECTIVE	
CEEEINNPT	PENITENCE	
CEEEINNSU	ESURIENCE	
CEEEINSTX	EXISTENCE	
CEEEIPRRV	PERCEIVER	
CEEEIPRTV	RECEPTIVE	
CEEEIRSSV	RECESSIVE	
CEEEIRSTV	SECRETIVE	

CEEEIRTVX	EXCRETIVE	
CEEEISSVX	EXCESSIVE	
CEEEITUVX	EXECUTIVE	
CEEEJMNTT	EJECTMENT	
CEEELLNTX	EXCELLENT	
CEEELMNTU	TEMULENCE	
CEEELNOQU	ELOQUENCE	
CEEELOPST	TELESCOPE	
CEEEMNRRT	RECREMENT	
CEEEMNRTX	EXCREMENT	
CEEENNRST	SECERNENT	
	SENTENCER	
CEEENNSST	SENESCENT	
CEEENRSST	ERECTNESS	
CEEEORRRV	RECOVERER	
CEEEPRRST	RESPECTER	
CEEEPRSTU	PERSECUTE	
CEEFFIINT	EFFICIENT	
CEEFFOOPT	COFFEE-POT	
CEEFGLNTU	GENUFLECT	
CEEFHIPSY	SPEECHIFY	
CEEFIINTV	INFECTIVE	
CEEFIIRRT	CERTIFIER	
	RECTIFIER	
CEEFILNNU	INFLUENCE	
CEEFILRTY	ELECTRIFY	
CEEFIMNOR	CONFIRMEE	
CEEFIMPRT	IMPERFECT	
CEEFINORR	REINFORCE	
CEEFINORT	REFECTION	
CEEFKLLSS	FLECKLESS	
CEEFLOORS	FORECLOSE	
CEEFLORRT	REFLECTOR	
CEEFLORSS	FORCELESS	
CEEFLPRTY	PERFECTLY	
CEEFNOPRU	FOURPENCE	
CEEFNORRR	CONFERRER	
CEEFNQRUY	FREQUENCY	
CEEFORRTY	REFECTORY	
CEEFORSTW	CROW'S-FEET	
CEEGHIMNO	HEGEMONIC	
CEEGILNRY	GLYCERINE	
CEEGIMORT	GEOMETRIC	
CEEGINNOS	CONSIGNEE	
CEEGINNRT	CENTERING	
CEEGINOPS	ENGISCOPE	
CEEGINORS	CONGERIES	
	RECOGNISE	
CEEGINPTX	EXCEPTING	
CEEGNOPSY	ENGYSCOPE	
CEEHHIRVW	WHICHEVER	
CEEHIKNRT	KITCHENER	
CEEHILRSV	CLEVERISH	
CEEHIMPTY	CHEMITYPE	
CEEHINNRY	INHERENCY	
CEEHINPRT	PHRENETIC	
CEEHINQTU	TECHNIQUE	
CEEHINRTT	THRENETIC	
CEEHIORSS	COHEIRESS	
CEEHIORTT	THEORETIC	
CEEHLORSU	LECHEROUS	

CEEHLPRSU	SEPULCHRE	CEEIOORTZ	OZOCERITE	CEGHILOOT	THEOLOGIC
CEEHRRSTT	STRETCHER	CEEIOPPRS	PERISCOPE	CEGHINOOT	THEOGONIC
CEEIILNRT	LIENTERIC	CEEIOPSST	CESPITOSE	CEGHLOOUY	EUCHOLOGY
CEEIILPPT	EPILEPTIC	CEEIORRSX	EXORCISER	CEGIIJNOR	REJOICING
CEEIIMMNN	IMMINENCE	CEEIORSSU	SERICEOUS	CEGIIKNNS	SICKENING
CEEIIMPRS	IMPRECISE	CEEIRRRTU	RECRUITER	CEGIINOTV	COGNITIVE
CEEIINNOR	EIRENICON	CEEIRRSUV	RECURSIVE	CEGIIOSTT	EGOTISTIC
CEEIINNRS	INSINCERE	CEEIRSUVX	EXCURSIVE	CEGIKNNOR	RECKONING
CEEIINNTV	INCENTIVE	CEEIRTUXX	EXECUTRIX	CEGILMMNO	COMMINGLE
CEEIINPRT	RECIPIENT	CEELLLOSU	CELLULOSE	CEGILNRSU	SURCINGLE
CEEIINPTV	INCEPTIVE	CEELLMNTY	CLEMENTLY	CEGILOOST	ECOLOGIST
CEEIINPTX	EXCIPIENT	CEELLRSUY	RECLUSELY	CEGIMNOUY	GYNOECIUM
CEEIINTVV	INVECTIVE	CEELMNOUW	UNWELCOME	CEGINNORS	CONSIGNER
CEEIJLSSU	JUICELESS	CEELNNNOP	PENNONCEL	CEGINOOPS	GEOPONICS
CEEIJNORT	REJECTION	CEELNORSU	ENCLOSURE	CEGINOPPR	COPPERING
CEEIJNRTT	INTERJECT	CEELNOSSS	CLOSENESS	CEGINOPRY	PYROGENIC
CEEIILNTT	INTELLECT	CEELNPRUU	PURULENCE	CEGINRRRU	RECURRING
CEEIILMNNT	INCLEMENT	CEELNSSST	SCENTLESS	CEGLNOORY	NECROLOGY
CEEIILMRSS	CRIMELESS	CEELOPRRT	PRELECTOR	CEGNNORTU	CONGRUENT
	MERCILESS	CEELOPSTY	TELESCOPY	CEGNORRSU	SCROUNGER
CEEIILNNOS	INSOLENCE	CEELRSSST	CRESTLESS	CEGNORSUY	SURGEONCY
CEEIILNOST	SELECTION	CEELRSSTU	TRUCELESS	CEGOOPRSY	GYROSCOPE
CEEIILNPST	SPLENETIC	CEEMMNORT	COMMENTER	CEHHHIIKT	HITCH-HIKE
CEEIILNRSY	SINCERELY	CEEMNNORT	CONTEMNER	CEHHIIMST	HEMISTICH
CEEIILNRTV	VENTRICLE	CEEMNOPTT	COMPETENT	CEHHOOPSU	CHOP-HOUSE
CEEIILNRUV	VIRULENCE	CEENNORRU	RENOUNCER	CEHIIKLRS	LICKERISH
CEEIILOPTU	POETICULE	CEENNORTU	ENCOUNTER	CEHIILMOT	HOMILETIC
CEEIILOSSS	ISOSCELES	CEENOOPST	COPE-STONE	CEHIILNOT	NEOLITHIC
CEEIILOSSV	VOICELESS	CEENOPRRT	PRECENTOR	CEHIILOST	ELOHISTIC
CEEIILPRSS	PRICELESS	CEENOPSTT	PENTECOST	CEHIIMNST	ETHNICISM
CEEIILPRSY	PRECISELY	CEENOQRRU	RECONQUER	CEHIINPRT	NEPHRITIC
CEEIILRSUV	RECLUSIVE	CEENORRSV	CONSERVER	CEHIINSST	ITCHINESS
CEEIILSSUV	SECLUSIVE	CEENORRTV	CONVERTER	CEHIIPPPT	PITCHPIPE
CEEIILSUVX	EXCLUSIVE	CEENRRRTU	RECURRENT	CEHIIPPTY	EPIPHYTIC
CEEIIMMOTT	COMMITTEE	CEENRRTUX	EXCURRENT	CEHIIRSTU	HEURISTIC
CEEIIMNNRT	INCREMENT	CEEOPPRRT	PRECEPTOR	CEHIKLPRS	CLERKSHIP
CEEIMNNOOS	ECONOMISE	CEEOPRSTU	PROSECUTE	CEHIKLSTY	SKETCHILY
CEEIMNOOZ	ECONOMIZE	CEEORRSSS	SORCERESS	CEHIKNSST	THICKNESS
CEEIMNOPT	IMPOTENCE	CEEORRSTY	SECRETORY	CEHIKPRSW	SHIPWRECK
CEEIMNSTU	INTUMESCE	CEEORRSUV	VERRUCOSE	CEHILLNSS	CHILLNESS
CEEIINNORS	RECENSION	CEEORRTUV	COVERTURE	CEHILNOSU	LICHENOUS
CEEIINNRTY	RENITENCY	CEEORRTXY	EXCRETORY	CEHILNPSU	SIPHUNCLE
CEEINOPRT	RECEPTION	CEEORTUXY	EXECUTORY	CEHIMNNOU	ICHNEUMON
CEEINOPTX	EXCEPTION	CEEPRRSSU	REPERCUSS	CEHIMRSTY	CHEMISTRY
CEEINORSS	RECESSION	CEERRRSTU	RESURRECT	CEHIMSTTY	METHYSTIC
CEEINORST	RESECTION	CEFGINORU	CONFIGURE	CEHINOPST	PHONETICS
	SECRETION	CEFHIILSS	FISH-SLICE	CEHINPRST	SPHINCTER
CEEINORSU	CINEREOUS	CEFHKLLOU	CHOKE-FULL	CEHINSTTY	SYNTHETIC
CEEINORTX	EXCRETION	CEFIINNOT	INFECTION	CEHIOOPRT	ORTHOEPIC
CEEINOSSS	SECESSION	CEFIMNORR	CONFIRMER	CEHIOOPPRS	COPPERISH
CEEINOTUX	EXECUTION	CEFIMNORU	CUNEIFORM	CEHIOPPRT	PROPHETIC
CEEINPRRU	PRURIENCE	CEFIOORSU	FEROCIOUS	CEHIOPRTY	HYPOCRITE
CEEINPRST	PRESCIENT	CEFIORRSS	CROSS-FIRE	CEHIORRST	CHORISTER
	REINSPECT	CEFIORSTU	FRUTICOSE	CEHIOSSST	SCHISTOSE
CEEINPRTT	INTERCEPT	CEFKLOPTU	POCKETFUL	CEHIPRRTY	CHERRY-PIT
CEEINQSTU	QUIESCENT	CEFLNNOTU	CONFLUENT	CEHIRSSTY	HYSTERICS
CEEINRRSV	SCRIVENER	CEFMNOORR	CONFORMER	CEHLMNOUU	HOMUNCUL
CEEINRSTT	INTERSECT	CEFNOORSS	CONFESSOR	CEHNNORTU	TRUNCHEON
CEEINRSTV	VIRESCENT	CEFOOORSU	FOURSCORE	CEHOOOPRS	HOROSCOPE
CEEINRSUY	ESURIENCY	CEFOORRTU	FORECOURT	CEIIILRSV	CIVILISER
CEEINSSTY	NECESSITY	CEGHILNTV	VETCHLING	CEIIILRVZ	CIVILIZER

136

CEIIIMSTV	VICTIMISE
CEIIIMTVZ	VICTIMIZE
CEIIINNPT	INCIPIENT
CEIIIPSTT	PIETISTIC
CEIIJNNOT	INJECTION
CEIIJNSSU	JUICINESS
CEIIJNSTU	INJUSTICE
CEIIKLMQU	QUICKLIME
CEIILMNSU	MINISCULE
CEIILNNOR	CRINOLINE
CEIILNPPR	PRINCIPLE
CEIIINSUV	INCLUSIVE
CEIILOPST	EPISTOLIC
CEIILOQRU	LIQUORICE
CEIILOSSU	SILICEOUS
CEIILPRTU	PLEURITIC
CEIIMNOST	SEMITONIC
CEIIMNRST	CRETINISM
CEIIMORST	EROTICISM
	ISOMETRIC
CEIIMPRSU	EPICURISM
CEIINNOPT	INCEPTION
CEIINOPRS	PRECISION
CEIINORRT	CRITERION
CEIINORTV	VICTORINE
CEIINPSSS	SPICINESS
CEIINRSTX	EXTRINSIC
CEIINRSTY	SINCERITY
CEIINSSTT	SCIENTIST
CEIIOOPTZ	EPIZOOTIC
CEIKLNOPV	CLOVE-PINK
CEIKLNORT	INTERLOCK
CEIKLNSSU	LUCKINESS
CEIKLOPST	STOCKPILE
CEIKMORST	TRICKSOME
CEIKNORSS	ROCKINESS
CEIKNQSSU	QUICKNESS
CEIKRRSTT	TRICKSTER
CEILLNOOR	COROLLINE
CEILLOSUV	COLLUSIVE
CEILMNOOS	SEMICOLON
CEILMNOTU	MONTICULE
CEILMOPRY	MICROPYLE
CEILMRTUU	RETICULUM
CEILNOOTU	ELOCUTION
CEILNORSU	INCLOSURE
CEILNOSSU	SECLUSION
CEILNOSUX	EXCLUSION
CEILNRSSU	CURLINESS
CEILOOPRT	COPROLITE
CEILOPPRT	PROLEPTIC
CEILORSSS	SCLEROSIS
CEILOSTVY	COSTIVELY
CEIMMNOTU	COMMINUTE
CEIMMNOTY	METONYMIC
CEIMMOORT	MICROTOME
CEIMMRSTY	SYMMETRIC
CEIMNNOPU	PNEUMONIC
CEIMNNORS	ENCRIMSON
CEIMNOOPT	COEMPTION
CEIMNOOST	ECONOMIST

CEIMNOPTY	IMPOTENCY
CEIMOOPST	COMPOSITE
CEIMOOSTX	EXOSMOTIC
CEIMOPSUU	PUMICEOUS
CEIMORSTU	COSTUMIER
CEIMOSTUV	MUSCOVITE
CEINNNOOX	CONNEXION
CEINNNOTT	CONTINENT
CEINNORTU	CENTURION
	CONTINUER
CEINOPPRU	PORCUPINE
CEINOPRRS	CONSPIRER
CEINOPRST	INSPECTOR
CEINOPSUU	PECUNIOUS
CEINORRRS	SERRICORN
CEINORRSU	RECURSION
CEINORRTV	CONTRIVER
CEINORSTT	CORNETIST
CEINORSUX	EXCURSION
CEINOTVXY	CONVEXITY
CEINPRRUY	PRURIENCY
CEINPRSSS	CRISPNESS
CEIOOPRST	PORTICOES
CEIOORRSV	CORROSIVE
CEIOORSTV	VORTICOSE
CEIORRSTU	SCRUTOIRE
CEIORSSSW	CROSSWISE
CEIORSSTV	VICTORESS
CEIPPRRST	PRESCRIPT
CEIPRRSTU	SCRIPTURE
CEIRRSTTU	STRICTURE
CEJOOPRRT	PROJECTOR
CEKOORSTV	OVERSTOCK
CELLMOPXY	COMPLEXLY
CELLMSTUU	SCUTELLUM
CELMNOTUY	CONTUMELY
CELMOOSSU	COLOSSEUM
CELMOPRUU	OPERCULUM
CELMOPSUX	COMPLEXUS
CELNOOTUV	CONVOLUTE
CELNOPRTU	CORPULENT
CELNORSSW	CROWNLESS
CELNORSTU	CONSULTER
CELNOSSTU	COUNTLESS
CELNPRUUY	PURULENCY
CELNRRTUY	CURRENTLY
CELNRTTUU	TRUCULENT
CELPRSTUU	SCULPTURE
CEMNNOOPT	COMPONENT
CEMNORTUY	EMUNCTORY
CEMOOPRSU	COMPOSURE
CEMORRSUU	MERCUROUS
CENNOOPRU	PRONOUNCE
CENNOSSSU	CONSENSUS
CENOOQRRU	CONQUEROR
CENORSSSS	CROSSNESS
CENORSSTW	CROW'S-NEST
CENRSSSTU	CURSTNESS
CEOOPRRST	PROSECTOR
CEOOPRRTT	PROTECTOR
CEOOORRSSV	CROSS-OVER

CEOORSTUU	COURTEOUS
CEOPRRRSU	PRECURSOR
CEOPRRRTU	CORRUPTER
CEORRSUUV	VERRUCOUS
CERRSTTUU	STRUCTURE
CFFFIISTU	FISTICUFF
CFFIIOOSU	OFFICIOUS
CFGIIIKNN	FINICKING
CFHIKOPRT	PITCHFORK
CFHLOOOTT	FOOT-CLOTH
CFIILMMOR	MICROFILM
CFIIMOPRS	PISCIFORM
CFIIOOPRS	SOPORIFIC
CFIKLLNOT	FLINT-LOCK
CFIKLMOSU	FOLK-MUSIC
CFIMORSTU	SCUTIFORM
CFIMORSTY	CYSTIFORM
CFINNOOSU	CONFUSION
CFIORSTUU	FRUTICOUS
CFLLOORUU	COLOURFUL
CFLNOORRU	CORN-FLOUR
CFLOOOSTT	COLTSFOOT
CFOOORSTW	CROW'S-FOOT
CGHIIMOST	GOTHICISM
CGHIINSTT	STITCHING
CGHILNOOS	SCHOOLING
CGHILNOOY	ICHNOLOGY
CGHILNOSU	SLOUCHING
CGHILOORY	CHIROLOGY
CGHIOPRTY	COPYRIGHT
CGHLOOPYY	PHYCOLOGY
CGIIKMMRY	GIMMICKRY
CGIINNOOT	COGNITION
	INCOGNITO
CGIKLMNOY	MOCKINGLY
CGILMOORY	MICROLOGY
CGILNNNUY	CUNNINGLY
CGILNNOOR	LONGICORN
CGILNOOOY	ICONOLOGY
CGILNOORU	COLOURING
CGILNORTU	COURTLING
CGILNTTUY	CUTTINGLY
CGILOOOSY	SOCIOLOGY
CGIMMNSSU	SCUMMINGS
CGIMNNOOS	GNOMONICS
CGIMNNOSU	CONSUMING
CGINNOOTT	COTTON-GIN
CGINORTUY	CONGRUITY
CGLMOOOSY	COSMOLOGY
CGLMOOSUY	MUSCOLOGY
CGLOOOPRY	COPROLOGY
CGMNOOOSY	COSMOGONY
CGNOORSUU	CONGRUOUS
CHHKLLOOY	HOLLYHOCK
CHIIILPPP	PHILIPPIC
CHIIILRTT	TRILITHIC
CHIIMPSSY	PHYSICISM
CHIIOPSST	SOPHISTIC
CHIIORRSS	CIRRHOSIS
CHIIPSSTY	PHYSICIST
CHIKLMOST	LOCKSMITH

CHIKOOPTT	TOOTHPICK	CIMMNOTUY	COMMUNITY
CHILOORSS	CHLOROSIS	CIMNNOOOT	MONOTONIC
CHILPRSUU	SULPHURIC	CIMNNOSYY	SYNONYMIC
CHIMNOPSY	SYMPHONIC	CIMNNOTUU	CONTINUUM
CHINOPRRY	PYRRHONIC	CINNOOSTU	CONTUSION
CHINOPSTU	COUNTSHIP	CINNOOSUU	INNOCUOUS
CHIOOPTYZ	ZOOPHYTIC	CINOOORRS	CORROSION
CHIOPRSTU	COURTSHIP	CINOPRRTU	INCORRUPT
CHIOPRSYY	HYPOCRISY	CINOSTUVY	VISCOUNTY
CHIOPSSSY	PSYCHOSIS	CIOPRRSTY	SCRIPTORY
CHIORRSSU	SCIRRHOUS	CKNOORRWW	CROWN-WORK
CHIOSSSTU	SCHISTOUS	CLLOORRTU	COURT-ROLL
CHKLMOOST	STOCKHOLM	CLMOOOORT	LOCOMOTOR
CHLNOOOPY	COLOPHONY	CLMOORSTU	COLOSTRUM
CHLNOTUUY	UNCOUTHLY	CLNOOPRSU	PROCONSUL
CHMOORRSU	CRUSH-ROOM	CLNORTUUY	UNCOURTLY
CHNNORSYY	SYNCHRONY	CLOPRRTUY	CORRUPTLY
CHNORSTUU	COTHURNUS	CMNOPRTYY	CRYPTONYM
CHOOOPPTY	PHOTOCOPY	CMOOSTTYY	CYSTOTOMY
CHOOOPRSY	HOROSCOPY	CNOPRRTUU	UNCORRUPT
CIIILLLTY	ILLICITLY	COOPRSSTY	SPOROCYST
CIIILMOPT	IMPOLITIC	DDDEIINUV	UNDIVIDED
CIIILOPST	PISOLITIC	DDEEELOPV	DEVELOPED
CIIILORTV	VITRIOLIC	DDEEEENNPT	DEPENDENT
CIIILOSSS	SILICOSIS	DDEEENPRT	PRETENDED
CIIIMSTTW	WITTICISM	DDEEEPRSS	DEPRESSED
CIIINNRST	INTRINSIC	DDEEERSWY	DYER'S-WEED
CIIKKRRST	RIKSTRICK	DDEEESTUU	DESUETUDE
CIILLNOOS	COLLISION	DDEEFGLNU	UNFLEDGED
CIILLNOOT	COTILLION	DDEEFINNU	UNDEFINED
CIILLNUVY	UNCIVILLY	DDEEFIRTW	DRIFT-WEED
CIILLOPTY	POLITICLY	DDEEGHILT	DELIGHTED
CIILNOPTU	PUNCTILIO	DDEEHNORU	DEER-HOUND
CIILOORST	SOLICITOR	DDEEIILMV	DEMI-DEVIL
CIILOSUVY	VICIOUSLY	DDEEIIOSX	DEOXIDISE
CIILSSTTY	STYLISTIC	DDEEIIOXZ	DEOXIDIZE
CIIMMSSTY	MYSTICISM	DDEEILMSX	MIDDLESEX
CIIMNORSU	CRIMINOUS	DDEEIMMNO	DEMI-MONDE
CIIMNORUZ	ZIRCONIUM	DDEEINOPS	DISPONDEE
CIINNORSU	INCURSION	DDEEINORW	EIDER-DOWN
CIINNOSSW	WISCONSIN	DDEEINRSU	UNDESIRED
CIINOPSSU	SUSPICION	DDEEIOORS	DEODORISE
CIINORSUU	INCURIOUS	DDEEIOORZ	DEODORIZE
CIIORSTUY	CURIOSITY	DDEELOTVY	DEVOTEDLY
CIIOSSTVY	VISCOSITY	DDEENNOUW	UNENDOWED
CIIRSTTUY	RUSTICITY	DDEENRSSU	UNDRESSED
CIKLLNUUY	UNLUCKILY	DDEFFIINT	DIFFIDENT
CILLMORUY	COLLYRIUM	DDEFGIIIN	DIGNIFIED
CILLNOOSU	COLLUSION	DDEFILOOT	FLOOD-TIDE
CILLOQRUW	CROW-QUILL	DDEFLLOOW	ODDFELLOW
CILMNOSTU	COLUMNIST	DDEFNNOUU	UNFOUNDED
CILOOPSUY	COPIOUSLY	DDEGIINSS	GIDDINESS
CILOORRTU	TRICOLOUR	DDEHHNRTU	HUNDREDTH
CILOORSTU	COLOURIST	DDEHIORXY	HYDROXIDE
CILOPRXYY	PYROXYLIC	DDEIINSST	DISSIDENT
CILORRSUY	CURSORILY	DDEILNTUU	UNDILUTED
CILORSUUY	CURIOUSLY	DDEILSTUY	STUDIEDLY
CIMMMNOSU	COMMUNISM	DDEIMNSSU	MUDDINESS
CIMMNNOOU	COMMUNION	DDEINRSSU	RUDDINESS
CIMMNOOOT	COMMOTION	DDEINSTUU	UNSTUDIED
CIMMNOSTU	COMMUNIST	DDEIORSTT	DISTORTED
DDENNORTU	UNTRODDEN		
DDENNOUUW	UNWOUNDED		
DDENOORUW	UNDERWOOD		
DDFIOORTW	DRIFT-WOOD		
DDGIILNRS	RIDDLINGS		
DDHIOOOWW	WIDOWHOOD		
DEEEFINSV	DEFENSIVE		
DEEEFMNRT	DEFERMENT		
DEEEGIMNR	REDEEMING		
DEEEGKLNT	KENTLEDGE		
DEEEGNRTT	DETERGENT		
DEEEHNPRR	REPREHEND		
DEEEILLMP	MILLEPEDE		
DEEEILLVW	WEEVILLED		
DEEEILPTV	DEPLETIVE		
DEEEILRRV	DELIVERER		
	REDELIVER		
DEEEILSSW	EDELWEISS		
DEEEIMNRT	DETERMINE		
DEEEIMSST	DISESTEEM		
DEEEINNSS	NEEDINESS		
DEEEINPTX	EXPEDIENT		
DEEEINSSS	SEEDINESS		
DEEEIRSTV	DETERSIVE		
DEEELLPSW	SPEEDWELL		
DEEELOPRV	DEVELOPER		
	REDEVELOP		
DEEEMNRTT	DETERMENT		
DEEEMOPRT	PEDOMETER		
DEEEMORSU	DEER-MOUSE		
DEEENNSSS	DENSENESS		
DEEENPRRT	PRETENDER		
DEEENRRTT	DETERRENT		
DEEEORSTV	STEVEDORE		
DEEEPRSSU	SUPERSEDE		
DEEEPRSTU	DESREPUTE		
DEEFFINRT	DIFFERENT		
DEEFGIILR	FILIGREED		
DEEFGILNY	FEIGNEDLY		
DEEFGINNU	UNFEIGNED		
DEEFGJORU	FOREJUDGE		
DEEFHLLUY	HEEDFULLY		
DEEFHLNUU	UNHEEDFUL		
DEEFHLOPS	SHEEPFOLD		
DEEFHLORT	THREEFOLD		
DEEFIILMN	MINE-FIELD		
DEEFIIPRT	PETRIFIED		
DEEFILNRY	REFINEDLY		
DEEFINNPR	PENFRIEND		
DEEFINNRU	UNREFINED		
DEEFINSST	FETIDNESS		
DEEFINSSX	FIXEDNESS		
DEEFIPRRV	PERFERVID		
DEEFLLNNU	FUNNELLED		
DEEFLLNUY	NEEDFULLY		
DEEFLLPSU	FULL-SPEED		
DEEFLNOSV	SEVENFOLD		
DEEFOPRSS	PROFESSED		
DEEGHILNW	WHEEDLING		
DEEGHINNU	UNHEEDING		
DEEGHINUW	UNWEIGHED		

138

DEEGIISTV	DIGESTIVE	DEEINRSST	DISSENTER	DEFIMORTY	DEFORMITY
DEEGILNRT	RINGLETED		TIREDNESS	DEFIORSST	DISFOREST
DEEGILSSU	GUIDELESS	DEEINRSSW	WEIRDNESS	DEFIORTTU	FORTITUDE
DEEGINRRR	DERRINGER	DEEIORRVV	OVERDRIVE	DEFLLLOUY	DOLEFULLY
DEEGINRSV	DESERVING	DEEIPRRSS	DISPERSER	DEFLNORUW	WONDERFUL
DEEGINRTV	DIVERGENT	DEEIRSTUV	SERVITUDE	DEFNORSSU	FOUNDRESS
DEEGINRUV	GERUNDIVE	DEEIRTTXY	DEXTERITY	DEGGIINNS	DESIGNING
DEEGIOSST	GEODESIST	DEEISTTTU	DESTITUTE	DEGHIJPSU	JUDGESHIP
DEEGJMNTU	JUDGEMENT	DEELLNRSU	UNDERSELL	DEGHMOORT	GODMOTHER
DEEGKLNNO	DOG-KENNEL	DEELLNRSY	SLENDERLY	DEGHNNRUU	UNDERHUNG
DEEGKLNOW	KNOWLEDGE	DEELLNSSY	ENDLESSLY	DEGHNORUY	GREYHOUND
DEEGNNORU	DUNGEONER	DEELMOORV	VELODROME	DEGIINNSS	DINGINESS
DEEIIIKRSW	WHISKERED	DEELNNPST	SPLENDENT	DEGIINOST	DIGESTION
DEEHILPRS	ELDERSHIP	DEELNNPTY	PENDENTLY	DEGIINRSS	RIGIDNESS
DEEHILRSS	DESRELISH	DEELNOOST	LODESTONE	DEGIINRTV	DIVERTING
DEEHIMOST	METHODISE	DEELNPRRU	PLUNDERER	DEGIIRRSV	VERDIGRIS
DEEHIMOTZ	METHODIZE	DEELNSTTU	UNSETTLED	DEGIIRSSU	DISGUISER
DEEHINRSW	SWINEHERD	DEELOPRTY	DEPLETORY	DEGILLMNO	MODELLING
DEEHMOORT	HODOMETER	DEELORRSS	ORDERLESS	DEGILNNRU	UNDERLING
DEEHNOOQU	QUEENHOOD	DEELORSSW	DOWERLESS	DEGILNNTU	INDULGENT
DEEHNORRT	DETHRONER	DEELPRTUY	REPUTEDLY	DEGILNNYY	DENYINGLY
DEEHNRRTU	THUNDERER	DEEMNNOTW	ENDOWMENT	DEGILNOOR	GONDOLIER
DEEHOOPRT	HETEROPOD	DEEMNOPRS	ENDOSPERM	DEGILNORS	SOLDERING
DEEHOORTX	HETERODOX	DEEMNOSTU	ENDOSTEUM	DEGILNOSS	GODLINESS
DEEIIKNRS	DIE-SINKER	DEEMRRSSU	MURDERESS	DEGILNOTU	LONGITUDE
DEEIIMPRS	EPIDERMIS	DEENOPRRV	PROVENDER	DEGINNRSU	UNDERSIGN
DEEIIRRSV	RIVERSIDE	DEENOPRUX	EXPOUNDER	DEGIOPRTY	PTERYGOID
DEEIJNORR	REJOINDER	DEENOPSUX	UNEXPOSED	DEGLLOSSY	GODLESSLY
DEEILLNRW	INDWELLER	DEENPRSSU	SUSPENDER	DEGLNOOUZ	ZEUGLODON
DEEILLRRV	DRIVELLER	DEENRRRSU	SURRENDER	DEGLNORSU	GROUNDSEL
DEEILLRSU	SLIDE-RULE	DEENRSTYY	DYSENTERY	DEGNOPRUW	GUNPOWDER
DEEILMNTV	DEVILMENT	DEEOOPRST	TORPEDOES	DEGORRSTU	DRUGSTORE
DEEILNNRU	UNDERLINE	DEEOOPRSS	DEPRESSOR	DEHHIOPPS	PHOSPHIDE
DEEILNOPT	DEPLETION	DEEOORRSV	OVERDRESS	DEHHLOOSU	HOUSEHOLD
DEEILNPTU	PLENITUDE	DEEOORRSU	TROUSERED	DEHHLORST	THRESHOLD
DEEILNRTU	INTERLUDE	DEEOORRSX	DEXTRORSE	DEHHNOORU	HOREHOUND
DEEILNTVY	EVIDENTLY	DEEOORRST	DESTROYER	DEHIILPSV	DEVILSHIP
DEEILOPPS	DISPEOPLE	DEEOORSTUX	DEXTEROUS	DEHIIMNSU	DISINHUME
DEEILOPRS	DESPOILER	DEFFIISUV	DIFFUSIVE	DEHIINNRU	HIRUNDINE
DEEILOSTT	DELOITTES	DEFFILNTU	DIFFLUENT	DEHILOSUY	HIDEOUSLY
DEEILPPRS	SLIPPERED	DEFFINOOT	FIN-FOOTED	DEHILRRUY	HURRIEDLY
DEEILRRTY	RETIREDLY	DEFFLNRUU	UNRUFFLED	DEHIMMOST	METHODISM
DEEILRSVY	DIVERSELY	DEFGGILLN	FLEDGLING	DEHIMOSTT	METHODIST
DEEILRTUY	ERUDITELY	DEFGHILOT	EIGHTFOLD	DEHINORRT	TRIHEDRON
DEEIMMNNPT	IMPENDENT	DEFGIILOR	GLORIFIED	DEHINOSST	DISHONEST
DEEIMNNRU	UNDERMINE	DEFGIIRSU	DISFIGURE	DEHLMNOPY	ENDOLYMPH
DEEIMNORS	MODERNISE	DEFHIILSV	DEVIL-FISH	DEHMNOOPR	ENDOMORPH
DEEIMNORZ	MODERNIZE	DEFHINRSU	FURNISHED	DEHNORSTU	UNDERSHOT
DEEIMNRTT	DETRIMENT	DEFIIIRTV	VITRIFIED	DEHNORSUY	ENHYDROUS
DEEIMNRTU	UNMERITED	DEFIIILRR	FIRE-DRILL	DEHOPRSTY	DYSTROPHE
DEEIMPRST	DISTEMPER	DEFIIMNNY	INDEMNIFY	DEIIILQSU	LIQUIDISE
DEEINNORT	INTERNODE	DEFIIMRWY	MIDWIFERY	DEIILLMPY	IMPLIEDLY
DEEINNOTT	DETENTION	DEFIIRSVY	DIVERSIFY	DEIILLMTY	LIMITEDLY
DEEINNRTU	INDENTURE	DEFIIRTVY	DEVITRIFY	DEIILLOPR	PILLORIED
DEEINORST	DESERTION		FERVIDITY	DEIILLOPS	ELLIPSOID
	DETERSION	DEFIKLORW	FIELD-WORK	DEIILLRST	DISTILLER
DEEINPRSS	DISPENSER	DEFILLRUY	DIREFULLY	DEIILMNTU	UNLIMITED
DEEINPRST	PRESIDENT	DEFILMNRU	REMINDFUL	DEIILMQUU	DELIQUIUM
DEEINPRUX	UNEXPIRED	DEFILNOUX	DEFLUXION	DEIILNSSV	LIVIDNESS
DEEINPSST	TEPIDNESS	DEFILRSST	DRIFTLESS	DEIILORSU	DELIRIOUS
DEEINRRTV	TRINERVED	DEFIMNORT	DENTIFORM	DEIILPPTU	LIPPITUDE

DEIILSUVV	DIVULSIVE
DEIIMNNOS	DIMENSION
DEIIMNNTY	INDEMNITY
DEIIMNOSS	DEMISSION
DEIIMNRTW	MIDWINTER
DEIIMNSST	TIMIDNESS
DEIIMORTV	DORMITIVE
DEIINNOOP	OPINIONED
DEIINNORS	DEINORNIS
DEIINNORT	RENDITION
DEIINNOTT	DENTITION
DEIINNSSW	WINDINESS
DEIINNTUV	UNINVITED
DEIINOPRT	PERDITION
DEIINOPSS	INDISPOSE
DEIINORSV	DIVERSION
DEIINORTT	DETRITION
DEIINORTU	ERUDITION
DEIINRSST	DIRTINESS
DEIINSSVV	VIVIDNESS
DEIINSSZZ	DIZZINESS
DEIINSTUV	UNVISITED
DEIIORSSZ	DISSEIZOR
DEIIOSSTU	SEDITIOUS
DEIIRSTVY	DIVERSITY
DEIJNNOTU	UNJOINTED
DEIJNNRUU	UNINJURED
DEIKLLNSU	UNSKILLED
DEIKNSSSU	DUSKINESS
DEILLMNOU	MULLIONED
DEILLNSUU	UNSULLIED
DEILLORSY	SOLDIERLY
DEILMNUXY	UNMIXEDLY
DEILMOOSU	MELODIOUS
DEILMTTUU	MULTITUDE
DEILNOPSU	UNSPOILED
DEILNOPTY	POINTEDLY
DEILNOSSS	SOLIDNESS
DEILNOTUV	INVOLUTED
DEILOSSTU	DISSOLUTE
DEILOSTUY	TEDIOUSLY
DEILOSUVY	DEVIOUSLY
DEIMMMRSU	MIDSUMMER
DEIMMNORS	MODERNISM
DEIMMOSTY	IMMODESTY
DEIMNOOSS	MOODINESS
DEIMNOPRU	IMPOUNDER
DEIMNORST	MODERNIST
DEIMNPRTU	IMPRUDENT
DEIMNSSTU	TUMIDNESS
DEIMOPSST	DESPOTISM
DEINNNOSU	INNUENDOS
DEINNOSSW	DOWNINESS
DEINNOSTU	TENDINOUS
DEINNSTTU	UNSTINTED
DEINOOSSW	WOODINESS
DEINOPRTV	PROVIDENT
DEINORSSW	WORDINESS
DEINORSTU	DETRUSION
DEINRSTTY	DENTISTRY
DEIOOPRST	DEPOSITOR

DEIOPRSSU	DISPOSURE
DEIOPRSTU	DIPTEROUS
DEIPRRSSU	SURPRISED
DEIPRTTUU	TURPITUDE
DEKLNNRUY	DRUNKENLY
DELNOPRSU	SPLENDOUR
DELNOPRTU	UNDERPLOT
DELNOPSUU	PENDULOUS
DELNOSSSU	SOUNDLESS
DELNPRTUY	PRUDENTLY
DELOORSSU	ODOURLESS
DELORSTUY	DESULTORY
DELOSTUUY	DUTEOUSLY
DEMNOPSUY	PSEUDONYM
DEMNORSTU	UNDERMOST
DEMORRSUU	MURDEROUS
DENNORSSU	ROUNDNESS
DENNOSSSU	SOUNDNESS
DENOOPPSU	UNOPPOSED
DENOOPRSU	PONDEROUS
DENOOPRTV	DEVONPORT
DENOPPRRU	UNDERPROP
DENOPRSSU	PROUDNESS
DENOPSTTU	UNSPOTTED
DENORTTUU	UNTUTORED
DEOPPRRSS	DROP-PRESS
DFFFOOSTU	FOODSTUFF
DFFIINOSU	DIFFUSION
DFGIIIRTY	FRIGIDITY
DFGILNNOU	FOUNDLING
DFHHINOSU	HOUNDFISH
DFIILORTY	FLORIDITY
DFIINPRST	SPINDRIFT
DFILLMNUY	MINDFULLY
DFILLTUUY	DUTIFULLY
DFILMNNUU	UNMINDFUL
DFILNTUUU	UNDUTIFUL
DFNOOOPTU	FOOT-POUND
DGGHINOOT	GOODNIGHT
DGHHIINST	HINDSIGHT
DGHHINOPT	DIPHTHONG
DGHILMOST	GOLDSMITH
DGHILOTUY	DOUGHTILY
DGHINORTW	DOWNRIGHT
DGHLOORYY	HYDROLOGY
DGIIINNTY	INDIGNITY
DGIILNNSW	SWINDLING
DGIILNNWY	WINDINGLY
DGIIRTTUY	TURGIDITY
DGILLNORW	WORLDLING
DGILMNOOO	MONGOLOID
DGLNOOPTY	GLYPTODON
DHIIIPSTY	HISPIDITY
DHIILNRWW	WHIRLWIND
DHILPRSUY	PRUDISHLY
DHINNOTUW	WHODUNNIT
DHINOORSU	DISHONOUR
DHLLOOPPY	PHYLLOPOD
DHLOPRTUY	HYDROPULT
DHNOOORYZ	HYDROZOON
DHNOORTWW	DOWNTHROW

DHOOOORTXY	ORTHODOXY
DIIILMPTY	LIMPIDITY
DIIILQTUY	LIQUIDITY
DIIINOSSU	INSIDIOUS
DIIINOSUV	INVIDIOUS
DIILLMNOO	MODILLION
DIILNOSUV	DIVULSION
DIILOSTTY	STOLIDITY
DIIMOPRSU	SPORIDIUM
DIIMORSSY	DIMISSORY
DIIOPRTTY	TORPIDITY
DIIORRTTY	TORRIDITY
DIIPRTTUY	PUTRIDITY
DIIPSTTUY	STUPIDITY
DILMOOPPY	POLYPIDOM
DIMOOOOSV	VOODOOISM
DIMOORRTY	DORMITORY
DINOOORSU	INODOROUS
DINORTTUY	ROTUNDITY
DIOOPRSST	PROSODIST
DLLNORUWY	UNWORLDLY
DLNNOSUUY	UNSOUNDLY
DLOOORSUY	ODOROUSLY
EEEEGNRRV	EVERGREEN
EEEEHLRSW	ELSEWHERE
EEEELMRTT	TELEMETER
EEEELNSSV	ELEVENSES
EEEELNTVV	VELVETEEN
EEEENNSST	TENNESSEE
EEEENNSTV	SEVENTEEN
EEEENPRST	PRESENTEE
EEEENRSTW	SWEETENER
EEEEPRRSV	PERSEVERE
EEEERSTVY	YESTEREVE
EEEFFMTTU	MUFFETTEE
EEEFGKNRU	FENUGREEK
EEEFHORRT	THEREFORE
EEEFHORRW	WHEREFORE
EEEFHRRRS	REFRESHER
EEEFILRVX	REFLEXIVE
EEEFINRRT	INTERFERE
EEEFLNSST	FLEETNESS
EEEFNORST	FREESTONE
EEEFPRRRR	PREFERRER
EEEGINNRV	VENEERING
EEEGISTTX	EXEGETIST
EEEGLLNTY	GENTEELLY
EEEGLMNNT	GENTLEMEN
EEEGLNNTU	UNGENTEEL
EEEGMNRSS	MESSENGER
EEEGNNRSS	GREENNESS
EEEHILLNZ	HELLENIZE
EEEHIMPRS	EPHEMERIS
EEEHIMPSU	EUPHEMISE
EEEHIMPUZ	EUPHEMIZE
EEEHLNOPT	TELEPHONE
EEEHMMNTY	ENTHYMEME
EEEHMNOPR	EPHEMERON
EEEHMORRT	RHEOMETER
EEEHMORSW	SOMEWHERE
EEEHNNPST	NEPENTHES

EEEHNRSSW	WHERENESS	EEFFINRST	STIFFENER	EEGILLSSU	GUILELESS
EEEHRSTTU	USHERETTE	EEFFIORRT	FORFEITER	EEGILMMSU	GELSEMIUM
EEEIKNNPR	INNKEEPER	EEFFJNORS	JEFFERSON	EEGILMNSY	SEEMINGLY
EEEILNNRV	ENLIVENER	EEFFOPRRR	PROFFERER	EEGILNNUY	GENUINELY
EEEILNSTX	EXTENSILE	EEFGHIRRT	FREIGHTER	EEGILNOOZ	NEOLOGIZE
EEEILPTVX	EXPLETIVE	EEFGILLNY	FEELINGLY	EEGILNPWY	WEEPINGLY
EEEILRSTX	EXSERTILE	EEFGILNNU	UNFEELING	EEGILNRTT	LETTERING
EEEIMMRSS	MESMERISE	EEFGIMRUV	VERMIFUGE	EEGILNRVY	VEERINGLY
EEEIMMRSZ	MESMERIZE	EEFGINORR	FOREIGNER	EEGILNTVV	VELVETING
EEEIMORRT	ERIOMETER	EEFGIPRRU	PREFIGURE	EEGILORST	SORTILEGE
EEEIMORTT	METEORITE	EEFGLNRTU	REFULGENT	EEGIMNPRT	TEMPERING
EEEIMPRRT	PERIMETER	EEFGLRRTU	REGRETFUL	EEGINORSS	EGRESSION
EEEINNRTV	INTERVENE	EEFHIOSUW	HOUSEWIFE	EEGINORSV	SOVEREIGN
EEEINNRTZ	NEOTERIZE	EEFHLLSSS	FLESHLESS	EEGINOSXY	OXYGENISE
EEEINPSVX	EXPENSIVE	EEFHMORRT	THEREFROM	EEGINOXYZ	OXYGENIZE
EEEINRTTV	RETENTIVE	EEFHNRSSS	FRESHNESS	EEGINRSTW	WESTERING
EEEINSSTV	SEVENTIES	EEFHRRRTU	FURTHERER	EEGLLOPRS	GOSPELLER
EEEINSTVX	EXTENSIVE	EEFIILNRT	INFERTILE	EEGLLORRV	GROVELLER
EEEIPRRTT	PRETERITE	EEFIILQRU	LIQUEFIER	EEGLNORTT	LORGNETTE
EEEIPRSTX	EXPERTISE	EEFIILRST	FERTILISE	EEGLNOTTU	TONGUELET
EEEIQTTTU	ETIQUETTE	EEFIILRTZ	FERTILIZE	EEGLNSSUY	GLUEYNESS
EEEIRRRTV	RETRIEVER	EEFIINRSS	FIERINESS	EEGNOORST	OESTROGEN
EEEIRSTTV	SERVIETTE	EEFIIRRSV	VERSIFIER	EEGNOORSU	EROGENOUS
EEEJLLRWY	JEWELLERY	EEFIIRSTT	TESTIFIER	EEGNOOSUX	EXOGENOUS
EEEKLNSSS	SLEEKNESS	EEFILLRTY	FERTILELY	EEGNORRSS	ENGROSSER
EEELLNPRT	REPELLENT	EEFILMPXY	EXEMPLIFY	EEGNORSSV	GOVERNESS
EEELLPSSS	SLEEPLESS	EEFILNORX	REFLEXION	EEGNRRSTU	RESURGENT
EEELMNOPT	ELOPEMENT	EEFILSTVY	FESTIVELY	EEGOQRSTU	GROTESQUE
EEELMRTTY	TELEMETRY	EEFIMNRTT	REFITMENT	EEHHIRTTW	THEREWITH
EEELMRTXY	EXTREMELY	EEFINORST	FORESTINE	EEHHIRTWW	WHEREWITH
EEELNORVW	WOLVERENE	EEFINPRSU	SUPERFINE	EEHHKOOPS	SHEEPHOOK
EEELNOTTV	NOVELETTE	EEFINRSTU	INTERFUSE	EEHHOORSS	HORSE-SHOE
EEELNRSSV	NERVELESS	EEFIOPRRT	PROFITEER	EEHIINNTT	NINETIETH
EEELNSSSS	SENSELESS	EEFIPRSTU	STUPEFIER	EEHILLNST	HELLENIST
EEELOPRSV	OVERSLEEP	EEFIRRRTU	FRUITEER	EEHILMOST	LITHESOME
EEELRRSVY	REVERSELY	EEFIRRTTU	FRUIT-TREE	EEHILNPRS	REPLENISH
EEEMNORRV	NEVERMORE	EEFKNOORT	FORETOKEN	EEHILNPSS	SPLEENISH
EEEMNRSTT	ENTREMETS	EEFLLNPSU	SPLEENFUL	EEHILNSST	LITHENESS
EEEMNRSTY	MESENTERY	EEFLNRSTU	RESENTFUL	EEHILOPTY	HELIOTYPE
EEEMNRTTV	REVETMENT	EEFLNRTVY	FERVENTLY	EEHILPSVY	PEEVISHLY
EEEMOPRTX	EXTEMPORE	EEFLOPRSU	REPOSEFUL	EEHILRSTW	ERSTWHILE
EEENNORST	SONNETEER	EEFMOPRRR	PERFORMER	EEHIMMPSU	EUPHEMISM
EEENNSSST	TENSENESS	EEFMPRRUY	PERFUMERY	EEHIMPRRW	WHIMPERER
EEENPRRST	REPRESENT	EEFOPRRTY	FERROTYPE	EEHINORTT	THEREINTO
EEENPRRTV	PREVENTER	EEGGILNNT	NEGLIGENT	EEHINORTW	WHEREINTO
EEENPRSUV	SUPERVENE	EEGGIORSU	EGREGIOUS	EEHINSSTW	WHITENESS
EEENPSSST	STEEPNESS	EEGGOORRV	OVERGORGE	EEHINSTTX	SIXTEENTH
EEENQRSSU	QUEERNESS	EEGGRSSTU	SUGGESTER	EEHINTTTW	TWENTIETH
EEENRRSTW	WESTERNER	EEGHHIITT	EIGHTIETH	EEHIORRST	THEORISER
EEENRSSST	TERSENESS	EEGHILMNT	METHEGLIN	EEHIORRTZ	THEORIZER
EEENSSSTW	SWEETNESS	EEGHILNNT	ENLIGHTEN	EEHIORSTW	OTHERWISE
EEEPPPRTU	PUPPETEER	EEGHIMOST	EGOTHEISM	EEHIPPRRY	PERIPHERY
EEEPRRRSS	REPRESSER	EEGHIORVW	OVERWEIGH	EEHIPRRSW	WHISPERER
EEEPRRRSV	PRESERVER	EEGHNNORR	GREENHORN	EEHIRRTTY	ERYTHRITE
EEEPRRRTV	PERVERTER	EEGIILNRV	RELIEVING	EEHLLORSV	SHOVELLER
EEEQRSSTU	SEQUESTER	EEGIILOPS	EPILOGISE	EEHLMOOSW	WHOLESOME
EEFFFMNOT	FEOFFMENT	EEGIILOPZ	EPILOGIZE	EEHLMORVW	OVERWHELM
EEFFGLNTU	EFFULGENT	EEGIILPRV	PRIVILEGE	EEHLMRSSY	RHYMELESS
EEFFHINTT	FIFTEENTH	EEGIJLNRY	JEERINGLY	EEHLNOPTY	POLYTHENE
EEFFHLRSU	RESHUFFLE	EEGIJNNNT	JENNETING		TELEPHONY
EEFFINOSV	OFFENSIVE	EEGILLLNV	LEVELLING	EEHLNOSSW	WHOLENESS

EEHLNSTVY	SEVENTHLY	EEILNOSSU	SELENIOUS	EEINPSSTT	PETTINESS
EEHLORSSS	SHORELESS	EEILNPSSS	SPINELESS	EEINQSSTU	QUIETNESS
EEHLOSSSU	HOUSELESS	EEILNPSTT	PESTILENT	EEINQTTTU	QUINTETTE
EEHMNORTY	HETERONYM	EEILNPSVY	PENSIVELY	EEINRRRSU	REINSURER
EEHNOPRTU	THEREUPON	EEILNRSVY	INVERSELY	EEINRSSSY	SYNERESIS
EEHNOPRUW	WHEREUPON	EEILNSSSW	SINEWLESS	EEINRSSTT	RESISTENT
EEHNOPSTU	PENTHOUSE	EEILOPRTX	EXPLOITER		TRITENESS
EEHNOPTTY	ENTOPHYTE	EEILOPSVX	EXPLOSIVE	EEINRSSTW	WITNESSER
EEHNORSST	OTHERNESS	EEILOTUVV	EVOLUTIVE	EEINSSSTT	TESTINESS
EEHNORTUW	WHEREUNTO	EEILPPRTU	PULPITEER	EEINSTTXY	EXTENSITY
EEHNOSTTW	WHETSTONE	EEILPRSTY	PERISTYLE	EEIOPRTTU	PIROUETTE
EEHOORSVW	HOWSOEVER	EEILPRSUV	PRELUSIVE	EEIOPSTTT	PETTITOES
	WHOSOEVER		PULVERISE	EEIOQQUUV	EQUIVOQUE
EEHOPSSTW	SWEETSHOP		REPULSIVE	EEIORRRST	ROISTERER
EEIILLNTV	VITELLINE	EEILPRUVZ	PULVERIZE		TERRORISE
EEIILNNRT	INTERLINE	EEILPSUVX	EXPULSIVE	EEIORRRSV	RESERVOIR
EEIILNRST	RESILIENT	EEILRSTVY	RESTIVELY	EEIORRRTZ	TERRORIZE
EEIILRSST	STERILISE	EEILRSUVV	REVULSIVE	EEIORSSUV	OVERISSUE
EEIILRSTZ	STERILIZE	EEILSSSSU	ISSUELESS	EEIPRSSST	PRIESTESS
EEIILRSVZ	SILVERIZE	EEIMMMRSS	MESMERISM	EEIPRSSUV	SUPERVISE
EEIIMMRST	EREMITISM	EEIMMNRRT	MERRIMENT	EEJMNNOTY	ENJOYMENT
EEIIMOPST	EPITOMISE	EEIMMOSST	SOMETIMES	EEJNORRUY	JOURNEYER
EEIIMOPTZ	EPITOMIZE	EEIMMRSST	MESMERIST	EEKLMOSSS	SMOKELESS
EEIIMRSSV	REMISSIVE	EEIMMRSTW	SWIMMERET	EEKLNOOTV	LOVE-TOKEN
EEIINNSTT	INTESTINE	EEIMMRSTX	EXTREMISM	EEKMRSTTU	MUSKETTER
EEIINNSTV	INTENSIVE	EEIMNNRTT	INTERMENT	EELLMPSSU	PLUMELESS
EEIINNTVV	INVENTIVE	EEIMNNRTU	INUREMENT	EELLOPPRR	PROPELLER
EEIINPRRS	REINSPIRE	EEIMNNSTT	SENTIMENT	EELLPSSSU	PULSELESS
EEIINRSTT	ENTERITIS	EEIMNOPTX	EXEMPTION	EELLSSSUY	USELESSLY
EEIINRTVW	INTERVIEW	EEIMNORSS	SERMONISE	EELMMNOTU	EMOLUMENT
EEIINSSST	SENSITISE	EEIMNORST	NEOTERISM	EELMNNORT	ENROLMENT
EEIINSSTV	SENSITIVE	EEIMNORSZ	SERMONIZE	EELMNOSSS	SOLEMNESS
EEIINSSTZ	SENSITIZE	EEIMNOSTX	SIXTEENMO	EELMNOSSY	MONEYLESS
EEIIOPQSU	EQUIPOISE	EEIMNPQTU	EQUIPMENT	EELMOPRTU	PETROLEUM
EEIIQRSTU	REQUISITE	EEIMNPSST	EMPTINESS	EELMORTTV	VOLTMETER
EEIIQSTUX	EXQUISITE	EEIMNRTTT	REMITTENT	EELMORTUV	VOLUMETER
EEIJNSSTT	JETTINESS	EEIMOPRST	PERISTOME	EELMPRSUY	SUPREMELY
EEIKLMORT	KILOMETER		TEMPORISE	EELNNOPRS	PERSONNEL
	KILOMETRE	EEIMORSST	ESOTERISM	EELNOOSSS	LOOSENESS
EEIKNRRTT	TRINKETER	EEIMPPRRS	PERISPERM	EELNOPSTU	PLENTEOUS
EEIKOORTZ	OZOKERITE	EEIMPRRTT	PERMITTER	EELNORSTV	RESOLVENT
EEILLMNOT	EMOLLIENT		PRETERMIT	EELNORTUV	VOLUNTEER
EEILLMNPT	IMPELLENT	EEIMQSTUU	EQUISETUM	EELNPRSTY	PRESENTLY
EEILLNNTY	LENIENTLY	EEIMRRSTT	TRIMESTER	EELOOPRSY	OPEROSELY
EEILLNRSV	SNIVELLER	EEIMRSSSU	MESSIEURS	EELOORSTV	ROOSEVELT
EEILLRSUY	LEISURELY	EEIMRSSTY	MYSTERIES	EELOPRRTU	POULTERER
EEILLRSVY	SERVILELY	EEIMRSSTX	EXTREMIST	EELOPRSSW	POWERLESS
EEILMMNPT	IMPLEMENT	EEIMRTTXY	EXTREMITY	EELOPRSTY	PROSELYTE
EEILMMNSY	IMMENSELY	EEIMSSSTY	SYSTEMISE	EELOPRTXY	EXPLETORY
EEILMNNTY	EMINENTLY	EEIMSSTYZ	SYSTEMIZE	EELORSSUV	OURSELVES
EEILMNOSS	SOLEMNISE	EEINNOPRS	PENSIONER	EELPRSSXY	EXPRESSLY
EEILMNOST	LIMESTONE	EEINNORTT	RETENTION	EELPRSTUU	SEPULTURE
	MILESTONE	EEINNOSTX	EXTENSION	EEMMNOORT	METRONOME
EEILMNOSZ	SOLEMNIZE	EEINNOSTZ	SONNETIZE	EEMMORTYZ	ZYMOMETER
EEILMNPPR	PIMPERNEL	EEINNPRST	SPINNERET	EEMMRSSTU	SUMMERSET
EEILMOSTT	MISTLETOE	EEINNPRTT	PERTINENT	EEMNOOSTT	TOMENTOSE
EEILNNPSS	PENNILESS	EEINNRSST	INERTNESS	EEMOOPRTT	OPTOMETER
EEILNNSTY	INTENSELY	EEINOPRST	INTERPOSE	EEMOPRRTY	PYROMETER
EEILNOPRT	INTERLOPE	EEINORRSV	REVERSION	EEMPRRTTU	TRUMPETER
	REPLETION	EEINOSSTV	OSTENSIVE	EEMPRSSTT	TEMPTRESS
EEILNOSSS	NOISELESS	EEINPRRTT	INTERPRET	EENNOPRSS	PRONENESS

EENNPRTUY	TRUEPENNY	EFIILLRST	FILLISTER	EGHINOSTY	HISTOGENY
EENOORRSU	ERRONEOUS	EFIILMNSS	FILMINESS	EGHINRSST	RIGHTNESS
EENOPPRTT	PREPOTENT	EFIILNNOX	INFLEXION	EGHINRTUW	WUTHERING
EEOOPRRVW	OVERPOWER	EFIILOSSS	FOSSILISE	EGHINSSTT	TIGHTNESS
EEOPPRSSU	SUPERPOSE	EFIILOSSZ	FOSSILIZE	EGHIOPRTT	TIGHT-ROPE
EEOPRRRTY	REPERTORY	EFIILRTTY	FERTILITY	EGHIORSTU	RIGHTEOUS
EEOPRRSTT	PROTESTER	EFIINNSTY	INTENSIFY	EGHIORSTV	OVERSIGHT
EEOPRSSSS	REPOSSESS	EFIINOPRX	PREFIXION	EGHIRSTTU	THEURGIST
EEOPSSTTU	POUSSETTE	EFIINORRS	FIRE-IRONS	EGHLMOOOU	HOMOLOGUE
EEORRSSTU	RETROUSSÉ	EFIISTTVY	FESTIVITY	EGHLNOOTY	ETHNOLOGY
EEORRTTVX	EXTROVERT	EFILLMOPU	FILOPLUME	EGHLOOORR	HOROLOGER
EEPRRSTTU	SPUTTERER	EFILLNPTU	PLENTIFUL	EGHLOOTYY	HYETOLOGY
EERRSTTTU	STUTTERER	EFILMNORT	LENTIFORM	EGHNOOOPR	GONOPHORE
EFFGGINOR	GOFFERING	EFILMORUZ	FORMULIZE	EGHNOOPRY	GYNOPHORE
EFFGINRSU	SUFFERING	EFILNOOSU	FELONIOUS	EGHNOPTYY	PHYTOGENY
EFFGLORTU	FORGETFUL	EFILNOSST	LOFTINESS	EGHNORSSU	ROUGHNESS
EFFGNRSSU	GRUFFNESS	EFILOSSTU	FISTULOSE	EGHNOSSTU	TOUGHNESS
EFFHILRSY	FLY-FISHER	EFILRSSTU	FRUITLESS	EGIILNRSV	SILVERING
EFFHINSSU	HUFFINESS	EFILRTUVY	FURTIVELY	EGIILNSUV	INGLUVIES
EFFIIORRT	FORTIFIER	EFIMMORRV	VERMIFORM	EGIILNTTY	GENTILITY
EFFILMUUV	EFFLUVIUM	EFIMORRST	RESTIFORM	EGIILORSU	RELIGIOUS
EFFILNOUX	EFFLUXION	EFINNNSSU	UNFITNESS	EGIIMNNPT	IMPINGENT
EFFINPSSU	PUFFINESS	EFINOPRSY	PERSONIFY	EGIIMNPRS	SIMPERING
EFFINSSST	STIFFNESS	EFINRRTUU	FURNITURE	EGIIMNRSS	GRIMINESS
EFFIOOPRR	FIRE-PROOF	EFINRSSTU	TURFINESS	EGIINNOSU	INGENIOUS
EFFIORRTY	REFORTIFY	EFINSSSSU	FUSSINESS	EGIINNTUY	INGENUITY
EFFLLRTUY	FRETFULLY	EFINSSSTU	FUSTINESS	EGIINORSY	SEIGNIORY
EFFNOORRT	FOREFRONT	EFINSSSTW	SWIFTNESS	EGIINRRTU	INTRIGUER
EFFOORRTY	OFFERTORY	EFIOORSUV	OVIFEROUS	EGIINRTTY	INTEGRITY
EFGGIINNR	FINGERING	EFIORTTTU	OUTFITTER	EGILLMNTY	MELTINGLY
EFGGILOOS	SOLFEGGIO	EFLLMOSUY	FULSOMELY	EGILLMOTU	GUILLEMOT
EFGGINOOR	FOREGOING	EFLLNTUUY	TUNEFULLY	EGILLNOTW	TOWELLING
EFGGINOSS	FOGGINESS	EFLLRSTUY	RESTFULLY	EGILLOSSY	SYLLOGISE
EFGHILNSS	FLESHINGS	EFLNORSST	FRONTLESS	EGILLOSYZ	SYLLOGIZE
EFGHIORST	FORESIGHT	EFLNORSUW	SUNFLOWER	EGILLSSTU	GUILTLESS
EFGIILLNT	FILLETING	EFLNOSSUW	WOFULNESS	EGILMNOOS	NEOLOGISM
EFGIINPRT	FINGERTIP	EFLOOPRTW	FLOWER-POT	EGILMOOSY	SEMIOLOGY
EFGILNORW	FLOWERING	EFLOPRSUY	PROFUSELY	EGILNOOST	NEOLOGIST
EFGILRTUU	FULGURITE	EFNOORSST	FOSTERSON	EGILNOOSU	SINOLOGUE
EFGIMNORR	REFORMING	EFOOPRRSS	PROFESSOR	EGILNORTV	REVOLTING
EFGINNOST	SOFTENING	EGGHIINTW	WEIGHTING	EGILNORVV	REVOLVING
EFGNOORTT	FORGOTTEN	EGGIILNNR	LINGERING	EGILNOTVY	LONGEVITY
EFHHKLOOS	FLESH-HOOK	EGGIINNSW	SWINGEING	EGILNPRST	SPRINGLET
EFHIIMSST	FETISHISM	EGGILOOST	GEOLOGIST	EGILNRSTW	WRESTLING
EFHIINSSS	FISHINESS	EGGIORRTU	OUTRIGGER	EGIMMNSSU	GUMMINESS
EFHIISSTT	FETISHIST	EGGLRRSTU	STRUGGLER	EGIMNORSV	MISGOVERN
EFHIJLLSY	JELLYFISH	EGHHINRST	THRESHING	EGIMNPRSU	PRESUMING
EFHILLSSY	SELFISHLY	EGHHMOTTU	METHOUGHT	EGIMNRTTU	MUTTERING
EFHILNSSU	UNSELFISH	EGHIILLMT	LIMELIGHT	EGINNOSUU	INGENUOUS
EFHILOSSU	FISH-LOUSE	EGHIILTWY	WEIGHTILY	EGINNRSTT	STRINGENT
EFHILSSST	SHIFTLESS	EGHIINRTW	WITHERING	EGINNRSTU	INSURGENT
EFHINRRSU	FURNISHER	EGHILLNTY	LENGTHILY		UNRESTING
	REFURNISH	EGHILMOST	LIGHTSOME	EGINOPRRT	REPORTING
EFHLLOPUY	HOPEFULLY	EGHILNNSU	UNENGLISH	EGINOPSUY	EPIGYNOUS
EFHLLOSUV	SHOVELFUL	EGHILNRSY	ENGLISHRY	EGINOSSTU	GOUTINESS
EFHLNOPUU	UNHOPEFUL	EGHILNSST	LIGHTNESS	EGIOORSUV	OVIGEROUS
EFHNORTUX	FOXHUNTER		NIGHTLESS	EGKORSSUW	GUESSWORK
EFHOOORTT	FORETOOTH	EGHILOORY	HIEROLOGY	EGLMNOOOU	MONOLOGUE
EFIIJRSTU	JUSTIFIER	EGHILSSST	SIGHTLESS	EGLMOOTYY	ETYMOLOGY
EFIILLMOR	MOLLIFIER	EGHIMNOST	SOMETHING	EGLNNPTUY	PUNGENTLY
EFIILLNRU	NULLIFIER	EGHINORTV	OVERNIGHT	EGLNOOOPY	POENOLOGY

EGLNOORUY	NEUROLOGY	EHMOOORSU	HOUSEROOM	EIINPPRST	PINSTRIPE
EGLNOOSUV	LONGEVOUS	EHMOOOSTT	TOOTHSOME	EIINPSSST	TIPSINESS
EGLOOOSTY	OSTEOLOGY	EHMOORRTY	HOROMETRY	EIINRSTUV	INTRUSIVE
EGLOOPRTY	PETROLOGY	EHMPRRTUY	PYRETHRUM	EIINRTTUV	NUTRITIVE
EGNNORSSW	WRONGNESS	EHNOOPPTY	PHONOTYPE	EIINSSSYZ	SYNIZESIS
EGNNOSSUY	YOUNGNESS	EHNOOTTTT	HOTTENTOT	EIINSSTTW	WITTINESS
EGNOORRVW	OVERGROWN	EHNOPSSTY	PYTHONESS	EIINSTTTU	INSTITUTE
EGNOOSUXY	OXYGENOUS	EHNORSSST	SHORTNESS	EIIPRRTUV	IRRUPTIVE
EGNORSSSS	GROSSNESS	EHNORSTTW	NORTH-WEST	EIJLLNOSS	JOLLINESS
EGNORSTUY	YOUNGSTER	EHOOOPRSU	POORHOUSE	EIKLMORSY	IRKSOMELY
EHHIIRTTT	THIRTIETH	EHOOORSTV	OVERSHOOT	EIKLNPRRS	SPRINKLER
EHHILLLSY	HELLISHLY	EHOOPPTTY	PHOTOTYPE	EIKLNSSSU	SULKINESS
EHHIOPRSW	HORSEWHIP	EHOORRTVW	OVERTHROW	EIKMMNOSY	MONKEYISM
EHHIPRSSU	USHERSHIP	EHORRSTTW	THROWSTER	EIKMNOSSS	SMOKINESS
EHHMNOOOP	HOMOPHONE	EHOSSTTUW	SOUTH-WEST	EIKNRRTTY	TRINKETRY
EHHOOPSTY	THEOSOPHY	EIIILNNQU	INQUILINE	EILLMNOST	MILLSTONE
EHIIKNSTT	KITTENISH	EIIIMPRTV	PRIMITIVE	EILLMPTUX	MULTIPLEX
EHIILLNSS	HILLINESS	EIIiNRSTT	RETINITIS	EILLNOSSW	LOWLINESS
EHIILPSYZ	SYPHILIZE	EIIINTTUV	INTUITIVE	EILLNOTVY	VIOLENTLY
EHIIMRSTI	TRITHEISM	EIIJMSSTU	JESUITISM	EILLNSSST	STILLNESS
EHIINORRT	INHERITOR	EIIKLMNSS	MILKINESS	EILLNSSSY	SINLESSLY
EHIINPRST	NEPHRITIS	EIIKLNSSS	SILKINESS	EILLOOPRV	LIVERPOOL
	PHRENITIS	EIILLMNRY	MILLINERY	EILLOPRSV	OVERSPILL
EHIINPSST	PITHINESS	EIILLMSST	LIMITLESS		SPILL-OVER
EHIIPPSSY	EPIPHYSIS	EIILLNSSS	SILLINESS	EILLOPRTY	PELLITORY
EHIKNSSSU	HUSKINESS	EIILMNOSU	LIMOUSINE	EILLSSTWY	WITLESSLY
EHIKORRSY	YORKSHIRE	EIILMNSSS	SLIMINESS	EILMMOPSY	MISEMPLOY
EHILLOSTY	HOSTILELY	EIILMPSUV	IMPULSIVE	EILMNOOSY	NOISOMELY
EHILLOSWY	YELLOWISH	EIILMRSST	LISTERISM	EILMNOPST	SIMPLETON
EHILMRSST	MIRTHLESS	EIILNPSST	SPLENITIS	EILMNORTT	TORMENTIL
EHILNOSUY	HEINOUSLY	EIILNPTUV	VULPINITE	EILMNOSTY	SOLEMNITY
EHILPSTTY	PETTISHLY	EIILNRTUY	NEURILITY	EILNNOSTV	INSOLVENT
EHIMNNOOS	MOONSHINE	EIILNSTTY	TENSILITY	EILNOOPSX	EXPLOSION
EHIMNOPRS	PREMONISH	EIILOQSSU	SILIQUOSE	EILNOOTUV	EVOLUTION
EHIMNOPUU	EUPHONIUM	EIILPRSTU	PLEURITIS	EILNOPRRU	PURLOINER
EHIMNRTUU	RUTHENIUM	EIILPRTUY	PUERILITY	EILNOPRSU	REPULSION
EHIMPRRTU	TRIUMPHER	EIILRSTTY	STERILITY	EILNOPSST	POINTLESS
EHINNOSTW	WHINSTONE	EIILRSTVY	SERVILITY	EILNOPSUX	EXPULSION
EHINOPRSW	OWNERSHIP	EIIMMNORS	IMMERSION	EILNORSUV	REVULSION
EHINOPSTY	HYPNOTISE	EIIMMNSTY	IMMENSITY	EILNOSSSU	LOUSINESS
EHINOPSVY	ENVOYSHIP	EIIMMORSS	ISOMERISM	EILNOSUVY	ENVIOUSLY
EHINOPTYZ	HYPNOTIZE	EIIMMORST	MEMOIRIST	EILNPPSSU	PULPINESS
EHINORRSU	NOURISHER	EIIMMPSSS	PESSIMISM	EILNPQTUU	QUINTUPLE
EHINOSSSW	SHOWINESS	EIIMNORSS	REMISSION	EILNPRSTY	SPLINTERY
EHINSSSTY	SYNTHESIS	EIIMNSSST	MISTINESS	EILNQTUUY	UNQUIETLY
EHIOPRSST	SOPHISTER	EIIMOPRSU	IMPERIOUS	EILNRSSSU	SURLINESS
EHIPRSTTY	PRETTYISH	EIIMOPRSV	IMPROVISE	EILNRSTTU	TURNSTILE
EHKOORSUW	HOUSEWORK	EIIMOPSTT	EPITOMIST	EILNRTUUV	VULTURINE
	WORKHOUSE	EIIMPSSST	PESSIMIST	EILNSSSTT	STINTLESS
EHLNOOPXY	XYLOPHONE	EIINNNOST	INTENSION	EILNSSSTU	LUSTINESS
EHLNORRTY	NORTHERLY	EIINNNOTT	INTENTION	EILOPPRSS	PROLEPSIS
EHLOOSSTT	TOOTHLESS	EIINNNOTV	INVENTION	EILOPRSTY	LEPROSITY
EHLOPRSTU	UPHOLSTER	EIINNORST	INSERTION	EILOPSTUY	PITEOUSLY
EHLOPSTYY	HYPOSTYLE	EIINNORSV	INVERSION	EILORRTVW	LIVERWORT
EHLORRTTT	THROTTLER	EIINNOSSS	NOISINESS	EILORSSUY	SERIOUSLY
EHLORSSTW	WORTHLESS	EIINNPSSS	SPININESS	EIMMNOORT	MORMONITE
EHLORSTUY	SOUTHERLY	EIINNSSTT	INSISTENT	EIMMNOPRS	PERSIMMON
EHLPRSTUU	SULPHURET	EIINNSTTY	INTENSITY	EIMMOOPRU	PROOEMIUM
EHLRSSTTU	TRUTHLESS	EIINOPRSV	PREVISION	EIMMNOPRT	PROMINENT
EHMNNOOOY	HONEYMOON	EIINOPTVW	VIEWPOINT	EIMMNORST	INNERMOST
EHMOOOPRS	SOPHOMORE	EIINORSTY	SENIORITY	EIMNNRTTU	NUTRIMENT

144

EIMNOORSS	ROOMINESS	
EIMNOPRTU	ENTROPIUM	
	IMPORTUNE	
EIMNORRTW	WORRIMENT	
EIMNORSST	MONITRESS	
EIMNORSSU	SENSORIUM	
EIMNORSUV	VERMINOUS	
EIMNOSSSS	MOSSINESS	
EIMNOSSST	MOISTNESS	
EIMNOSTTY	TESTIMONY	
EIMNOSTUU	UNTIMEOUS	
EIMNOTTZZ	MEZZOTINT	
EIMOOPRTV	PROMOTIVE	
EIMOOSEOX	EXOSMOSIS	
EIMOPRRST	MISREPORT	
EIMOPRSTU	IMPOSTURE	
EIMOPSTUU	IMPETUOUS	
EIMORRRST	TERRORISM	
EIMORRSSY	REMISSORY	
EIMORRSTU	TRIMEROUS	
EINNNOTTY	NONENTITY	
EINNNSSSU	SUNNINESS	
EINNOOPRT	PONTONIER	
EINNORTVY	INVENTORY	
EINNOSSST	STONINESS	
EINNPRSTW	NEWSPRINT	
EINNRTTUW	UNWRITTEN	
EINOOPRRT	PORTIONER	
EINOORTTX	EXTORTION	
EINOORTTY	NOTORIETY	
EINOOSSST	SOOTINESS	
EINOPRSSS	PROSINESS	
EINOPRSTU	PERTUSION	
EINOPRSUU	PENURIOUS	
EINORRSSS	SORRINESS	
EINORRTTV	INTROVERT	
EINORSTUX	EXTRUSION	
EINPRRTTU	INTERRUPT	
EINRSSSTU	RUSTINESS	
EIOOPRRST	POSTERIOR	
EIOOPRSTX	EXPOSITOR	
EIOOPRSTY	OPEROSITY	
EIOPPRRTY	PROPRIETY	
EIOPPRSUV	PURPOSIVE	
EIOPRSTTY	POSTERITY	
EIOQRSTUU	TURQUOISE	
EIORRRSTT	TERRORIST	
EIORRRTTY	TERRITORY	
EJLLOSSYY	JOYLESSLY	
EJNOORRSU	SOJOURNER	
EKLLNNOWW	WELL-KNOWN	
EKMNOOSTU	MUSKETOON	
EKNOOPSTU	OUTSPOKEN	
EKNORSSTU	SUNSTROKE	
ELLMORSTU	ROSTELLUM	
ELLMOSUUY	EMULOUSLY	
ELLMRSTUU	SURMULLET	
ELLNOPTUY	OPULENTLY	
ELLOPSTYY	POLYSTYLE	
ELMNNOOST	SOMNOLENT	
ELMNPPSSU	PLUMPNESS	

ELMOORSTW	LOWERMOST	
ELMORSTUU	TREMULOUS	
ELNOORSUY	ONEROUSLY	
ELNORSUVY	NERVOUSLY	
ELOORSTVY	LOVE-STORY	
ELOPPRSSY	PURPOSELY	
ELOPRSUUV	PULVEROUS	
ELOPSSSTU	SPOUTLESS	
ELOQRSUUU	QUERULOUS	
ELRSSSTTU	TRUSTLESS	
EMMNOOSTU	MOMENTOUS	
EMMNRSTUU	MENSTRUUM	
EMNNOUOOST	MOONSTONE	
EMNOOOPTT	MONOPTOTE	
EMNOOPSUY	EPONYMOUS	
EMNOORRTT	TORMENTOR	
EMNOOSTTU	TOMENTOUS	
EMNORSSTT	STERNMOST	
EMOOOSTTY	OSTEOTOMY	
EMOORSTTU	OUTERMOST	
EMOPPRSTU	UPPERMOST	
EMORSTTTU	UTTERMOST	
ENNOOPPRT	PROPONENT	
ENNORSTTU	TURNSTONE	
ENOOPPRTU	OPPORTUNE	
ENOPRSSSU	SUSPENSOR	
ENORSSTUU	STRENUOUS	
ENORSTUUV	VENTUROUS	
ENOSSSTTU	STOUTNESS	
EOOPPRRSS	OPPRESSOR	
EOOPPRTTY	PROTOTYPE	
EOOPRSSSS	POSSESSOR	
EOPPRRSTU	SUPPORTER	
EOPPRSSST	STOP-PRESS	
FFGHILNSU	SHUFFLING	
FFGHILRTU	FRIGHTFUL	
FFGIMNORU	FUNGIFORM	
FFGINOPRS	OFFSPRING	
FFINOSSUU	SUFFUSION	
FFLOOOOPR	FOOLPROOF	
FFORRSUUU	FURFUROUS	
FGGIINORV	FORGIVING	
FGHIILLTY	FLIGHTILY	
FGHILOOTT	FOOTLIGHT	
FGHINORTT	FORTNIGHT	
FGIILNPTU	UPLIFTING	
FGIILNRST	FIRSTLING	
FGIILNTTY	FITTINGLY	
FGIINNTTU	UNFITTING	
FGILLNOOW	FOLLOWING	
FGIMNORUU	UNGUIFORM	
FGLORSUUU	FULGUROUS	
FHHIORTTW	FORTHWITH	
FHIIJNOST	FISH-JOINT	
FHIILRTTY	THRIFTILY	
FHILLOOSY	FOOLISHLY	
FHILLOSWY	WOLFISHLY	
FHILOPPSY	FOPPISHLY	
FHINRTTUY	UNTHRIFTY	
FHLLRTUUY	HURTFULLY	
FIIIMNRTY	INFIRMITY	

FIIKLNNST	SKINFLINT	
FIILLMORV	VILLIFORM	
FIILLMOTU	MULTIFOIL	
FIILLPTUY	PITIFULLY	
FIILNNOUX	INFLUXION	
FIILOPRST	PROFILIST	
FIILORTVY	FRIVOLITY	
FIIMMNORS	MISINFORM	
FIIMMORRT	MITRIFORM	
FIIMORRTU	TRIFORIUM	
FIIMORRTV	VITRIFORM	
FIKLLLSUY	SKILFULLY	
FIKLLNSUU	UNSKILFUL	
FILLSTUWY	WISTFULLY	
FILMMORTU	MULTIFORM	
FILMNORUY	UNIFORMLY	
FILOOOPRT	PORTFOLIO	
FILOORSUV	FRIVOLOUS	
FILORSUUY	FURIOUSLY	
FILOSSTUU	FISTULOUS	
FINOOPRSU	PROFUSION	
FINOOPRTT	FOOTPRINT	
FKLNOOSTW	TOWNSFOLK	
FKOORRSTW	FROSTWORK	
FLLLSTUUY	LUSTFULLY	
FLLNOORRY	FORLORNLY	
FLOOOOSTT	FOOTSTOOL	
FLOORRSUW	SORROWFUL	
FOOPRRSTU	RUST-PROOF	
GGGILMNSU	SMUGGLING	
GGHHHIILT	HIGHLIGHT	
GGHIIILRW	WHIRLIGIG	
GGHIILNNS	SHINGLING	
GGHIILNNT	LIGHTNING	
GGHIILNSY	SIGHINGLY	
GGHIINRTW	RIGHT-WING	
GGHILNSUY	GUSHINGLY	
GGIIIMNSV	MISGIVING	
GGIILNPRY	GRIPINGLY	
GGIINNPRS	SPRINGING	
GGILLNNOY	LONGINGLY	
GGILLNOWY	GLOWINGLY	
GGILMNSUY	GINGLYMUS	
GGILNNOUY	YOUNGLING	
GGILNOPRY	GROPINGLY	
GHHNOTTUU	UNTHOUGHT	
GHIILLNRT	THRILLING	
GHIILNNWY	WHININGLY	
GHIINNPSU	PUNISHING	
GHILLOOPY	PHILOLOGY	
GHILLOOTY	LITHOLOGY	
GHILMNOOT	MOONLIGHT	
GHILNOPYY	PHILOGYNY	
GHILNPSUY	PUSHINGLY	
GHILNSTUY	UNSIGHTLY	
GHILOOOPY	OPHIOLOGY	
GHILOOSTY	HISTOLOGY	
GHILOPSTT	SPOTLIGHT	
GHILORSUY	ROGUISHLY	
GHILPRSTY	SPRIGHTLY	
GHILPRTUY	UPRIGHTLY	

GHINORTUW	INWROUGHT	GLOOOPRTY	TROPOLOGY	IILNOOPST	POSTILION
GHLMNOOYY	HYMNOLOGY	HHIILNORT	RHINOLITH	IILOPRTXY	PROLIXITY
GHLMOOTYY	MYTHOLOGY	HIILLMNOT	MILLIONTH	IILORTTTY	TORTILITY
GHLNOOOPY	PHONOLOGY	HIILNORTT	TRILITHON	IIMOPRTXY	PROXIMITY
GHNORTUUW	UNWROUGHT	HIILNSSWY	SWINISHLY	IIMOQSTUZ	QUIZOTISM
GHOOORSTT	OSTROGOTH	HIILOQRSU	LIQUORISH	IINNOORTT	INTORTION
GHOORTTUW	OUTGROWTH	HIILOSTTY	HOSTILITY	IINNORSTU	INTRUSION
GIIINNQRU	INQUIRING	HIILRSTTY	THIRSTILY	IINNORTTU	NUTRITION
GIIINRTVY	VIRGINITY	HIIMNOPRS	MINORSHIP	IINOOPRSV	PROVISION
GIIKLNNTW	TWINKLING	HIIMNORST	IRONSMITH	IINOPRRTU	IRRUPTION
GIIKNNNUW	UNWINKING	HIIOPPRRS	PRIORSHIP	IINOPSSTY	SPINOSITY
GIILLLNWY	WILLINGLY	HILLMPSUY	LUMPISHLY	IINOSSTUY	SINUOSITY
GIILLMNPY	LIMPINGLY	HILLOOPRW	WHIRLPOOL	ILLNOOPTU	POLLUTION
GIILLMNSY	SMILINGLY	HILLSSTYY	STYLISHLY	ILLOOQSUY	SOLILOQUY
GIILLNNUW	UNWILLING	HILMMPSUY	MUMPISHLY	ILMNOOSUY	OMINOUSLY
GIILNNNWY	WINNINGLY	HILMOOSYZ	HYLOZOISM	ILMNOPTUU	PLUTONIUM
GIILNNSTU	INSULTING	HILMOOTTY	LITHOTOMY	ILNOOPRSU	PROLUSION
GIILNOSUU	ULIGINOUS	HILMOPRSY	ROMPISHLY	ILNOOSUXY	NOXIOUSLY
GIILNPRST	STRIPLING	HILOSSTTY	SOTTISHLY	ILNOPSTTU	PLUTONIST
GIILNPTYY	PITYINGLY	HILRSTUUV	VULTURISH	ILNORSUUY	RUINOUSLY
GIILNTTWY	WITTINGLY	HIMNNOOSY	MOONSHINY	ILNOSSUUY	SINUOUSLY
GIILRSTTU	LITURGIST	HIMNOPSTY	HYPNOTISM	ILOORSTUY	RIOTOUSLY
GIIMNOPRS	PROMISING	HIMORSTUU	HUMOURIST	ILORSUUUX	LUXURIOUS
GIIMNOPRV	IMPROVING	HIMPSSSYY	SYMPHYSIS	IMMMNOORS	MORMONISM
GIIMNRSSU	SURMISING	HIOPRSSTY	SOPHISTRY	IMMOPPRTU	IMPROMPTU
GIINNPTUY	UNPITYING	HIOPRSTTU	TUTORSHIP	IMMOPSSUY	SYMPOSIUM
GIINNRSSU	SUNRISING	HKMMNORRU	KRUMMHORN	IMNOOOPRT	PROMOTION
GIINNTTUW	UNWITTING	HLMOOPPXY	POMPHOLYX	IMNORSTTU	STRONTIUM
GIIORRSUU	IRRIGUOUS	HLNOOPPYY	POLYPHONY	IMOOOSTTZ	ZOOTOMIST
GIKLNNOWY	KNOWINGLY	HMOOPTTYY	PHYTOTOMY	IMOOPPSTY	POMPOSITY
GIKNNNOUW	UNKNOWING	HMOOSSTTU	SOUTHMOST	INNOOSSUU	UNISONOUS
GIKNOOPRV	PROVOKING	HNOOPPTYY	PHONOTYPY	INOOOPSSU	POISONOUS
GILLMOSSY	SYLLOGISM	HOOPPTTYY	PHOTOTYPY	INOOORSTU	NOTORIOUS
GILLOOOPY	OLIGOPOLY	IIIKLLNPS	SPILLIKIN	IOOPRRSVY	PROVISORY
GILNORTTU	TROUTLING	IIILNOSTV	VIOLINIST	IOPRSSTTU	POSTURIST
GILNOSTUU	GLUTINOUS	IIILNTTUY	INUTILITY	LMOOPPSUY	POMPOUSLY
GILOOOSTT	OTOLOGIST	IIILOSUVX	LIXIVIOUS	LOPSSTUUU	PUSTULOUS
GILOOOSTZ	ZOOLOGIST	IIINNOTTU	INTUITION	LORSTUUUV	VULTUROUS
GIMMNRRUU	MURMURING	IIJNORSUU	INJURIOUS	MNOORSSTU	MONSTROUS
GIMNNOORS	MONSIGNOR	IIJNORTUY	JUNIORITY	MNOORSSTW	SNOWSTORM
GIMNNOOST	GNOMONIST	IILLMPRSU	SPIRILLUM	MOPSSTUUU	SUMPTUOUS
GINOOPRSS	PROGNOSIS	IILLOSTVY	VILLOSITY	NOOOOPRTZ	PROTOZOON
GINOORSTU	TRIGONOUS	IILMNOOPS	IMPLOSION		
GINORSTUY	TRIGYNOUS	IILMNOPSU	IMPULSION		

Ten Letter Words

AAAAEGLMMT	AMALGAMATE	AAADEIMNNT	ADAMANTINE
AAAAHINNST	ATHANASIAN	AAADELMNRS	SALAMANDER
AAARBCILGT	SABBATICAL	AAADELMPPS	ADAM'S-APPLE
AAABCCKNSV	CANVAS-BACK	AAADGILLNR	GRANADILLA
AAABCEHLTT	ATTACHABLE	AAADGNOPPR	PROPAGANDA
AAABCEKLTT	ATTACKABLE	AAADGNRTUV	AVANT-GUARD
AAABCHINRT	BATRACHIAN	AAADINOPTT	ADAPTATION
AAABCIKRSS	CASSIA-BARK	AAADLMNRTU	LAUNDRAMAT
AAABDEEGLM	DAMAGEABLE	AAADLNQRTU	QUADRANTAL
AAABDMORSS	AMBASSADOR	AAADMNQRUU	QUADRUMANA
AAABEEGLMN	MANAGEABLE	AAAEEILMMN	MELANAEMIA
AAABEELLPP	APPEALABLE	AAAEGHLLNP	PHALANGEAL
AAABEELPPS	APPEASABLE	AAAEGILMNR	MANAGERIAL
AAABEGGMNR	GARBAGEMAN	AAAEGILPPR	PARAPLEGIA
AAABEILLSS	ASSAILABLE	AAAEHIMRTU	HAEMATURIA
AAABEILNTT	ATTAINABLE	AAAEHINSTU	EUTHANASIA
AAABELLNSY	ANALYSABLE	AAAEHPPRRS	PARAPHRASE
AAABIMNPST	ANABAPTISM	AAAEILLPTZ	PALATALIZE
AAABINPSTT	ANABAPTIST	AAAEILNPTT	PALATINATE
AAACCDEILM	ACADEMICAL	AAAEIMNQRU	AQUAMARINE
AAACCEIPTT	CAPACITATE	AAAELMNRTT	ATRAMENTAL
AAACCHKKMT	HACKMATACK	AAAELMRSTT	METATARSAL
AAACCHPRTT	CATAPHRACT	AAAGGILRST	GASTRALGIA
AAACCILLRS	CASCARILLA	AAAGGNNRTU	GARGANTUAN
AAACCILNST	ANACLASTIC	AAAGIILMST	GALIMATIAS
AAACCIMORT	ACROAMATIC	AAAGILMNNO	ANGLOMANIA
AAACCINRTT	ANTARCTICA	AAAHLMNPST	PHANTASMAL
AAACDEIMMZ	MACADAMIZE	AAAIINNRST	SANITARIAN
AAACDGIILR	CARDIALGIA	AAAILNORTT	NATATORIAL
AAACDHINNR	ARACHNIDAN	AAAILNRSTU	AUSTRALIAN
AAACDIKLSY	LACKADAISY		SATURNALIA
AAACDILMRT	DRAMATICAL	AAAINNPRSS	PARNASSIAN
AAACEENPPR	APPEARANCE	AABBBELORS	ABSORBABLE
AAACEENRRV	CARAVANEER	AABBCDEEKR	BAREBACKED
AAACEFLQTU	CATAFALQUE	AABBCDKLOR	BLACK-BOARD
AAACEILMNT	CATAMENIAL	AABBCEILRS	ASCRIBABLE
AAACEINNRT	CATENARIAN	AABBCELMOT	COMBATABLE
AAACEJKNPS	JACKANAPES	AABBCIILNR	RABBINICAL
AAACELLNPT	APLACENTAL	AABBDEGORR	BARGE-BOARD
AAACELMPRT	METACARPAL	AABBDEOORV	ABOVE-BOARD
AAACGGILNO	ANAGOGICAL	AABBEEHLRT	BREATHABLE
AAACGHNRTT	TRAGACANTH	AABBEEIRTV	ABBREVIATE
AAACGILLNO	ANALOGICAL	AABBEELLRS	BASEBALLER
AAACILLMNY	MANIACALLY	AABBEELNRU	UNBEARABLE
AAACILLNTY	ANALYTICAL	AABBEELNTU	UNBEATABLE
AAACILMNOT	ANATOMICAL	AABBEFMRRY	BABY-FARMER
AAACILNPST	ANAPLASTIC	AABBEILMNO	ABOMINABLE
AAACILNRST	SCARLATINA	AABBEILNOT	OBTAINABLE
AAACINRRTT	TRACTARIAN	AABBEKLLST	BASKETBALL
AAADEEGHNP	PHAGEDAENA	AABBILMNOY	ABOMINABLY

AABBILNNOY	BABYLONIAN	AABCHINOTT	COHABITANT
AABBIORSSU	BABIROUSSA	AABCHLRRUY	BRACHYURAL
AABCCEELPT	ACCEPTABLE	AABCIILPTY	CAPABILITY
AABCCEHILN	CHAIN-CABLE	AABCILLLSY	SYLLABICAL
AABCCEILLN	CALCINABLE	AABCILLMPY	IMPLACABLY
AABCCELLLU	CALCULABLE	AABCILNSUV	SUBCLAVIAN
AABCCELPTY	ACCEPTABLY	AABCIQSTUU	SUBAQUATIC
AABCCINOTU	ACCUBATION	AABCKLMOOR	BLACKAMOOR
AABCCIORST	ACROBATICS	AABCLLNNNO	CANNON-BALL
AABCCIORTZ	CARBAZOTIC	AABCLMMRUU	AMBULACRUM
AABCDEEILR	ERADICABLE	AABCLMOPRY	COMPARABLY
AABCDEELLR	DECLARABLE	AABCLORUVY	VOCABULARY
AABCDEELNS	ASCENDABLE	AABCLRSTTY	ABSTRACTLY
AABCDEHKNR	BACKHANDER	AABDDEEEHR	BAREHEADED
AABCDEIILT	DIABETICAL	AABDDEELMN	DEMANDABLE
AABCDELNNU	UNBALANCED	AABDDEHLMO	HEBDOMADAL
AABCDERSTT	ABSTRACTED	AABDDEHLRS	BALDERDASH
AABCDGKLRU	BLACKGUARD	AABDDEILRR	AIR-BLADDER
AABCDIILLO	DIABOLICAL	AABDDILLMO	LAMBDOIDAL
AABCDIINOT	ABDICATION	AABDEEGNRR	BEAR-GARDEN
AABCDILMMS	LAMBDACISM	AABDEEHRRT	THREADBARE
AABCDKLRWY	BACKWARDLY	AABDEELNRU	UNREADABLE
AABCDNNORT	CONTRABAND	AABDEELRRW	REWARDABLE
AABCEEEFFL	EFFACEABLE	AABDEFINRT	FAT-BRAINED
AABCEEERTT	EBRACTEATE	AABDEGGINR	BRIGANDAGE
AABCEEERTX	EXACERBATE	AABDEGHLNS	BANGLADESH
AABCEEGHLN	CHANGEABLE	AABDEGORSW	BOARD-WAGES
AABCEEGHLR	CHARGEABLE	AABDEGRRSS	BEARD-GRASS
AABCEEHILV	ACHIEVABLE	AABDEILMTT	ADMITTABLE
AABCEEHLRS	SEARCHABLE	AABDEILNOR	ORDAINABLE
AABCEEHLTY	CHALYBEATE	AABDEIRSTZ	BASTARDIZE
AABCEEINRR	CARABINEER	AABDEJLSTU	ADJUSTABLE
AABCEELLLR	RECALLABLE	AABDELLNNO	BELLADONNA
AABCEELLNS	CLEANSABLE	AABDELNOPR	PARDONABLE
AABCEELNRT	TABERNACLE	AABDELRSTU	BALUSTRADE
AABCEFIILP	PACIFIABLE	AABDEMORSS	EMBASSADOR
AABCEGHLNY	CHANGEABLY	AABDEOPRST	PASTEBOARD
AABCEGLLOU	COAGULABLE	AABDGHRRTU	DRAUGHT-BAR
AABCEGLMNN	BLANC-MANGE	AABDHMNNSU	HUSBANDMAN
AABCEHILPT	ALPHABETIC	AABDILMNRU	MANDIBULAR
AABCEHILRT	CHARITABLE	AABDLNNTUY	ABUNDANTLY
AABCEHINRT	BRANCHIATE	AABDLNOPRY	PARDONABLY
AABCEIINTU	BEAUTICIAN	AABEEELLPR	REPEALABLE
AABCEILLMP	IMPLACABLE	AABEEEELLRS	RELEASABLE
AABCEILLPP	APPLICABLE	AABEEEELLRV	REVEALABLE
AABCEILMST	MASTICABLE	AABEEELPRT	REPEATABLE
AABCEILNOT	ACTIONABLE	AABEEFLLLT	FLABELLATE
AABCEILOSS	ASSOCIABLE	AABEEGLMSS	ASSEMBLAGE
AABCEILQRU	ACQUIRABLE	AABEEGLOVY	VOYAGEABLE
AABCEIORST	AEROBATICS	AABEEILLRZ	REALIZABLE
AABCELLLOT	COLLATABLE	AABEEILMNX	EXAMINABLE
AABCELLMOR	COLLAR-BEAM	AABEEILNRT	RETAINABLE
AABCELLORR	BARCAROLLE	AABEEILPRR	REPAIRABLE
AABCELMOPR	COMPARABLE	AABEEKLMRR	REMARKABLE
AABCELMTUU	ACETABULUM	AABEEKLMRT	MARKETABLE
AABCELRRTU	TRABECULAR	AABEEKRRTW	BREAKWATER
AABCERRTUU	BUREAUCRAT	AABEELLMNT	LAMENTABLE
AABCFIORRT	FABRICATOR	AABEELLNSU	UNSALEABLE
AABCGKMMNO	BACKGAMMON	AABEELMNTU	UNTAMEABLE
AABCHHIMPR	AMPHIBRACH	AABEELMRSU	MEASURABLE
AABCHILRTY	CHARITABLY	AABEELNNTT	TENANTABLE

AABEELNORS	REASONABLE	AABIINNSSY	ABYSSINIAN
AABEELNOSS	SEASONABLE	AABIINPRST	BIPARTISAN
AABEELNPTT	PATENTABLE	AABIJNORTU	ABJURATION
AABEELNRSW	ANSWERABLE	AABILLMPPY	IMPALPABLY
AABEELNRUW	UNWEARABLE	AABILLNRUY	BINAURALLY
AABEELOPRV	EVAPORABLE	AABILMNOTU	AMBULATION
AABEELSSSS	ASSESSABLE	AABILNOTTU	TABULATION
AABEERRTTV	VERTEBRATA	AABIORRRTT	ARBITRATOR
AABEFFIILL	AFFILIABLE	AABLLMNORY	ABNORMALLY
AABEFFILMR	AFFIRMABLE	AABLMORTUY	AMBULATORY
AABEFHLMOT	FATHOMABLE	AABLOORRTY	LABORATORY
AABEFILLNT	INFLATABLE	AABLSTTTUY	STATUTABLY
AABEFIMORS	FRAMDOESIA	AACCCDENOR	ACCORDANCE
AABEFIORUV	FAVOURABLE	AACCCEENPT	ACCEPTANCE
AABEFNORRT	FORBEARANT	AACCCEILTT	CATALECTIC
AABEGHORRU	HARBOURAGE	AACCCENPTY	ACCEPTANCY
AABEGIILMN	IMAGINABLE	AACCCINRUY	INACCURACY
AABEGILNSS	ASSIGNABLE	AACCDDIILT	DIDACTICAL
AABEGILRST	ALGEBRAIST	AACCDEEFMR	CREAM-FACED
AABEGINNOT	ABNEGATION	AACCDEENNS	ASCENDANCE
AABEGIORTV	ABROGATIVE	AACCDEHNOR	ARCHDEACON
AABEGLNRUU	UNARGUABLE	AACCDEILNT	ACCIDENTAL
AABEHIILTT	HABILITATE	AACCDEIORT	CO-RADICATE
AABEIILNRV	INVARIABLE	AACCDELLNO	CANDLE-COAL
AABEIILNST	INSATIABLE	AACCDELLTU	CALCULATED
AABEIILSST	ASSIBILATE	AACCDENNSY	ASCENDANCY
AABEIKLMST	MISTAKABLE	AACCDHNOST	COACH-STAND
AABEILLMPP	IMPALPABLE	AACCDIISTU	DIACAUSTIC
AABEILLNUV	INVALUABLE	AACCEEEELRT	ACCELERATE
AABEILMNTV	AMBIVALENT	AACCEEIMNR	CINE-CAMERA
AABEILMPSS	IMPASSABLE	AACCEEELLNT	CANCELLATE
AABEILQRRU	QUARRIABLE	AACCEENTTU	ACCENTUATE
AABEILRTUZ	TABULARIZE	AACCEFPRST	SPACECRAFT
AABEINORRT	ABERRATION	AACCEGHOST	STAGECOACH
AABEKLMRRY	REMARKABLY	AACCEHILMN	MECHANICAL
AABELLMNTY	LAMENTABLY	AACCEHINRS	SACCHARINE
AABELLRSTW	BREAST-WALL	AACCEHINRU	CHAUCERIAN
AABELMNORS	RANSOMABLE	AACCEILPTT	CATALEPTIC
AABELMRSUY	MEASURABLY	AACCEINOSU	ACINACEOUS
AABELNORSY	REASONABLY	AACCEINPRT	PANCREATIC
AABELNOSSY	SEASONABLY	AACCEINRTT	CANTATRICE
AABELNRSWY	ANSWERABLY	AACCEINRTU	INACCURATE
AABELOORRT	ELABORATOR	AACCEIRRTU	CARICATURE
AABELOPPRV	APPROVABLE	AACCEISTUV	ACCUSATIVE
AABELSTTTU	STATUTABLE	AACCEKLLVV	CLACK-VALVE
AABEMRSTTU	MASTURBATE	AACCELLNNO	CANNEL-COAL
AABFFIILTY	AFFABILITY	AACCELMTUU	ACCUMULATE
AABFLMNOTY	FLAMBOYANT	AACCELORSU	CALCAREOUS
AABFLORUVY	FAVOURABLY	AACCELRTUY	ACCURATELY
AABGIILMNY	IMAGINABLY	AACCENRSTU	CRUSTACEAN
AABGIILNOR	ABORIGINAL	AACCFHIRSY	SACCHARIFY
AABGINOORT	ABROGATION	AACCFILLRY	FARCICALLY
AABHIINNTT	INHABITANT	AACCFILRSU	FASCICULAR
AABHIINOTT	HABITATION	AACCFINNRS	FRANCISCAN
AABHILLTUY	HABITUALLY	AACCGHIORY	HAGIOCRACY
AABHIMMNRS	BRAHMANISM	AACCGHOPRY	CACOGRAPHY
AABHLLLOOU	HULLABALOO	AACCHILNPY	CHAPLAINCY
AABIIILMTY	AMIABILITY	AACCHIMORT	ACHROMATIC
AABIILNRVY	INVARIABLY	AACCHLNORY	ACRONYCHAL
AABIILRTTY	RATABILITY	AACCHMORSU	SCARAMOUCH
AABIILTTXY	TAXABILITY	AACCIILLMT	CLIMATICAL

AACCIINPTY	INCAPACITY
AACCILLRUV	CLAVICULAR
AACCILLTTY	TACTICALLY
AACCILNNOS	CANONICALS
AACCILNOOS	OCCASIONAL
AACCILORST	SOCRATICAL
AACCINOSTU	ACCUSATION
AACCIORTTU	AUTOCRATIC
AACCLLORTU	CALCULATOR
AACCLNOTTU	CONTACTUAL
AACCMNNOPY	CAPNOMANCY
AACCNNOTTU	ACCOUNTANT
AACCNORSST	SACROSANCT
AACDDEEHLR	DECAHEDRAL
AACDDEEIMP	AIDE-DE-CAMP
AACDDEIJTU	ADJUDICATE
AACDDEINNR	DECANDRIAN
AACDEEEFNS	DEFEASANCE
AACDEEFHMS	SHAMEFACED
AACDEEHNRS	CASE-HARDEN
AACDEEILRT	DILACERATE
AACDEEINRT	DERACINATE
AACDEEIPTT	DECAPITATE
AACDEEITTV	DEACTIVATE
AACDEENNTT	ATTENDANCE
AACDEFINRR	AFRICANDER
AACDEFINRU	FRICANDEAU
AACDEFLORT	DEFALCATOR
AACDEGINNY	DECAGYNIAN
AACDEHHTTW	DEATH-WATCH
AACDEHLORT	OCTAHEDRAL
AACDEHNTTU	UNATTACHED
AACDEHORTY	CATHODE-RAY
AACDEIINRR	IRRADIANCE
AACDEIIPRT	PAEDIATRIC
AACDEIIRTV	DIVARICATE
AACDEIJLTV	ADJECTIVAL
AACDEILMNR	ALDERMANIC
AACDEILMNT	DECLAIMANT
AACDEILNNO	CALEDONIAN
AACDEILNPT	PEDANTICAL
AACDEILNSZ	SCANDALIZE
AACDEIMNTT	ADMITTANCE
AACDEINQTU	ACQUAINTED
AACDEIORRT	ERADICATOR
AACDEJLNTY	ADJACENTLY
AACDELMOPR	CAMELOPARD
AACDELORRT	DECLARATOR
AACDELORST	SACERDOTAL
AACDELORSU	LARDACEOUS
AACDEORSUV	CADAVEROUS
AACDFHINRT	HANDICRAFT
AACDFIINOO	AFICIONADO
AACDFIMORR	MICROFARAD
AACDGIMORR	CARDIOGRAM
AACDGORSTU	COAST-GUARD
AACDIILMRS	RADICALISM
AACDIINRRY	IRRADIANCY
AACDIJLLUY	JUDAICALLY
AACDILLMTU	TALMUDICAL
AACDINNORT	OCTANDRIAN
AACDLNOSSU	SCANDALOUS
AACDMMNNOT	COMMANDANT
AACDNOORWY	CANARY-WOOD
AACDORSSTW	COASTWARDS
AACEEELMNP	ELECAMPANE
AACEEGILLN	ALLEGIANCE
AACEEHILNT	CHÂTELAINE
AACEEHKPST	CHEAPSKATE
AACEEHLMNO	CHAMAELEON
AACEEHLNPT	ANTE-CHAPEL
AACEEHLORV	COAL-HEAVER
AACEEHNNRT	ANTHRACENE
AACEEILPRT	ALTAR-PIECE
AACEEILSTT	ELASTICATE
AACEEIMNPT	EMANCIPATE
AACEEIPPRT	APPRECIATE
AACEEIRTTV	REACTIVATE
AACEELLNOT	LANCEOLATE
AACEELMSTU	EMASCULATE
AACEENORSU	ARENACEOUS
AACEFGLMOU	CAMOUFLAGE
AACEFHLLNP	CHAPFALLEN
AACEFIILTT	FACILITATE
AACEFIINTZ	FANATICIZE
AACEFINORT	AREFACTION
AACEFLMORT	MALEFACTOR
AACEFMNRSU	SURFACEMAN
AACEGHNORT	COAT-HANGER
AACEGILMNN	MALIGNANCE
AACEGIMNPR	CAMPAIGNER
AACEHHILRR	HIERARCHAL
AACEHILMMS	MICHAELMAS
AACEHILMPT	EMPHATICAL
AACEHILNRS	LANCASHIRE
AACEHILRTT	THEATRICAL
AACEHIMMPR	AMPHIMACER
AACEHIMMTT	MATHEMATIC
AACEHINRRT	CATARRHINE
AACEHINSTU	EUSTACHIAN
AACEHIRRTV	ARCHITRAVE
AACEHKLMRS	RAMSHACKLE
AACEHKMMRT	MATCHMAKER
AACEHLMMRW	CLAW-HAMMER
AACEHLOPSU	ACEPHALOUS
AACEHLPRTY	ARCHETYPAL
AACEHMNPRY	PARENCHYMA
AACEHMNTTT	ATTACHMENT
AACEHMOPRT	CAMPHORATE
AACEHOPRTY	APOTHECARY
AACEIILLPR	CAPILLAIRE
AACEIILPST	CAPITALISE
AACEIILPTZ	CAPITALIZE
AACEIIMNOT	EMACIATION
AACEIINPTT	ANTICIPATE
AACEIINTTV	VATICINATE
AACEIIOPSS	CASSIOPEIA
AACEIIPRTT	PATRICIATE
AACEILLMNU	ANIMALCULE
AACEILLNRT	CARNALLITE
AACEILLOSU	ALLIACEOUS
AACEILLPRT	PRELATICAL

AACEILLRVY	CAVALIERLY	AACHILLOPT	ALLOPATHIC
AACEILMMTU	IMMACULATE	AACHIMNORS	MARASCHINO
AACEILMNTU	CALUMNIATE	AACHIMNORT	MACHINATOR
AACEILNORT	CREATIONAL	AACHIMNORW	CHAIRWOMAN
	LACERATION	AACHIMPRST	PHARMACIST
AACEILNOST	ESCALATION	AACHIMRRTY	MATRIARCHY
AACEILNPTU	PANICULATE	AACHINPSWW	WAPINSCHAW
AACEILOOPZ	PALAEOZOIC	AACHINRSTU	CARTHUSIAN
AACEILPTTU	CAPITULATE	AACHIPRRTY	PATRIARCHY
AACEILRTTU	ARTICULATE	AACHLLORTT	ALTAR-CLOTH
AACEILRTUU	AURICULATE	AACHLOPPRY	APOCRYPHAL
AACEILSTTT	STALACTITE	AACHLRRTUY	CHARTULARY
AACEIMNNOR	CAMERONIAN	AACIILLNNT	ANTICLINAL
AACEIMNURT	MACERATION	AACIILLOPT	APOLITICAL
AACEINNNTU	ANNUNCIATE	AACIILMNOS	SIMONIACAL
AACEINNOTT	CATENATION	AACIILMNORT	TALISMANIC
AACEINNRTU	CENTAURIAN	AACIILMNTX	ANTI-CLIMAX
AACEINORTU	AERONAUTIC	AACIILMPST	CAPITALISM
AACEINOTUV	EVACUATION	AACIILNOST	ANTISOCIAL
AACEINOTVX	EXCAVATION	AACIILPPST	PAPISTICAL
AACEINSSST	ASSISTANCE	AACIILPSTT	CAPITALIST
AACEIORSTT	AEROSTATIC	AACIIMNSTV	VATICANISM
AACEIRTTTV	ATTRACTIVE	AACIINOPTT	CAPITATION
AACEJKNRTT	NATTERJACK	AACIINOTTV	ACTIVATION
AACEILLORT	COLLATERAL	AACIIORSUV	AVARICIOUS
AACELLLRST	SALT-CELLAR	AACILLMOSY	MOSAICALLY
AACELLPRRY	CARPELLARY	AACILLNOOT	ALLOCATION
AACELMMORS	SARCOLEMMA	AACILLNTUY	NAUTICALLY
AACELMOPSU	PALMACEOUS	AACILLSTTY	STATICALLY
AACELMORST	COAL-MASTER	AACILMNOTU	MACULATION
AACELMOSUV	MALVACEOUS	AACILMOSTU	CALAMITOUS
AACELMOSUY	AMYLACEOUS	AACILNNRTY	TYRANNICAL
AACELMPRST	CAMPESTRAL	AACILNOOTV	VOCATIONAL
AACELNRRUV	VERNACULAR	AACILNOPTY	NYCTALOPIA
AACELNRTTU	TENTACULAR	AACILOORRT	ORATORICAL
AACELOPPSY	APOCALYPSE	AACILOPTTU	AUTOPTICAL
AACELPRTTY	CALYPTRATE	AACILPRRTU	PARTICULAR
AACEMPRSTU	METACARPUS	AACIMMNNOO	MONOMANIAC
AACFGIILMN	MAGNIFICAL	AACIMNOPRY	PYROMANIAC
AACFHKNRST	CRANKSHAFT	AACIMNPRTU	PANCRATIUM
AACFHLLOTW	FALLOW-CHAT	AACIMORSTT	MASTICATOR
AACFIIILRT	ARTIFICIAL	AACINORSTT	CASTRATION
AACFIILNOR	CALIFORNIA	AACINORTTT	ATTRACTION
AACFIILSTT	FATALISTIC	AACINORTUY	CAUTIONARY
AACFIIMNST	FANATICISM	AACIORRSTT	ARISTOCRAT
AACFIINOST	FASCIATION	AACIOSSUVX	SAXICAVOUS
AACFILLOSU	FALLACIOUS	AACLLORRUY	ORACULARLY
AACFILNORT	FRACTIONAL	AACLNNORTU	CONNATURAL
AACFINORTY	FACTIONARY	AACMOORRTU	COAT-ARMOUR
AACGHIOPRS	SARCOPHAGI	AACMOPSSSW	COMPASS-SAW
AACGIILLST	GLACIALIST	AACNORRSTT	TRANSACTOR
AACGIILNOT	GLACIATION	AACOOPPRSU	APOCARPOUS
AACGIIMSTT	ASTIGMATIC	AADDDEEHHR	HARD-HEADED
AACGILLRTY	TRAGICALLY	AADDEEHHST	DEATH'S-HEAD
AACGIMNORT	MORGANATIC	AADDEEHIMN	MAIDENHEAD
AACGIMRSTY	MAGISTRACY	AADDEEMRRY	DAY-DREAMER
AACGIORSTT	CASTIGATOR	AADDEGIRRT	TARDIGRADE
AACGLLMOOY	MALACOLOGY	AADDEGMNOR	ARMAGEDDON
AACGLNORTU	OCTANGULAR	AADDEHIMNN	HANDMAIDEN
AACGLOORTU	COAGULATOR	AADDEIILPT	DILAPIDATE
AACHHILNPT	NAPHTHALIC	AADDGILMOY	AMYGDALOID

AADDGNNRST	GRANDSTAND	AADHOOPRRT	ARTHROPODA
AADDIILNOT	ADDITIONAL	AADIILNOTT	DILATATION
AADDIMNRTY	DYNAMITARD	AADIILQRUV	QUADRIVIAL
AADEEFGLRT	DEFLAGRATE	AADIIMNOPS	DIPSOMANIA
AADEEFMNOR	AFORENAMED	AADIIMNORT	ADMIRATION
AADEEGIRTV	VARIEGATED	AADIIPRSST	ASPIDISTRA
AADEEHHLRX	HEXAHEDRAL	AADIJNORTU	ADJURATION
AADEEHMRST	HEADMASTER	AADILNSSUW	DUNIWASSAL
AADEEHNRVW	HEAVENWARD	AADIMOPPRU	PARAPODIUM
AADEEILNST	DESALINATE	AADIMRTTTU	ADMITTATUR
AADEEIMPRT	PREADAMITE	AADIOPRSSU	SAUROPSIDA
AADEEINQTU	INADEQUATE	AADJORRTUY	ADJURATORY
AADEEIPRST	DEASPIRATE	AADMNOORSU	ANADROMOUS
AADEELNRSX	ALEXANDERS	AAEEEGGRTX	EXAGGERATE
AADEELQTUY	ADEQUATELY	AAEEELNPRS	PARASELENE
AADEELRTTU	ADULTERATE	AAEEEPRSTX	EXASPERATE
AADEEMNSSZ	AMAZEDNESS	AAEEERSSTV	ASSEVERATE
AADEEMQRSU	MASQUERADE	AAEEFGIMRT	AFTER-IMAGE
AADEEMQSTU	DESQUAMATE	AAEEFGLLLT	FLAGELLATE
AADEFHIIRR	FAIR-HAIRED	AAEEFRSTTT	AFTER-TASTE
AADEFHLNRT	FATHERLAND	AAEEGILNTT	GELATINATE
AADEFIMNOT	DEFAMATION	AAEEGIMNRT	EMARGINATE
AADEFINTTU	INFATUATED	AAEEGIMRRR	REMARRIAGE
AADEFMORTY	DEFAMATORY	AAEEGINRTV	VEGETARIAN
AADEFRRSTW	AFTERWARDS	AAEEGIOPRT	AREOPAGITE
AADEGGILLT	DAGGLE-TAIL	AAEEGMMNNT	MANAGEMENT
AADEGGINRS	AGGRANDISE	AAEEGMNRSS	MANAGERESS
AADEGGINRZ	AGGRANDIZE	AAEEGNPRRR	PREARRANGE
AADEGHNOTY	DEATH-AGONY	AAEEGNRSXY	SEXAGENARY
AADEGINRRS	DISARRANGE	AAEEGNSSSV	SAVAGENESS
AADEGIPRRS	DISPARAGER	AAEEHILRTX	EXHILARATE
AADEGLNQRU	QUADRANGLE	AAEEHIPRSS	APHAERESIS
AADEHIIMNR	MAIDENHAIR	AAEEHKQRTU	EARTHQUAKE
AADEHILMRT	DIATHERMAL	AAEEHLPRTT	EARTH-PLATE
AADEHINNRX	HEXANDRIAN	AAEEHMPRST	METAPHRASE
AADEHMMMNO	MOHAMMEDAN	AAEEILLRTT	ALLITERATE
AADEIILNTV	INVALIDATE	AAEEILMORT	AMELIORATE
AADEIIMNST	DISANIMATE	AAEEILNPRT	PENETRALIA
AADEIIRRTT	TRIRADIATE	AAEEILRTTV	ALTERATIVE
AADEIKSSTU	DIASKEUAST	AAEEILRTVX	RELAXATIVE
AADEILMNNT	NIDAMENTAL	AAEEIPRRTT	REPATRIATE
AADEILORST	ASTEROIDAL	AAEEIPRRTV	REPARATIVE
AADEILPPRS	DISAPPAREL	AAEEIPRTTX	EXPATRIATE
AADEIMNRTV	ANIMADVERT	AAEELLPRTY	PLATELAYER
AADEINNOPT	ANTIPODEAN	AAEELPRSTY	SEPARATELY
AADEINPQSU	PASQUINADE	AAEFGIISTT	FASTIGIATE
AADEINQTTU	ANTIQUATED	AAEFGLLLNT	FLAGELLANT
AADELLMNRY	ALDERMANLY	AAEFGLMNRT	FRAGMENTAL
AADELNRTTU	ADULTERANT	AAEFGRRSST	AFTER-GRASS
AADEMNORTY	AMENDATORY	AAEFINPRST	AFTER-PAINS
AADEQRRTUU	QUADRATURE	AAEGGILOSU	SIALAGOGUE
AADFFGHNSY	SHANDYGAFF	AAEGHILMPS	PHLEGMASIA
AADGIINNOT	INDAGATION	AAEGHINNXY	HEXAGYNIAN
AADGIINOTV	DIVAGATION	AAEGHLNOPT	HEPTAGONAL
AADGILLNOY	DIAGONALLY	AAEGHLNPRY	PHARYNGEAL
AADGILMNSU	SALMAGUNDI	AAEGHMNOPR	ANEMOGRAPH
AADGINORTU	GRADUATION		PHANEROGAM
AADGLMNSUY	SALMAGUNDY	AAEGIILPRZ	PLAGIARIZE
AADGMRRTUY	DRAMATURGY	AAEGIINNTV	INVAGINATE
AADHILRTWW	WITHDRAWAL	AAEGILLMNT	LIGAMENTAL
AADHINOPSU	DIAPHANOUS	AAEGILLNOT	ALLEGATION

AAEGILMNRT	MARTINGALE	AAEIMNOORT	EROTOMANIA
AAEGILMSTT	STALAGMITE	AAEIMNORTX	EXAMINATOR
AAEGILNNTT	TANGENTIAL	AAEIMPRSST	SEPARATISM
AAEGILNRVZ	GALVANIZER	AAEIMQRSTU	MARQUISATE
AAEGILNSWX	SEALING-WAX	AAEIMRTTUV	MATURATIVE
AAEGIMNRRS	MISARRANGE	AAEIMSSSTT	METASTASIS
AAEGIMNRRV	MARGRAVINE	AAEINNNOTX	ANNEXATION
AAEGIMRSTT	MAGISTRATE	AAEINNQRTU	QUARANTINE
AAEGINNOST	ANTAGONISE	AAEINNRTUV	AVANTURINE
AAEGINNSTU	NAUSEATING	AAEINOPRRT	REPARATION
AAEGINRTUU	INAUGURATE	AAEINOPRST	SEPARATION
AAEGLMORSU	MEGALOSAUR	AAFINOPSST	PASSIONATE
AAEGLNNOPT	PENTAGONAL	AAEIOPRTTX	EXPATIATOR
AAEGLNORTT	TETRAGONAL	AAEIOPSTTZ	APOSTATIZE
AAEHHILLLU	HALLELUIAH	AAEIPRSSTT	SEPARATIST
AAEHHJLLLU	HALLELUJAH	AAELLLLPRY	PARALLELLY
AAEHHLPRTY	HYPAETHRAL	AAELLMNRTY	MATERNALLY
AAEHIILNNT	ANNIHILATE	AAELLNPSTY	PLEASANTLY
AAEHIIINPPT	EPITAPHIAN	AAELMNNORT	ORNAMENTAL
AAEHILNOTX	EXHALATION	AAELMNOSSW	SALESWOMAN
AAEHILNRTX	EXHILARANT	AAELMRRTUX	EXTRAMURAL
AAEHIMOSST	HAEMATOSIS	AAELNNNPRU	PENANNULAR
AAEHIMRSTU	AMATEURISH	AAELNNPSTU	UNPLEASANT
AAEHIPSTXY	ASPHYXIATE	AAELNORRTT	ALTERNATOR
AAEHLLMRRS	MARSHALLER	AAELNPPRTY	APPARENTLY
AAEHMNRSST	HARASSMENT	AAELNPRRSU	SUPRARENAL
AAEHMORTTX	METATHORAX	AAELNPRSTY	PLEASANTRY
AAEHMPRSTT	METAPHRAST	AAELOOPSTT	APOSTOLATE
AAEHNPRSTY	PHEASANTRY	AAEMNNORTT	TRAMONTANE
AAEIILLPTV	PALLIATIVE	AAEMNOOSST	ANASTOMOSE
AAEIILMMRT	IMMATERIAL	AAEMRSSTTU	METATARSUS
AAEIILMSST	ASSIMILATE	AAENQRRTUY	QUATERNARY
AAEIILNNOT	ALIENATION	AAENRRSTTU	RESTAURANT
	ALINEATION	AAEORRSTTU	TARTAREOUS
AAEIIMNNRT	MAINTAINER	AAFFGIMNRU	RAGAMUFFIN
AAEIKNPRST	PAINSTAKER	AAFGLLNRTY	FLAGRANTLY
AAEIILLMRTY	MATERIALLY	AAFGLNRRTY	FRAGRANTLY
AAEIILLNORT	RELATIONAL	AAFIILLMRY	FAMILIARLY
AAEIILLNRTU	UNILATERAL	AAFIILMNRU	UNFAMILIAR
AAEIILLORTV	ALLEVIATOR	AAFILNOOTT	FLOATATION
AAEIILLRRTT	TRILATERAL	AAGHHIMNWY	HIGHWAYMAN
AAEIILMNPRT	PARLIAMENT	AAGHIILMNP	MALPIGHIAN
AAEIILMNPTU	MANIPULATE	AAGHILNPST	PHALANGIST
AAEIILMNRTY	ALIMENTARY	AAGHIPPRSY	PASIGRAPHY
AAEIILNNOPT	NEAPOLITAN	AAGHNOPPRT	PANTOGRAPH
AAEIILNOORT	AREOLATION	AAGHOPRTUY	AUTOGRAPHY
AAEIILNORST	SENATORIAL	AAGIIILLRS	SIGILLARIA
AAEIILNORTT	ALTERATION	AAGIILLNOT	ALLIGATION
AAEIILNORTU	LAUREATION	AAGIILMPRS	PLAGIARISM
AAEIILNORTX	RELAXATION	AAGIILNNUV	UNAVAILING
AAEIILNOTTX	EXALTATION	AAGIILPRST	PLAGIARIST
AAEIILNOTUV	EVALUATION	AAGIINNOPT	PAGINATION
AAEIILNRTUZ	NATURALIZE	AAGIINNOTV	NAVIGATION
AAEIILOQRTU	EQUATORIAL	AAGIJKLNWY	JAYWALKING
AAEIILPPSUV	APPLAUSIVE	AAGILLMNRY	ALARMINGLY
AAEIILSTUXY	ASEXUALITY		MARGINALLY
AAEIMMNRST	MAINSTREAM	AAGILLORSS	GLOSSARIAL
AAEIMMRSTU	AMATEURISM	AAGILMOPRS	PARALOGISM
AAEIMNNOSY	MAYONNAISE	AAGILNORTY	GYRATIONAL
AAEIMNNSSU	AMANUENSIS	AAGILNPRTU	TARPAULING
AAEIMNNTTT	ATTAINMENT	AAGILNRRTU	TRIANGULAR

AAGILNRTUY	ANGULARITY	AALMOOPPRS	MALAPROPOS
AAGILOSUVY	YUGOSLAVIA	AALMOPRSXY	PAROXYSMAL
AAGIMMPRST	PRAGMATISM	AALNNPRSTT	TRANSPLANT
AAGIMNNOST	ANTAGONISM	AALNNRRSTU	TRANSLUNAR
AAGIMPRSTT	PRAGMATIST	AALNOPRSST	TRANSPOSAL
AAGINNOSTT	ANTAGONIST	AALNORRSTT	TRANSLATOR
	STAGNATION	AALORRSTTY	ASTROLATRY
AAGINNRSUY	SANGUINARY	AALORSTTUY	SALUTATORY
AAGINOORRT	ARROGATION	AAMNNOTTTU	TANTAMOUNT
AAGLNNOOSX	ANGLO-SAXON	AAMNOOPRSY	PARONOMASY
AAGLNNSTTY	STAGNANTLY	AAMOOSSTTU	ASTOMATOUS
AAGLNORRTY	ARROGANTLY	ABBBCIKRTU	BUCK-RABBIT
AAGOOPPRRT	PROPAGATOR	ABBBEELMNT	BABBLEMENT
AAHHILMOPT	OPHTHALMIA	ABBCDEEHMR	BEDCHAMBER
AAHIILNNOT	INHALATION	ABBCEINSSS	SCABBINESS
AAHIIMPRSS	PHARISAISM	ABBCEKKSTU	BUCK-BASKET
AAHILMTTUZ	ALTAZIMUTH	ABBCEKLRRY	BLACKBERRY
AAHILNNOPT	ANTIPHONAL	ABBCENORSY	ABSORBENCY
AAHLMOPSTY	STAPHYLOMA	ABBCGIIKNT	BACKBITING
AAHNORRSTU	ANARTHROUS	ABBCIILLLY	BIBLICALLY
AAIIILMMNT	MILITIAMAN	ABBDDEEILO	ABLE-BODIED
AAIIKLLNTY	ALKALINITY	ABBDEIMORR	BOMBARDIER
AAIILLNOPT	PALLIATION	ABBDELLNRU	LANDLUBBER
AAIILMNNOT	ANTIMONIAL	ABBDELORSY	ABSORBEDLY
	LAMINATION	ABBDELOSSU	DOUBLE-BASS
AAIILNORRT	IRRATIONAL	ABBEEEILLV	BELIEVABLE
AAIILNOSTV	SALIVATION	ABBEELMNRT	RABBLEMENT
AAIILPRTTY	PARTIALITY	ABBEELORSV	OBSERVABLE
AAIIMMNNOT	IMMANATION	ABBEENORST	BREAST-BONE
AAIIMNNOPT	IMPANATION	ABBEFILNSS	FLABBINESS
AAIIMNRSTU	SANITARIUM	ABBEILLMSU	SUBLIMABLE
AAIIMPRSST	PARASITISM	ABBEILMOPR	IMPROBABLE
AAIINNOSTT	SANITATION	ABBEIRSTTY	BABY-SITTER
AAIINNRSTY	INSANITARY	ABBEKLLRRU	BARREL-BULK
AAIINOPPRT	APPARITION	ABBELORSVY	OBSERVABLY
AAIINOPRST	ASPIRATION	ABBEORTTTU	BUTTER-BOAT
AAIIRSSSTY	SATYRIASIS	ABBERRTTUY	BUTTERY-BAR
AAILLNNOTY	NATIONALLY	ABBGHINOTX	BATHING-BOX
AAILLNORTY	NOTARIALLY	ABBILMOPRY	IMPROBABLY
	RATIONALLY	ABCCDELNRU	CARBUNCLED
AAILLRSTUY	SALUTARILY	ABCCEEEELNS	ALBESCENCE
AAILMNPSSV	PANSLAVISM	ABCCEEILMP	IMPECCABLE
AAILMNRRTU	INTRAMURAL	ABCCEEILSS	ACCESSIBLE
AAILMNRSTU	NATURALISM	ABCCEILLRU	CIRCULABLE
AAILMORRTY	MARIOLATRY	ABCCEILSSY	ACCESSIBLY
AAILNHNNOTU	ANNULATION	ABCCHIKSTW	SWITCHBACK
AAILNNOPTT	PLANTATION	ABCCILRTUU	CUCURBITAL
AAILNOORTT	ROTATIONAL	ABCCINORTU	BUCCINATOR
AAILNOSTTU	SALUTATION	ABCDEEEELR	DECREEABLE
AAILNRSTTU	NATURALIST	ABCDEEEILV	DECEIVABLE
AAILNRSTUY	INSALUTARY	ABCDEEELLT	DELECTABLE
AAIMMRSTTU	TRAUMATISM	ABCDEEELRT	CELEBRATED
AAIMNOOTTU	AUTOMATION	ABCDEEELTT	DETECTABLE
AAIMNOPTTU	AMPUTATION	ABCDEEHRUY	DEBAUCHERY
AAIMNORSTU	SANATORIUM	ABCDEEILLN	DECLINABLE
AAIMNORTTU	MATURATION	ABCDEEILPR	PREDICABLE
AAINNNOOTT	ANNOTATION	ABCDEEILPS	DESPICABLE
AAINOPRSSY	PASSIONARY	ABCDEEILRT	CREDITABLE
AAINORSTTU	SATURATION	ABCDEELLNY	BELLY-DANCE
AAINORSTTV	STARVATION	ABCDEELLTY	DELECTABLY
AAINORSTTY	STATIONARY	ABCDEHKMPU	HUMPBACKED

ABCDEHORSS	CHESS-BOARD	ABCEINRRST	TRANSCRIBE
ABCDEIILNT	INDICTABLE	ABCEJKLMRU	LUMBER-JACK
ABCDEIKLRS	BACKSLIDER	ABCEKKORST	BACKSTROKE
ABCDEILPSY	DESPICABLY	ABCEKLNORU	COAL-BUNKER
ABCDEILRTY	CREDITABLY	ABCELLNOOS	CONSOLABLE
ABCDELMNNRU	CUMBERLAND	ABCELLOORU	COLOURABLE
ABCDEOORRS	SCORE-BOARD	ABCELLRTUU	CULTURABLE
ABCDGKNORU	BACKGROUND	ABCELMMNOO	COMMONABLE
ABCDHIILNR	BRAINCHILD	ABCELMMOTU	COMMUTABLE
ABCDHIOOPR	BRACHIOPOD	ABCELMNOSU	CONSUMABLE
ABCDHLOORT	BROAD-CLOTH	ABCELMOPTU	COMPUTABLE
ABCEEEFFNO	COFFEE-BEAN	ARCELMOSTU	CUSTOMABLE
ABCEEEILNT	ENTICEABLE	ABCELNORRY	BARLEY-CORN
ABCEFEILPR	PIERCEABLE	ABCELNRSUY	CENSURABLY
ABCEEEILRV	RECEIVABLE	ABCELOPRRU	PROCURABLE
ABCEEEELLRR	CEREBELLAR	ABCELRRTUU	TUBERCULAR
ABCEEEELTUX	EXECUTABLE	ABCENRRTUY	CANTERBURY
ABCEEENRUX	EXUBERANCE	ABCGHIIOPR	BIOGRAPHIC
ABCEEFIILN	BENEFICIAL	ABCGHLORYY	BRACHYLOGY
ABCEEFNORT	BENEFACTOR	ABCGIILLOO	BIOLOGICAL
ABCEEGILLR	CLERGIABLE	ABCGILMNRS	SCRAMBLING
ABCEEHLNQU	QUENCHABLE	ABCGILNOYZ	COGNIZABLY
ABCEEHNORR	ABHORRENCE	ABCHHIOPRS	ARCHBISHOP
ABCEEIILLPX	EXPLICABLE	ABCHIKLMST	BLACKSMITH
ABCEEILMMT	EMBLEMATIC	ABCHIKLRST	BLACKSHIRT
ABCEEILNNU	ENUNCIABLE	ABCHKLNORT	BLACKTHORN
ABCEEILNOT	NOTICEABLE	ABCIILLSST	BALLISTICS
ABCEEILRTX	EXTRICABLE	ABCIILRTUY	CURABILITY
ABCEEINNST	ABSTINENCE	ABCIINNOTU	INCUBATION
ABCEEJKLTU	BLUE-JACKET	ABCIINOSSS	ABSCISSION
ABCEEJNSST	ABJECTNESS	ABCIKLLORY	ROCKABILLY
ABCEELNNOV	CONVENABLE	ABCILLMOSY	SYMBOLICAL
ABCEELNOVY	CONVEYABLE	ABCILMOPTY	COMPATIBLY
ABCEELNRSU	CENSURABLE	ABCILMRUUV	VIBRACULUM
ABCEELOSTT	CASE-BOTTLE	ABCILNOSUY	UNSOCIABLY
ABCEENORSV	OBSERVANCE	ABCILORRTU	LUBRICATOR
ABCEENRUXY	EXUBERANCY	ABCIORRRTU	RUBRICATOR
ABCEFILNNO	CONFINABLE	ABCKNPRTUY	BANKRUPTCY
ABCEFLNOTU	CONFUTABLE	ABCLLOORUY	COLOURABLY
ABCEGILNOZ	COGNIZABLE	ABCNOORRTU	COURT-BARON
ABCEGLNOOT	CONGLOBATE	ABDDEEEFLN	DEFENDABLE
ABCEHILORW	ELBOW-CHAIR	ABDDEEELNP	DEPENDABLE
ABCEHILPRT	BIRTHPLACE	ABDDEEIMNS	BASE-MINDED
ABCEHIMNRT	CHAMBERTIN	ABDDEGINRU	UNABRIDGED
ABCEHIMORT	BICHROMATE	ABDDEGIRRW	DRAWBRIDGE
ABCEHLNRSS	BRANCHLESS	ABDDEHHINN	BEHINDHAND
ABCEHMOPRT	CHAMBER-POT	ABDDEHILNR	BRIDLE-HAND
ABCEHORTTX	CHATTER-BOX	ABDDEIIMRS	BRIDESMAID
ABCEIILLMT	BIMETALLIC	ABDDEILORR	BRIDLE-ROAD
ABCEIILLNN	INCLINABLE	ABDDELNORR	BORDER-LAND
ABCEIILLNR	BRILLIANCE	ABDDOORRSW	BROADSWORD
ABCEIINTUV	INCUBATIVE	ABDEEEELMR	REDEEMABLE
ABCEIKLRRY	BRICKLAYER	ABDEEEFILS	DEFEASIBLE
ABCEILLNOU	INOCULABLE	ABDEEEILRT	DELIBERATE
ABCEILLNRS	CRANES-BILL	ABDEEEINRV	ABERDEVINE
ABCEILLTUV	CULTIVABLE	ABDEEELNRR	RENDERABLE
ABCEILMOPT	COMPATIBLE	ABDEEELSTT	DETESTABLE
ABCEILNOSU	UNSOCIABLE	ABDEEEMNST	DEBASEMENT
ABCEILNOTY	NOTICEABLY	ABDEEEPRST	BREAST-DEEP
ABCEILNPRU	REPUBLICAN	ABDEEERSTW	SWEETBREAD
ABCEIMORRT	BAROMETRIC	ABDEEFHNOR	BEFOREHAND

ABDEEHILLS	DÉSHABILLÉ	ABDNOORTUU	ROUNDABOUT
ABDEEHILPS	BEADLESHIP	ABDOORRTUU	TROUBADOUR
ABDEEHILRR	HALBERDIER	ABEEEFLPRR	PREFERABLE
ABDEEIILTT	DEBILITATE	ABEEEILLRV	RELIEVABLE
ABDEEILNNU	UNDENIABLE	ABEEEILMRR	IRREMEABLE
ABDEEILPSS	DESPISABLE	ABEEEILRVW	REVIEWABLE
ABDEEIMRTX	AMBIDEXTER	ABEEELMPRT	TEMPERABLE
ABDEELLOPR	DEPLORABLE	ABEEELMRSS	REASSEMBLE
ABDEELMRRU	DEMURRABLE	ABEEELNPRT	PENETRABLE
ABDEELNOPR	PONDERABLE	ABEEELQSUZ	SQUEEZABLE
ABDEELNORS	ENDORSABLE	ABEEERRTTV	VERTEBRATE
ABDEELORTT	BATTLEDORE	ABEEFFLRSU	SUFFERABLE
ABDEELPRRU	PERDURABLE	ABEEFIILRV	VERIFIABLE
ABDEELSTTY	DETESTABLY	ABEEFIIRTU	BEAUTIFIER
ABDEENPRRY	PREBENDARY	ABEEFIILNTT	FLEABITTEN
ABDEFFRSTU	BREADSTUFF	ABEEFILRSS	BASS-RELIEF
ABDEFIILMO	MODIFIABLE	ABEEFINRRV	BRAIN-FEVER
ABDEFIIMRT	FIMBRIATED	ABEEFLMORR	REFORMABLE
ABDEFILMOR	FORMIDABLE	ABEEFLPRRY	PREFERABLY
ABDEFIRRTU	BREADFRUIT	ABEEFLSTTY	SAFETY-BELT
ABDEGGIRRU	BUDGERIGAR	ABEEGHLLNR	BELL-HANGER
ABDEGHINSU	SUBHEADING	ABEEGILNOT	NEGOTIABLE
ABDEGHORTU	DEAR-BOUGHT	ABEEGILRTW	BILGE-WATER
ABDEGIMNRT	ABRIDGMENT	ABEEGLNORV	GOVERNABLE
ABDEHIILLS	DISHABILLE	ABEEGNRSTT	ABSTERGENT
ABDEHILPRT	BRIDLE-PATH	ABEEHILLRS	RELISHABLE
ABDEHNORTU	EARTH-BOUND	ABEEHILPRS	PERISHABLE
ABDEHNRSTU	SUBTRAHEND	ABEEHLMPRS	BLASPHEMER
ABDEHORRST	SHORTBREAD	ABEEHLRSST	BREATHLESS
ABDEIILMSS	ADMISSIBLE	ABEEHMORTT	BATHOMETER
ABDEIILOXZ	OXIDIZABLE	ABEEHORSTU	HEREABOUTS
ABDEILNNUY	UNDENIABLY	ABEEHORTTU	THEREABOUT
ABDEILNORY	DEBONAIRLY	ABEEHORTUW	WHEREABOUT
ABDEILOPSS	DISPOSABLE	ABEEHQRSUU	HARQUEBUSE
ABDEILPSTU	DISPUTABLE	ABEEIILLMN	ELIMINABLE
ABDEIMRTUW	DUMB-WAITER	ABEEIILLRZ	LIBERALIZE
ABDEKLLOTU	DOUBLE-TALK	ABEEIILNPX	INEXPIABLE
ABDELLOPRY	DEPLORABLY	ABEEIILNTV	INEVITABLE
ABDELMORST	BLASTODERM	ABEEIILSTZ	BESTIALIZE
ABDELORTUY	OBDURATELY	ABEEIKNNRT	BARKENTINE
ABDELPRRUY	PERDURABLY	ABEEILLNRU	UNRELIABLE
ABDENRSSSU	ABSURDNESS	ABEEILMNRT	TERMINABLE
ABDFILMORY	FORMIDABLY	ABEEILNNUV	UNENVIABLE
ABDGIIMNRS	BRIGANDISM	ABEEILNOPR	INOPERABLE
ABDGIINPRU	UPBRAIDING	ABEEILNORX	INEXORABLE
ABDHIIINOT	ADHIBITION	ABEEILNPSX	EXPANSIBLE
ABDHILMOOR	RHOMBOIDAL	ABEEILNRSS	BLEARINESS
ABDIIILSTY	DISABILITY	ABEEILORTT	OBLITERATE
ABDIIILTUY	AUDIBILITY	ABEEILPRRS	RESPIRABLE
ABDIIIRSTT	DIATRIBIST	ABEEILPRTX	EXTIRPABLE
ABDIILMNOU	ALBUMINOID	ABEEILQRTU	REQUITABLE
ABDIILNOOS	OBSIDIONAL	ABEEKMMNNT	EMBANKMENT
ABDIILPTUY	DUPABILITY	ABEELLMOPY	EMPLOYABLE
ABDIILRTUY	DURABILITY	ABEELLNRUV	VULNERABLE
ABDIINOTTU	DUBITATION	ABEELLOPRX	EXPLORABLE
ABDIIRSSUY	SUBSIDIARY	ABEELMNORZ	EMBLAZONER
ABDILNOOST	BLOODSTAIN	ABEELMNRSU	LEBENSRAUM
ABDILOORWZ	BRAZIL-WOOD		MENSURABLE
ABDILPSTUY	DISPUTABLY	ABEELMNTTT	BATTLEMENT
ABDIMNOOSU	ABDOMINOUS	ABEELMPRSU	PRESUMABLE
ABDMNNOOSW	BONDS-WOMAN	ABEELNOPRS	PERSONABLE

ABEELNOSST	OBLATENESS	ABEIINNRSS	BRAININESS
ABEELNRRTU	RETURNABLE	ABEIKLNNSU	UNSINKABLE
ABEELNSSST	STABLENESS	ABEILLLNTU	UNTILLABLE
ABEELOPRRT	REPORTABLE	ABEILLMMOS	EMBOLISMAL
ABEELOPRTX	EXPORTABLE	ABEILLNOSV	INSOLVABLE
ABEELORRST	RESTORABLE	ABEILMMOST	METABOLISM
ABEENNNRRU	RUNNER-BEAN	ABEILMOOTU	AUTOMOBILE
ABEENNRRSS	BARRENNESS	ABEILMOPRT	IMPORTABLE
ABEENNRSSZ	BRAZENNESS	ABEILNSTUU	UNSUITABLE
ABEEOPRRRT	REPROBATER	ABEILOPRRV	PROVERBIAL
ABEFFGILRU	FEBRIFUGAL	ABEILORRTY	LIBERATORY
ABEFFLRSUY	SUFFERABLY	ABEILORTVY	ABORTIVELY
ABEFGILORV	FORGIVABLE	ABEILRSTUV	VESTIBULAR
ABEFGILRSS	FIBREGLASS	ABEIMMOQUZ	MOZAMBIQUE
ABEFGINORR	FORBEARING	ABEIMNNOTT	OBTAINMENT
ABEFHIRRTT	AFTER-BIRTH	ABEIMNORTU	TAMBOURINE
ABEFIILLLN	INFALLIBLE	ABEIMOSSTU	ABSTEMIOUS
ABEFILOPRT	PROFITABLE	ABEINNOPSV	BONE-SPAVIN
ABEFLLLMUY	BLAMEFULLY	ABEINNOSTT	ABSTENTION
ABEFLLOORT	FOOTBALLER	ABEINNRSSW	BRAWNINESS
ABEGHIOPRR	BIOGRAPHER	ABEINORSST	ABSTERSION
ABEGHLLOPU	PLOUGHABLE	ABEINORTTX	EXORBITANT
ABEGHNRRSU	BUSH-RANGER	ABEIOPRSTV	ABSORPTIVE
ABEGIILNNT	INTANGIBLE	ABEIORRSTT	BIROSTRATE
ABEGIINNRT	BRIGANTINE	ABEIPRSTTY	BAPTISTERY
ABEGIINORS	ABORIGINES	ABEKLNORUW	UNWORKABLE
ABEGIINOST	ABIOGENIST	ABEKMNNOTU	MOUNTEBANK
ABEGIKLNNT	BLANKETING	ABEKNOPRRW	PAWNBROKER
ABEGILMNPU	IMPUGNABLE	ABEKNORSTT	BREAST-KNOT
ABEGLLNOOY	BALNEOLOGY	ABEKORRSTW	BREAST-WORK
ABEGMORRSS	BROME-GRASS	ABELLLLOVY	VOLLEY-BALL
ABEGMORSUU	UMBRAGEOUS	ABELLOSTUY	ABSOLUTELY
ABEGNNSTTU	SUBTANGENT	ABELMNNOOW	NOBLEWOMAN
ABEGNOORST	BRANT-GOOSE	ABELMPRSUY	PRESUMABLY
ABEHIILMNT	HABILIMENT	ABELNOOPST	TABLESPOON
ABEHIKLNRS	SHRINKABLE	ABELNOPRUV	UNPROVABLE
ABEHIKLSTT	BASKET-HILT	ABELOOSSTT	OSTEOBLAST
ABEHILNPSU	PUNISHABLE	ABELOPPSSU	SUPPOSABLE
ABEHILOPST	HOSPITABLE	ABELRSSTUY	ABSTRUSELY
ABEHILPSTT	BATTLE-SHIP	ABEMMNORSU	MEMBRANOUS
ABEHILPSTU	BISULPHATE	ABENPRSSTU	ABRUPTNESS
ABEHIMNNST	BANISHMENT	ABEOPSTTUY	BEAUTY-SPOT
ABEHINOOPX	XENOPHOBIA	ABEOQSSUUU	SUBAQUEOUS
ABEHLNOORU	HONOURABLE	ABERRRSTWY	STRAWBERRY
ABEHMMNSTU	AMBUSHMENT	ABFFGILLNY	BAFFLINGLY
ABEHMRTTYY	BATHYMETRY	ABFFMOORST	BROOMSTAFF
ABEHNORSST	BASSET-HORN	ABFGILNOTW	BAT-FOWLING
ABEIIILMNT	INIMITABLE	ABFIILLLNY	INFALLIBLY
ABEIIILLMRS	LIBERALISM	ABFILOPRTY	PROFITABLY
ABEIIILLNNY	BIENNIALLY	ABFILOSTUY	FABULOSITY
ABEIIILLNOV	INVIOLABLE	ABFLLOSTUY	BOASTFULLY
ABEIIILLRTY	LIBERALITY	ABFLLOSUUY	FABULOUSLY
ABEIIILLSTU	UTILISABLE	ABGGGILNRY	BRAGGINGLY
ABEIIILMNSS	LESBIANISM	ABGHIIMMNR	BIRMINGHAM
ABEIIILMPSS	IMPASSIBLE	ABGHINNSTU	SUNBATHING
ABEIIILNORT	LIBERATION	ABGIILNNTY	INTANGIBLY
ABEIIILNPRS	INSPIRABLE	ABGIILNOOT	OBLIGATION
ABEIIILNTTY	TENABILITY	ABGILLMNRY	RAMBLINGLY
ABEIIILQTUY	EQUABILITY	ABGILLNNOO	BALLOONING
ABEIIILRSST	STABILISER	ABGILLNSUU	SUBLINGUAL
ABEIIILSTTY	BESTIALITY	ABGILOORTY	OBLIGATORY

ABGINOORTW	ROWING-BOAT	ACCDIIOSTU	DIACOUSTIC
ABGJORSTUU	SUBJUGATOR	ACCDINORTT	CONTRADICT
ABGLLLORUY	GLOBULARLY	ACCDNNOORT	CONCORDANT
ABHHORRSUW	BUSH-HARROW	ACCEEEEHKS	CHEESE-CAKE
ABHIIMOPSU	AMPHIBIOUS	ACCEEELPRT	RECEPTACLE
ABHILOPSTY	HOSPITABLY	ACCEEENNRS	RENASCENCE
ABHLNOORUY	HONOURABLY	ACCEEENPTX	EXPECTANCE
ABIIJLNOTU	JUBILATION	ACCEEHILNP	ENCEPHALIC
ABIILLMNSU	SUBLIMINAL	ACCEEHMNTU	CATECHUMEN
ABIILMOTVY	MOVABILITY	ACCEEHNORR	ENCROACHER
ABIILMTTUY	MUTABILITY	ACCEEILLRT	ELECTRICAL
ABIILNOTTY	NOTABILITY	ACCEEILMNU	ECUMENICAL
ABIILORSTY	SIBILATORY	ACCEEILSST	ECCLESIAST
ABIIMRSSTY	SYBARITISM	ACCEEINPQU	CINQUE-PACE
ABIJNOORTU	OBJURATION	ACCEEIORSU	ERICACEOUS
ABILLNOOST	BALLOONIST	ACCEEIRTUX	EXCRUCIATE
ABILMNOSUU	ALBUMINOUS	ACCEELNOST	COALESCENT
ABILMOSSTU	ABSOLUTISM	ACCEELNOSV	CONVALESCE
ABILNOOSTU	ABSOLUTION	ACCEELNPRU	CRAPULENCE
ABILNSTUUY	UNSUITABLY	ACCEELNRTU	RELUCTANCE
ABILORSSUU	SALUBRIOUS	ACCEELNRUX	CLARENCEUX
ABIMNORRST	BRAINSTORM	ACCEELNSTU	CAULESCENT
ABIMRSSSTU	STRABISMUS	ACCEELPSST	SPECTACLES
ABINOOPRST	ABSORPTION	ACCEEMNRST	MARCESCENT
ABINOORTTU	OBTURATION	ACCEENNNOV	CONVENANCE
ABINOOSSST	BASSOONIST	ACCEENNOVY	CONVEYANCE
ABLOORSTUY	ABSOLUTORY	ACCEENOPRR	COPARCENER
ABMOORSTTY	STRABOTOMY	ACCEENORST	CONSECRATE
ABMRSSTTUU	SUBSTRATUM	ACCEENPTXY	EXPECTANCY
ABOORSTTUU	ROUSTABOUT	ACCEENRSSS	SCARCENESS
ACCCEEHITT	CATECHETIC	ACCEEORRSU	RACECOURSE
ACCCEENRST	ACCRESCENT	ACCEEORSTU	CRETACEOUS
ACCCEFHKOR	COCKCHAFER	ACCEFFIITY	EFFICACITY
ACCCEHORTW	COW-CATCHER	ACCEFIIRRS	SACRIFICER
ACCCEHORUU	ACCOUCHEUR	ACCEFINOST	CONFISCATE
ACCCEIKORT	COCKATRICE	ACCEGILLOO	ECOLOGICAL
ACCCEILLNY	ENCYCLICAL	ACCEGINNOZ	COGNIZANCE
ACCCEILMOP	ACCOMPLICE	ACCEHHIPRT	HEPTARCHIC
ACCCHLOORY	OCHLOCRACY	ACCEHHRRTU	CHURCH-RATE
ACCCHOOTUU	CAOUTCHOUC	ACCEHIILMR	CHIMERICAL
ACCCILMOPY	COMPLICACY	ACCEHIINNT	TECHNICIAN
ACCDEEENNS	ASCENDENCE	ACCEHILLMY	CHEMICALLY
ACCDEELPST	SPECTACLED	ACCEHIMNNY	CHIMNEY-CAN
ACCDEENNST	CANDESCENT	ACCEHINORT	ANCHORETIC
ACCDEHLNOY	CHALCEDONY	ACCEHIORST	ESCHAROTIC
ACCDEIILST	DIALECTICS	ACCEHIRTVZ	CZAREVITCH
ACCDEIIOPT	APODEICTIC	ACCEHLLNOR	CHANCELLOR
ACCDEIKLNW	CANDLEWICK	ACCEHNNPTY	CATCH-PENNY
ACCDEILLOP	PECCADILLO	ACCEHOORSU	OCHRACEOUS
ACCDEILNOT	OCCIDENTAL	ACCEIILNOT	CONCILIATE
ACCDEILOPY	CYCLOPEDIA	ACCEIIMSST	ASCETICISM
ACCDEIMNNY	MENDICANCY	ACCEIINNOR	CICERONIAN
ACCDEIMORT	DEMOCRATIC	ACCEIINNRS	CIRCENSIAN
ACCDEIORST	DESICCATOR	ACCEIINRST	CISTERCIAN
ACCDEMOSTU	ACCUSTOMED	ACCEILLNRU	UNCLERICAL
ACCDENORTT	CONTRACTED	ACCEILMMOR	COMMERCIAL
ACCDFIILTY	FLACCIDITY	ACCEILMNOO	ECONOMICAL
ACCDHHRRUY	CHURCHYARD	ACCEILMNOP	COMPLIANCE
ACCDHILNOO	CONCHOIDAL	ACCEILMOPT	COMPLICATE
ACCDHILORV	CLAVICHORD	ACCEILNRST	CALC-SINTER
ACCDIIMOST	DOCIMASTIC	ACCEILOPPT	APOPLECTIC

ACCEILOPRR	RECIPROCAL	ACCINOOPTU	OCCUPATION
ACCEINNNOV	CONNIVANCE	ACCINOPRSY	CONSPIRACY
ACCEINNOPR	COPERNICAN	ACCIOPRSTT	CATOPTRICS
ACCEINNORT	CONCERTINA	ACCLOPRTUY	PLUTOCRACY
ACCEINOOST	CONSOCIATE	ACCNOORRTT	CONTRACTOR
ACCEINORST	CESTRACION	ACDDEEENNP	DEPENDANCE
ACCEIOORSU	CORIACEOUS	ACDDEEHLOO	COOL-HEADED
ACCEIOPPSY	EPISCOPACY	ACDDEEHNOR	DECAHEDRON
ACCEIORSTX	EXSICCATOR	ACDDEELLRY	DECLAREDLY
ACCEJKKORT	CORK-JACKET	ACDDEENNRU	REDUNDANCE
ACCEJNOSUU	JUNCACEOUS	ACDDEENNST	DESCENDANT
ACCEKKLMOR	CLOCKMAKER	ACDDEENTUU	UNEDUCATED
ACCEKNRRTU	NUTCRACKER	ACDDEHNNOS	SECOND-HAND
ACCELLNOSU	CANCELLOUS	ACDDEHNOOO	DEACONHOOD
ACCELMNOPT	COMPLACENT	ACDDEIILTU	DILUCIDATE
ACCELNOPTU	CONCEPTUAL	ACDDEIINNOT	DEDICATION
ACCELNRTUY	RELUCTANCY	ACDDEILMOU	DUODECIMAL
ACCEMNNORY	NECROMANCY	ACDDEINNSS	CANDIDNESS
ACCENNNOOS	CONSONANCE	ACDDEIORTY	DEDICATORY
ACCENNNOST	CONNASCENT	ACDDEIRSTT	DISTRACTED
ACCENORTTU	COUNTERACT	ACDDEKLLNO	LANDLOCKED
ACCEORSUUV	CURVACEOUS	ACDDENNRUY	REDUNDANCY
ACCFHIRTTW	WITCHCRAFT	ACDDENORSU	DECANDROUS
ACCFIINNOT	FANTOCCINI	ACDDEOOPSU	DECAPODOUS
ACCFILMORY	CALYCIFORM	ACDDGHILNR	GRANDCHILD
ACCFILSSUU	FASCICULUS	ACDDINORST	DISCORDANT
ACCFNOORRT	CORN-FACTOR	ACDEEEELRT	DECELERATE
ACCGHIILOR	OLIGARCHIC	ACDEEEEPRS	PREDECEASE
ACCGHORSSU	COUCH-GRASS	ACDEEEFLNR	FER-DE-LANCE
ACCGINNOTU	ACCOUNTING	ACDEEEFMNT	DEFACEMENT
ACCHHIILLN	CHINCHILLA	ACDEEEGNRY	DEGENERACY
ACCHIIMSST	SCHISMATIC	ACDEEEIPRT	DEPRECIATE
ACCHILMOPS	ACCOMPLISH	ACDEEEMNST	CASEMENTED
ACCHILNNPS	SPLANCHNIC	ACDEEENNTT	ANTECEDENT
ACCHILNOOT	CATHOLICON	ACDEEENRTV	ADVERTENCE
ACCHILOSST	SCHOLASTIC	ACDEEERRST	DESECRATER
ACCHIMNORY	CHIROMANCY	ACDEEFFHRT	FAR-FETCHED
ACCHIMORST	CHROMATICS	ACDEEFFLTY	AFFECTEDLY
ACCHIOSSTT	STOCHASTIC	ACDEEFFNTU	UNAFFECTED
ACCHNOPSYY	SYCOPHANCY	ACDEEFINOT	DEFECATION
ACCIILLLNY	CLINICALLY	ACDEEFKOPR	POKER-FACED
ACCIILLRTY	CRITICALLY	ACDEEGIMMR	DECIGRAMME
ACCIILMNOS	LACONICISM	ACDEEGINNR	GRANDNIECE
ACCIILMOTY	COMICALITY	ACDEEGINRT	CENTIGRADE
ACCIILMSSS	CLASSICISM	ACDEEHILNR	CHANDELIER
ACCIILNRTU	UNCRITICAL	ACDEEHINNR	HINDERANCE
ACCIILPTTY	PLACTICITY	ACDEEHINOT	THEODICEAN
ACCIILSSST	CLASSICIST	ACDEEHLLNN	CHANNELLED
ACCIINNOTY	CANONICITY	ACDEEHMNTT	DETACHMENT
ACCIIOPRSU	CAPRICIOUS	ACDEEHOPPR	COPPER-HEAD
ACCIISTTUY	CAUSTICITY	ACDEEHPRST	DESPATCHER
ACCILLMOSY	COSMICALLY	ACDEEIILMP	EPIDEMICAL
ACCILLRRUY	CIRCULARLY	ACDEEIILMS	DECIMALISE
ACCILMNNOU	COUNCIL-MAN	ACDEEIILNT	INDELICATE
ACCILMNOOS	ICONOCLASM	ACDEEIILTT	DIETETICAL
ACCILNOOST	ICONOCLAST	ACDEEIIMRT	ACIDIMETER
ACCILNOSTV	CONCLAVIST	ACDEEILLNR	CINDERELLA
ACCILOPPRY	POLYCARPIC	ACDEEILLTY	DELICATELY
ACCILORRTU	CIRCULATOR	ACDEEILMRV	DECEMVIRAL
ACCIMMOORS	COSMORAMIC	ACDEEILNRT	CREDENTIAL
ACCINOOPRU	CORNUCOPIA	ACDEEIMMNT	MEDICAMENT

ACDEEIMNRT	ENDERMATIC	ACDEILNORT	DECLINATOR
ACDEEIMOTT	COMEDIETTA	ACDEILORTU	ELUCIDATOR
ACDEEINNTU	DENUNCIATE	ACDEILOSUY	EDACIOUSLY
ACDEEINOST	CESTIODEAN	ACDEIMNORU	ANDROECIUM
ACDEEIORTV	DECORATIVE	ACDEIMNOSU	MENDACIOUS
ACDEEIRTTV	DETRACTIVE	ACDEINNNTY	INTENDANCY
ACDEEITTUX	EXACTITUDE	ACDEINNOSS	DISSONANCE
ACDEELLLTU	CELLULATED	ACDEINNRSS	RANCIDNESS
ACDEELNOST	ADOLESCENT	ACDEINOORT	CO-ORDINATE
ACDEELOORT	DECOLORATE		DECORATION
ACDEELORTU	EDULCORATE	ACDEINORRW	CORDWAINER
ACDEEMMNOR	COMMANDEER	ACDEINORTT	DETRACTION
ACDEEMMNPT	DECAMPMENT	ACDEINOSTT	ANECDOTIST
ACDEENORST	SECOND-RATE	ACDEINPRST	DISCREPANT
ACDEENRSSS	SACREDNESS	ACDEIOPSSU	SPADICEOUS
ACDEENRTTU	DETRUNCATE	ACDEIRSSTT	DICTATRESS
ACDEEOPRRT	DEPRECATOR	ACDEIRSSTU	CRASSITUDE
ACDEEOPRSU	PREDACEOUS	ACDELMNOTU	DOCUMENTAL
ACDEFHILNS	CANDLE-FISH	ACDELNOORT	DECOLORANT
ACDEFIIINT	NIDIFICATE	ACDELNOOTY	ACOTYLEDON
ACDEFIILSS	CLASSIFIED	ACDELNPRUU	PEDUNCULAR
ACDEFIINST	SANCTIFIED	ACDELOPRRU	PROCEDURAL
ACDEFIIRRT	FRATRICIDE	ACDEMMOSTU	CUSTOM-MADE
ACDEFINNOT	CONFIDANTE	ACDENOPSTY	SYNCOPATED
ACDEFIOPRT	FORCIPATED	ACDENRSTTU	CRUET-STAND
ACDEGHIRRS	DISCHARGER	ACDEOPRSUU	DRUPACEOUS
ACDEGILOST	DECALOGIST	ACDEORRTTY	DETRACTORY
ACDEGINORR	CORRIGENDA	ACDGIINOST	DIAGNOSTIC
ACDEGIORSU	DISCOURAGE	ACDGILNOOT	ODONTALGIC
ACDEGLNNRU	GRANDUNCLE	ACDGIMMNNO	COMMANDING
ACDEGNOSUY	DECAGYNOUS	ACDGLNORUY	CLAY-GROUND
ACDEGORRTU	CORRUGATED	ACDHHLNOOR	ANCHOR-HOLD
ACDEHIILLO	HELICOIDAL	ACDHIIIOPT	IDIOPATHIC
ACDEHIIMRT	DIATHERMIC	ACDHILRSST	THIRD-CLASS
ACDEHILMOT	METHODICAL	ACDHILRSUY	HYDRAULICS
ACDEHILORT	CHLORIDATE	ACDHIOOPRS	DISCOPHORA
ACDEHINNST	DISENCHANT	ACDHMNORYY	HYDROMANCY
ACDEHINOPS	DEACONSHIP	ACDIIIJLNU	INJUDICIAL
ACDEHINOPT	DICTAPHONE	ACDIIINNOT	INDICATION
ACDEHLOOPP	CEPHALOPOD	ACDIIJLLUY	JUDICIALLY
ACDEHNOORT	OCTAHEDRON	ACDIILLSUY	SUICIDALLY
ACDEHNOPRT	PENTACHORD	ACDIILMOPT	DIPLOMATIC
ACDEHORRTT	TETRACHORD	ACDIILOPRT	DIOPTRICAL
ACDEIIILST	IDEALISTIC	ACDIILORTY	CORDIALITY
ACDEIIINTV	INDICATIVE	ACDIIMNOSY	ISODYNAMIC
ACDEIIKNNR	KINCARDINE	ACDIINORTV	VINDICATOR
ACDEIIKNNS	DICKENSIAN	ACDIINORTY	DICTIONARY
ACDEIILMRS	DISCLAIMER	ACDIJNNOTU	ADJUNCTION
ACDEIILNNT	INCIDENTAL	ACDIJORTUX	COADJUTRIX
ACDEIILOPR	PERIODICAL	ACDILLOOST	IDOLOCLAST
ACDEIILOPS	EPISODICAL	ACDILNRSTU	TRANSLUCID
ACDEIILPST	SEPTICIDAL	ACDILOPRTU	DUPLICATOR
ACDEIIMNOT	DECIMATION	ACDIMOORSU	MORDACIOUS
	MEDICATION	ACDIOOPRSY	RADIOSCOPY
ACDEIIMRTX	TAXIDERMIC	ACDLLOOPSW	CODSWALLOP
ACDEIINNRY	INCENDIARY	ACDOORRSSS	CROSSROADS
ACDEIIOSST	DISSOCIATE	ACEEEFFMNT	EFFACEMENT
ACDEIIPSTU	PAIDEUTICS	ACEEEFFTTU	EFFECTUATE
ACDEIJNTUV	ADJUNCTIVE	ACEEEFIPRS	FIRE-ESCAPE
ACDEILLORR	CORDILLERA	ACEEEFIPRT	AFTER-PIECE
ACDEILNNOR	ENDOCRINAL	ACEEEGILNN	INELEGANCE

ACEEEGNPRT	PERCENTAGE	ACEEHLLNOP	CELLOPHANE
ACEEEGNRRY	REGENERACY	ACEEHLNNOP	ENCEPHALON
ACEEEHRRRS	RESEARCHER	ACEEHLNPRU	LEPRECHAUN
ACEEEIRRTV	RECREATIVE	ACEEHLRSSS	SEARCHLESS
ACEEEIRSTV	EVISCERATE	ACEEHLSSST	SCATHELESS
ACEEEIRTVX	EXECRATIVE	ACEEHMMRSU	MEERSCHAUM
ACEEELLNRT	CRENELLATE	ACEEHMNRST	MANCHESTER
ACEEELMNNT	ENLACEMENT	ACEEHMORTT	TACHOMETER
ACEEELNPRV	PREVALENCE	ACEEHMPRTY	PACHYMETER
ACEEELORTT	ELECTORATE	ACEEHNPTTU	PENTATEUCH
ACEEELRTUX	EXULCERATE	ACEEHNSSST	CHASTENESS
ACEEEMMNRT	AMERCEMENT	ACEEHOPRRR	REPROACHER
ACEEEMNNPR	PERMANENCE	ACEEHPRRSU	REPURCHASE
ACEEEMNPRT	TEMPERANCE	ACEEHRRSTU	CHARTREUSE
ACEEEMNPST	ESCAPEMENT	ACEEIILMRT	EREMITICAL
ACEEEMNRTT	METACENTRE	ACEEIILNTT	LICENTIATE
ACEEENNOTV	COVENANTEE	ACEEIILPSZ	SPECIALIZE
ACEEENNPRT	REPENTANCE	ACEEIIMNPT	IMPATIENCE
ACEEENNSTV	EVANESCENT	ACEEIINNRT	INCINERATE
ACEEEPRRTU	RECUPERATE	ACEEIIITVX	EXCITATIVE
ACEEFFHSUU	CHAUFFEUSE	ACEEIILLMTY	EMETICALLY
ACEEFFIMNY	EFFEMINACY	ACEEIILPSY	ESPECIALLY
ACEEFFNRSU	SUFFERANCE	ACEEFILMNOR	CEREMONIAL
ACEEFIILTT	FELICITATE	ACEEILMNRT	MERCANTILE
ACEEFILNRT	FRENETICAL	ACEEILMNST	CENTESIMAL
ACEEFILNSS	FACILENESS	ACEEILNNNT	CENTENNIAL
ACEEFIORTV	VOCIFERATE	ACEEILNORT	NEOTERICAL
ACEEFIRRTV	REFRACTIVE	ACEEILNRST	CENTRALISE
ACEEFLLNTU	FLATULENCE	ACEEILNRTV	CANTILEVER
ACEEFLLPUY	PEACEFULLY	ACEEILNRTZ	CENTRALIZE
ACEEFLNSTV	FLAVESCENT	ACEEILORTV	CORELATIVE
ACEEFLORST	FORECASTLE	ACEEILORTX	EXOTERICAL
ACEEFORRST	FORECASTER	ACEEILRRTT	RETRACTILE
ACEEGGNORT	CONGREGATE	ACEEILRSUZ	SECULARIZE
ACEEGHILNT	GENETHLIAC	ACEEILRTTU	RETICULATE
ACEEGHLLNR	CHALLENGER	ACEEILRTVY	CREATIVELY
ACEEGHLNSS	CHANGELESS		REACTIVELY
ACEEGHNNOP	COPENHAGEN	ACEEILSTUV	VESICULATE
ACEEGHNORV	CHANGEOVER	ACEEIMNNST	INCASEMENT
ACEEGHORRV	OVERCHARGE	ACEEIMNRSS	CREAMINESS
ACEEGIILTX	EXEGITICAL	ACEEIMNRSV	SERVICEMAN
ACEEGILLOT	COLLEGIATE	ACEEIMNRTT	REMITTANCE
ACEEGILNTU	GENICULATE	ACEEIMPRST	SPERMACETI
ACEEGIORST	CATEGORISE	ACEEINNRST	TRANSIENCE
ACEEGIORTZ	CATEGORIZE	ACEEINORRT	RECREATION
ACEEGIOTTX	EXCOGITATE	ACEEINORTU	AUCTIONEER
ACEEGMMOSU	GEMMACEOUS	ACEEINORTX	EXECRATION
ACEEGNNORV	GOVERNANCE	ACEEINPPRT	APPRENTICE
ACEEGNNPRU	REPUGNANCE	ACEEINPRST	INTERSPACE
ACEEGNORRU	ENCOURAGER	ACEEINRSST	RESISTANCE
ACEEGOPRST	CORPSE-GATE	ACEEINSSTV	ACTIVENESS
ACEEHHIRRS	HERESIARCH	ACEEIOPPST	EPISCOPATE
ACEEHHPTTU	HEPTATEUCH	ACEEIOPSST	CAESPITOSE
ACEEHILMNN	MANCHINEEL	ACEEIOQTUV	EQUIVOCATE
ACEEHILMRT	HERMETICAL	ACEEIRRTTV	RETRACTIVE
ACEEHILPTT	TELEPATHIC	ACEEIRTTVX	EXTRACTIVE
ACEEHIMNPZ	CHIMPANZEE	ACEELLRSSY	CARELESSLY
ACEEHIMRTX	HEXAMETRIC	ACEELMNOST	SOLACEMENT
ACEEHIMSTZ	SCHEMATIZE	ACEELNOPST	OPALESCENT
ACEEHIORRT	CHARIOTEER	ACEELNRRTY	RECREANTLY
ACEEHISSTT	AESTHETICS	ACEELOOPRT	COLEOPTERA

ACEELOORSU	OLERACEOUS	ACEHIILLPT	PHILATELIC
ACEELOSSTT	CASSOLETTE	ACEHIILMPT	MEPHITICAL
ACEEMMNNNPT	ENCAMPMENT	ACEHIILPST	CEPHALITIS
ACEEMNOPST	COMPENSATE	ACEHIIMRTT	ARITHMETIC
ACEEMNPRST	ESCARPMENT	ACEHIINNOP	PHOENICIAN
ACEENNOPRV	PROVENANCE	ACEHIINOTV	INCHOATIVE
ACEENNORTV	CONTRAVENE	ACEHIINTTT	ANTITHETIC
	COVENANTER	ACEHIIRSTT	TRACHEITIS
ACEENNSSTU	SUSTENANCE	ACEHIKLNSS	CHALKINESS
ACEENOOSTU	COETANEOUS	ACEHILLOOZ	ALCOHOLIZE
ACEENORSSS	COARSENESS	ACEHILNOPT	PHONETICAL
ACEENRSSST	ANCESTRESS	ACEHILNORT	CHLORINATE
ACEENRSSTW	NEWSCASTER	ACEHILNOTY	INCHOATELY
ACEENRSUVY	SURVEYANCE	ACEHILOORZ	COLEORHIZA
ACEEORRSTT	STERCORATE	ACEHILORRT	RHETORICAL
ACEEORRTXY	EXECRATORY	ACEHILRSTY	HYSTERICAL
ACEFFIILTV	AFFLICTIVE	ACEHIMNNOR	ENHARMONIC
ACEFFIKRRT	TRAFFICKER	ACEHIMOPRT	METAPHORIC
ACEFGINRRT	REFRACTING	ACEHIMOPTU	APOTHECIUM
ACEFGLLRUY	GRACEFULLY	ACEHIMPSTY	METAPHYSIC
ACEFGLNRUU	UNGRACEFUL	ACEHINOPSS	POACHINESS
ACEFHHIRRS	ARCHER-FISH	ACEHIPPSTT	PETTICHAPS
ACEFHILPST	FELSPATHIC	ACEHIPRSTU	CURATESHIP
ACEFHIRRSV	FISH-CARVER	ACEHIRSTTT	TETRASTICH
ACEFHLLNOP	CHOP-FALLEN	ACEHLLMNOY	MELANCHOLY
ACEFHORRTV	HOVERCRAFT	ACEHLLNORS	ACORN-SHELL
ACEFIIILST	FACILITIES	ACEHLLPRSU	SEPULCHRAL
ACEFIINRST	SANCTIFIER	ACEHLMORSY	LACHRYMOSE
ACEFIKLNPS	CLASP-KNIFE	ACEHLNNNOT	NONCHALENT
ACEFILOOSU	FOLIACEOUS	ACEHLNSSST	STANCHLESS
ACEFINORRT	REFRACTION	ACEHLOORST	ORTHOCLASE
ACEFINRSST	CRAFTINESS	ACEHLORRST	ORCHESTRAL
ACEFIRRTTU	TRIFURCATE	ACEHLOSTTW	CATTLE-SHOW
ACEFLLNTUY	FLATULENCY	ACEHMNRRTY	MERCHANTRY
ACEGGHILNN	CHANGELING	ACEHNNSSST	STANCHNESS
ACEGGHLOOU	CHOLAGOGUE	ACEHNOOPRT	CTENOPHORA
ACEGGILLOO	GEOLOGICAL	ACEHNOPRSU	CANEPHORUS
ACEGGINRSS	CRAGGINESS	ACEHNORRTT	TROCHANTER
ACEGHIILMT	MEGALITHIC	ACEHOORRST	ORTHOCERAS
ACEGHIIPPR	EPIGRAPHIC	ACEHOPRSUY	CORYPHAEUS
ACEGHILMPT	PHLEGMATIC	ACEHPPSTTY	PETTYCHAPS
ACEGHIMNNU	MACHINE-GUN	ACEIIILRST	ISRAELITIC
ACEGHINNNT	ENCHANTING	ACEIIJLSTU	JESUITICAL
ACEGIILMTY	LEGITIMACY	ACEIIKMNST	KINEMATICS
ACEGIIOTTV	COGITATIVE	ACEIILLLPT	ELLIPTICAL
ACEGIIPRST	EPIGASTRIC	ACEIILLRTY	ILLITERACY
ACEGIIRRST	GERIATRICS	ACEIILMPSS	SPECIALISM
ACEGILLNOO	NEOLOGICAL	ACEIILNNRT	ENCRINITAL
ACEGILLOOS	OLIGOCLASE	ACEIILNOTT	ACTINOLITE
ACEGILMNNY	MENACINGLY	ACEIILNPST	PLASTICINE
ACEGILNNOT	CONGENITAL	ACEIILNTVY	INACTIVELY
ACEGILNOOP	GEOPONICAL	ACEIILPPRT	PARTICIPLE
ACEGILNOPY	CLAY-PIGEON	ACEIILPRTT	TRIPLICATE
ACEGILOOPT	APOLOGETIC	ACEIILPSST	SPECIALIST
ACEGLMOSUU	GLUMACEOUS	ACEIILPSTY	SPECIALITY
ACEGLOOPSY	ESCAPOLOGY	ACEIILSTTY	ELASTICITY
ACEGNOORSU	ACROGENOUS	ACEIINORTT	RECITATION
ACEGNOORTY	OCTOGENARY	ACEIINOSTV	VESICATION
ACEGOORSUU	COURAGEOUS	ACEIINOTTX	EXCITATION
ACEGOPRRSU	SUPERCARGO		INTOXICATE
ACEHHINOPT	THEOPHANIC	ACEIINPSTT	ANTISEPTIC

	PSITTACINE	ACEIOQSSUU	SEQUACIOUS
ACEIIORRRT	CERTIORARI	ACEIORSTTT	TRICOSTATE
ACEIIPPSST	EPISPASTIC	ACEIORSTVY	VESICATORY
ACEIIRRSSU	CUIRASSIER	ACEIORTTXY	EXCITATORY
ACEIIRTTVY	CREATIVITY	ACEJORRTTY	TRAJECTORY
ACEIISSSTY	ESSAYISTIC	ACEKLNOPST	ALPENSTOCK
ACEILLLPRU	PELLICULAR	ACEKMNORRW	CANKER-WORM
ACEILLMNSY	MISCELLANY	ACEKPRRSSY	SKYSCRAPER
ACEILLMRTY	METRICALLY	ACELLLORSS	COLLARLESS
ACEILLNOOT	OCELLATION	ACELLMNOTU	LOCULAMENT
ACEILLNRTU	LENTICULAR	ACELLOPTUY	EUCALYPTOL
ACEILLOPTY	POETICALLY	ACELLPRSTY	SPECTRALLY
ACEILLOQTU	COLLIQUATE	ACELMMNOOW	COMMONWEAL
ACEILLPRUY	PECULIARLY	ACELMNNOTT	MALCONTENT
ACEILLRTUV	VICTUALLER	ACELNNOSSU	CONSENSUAL
ACEILLRTVY	VERTICALLY	ACELNNOTUV	CONVENTUAL
ACEILMMNNO	MNEMONICAL	ACELNORRTY	NECROLATRY
ACEILMMNSS	CLAMMINESS	ACELNOTTUX	CONTEXTUAL
ACEILMNOPR	COMPLAINER	ACELOOPRRT	PERCOLATOR
ACEILMNRST	CENTRALISM	ACELOPRSTU	SPECULATOR
ACEILMRRUV	VERMICULAR	ACELOPRSWY	COW-PARSLEY
ACEILMTUUV	CUMULATIVE	ACELORRSTY	CLEAR-STORY
ACEILNOORT	CO-RELATION	ACELPSTUUY	EUCALYPTUS
ACEILNOPST	PLEONASTIC	ACEMMNORTY	COMMENTARY
ACEILNOPTU	PECULATION	ACEMMNOSTU	CONSUMMATE
	UNPOETICAL	ACEMMOSTTY	MASTECTOMY
ACEILNORTU	ULCERATION	ACEMNNNOTT	CANTONMENT
ACEILNOSTU	INOSCULATE	ACENNOORTV	COVENANTOR
ACEILNPPSU	SUPPLIANCE	ACENNORSTV	CONVERSANT
ACEILNRSTU	LACUSTRINE	ACENNOSTTT	CONTESTANT
ACEILNRTTY	CENTRALITY	ACENOOPRVY	OVERCANOPY
ACEILNRUUX	LUXURIANCE	ACENOORRSZ	SCORZONERA
ACEILOOSUV	OLIVACEOUS	ACEOOOPRRT	CO-OPERATOR
	VIOLACEOUS	ACEOOPRRRT	PROCREATOR
ACEILOPTUV	COPULATIVE	ACEOOPRRSU	PORRACEOUS
ACEILOQTUY	COEQUALITY	ACEORSTUXY	EXCUSATORY
ACEILPPSTU	SUPPLICATE	ACFFGIILNT	AFFLICTING
ACEILPRTUU	APICULTURE	ACFFIILLOY	OFFICIALLY
ACEILRSSTU	SECULARIST	ACFFIILNOT	AFFLICTION
ACEILRSTTU	TESTICULAR	ACFFIILNOU	UNOFFICIAL
	TRISULCATE	ACFFIIOORT	OFFICIATOR
ACEILRTUUV	AVICULTURE	ACFFILLNUY	FANCIFULLY
ACEIMMRSTY	ASYMMETRIC	ACFFORSSST	CROSS-STAFF
ACEIMNNOST	CISMONTANE	ACFGILOPRY	PROFLIGACY
ACEIMNOPRT	IMPORTANCE	ACFHIMORTY	CYATHIFORM
ACEIMNPSTU	PNEUMATICS	ACFHIOPRST	FACTORSHIP
ACEIMORRTU	ACROTERIUM	ACFHLLTUWY	WATCHFULLY
ACEIMSSTTY	SYSTEMATIC	ACFIIILNTY	FINICALITY
ACEINNNOSU	UNISONANCE	ACFIILNOPT	PONTIFICAL
ACEINNORTU	ENUNCIATOR	ACFIILNORT	FRICTIONAL
ACEINNRSTY	TRANSIENCY	ACFIINNORT	INFRACTION
ACEINNSSST	SCANTINESS	ACFIINOSTT	FACTIONIST
ACEINOORTV	REVOCATION	ACFIIOSTTU	FACTITIOUS
ACEINOPRTU	PRECAUTION	ACFILNNOTU	FUNCTIONAL
ACEINOPSTT	CONSTIPATE	ACFILOSTUY	FACTIOUSLY
ACEINORRTT	RETRACTION	ACFILRSSST	FIRST-CLASS
ACEINORSSY	CESSIONARY	ACFINOORRT	FORNICATOR
ACEINORTTU	ERUCTATION	ACGGHINNNU	UNCHANGING
ACEINORTTX	EXTRACTION	ACGGIILNNO	GANGLIONIC
ACEINOSTTU	UNICOSTATE	ACGGILLNNY	GLANCINGLY
ACEIOPRRSU	PRECARIOUS	ACGHHIOPRR	CHIROGRAPH

ACGHILMNRY	CHARMINGLY	ACIILLMNRY	CRIMINALLY
ACGHILNSTY	SCATHINGLY	ACIILNOORT	LORICATION
ACGHIMNNOP	CHAMPIGNON	ACIILNOPRV	PROVINCIAL
ACGHINOPRT	PROGNATHIC	ACIILNORTT	TINCTORIAL
ACGHINOPRZ	ZINCOGRAPH	ACIILNOSTT	SOLICITANT
ACGHIRRTTW	CARTWRIGHT	ACIILOPTTY	TOPICALITY
ACGHMNOORR	CHRONOGRAM	ACIILOSSUV	LASCIVIOUS
ACGIILLOST	LOGISTICAL	ACIILRSTTU	ALTRUISTIC
ACGIILLRTU	LITURGICAL	ACIIMMNNSTU	NUMISMATIC
ACGIILNOSU	CALIGINOUS	ACIIMNPTTY	TYMPANITIC
ACGIINOOTT	COGITATION	ACIIMNRSSS	NARCISSISM
ACGIINPRST	PRACTISING	ACIINNOOTV	INVOCATION
ACGILLOOOR	OROLOGICAL	ACIINNOSTU	INSOUCIANT
ACGILLOOOZ	ZOOLOGICAL	ACIINOPRST	ASCRIPTION
ACGILLRSUY	SURGICALLY		CRISPATION
ACGILMNNOO	COGNOMINAL	ACIINORTTU	URTICATION
ACGILNOORY	CRANIOLOGY	ACIINRSSST	NARCISSIST
ACGILOOTTU	TAUTOLOGIC	ACIIOPSSUU	AUSPICIOUS
ACGILORSUU	GLUCOSURIA	ACIIORSTVY	VARICOSITY
ACGILORSUY	GRACIOUSLY	ACIIPRSSTT	PATRISTICS
ACGIMNSSTY	GYMNASTICS	ACIISSSTTT	STATISTICS
ACGINOOSTU	CONTAGIOUS	ACIJLORTUY	JOCULARITY
ACGINOPSUU	PUGNACIOUS	ACILLLOOQU	COLLOQUIAL
ACGINORSUU	UNGRACIOUS	ACILLMOORT	COLLIMATOR
ACGJLLNOUY	CONJUGALLY	ACILLNOOTU	ALLOCUTION
ACGLNOORSU	CLANGOROUS	ACILLNORUU	UNILOCULAR
ACGMOPRRTY	CRYPTOGRAM	ACILLNORUV	INVOLUCRAL
ACGMOPRTYY	CRYPTOGAMY	ACILLNOUVY	UNIVOCALLY
ACGNNOPPUY	OPPUGNANCY	ACILLOPRTY	TROPICALLY
ACGOORRRTU	CORRUGATOR	ACILLORRTU	TRILOCULAR
ACHHILMOPT	OPHTHALMIC	ACILMMRSUU	SIMULACRUM
ACHHILMRTY	RHYTHMICAL	ACILMNOSUU	CALUMNIOUS
ACHHNOOTTU	AUTOCHTHON	ACILMNOTUU	CUMULATION
ACHHOPPSTY	PSYCHOPATH	ACILMOOOTZ	ZOOTOMICAL
ACHIILORST	HISTORICAL	ACILMORSUU	MIRACULOUS
ACHIIMNSUV	CHAUVINISM	ACILNOOORT	COLORATION
ACHIINNORT	CORINTHIAN	ACILNOOPTU	COPULATION
ACHIINORSU	AIR-CUSHION	ACILNOORTU	INOCULATOR
ACHIINRSTT	ANTICHRIST	ACILNOORTY	ICONOLATRY
ACHIINSTUV	CHAUVINIST	ACILNOOSTU	OSCULATION
ACHIIOPRST	APHORISTIC	ACILNORRTY	CONTRARILY
ACHIKMNOST	MACKINTOSH	ACILNORSTU	ULTRASONIC
ACHILLMOOS	ALCOHOLISM	ACILNRTTUY	TACITURNLY
ACHILLMORS	CHLORALISM	ACILOOPRRT	PROCTORIAL
ACHILLMTYY	MYTHICALLY	ACILOOQSUU	LOQUACIOUS
ACHILLNNSY	CLANNISHLY	ACILOOSSUX	SAXICOLOUS
ACHILLPSYY	PHYSICALLY	ACILOPSSUY	SPACIOUSLY
ACHILNOORS	ISOCHRONAL	ACILOPSTUY	CAPTIOUSLY
ACHILORSUV	CHIVALROUS	ACILORTTUV	CULTIVATOR
ACHIMMNNORS	MONARCHISM	ACILOSTUUY	CAUTIOUSLY
ACHIMNORST	MONARCHIST	ACILPRRSTU	SCRIPTURAL
ACHINSTTUY	UNCHASTITY	ACIMMORSSY	COMMISSARY
ACHIPRSTYY	PSYCHIATRY	ACIMNNORTU	UNROMANTIC
ACHIRSTTWW	WRIST-WATCH	ACIMNNOSTY	SANCTIMONY
ACHLNNORSY	SYNCHRONAL	ACIMNOOPRS	COMPARISON
ACHNNNOOST	CANNON-SHOT	ACIMNOOPSS	COMPASSION
ACIIILLMNY	INIMICALLY	ACIMNOORST	ASTRONOMIC
ACIIILNOPT	POLITICIAN	ACIMNOPRTY	PATRONYMIC
ACIIILORTV	VARIOLITIC	ACIMNPRSTU	MANUSCRIPT
ACIIINTTVY	INACTIVITY	ACIMOOPRTT	COMPATRIOT
ACIIKNNNPY	PICKANINNY	ACIMOPSTTY	ASYMPTOTIC

ACINNNOSTT	INCONSTANT	ADDEOORRSTW	ADDER'S-WORT
ACINNOOORT	CORONATION	ADDFIILNSU	DISDAINFUL
ACINNORSTT	CONSTRAINT	ADDIIILNUV	INDIVIDUAL
ACINNORRTTU	TRUNCATION	ADDILLLLYY	DILLY-DALLY
ACINOORSTT	CARTOONIST	ADDIMNOSUY	DIDYNAMOUS
ACINOORTVY	INVOCATORY	ADDNNOOTUW	DOWN-AND-OUT
ACINOPPRSW	COW-PARSNIP	ADEEEEGNRT	DEGENERATE
ACINORSTTU	CRUSTATION	ADEEEELRTT	LEADERETTE
ACINPRRSTT	TRANSCRIPT	ADEEEFILRZ	FEDERALIZE
ACLLNPTUUY	PUNCTUALLY	ADEEEFIRTV	FEDERATIVE
ACLLOOPRRY	CORPORALLY	ADEEEHLRTT	LETTERHEAD
ACLLPRSTUU	SCULPTURAL	ADEEEHLRTW	TREADWHEEL
ACLMMNOOTY	COMMUNALTY	ADEEEIRSTT	EASTERTIDE
ACLNNOSTTU	CONSULTANT	ADEEELNNUV	UNLEAVENED
ACLNNOSTTY	CONSTANTLY	ADEEELNPRU	UNREPEALED
ACLNNPTUUU	UNPUNCTUAL	ADEEELPRTY	REPEATEDLY
ACLOOPRTUY	COPULATORY	ADEEEMNNRT	ENDEARMENT
ACLOORSTUY	OSCULATORY	ADEEENRRSW	NEWSREADER
ACLRRSTTUU	STRUCTURAL	ADEEENRSSS	SEAREDNESS
ACMNNORTUY	COUNTRYMAN	ADEEENSSST	SEDATENESS
ACNOPRSSUY	SYNCARPOUS	ADEEFGHIRU	FIGURE-HEAD
ACOOPRRRTT	PROTRACTOR	ADEEFHNRTU	UNFATHERED
ACOOPRRRTU	PROCURATOR	ADEEFILLNS	SELF-DENIAL
ADDDEEGILM	MIDDLE-AGED	ADEEFILMRS	FEDERALISM
ADDDEEHNRU	DUNDERHEAD	ADEEFILRST	FEDERALIST
ADDEEEFHNR	FREEHANDED	ADEEFINORT	FEDERATION
ADDEEEFNTU	UNDEFEATED	ADEEFIRSTU	DISFEATURE
ADDEEEHNNV	EVEN-HANDED	ADEEFLORUV	FOUR-LEAVED
ADDEEEIRST	DESIDERATE	ADEEFMNRTY	DEFRAYMENT
ADDEEELNTT	DEAD-NETTLE	ADEEGGHLOR	LOGGERHEAD
ADDEEELRTT	DEAD-LETTER	ADEEGGJNSS	JAGGEDNESS
ADDEEFHLNT	LEFT-HANDED	ADEEGILNOT	DELEGATION
ADDEEFHNOR	FOREHANDED	ADEEGILNRR	RINGLEADER
ADDEEGGINS	DISENGAGED	ADEEGLPPRY	DAPPLE-GREY
ADDEEGHITW	DEAD-WEIGHT	ADEEGLRRSS	REGARDLESS
ADDEEGHLNO	LONGHEADED	ADEEGNORRS	ROSE-GARDEN
ADDEEGNRRU	UNREGARDED	ADEEGNORRT	DRAGON-TREE
ADDEEIIPSS	DIAPEDESIS	ADEEGORRRT	RETROGRADE
ADDEEILNSS	DEADLINESS	ADEEHHILMR	HEMIHEDRAL
ADDEEILPSS	DISPLEASED	ADEEHHNORX	HEXAHEDRON
ADDEEIPRSW	WIDESPREAD	ADEEHILOPP	PAEDOPHILE
ADDEELPRVY	DEPRAVEDLY	ADEEHILPRS	LEADERSHIP
ADDEENNTTU	UNATTENDED	ADEEHILSVY	ADHESIVELY
ADDEENORST	ADDER-STONE	ADEEHIMNUZ	DEHUMANIZE
ADDEENRRUW	UNREWARDED	ADEEHINRST	DISHEARTEN
ADDEEOPRRT	DEPREDATOR	ADEEHIPRRS	READERSHIP
ADDEFIIMNR	FAIR-MINDED	ADEEHIRRTY	HEREDITARY
ADDEFLLRUY	DREADFULLY	ADEEHJLORT	JOLTERHEAD
ADDEGJMNTU	ADJUDGMENT	ADEEHKNOTT	DEATH-TOKEN
ADDEHIILNP	DIDELPHIAN	ADEEHLMTTY	METHYLATED
ADDEHIMNOO	MAIDENHOOD	ADEEHMNPRU	UNHAMPERED
ADDEHLLNOR	LANDHOLDER	ADEEHNNRTU	UNDERNEATH
ADDEIIMSSV	MISADVISED	ADEEIIJNRR	JARDINIÈRE
ADDEIIPSST	DISSIPATED	ADEEIILNTV	EVIDENTIAL
ADDEILMTTY	ADMITTEDLY	ADEEIILTVZ	DEVITALIZE
ADDEIMNSUY	UNDISMAYED	ADEEIIMTTV	MEDITATIVE
ADDEINNOTU	DENUDATION	ADEEIINRVV	VIVANDIÈRE
ADDEINNRRU	UNDERDRAIN	ADEEIIRTVV	DERIVATIVE
ADDELNOORW	WOODLANDER	ADEEIJOPRZ	JEOPARDIZE
ADDENNRSTU	UNDERSTAND	ADEEILLMRY	REMEDIALLY
ADDENOQRSU	SQUADRONED	ADEEILLUVV	VAUDEVILLE

ADEEILMORZ	DEMORALIZE	ADEGIILMNS	MISLEADING
ADEEILNORT	DELINEATOR	ADEGIILTTY	DIGITATELY
ADEEILNRTU	ADULTERINE	ADEGIIMNNU	UNIMAGINED
ADEEILNSSV	DISENSLAVE	ADEGIINPRS	DESPAIRING
ADEEILNTTT	DILETTANTE	ADEGILLNPY	PLEADINGLY
ADEEILOPRZ	DEPOLARIZE	ADEGILNNRS	SANDERLING
ADEEILPRRV	PEARL-DIVER	ADEGIMNOPU	IMPOUNDAGE
ADEEIMMORT	IMMODERATE	ADEGIMNORZ	GORMANDIZE
ADEEIMNNOT	DENOMINATE	ADEGIMORTZ	DOGMATIZER
	EMENDATION	ADEGINOORT	DEROGATION
ADEEIMNNTT	DETAINMENT	ADEGINORRT	DENIGRATOR
ADEEIMNNUX	UNEXAMINED	ADEGINORST	DESIGNATOR
ADEEIMNRSS	DREAMINESS	ADEGLOPRSY	DOG-PARSLEY
ADEEIMORRT	RADIOMETER	ADEGMNOOSU	ENDOGAMOUS
ADEEIMORTU	AUDIOMETER	ADEGOOPRST	GASTEROPOD
ADEEINORTT	ORIENTATED	ADEGOORRTY	DEROGATORY
ADEEINOTTV	DENOTATIVE	ADEHHIIPRT	DIPHTHERIA
ADEEINPRST	PEDESTRIAN	ADEHHIRRTW	HITHERWARD
ADEEINRRSS	DREARINESS	ADEHHNOPRY	HYDROPHANE
ADEEINRTTT	TRIDENTATE	ADEHIILOPU	AUDIOPHILE
ADEEINSSST	STEADINESS	ADEHILNOPS	SPHENOIDAL
ADEEIRRSTV	ADVERTISER	ADEHILNORZ	ENDORHIZAL
ADEEKMRRSS	DRESSMAKER	ADEHILOPRS	SPHEROIDAL
ADEEKNRRTU	UNDERTAKER	ADEHILPRUY	HYPERDULIA
ADEELLMMRT	TRAMMELLED	ADEHINOOPR	RADIOPHONE
ADEELLOSTY	DESOLATELY	ADEHINOSST	ASTONISHED
ADEELMNNTU	UNLAMENTED	ADEHINPRSW	WARDENSHIP
ADEELMNORT	ALMOND-TREE	ADEHINPSSU	DAUPHINESS
ADEELMORTY	MODERATELY	ADEHIOOPRT	ORTHOPEDIA
ADEELNOPRU	ENDOPLEURA	ADEHIOPRSZ	RHAPSODIZE
ADEELNRUUV	UNDERVALUE	ADEHLLNOUW	UNHALLOWED
ADEELOPPTU	DEPOPULATE	ADEHLLOPRY	POLYHEDRAL
ADEELRSSTU	ADULTERESS	ADEHLMOPRY	HYPODERMAL
ADEEMNORTY	EMENDATORY	ADEHLNRSTU	SUTHERLAND
ADEEMNPRTT	DEPARTMENT	ADEHLOSSSW	SHADOWLESS
ADEEMNRRTT	RETARDMENT	ADEHMMOPRR	DROP-HAMMER
ADEEMNRSUU	UNMEASURED	ADEHMNNOSU	UNHANDSOME
ADEENNNTTU	UNTENANTED	ADEHOORSVW	OVERSHADOW
ADEENNOSSU	UNSEASONED	ADEIIIMNTT	INTIMIDATE
ADEENPPRRU	UNPREPARED	ADEIILLMPX	MAXILLIPED
ADEENPRRTU	ENRAPTURED	ADEIILLSTT	DISTILLATE
ADEENRRTUV	ADVENTURER	ADEIILNOPT	DEPILATION
ADEENRSTTU	UNDERSTATE	ADEIIMNOTT	MEDITATION
ADEENSTTTU	UNATTESTED	ADEIIMNOTV	ADMONITIVE
ADEERSSSTW	STEWARDESS	ADEIIMNPRU	UNIMPAIRED
ADEFGHIRST	FAR-SIGHTED	ADEIIMNRST	ADMINISTER
ADEFHHOORT	FATHERHOOD	ADEIIMRSTT	DERMATITIS
ADEFHILTTW	HALF-WITTED	ADEIINNORT	INORDINATE
ADEFHINPRT	PATHFINDER	ADEIINNOTW	NATIONWIDE
ADEFHOORSW	FORESHADOW	ADEIINNOTZ	DENIZATION
ADEFIIRSTT	STRATIFIED	ADEIINNSST	DAINTINESS
ADEFINOORR	FOREORDAIN	ADEIINORTV	DERIVATION
ADEFKLORST	TRADESFOLK	ADEIINPTTU	INAPTITUDE
ADEFLNRTUU	FRAUDULENT	ADEIINRRST	DISTRAINER
ADEGGIMMOS	DEMAGOGISM	ADEIISSSUV	DISSUASIVE
ADEGHHINST	NIGHTSHADE	ADEIJMMNRW	WINDJAMMER
ADEGHILNOR	LONG-HAIRED	ADEIKLLNUY	UNLADYLIKE
ADEGHIOPRY	IDEOGRAPHY	ADEILLNPSS	PALLIDNESS
ADEGHLRTUY	DAUGHTERLY	ADEILLNRUV	UNRIVALLED
ADEGHMOPRY	DEMOGRAPHY	ADEILMNOPR	PALINDROME
ADEGHNORST	HEADSTRONG	ADEILMNRTU	RUDIMENTAL
ADEGIILLSU	SEGUIDILLA		

166

ADEILMNSSS	DISMALNESS	ADGMNNORSU	GROUNDSMAN
ADEILMOPSZ	PSALMODIZE	ADGNNORSUY	GYNANDROUS
ADEILNOOST	DESOLATION	ADHHNOOOPR	ORPHANHOOD
ADEILNOOTV	DEVOTIONAL	ADHHNOSTTU	THOUSANDTH
ADEILNPRTU	PRUDENTIAL	ADHHOPRTYY	HYDROPATHY
ADEILNSTUY	UNSTEADILY	ADHIILMNOT	MIDLOTHIAN
ADEILOPRTY	DEPILATORY	ADHIIMMNPS	MIDSHIPMAN
ADEILOPSTU	DIPETALOUS	ADHIINNSTU	HINDUSTANI
ADEIMMNNRST	MASTER-MIND	ADHILNOSTU	OUTLANDISH
ADEIMMORST	MODERATISM	ADHINOOPRT	ANTHROPOID
ADEIMNNORT	ORDAINMENT	ADHINSTUWY	WHITSUNDAY
ADEIMNOORT	MODERATION	ADIIIOPRSST	RHAPSODIST
ADEIMRTUUV	DUUMVIRATE	ADHLNOPSSW	SPLASHDOWN
ADEINNOOTT	DENOTATION	ADHMNOOORT	MATRONHOOD
	DETONATION	ADHNORRSTW	NORTHWARDS
ADEINNOPVWW	WINDOW-PANE	ADHOORRTWY	ROADWORTHY
ADEINNRSSW	INWARDNESS	ADIIILMRSS	DISSIMILAR
ADEINNRSTU	UNSTRAINED	ADIIILNOSV	DIVISIONAL
ADEINOPRTU	DEPURATION	ADIIINNOTV	DIVINATION
ADEINOPTTU	DEPUTATION	ADIIILLORTY	DILATORILY
ADEINORSST	ADROITNESS	ADIILMOPRR	PRIMORDIAL
ADEINPRSSY	DISPENSARY	ADIILNORRY	ORDINARILY
ADEINRSSTW	TAWDRINESS	ADIILNRSTU	INDUSTRIAL
ADEINSSSTU	UNASSISTED	ADIILOQRTU	LIQUIDATOR
ADEIOPPRSV	DISAPPROVE	ADIILORSTY	SOLIDARITY
ADEIOPRRTU	REPUDIATOR	ADIILQSTUY	SQUALIDITY
ADEIOPRSTY	DEPOSITARY	ADIIMNNOOT	ADMONITION
ADEIORSSTT	SIDEROSTAT		DOMINATION
ADEJMNSTTU	ADJUSTMENT	ADIIMNOPRY	PYRAMIDION
ADEJOOPRSU	JEOPARDOUS	ADIIMORTUU	AUDITORIUM
ADELNORSSU	SLANDEROUS	ADIINNNOTU	INUNDATION
ADELNRSTUW	WANDERLUST	ADIINNOORT	ORDINATION
ADELORSTUU	ADULTEROUS	ADIINNORTU	INDURATION
ADELPQRTUU	QUADRUPLET	ADIINOPPST	DISAPPOINT
ADELRRSTYY	DRYSALTERY	ADIINOPSSS	DISPASSION
ADELRSTWWY	WESTWARDLY	ADIINORRST	DISTRAINOR
ADEMMMNORU	MEMORANDUM	ADIINOSSSU	DISSUASION
ADENNORRRU	ROAD-RUNNER	ADILLLMORS	LOLLARDISM
ADEOPRRTUY	DEPURATORY	ADILLLOSYY	DISLOYALLY
ADFFLLRUUY	FRAUDFULLY	ADILLNSSTT	STANDSTILL
ADFGILMNOR	GLANDIFORM	ADILLOSTYY	DISLOYALTY
ADFGINORRU	FAIRGROUND	ADILMNOOTU	MODULATION
ADFHILRSWY	DWARFISHLY	ADILMOPSST	PSALMODIST
ADFIIINNPT	PINNATIFID	ADILNNOTUU	UNDULATION
ADFIILQSUY	DISQUALIFY	ADILNOPSUU	PALUDINOUS
ADFIIOSSTU	FASTIDIOUS	ADILOORSTU	IDOLATROUS
ADFIISSSTY	DISSATISFY	ADILOPRTUY	PLAUDITORY
ADFILLMNOY	MANIFOLDLY	ADIMNOORTY	ADMONITORY
ADFINNOOTU	FOUNDATION	ADIMORSTUU	SUDATORIUM
ADGHIRSTTU	DISTRAUGHT	ADINNOPSTT	STANDPOINT
ADGIIINOTT	DIGITATION	ADINORSSTW	DOWN-STAIRS
ADGIIKNNPP	KIDNAPPING	ADIORSSSTU	DISASTROUS
ADGIILMNRY	ADMIRINGLY	ADLMOOORSU	MALODOROUS
ADGILLNRWY	DRAWLINGLY	ADLNORTUUY	UNDULATORY
ADGILLNYZZ	DAZZLINGLY	ADLNORTUWY	UNTOWARDLY
ADGILNNPRS	LANDSPRING	AEEEEGKMPR	GAMEKEEPER
ADGILNNTUU	UNDULATING	AEEEEGNRRT	REGENERATE
ADGINNOSTU	ASTOUNDING	AEEEFFIMNT	EFFEMINATE
ADGINNPSTU	UPSTANDING	AEEEFHRRTT	THEREAFTER
ADGLLNOSUU	GLANDULOUS	AEEEFINRTZ	ANTIFREEZE
ADGLNOPRUY	PLAYGROUND	AEEEFNRRST	TRANSFEREE

AEEEFNRSTT	FENESTRATE	AEEGILMNRR	MALINGERER
AEEEGGMNNT	ENGAGEMENT	AEEGILMNRT	REGIMENTAL
AEEEGHLPRT	TELPHERAGE	AEEGILMNSV	EVANGELISM
AEEEGILNRZ	GENERALIZE	AEEGILNNSS	GENIALNESS
AEEEGILNVZ	EVANGELIZE	AEEGILNORT	REGELATION
AEEEGINNOR	AEROENGINE		RELEGATION
AEEEGINRTV	GENERATIVE	AEEGILNRST	EASTERLING
AEEEGITTVV	VEGETATIVE	AEEGILNRTY	GENERALITY
AEEEGKLOPR	GOAL-KEEPER	AEEGILNSTV	EVANGELIST
AEEEGLMNRT	REGALEMENT	AEEGILNTVY	NEGATIVELY
AEEEGMNRSS	MEAGRENESS	AEEGILOPTX	EXPLOITAGE
AEEEHHINST	HEATHENISE	AEEGILRRSU	REGULARISE
AEEEHLLRTY	ETHEREALLY	AEEGILRTUV	REGULATIVE
AEEEHNRRTT	THREATENER	AEEGIMNPRT	IMPREGNATE
AEEEHRSTTW	SWEETHEART	AEEGIMNRTZ	MAGNETIZER
AEEEILNRTZ	ETERNALIZE	AEEGIMRRTV	GRAVIMETER
AEEEINRTTV	INVETERATE	AEEGINNNSU	ENSANGUINE
AEEEINRTVW	INTERWEAVE	AEEGINNORT	GENERATION
AEEEJNRTUV	REJUVENATE	AEEGINNPSS	PANGENESIS
AEEEKPSSTW	SWEEPSTAKE	AEEGINORRS	REORGANISE
AEEELLSSTT	TESSELLATE	AEEGINOTTV	VEGETATION
AEEELMNNTT	TENEMENTAL	AEEGINPRYZ	PANEGYRIZE
AEEELMNPTU	EPAULEMENT	AEEGINRRTX	GENERATRIX
AEEELMNRTY	ELEMENTARY	AEEGINRSSS	GREASINESS
AEEELNOSTT	TELEOSTEAN	AEEGJLLNOR	JARGONELLE
AEEEMMNORT	ANEMOMETER	AEEGLLORTT	ALLEGRETTO
AEEEMNPRTT	PENTAMETER	AEEGLNORTV	GRAVEOLENT
AEEEMNRRTU	REMUNERATE	AEEGMNNOST	MANGOSTEEN
AEEEMRRTTT	TETRAMETER	AEEGMORRST	STEREOGRAM
AEEENRSSSV	AVERSENESS	AEEGNORSTV	GRAVESTONE
AEEENRSTVY	EYE-SERVANT	AEEHHINRST	EARTH-SHINE
AEEEPPRRTT	PERPETRATE	AEEHHLMSTU	METHUSELAH
AEEEPPRTTU	PERPETUATE	AEEHIILLPT	EPITHELIAL
AEEERRSTYY	YESTERYEAR	AEEHIILMST	ISHMAELITE
AEEFFHORRT	FOREFATHER	AEEHIMSSTT	METATHESIS
AEEFFORRST	REAFFOREST	AEEHINRSST	EARTHINESS
AEEFGGHIRT	FREIGHTAGE		HEARTINESS
AEEFGHINRT	FEATHERING	AEEHIPPRRS	PERIPHRASE
AEEFGILPRS	PERSIFLAGE	AEEHISTUVX	EXHAUSTIVE
AEEFHHINRT	FAHRENHEIT	AEEHLLORSW	WHOLESALER
AEEFHLRSST	FATHERLESS	AEEHLMNNOP	PHENOMENAL
AEEFHPRSTT	STEPFATHER	AEEHMOPRST	ATMOSPHERE
AEEFHRRSTW	FRESHWATER	AEEHNORSSS	HOARSENESS
AEEFIMNRRT	FREEMARTIN	AEEHORSTVW	WHATSOEVER
AEEFINRRST	FRATERNISE	AEEIILLRTT	ILLITERATE
AEEFLLRSSY	FEARLESSLY	AEEIILLRTZ	LITERALIZE
AEEGGHOPRR	GEOGRAPHER	AEEIILMNRZ	MINERALIZE
AEEGGIRSSV	AGGRESSIVE	AEEIILNNSU	ELEUSINIAN
AEEGHHMORR	HEMORRHAGE	AEEIILRSTV	REVITALISE
AEEGHILPST	LEGATESHIP	AEEIIMNNST	INSEMINATE
AEEGHILRTZ	LETHARGIZE	AEEIIMPRTV	IMPERATIVE
AEEGHINRTW	WEATHERING	AEEIINNPRS	PARISIENNE
	GEOTHERMAL	AEEIIPPTTV	APPETITIVE
AEEGHLNTVW	WAVELENGTH	AEEIJOPRTV	PEJORATIVE
AEEGHLORTT	ALTOGETHER	AEEILLMNST	ENAMELLIST
AEEGHLPRTY	TELEGRAPHY	AEEILLRSSV	VERSAILLES
AEEGIILLLS	ILLEGALISE	AEEILLRTVY	RELATIVELY
AEEGIILLNV	VILLEINAGE	AEEILMNNTT	ENTAILMENT
AEEGIILMTT	LEGITIMATE	AEEILMNPRT	PLANIMETER
AEEGIILNTZ	GELATINIZE	AEEILMNRST	STREAMLINE
AEEGILLORZ	ALLEGORIZE	AEEILNNPST	SEPTENNIAL

AEEILNNTTU	LIEUTENANT	AEELNRSSSW	ANSWERLESS
AEEILNOPRT	PERITONEAL	AEELOQRRUU	ROQUELAURE
AEEILNORTV	REVELATION	AEELPRRSSY	PRAYERLESS
AEEILNQTUV	EQUIVALENT	AEELRSTTTY	TETRASTYLE
AEEILNRRTV	IRRELEVANT	AEEMMNORTY	ANEMOMETRY
AEEILNRSTT	ETERNALIST	AEEMNNORRT	ORNAMENTER
AEEILNRTUZ	NEUTRALIZE	AEEMNOQRSU	ROMANESQUE
AEEILNSSUZ	SENSUALIZE	AEEMNORRTU	ENUMERATOR
AEEILOPRST	PERIOSTEAL	AEEMNORRUV	MANOEUVRER
AEEILPPRRT	PERIPTERAL	AEEMNPPRTY	PREPAYMENT
AEEILPRSSY	ERYSIPELAS	AEEMNRRSTT	ARRESTMENT
AEEILRRTTU	LITERATURE	AEEMNRSSTU	MATURENESS
AEEIMMOPRT	EMMETROPIA	AEEMNRSTTU	MENSTRUATE
AEEIMMRSSU	MISMEASURE	AEEMNSSSST	ASSESSMENT
AEEIMNNPRT	PINEMARTEN	AEEMOSTUXZ	EXEZEMATOUS
AEEIMNOPRT	PERMEATION	AEEMPRRTTU	EAR-TRUMPET
AEEIMNORTT	MARIONETTE	AEENOPRRTT	PENETRATOR
AEEIMNOSTT	MAISONETTE	AEENORSTUX	EXTRANEOUS
AEEIMNPRRU	PRAEMUNIRE	AEENORTTUX	EXTENUATOR
AEEIMNSSST	STEAMINESS	AEENPRSSSS	SPARSENESS
AEEINNNSSS	INSANENESS	AEENQRSSSU	SQUARENESS
AEEINNNSST	INNATENESS	AEENRRSSTV	TRANSVERSE
AEEINNORTV	ENERVATION	AEENSSSTTU	ASTUTENESS
	VENERATION	AEEQSSTTUU	STATUESQUE
AEEINNRTUV	AVENTURINE	AEFGGILNSS	FLAGGINESS
AEEINNSSSU	UNEASINESS	AEFGHINRRW	WHARFINGER
AEEINNSSTT	ASSENTIENT	AEFGHLSTTU	SELF-TAUGHT
AEEINNSSTV	NATIVENESS	AEFGIILNNR	FINGERNAIL
AEEINQRSTU	EQUESTRIAN	AEFGIIRTUV	FIGURATIVE
AEEINQSSSU	QUEASINESS	AEFGILMNNU	MEANINGFUL
AEEINRRRST	RESTRAINER	AEFGILNRTT	FLATTERING
AEEINRRTTT	TRITERNATE	AEFGILOPRT	PROFLIGATE
AEEINRRTVY	VETERINARY	AEFGIPRRTU	GRAPEFRUIT
AEEINRSSTW	EAR-WITNESS	AEFGLLRTUY	GRATEFULLY
	WATERINESS	AEFGLNRTUU	UNGRATEFUL
AEEINRSTTT	INTERSTATE	AEFGLPSTUY	SAFETY-PLUG
AEEINSSSTW	SWEATINESS	AEFHHIPRST	FATHERSHIP
AEEINSSSTY	YEASTINESS	AEFHIKLRSY	FREAKISHLY
AEEIOPRRSV	OVERPRAISE	AEFHIMMNST	FAMISHMENT
AEEIPPRRST	PERSPIRATE	AEFHLLMSUY	SHAMEFULLY
AEEIPRSSTT	STRIP-TEASE	AEFHLMOSST	FATHOMLESS
AEEIPRSSTU	PASTEURISE	AEFHLNRTUY	UNFATHERLY
AEEIPRSSUV	PERSUASIVE	AEFIILLTUV	FLUVIATILE
AEEIPRTTUV	VITUPERATE	AEFIILNRTT	INFILTRATE
AEEJLNORSU	JOURNALESE	AEFIILORTT	TRIFOLIATE
AEELLMMRRT	TRAMMELLER	AEFIKNOPRS	FAIR-SPOKEN
AEELLMNOTV	MALEVOLENT	AEFILMNSTY	MANIFESTLY
AEELLMNRTU	ALLUREMENT	AEFILNORSU	LANIFEROUS
AEELLMNSSY	NAMELESSLY	AEFILNSSTU	FAULTINESS
AEELLNRTXY	EXTERNALLY	AEFINNRSSU	UNFAIRNESS
AEELLNTUVY	EVENTUALLY	AEFINOOPRT	PIANOFORTE
AEELMNOPRT	PLANOMETER	AEFINORTTU	REFUTATION
AEELMNORTW	WATER-MELON	AEFINRRTTY	FRATERNITY
AEELMORTTV	VOLTAMETER	AEFIORRSUU	AURIFEROUS
AEELMRSSST	MASTERLESS	AEFLLLORWW	WALLFLOWER
AEELNNPTTU	ANTEPENULT	AEFLLNSSUW	LAWFULNESS
AEELNNQSTU	LANSQUENET	AEFLLSITUY	TASTEFULLY
AEELNNSSTT	TENANTLESS	AEFLLSTUWY	WASTEFULLY
AEELNOSSSS	SEASONLESS	AEFLMNNSSU	MANFULNESS
AEELNPRSST	PARENTLESS	AEFLNRSSTU	ARTFULNESS
AEELNPSTTY	PENTASTYLE	AEFOOPRRRT	PERFORATOR

AEFOOPRRTW	WATERPROOF	AEGILNRVWY	WAVERINGLY
AEFOQRRSUU	FOURSQUARE	AEGILNSSSS	GLASSINESS
AEGGGILNNY	ENGAGINGLY	AEGILOORST	AEROLOGIST
AEGGGINRSW	SWAGGERING	AEGILOPRTT	GRAPTOLITE
AEGGHIMOPS	GEOPHAGISM	AEGILORRSS	GRESSORIAL
AEGGHINSSS	SHAGGINESS	AEGILRRTUY	REGULARITY
AEGGIILMPR	PILGRIMAGE	AEGIMMNRST	STAMMERING
AEGGILOOSU	SIALOGOGUE	AEGIMNNSST	ASSIGNMENT
AEGGIMNRRS	GRANGERISM	AEGIMNOPRS	ANGIOSPERM
AEGGINORSS	AGGRESSION	AEGIMNRRST	RING-MASTER
AEGGIORRSU	GREGARIOUS	AEGIMNRSTT	SMATTERING
AEGGJNRTUU	JUGGERNAUT	AEGINNNPRT	TREPANNING
AEGGMOSTUY	MYSTAGOGUE	AEGINNRSTT	ASTRINGENT
AEGGNNOORY	ORGANOGENY	AEGINNRUVW	UNWAVERING
AEGGNNORSU	GANGRENOUS	AEGINOORTT	NEGOTIATOR
AEGHHILOPR	HELIOGRAPH	AEGINORSUU	AERUGINOUS
AEGHHMOPPT	APOPHTHEGM	AEGINPRSTY	PANEGYRIST
AEGHIKMNOS	SHOEMAKING	AEGINQRRTU	QUARTERING
AEGHILMNNS	ENGLISHMAN	AEGINRSSSS	GRASSINESS
AEGHILNOOT	THEOLOGIAN	AEGINRSSSU	SUGARINESS
AEGHIMMOPR	MIMEOGRAPH	AEGIRSSTTT	STRATEGIST
AEGHINPRRS	RANGERSHIP	AEGLLMRTUY	METALLURGY
AEGHINRSSS	GARISHNESS	AEGLMOPRTU	PROMULGATE
AEGHINRSTT	STRAIGHTEN	AEGLOORRST	ASTROLOGER
AEGHINSTUX	EXHAUSTING	AEGLOORTTY	TERATOLOGY
AEGHIRTTTW	WATERTIGHT	AEGLORRTUY	REGULATORY
AEGHLNOORS	ALONGSHORE	AEGLPRSSUU	SURPLUSAGE
AEGHMNOOPR	GRAMOPHONE	AEGMNOORST	GASTRONOME
AEGHMNOPRS	SPHENOGRAM	AEGNOOSTUU	AUTOGENOUS
AEGHNOOORR	GONORRHOEA	AEGNRRSSST	TRANSGRESS
AEGHNOPRST	STENOGRAPH	AEGNSSSTUU	AUGUSTNESS
AEGHOOPRRY	OREOGRAPHY	AEGOORSTUU	OUTRAGEOUS
AEGHOOPSSU	OESOPHAGUS	AEGOPRRTUX	EXPURGATOR
AEGHORRTUV	OVERRAUGHT	AEHHINOPRT	HIEROPHANT
AEGIIILNTV	INVIGILATE	AEHHMOOPTY	HOMEOPATHY
AEGIIILLTY	ILLEGALITY	AEHIINOSTT	HESITATION
AEGIILMNRT	TRIGEMINAL	AEHIINPPRS	SAPPHIRINE
AEGIILNOTV	LEVIGATION	AEHIINSSTT	ANTITHESIS
AEGIILNPRV	PREVAILING	AEHIIPPSTT	EPITAPHIST
AEGIIMNNOT	GEMINATION	AEHILLSTTY	STEALTHILY
AEGIIMNORT	EMIGRATION	AEHILMORST	ISOTHERMAL
AEGIIMNSTT	ENIGMATIST	AEHILRSTVY	SHRIEVALTY
AEGIIMSTTZ	STIGMATIZE	AEHIMMRSTU	RHEUMATISM
AEGIINORTV	INVIGORATE	AEHIMNOTUX	EXHUMATION
AEGIINPPST	APPETISING	AEHIMNRSSS	MARSHINESS
AEGIKLMMOR	KILOGRAMME	AEHIMNRSTV	RAVISHMENT
AEGIKLNNSY	SNEAKINGLY	AEHIMNSSTU	ENTHUSIASM
AEGILLNRTV	TRAVELLING	AEHIMPRSST	MASTERSHIP
AEGILLORST	ALLEGORIST	AEHIMPSSTY	SYMPATHISE
	LEGISLATOR	AEHINOSTUX	EXHAUSTION
AEGILMNORY	MINERALOGY	AEHINQRSUV	VANQUISHER
AEGILNNOOT	ELONGATION	AEHINRSSST	TRASHINESS
AEGILNNPSU	UNPLEASING	AEHINSSTTU	ENTHUSIAST
AEGILNNRYY	YEARNINGLY	AEHIOOPSST	APOTHEOSIS
AEGILNNSUY	SANGUINELY	AEHLLMRSSY	HARMLESSLY
AEGILNOOSU	OLEAGINOUS	AEHLLMSTUU	HAUSTELLUM
AEGILNORSU	LANIGEROUS	AEHLLOPRXY	PHYLLOXERA
AEGILNORTU	REGULATION	AEHLMOOSUX	HOMOSEXUAL
AEGILNOSTU	GELATINOUS	AEHLNNOPTT	PENTATHLON
AEGILNPRST	PLASTERING	AEHLPRSTUU	SULPHURATE
AEGILNRSTV	STARVELING	AEHMNORRTT	MATTERHORN

AEHMNPRSUU	SUPERHUMAN	AEILMNNSTT	INSTALMENT
AEHMOORSTX	MESOTHORAX	AEILMNOPRS	IMPERSONAL
AEHMORSTTT	THERMOSTAT	AEILMNOPRT	TRAMPOLINE
AEHNOPRTUY	NEUROPATHY	AEILMNORTU	TOURMALINE
AEHOOPPRST	APOSTROPHE	AEILMNPRTY	PLANIMETRY
AEHOOPSTTT	TOOTHPASTE	AEILMPPSST	PALIMPSEST
AEHOOPSTTY	OSTEOPATHY	AEILMPRSST	SLIPSTREAM
AEHOORSSTY	SOOTHSAYER	AEILMPRSSU	PLUMASSIER
AEHORRRSTW	RESTHARROW	AEILMRRSSU	SURREALISM
AEHPRSSTTY	STRATHSPEY	AEILNNNSTW	LAWN-TENNIS
AEIIIINTTV	INITIATIVE	AEILNNORTT	INTOLERANT
AEIIILMRST	MILITARISE	AEILNNPRSU	PENINSULAR
AEIIILRSTV	TRIVIALISE	AEILNNRRTU	INTERLUNAR
AEIIILLLMMS	MILLESIMAL	AEILNOORTT	TOLERATION
AEIIILLLMNN	MILLENNIAL	AEILNOPRTU	ERUPTIONAL
AEIIILLTVY	ILLATIVELY	AEILNORRTT	TORRENTIAL
AEIIILLMNTU	ILLUMINATE	AEILNORRTY	ANTERIORLY
AEIIILLMPRY	IMPERIALLY	AEILNORTTV	VENTILATOR
AEIIILLMRST	LITERALISM	AEILNOTTUX	EXULTATION
AEIIILLOTVZ	VOLATILIZE	AEILNPRSST	PALTRINESS
AEIIILLPSTT	PISTILLATE	AEILNRTTUY	NEUTRALITY
AEIIILLRRTT	TRILITERAL	AEILNSSSTU	SENSUALIST
AEIIILLRSTT	LITERALIST	AEILNSSTUY	SENSUALITY
AEIIILLRTTY	LITERALITY	AEILOOPTTZ	TOPAZOLITE
AEIIILMMMOR	IMMEMORIAL	AEILOPPRUZ	POPULARIZE
AEIIILMNORT	ELIMINATOR	AEILOPPSTY	APPOSITELY
AEIIILMNTTY	INTIMATELY	AEILOPTTVY	OPTATIVELY
AEIIILMRSVV	REVIVALSIM	AEILORSTTU	STAUROLITE
AEIIILNNORS	ROSANILINE	AEILPRSSUV	SUPERVISAL
AEIIILNNSTT	INTESTINAL	AEILRRSSTU	SURREALIST
AEIIILNOOTT	ETIOLATION	AEILSTTTUX	TEXTUALIST
AEIIILNOTTV	LEVITATION	AEIMMNNNOTT	ANOINTMENT
AEIIILNQTUY	INEQUALITY	AEIMNNORTU	NUMERATION
AEIIILORTTV	VITRIOLATE	AEIMNOPRTT	ARMIPOTENT
AEIIILRSTVV	REVIVALIST	AEIMNOPTTT	TEMPTATION
AEIIILRTTVY	RELATIVITY	AEIMNOQSUU	EQUANIMOUS
AEIIIMNNNOT	INNOMINATE	AEIMNOSSTU	STAMINEOUS
AEIIIMNNOTV	NOMINATIVE	AEIMNRRRTY	INTERMARRY
AEIIIMNOSTT	ESTIMATION	AEIMOPRRTU	PRAETORIUM
AEIIIMNQTUY	EQUANIMITY	AEIMPSSTUV	ASSUMPTIVE
AEIIIMOPRRS	IMPRESARIO	AEINNOORTV	RENOVATION
AEIIIMPRSTT	TEAM-SPIRIT	AEINNOPRSY	PENSIONARY
AEIIIMPTTUV	IMPUTATIVE	AEINNOQRTU	QUATERNION
AEIIINNOSST	ENANTIOSIS	AEINNORSTT	STENTORIAN
AEIIINNPRTT	TRIPINNATE	AEINNRSSUW	UNWARINESS
AEIIINOPRTX	EXPIRATION	AEINOPRRTZ	PATRONIZER
AEIIINOQTTU	EQUITATION	AEINOPRSSU	PERSUASION
AEIIINOTUVX	EXUVIATION	AEINOPRTTU	REPUTATION
AEIIINPSSST	INSPISSATE	AEINORRSTV	OVERSTRAIN
AEIIINQTTUV	QUANTITIVE	AEINORSTTY	STATIONERY
AEIIINRSTTV	TRANSITIVE	AEINPRRTTU	PARTURIENT
AEIIOPPSTV	APPOSITIVE	AEINRRSSST	STARRINESS
AEIIPRRTTT	TRIPARTITE	AEINRSTUYZ	SUZERAINTY
AEIJLNOSSV	JOVIALNESS	AEIOPRRRST	RESPIRATOR
AEIKLMNSTY	MISTAKENLY	AEIOPRRTTX	EXTIRPATOR
AEILLLSUVY	ALLUSIVELY	AEIOPRRTXY	EXPIRATORY
AEILLMTTUY	ULTIMATELY	AEJMNNORUY	JOURNEYMAN
AEILLNNRTY	INTERNALLY	AELLMORSUV	MARVELLOUS
AEILLRSTTU	ILLUSTRATE	AELLNOPRSY	PERSONALLY
AEILMMRTUY	IMMATURELY	AELLNORTTY	TOLERANTLY
AEILMNNOTY	NOMINATELY	AELLNOSSSW	SALLOWNESS

AELLNPTTUY	PETULANTLY
AELMMNNOTU	MONUMENTAL
AELMNNNRUY	UNMANNERLY
AELMNOOPRY	LAMPOONERY
AELMNORSSS	RANSOMLESS
AELMOOPRTU	TROPAEOLUM
AELMORRSSW	MARROWLESS
AELMORSSTU	SOMERSAULT
AELMRSSTTU	MULATTRESS
AELNNOPRYY	PENNYROYAL
AELNNORSTY	RESONANTLY
AELNOPRSTY	PERSONALTY
AELNORSUVY	RAVENOUSLY
AELNPPRSTU	SUPPLANTER
AELNPRRSUU	SUPERLUNAR
AELOPPRRRU	POURPARLER
AELORSSSUV	SAVOURLESS
AEMNNORTTU	TOURNAMENT
AEMNNRRSUY	NURSERYMAN
AEMNOORRST	ASTRONOMER
AEMNORSSTT	ASSORTMENT
AEMOPRSSTT	POSTMASTER
AENOOPRRST	PERSONATOR
AENOOPRTXY	PAROXYTONE
AENOORSSTU	TREASONOUS
AENOPRRSST	TRANSPOSER
AENOPRSTTT	PROTESTANT
AEOOQRRSTU	SQUARE-ROOT
AFFGINNORT	AFFRONTING
AFFGIRSSTU	SUFFRAGIST
AFFHIINRSU	RUFFIANISH
AFFHILLTUY	FAITHFULLY
AFFHILNTUU	UNFAITHFUL
AFFIIMNRSU	RUFFIANISM
AFGGGILNNU	UNFLAGGING
AFGGIINRTY	GRATIFYING
AFGHHILLST	FLASHLIGHT
AFGIILNQUY	QUALIFYING
AFGIILOSTU	FLAGITIOUS
AFGIIMNOTU	FUMIGATION
AFGIINORTU	FIGURATION
AFGIINSSTY	SATISFYING
AFGILNORUV	FLAVOURING
AFHKLLNTUY	THANKFULLY
AFHKLNNTUU	UNTHANKFUL
AFHLLRTUWY	WRATHFULLY
AFIILLRRTY	FRITILLARY
AFIILNORSU	INFUSORIAL
AFIILNORTT	FILTRATION
	FLIRTATION
AFIINNORSU	INFUSORIAN
AFIIORRSTU	TRIFARIOUS
AFILLMNORY	INFORMALLY
AFILLNPPTY	FLIPPANTLY
AFILMNOSUY	INFAMOUSLY
AFILNORUXY	FLUXIONARY
AFIMNOORSU	FORAMINOUS
AFIMORRSTT	STRATIFORM
AGGHIINNRS	GARNISHING
AGGHILLNUY	LAUGHINGLY
AGGHLOOPRY	GRAPHOLOGY
	LOGOGRAPHY
AGGLNOOORZ	GORGONZOLA
AGHHILOPRT	LITHOGRAPH
AGHHIOPPPY	HIPPOPHAGY
AGHHLOOPRY	HOLOGRAPHY
AGHHOOPPRT	PHOTOGRAPH
AGHHOOPRRY	HOROGRAPHY
AGHIILNORS	ANGLO-IRISH
AGHIINRTWW	WAINWRIGHT
AGHIKMRTTU	KHITMUTGAR
AGHILPRTWY	PLAYWRIGHT
AGHINNOSTW	WASHINGTON
AGHIOPPRRS	SPIROGRAPH
AGHLOPPRYY	POLYGRAPHY
AGHLOPRXYY	XYLOGRAPHY
AGHOOOPSUZ	ZOOPHAGOUS
AGHOOPPRTY	TOPOGRAPHY
AGHOPPRTYY	TYPOGRAPHY
AGHOPRSTUY	PYTHAGORUS
AGIIILNOTT	LITIGATION
AGIIIMNOTT	MITIGATION
AGIIINOORRT	IRRIGATION
AGIIINRRTT	IRRITATING
AGIILLNORY	ORIGINALLY
AGIILLNRTU	TRILINGUAL
AGIILLNTVY	VIGILANTLY
AGIILNPRSY	ASPIRINGLY
AGIILNRSTY	LARYNGITIS
AGIIMMOSST	MISOGAMIST
AGIIMSSTTT	STIGMATIST
AGIINNPRSU	UNASPIRING
AGIINOORRT	ORIGINATOR
AGIINORSTT	INSTIGATOR
AGILLLNRUY	ALLURINGLY
AGILLNNSTY	SLANTINGLY
AGILLNRSUY	SINGULARLY
AGILMOPSTY	POLYGAMIST
AGILNNOPTY	POIGNANTLY
AGILNNORTY	IGNORANTLY
AGILNNTTUY	TAUNTINGLY
AGILNNTUVY	VAUNTINGLY
AGILORSSST	GLOSSARIST
AGIMMNOOST	MONOGAMIST
AGIMNNSSUU	UNASSUMING
AGIMNOORST	AGRONOMIST
AGINPRSSSU	SURPASSING
AGIORSTTUU	GRATUITOUS
AGLLRTTUUY	GUTTURALLY
AGLMOOOSTY	SOMATOLOGY
AGLMOOPSUY	POLYGAMOUS
AGLNOORSUU	LANGUOROUS
AGMMNOOOSU	MONOGAMOUS
AGMNOORSTY	GASTRONOMY
AGOORRSSST	GRASS-ROOTS
AHHIOPRSTU	AUTHORSHIP
AHHLLOOOPT	HOLOPHOTAL
AHIIIJKNRS	JINRIKISHA
AHIIMNNOTU	INHUMATION
AHIIMNNTUY	INHUMANITY
AHIKKMNRSS	SKRIMSHANK
AHILMMORSU	HUMORALISM

AHILMNOSWY	WOMANISHLY	AIINNNOOTV	INNOVATION
AHILMORSTU	HUMORALIST	AIINNOPSTU	SUPINATION
AHILNOORTZ	HORIZONTAL	AIINNORSTT	TRANSITION
AHILNPPSSY	SNAPPISHLY	AIINNORSTU	INSINUATOR
AHILNPSSTU	SULTANSHIP	AIINOOPPST	APPOSITION
AHIMNOORRU	HONORARIUM	AIINORTTUY	TUITIONARY
AHIMNOORSU	HARMONIOUS	AIINORTTVY	INVITATORY
AHIMNPRTTU	TRIUMPHANT	AIJLMNORSU	JOURNALISM
AHLLOPRSTU	PROTHALLUS	AIJLNORSTU	JOURNALIST
AHLNOPSTUY	POLYANTHUS	AILLMNOOPY	POLYNOMIAL
AIIIINNOTT	INITIATION	AILLNOOPTY	OPTIONALLY
AIIILI MNTU	ILLUMINATI	AILLNQRTUY	TRANQUILLY
AIIILMMNST	MINIMALIST	AILMNNOOPR	PRONOMINAL
AIIILMMRST	MILITARISM	AILMORSTTU	STIMULATOR
AIIILMNOTT	LIMITATION	AILMORSTUY	SIMULATORY
AIIILMRSTT	MILITARIST	AILNOOPPTU	POPULATION
AIIILMRSTY	SIMILARITY	AILNOOPRSS	SPONSORIAL
AIIILRTTVY	TRIVIALITY	AILNORSTTU	LUSTRATION
AIIIMNNOTT	INTIMATION	AILNPSSTUY	PUISSANTLY
AIIIMNOPSS	PIANISSIMO	AILOPPRTUY	POPULARITY
AIIINNOOST	IONISATION	AILOPRSTTU	STIPULATOR
AIIINNOTTV	INVITATION	AIMMNNORSTU	STRAMONIUM
AIIINORRTT	IRRITATION	AIMMOORRTU	MORATORIUM
AIIINORTTY	INITIATORY	AIMNOPSSTU	ASSUMPTION
AIIINOSTTV	VISITATION	AIMNRSTTUU	NASTURTIUM
AIIINOTTTV	TITIVATION	AIMOOORTVY	OVARIOTOMY
AIIIPRSSTY	PITYRIASIS	AINOPRSTUU	USURPATION
AIIIPRTVVY	VIVIPARITY	AINORRSTTY	TRANSITORY
AIILLMNNTU	ILLUMINANT	AIOOPRRSUU	UPROARIOUS
AIILLNOOTV	VOLITIONAL	AIOORRSTTU	TRAITOROUS
AIILLNOSUV	VILLAINOUS	AIOPPPRSUU	PUPIPAROUS
AIILLORSTY	SOLITARILY	ALLOORSUVY	VALOROUSLY
AIILLOSSTT	SOLSTITIAL	ALMMNSSSUU	MUSSULMANS
AIILLOTTVY	VOLATILITY	ALMOOPPRST	PROTOPLASM
AIILLPRSTY	PISTILLARY	ALOOPPRSTT	PROTOPLAST
AIILMMNNOS	NOMINALISM	ALOPRTUUVY	VOLUPTUARY
AIILMMNOOT	IMMOLATION	AMNOOOSTUU	AUTONOMOUS
AIILMMORTY	IMMORALITY	AMNOOPRSUY	PARONYMOUS
AIILMNOORT	MONITORIAL	BBCEHINSSU	CHUBBINESS
AIILMNOSTU	SIMULATION	BBCEIRRSSU	SUBSCRIBER
AIILMNOTTU	MUTILATION	BBCHMRRSUU	CRUMB-BRUSH
AIILNNOOST	INSOLATION	BBDEIRRTTU	BUTTER-BIRD
AIILNNOSTU	INSULATION	BBEELLOTTU	BLUE-BOTTLE
AIILNOOPST	POSITIONAL	BBEELMOSSV	BOMB-VESSEL
	SPOLIATION	BBEEMMNNTU	BENUMBMENT
AIILNRSTUY	INSULARITY	BBEGIILOPY	BIBLIOPEGY
AIILPPRTUY	PUPILARITY	BBEHHILOST	SHIBBOLETH
AIILRTTTUY	TITULARITY	BBEIKLLORR	BILL-BROKER
AIIMMNNOTU	AMMUNITION	BBGHIINRSU	RUBBISHING
AIIMMRTTUY	IMMATURITY	BBGIILLOOY	BIBLIOLOGY
AIIMNNNOOT	NOMINATION	BBLNORSTUY	STUBBORNLY
AIIMNNORTU	RUMINATION	BCCDEEEMNU	DECUMBENCE
AIIMNNRSTT	MINISTRANT	BCCDEEMNUY	DECUMBENCY
AIIMNOOTTV	MOTIVATION	BCCEEENPSU	PUBESCENCE
AIIMNOPTTU	IMPUTATION	BCCEEINRTY	CYBERNETIC
AIIMNORSSY	MISSIONARY	BCCEEMNRUY	RECUMBENCY
AIIMNPRSTU	PURITANISM	BCCEHIIMRU	CHERUBIMIC
AIIMNPSTTY	TYMPANITIS	BCCEIMNNUY	INCUMBENCY
AIIMOPRSTT	PATRIOTISM	BCCHIINORT	BRONCHITIC
AIIMOSSTTT	STOMATITIS	BCCHLMORTU	CRUMB-CLOTH
AIINNNOOTT	INTONATION	BCDDEEILTU	DEDUCTIBLE

BCDDEIKLLU	DUCK-BILLED	BCEINOSSTU	SUBSECTION
BCDDHIISTU	BUDDHISTIC	BCEIOPRRRS	PROSCRIBER
BCDEEEEHMR	BÊCHE-DE-MER	BCEJKMPRUU	BUCK-JUMPER
BCDEEEIINT	BENEDICITE	BCELNRTUUY	TURBULENCY
BCDEEEELMRY	DECEMBERLY	BCEMNOPRTU	PROCUMBENT
BCDEEHORUU	DEBOUCHURE	BCENOORSSS	CROSS-BONES
BCDEEIILNR	INCREDIBLE	BCFIIMORRR	CRIBRIFORM
BCDEEINSSU	SUBSIDENCE	BCHIINORST	BRONCHITIS
BCDEEINSTU	BENEDICTUS	BCHIIOPSSY	BIOPHYSICS
BCDEEORRSS	CROSS-BREED	BCIKMOORST	BROOMSTICK
BCDEFLOOTU	CLUB-FOOTED	BCIMNOOSTU	COMBUSTION
BCDEHIRRRY	BIRD-CHERRY	BCINOSSSTU	CONSUBSIST
BCDEIILLNU	INCLUDIBLE	BCLMORSUUY	CUMBROUSLY
BCDEIILNRY	INCREDIBLY	BCOORRSTTU	OBSTRUCTOR
BCDEILOORR	CORRODIBLE	BDDDEELOOR	REDBLOODED
BCDEILOPRU	PRODUCIBLE	BDDDEELOUY	DOUBLE-DYED
BCDELORRUY	CLOUDBERRY	BDDEEEENRTU	DEBENTURED
BCDEMMNRUU	CUMMER-BUND	BDDEHLNOOR	BOND-HOLDER
BCDHHIILRT	CHILDBIRTH	BDDEIIPRRS	BIRD-SPIDER
BCDILLOTUU	CLOUD-BUILT	BDDFGIINOR	FORBIDDING
BCDINOSTUU	SUBDUCTION	BDDHLNOOOU	BLOOD-HOUND
BCDKORRUUW	BURROW-DUCK	BDEEEFILNS	DEFENSIBLE
BCDLOOORUY	BODY-COLOUR	BDEEEIILSV	DISBELIEVE
BCDLORSTUU	CLOUD-BURST	BDEEEEILNSS	EDIBLENESS
BCEEEFFILT	EFFECTIBLE	BDEEEILNTX	EXTENDIBLE
BCEEEFINNT	BENEFICENT	BDEEEINNRT	INTERBREED
BCEEEIILLNU	EBULLIENCE	BDEEEELRRRY	ELDER-BERRY
BCEEEELLMRU	CEREBELLUM	BDEEGIILST	DIGESTIBLE
BCEEENRSTU	ERUBESCENT	BDEEGIMOSU	DISEMBOGUE
BCEEFIINRT	TENEBRIFIC	BDEEGIORRV	OVERBRIDGE
BCEEFIKRTU	FIRE-BUCKET	BDEEHIMRSU	HUMBERSIDE
BCEEFILNOR	ENFORCIBLE	BDEEIILMOS	DEMOBILISE
BCEEFPRSTU	SUBPREFECT	BDEEIILNRR	BRIDLE-REIN
BCEEHIRTWY	BEWITCHERY	BDEEILMOSW	DISEMBOWEL
BCEEHKOOQU	CHEQUE-BOOK	BDEEILMRSS	DISSEMBLER
BCEEHMORUU	EMBOUCHURE	BDEEILNNOS	DISENNOBLE
BCEEIILPST	PLEBISCITE	BDEEILNOTY	OBEDIENTLY
BCEEIIRRST	CEREBRITIS	BDEEILORWZ	BOWDLERIZE
BCEEIJSTUV	SUBJECTIVE	BDEEIMMNOT	EMBODIMENT
BCEEILLNPU	BLUE-PENCIL	BDEEIMORRY	EMBROIDERY
BCEEILLNUY	EBULLIENCY	BDEELLNRUY	UNDERBELLY
BCEEILMOST	COMESTIBLE	BDEELNOSSU	DOUBLENESS
BCEEILNOTY	BY-ELECTION	BDEELOSTTY	BESOTTEDLY
BCEEIPSSSU	SUBSPECIES	BDEEMNNRUU	UNNUMBERED
BCEEJLOSST	OBJECTLESS	BDEEMNORSU	BURDENSOME
BCEELMRSSU	CUMBERLESS	BDEENORRUV	OVERBURDEN
BCEELNOTTU	CUTTLE-BONE	BDEENORSUV	UNOBSERVED
BCEELNRTUU	TURBULENCE	BDEFFIILSU	DIFFUSIBLE
BCEEMMORSU	CUMBERSOME	BDEFGINOOR	FOREBODING
BCEGHIINTW	BEWITCHING	BDEFGIOORT	FOOTBRIDGE
BCEGIILORR	CORRIGIBLE	BDEGIILLNV	DIVING-BELL
BCEGILMNOY	BECOMINGLY	BDEGIMOORR	BRIDEGROOM
BCEHIIMOST	BIOCHEMIST	BDEHINRSTU	DISBURTHEN
BCEHILOPRY	HYPERBOLIC	BDEHLOOORS	BLOOD-HORSE
BCEHKLOOSU	BLOCK-HOUSE	BDEHNRRSUU	UNDERBRUSH
BCEIIILNNV	INVINCIBLE		UNDERSHRUB
BCEIILMMOS	EMBOLISMIC	BDEIILMORS	DISEMBROIL
BCEIIMORST	BIOMETRICS	BDEIIRSTTU	DISTRIBUTE
BCEIJNOSTU	SUBJECTION	BDEIJNORSU	SUBJOINDER
BCEILNPSSU	PUBLICNESS	BDEILLOSSU	DISSOLUBLE
BCEINORTTU	CONTRIBUTE	BDEILLOTUX	BILLET-DOUX

BDEILNOOSS	BLOODINESS
BDEIMMOOSS	DISEMBOSOM
BDEIMNORSS	MORBIDNESS
BDEINRSSTU	TURBIDNESS
BDEKNNOORW	BROKEN-DOWN
BDELLNOPSU	SPELLBOUND
BDELMMNOUY	MOLYBDENUM
BDELMNOOOY	BLOOD-MONEY
BDELNOOOST	BLOOD-STONE
BDELNORTUU	UNTROUBLED
BDFLLOTUUY	DOUBTFULLY
BDGIKMNOSU	SUBKINGDOM
BDIIIILNST	LIBIDINIST
BDILLNPRUY	PURBLINDLY
BDNOOOTTUW	BUTTON-WOOD
BEEEEFLNSS	FEEBLENESS
BEEEEGIKNP	BEEKEEPING
BEEEEGINNR	BEER-ENGINE
BEEEEHLLVW	BEVEL-WHEEL
BEEEEMMRRR	REMEMBERER
BEEEFILLRX	REFLEXIBLE
BEEEFILRRR	REFERRIBLE
BEEEFOORRT	FREEBOOTER
BEEEGGINRR	GINGERBEER
BEEEGMOORS	EMBER-GOOSE
BEEEHLLRTW	BELL-WETHER
BEEEIILMSV	MISBELIEVE
BEEEILNSTX	EXTENSIBLE
BEEEILRRSV	REVERSIBLE
BEEEILRRTV	REVERTIBLE
BEEEKKOOPR	BOOK-KEEPER
BEEELLRSST	BESTSELLER
BEEELMNOTU	ÉBOULEMENT
BEEELNNOTV	BENEVOLENT
BEEELORTTT	BOTTLE-TREE
BEEEMNRTTT	BETTERMENT
BEEENORSTT	BONE-SETTER
BEEENRSSTT	BETTERNESS
BEEERRTTTU	BUTTER-TREE
BEEFGRSTUU	SUBTERFUGE
BEEFIIKNOW	BOWIE-KNIFE
BEEFIILLNX	INFLEXIBLE
BEEFIILNRR	INFERRIBLE
BEEFILLMRU	UMBELLIFER
BEEFIORSSU	SEBIFEROUS
BEEFLLLORW	BELL-FLOWER
BEEGGIILLN	NEGLIGIBLE
BEEGGLOORT	BOOTLEGGER
BEEGIIILLN	INELIGIBLE
BEEGIINOSS	BIOGENESIS
BEEGILLNRR	BELL-RINGER
BEEGILMNOT	OBLIGEMENT
BEEGILMNRS	RESEMBLING
BEEGMNORYY	EMBRYOGENY
BEEGNOORST	BRENT-GOOSE
BEEGOORRSY	GOOSEBERRY
BEEHIIITVX	EXHIBITIVE
BEEHILMOST	BLITHESOME
BEEHILNSST	BLITHENESS
BEEHIMMPRS	MEMBERSHIP
BEEHLMNSSU	HUMBLENESS
BEEIIJORTU	BIJOUTERIE
BEEIILMRSS	REMISSIBLE
BEEIILNNSS	INSENSIBLE
BEEIILNNTV	INVENTIBLE
BEEIILRSST	RESISTIBLE
BEEIILSSTX	BISSEXTILE
BEEIKKNORR	KNOBKERRIE
BEEIKLNPRS	BESPRINKLE
BEEILLORSU	REBELLIOUS
BEEILMNNSS	NIMBLENESS
BEEILNOSST	OSTENSIBLE
BEEINRSSTT	BITTERNESS
BEEIQRRSUU	BRUSQUERIE
BEEIRSSUVV	SUBVERSIVE
BEEKLLOORS	BOOKSELLER
BEEKNNORSS	BROKENNESS
BEELLOOSTY	OBSOLETELY
BEELLRRTTU	BELL-TURRET
BEELNOOSTT	BOTTLE-NOSE
BEELNSSSTU	SUBTLENESS
BEEMMNNOTT	ENTOMBMENT
BEEMMNOSST	EMBOSSMENT
BEEMNORSSS	SOMBRENESS
BEEMORSTTT	BETTERMOST
BEENOSSSTU	OBTUSENESS
BEENQSSTUU	SUBSEQUENT
BEEPRRSTYY	PRESBYTERY
BEFFNOORUY	BUFFOONERY
BEFHILLMTU	THIMBLEFUL
BEFHILOSTT	BOTTLE-FISH
BEFIILRSTU	FILIBUSTER
BEFINORSUU	NUBIFEROUS
BEFLLMRTUU	TUMBLERFUL
BEGHIILNRT	BLITHERING
BEGHIMORST	BRIGHTSOME
BEGHINRSST	BRIGHTNESS
BEGIIILLTY	LEGIBILITY
BEGIKLNRUY	REBUKINGLY
BEGILNRSTU	BLUSTERING
BEGLMOORYY	EMBRYOLOGY
BEGLMORUUX	LUXEMBOURG
BEGOORRTTT	BOG-TROTTER
BEHHIKRSSU	BUSH-SHRIKE
BEHIIINOTX	EXHIBITION
BEHIIORTXY	EXHIBITORY
BEHILPRSTU	BUTLERSHIP
BEHIMOPRUU	EUPHORBIUM
BEHINOSSSY	BOYISHNESS
BEHKNOORTU	BOOK-HUNTER
BEHLMOOPTY	PHLEBOTOMY
BEHLNOOTTU	BUTTON-HOLE
BEIIILMMOS	IMMOBILISE
BEIIIMNTUZ	BITUMINIZE
BEIILLNOTU	EBULLITION
BEIILMOPSS	IMPOSSIBLE
BEIILNNSSY	INSENSIBLY
BEIILRSTTT	LIBRETTIST
BEIIMSSSUV	SUBMISSIVE
BEIINORSTY	INSOBRIETY
BEIKLMRTTU	BUTTERMILK
BEILNOSSTY	OSTENSIBLY

BEILNOSTUY   NEBULOSITY
BEIMNNOOPT   EMBONPOINT
BEIMNORSSU   SUBMERSION
BEINNOSTUV   SUBVENTION
BEINORSSUV   SUBVERSION
BEINSSSTTU   SUBSISTENT
BEIOOQSSUU   OBSEQUIOUS
BEIOORSSTU   BOISTEROUS
BEIORSTTUY   TUBEROSITY
BEISSTTTUU   SUBSTITUTE
BELLOOSSTY   BOOTLESSLY
BELMOOSSTT   BOTTOMLESS
BELMORSSUU   SLUMBEROUS
BELORSSTUU   BLUSTEROUS
BEMMOORTYY   EMBRYOTOMY
BENORSSSTU   ROBUSTNESS
BEORRTTTUW   BUTTERWORT
BFIILLORSU   FIBRILLOUS
BFILLLSSUY   BLISSFULLY
BGGIILLNOY   OBLIGINGLY
BGGIINNPRU   UPBRINGING
BGGILLNNUY   BUNGLINGLY
BGHHIINRTT   BIRTHNIGHT
BGHHIIRRTT   BIRTHRIGHT
BGHILLNSUY   BLUSHINGLY
BGHILNNSUU   UNBLUSHING
BGIIILNSTU   BILINGUIST
BGIINORSUU   RUBIGINOUS
BGILLMMNUY   MUMBLINGLY
BGILORSUUU   LUGUBRIOUS
BHHOORSTTU   TOOTHBRUSH
BHIIIINNOT   INHIBITION
BHIIINORTY   INHIBITORY
BHIMOORSST   THROMBOSIS
BHKNOOOTTU   BUTTON-HOOK
BIIIILRSTY   RISIBILITY
BIIIILSTVY   VISIBILITY
BIIILMMOTY   IMMOBILITY
BIILLNOSTU   BULLIONIST
BIILLOSTUY   SOLUBILITY
BIILLOTUVY   VOLUBILITY
BIIMNOSSSU   SUBMISSION
BIIMNOSTUU   BITUMINOUS
BIIOQSTUUU   UBIQUITOUS
BIKLMNOOSU   BOOK-MUSLIN
BIMNOORSTT   TROMBONIST
BIMOOPPRRU   OPPROBRIUM
CCCEEINNOS   CONSCIENCE
CCCEEINRST   CRESCENTIC
CCCEELNSUU   SUCCULENCE
CCCEENORRU   OCCURRENCE
CCCEIIMRSU   CIRCUMCISE
CCCEINNORT   CONCENTRIC
CCCEIOOPRT   ECCOPROTIC
CCCEKLNOOR   CORN-COCKLE
CCCELNSUUY   SUCCULENCY
CCCILNSTUY   SUCCINCTLY
CCCINNOOOT   CONCOCTION
CCDDEEENOS   CONDESCEND
CCDEEEENPR   PRECEDENCE
CCDEEEFIIN   DEFICIENCE

CCDEEEHINS   DEHISCENCE
CCDEEENPRY   PRECEDENCY
CCDEEEENRST   CRESCENTED
    DECRESCENT
CCDEEEERRSU   RECRUDESCE
CCDEEFIINY   DEFICIENCY
CCDEEFINNO   CONFIDENCE
CCDEEGINSU   SUCCEEDING
CCDEEHNOSY   SYNECDOCHE
CCDEEHORTT   CROTCHETED
CCDEEIIIPT   EPIDEICTIC
CCDEELNNOO   CONDOLENCE
CCDEENRRUY   DECURRENCY
CCDEHILLOS   COLD-CHISEL
CCDEIILOPY   EPICYCLOID
CCDEIINNOT   COINCIDENT
CCDEIJKOSY   DISC-JOCKEY
CCDEINNOST   DISCONNECT
CCDEINORST   DISCONCERT
CCDEINOTUV   CONDUCTIVE
CCDEKMNOOY   COCKNEYDOM
CCDGILNNOU   CONCLUDING
CCDIMNOSTU   MISCONDUCT
CCDINNOOTU   CONDUCTION
CCEEEELLNX   EXCELLENCE
CCEEEFNNOR   CONFERENCE
CCEEEINPRS   PRESCIENCE
CCEEEINQSU   QUIESCENCE
CCEEELLNXY   EXCELLENCY
CCEEEMMNOR   RECOMMENCE
CCEEEMNOPT   COMPETENCE
CCEEENRRRU   RECURRENCE
CCEEENRSTX   EXCRESCENT
CCEEFFIINY   EFFICIENCY
CCEEFLNNOU   CONFLUENCE
CCEEGINNOR   CONGENERIC
CCEEGINORT   EGOCENTRIC
    GEOCENTRIC
CCEEGNNORU   CONGRUENCE
CCEEHHKOPU   CHEEK-POUCH
CCEEHIOPTU   TOUCH-PIECE
CCEEHNOSTU   ESCUTCHEON
CCEEIILMRS   SEMICIRCLE
CCEEIINPRY   RECIPIENCY
CCEEIIPSTZ   SCEPTICIZE
CCEEILLOTV   COLLECTIVE
CCEEILNORR   RECONCILER
CCEEILNORT   ELECTRONIC
CCEEILOPST   TELESCOPIC
CCEEILORVY   COERCIVELY
CCEEINNNOT   CONTINENCE
CCEEINNNOV   CONNIVENCE
CCEEINNOTV   CONNECTIVE
CCEEINNRST   INCRESCENT
CCEEINOSSV   CONCESSIVE
CCEEINOTVV   CONVECTIVE
CCEEIORRTV   CORRECTIVE
CCEEISSSUV   SUCCESSIVE
CCEEJNORTU   CONJECTURE
CCEELMORTY   CYCLOMETER
CCEELNOPRU   CORPULENCE

CCEELNORTY	CONCRETELY	CCIKOOPSTU	CUCKOO-SPIT
CCEELNRTUU	TRUCULENCE	CCILLNOORU	COUNCILLOR
CCEENOPRRT	PRECONCERT	CCILMRRUUU	CURRICULUM
CCEFIIINST	SCIENTIFIC	CCILNNOOSU	CONCLUSION
CCEFILMRUX	CIRCUMFLEX	CCIMOOPRSY	MICROSCOPY
CCEFILNOTU	CONCEITFUL	CCINNOOSSU	CONCUSSION
CCEFIMRSUU	CIRCUMFUSE	CCINOSSSUU	SUCCUSSION
CCEFINNOOT	CONFECTION	CCIORRSSSS	CRISS-CROSS
CCEFLLNOTU	FLOCCULENT	CCJLNNOTUY	CONJUNCTLY
CCEFLSSSUU	SUCCESSFUL	CCLLOOORTU	COLLOCUTOR
CCEGHHORRU	CHURCH-GOER	CDDEEEFFNNP	DEPENDENCE
CCEGILLNOT	COLLECTING	CDDEEEEJLTY	DEJECTEDLY
CCEGIINNNOR	CONCERNING	CDDEEEENNPY	DEPENDENCY
CCEHHLRSSU	CHURCH-LESS	CDDEEEENNST	DESCENDENT
CCEHIKNOPX	CHICKEN-POX	CDDEEFFIIN	DIFFIDENCE
CCEHIKNOSY	COCKNEYISH	CDDEEGINNS	DESCENDING
CCEHILNORR	CHRONICLER	CDDEEIINSS	DISSIDENCE
CCEHILOPRR	PERCHLORIC	CDDEENNOSU	UNSECONDED
CCEHILORVW	COW-CHERVIL	CDDEENORRU	UNRECORDED
CCEHIMOSSY	ECCHYMOSIS	CDDEFNNOOU	CONFOUNDED
CCEIIINNRT	ENCRINITIC	CDDEIMMNOS	DISCOMMEND
CCEIILOSST	SOLECISTIC	CDDEMNOOPU	DECOMPOUND
CCEIIMPSST	SCEPTICISM	CDDIILNORY	CYLINDROID
CCEIINRTTY	CENTRICITY	CDDILNSUUU	DIDUNCULUS
CCEIKKOPPT	PICKPOCKET	CDDILOOPSU	DIPLODOCUS
CCEIKMNOSY	COCKNEYISM	CDEEEEGNRT	DETERGENCE
CCEILLNOOT	COLLECTION	CDEEEEINPX	EXPEDIENCE
CCEILNOSUV	CONCLUSIVE	CDEEEFFINR	DIFFERENCE
CCEIMMRRUU	CIRCUMMURE	CDEEEFHIKR	KERCHIEFED
CCEIMNRTUV	CIRCUMVENT	CDEEEFILST	SELF-DECEIT
CCEIMOOPRS	MICROSCOPE	CDEEEGINRV	DIVERGENCE
CCEINNNOOT	CONNECTION	CDEEEGNRTY	DETERGENCY
CCEINNOOPT	CONCEPTION	CDEEEILOPV	VELOCIPEDE
CCEINNOORT	CONCRETION	CDEEEILQSU	DELIQUESCE
CCEINNOOSS	CONCESSION	CDEEEIMNNO	COMÉDIENNE
CCEINNOOTV	CONVECTION	CDEEEINPXY	EXPEDIENCY
CCEINOORRT	CORRECTION	CDEEEMNSTU	SEDUCEMENT
CCEINOSSSU	SUCCESSION	CDEEENPTUX	UNEXPECTED
CCEINOSSUV	CONCUSSIVE	CDEEENTUUX	UNEXECUTED
CCEIOOPRSU	PRECOCIOUS	CDEEFIINRT	DENTIFRICE
CCEISSSUUV	SUCCUSSIVE	CDEEFILNOT	DEFLECTION
CCEKORRTTU	CORK-CUTTER	CDEEGILNNU	INDULGENCE
CCELNOSSTU	OCCULTNESS	CDEEGINOPR	PROCEEDING
CCELNRTUUY	TRUCULENCY	CDEEGINRVY	DIVERGENCY
CCENNORRTU	CONCURRENT	CDEEHIMNOR	ECHINODERM
CCENOPSSTU	CONSPECTUS	CDEEHLRTWY	WRETCHEDLY
CCEOORRRTY	CORRECTORY	CDEEHMNOPR	COMPREHEND
CCGHLNOOOY	CONCHOLOGY	CDEEIIINSV	INDECISIVE
CCGIILOOOS	SOCIOLOGIC	CDEEIILSVY	DECISIVELY
CCGIINNNOV	CONVINCING	CDEEIIMNTY	ENDEMICITY
CCHHHOOPTT	HOTCHPOTCH	CDEEIINOPW	COWDIE-PINE
CCHIIMNNOS	CINCHONISM	CDEEIINRST	INDISCREET
CCHIKOPSST	CHOPSTICKS		IRIDESCENT
CCHIOOOPRS	HOROSCOPIC	CDEEIIPRTV	PREDICTIVE
CCIIILOSST	SCIOLISTIC	CDEEIIRSSV	DISSERVICE
CCIILMOPTY	COMPLICITY	CDEEIIRSTV	DISCRETIVE
CCIILOOPRT	COPROLITIC	CDEEIKNSSW	WICKEDNESS
CCIIMOSSTT	SCOTTICISM	CDEEILNNOS	DECLENSION
CCIINNNOTY	CONCINNITY	CDEEILNNSU	UNLICENSED
CCIINNOOTV	CONVICTION	CDEEILNNTY	INDECENTLY
CCIIORSTUU	CIRCUITOUS	CDEEILOORZ	DECOLORIZE

CDEEILORST	CLOISTERED
CDEEILRSTY	DISCREETLY
CDEEIMNNNTU	INDUCEMENT
CDEEIMNPRU	IMPRUDENCE
CDEEINNOSS	DESCENSION
CDEEINNRSW	WINDSCREEN
CDEEINOPRV	PROVIDENCE
CDEEINORRS	RECONSIDER
CDEEINPRSY	PRESIDENCY
CDEEINRSST	DIRECTNESS
CDEEINRSTY	DYSENTERIC
CDEEIORRSV	DISCOVERER
	REDISCOVER
CDEEIPRSST	DISRESPECT
CDEEIRRSST	DIRECTRESS
CDEEKOOPRW	WOODPECKER
CDEEMOPRSS	COMPRESSED
	DECOMPRESS
CDEENOOSTT	COTTON-SEED
CDEENORRUV	UNDERCOVER
CDEEENOSTUU	CONSUETUDE
CDEENRSSSU	CURSEDNESS
CDEEOPRRRU	REPRODUCER
CDEERSSSTU	SEDUCTRESS
CDEFINNNOU	UNCONFINED
CDEFINOORV	CONFERVOID
CDEFLNOSUY	CONFUSEDLY
CDEGIINNRS	DISCERNING
CDEGIINSST	DISSECTING
CDEGMNORUU	CURMUDGEON
CDEHIIISTT	DITHEISTIC
CDEHIILOPS	DISCOPHILE
CDEHIILORZ	CHLORIDIZE
CDEHIMNRSU	UNSMIRCHED
CDEHIMOPRY	HYPODERMIC
CDEHIOOPRT	ORTHOPEDIC
CDEHIOORSU	ORCHIDIOUS
CDEHLNOORY	CHLORODYNE
CDEHLNOOSU	UNSCHOOLED
CDEHLOOPPR	CLODHOPPER
CDEHLOOPRY	COPYHOLDER
CDEHNOOORT	OCTOHEDRON
CDEIIILNNS	DISINCLINE
CDEIIILNPS	DISCIPLINE
CDEIIINNOS	INDECISION
CDEIIINTVV	VINDICTIVE
CDEIILNPPR	PRINCIPLED
CDEIILNRTY	INDIRECTLY
CDEIILOSTU	SOLICITUDE
CDEIIMNNTT	INDICTMENT
CDEIIMORTY	MEDIOCRITY
CDEIINOPRT	PREDICTION
CDEIINORST	DISCRETION
CDEIINOSST	DISSECTION
CDEIINSTTU	DISCUTIENT
CDEIIOORRS	SORORICIDE
CDEIIRSSUV	DISCURSIVE
CDEIISSSUV	DISCUSSIVE
CDEILNNOSU	UNINCLOSED
CDEILNOSSU	CLOUDINESS
CDEILOPRTU	PRODUCTILE

CDEILORSSU	DISCLOSURE
CDEIMMNOPU	COMPENDIUM
CDEIMNOOST	ENDOSMOTIC
CDEIMNOSUU	MUCEDINOUS
CDEIMOOPSS	DISCOMPOSE
CDEINNOSTT	DISCONTENT
CDEINOORSU	INDECOROUS
CDEINORRTU	INTRODUCER
CDEINORSTU	DISCOUNTER
CDEIOPRTUV	PRODUCTIVE
CDEIORRSSU	DISCOURSER
CDELMNOSUY	CONSUMEDLY
CDELMOOPSY	COMPOSEDLY
CDELNOORUU	UNCOLOURED
CDELNOOTUV	CONVOLUTED
CDELOORSUY	DECOROUSLY
CDELPRSTUU	SCULPTURED
CDEMNOOPRU	COMPOUNDER
CDENOOPRRS	CORRESPOND
CDEOORTTUW	WOODCUTTER
CDEORRSSTU	COURT-DRESS
CDERRSTTUU	STRUCTURED
CDFFIILTUY	DIFFICULTY
CDFIMOORST	DISCOMFORT
CDHHIILLSY	CHILDISHLY
CDHHIOORST	CHRISTHOOD
CDHIIOSSTU	DISTICHOUS
CDHINOOOSU	COUSINHOOD
CDHIOOPRST	DOCTORSHIP
CDIIILNOTY	INDOCILITY
CDIIINNSTT	INDISTINCT
CDIILNSTTY	DISTINCTLY
CDIILORSUU	RIDICULOUS
CDIINOSSSU	DISCUSSION
CDILMOOORX	LOXODROMIC
CDIMMOOOSU	COMMODIOUS
CDINOOPRTU	PRODUCTION
CDNOOOOTTW	COTTON-WOOD
CDOORRSTUW	COURT-SWORD
CEEEEFFRSV	EFFERVESCE
CEEEEFNPRR	PREFERENCE
CEEEEHNPRT	THREEPENCE
CEEEEINPRX	EXPERIENCE
CEEEEIRSVY	EYE-SERVICE
CEEEELLNPR	REPELLENCE
CEEEELNORT	ENTEROCELE
CEEEENRRRV	REVERENCER
CEEEFFGLNU	EFFULGENCE
CEEEFFLORS	EFFLORESCE
CEEEFFLSST	EFFECTLESS
CEEEFGLNRU	REFULGENCE
CEEEFILRTV	REFLECTIVE
CEEEFINRRS	FIRE-SCREEN
CEEEFINRSS	FIERCENESS
CEEEFPRRTU	PREFECTURE
CEEEGGILNN	NEGLIGENCE
CEEEGIINPT	EPIGENETIC
CEEEGINRTV	VICEREGENT
CEEEGNRRSU	RESURGENCE
CEEEHIMSTT	CHEMISETTE
CEEEHINPTT	EPENTHETIC

CEEEHINRSS	CHEERINESS	CEEIILLMRV	VERMICELLI
CEEEHINSSS	CHEESINESS	CEEIILNRSY	RESILIENCY
CEEEHLPSSS	SPEECHLESS	CEEIILNRTT	CENTILITRE
CEEEHNORSS	CHERSONESE	CEEIILRTTY	ERECTILITY
CEEEHORRST	THREESCORE	CEEIIMNNTT	INCITEMENT
CEEEIILNRS	RESILIENCE	CEEIIMOSST	SEMEIOTICS
CEEEILNPST	PESTILENCE	CEEIINOPRW	COWRIE-PINE
CEEEIMNNTT	ENTICEMENT	CEEIINPPRT	PERCIPIENT
CEEEIMNRST	MESENTERIC	CEEIIORRST	ESCRITOIRE
CEEEIMNRTT	CENTIMETRE	CEEIJLOPRT	PROJECTILE
CEEEIMNTTX	EXCITEMENT	CEEILLNRST	STENCILLER
CEEEINNPRT	PERTINENCE	CEEILMNOPT	INCOMPLETE
CEEEIPPRTV	PERCEPTIVE	CEEILMNORT	CLINOMETER
CEEEIPRSTV	RESPECTIVE	CEEILMNOSS	COMELINESS
CEEELLNPRY	REPELLENCY	CEEILMOPTV	COMPLETIVE
CEEELNRSSV	CLEVERNESS	CEEILNORST	ENCLOISTER
CEEELNSSST	SELECTNESS	CEEILNQSTU	LIQUESCENT
CEEEMNOPRS	RECOMPENSE	CEEILNRSUY	INSECURELY
CEEENNRSST	RECENTNESS	CEEILNRTUV	VENTRICULE
CEEENRSSST	SECRETNESS	CEEILORRST	CLOISTERER
CEEENRSSSU	SECURENESS	CEEILOSSUV	VESICULOSE
CEEFFILLMO	COFFEE-MILL	CEEILPRSUV	PRECLUSIVE
CEEFFMOOOR	COFFEE-ROOM	CEEIMMORRT	MICROMETER
CEEFGILNRT	REFLECTING	CEEIMNNOPR	PROMINENCE
CEEFGINRTU	CENTRIFUGE	CEEINNNOTV	CONVENIENT
CEEFGLLNTU	NEGLECTFUL	CEEINNPSST	SPINESCENT
CEEFGLNRUY	REFULGENCY	CEEINOPPRT	PERCEPTION
CEEFHHNORT	HENCEFORTH	CEEINOPRSS	PRECESSION
CEEFHLLRUY	CHEERFULLY	CEEINOPRTX	EXCERPTION
CEEFHNOORS	FORECHOSEN	CEEINORRSW	CORNERWISE
CEEFHORTTU	FOURCHETTE	CEEINORSTV	VENTRICOSE
CEEFIILNTV	INFLECTIVE	CEEINORTTY	COETERNITY
CEEFIKLNSS	FICKLENESS	CEEINOSTTX	COEXISTENT
CEEFILNORT	REFLECTION	CEEINPRTTU	PERCUTIENT
CEEFILRTTU	FILE-CUTTER	CEEINRRSTU	SCRUTINEER
CEEFINOPRT	PERFECTION	CEEINRSTTV	VITRESCENT
CEEFKLORTT	FETTERLOCK	CEEIOPRTTV	PROTECTIVE
CEEFLPPRTU	PLUPERFECT	CEEIPRSSUV	PERCUSSIVE
CEEFLPRSTU	RESPECTFUL	CEEIPSSTUV	SUSCEPTIVE
CEEGINNRSS	SCREENINGS	CEEKLLRSSY	RECKLESSLY
CEEGINNRST	NIGRESCENT	CEELLMOPTY	COMPLETELY
CEEGINNSTY	SYNGENETIC	CEELMMNOPT	COMPLEMENT
CEEGINOSTV	CONGESTIVE	CEELMNNOOS	SOMNOLENCE
CEEGINPRST	RESPECTING	CEELNORSVY	CONVERSELY
CEEGNNORTV	CONVERGENT	CEELORRSTY	CLERESTORY
CEEGNPRSUU	UPSURGENCE	CEEMNNSTTY	ENCYSTMENT
CEEGNRSTTU	TURGESCENT	CEEMNOPRTU	RECOUPMENT
CEEHHKOOTT	CHEEK-TOOTH	CEEMNPSSTU	SPUMESCENT
CEEHIIRSTT	ERETHISTIC	CEENNOQSTU	CONSEQUENT
CEEHILNOPR	NECROPHILE	CEENNORRTU	RENCOUNTER
CEEHILOPRT	HELICOPTER	CEENNOSSVX	CONVEXNESS
CEEHILOSVY	COHESIVELY	CEENOORTTT	COTTON-TREE
CEEHIMNNRT	ENRICHMENT	CEENOQRSTU	RECONQUEST
CEEHIMOPTU	MOUTHPIECE	CEENORTTUX	CONTEXTURE
CEEHINNORT	INCOHERENT	CEENPRRRTU	PERCURRENT
CEEHINSSTT	TETCHINESS	CEENPRSSSU	SPRUCENESS
CEEHLMORTY	EMERY-CLOTH	CEENPRSTTU	PUTRESCENT
CEEHLNORTY	COHERENTLY	CEEOPRRSTT	RETROSPECT
CEEHLNORWW	CROWN-WHEEL	CEFFHIINOR	CHIFFONIER
CEEHLNQSSU	QUENCHLESS	CEFFIINSTU	SUFFICIENT
CEEIIINTZZ	CITIZENIZE	CEFFIOOPST	POST-OFFICE

CEFFLLORUY	FORCEFULLY	CEHIMOPRTY	MICROPHYTE
CEFGLOORSU	GOLF-COURSE	CEHIMORSTT	THERMOTICS
CEFHILSTTU	CUTTLE-FISH	CEHINNNPPY	PINCHPENNY
CEFIIILNTV	INFLICTIVE	CEHINNRSTY	STRYCHNINE
CEFIIILNTY	INFELICITY	CEHINOOPRS	RHINOSCOPE
CEFIILNNOT	INFLECTION	CEHINOORRS	RHINOCEROS
CEFIILNOQU	CINQUE-FOIL	CEHINOPRSS	CENSORSHIP
CEFIILOSTU	FELICITOUS	CEHINOPRSY	HYPERSONIC
CEFIINOPRT	PROFICIENT	CEHINOPTTY	ENTOPHYTIC
CEFIINOSTU	INFECTIOUS	CEHINOSSTU	TOUCHINESS
CEFILLMRUY	MERCIFULLY	CEHIOORRRT	RETROCHOIR
CEFILMNRUU	UNMERCIFUL	CEHIOPRRST	RECTORSHIP
CEFILMOORS	FROLICSOME	CEHIOQSTTU	COQUETTISH
CEFINNOOSS	CONFESSION	CEHLMOOPRY	POLYCHROME
CEFINOORSU	CONIFEROUS	CEHLMOORST	SCHOOL-TERM
CEFINORSUU	NUCIFEROUS	CEHMMNOOOR	MONOCHROME
CEFIOORSUV	VOCIFEROUS	CEHMMOOORS	CHROMOSOME
CEFLNOORRW	CORN-FLOWER	CEHNOOSTTU	TOUCHSTONE
CEFLOORRWW	CROW-FLOWER	CEHNOPRTYY	PYROTECHNY
CEGGIILNNR	CRINGELING	CEHOORSTUU	COURTHOUSE
CEGGINOOST	GEOGNOSTIC	CEHORSTTTU	OUTSTRETCH
CEGHIIKNNT	THICKENING	CEIIILLNNP	PENICILLIN
CEGHIILLNS	CHISELLING	CEIIILOPST	POLITICISE
CEGHILNOOT	ETHNOLOGIC	CEIIIMMPRS	EMPIRICISM
CEGHINOOPT	PHOTOGENIC	CEIIKLNSSS	SICKLINESS
CEGHINOPTY	PYTHOGENIC	CEIIKNRSST	TRICKINESS
CEGHINORRU	CHIRURGEON	CEIIKNSSST	STICKINESS
CEGHLNOOTY	TECHNOLOGY	CEIILLPTXY	EXPLICITLY
CEGIIKNNQU	QUICKENING	CEIILNOSTU	LICENTIOUS
CEGIILNNTY	ENTICINGLY	CEIIMMORSS	MICROSEISM
CEGIILNPRY	PIERCINGLY	CEIIMMNNOST	OMNISCIENT
CEGIILOPTT	EPIGLOTTIC	CEIIMORSST	ISOMETRICS
CEGIILOSTU	EULOGISTIC	CEIIMORSTT	COTTIERISM
CEGIINNTUX	UNEXCITING	CEIINNOPST	INSPECTION
CEGIINRRTU	RECRUITING	CEIINNOTTX	EXTINCTION
CEGILLOOXY	LEXICOLOGY	CEIINOPRSU	PERNICIOUS
CEGILNNOST	CLINGSTONE	CEIINORSSS	RESCISSION
CEGILNOTVY	COVETINGLY	CEIINORSTT	TRISECTION
CEGIMNOORS	ERGONOMICS	CEIINPSSTU	SUSCIPIENT
CEGINNNOTT	CONTINGENT	CEIINRSSTU	SINECURIST
CEGINNOOST	CONGESTION	CEIINRSTUY	INSECURITY
CEGINNOQRU	CONQUERING	CEIINRSTUZ	SCRUTINIZE
CEGINNORST	CONSTRINGE	CEIIORSTVV	VIVISECTOR
CEGINNRSTY	STRINGENCY	CEIJNOOPRT	PROJECTION
CEHHHIIKRT	HITCH-HIKER	CEIKLNNOST	CLINK-STONE
CEHHIILMNT	HELMINTHIC	CEILLOOQUZ	COLLOQUIZE
CEHHIOOPST	THEOSOPHIC	CEILMMNNOPT	COMPLIMENT
CEHHKLLOSS	SHELLSHOCK	CEILMNOOPT	COMPLETION
CEHIIKLRST	CHRISTLIKE	CEILMNOOPX	COMPLEXION
CEHIILLNSS	CHILLINESS	CEILMNSSSU	CLUMSINESS
CEHIILMOST	HOMILETICS	CEILMOOOTV	LOCOMOTIVE
CEHIILNPST	CLIENTSHIP	CEILMOPSUV	COMPULSIVE
CEHIILPSST	ECTHLIPSIS	CEILMOPTXY	COMPLEXITY
CEHIINOPSV	NOVICESHIP	CEILMORTUV	VOLUMETRIC
CEHIINPSST	PITCHINESS	CEILMOSTUU	METICULOUS
CEHIIPRSTY	SPHERICITY	CEILNNNOTY	INNOCENTLY
CEHIIPSTUU	EUPHUISTIC	CEILNNOSVY	INSOLVENCY
CEHILORSTY	CHRYSOLITE	CEILNOOPRS	NECROPOLIS
CEHILRSSST	CHRISTLESS	CEILNOPRSU	PRECLUSION
CEHIMNOOPR	MICROPHONE	CEILNORTTY	CONTRITELY
CEHIMNOPTY	CHIMNEY-TOP	CEILNOSSST	COSTLINESS

CEILNOSTUV	CONSULTIVE	CFGIMNOORT	COMFORTING
CEILNOSUVV	CONVULSIVE	CFHLMOOOORR	CHLOROFORM
CEILOPRSUY	PRECIOUSLY	CFIIILNNOT	INFLICTION
CEILOPSSUY	SPECIOUSLY	CFIIINOSTT	FICTIONIST
CEIMMMNOTT	COMMITMENT	CFIIIOSTTU	FICTITIOUS
CEIMMNOQUU	COMMUNIQUE	CFIIRSTTUU	FUTURISTIC
CEIMMNORTY	METRONYMIC	CFILMOOPRU	POCULIFORM
CEIMMOOPRS	COMPROMISE	CFILMOORTY	COTYLIFORM
CEIMMORRTY	MICROMETRY	CFIMNOORST	CONFORMIST
CEIMMORSSU	COMMISSURE	CFIMNOORTY	CONFORMITY
CEIMMORTUX	COMMIXTURE	CFLLNORSUY	SCORNFULLY
CEIMNOOOSU	MONOECIOUS	CFLLOOSSUU	FLOSCULOUS
CEIMNOPRSU	PROSCENIUM	CFLOORSSUU	SCROFULOUS
CEIMNORSUU	CERUMINOUS	CGHIILLOOT	LITHOLOGIC
CEIMNPRSSS	SCRIMPNESS	CGHIILOPST	PHLOGISTIC
CEIMNRSSTY	SYNCRETISM	CGHIKLNOSY	SHOCKINGLY
CEIMOOPRTT	COMPETITOR	CGHILLOORS	SCHOOLGIRL
CEIMOPRRTY	PYROMETRIC	CGHILMOOTY	MYTHOLOGIC
CEINNNOOTT	CONTENTION	CGHILNOTUY	TOUCHINGLY
CEINNNOOTV	CONVENTION	CGHILORRSU	CHORUS-GIRL
CEINNOORSV	CONVERSION	CGHIMNOORY	CHIROGNOMY
CEINNOSSTT	CONSISTENT	CGHLNOOORY	CHRONOLOGY
CEINOOPRTT	PROTECTION	CGHLOOPSYY	PSYCHOLOGY
CEINOORSSU	CENSORIOUS	CGIIILNSTU	LINGUISTIC
CEINOPRSSU	PERCUSSION	CGIIILPSTU	PUGILISTIC
	SUPERSONIC	CGIIKLLNOR	ROLLICKING
CEINOPRSTT	INTROSPECT	CGIIKNNOPR	CORKING-PIN
CEINOPRSTU	SUPERTONIC	CGIIMNOSST	GNOSTICISM
CEINOQRRTU	QUERCITRON	CGIINOTTUY	CONTIGUITY
CEINORRSST	INTERCROSS	CGILLNOSWY	SCOWLINGLY
CEINORSTUV	VENTRICOUS	CGILMOOSTY	MYCOLOGIST
CEINOSSTUU	INCESTUOUS	CGILMOOSUY	MUSICOLOGY
CEINOSTTTU	CONSTITUTE	CGILNNOSTU	CONSULTING
CEINRSSSTT	STRICTNESS	CGILOOOTXY	TOXICOLOGY
CEINRSSSTU	CRUSTINESS	CGINOOSTUU	CONTIGUOUS
CEINRSSSUV	SCURVINESS	CGLOOPRTYY	CRYPTOLOGY
CEIOOPRRTY	CORPOREITY	CHHILLRSUY	CHURLISHLY
CEIOPRRTTX	PROTECTRIX	CHHIOOPPRS	PHOSPHORIC
CEIOPRRTUV	CORRUPTIVE	CHHLLOOPRY	CHLOROPHYL
CEIPPRSTTY	TYPESCRIPT	CHIIILLNST	NIHILISTIC
CEKLLLSSUY	LUCKLESSLY	CHIIILPSTY	SYPHILITIC
CEKLMPRSUU	LUMPSUCKER	CHIIINORST	HISTRIONIC
CELLLNTUUY	LUCULENTLY	CHIIKLLSTY	TICKLISHLY
CELLNOORRT	CONTROLLER	CHIILMNOOT	MONOLITHIC
CELLNOORSU	COUNSELLOR	CHIIMOPRRT	TRIMORPHIC
CELLOOOSST	CLOSE-STOOL	CHIIMORSTU	HUMORISTIC
CELLOORSSU	COLOURLESS	CHIINOPRSX	CRIO-SPHINX
CELMOOPRTY	COMPLETORY	CHIINOPSSU	COUSINSHIP
CELOOPRRTU	COLPORTEUR	CHIINORSTU	UNHISTORIC
CELOOSTUVY	COVETOUSLY	CHILLNOSWY	CLOWNISHLY
CEMMNNOOSS	COMMONNESS	CHILNOPSSU	CONSULSHIP
CEMOOPRRSS	COMPRESSOR	CHIMOOOPRZ	ZOOMORPHIC
CENOORRTTV	CONTROVERT	CHIMOORTTY	TRICHOTOMY
CENOORSSST	CROSS-STONE	CHLMOOOORS	SCHOOLROOM
CEOOPRRSTU	PROSECUTOR	CHLMOOPRYY	POLYCHROMY
CEOPPRSSTU	PROSPECTUS	CHIMMNOOORY	MONOCHROMY
CEOPRRRSUY	PRECURSORY	CHOOPRRSUY	CRYOPHORUS
CFFIISSTU	FISTICUFFS	CIIILLMPTY	IMPLICITLY
CFFGIIIORR	FRIGORIFIC	CIIILMNRTU	TRICLINIUM
CFFGIILNOSY	SCOFFINGLY	CIIILMPSST	SIMPLISTIC
CFGILOSUUU	LUCIFUGOUS	CIIILMPSTY	SIMPLICITY

CIIIMOPSTT	OPTIMISTIC	DDEIIIPRST	DISPIRITED
CIIJNNNOTU	INJUNCTION	DDEIIJNOST	DISJOINTED
CIILOPRTVY	PROCLIVITY	DDEIIMMNOU	DIMINUENDO
CIILRRSTUY	SCURRILITY	DDEILLNPSY	SPLENDIDLY
CIIMMNOOSS	COMMISSION	DDEILLTTUW	DULL-WITTED
CIINNOORTT	CONTRITION	DDEILORRSY	DISORDERLY
CIINNOTTUY	CONTINUITY	DDEINOPRUV	UNPROVIDED
CIIOORSTUV	VICTORIOUS	DDEINOPSSU	UNDISPOSED
CIIOPSSSUU	SUSPICIOUS	DDEINORSSS	SORDIDNESS
CIJLNNOOTY	CONJOINTLY	DDEINPSTUU	UNDISPUTED
CILLOOQSTU	COLLOQUIST	DDELNORRUW	UNDERWORLD
CILLOPRSTU	PORTCULLIS	DDENRSTUUY	UNDERSTUDY
CILLOSSUUY	LUSCIOUSLY	DDGGILNRUY	DRUDGINGLY
CILMNOOOOT	LOCOMOTION	DDGHIINOOR	RIDING-HOOD
CILMNOOPSU	COMPULSION	DDGILLNOPY	PLODDINGLY
CILMNORUUV	INVOLUCRUM	DDHINOOPTY	DIPHYODONT
CILNNOOSUV	CONVULSION	DDINOOOPRT	DIPROTODON
CILORRSSUU	SCURRILOUS	DEEEEEFPRZ	DEEP-FREEZE
CIMNNOOOPP	NINCOMPOOP	DEEEFHLORR	FREEHOLDER
CIMOOOPRST	COMPOSITOR	DEEEFILMNT	DEFILEMENT
CINNOOOORTT	CONTORTION	DEEEFLORRW	DEFLOWERER
CINNOOSTUU	CONTINUOUS	DEEEFMNRRU	REFERENDUM
CINOOPRRTU	CORRUPTION	DEEEFNRTTU	UNFETTERED
CINOOPRSUY	URINOSCOPY	DEEEGIRRST	REGISTERED
CINOORSSTY	CONSISTORY	DEEEGNNRUV	UNREVENGED
CINORRSTTU	INSTRUCTOR	DEEEHLLSSY	HEEDLESSLY
CINORSSTUU	SCRUTINOUS	DEEEHNRRTU	THEREUNDER
CINOSTTUUY	UNCTUOSITY	DEEEIKLLRW	WEEDKILLER
CIOPPRSSTT	POST-SCRIPT	DEEEILLMOS	DEMOISELLE
CLMMNNOOUY	UNCOMMONLY	DEEEILMRSS	REMEDILESS
CLMNOOOSUU	MONOCULOUS	DEEEILNRUV	UNRELIEVED
CLMOOPRSUY	COMPULSORY	DEEEILRRVY	REDELIVERY
CLNOOOOTTW	COTTON-WOOL	DEEEIMNOTZ	DEMONETIZE
CLNOORSTUY	CONSULTORY	DEEEIMNRST	DENSIMETER
CLOOOPRRTU	PROLOCUTOR	DEEEIMORTU	EUDIOMETER
CLOPRSSUUU	SCRUPULOUS	DEEEIMRSSY	MERSEYSIDE
DDDEEEFNNU	UNDEFENDED	DEEEINNPTV	PENDENTIVE
DDDEEFIOST	EISTEDDFOD	DEEEINPRST	PREDESTINE
DDDEEIORRS	DISORDERED	DEEEINPSSS	SPEEDINESS
DDDEFILOOW	FIDDLE-WOOD	DEEEINRRST	RESIDENTER
DDEEEEMNRU	UNREDEEMED	DEEEINRSTT	INTERESTED
DDEEEIMNRT	DETERMINED	DEEEIPRSSV	DEPRESSIVE
DDEEELMMOS	MEDDLESOME	DEEEIRRSSV	REDRESSIVE
DDEEELRSVY	DESERVEDLY	DEEEKLNORW	NEEDLEWORK
DDEEENRRTU	UNDETERRED	DEEEKOOPRR	DOOR-KEEPER
DDEEFLMORY	DEFORMEDLY	DEEELNRTTU	UNLETTERED
DDEEGGNOSS	DOGGEDNESS	DEEELRRSVY	RESERVEDLY
DDEEGILNSY	DESIGNEDLY	DEEEMNNOTU	DÉNOUEMENT
DDEEHINNSS	HIDDENNESS	DEEEMNPRTU	UNTEMPERED
DDEEILLNRT	TENDRILLED	DEEEMNRSSU	DEMURENESS
DDEEIMNNOP	OPEN-MINDED	DEEENNPRTU	UNREPENTED
DDEEIOORRZ	DEODORIZER	DEEENNRSST	TENDERNESS
DDEEIRSSST	DISTRESSED	DEEENRRSUV	UNRESERVED
DDEENNOPST	DESPONDENT	DEEFGGILLN	FLEDGELING
DDEENNSSSU	SUDDENNESS	DEEFGHINRT	FRIGHTENED
DDEFIMNORR	DENDRIFORM	DEEFIIINNT	INDEFINITE
DDEGHINRSU	SHUDDERING	DEEFIIINTV	DEFINITIVE
DDEGIILNRY	DERIDINGLY	DEEFIILNTY	DEFINITELY
DDEGLNOORY	DENDROLOGY	DEEFILMOSU	FIELD-MOUSE
DDEGNNORUU	UNGROUNDED	DEEFILNRSS	FRIENDLESS
DDEHIILNSW	WINDSHIELD	DEEFILPSTU	DESPITEFUL

DEEFINRSSV	FERVIDNESS	DEFGIILNYY	EDIFYINGLY
DEEFMNORRU	UNREFORMED	DEFGIINNUY	UNEDIFYING
DEEGGNRSSU	RUGGEDNESS	DEFGNOORRU	FOREGROUND
DEEGIINNRT	INGREDIENT	DEFHIINNSU	UNFINISHED
DEEGIIRSSV	DIGRESSIVE	DEFHIINPRS	FRIENDSHIP
DEEGINPRSS	DEPRESSING	DEFIIILMPS	SIMPLIFIED
DEEGNNOOSU	ENDOGENOUS	DEFIIILNTY	INFIDELITY
DEEGNNORUV	UNGOVERNED	DEFIIINNOT	DEFINITION
DEEHHIMNOR	HEMIHEDRON	DEFIIINNTU	INFINITUDE
DEEHILLSSS	SHIELDLESS	DEFIIOPRSU	PERFIDIOUS
DEEHILOOTT	THEODOLITE	DEFILNNRUY	UNFRIENDLY
DEEHMURRTY	HYDROMETER	DEFILNORSS	FLORIDNESS
DEEHNRSSSW	SHREWDNESS	DEGGMNOOOR	DEMOGORGON
DEEHOORTXY	HETERODOXY	DEGHINNRTU	THUNDERING
DEEIILNSTT	DISENTITLE	DEGHINRSST	NIGHTDRESS
DEEIILRSVY	DERISIVELY	DEGIIKNNS	DIE-SINKING
DEEIIMMNPT	IMPEDIMENT	DEGIILLNTY	DILIGENTLY
DEEIIMNNRT	DINNER-TIME	DEGIILNNUY	UNYIELDING
DEEIIMNNTT	INDITEMENT	DEGIILNORS	SOLDIERING
DEEIINNRTT	TRIDENTINE	DEGIILOOST	IDEOLOGIST
DEEIINNSSV	DIVINENESS	DEGIINNOSU	INDIGENOUS
DEEIINOPTX	EXPEDITION	DEGIINNPSS	DISPENSING
DEEIINQTUU	INQUIETUDE	DEGIINNSST	DISSENTING
DEEIINSSTV	DISTENSIVE	DEGIINORSS	DIGRESSION
DEEIIPRSSV	DISPERSIVE	DEGILNNRUY	ENDURINGLY
DEEIILLSUVY	DELUSIVELY	DEGILNOOSS	GOODLINESS
DEEILMNRTW	WILDERMENT	DEGINNORSU	RESOUNDING
DEEILNNQTU	DELINQUENT	DEGINRSSTU	TURGIDNESS
DEEILNNRSS	DINNERLESS	DEGLMNOOOY	DEMONOLOGY
DEEILNRSSW	WILDERNESS	DEGLNOOOTY	DEONTOLOGY
DEEIMMNOSU	EUDEMONISM	DEGLNORSSU	GROUNDLESS
DEEIMNOOTV	MONTEVIDEO	DEGLOORTTY	TROGLODYTE
DEEIMNOPRT	REDEMPTION	DEHHILORTW	WITHHOLDER
DEEIMNORRZ	MODERNIZER	DEHHMOOORT	MOTHERHOOD
DEEIMNOSTU	EUDEMONIST	DEHHOPRTYY	HYDROPHYTE
DEEIMNSTTV	DIVESTMENT	DEHIIINRST	DISINHERIT
DEEINNNOSU	INNUENDOES	DEHIIKLLOO	LIKELIHOOD
DEEINOPRSS	DEPRESSION	DEHIILLOOV	LIVELIHOOD
DEEINPRRST	RINDERPEST	DEHIILLSVY	DEVILISHLY
DEEINQRTUU	UNREQUITED	DEHIILMNPU	DELPHINIUM
DEEINRRTUW	UNDERWRITE	DEHIIOPRST	EDITORSHIP
DEEINRSSTU	UNRESISTED	DEHILNOPSU	UNPOLISHED
DEEIOPPRRT	PROPERTIED	DEHIMNOSSS	MODISHNESS
DEEKLMRTTU	KETTLEDRUM	DEHIMOOPPR	HIPPODROME
DEELMNOPTY	DEPLOYMENT	DEHINNORRU	DINNER-HOUR
DEELMNOPUY	UNEMPLOYED	DEHINNPSUU	UNPUNISHED
DEELMNOSTU	UNMOLESTED	DEHINOSSTY	DISHONESTY
DEELNOPRUX	UNEXPLORED	DEHIOOPRST	PRIESTHOOD
DEELNORSUV	UNRESOLVED	DEHIOOQRSU	SQUIREHOOD
DEELNOSTUU	EDENTULOUS	DEHIOORSST	SISTERHOOD
DEEMNNORSS	MODERNNESS	DEHLNOOPRY	POLYHEDRON
DEEMNNORTW	WONDERMENT	DEHNNOORUU	UNHONOURED
DEEMNOPRTT	DEPORTMENT	DEHNOORRSU	HORRENDOUS
DEEMNORSTU	TREMENDOUS	DEHNORSTUU	THUNDEROUS
DEEMOORRST	DROSOMETER	DEIIILMSTU	SIMILITUDE
DEENNOPRST	RESPONDENT	DEIIILNSST	DISSILIENT
DEENOORSST	ROOTEDNESS	DEIIIMNTUV	DIMINUTIVE
DEENORRSTU	UNRESTORED	DEIIIMSSSV	DISMISSIVE
DEENORSUVZ	RENDEZVOUS	DEIIKLNNSS	KINDLINESS
DEFGHILLTU	DELIGHTFUL	DEIIILNUWY	UNWIELDILY
DEFGIILNRR	GIRLFRIEND	DEIILLRSTY	DISTILLERY

DEIILMNOOT	DEMOLITION	DHINOOPSWW	SHOP-WINDOW
DEIILNPRTY	INTREPIDLY	DHNOOORTUX	UNORTHODOX
DEIILPRSTY	SPIRITEDLY	DIIIINPSTY	INSIPIDITY
DEIINNOSSS	DISSENSION	DIIIMNNOTU	DIMINUTION
DEIINNOSTT	DISTENTION	DIIIMNOSSS	DISMISSION
DEIINNPRSU	UNINSPIRED	DIIMORSSSY	DISMISSORY
DEIINNSSTU	UNTIDINESS	DIINOORSTT	DISTORTION
DEIINOOPST	DEPOSITION	DIINOPRSTU	DISRUPTION
DEIINOPRSS	DISPERSION	DILORSSTUU	STRIDULOUS
DEIIORSTTV	DISTORTIVE	DILOSSTUUY	STUDIOUSLY
DEIIPRSTUV	DISRUPTIVE	DLLOOORSUY	DOLOROUSLY
DEIIPSSSTU	SPISSITUDE	DLNOORSUWY	WONDROUSLY
DEIKNNNSSU	UNKINDNESS	EEEEGIPSSX	EPEXEGESIS
DEILLNORSS	LORDLINESS	EEEEHLLOTY	EYELET-HOLE
DEILMMOSTY	IMMODESTLY	EEEEHRRVWY	EVERYWHERE
DEILMNOSSU	MOULDINESS	EEEEKMRRSY	KERSEYMERE
DEILMNPTUY	IMPUDENTLY	EEEELLSSSV	SLEEVELESS
DEILNOOTUV	DEVOLUTION	EEEENNRSSS	SERENENESS
DEILNOSSST	STOLIDNESS	EEEEENRSTVY	YESTEREVEN
DEILNOSSTV	DISSOLVENT	EEEFGIINNR	FIRE-ENGINE
DEIMNNOSTW	DISOWNMENT	EEEEFGLNRUV	REVENGEFUL
DEIMNOOSSS	ENDOSMOSIS	EEEFIMNNRT	REFINEMENT
DEIMNOPRUV	UNIMPROVED	EEEFLLORRT	FORETELLER
DEINNNORTU	TRUNNIONED	EEEFLRSSTT	FETTERLESS
DEINOOSSSU	ODIOUSNESS	EEEFMNPRRT	PREFERMENT
DEINOPRSST	TORPIDNESS	EEEFNNORSU	UNFORESEEN
DEINORRSST	TORRIDNESS	EEEFNQRRTU	FREQUENTER
DEINORSSSS	DROSSINESS	EEEGHHINTT	EIGHTEENTH
DEINORSSSW	DROWSINESS	EEEGHIMNOT	EIGHTEENMO
DEINPSSSTU	STUPIDNESS	EEEGIINPSS	EPIGENESIS
DEINRSSSTU	STURDINESS	EEEGINNSTW	SWEETENING
DEIOPSSSSS	DISPOSSESS	EEEGIRRSSV	REGRESSIVE
DEKKNOORWY	DONKEY-WORK	EEEGLMNRTY	EMERGENTLY
DEKNOOPRUV	UNPROVOKED	EEEGLNNSST	GENTLENESS
DELLLOPTUY	POLLUTEDLY	EEEHHIMPRS	HEMISPHERE
DELLNOPTUU	UNPOLLUTED	EEEHHORRTW	OTHERWHERE
DELLOSSUUY	SEDULOUSLY	EEEEHILNPRS	PREHENSILE
DELNNOPSSU	NONPLUSSED	EEEHIMMRSU	EUHEMERISM
DELNNOTUWY	UNWONTEDLY	EEEHIMPRST	EPHEMERIST
DENOPSSTUU	STUPENDOUS	EEEHINNNTT	NINETEENTH
DFFIIMORTY	DIFFORMITY	EEEHINPSST	EPENTHESIS
DFGHIINORS	FISHING-ROD	EEEHINSTTV	SEVENTIETH
DFGHILLOOT	FLOODLIGHT	EEEHKOPPRS	SHOPKEEPER
DFGIIIMORT	DIGITIFORM	EEEHLMNTVY	VEHEMENTLY
DFGILSSTUU	DISGUSTFUL	EEEHLMSSTV	THEMSELVES
DFHIINRSSU	DISFURNISH	EEEHMPRRTY	HYPERMETER
DFINOPRTUY	PROFUNDITY	EEEHNNPRTY	THREEPENNY
DFNOOOPRSU	SOUNDPROOF	EEEHNORSVW	WHENSOEVER
DGGGILNRUY	GRUDGINGLY	EEEIIPRTTV	REPETITIVE
DGGGINNRUU	UNGRUDGING	EEEILMNRTV	REVILEMENT
DGGIINSSTU	DISGUSTING	EEEILMNSSS	SEEMLINESS
DGHHIKNOOT	KNIGHTHOOD	EEEILMPRTX	PLEXIMETER
DGHLNOORST	STRONGHOLD	EEEILNSSST	SLEETINESS
DGIIIMORTU	DIGITORIUM	EEEIMMRRSZ	MESMERIZER
DGIIMNNOOR	DINING-ROOM	EEEIMNNPRT	PRE-EMINENT
DGILLNORSU	GROUNDSILL	EEEIMNNORTZ	REMONETIZE
DGILNOOPRY	DROOPINGLY	EEEIMNPRTX	EXPERIMENT
DGKNOORRUW	GROUNDWORK	EEEIMNRRTT	RETIREMENT
DGLNOOOOTY	ODONTOLOGY	EEEIMOPRTZ	PIEZOMETER
DHIIMMOPRS	DIMORPHISM	EEEINNRSST	ENTIRENESS
DHIMOOPRSU	DIMORPHOUS	EEEINPRRST	ENTERPRISE

EEEINPRSTV	PRESENTIVE
	VESPERTINE
EEEINPRTVV	PREVENTIVE
EEEINRRRTV	IRREVERENT
EEEINRSSTW	WESTERNISE
EEEINSSTWY	EYE-WITNESS
EEEIOPRRRT	REPERTOIRE
EEEIPRRSSV	REPRESSIVE
EEEIPRRSVV	PERVERSIVE
EEEIPRSSVX	EXPRESSIVE
EEELLNRSST	RELENTLESS
EEELLORTTV	LOVE-LETTER
EEELLPRSSY	PEERLESSLY
EEELMMOSTT	METTLESOME
EEELMNNRTT	RELENTMENT
EEELMNOTVV	EVOLVEMENT
EEELMNSTTT	SETTLEMENT
EEEMNNRSTT	RESENTMENT
EEEMNORSST	REMOTENESS
EEENNNSSUV	UNEVENNESS
EEENPRSSTX	EXPERTNESS
EEEOOPRSVX	OVEREXPOSE
EEEOPRSTTY	STEREOTYPE
EEEOPRTTUV	ÉPROUVETTE
EEFFGINORR	FOREFINGER
EEFFILSUVY	EFFUSIVELY
EEFFIMNNTT	INFEFTMENT
EEFFIORRTU	FORFEITURE
EEFFLORSST	EFFORTLESS
EEFFNORRTY	EFFRONTERY
EEFGHINRRS	REFRESHING
EEFGINNRRT	REFRINGENT
EEFGKLLNOT	GENTLEFOLK
EEFGLLMNOR	FELLMONGER
EEFGLLNUVY	VENGEFULLY
EEFHILLORW	FELLOW-HEIR
EEFHILNSSS	FLESHINESS
EEFHILRSVY	FEVERISHLY
EEFHIMORRT	ETHERIFORM
EEFHNORTTU	FOURTEENTH
EEFIILMNNY	FEMININELY
EEFIILRRTZ	FERTILIZER
EEFIIMNNNU	UNFEMININE
EEFIINNSST	FINITENESS
EEFIKNNOPS	FINE-SPOKEN
EEFILLLSSY	LIFELESSLY
EEFILLNOTU	FEUILLETON
EEFILNNORT	FLORENTINE
EEFIMNOSTT	OFTENTIMES
EEFINNQRTU	INFREQUENT
EEFIRRSSTU	FRUITERESS
EEFLMORRSU	REMORSEFUL
EEFLNNTUUV	UNEVENTFUL
EEFLNOSSUW	WOEFULNESS
EEFLNQRTUY	FREQUENTLY
EEFLNRSSUU	RUEFULNESS
EEFLNSSSUU	USEFULNESS
EEFNNORRRU	FORERUNNER
EEGGISSTUV	SUGGESTIVE
EEGHILOOTZ	THEOLOGIZE
EEGHIMNOOS	HOMOGENISE

EEGHINPRST	REGENTSHIP
EEGHINRTVY	EVERYTHING
EEGHIORTVW	OVERWEIGHT
EEGHMORRTY	HYGROMETER
EEGHNNRSTT	STRENGTHEN
EEGIIILMTZ	LEGITIMIZE
EEGIIKLPRS	KRIEGSPIEL
EEGIILNRVV	EVERLIVING
EEGIILOPUZ	EPILOGUIZE
EEGILMOOSY	SEMEIOLOGY
EEGILNNRGY	SNEERINGLY
EEGILNPPRX	PERPLEXING
EEGILNPSWY	SWEEPINGLY
EEGIMNNOTT	MIGNONETTE
EEGIMNNTTU	INTEGUMENT
EEGIMNOORT	GONIOMETER
EEGINORRSS	REGRESSION
EEGINORSTY	GENEROSITY
EEGINPRRST	PERSTRINGE
EEGLNORSUY	GENEROUSLY
EEGLNOSSTU	TONGUELESS
EEGMNNORSW	NEWSMONGER
EEGMNNORTV	GOVERNMENT
EEGNNORSUU	UNGENEROUS
EEGOPRSTUU	PORTUGUESE
EEGORRRSST	RETROGRESS
EEHHIMNOST	HENOTHEISM
EEHHINRTTT	THIRTEENTH
EEHHOOPRST	THEOSOPHER
EEHIILMPTU	EPITHELIUM
EEHIILNOPR	PERIHELION
EEHILLPRST	TELLERSHIP
EEHILMNOSS	HOMELINESS
EEHILNNRTY	INHERENTLY
EEHILNORTT	ENTEROLITH
EEHILOOPRT	HELIOTROPE
EEHILOSTTU	SILHOUETTE
EEHIMNPRST	RESHIPMENT
EEHINNORTZ	ENTHRONIZE
EEHINSSSTY	SYNTHESISE
EEHKNOORTT	TENTERHOOK
EEHLLOPSSY	HOPELESSLY
EEHLMORSST	MOTHERLESS
EEHLNORSST	THRONELESS
EEHMNNNOOP	PHENOMENON
EEHMNOOPRT	PHONOMETER
EEHMNOPRTY	HYMENOPTER
EEHMNORSTT	NETHERMOST
EEHMOOPRTT	PHOTOMETER
EEHMOPRSTT	STEPMOTHER
EEHMOPRSTY	HYPSOMETER
EEHNNORRRT	NORTHERNER
EEHNOPSTUY	HYPOTENUSE
EEHNORRSTU	SOUTHERNER
EEHOORSSTU	STOREHOUSE
EEIIKLLNSS	LIKELINESS
EEIIKLNPRW	PERIWINKLE
EEIIKLPRST	PRIESTLIKE
EEIILLNSSV	LIVELINESS
EEIILMNSST	TIMELINESS
EEIILNOSTV	TELEVISION

EEIILOPSTZ	EPISTOLIZE	EEIPRRSSSU	PRESSURISE
EEIILRRSTZ	STERILIZER	EEIPRRSTVY	PERVERSITY
EEIIMNNPTT	IMPENITENT	EEIPRRTTWY	TYPEWRITER
EEIIMOPRTZ	EPITOMIZER	EELLMNOOSY	LONESOMELY
EEIIMPRSSV	IMPRESSIVE	EELLNNSSSU	SULLENNESS
	PERMISSIVE	EELLNOQTUY	ELOQUENTLY
EEIINOPRTT	PETITIONER	EELLNOSSWY	YELLOWNESS
	REPETITION	EELLORSTUY	RESOLUTELY
EEIIOPSTVX	EXPOSITIVE	EELLRSSSTU	LUSTRELESS
EEIIPQRSTU	PERQUISITE		RESULTLESS
EEIIPRSSTV	PERSISTIVE	EELLRSSSTY	RESTLESSLY
EEIJMNNNOT	ENJOINMENT	EELMMNOPTY	EMPLOYMENT
EEILLMMORT	IMMORTELLE	EELMNPPSTU	SUPPLEMENT
EEILLNNOSS	LONELINESS	EELMNPTUZZ	PUZZLEMENT
EEILLNOSSV	LOVELINESS	EELMOPRSTU	PULSOMETER
EEILLNSSTT	LITTLENESS	EELMSSSSTY	SYSTEMLESS
EEILMNNSTT	ENLISTMENT	EELNOPRSTW	SPLEENWORT
EEILMNORSZ	SOLEMNIZER	EELNPPSSSU	SUPPLENESS
EEILMORSTY	TIRESOMELY	EELORSSUVY	YOURSELVES
EEILNNOQTU	INELOQUENT	EELPPRSSSU	SUPPERLESS
EEILNNSSST	SILENTNESS	EEMNOORSSS	MOROSENESS
EEILNOPRRT	INTERLOPER	EEMNOORTTY	ENTEROTOMY
EEILNOPSST	POLITENESS	EEMNORRSTY	YESTERMORN
EEILORRSTU	IRRESOLUTE	EEMOPPRRTY	PEREMPTORY
EEILORRTXY	EXTERIORLY	EEMPRSSSST	SEMPSTRESS
EEILORSVWY	OVERWISELY	EENNORSSTT	ROTTENNESS
EEILPPRTXY	PERPLEXITY	EENOPPRRSS	PROPERNESS
EEILPRRUVZ	PULVERIZER	EENORRRTUV	OVERTURNER
EEILRSSSST	SISTERLESS	EEOPPPRSSU	PRESUPPOSE
EEILRSSTUV	VIRTUELESS	EFFGIINNST	STIFFENING
EEIMMMRSTU	SUMMERTIME	EFFILLMNTU	FULFILMENT
EEIMMRSTYZ	SYMMETRIZE	EFFILNSSTU	FITFULNESS
EEIMNNORST	MINESTRONE	EFFINSSSTU	STUFFINESS
EEIMNNSSTU	MINUTENESS	EFGGHINRTU	GUNFIGHTER
EEIMNNSTTV	INVESTMENT	EFGHIIKNRS	KINGFISHER
EEIMNOPRTU	PERITONEUM	EFGHILLSST	FLIGHTLESS
EEIMNORTZZ	INTERMEZZO	EFGHIMNORS	FISHMONGER
EEIMNPPPRT	PEPPERMINT	EFGIILTUVY	FUGITIVELY
EEIMNRSSSS	REMISSNESS	EFGIINPRSY	PRESIGNIFY
EEIMOOPRST	OPSIOMETER	EFGIINRRTY	TERRIFYING
EEIMOPRRST	SPIROMETER	EFGILNORST	FOSTERLING
EEIMOPRRTZ	TEMPORIZER	EFGIMNOPRR	PERFORMING
EEIMOPRSTU	PERIOSTEUM	EFGINNORUV	UNFORGIVEN
EEIMPRSTUV	RESUMPTIVE	EFGINOPRST	FINGER-POST
EEINNOPRST	PRETENSION	EFGINPRTUY	PUTREFYING
EEINNOPRTV	PREVENTION	EFHIILNSST	FILTHINESS
EEINNPRTTU	TURPENTINE	EFHILLOPSW	FELLOWSHIP
EEINNRSSTV	INVENTRESS	EFHILRSSTT	THRIFTLESS
EEINOPRRSS	REPRESSION	EFHINORSST	FROTHINESS
EEINOPRRSV	PERVERSION	EFIIIINNTV	INFINITIVE
EEINOPRSSV	RESPONSIVE	EFIIILNNTY	INFINITELY
EEINOPRSSX	EXPRESSION	EFIIIMMNNS	FEMININISM
EEINOOQRSTU	QUESTIONER	EFIIIMNNTY	FEMININITY
EEINPRSSTT	PERSISTENT	EFIIKNRSSS	FRISKINESS
	PRETTINESS	EFIILNSSST	FLINTINESS
EEINPSSSSUV	SUSPENSIVE	EFIILNORRY	INFERIORLY
EEIOPPRSSV	OPPRESSIVE	EFIILNORSU	FLUORINISE
EEIOPRSTTT	OPERETTIST	EFIILOPRSU	PILIFEROUS
EEIOPSSSSV	POSSESSIVE	EFIILRSTTU	STULTIFIER
EEIPPRTTUY	PERPETUITY	EFIKLMNSUY	FLUNKEYISM
EEIPQRRRUU	PERRUQUIER	EFILLMORST	STELLIFORM

EFILLNSSUW	WILFULNESS	EGIMOOPRST	GEOTROPISM
EFILNNSSSU	SINFULNESS	EGINNOPSSS	SPONGINESS
EFIMNOORSU	OMNIFEROUS	EGINNRSUVW	UNSWERVING
EFIMNORSTU	MISFORTUNE	EGINNSSTTU	SUNSETTING
EFIMOOPRSU	POMIFEROUS	EGINOOPRRT	PROGENITOR
EFINOOPRSS	PROFESSION	EGINORRSTU	TROUSERING
EFINORSSST	FROSTINESS	EGLMNOOOTY	ENTOMOLOGY
EFIOORSSSU	OSSIFEROUS	EGLNOOPSUY	POLYGENOUS
EFJLNOSSUY	JOYFULNESS	EGMMNOPRSY	GYMNOSPERM
EFLLOPRUWY	POWERFULLY	EHHIILSTVY	THIEVISHLY
EFLMOOOORTY	TOMFOOLERY	EHHILMOSTY	XYLOTHEISM
EFLOPPRSUU	PURPOSEFUL	EHHILOOPPS	PHILOSOPHE
EFOOPRRSTU	FOUR-POSTER	EHHILOPTTY	LITHOPHYTE
EGGGINORSS	GROGGINESS	EHHILORTWW	WORTHWHILE
EGGHIINNUW	UNWEIGHING	EHHILRSSWY	SHREWISHLY
EGGIILMMNR	GLIMMERING	EHHIMORSTT	HITHERMOST
EGGILLNORV	GROVELLING	EHHIOPSSTY	HYPOTHESIS
EGGINNOOOR	GORGONEION	EHHNOOOPPT	PHOTOPHONE
EGGINNORSS	ENGROSSING	EHIIILNPST	PHILISTINE
EGGINOSSTU	SUGGESTION	EHIIINRRTX	INHERITRIX
EGGLOOPTYY	EGYPTOLOGY	EHIILNQRSU	RELINQUISH
EGGLOORSUY	GORGEOUSLY	EHIIMOPRSV	IMPOVERISH
EGHHILOSTU	LIGHTHOUSE	EHIIPQRSSU	SQUIRESHIP
EGHIIMNPRW	WHIMPERING	EHIIPRRSTW	WRITERSHIP
EGHIIMNSST	MIGHTINESS	EHILLNRSSS	SHRILLNESS
EGHIINNPSS	ENSIGNSHIP	EHILMNSSSU	MULISHNESS
EGHIINPRSW	WHISPERING	EHILMOPSTY	POLYTHEISM
EGHIINSTUX	EXTINGUISH	EHILNNOSSU	UNHOLINESS
EGHILNSSST	SLIGHTNESS	EHILOPSTTY	POLYTHEIST
EGHINOOSTT	THEOGONIST	EHIMMNOOST	MONOTHEISM
EGHLNOOPRY	PHRENOLOGY	EHIMMOPSTU	IMPOSTHUME
EGHMNOOOSU	HOMOGENOUS	EHIMNNPSTU	PUNISHMENT
EGHOORRTVW	OVERGROWTH	EHIMNOOSTT	MONOTHEIST
EGIIILNORR	IRRELIGION	EHIMNOPSSS	MOPISHNESS
EGIIKLNNSS	KINGLINESS	EHINOOPSUU	EUPHONIOUS
EGIILLNNSV	SNIVELLING	EHINOPRTYZ	HYPNOTIZER
EGIILLNOTU	GUILLOTINE	EHINORSSTW	WORTHINESS
EGIILNNPRY	REPININGLY	EHINPPSSSU	UPPISHNESS
EGIILNSSTU	GUILTINESS	EHIOOPRSTT	ORTHOEPIST
EGIILOPSTT	EPIGLOTTIS	EHIOPPRRSW	WORSHIPPER
EGIINNOPTT	IGNIPOTENT	EHIOPPRRTY	PORPHYRITE
EGIINRSSTT	GRITTINESS	EHIOPRRSTY	PREHISTORY
EGIINRTTTW	TWITTERING	EHIPRSSTUY	SURETYSHIP
EGILLNNOTW	WELLINGTON	EHLLNOOSSW	HOLLOWNESS
EGILLNORWY	LOWERINGLY	EHLLRSSTUY	RUTHLESSLY
EGILMNOOSS	GLOOMINESS	EHLMNOPPTY	NYMPHOLEPT
EGILMNOSUU	LEGUMINOUS	EHLMNORTUY	UNMOTHERLY
EGILMNPTTY	TEMPTINGLY	EHLOPRSTUY	UPHOLSTERY
EGILMOOSSY	SEISMOLOGY	EHMMNOOTYY	HYMENOTOMY
EGILNNRRUY	UNERRINGLY	EHMMOORSUU	HUMOURSOME
EGILNOOORY	ONEIROLOGY	EHMNOOPRTY	NEPHROTOMY
EGILNOSSSS	GLOSSINESS	EHMNOOSSST	SMOOTHNESS
EGILNOTTUZ	GLUTTONIZE	EHMOPRSTYY	HYPSOMETRY
EGILNPRSSY	PRESSINGLY	EHNNOPRTWY	PENNYWORTH
EGILNRSTTU	LUTESTRING	EHNOORTTWY	NOTEWORTHY
EGILORSUVY	GRIEVOUSLY	EHOOPPRTTY	PROTOPHYTE
EGIMNNOORR	IRONMONGER	EIIILORTVZ	VITRIOLIZE
EGIMNNOORS	MONSIGNORE	EIIJLNTUVY	JUVENILITY
EGIMNNOOSU	OMNIGENOUS	EIILLMMNNU	MILLENNIUM
EGIMNNORTT	TORMENTING	EIILLMPRTU	MULTIPLIER
EGIMNOORST	ERGONOMIST	EIILLNOPST	SEPTILLION

EIILLNOSTX	SEXTILLION	EJNOOSSSUY	JOYOUSNESS
EIIILLPPRSY	SLIPPERILY	ELLNPRTUUY	PURULENTLY
EIILLPSSTY	PITILESSLY	ELLOPSSSTY	SPOTLESSLY
EIILMNNSTT	INSTILMENT	ELMNOORSUY	ENORMOUSLY
EIILNRSSTY	SINISTERLY	ELMNOOSUVY	VENOMOUSLY
EIILOPSSTT	EPISTOLIST	ELMNORSUUY	NUMEROUSLY
EIILOPSTVY	POSITIVELY	ELNOORSTUU	ULTRONEOUS
EIILPRSSST	SPIRITLESS	ELOPPRSTUY	SUPPLETORY
EIIMNOPRSS	IMPRESSION	EMMOOPRSTT	POST-MORTEM
	PERMISSION	EMNOPPRSST	PROMPTNESS
EIIMOPRSUV	IMPERVIOUS	ENOOPRRSSY	RESPONSORY
EIIMORSSTU	MOISTURISE	ENOOPRSSSU	POROUSNESS
EIINOOPRST	REPOSITION	ENOOPRSTTU	PORTENTOUS
EIINOOPSTX	EXPOSITION	ENOPRSSSUY	SUSPENSORY
EIINOORSUV	EUROVISION	EOOPPRRSSU	PROSPEROUS
EIINRSTUVY	UNIVERSITY	EOOPRSSSSY	POSSESSORY
EIKNNOSSTT	KNOTTINESS	EOORRSSTTU	STERTOROUS
EIKORSTTTY	TROTSKYITE	EOPPRRSSSU	SUPPRESSOR
EILLMOOSTY	TOILSOMELY	FFGIILLLNU	FULFILLING
EILLNNOSTY	INSOLENTLY	FFIIRRSTTU	FIRST-FRUIT
EILLNRTUVY	VIRULENTLY	FFILLRTUUY	FRUITFULLY
EILLOPRSUY	PERILOUSLY	FGGHINOORT	FORTHGOING
EILMMOPRSY	POLYMERISM	FGHHIORRTT	FORTHRIGHT
EILMNOOOPZ	MONOPOLIZE	FGHHLOTTUU	THOUGHTFUL
EILMNOOSST	MOTIONLESS	FGHIINORRY	HORRIFYING
EILMNRSSTY	MINSTRELSY	FGHILLRTUY	RIGHTFULLY
EILMOOPRST	METROPOLIS	FGHILOOSTT	FOOTLIGHTS
EILMOPPRRY	IMPROPERLY	FGIILLNRTY	TRIFLINGLY
EILNNRSSUU	UNRULINESS	FGIILMNORU	LINGUIFORM
EILNOORSTU	RESOLUTION	FGIIMNORTY	MORTIFYING
EILNOORTUV	REVOLUTION	FGIIMNSTYY	MYSTIFYING
EILNOPPSSS	SLOPPINESS	FGILNNORWY	FROWNINGLY
EILNOPRSST	PORTLINESS	FGLLNORUWY	WRONGFULLY
EILNOSTUUV	VELUTINOUS	FHILLMRTUY	MIRTHFULLY
EILNPQTTUU	QUINTUPLET	FHILOPRSUW	WORSHIPFUL
EILNRSSSTU	SULTRINESS	FHLLLOSTUY	SLOTHFULLY
EILNRSSTUY	UNSISTERLY	FHLLOTUUYY	YOUTHFULLY
EILOOPPSTY	OPPOSITELY	FHLLRTTUUY	TRUTHFULLY
EILOPPRSUV	PROPULSIVE	FHLNRTTUUU	UNTRUTHFUL
EIMNNOOPTT	OMNIPOTENT	FIILMMNOOR	MONILIFORM
EIMNNRSTTU	INSTRUMENT	FIIMNORTUY	UNIFORMITY
EIMNOOPRRT	PREMONITOR	FIIMOORSST	FORTISSIMO
EIMNOOPRSS	SPOONERISM	FILNOORSUU	UNIFLOROUS
EIMNOPRSTU	RESUMPTION	FIOORSTTUU	FORTUITOUS
EIMNSSSTTU	SMUTTINESS	FLLMNORUUY	MOURNFULLY
EIMORSSTUY	MYSTERIOUS	FLLRSTTUUY	TRUSTFULLY
EINNOPSSSU	SUSPENSION	GGHILLSSUY	SLUGGISHLY
EINOOPPRSS	OPPRESSION	GGLLOOOSSY	GLOSSOLOGY
EINOOPSSSS	POSSESSION	GGLLOOOTTY	GLOTTOLOGY
EINOPPRSTY	PROPENSITY	GHHIIPRSTW	SHIPWRIGHT
EINOQRTTUU	TOURNIQUET	GHHINOPRTT	TRIPHTHONG
EINRSSSTTU	TRUSTINESS	GHHIOPPPRY	HIPPOGRYPH
EIOOPPRRRT	PROPRIETOR	GHHLOORTUY	THOROUGHLY
EIOOPRRSTY	REPOSITORY	GHHOORTTUU	THROUGHOUT
EIOOPRSTXY	EXPOSITORY	GHIIKLNNTY	THINKINGLY
EIOORRSSTU	ROISTEROUS	GHIIKNNNTU	UNTHINKING
EIOPPRRSTY	PROSPERITY	GHIILNRTVY	THRIVINGLY
EIOPPRSTUV	SUPPORTIVE	GHIILNWYZZ	WHIZZINGLY
EIOPPRRSSUV	SUPERVISOR	GHIINNORSU	NOURISHING
EIOPRRSTUV	PROTRUSIVE	GHILNOOPST	PHLOGISTON
EIOPRSTTTU	PROSTITUTE	GHILNOOSTY	SOOTHINGLY

GHILOOOORST	HOROLOGIST	IIIMNOOPST	IMPOSITION
GHILOOPSYY	PHYSIOLOGY	IIIMNOPRSS	MISPRISION
GHLMOOOOPRY	MORPHOLOGY	IIIMOPSSTV	POSITIVISM
GHNOOPSUYY	HYPOGYNOUS	IIINOQRSTU	INQUISITOR
GIIILNNTVY	INVITINGLY	IIINOQSTUU	INIQUITOUS
GIIINNNTUV	UNINVITING	IIIOPSSTTV	POSITIVIST
GIIKLNNPRS	SPRINKLING	IILLNOOPST	POSTILLION
GIILMMNRTY	TRIMMINGLY	IILMNOSTUY	LUMINOSITY
GIILMMNSWY	SWIMMINGLY	IILNNOOTUV	INVOLUTION
GIILMNOORV	LIVING-ROOM	IINOOOPPST	OPPOSITION
GIILMNOPSY	IMPOSINGLY	IINORSSSTU	SINISTROUS
GIILNOORGU	INGLORIOUS	IINORSTTTU	INSTITUTOR
GIILNOOSST	SINOLOGIST	IINORSTTUU	NUTRITIOUS
GIILNPPRTY	TRIPPINGLY	IIOOOPRSTV	OVIPOSITOR
GIILNTTTWY	TWITTINGLY	IIOOPPRSTU	PROPITIOUS
GIIMNNNOPSU	UNIMPOSING	IIOPRSSTUU	SPIRITUOUS
GIIMNOSSTY	MISOGYNIST	IKORSSTTTY	TROTSKYIST
GIINPRRSSU	SURPRISING	ILLMNOSUUY	LUMINOUSLY
GIKKLLNSUY	SKULKINGLY	ILMNOOOPST	MONOPOLIST
GILLOORSUY	GLORIOUSLY	ILMNOOSUUV	VOLUMINOUS
GILMNOOOST	MONOLOGIST	ILMNOSTUUY	MUTINOUSLY
GILMOOOPST	POMOLOGIST	ILMOORSTUY	TIMOROUSLY
GILNOOOSST	NOSOLOGIST	ILNOOPPRSU	PROPULSION
GILNOOOSTT	ONTOLOGIST	ILOOPPRSST	SPOILSPORT
GILNOOPSTY	STOOPINGLY	ILOORSUUXY	UXORIOUSLY
GILNOPRSTY	SPORTINGLY	ILOPRSSUUY	SPURIOUSLY
GILNORRWYY	WORRYINGLY	ILORSTUUVY	VIRTUOUSLY
GILNRSTTUY	TRUSTINGLY	IMNNOSSTYY	SYNONYMIST
GILOOORRSUY	RIGOROUSLY	IMNOOORSUV	OMNIVOROUS
GILOORSUVY	VIGOROUSLY	IMOOPRRSSY	PROMISSORY
HHILOOPPSY	PHILOSOPHY	INOOOPPRRT	PROPORTION
HHOOPPRSSU	PHOSPHORUS	INOOPRRSTU	PROTRUSION
HIIKLSSTTY	SKITTISHLY	IOOORSSSUV	OSSIVOROUS
HIILORTTTY	LITHOTRITY	LLOOPPSUUY	POPULOUSLY
HILLSSTTUY	SLUTTISHLY	LMOSTTUUUU	TUMULTUOUS
HILNORTUWY	UNWORTHILY	LNOOORSSUY	SONOROUSLY
HIMNOPRRSY	PYRRHONISM	LOOPSTUUUV	VOLUPTUOUS
HINOPRRSTY	PYRRHONIST	LOORSTTUUY	TORTUOUSLY
HLMOORSUUY	HUMOROUSLY	MNNOOOOSTU	MONOTONOUS
HMNOOOOSTU	HOMOTONOUS	MNNOOSSUYY	SYNONYMOUS
HMOOPSSTUU	POSTHUMOUS	MNOOOPRRTY	PROMONTORY
IIILNOSSTT	TONSILITIS		

Eleven Letter Words

AAAAABBCDRR	ABRACADABRA	AAADEFFNNOR	FANFARONADE
AAAAABBINRST	SABBATARIAN	AAADEFIOSST	ASSAFOETIDA
AAAABCCHILN	BACCHANALIA	AAADEILNNRX	ALEXANDRIAN
AAAACNRRSVY	CARAVANSARY	AAADEIMNNRT	MANDARINATE
AAAAILRSSTU	AUSTRALASIA	AAADGILNORT	GRADATIONAL
AAABBCEGLMP	CABBAGE-PALM	AAAEEHINSST	ANAESTHESIA
AAABCDEEINR	ABECEDARIAN	AAAEERSTTVX	EXTRAVASATE
AAABCEHINRT	ABRANCHIATE	AAAEGIILNRT	EGALITARIAN
AAABCELRTTT	ATTRACTABLE	AAAEGILMMNO	MEGALOMANIA
AAABCILLOPR	PARABOLICAL	AAAEGNRTTVX	EXTRAVAGANT
AAABCILNOTT	ABLACTATION	AAAEHIMNNRT	AMARANTHINE
AAABDEGGNOV	VAGABONDAGE	AAAEILPPRRS	REAPPRAISAL
AAABEHIMNPS	AMPHISBAENA	AAAEIMMNNOO	AMOENOMANIA
AAABEILLNUV	UNAVAILABLE	AAAEINSSSST	ASSASSINATE
AAABELLNPTU	UNPALATABLE	AAAGGGINRTV	AGGRAVATING
AAABLNRRTWY	WARRANTABLY	AAAGGINORTV	AGGRAVATION
AAACCCEILTT	ACATALECTIC	AAAGIIMNRRS	AGRARIANISM
AAACCCISTTU	CATACAUSTIC	AAAHINNORTZ	ZOANTHARIAN
AAACCDEIIMN	ACADEMICIAN	AAAIINNQRTU	ANTIQUARIAN
AAACCEHINPU	IPECACUANHA	AAAILNNRSTU	SATURNALIAN
AAACCEILLOR	CALCEOLARIA	AAAIMNNOOST	ANTONOMASIA
AAACCEILPRT	PALAEARCTIC	AAAIMNOOPRS	PARONOMASIA
AAACCGLLMNO	CLOG-ALMANAC	AABBCCIILST	CABBALISTIC
AAACCHILNRT	CHARLATANIC	AABBCEEEGRT	CABBAGE-TREE
AAACCILLPRT	PARALLACTIC	AABBCEEGORS	CABBAGE-ROSE
AAACCILLSTT	STALACTICAL	AABBCEGHMOT	CABBAGE-MOTH
AAACCILMNOT	ACCLAMATION	AABBCEGMORW	CABBAGE-WORM
AAACCILRSST	SARCASTICAL	AABBCEINORT	BICARBONATE
AAACCLMORTY	ACCLAMATORY	AABBEEKLNRU	UNBREAKABLE
AAACDEEIMRR	CAMARADERIE	AABBEFGLRST	FLABBERGAST
AAACDEILNRT	CARDINALATE	AABBEGIINRT	BEAR-BAITING
AAACDIINNSV	SCANDINAVIA	AABBEHIILNT	INHABITABLE
AAACDILOPRX	PARADOXICAL	AABBEHILLOS	ABOLISHABLE
AAACEEFLMNS	MALFEASANCE	AABBEIORRTV	ABBREVIATOR
AAACEGIRRWY	CARRIAGE-WAY	AABBIIILMNO	BIBLIOMANIA
AAACEILNPSU	AESCULAPIAN	AABBLORRSUY	BARBAROUSLY
AAACELMNPTU	CAMPANULATE	AABCCEELLNO	CONCEALABLE
AAACELMNRST	SACRAMENTAL	AABCCEILPRT	PRACTICABLE
AAACFILLNTY	FANATICALLY	AABCCELNOTU	ACCOUNTABLE
AAACFILNSTT	FANTASTICAL	AABCCERRUUY	BUREAUCRACY
AAACGHIPPRR	PARAGRAPHIC	AABCCGILLNR	CALLING-CRAB
AAACGILMMRT	GRAMMATICAL	AABCCIIJLOT	JACOBITICAL
AAACGILMPRT	PRAGMATICAL	AABCCILPRTY	PRACTICABLY
AAACGNRRSSY	CANARY-GRASS	AABCCLNOTUY	ACCOUNTABLY
AAACHIILPRS	PHARISAICAL	AABCCLNRRUU	CARBUNCULAR
AAACHILMRRT	MATRIARCHAL	AABCDEEFLRY	BAREFACEDLY
AAACHLNRRTY	CHARLATANRY	AABCDEEFNRZ	BRAZEN-FACED
AAACIILPRST	PARASITICAL	AABCDEFIIIL	ACIDIFIABLE
AAACILLMNRU	ANIMALCULAR	AABCDEHIMMR	CHAMBER-MAID
AAACILLNSTY	SATANICALLY	AABCDELMNRU	CANDELABRUM

191

AABCDEORRST	BROADCASTER
AABCDGGIOOR	BRAGGADOCIO
AABCDHIOOPR	BRACHIOPODA
AABCDHMNORY	RHABDOMANCY
AABCDIIQRTU	BIQUADRATIC
AABCEEEHLST	ESCHEATABLE
AABCEEEELLPR	REPLACEABLE
AABCEEFLRRT	REFRACTABLE
AABCEEFNORR	FORBEARANCE
AABCEEGLLNO	CONGEALABLE
AABCEEHILMP	IMPEACHABLE
AABCEEHLNRU	UNREACHABLE
AABCEEHLNTU	UNTEACHABLE
AABCEEHMNRT	ANTE-CHAMBER
AABCEEILLMR	RECLAIMABLE
AABCEEILMNV	AMBIVALENCE
AABCEEILNPS	INESCAPABLE
AABCEEILNRS	INCREASABLE
AABCEEILPPR	APPRECIABLE
AABCEELNORV	OVERBALANCE
AABCEELRRTT	RETRACTABLE
AABCEFILNOT	LABEFACTION
AABCEFINOTT	TABEFACTION
AABCEFLMNOY	FLAMBOYANCE
AABCEFLNOTU	CONFABULATE
AABCEHIINNT	INHABITANCE
AABCEHILMNR	CHAMBERLAIN
AABCEHILSST	CHASTISABLE
AABCEHLPRSU	PURCHASABLE
AABCEIILNNS	CANNIBALISE
AABCEIINNNR	CINNABARINE
AABCEIKLLMR	BLACKMAILER
AABCEILNNOT	CONTAINABLE
AABCEILNRTT	INTRACTABLE
AABCEILPPRY	APPRECIABLY
AABCEIRSTTV	ABSTRACTIVE
AABCEKKLMRT	BLACK-MARKET
AABCELLOORT	COLLABORATE
AABCELMOPSS	COMPASSABLE
AABCELNRTTU	UNTRACTABLE
AABCFIINORT	FABRICATION
AABCIILLPTY	PLACABILITY
AABCIILMNNS	CANNIBALISM
AABCIILNORT	CALIBRATION
AABCILLNOTY	BOTANICALLY
AABCILNRTTY	INTRACTABLY
AABCINORSTT	ABSTRACTION
AABCLPRSSUU	SUBSCAPULAR
AABCNOORSST	CONTRABASSO
AABDDEGLLLR	GALL-BLADDER
AABDDEHHNRT	HANDBREADTH
AABDDEHMORY	HEBDOMADARY
AABDDNRSSTU	SUBSTANDARD
AABDEEHHRRS	HABERDASHER
AABDEELPRSU	PERSUADABLE
AABDEEMRRSS	EMBARRASSED
AABDEHRSTWY	BREADTHWAYS
AABDEIILNSV	INADVISABLE
AABDEIILRTY	READABILITY
AABDEIKNORT	DEBARKATION
AABDEILLRVY	ADVERBIALLY
AABDEILMNTU	MANDIBULATE
AABDEILNOUV	UNAVOIDABLE
AABDEILNSUV	UNADVISABLE
AABDEILORRT	LABRADORITE
AABDELORRUY	DAY-LABOURER
AABDEMNNNOT	ABANDONMENT
AABDGIMNOSV	VAGABONDISM
AABDGINRSTW	BASTARD-WING
AABDHIKLNOY	BANK-HOLIDAY
AABDIILMQRU	LIQUIDAMBAR
AABDILNSUVY	UNADVISABLY
AABDIMNORTU	ADUMBRATION
AABEEELNRTT	ENTREATABLE
AABEEHILNTZ	ELIZABETHAN
AABEEHKLNSU	UNSHAKEABLE
AABEEIILLNN	INALIENABLE
AABEEIILNPX	EXPLAINABLE
AABEEIILNRT	INALTERABLE
AABEEILMNSS	AMIABLENESS
AABEEILNPRS	INSEPARABLE
AABEEILORTV	ELABORATIVE
AABEEILPRRR	IRREPARABLE
AABEEKLNPSU	UNSPEAKABLE
AABEELLNRTU	UNALTERABLE
AABEELLORTY	ELABORATELY
AABEELLPRSU	PLEASURABLE
AABEELMPRTU	PERAMBULATE
AABEELMPTTT	ATTEMPTABLE
AABEELNORST	TREASONABLE
AABEELNRTTU	ENTABLATURE
AABEELPRSTT	BREAST-PLATE
AABEELRRTTU	TEREBRATULA
AABEELRRTWY	BARLEY-WATER
AABEFGIILMN	MAGNIFIABLE
AABEFHILNOS	FASHIONABLE
AABEFILLMMN	INFLAMMABLE
AABEFLLNPPU	UNFLAPPABLE
AABEGIILNNV	INNAVIGABLE
AABEGILNORZ	ORGANIZABLE
AABEGLNORRR	BARREL-ORGAN
AABEGLRRSUY	BARLEY-SUGAR
AABEHILORUV	BEHAVIOURAL
AABEIILLNNY	INALIENABLY
AABEIILLSTY	SALEABILITY
AABEIILMMOR	MEMORABILIA
AABEIILNRRT	LIBERTARIAN
AABEIKMNORT	EMBARKATION
AABEILNOORT	ELABORATION
AABEILNPRSY	INSEPARABLY
AABEILNSSTU	SUSTAINABLE
AABEILPRRRY	IRREPARABLY
AABEIMNRRTT	ARBITRAMENT
AABEKLNPSUY	UNSPEAKABLY
AABELLORSUV	SLAVE-LABOUR
AABELLPRSUY	PLEASURABLY
AABELNORSTY	TREASONABLY
AABFILLMMNY	INFLAMMABLY
AABGHILNOOP	ANGLOPHOBIA
AABGHIOOOPR	AGOROPHOBIA
AABHIINOTTU	HABITUATION
AABIIILRTVY	VARIABILITY

AABIIILSTTY	SATIABILITY	AACCGILLNTU	CALCULATING
AABIILLPPTY	PALPABILITY	AACCHIIMRST	CHARISMATIC
AABIILLSTVY	SALVABILITY	AACCHIINRTT	ANTHRACITIC
AABIILMNRUU	ALBUMINURIA	AACCHILLOTY	CHAOTICALLY
AABIILORSTU	ATRABILIOUS	AACCHILMNOR	MONARCHICAL
AABIILRRRTY	ARBITRARILY	AACCHINOPST	CATAPHONICS
AABIIMNNOOT	ABOMINATION	AACCIILMPRT	IMPRACTICAL
AABIINORRTT	ARBITRATION	AACCIILNNOT	CALCINATION
AABILLMORSY	AMBROSIALLY	AACCIILSTTT	STALACTITIC
AABILLMRSUY	SYLLABARIUM	AACCIINNOTV	VACCINATION
AABILLRSUXY	SUBAXILLARY	AACCIINOSTU	ACOUSTICIAN
AABILMNORTY	ABNORMALITY	AACCILLLNOY	LACONICALLY
AABILNOOPRT	PROBATIONAL	AACCILLLSSY	CLASSICALLY
AABILNSSTTU	SUBSTANTIAL	AACCILLNNOY	CANONICALLY
AABINOOPPRT	APPROBATION	AACCILLNOTU	CALCULATION
AABINOPRSTT	BONAPARTIST	AACCILLPRTY	PRACTICALLY
AACCCDEOSUY	CYCADACEOUS	AACCILLSTUY	CAUSTICALLY
AACCCGIORST	CACOGASTRIC	AACCILNNNOU	UNCANONICAL
AACCCILMSTY	CATACLYSMIC	AACCILNPRTU	UNPRACTICAL
AACCCNNOTUY	ACCOUNTANCY	AACCILNSTTY	SYNTACTICAL
AACCDDEEINOR	ENDOCARDIAC	AACCILOPPTY	APOCALYPTIC
AACCDEHIRTT	CATHEDRATIC	AACCILOPSUY	CAPACIOUSLY
AACCDEIILLT	DIALECTICAL	AACCIMNOPST	ACCOMPANIST
AACCDEIIPRR	PERICARDIAC	AACCIORRSTY	ARISTOCRACY
AACCDEILNOT	ANECDOTICAL	AACCLMORTUU	ACCUMULATOR
AACCDEILOPY	CYCLOPAEDIA	AACDDEEEHLR	CLEAR-HEADED
AACCDEMMOOT	ACCOMMODATE	AACDDEINRTU	CANDIDATURE
AACCDIIILRT	DIACRITICAL	AACDDIJORTU	ADJUDICATOR
AACCDLNORTY	ACCORDANTLY	AACDEEGHINP	PHAGEDAENIC
AACCDMOPRSS	COMPASS-CARD	AACDEEHIMNR	ARCHIMEDEAN
AACCEEFILNT	CALEFACIENT	AACDEEIIRTV	ERADICATIVE
AACCEEINRRT	INCARCERATE	AACDEEILRTV	DECLARATIVE
AACCEELLNOT	COLLECTANEA	AACDEEILSTT	ELASTICATED
AACCEELORRT	ACCELERATOR	AACDEELLNOT	LANCEOLATED
AACCEENNOTT	CONCATENATE	AACDEELLSTT	CASTELLATED
AACCEFILNOT	CALEFACTION	AACDEEMNNTV	ADVANCEMENT
AACCEFLORTY	CALEFACTORY	AACDEFILNOT	DEFALCATION
AACCEGHILLP	CEPHALALGIC	AACDEGGILOP	PEDAGOGICAL
AACCEGHILNR	ARCHANGELIC	AACDEGIIMNT	DIAMAGNETIC
AACCEGILORT	CATEGORICAL	AACDEHIIMRT	ADIATHERMIC
AACCEHHPRST	CATCH-PHRASE	AACDEHILORS	ICOSAHEDRAL
AACCEHIIMNN	MECHANICIAN	AACDEHINPPR	HANDICAPPER
AACCEHIRSST	CATACHRESIS	AACDEHINRST	CANTHARIDES
AACCEHLNNNO	NONCHALANCE	AACDEHPRRRS	CARD-SHARPER
AACCEHORSTU	CHARTACEOUS	AACDEIILMRT	DIAMETRICAL
AACCEIILMTZ	ACCLIMATIZE	AACDEIILPRR	PERICARDIAL
AACCEIILLTUV	CALCULATIVE	AACDEIINNNR	INCARNADINE
AACCEIILMPRT	MALPRACTICE	AACDEIINORT	ERADICATION
AACCEIILORSS	ACCESSORIAL	AACDEIIORTV	RADIOACTIVE
AACCEIMNOPR	ACCOMPANIER	AACDEIIPRST	PAEDIATRICS
AACCEINNORT	ANACREONTIC	AACDEILMNOT	DECLAMATION
	CANCERATION	AACDEILNORT	DECLARATION
AACCEINOPTT	ACCEPTATION	AACDEILNOTU	EDUCATIONAL
AACCEINOQTTU	ACQUITTANCE	AACDEILNRRU	RURIDECANAL
AACCELNRTUU	CARUNCULATE	AACDEILRTTU	ARTICULATED
AACCELPRSTU	SPECTACULAR	AACDEIMNORT	DEMARCATION
AACCENOPRRY	COPARCENARY	AACDEIMNORY	AERODYNAMIC
AACCFIIILRS	SACRIFICIAL	AACDEINNORT	CARNATIONED
AACCFIILLPY	PACIFICALLY	AACDELMORTY	DECLAMATORY
AACCFIIMNOR	ACINACIFORM	AACDELORRTY	DECLARATORY
AACCFIIOPRT	PACIFICATOR	AACDFIILRRT	FRATRICIDAL

AACDGHIOPRR	CARDIOGRAPH
AACDGIMRRTU	DRAMATURGIC
AACDHIIOPRS	APHRODISIAC
AACDHILOPRS	RHAPSODICAL
AACDIIILMOT	IDIOMATICAL
AACDIILMNRU	ADMINICULAR
AACDIILORTT	DICTATORIAL
AACDIIMNOPS	DIPSOMANIAC
AACDILLMNYY	DYNAMICALLY
AACDILMOPSS	SPASMODICAL
AACDILOSUUY	AUDACIOUSLY
AACDIMNNOTU	MANDUCATION
AACDKLNOORT	COOL-TANKARD
AACDKNORRTW	DOCK-WARRANT
AACDMNORTUY	MANDUCATORY
AACEEFIMNSS	MISFEASANCE
AACEEGHNOPR	CHAPERONAGE
AACEEGHRRST	GATECRASHER
AACEEGILLNV	EVANGELICAL
AACEEHILMNR	AMELANCHIER
AACEEHILSTT	AESTHETICAL
AACEEHINSTT	ANAESTHETIC
AACEEHLNNSV	CLEAN-SHAVEN
AACEEIIMNRZ	AMERICANIZE
AACEEIIMPST	SEPTICAEMIA
AACEEIILLMNS	MÉSALLIANCE
AACEEILNRTT	INTERCALATE
AACEEILRRST	SECRETARIAL
AACEEIMNNNT	MAINTENANCE
AACEEIMRSSU	EREMACAUSIS
AACEEINNNRT	CENTENARIAN
AACEEINNRSS	RENAISSANCE
AACEEIPRRTV	PREVARICATE
AACEEIRRSTT	SECRETARIAT
AACEEKLLNST	ALKALESCENT
AACEEKLMPRT	MARKET-PLACE
AACEELNPSTU	ENCAPSULATE
AACEEMNOSTU	AMENTACEOUS
AACEENRRSSU	REASSURANCE
AACEFFHINRS	AFFRANCHISE
AACEFFINOTT	AFFECTATION
AACEFGHINRR	FAR-REACHING
AACEFGLNORT	CONFLAGRATE
AACEFILTTUV	FACULTATIVE
AACEFINORRT	RAREFACTION
AACEFINORTT	FRACTIONATE
AACEFMNRTUU	MANUFACTURE
AACEGHILLRT	LETHARGICAL
AACEGHILOPR	ARCHIPELAGO
AACEGHLLSSV	CHEVAL-GLASS
AACEGHLOORY	ARCHAEOLOGY
AACEGIILMNT	ENIGMATICAL
AACEGIIMNNT	MAGNETICIAN
AACEGIIMRRS	MISCARRIAGE
AACEGILLLNY	ANGELICALLY
AACEGILLLOR	ALLEGORICAL
AACEGILLOOR	AEROLOGICAL
AACEGILNPRY	PANEGYRICAL
AACEGILOTUV	COAGULATIVE
AACEGILRSTT	STRATEGICAL
AACEGLNRRTU	RECTANGULAR

AACEHIILMPT	EPITHALAMIC
AACEHILLMNO	MELANCHOLIA
AACEHILPPSS	CEPHALASPIS
AACEHILRSTT	THEATRICALS
AACEHIMMSTT	MATHEMATICS
AACEHMMNNRT	MERCHANTMAN
AACEHNOPRVY	ANCHOVY-PEAR
AACEHOPRSTT	CATASTROPHE
AACEHOPSSTU	SPATHACEOUS
AACEIIKLMNT	KINEMATICAL
AACEIILLMNS	MISALLIANCE
AACEIILPPTV	APPLICATIVE
AACEIIMMNRS	AMERICANISM
AACEIIMNRTV	CARMINATIVE
AACEIINORTT	RATIOCINATE
AACEIIOSSTV	ASSOCIATIVE
AACEIIPPRTT	PARTICIPATE
AACEIJLNOTU	EJACULATION
AACEILLLSTY	ELASTICALLY
AACEILLMNPT	IMPLACENTAL
AACEILLMPUX	AMPLEXICAUL
AACEILLPRRT	CATERPILLAR
AACEILLRRTY	ERRATICALLY
AACEILMNORT	RECLAMATION
AACEILMNOTX	EXCLAMATION
AACEILMRTTU	MATRICULATE
AACEILNOPRT	ANAPLEROTIC
AACEILNORTT	ALTERCATION
AACEILNRRTY	INTERCALARY
AACEILPRTTU	PARTICULATE
AACEILSTUVY	CAUSATIVELY
AACEIMNNOTT	CONTAMINATE
AACEIMNOPRT	EMANCIPATOR
AACEIMOPRTV	COMPARATIVE
AACEINNORTT	RECANTATION
AACEINNRSTU	UNSECTARIAN
AACEINORRTY	REACTIONARY
AACEINORSTU	AERONAUTICS
AACEIORSSTT	AEROSTATICS
AACEIPRRSTT	STAIR-CARPET
AACEKLQRSUV	QUACKSALVER
AACELMORTXY	EXCLAMATORY
AACELNOOSSU	SOLANACEOUS
AACENOOPSSU	SAPONACEOUS
AACENORRTVY	CONTRAYERVA
AACEOPPRSUY	PAPYRACEOUS
AACFGIINNST	FASCINATING
AACFIILLNNY	FINANCIALLY
AACFIINNOST	FASCINATION
AACFILLNRTY	FRANTICALLY
AACFILNORST	INFRACOSTAL
AACFKLMSUUV	VACUUM-FLASK
AACFMNORTUY	MANUFACTORY
AACFNORSTUU	ANFRACTUOUS
AACGHHILNOT	CHILOGNATHA
AACGHHPRTYY	TACHYGRAPHY
AACGHILLPRY	CALLIGRAPHY
	GRAPHICALLY
AACGHIOPRTU	AUTOGRAPHIC
AACGHOPRRTY	CARTOGRAPHY
AACGHOPRSSU	SARCOPHAGUS

AACGIILLNTV	VACILLATING	AACLMORRTYY	LACRYMATORY
AACGIILMNNS	ANGLICANISM	AACLNNNOOST	CONSONANTAL
AACGIILMSTT	STIGMATICAL	AACLOPRSSTU	SUPRACOSTAL
AACGIILNNNT	LANCINATING	AACLORSTTUU	AUSCULTATOR
AACGIILNNOR	CAROLINGIAN	AACMOORSSTU	SARCOMATOUS
AACGIIMRSTT	MAGISTRATIC	AADDDDEEEHL	ADDLE-HEADED
AACGIINOSTT	CASTIGATION	AADDDEIILPT	DILAPIDATED
AACGIINPTTV	CAPTIVATING	AADDEEHORRW	ARROW-HEADED
AACGILLNORY	ORGANICALLY	AADDEGINORT	DEGRADATION
AACGILNOOTU	COAGULATION	AADDEINRSST	STANDARDISE
AACGILOSSUY	SAGACIOUSLY	AADDEJLMSTU	MALADJUSTED
AACGINNOTTV	NOCTIVAGANT	AADDIILOPRT	DILAPIDATOR
AACGIORSTTY	CASTIGATORY	AADEEEHKRTW	WEAK-HEARTED
AACGLMNOOPY	CAMPANOLOGY	AADEEEHLNNR	ENNEAHEDRAL
AACHIILLNRV	ARCH-VILLAIN	AADEEEPPRTU	DEPAUPERATE
AACHIIMNNOT	MACHINATION	AADEEFHHLRT	HALF-HEARTED
AACHIINPPST	CAPTAINSHIP	AADEEFILNRT	ANTIFEDERAL
AACHILLOPRY	PAROCHIALLY	AADEEGINRTU	AGUARDIENTE
AACHILNORST	THRASONICAL	AADEEHLNNRT	NEANDERTHAL
AACHIMNNORS	ANACHRONISM	AADEEHLRRTT	TETRAHEDRAL
AACHIMNOPTT	PHANTOMATIC	AADEEHLRTTT	DEATH-RATTLE
AACHIPRSTTU	PARACHUTIST	AADEEHNRSVW	HEAVENWARDS
AACHILNNOOTU	ANACOLUTHON	AADEEILNNRX	ALEXANDRINE
AACIIILPPRT	PARTICIPIAL	AADEEIRRTTV	RETARDATIVE
AACIIJNOTTT	JACTITATION	AADEEIRSTVV	ADVERSATIVE
AACIILLMRTU	MULTIRACIAL	AADEEMNNNTU	ANTEMUNDANE
AACIILLNOTV	VACILLATION	AADEEMQRRSU	MASQUERADER
AACIILLPRTY	CAPILLARITY	AADEFGHNRRT	GRANDFATHER
	PIRATICALLY	AADEFGIISTT	FASTIGIATED
AACIILLRSTY	SATIRICALLY	AADEFGLORRT	DEFLAGRATOR
AACIILMNOST	ANOMALISTIC	AADEFIMNORT	FORAMINATED
AACIILMPRST	PRISMATICAL	AADEFLMNNTU	FUNDAMENTAL
AACIILNNNOT	LANCINATION	AADEFLSSTTY	STEADFASTLY
AACIILNOPPT	APPLICATION	AADEGILNPRT	PLANTIGRADE
AACIILNPRTU	PURITANICAL	AADEGIMNTTU	UNMITAGATED
AACIILNPTTY	ANTITYPICAL	AADEGNNOPRU	UNPARAGONED
AACIILOPRST	PISCATORIAL	AADEGNNPRRT	GRANDPARENT
AACIILSSTTT	STATISTICAL	AADEIILMORT	MEDIATORIAL
AACIIMNNOTU	ACUMINATION	AADEIILNOPT	PLANETOIDAL
AACIIMNOSTT	MASTICATION	AADEILNOTUV	DEVALUATION
AACIINNNORT	INCARNATION	AADEILOPRTZ	TRAPEZOIDAL
AACIINNNOTT	INCANTATION	AADEIMMNNRST	DISARMAMENT
AACIINOOSST	ASSOCIATION	AADEINOPRTV	DEPRAVATION
AACIINORTTV	VATICINATOR	AADEINORRTT	RETARDATION
AACIINPPRTT	PARTICIPANT	AADEINOSTTV	DEVASTATION
AACIINPSSTT	ANTISPASTIC	AADEINPRSTU	UNASPIRATED
AACILLNOPRS	RAPSCALLION	AADEKNRSSWW	AWKWARDNESS
AACILLOPRSY	PROSAICALLY	AADELLNNORT	RALLENTANDO
AACILLRRUUY	AURICULARLY	AADENNRRTUW	UNWARRANTED
AACILMNNOPT	COMPLAINANT	AADENRSSWWY	WAYWARDNESS
AACILMNOPST	COMPLAISANT	AADGHIOPRRY	RADIOGRAPHY
AACILMNORTU	CALUMNIATOR	AADGHMNRSTU	DRAUGHTSMAN
AACILNORTVY	CLAIRVOYANT	AADGIILNNNO	ANGLO-INDIAN
AACILOPPRTY	APPLICATORY	AADHIILMPRS	ADMIRALSHIP
AACILOPRSUY	RAPACIOUSLY	AADHIOOPRSU	ADIAPHOROUS
AACILRSTUVY	VASCULARITY	AADHLORSUYZ	HAZARDOUSLY
AACIMNOOSTT	ANASTOMOTIC	AADIIINORRT	IRRADIATION
AACIMORSTTY	MASTICATORY	AADIILLNTTU	LATITUDINAL
AACINNNORTU	ANNUNCIATOR	AADIILNORTT	TRADITIONAL
AACINNORSTT	TRANSACTION	AADIILNTTTU	ATTITUDINAL
AACINNORTTY	INCANTATORY	AADIILOSUUV	AUDIO-VISUAL

195

AADILLMNOOT	AMONTILLADO	AAEGILNRTTU	TRIANGULATE
AADILLMPRYY	PYRAMIDALLY	AAEGIMNNRRT	ARRAIGNMENT
AADILOPPRSV	DISAPPROVAL	AAEGINNNPTY	PENTAGYNIAN
AADMNORSSTU	NOSTRADAMUS	AAEGIOPPRTV	PROPAGATIVE
AAEEEHKPRSS	SHAKESPEARE	AAEGLLNORTY	ANGELOLATRY
AAEEEHNRRTW	EARTHENWARE	AAEGLNNPRTU	PENTANGULAR
AAEEEMNPPST	APPEASEMENT	AAEGLNRSTTU	STRANGULATE
AAEEFHHILRT	FAITH-HEALER	AAEHHIILMOP	HAEMOPHILIA
AAEEGGGLRTY	AGGREGATELY	AAEHMNORSWW	WASHERWOMAN
AAEEGGLMORT	AGGLOMERATE	AAEHMOPRTTU	THAUMATROPE
AAEEGGORRTX	EXAGGERATOR	AAEIILLMNNR	MILLENARIAN
AAEEGHHMORR	HAEMORRHAGE	AAEIILLNOTV	ALLEVIATION
AAEEGHLOOPS	OESOPHAGEAL	AAEIILMMRST	MATERIALISM
AAEEGIKNNRW	REAWAKENING	AAEIILMRSTT	MATERIALIST
AAEEGILMSSX	SEXAGESIMAL	AAEIILNNOST	NATIONALISE
AAEEGMNNRRT	ARRANGEMENT	AAEIILNORST	RATIONALISE
AAEEGMNOPRT	POMEGRANATE	AAEIILNORTT	RETALIATION
AAEEGMNSSTU	ASSUAGEMENT	AAEIILNORTZ	REALIZATION
AAEEHILMOPR	HEMERALOPIA	AAEIILQTTUV	QUALITATIVE
AAEEHIMMNPT	AMPHETAMINE	AAEIIMNNORT	REANIMATION
AAEEHLLSTTU	HAUSTELLATE	AAEIIMNNOTX	EXAMINATION
AAEEHMNOORR	AMENORRHOEA	AAEIIMNRSST	ERASTIANISM
AAEEIILMRTZ	MATERIALIZE	AAEIINNPPRT	PARIPINNATE
AAEEIILRRTZ	ARTERIALIZE	AAEIINOPTTX	EXPATIATION
AAEEIILRTTV	RETALIATIVE	AAEIINOSTTV	AESTIVATION
AAEEIKLLMRT	ALKALIMETER	AAEIKLLMRTY	ALKALIMETRY
AAEEIILLPPTV	APPELLATIVE	AAEIKLLTTVY	TALKATIVELY
AAEEIILLQRTU	EQUILATERAL	AAEIKLMNOPT	KLEPTOMANIA
AAEEILNOPRT	PERITONAEAL	AAEILLLMPRS	PARALLELISM
AAEEILNRTTV	ALTERNATIVE	AAEILLNOPPT	APPELLATION
AAEEIMNSSTV	AMATIVENESS	AAEILMNNOTT	LAMENTATION
AAEEIOPRTVV	EVAPORATIVE	AAEILMNPRST	PATERNALISM
AAEEIPPRRTV	PREPARATIVE	AAEILMNPRTU	PLANETARIUM
AAEEKLNRSTT	RATTLESNAKE	AAEILMNRRTU	ULTRAMARINE
AAEELLNRTTY	ALTERNATELY	AAEILNNOPTX	EXPLANATION
AAEELMNSTTT	TESTAMENTAL	AAEILNNORTT	ALTERNATION
AAEELNRRSTT	RETRANSLATE	AAEILNNOSST	SENSATIONAL
AAEFFIIMRTV	AFFIRMATIVE	AAEILNNPRST	TRANSALPINE
AAEFGHILNRT	FARTHINGALE	AAEILNNPTTU	ANTENUPTIAL
AAEFGMNRRTY	FRAGMENTARY	AAEILNOOPRT	OPERATIONAL
AAEFHILNRTW	FATHER-IN-LAW	AAEILNOPRRT	PROLETARIAN
AAEFIIILMRZ	FAMILIARIZE	AAEILNORTUV	REVALUATION
AAEFIIORRSV	SAVOIR-FAIRE	AAEILNRRTVY	NARRATIVELY
AAEFILMMNRT	FIRMAMENTAL	AAEILOPRRTT	PROLETARIAT
AAEFILMNRTY	FILAMENTARY	AAEILORRTTY	RETALIATORY
AAEFLLNRRTY	FRATERNALLY	AAEILORSSSS	ASSESSORIAL
AAEGGGINORT	AGGREGATION	AAEIMNNRRST	TRANSMARINE
AAEGGILNTTU	AGGLUTINATE	AAEIMOPPRTX	APPROXIMATE
AAEGHLLNOXY	HEXAGONALLY	AAEINNOTTTU	ATTENUATION
AAEGHLNNOPY	ANGELOPHANY	AAEINNRRSVY	ANNIVERSARY
AAEGHMRTTUU	THAUMATURGE	AAEINOOPRTV	EVAPORATION
AAEGHNOPRTY	PYTHAGOREAN	AAEINOORSTT	AEROSTATION
AAEGHOPPRRT	TOPAGRAPHER	AAEINOPPRRT	PREPARATION
AAEGIIIMNTV	IMAGINATIVE	AAEINOSTTTT	ATTESTATION
AAEGIILMNPS	PELAGIANISM	AAEIOPPPRRT	APPROPRIATE
AAEGIILMRST	MAGISTERIAL	AABIOPRTTXY	EXPATIATORY
AAEGIINORTV	VARIEGATION	AAELMOPRRTU	ARMOUR-PLATE
AAEGIIRTTVV	GRAVITATIVE	AAELNNRSSTU	NATURALNESS
AAEGILNNRTT	ALTERNATING	AAELNOPRTXY	EXPLANATORY
AAEGILNPRSV	PALSGRAVINE	AAELNRRSSTV	TRANSVERSAL
AAEGILNQRUU	EQUIANGULAR	AAELNRSSTUX	TRANS-SEXUAL

AAEMMNOORTT	MONOTREMATA	AAILLNRUUVY	UNIVALVULAR
AAEMMNOPRTTU	PORTMANTEAU	AAILMMOPPRS	MALAPROPISM
AAENNPRRSTT	TRANSPARENT	AAILMNOPRTU	MANIPULATOR
AAENNPRSTTU	SUPERNATANT	AAILMNRSTTT	TRANSMITTAL
AAEOOPPRRRT	PARATROOPER	AAILNNORSTT	TRANSLATION
AAEOPPRRRTY	PREPARATORY	AAILOORSTTT	TOTALISATOR
AAFFIIILNOT	AFFILIATION	AAILOPRRSUV	LARVIPARDUS
AAFFIIMNORT	AFFIRMATION	AAIMNOOSSST	ANASTOMOSIS
AAFGILLMRUY	GALLIMAUFRY	AAINOOPRSTT	ASPORTATION
AAFIIILMRTY	FAMILIARITY	AAINOORRSTZ	ZOROASTRIAN
AAFIINNOTTU	INFATUATION	AALLNNRTUUY	UNNATURALLY
AAFINNOOPRT	PROFANATION	AALNORRSTTY	TRANSLATORY
AAGGHHIOPRY	HAGIOGRAPHY	ABBBEELMNRT	BRABBLEMENT
AAGGILNNTTU	AGGLUTINANT	ABBCCDEHKNU	BUNCH-BACKED
AAGGLLLOSSW	GALLOWGLASS	ABBCCEEHKNR	BACKBENCHER
AAGHILLMNRS	MARSHALLING	ABBCDEEILRS	DESCRIBABLE
AAGHIRSTTWY	STRAIGHTWAY	ABBCDEENRSS	CRABBEDNESS
AAGHLNOOTTY	THANATOLOGY	ABBCEEEKLLT	BLACK-BEETLE
AAGHNOPRRUY	URANOGRAPHY	ABBCEELLORT	CORBEL-TABLE
AAGIIIMNNOT	IMAGINATION	ABBCEHIILOT	BIBLIOTHECA
AAGIIKNNPST	PAINSTAKING	ABBCIILMNOY	BIBLIOMANCY
AAGIILMNNTY	ANIMATINGLY	ABBDEELORTU	REDOUBTABLE
AAGIILNNSTT	TANTALISING	ABBDEIILNTU	INDUBITABLE
AAGIIMMNNTY	MAGNANIMITY	ABBDEMMNORT	BOMBARDMENT
AAGIIMMSSTT	ASTIGMATISM	ABBDIILNTUY	INDUBITABLY
AAGIINNOSST	ASSIGNATION	ABBEELPRRTU	PERTURBABLE
AAGIINORTTV	GRAVITATION	ABBEFFLOORU	BUFFALO-ROBE
AAGIIRSSTTU	SAGITTARIUS	ABBEHILLPSU	PUBLISHABLE
AAGILLLNPPY	APPALLINGLY	ABBEIILLORT	BIBLIOLATOR
AAGILLMNNTY	MALIGNANTLY	ABBEINRSTUU	SUBURBANITE
AAGILNNORTU	GRANULATION	ABBEMPRRSTU	RUBBER-STAMP
AAGILNORTTU	GRATULATION	ABBGIILLNTU	BULL-BAITING
AAGILOPRRTU	PURGATORIAL	ABBGLLORSUU	SUBGLOBULAR
AAGIMMNNOSU	MAGNANIMOUS	ABBIILLORTY	BIBLIOLATRY
AAGINOOPPRT	PROPAGATION	ABBIILOPRTY	PROBABILITY
AAGINOPRRTU	PURGATORIAN	ABCCCILMOOX	COXCOMBICAL
AAGINORRTUU	INAUGURATOR	ABCCDEHHKNU	HUNCHBACKED
AAGLLLNNTUY	UNGALLANTLY	ABCCDEIIILL	BACILLICIDE
AAGLLMNRTUU	MULTANGULAR	ABCCDEKKOOR	CROOK-BACKED
AAGLLNOOSUY	ANALOGOUSLY	ABCCDKLLNOU	COCK-AND-BULL
AAGLORRTTUY	GRATULATORY	ABCCEEILNOV	CONCEIVABLE
AAHHILMPRSS	MARSHALSHIP	ABCCEELLLOT	COLLECTABLE
AAHIILNNORT	ANNIHILATOR	ABCCEEELORRT	CORRECTABLE
AAHIINPRSST	ANTIPHRASIS	ABCCEEMNNRU	ENCUMBRANCE
AAHIMMNNOPY	NYMPHOMANIA	ABCCEFILNOS	CONFISCABLE
AAHLLMMORSW	MARSHMALLOW	ABCCEFIORSU	BACCIFEROUS
AAIIILNRTTU	UTILITARIAN	ABCCEGINNOU	CONCUBINAGE
AAIIIMMNNRS	ARMINIANISM	ABCCEHIILMO	BIOCHEMICAL
AAIIINNRRTT	TRINITARIAN	ABCCEIILLNO	CONCILIABLE
AAIILLMPRTY	IMPARTIALLY	ABCCEIILPTY	PECCABILITY
AAIILMMNORT	MATRIMONIAL	ABCCEIKKLST	STICKLEBACK
AAIILMNNOST	NATIONALISM	ABCCEILNOVY	CONCEIVABLY
AAIILNNOSTT	NATIONALIST	ABCCEILNSSU	CUBICALNESS
AAIILNNOTTY	NATIONALITY	ABCCEINORRT	CENTROBARIC
AAIILNOPPTT	PALPITATION	ABCCEINRRTY	BARYCENTRIC
AAIILNORSTT	RATIONALIST	ABCCIIMOORT	MACROBIOTIC
AAIILNORTTY	RATIONALITY	ABCCINNORUY	CONCUBINARY
AAIIMMNORSV	MORAVIANISM	ABCCINOOSTT	TOBACCONIST
AAIIMNOOTTZ	ATOMIZATION	ABCCIOORSUV	BACCIVOROUS
AAIIMNOPRTT	IMPARTATION	ABCCNORSTTU	SUBCONTRACT
AAIIMNPRTVY	PARVANIMITY	ABCDDEEEELNS	DESCENDABLE

ABCDDEEFLOU	DOUBLE-FACED	ABCEENPRRTU	PERTURBANCE
ABCDEEFHILL	BLEACHFIELD	ABCEFILMNOR	CONFIRMABLE
ABCDEEHMNTU	DEBAUCHMENT	ABCEFLMNOOR	CONFORMABLE
ABCDEEILLMN	CLEAN-LIMBED	ABCEFLMOORT	COMFORTABLE
ABCDEEILORV	DIVORCEABLE	ABCEGIILNOT	INCOGITABLE
ABCDEEILPRT	PREDICTABLE	ABCEHLNOTUU	UNTOUCHABLE
ABCDEEINORZ	DECARBONIZE	ABCEHLORTTT	BOTTLE-CHART
ABCDEELMMNO	COMMENDABLE	ABCEIILRTUV	LUBRICATIVE
ABCDEELMNNO	CONDEMNABLE	ABCEILLLOPS	COLLAPSIBLE
ABCDEELNNOS	CONDENSABLE	ABCEILLRTUV	CARVEL-BUILT
ABCDEELNRRY	CANDLE-BERRY	ABCEILMOPRT	PROBLEMATIC
ABCDEENORRT	CENTRE-BOARD	ABCEILNNOTU	CONTINUABLE
ABCDEERRTTU	CARBURETTED	ABCEILNORTV	CONTRIVABLE
ABCDEGHIINR	CHAIN-BRIDGE	ABCEILNRSTU	INSCRUTABLE
ABCDEILSSSU	DISCUSSABLE	ABCEILNSUXY	INEXCUSABLY
ABCDEINOORT	NOTICE-BOARD	ABCEILORRVY	IRREVOCABLY
ABCDEINRSTU	DISTURBANCE	ABCEILORSTT	OBSTETRICAL
ABCDELLORUY	BOULDER-CLAY	ABCEIMNOORT	EMBROCATION
ABCDELMMNOY	COMMENDABLY	ABCEINOORST	OBSECRATION
ABCDENORSUY	SUBDEACONRY	ABCEINORTXY	EXORBITANCY
ABCDGIIKLNS	BACKSLIDING	ABCEINRRRST	TRANSCRIBER
ABCDHIIMRTY	DITHYRAMBIC	ABCELNORSVY	CONVERSABLY
ABCDHINOOPR	BRANCHIOPOD	ABCEOOOORRRT	CORROBORATE
ABCDHIORSTW	SWITCHBOARD	ABCEORRRTTU	CARBURETTOR
ABCDHLOOORS	BOARD-SCHOOL	ABCFHINOOST	SONOFABITCH
ABCDHNOORRY	HYDROCARBON	ABCFIINORTU	BIFURCATION
ABCDIIMNOSY	BIODYNAMICS	ABCFINOOSTU	OBFUSCATION
ABCEEEFFLOT	COFFEE-TABLE	ABCFLMNOORY	CONFORMABLY
ABCEEEFLNOR	ENFORCEABLE	ABCFLMOORTY	COMFORTABLY
ABCEEEILNRX	INEXECRABLE	ABCGHIMNOTX	BOXING-MATCH
ABCEEEILPRV	PERCEIVABLE	ABCGIIKLNRY	BRICKLAYING
ABCEEEILRSV	SERVICEABLE	ABCIIILOSTY	SOCIABILITY
ABCEEELMNRS	RESEMBLANCE	ABCIIIMNORT	IMBRICATION
ABCEEELORRV	RECOVERABLE	ABCIILLPTUY	CULPABILITY
ABCEEELPRST	RESPECTABLE	ABCIILNOPTU	PUBLICATION
ABCEEEMMNRR	REMEMBRANCE	ABCIILNORTU	LUBRICATION
ABCEEEMMNRT	EMBRACEMENT	ABCIIMNNOOT	COMBINATION
ABCEEFIILRT	CERTIFIABLE	ABCILLNNOUY	CONNUBIALLY
	RECTIFIABLE	ABCILLORRUY	ORBICULARLY
ABCEEFIINRY	BENEFICIARY	ABCILMMNOSU	SOMNAMBULIC
ABCEEFINNOT	BENEFACTION	ABCILMMORUU	COLUMBARIUM
ABCEEFINRTU	RUBEFACIENT	ABCILNRSTUY	INSCRUTABLY
ABCEEFLNORR	CONFERRABLE	ABCILOPRSTU	SUBTROPICAL
ABCEEILMRRS	CEREBRALISM	ABCINNOOPRT	CARBON-POINT
ABCEEILNORT	CELEBRATION	ABCINOORSTU	OBSCURATION
ABCEEILNSUX	INEXCUSABLE	ABCINORSTTU	SUBTRACTION
ABCEEIILORRV	IRREVOCABLE	ABCNOOOORRRT	CORROBORANT
ABCEEILPRVY	PERCEIVABLY	ABCNORRSTUY	SUBCONTRARY
ABCEEILRSVY	SERVICEABLY	ABDDEEGGLNY	BANDY-LEGGED
ABCEEILRTTX	EXTRACTIBLE	ABDDEIMNNST	DISBANDMENT
ABCEEINNRTY	BICENTENARY	ABDDELMOORW	WARM-BLOODED
ABCEEINORRT	CEREBRATION	ABDDELORRTW	BLADDERWORT
ABCEEINORTX	EXORBITANCE	ABDDGIINORV	DIVING-BOARD
ABCEELLLMOP	COMPELLABLE	ABDEEEGLNUW	UNWEDGEABLE
ABCEELNOQRU	CONQUERABLE	ABDEEEHILRT	HEREDITABLE
ABCEELNORSV	CONSERVABLE	ABDEEEILLRV	DELIVERABLE
	CONVERSABLE	ABDEEELLOPV	DEVELOPABLE
ABCEELNOSTT	CONTESTABLE	ABDEEERRTTV	VERTEBRATED
ABCEELPRSTY	RESPECTABLY	ABDEEFGIIRR	FIRE-BRIGADE
ABCEELRTTUU	TUBERCULATE	ABDEEFIILNN	INDEFINABLE
ABCEENORRST	ARBORESCENT	ABDEEFIINRT	DEFIBRINATE

ABDEEFILNNU	UNDEFINABLE	ABEEHILRSST	ESTABLISHER
ABDEEGGINRR	GINGERBREAD	ABEEHILSTUX	EXHAUSTIBLE
ABDEEHILSST	ESTABLISHED	ABEEHLORRVWW	WHEELBARROW
ABDEEIIKLLS	DISLIKEABLE	ABEEHNOPRRY	HYPERBOREAN
ABDEEIILNOT	OBEDIENTIAL	ABEEHORSTUW	WHEREABOUTS
ABDEEILMNNO	DENOMINABLE	ABEEIILMNPS	PLEBEIANISM
ABDEEILMNST	DISABLEMENT	ABEEIILMNST	INESTIMABLE
ABDEEILNNRT	DINNER-TABLE	ABEEIILNQTU	INEQUITABLE
ABDEEILNPSS	DISPENSABLE	ABEEIILQRTU	EQUILIBRATE
ABDEEILNRSU	UNDESIRABLE	ABEEIILNORT	INTOLERABLE
ABDEEILNSSU	AUDIBLENESS	ABEEIILNPGS	PLIABLENESS
ABDEEINNRRW	BREAD-WINNER	ABEEIILLOPTX	EXPLOITABLE
ABDEELMNNRUU	UNENDURABLE	ABEEILMMPRY	IMPERMEABLY
ABDEGNOORUV	ABOVE-GROUND	ABEEILMMSTT	EMBLEMATIST
ABDEHIINNTU	UNINHABITED	ABEEILMNNOT	MENTIONABLE
ABDEHILNOSU	UNABOLISHED	ABEEILMNNRU	INNUMERABLE
ABDEHNORRUU	UNHARBOURED	ABEEILMORRV	IRREMOVABLE
ABDEIILLLST	DISTILLABLE	ABEEILNNSTT	TABLE-TENNIS
ABDEIILMNOT	INDOMITABLE	ABEEILNSSST	BEASTLINESS
ABDEIIMNOST	DEMI-BASTION	ABEEILPPRRS	PERSPIRABLE
ABDEILLOSSV	DISSOLVABLE	ABEEILPRSSU	PERSUASIBLE
ABDEINORSTU	SUBORDINATE	ABEEILPRTVU	VITUPERABLE
ABDELMOORST	BLOODSTREAM	ABEEILRRTVY	RETRIEVABLY
ABDENOPRSUU	SUPERABOUND	ABEEINNQRTU	BARQUENTINE
ABDENORSTVY	BODY-SERVANT	ABEEINSSSUV	ABUSIVENESS
ABDFILMOORR	DOLABRIFORM	ABEEIORSTVV	OBSERVATIVE
ABDHHIIOOPRY	HYDROPHOBIA	ABEEIQRRSUU	ARQUEBUSIER
ABDIILMNOTY	INDOMITABLY	ABEELLLMSSY	BLAMELESSLY
ABDIMNNOSTU	SUBDOMINANT	ABEELMNOSSV	MOVABLENESS
ABEEEEMNRTV	BEREAVEMENT	ABEELMNSSTU	MUTABLENESS
ABEEEERRRTV	REVERBERATE	ABEELNNOSST	NOTABLENESS
ABEEEFLMNRT	FERMENTABLE	ABEELNNSSTU	TUNABLENESS
ABEEEFLPRRR	PREFERRABLE	ABEELNRTTUU	UNUTTERABLE
ABEEEGLORSW	ELBOW-GREASE	ABEELNRTUXY	EXUBERANTLY
ABEEEGLRRTT	REGRETTABLE	ABEELORTTTW	WATER-BOTTLE
ABEEEHLRSTW	BREAST-WHEEL	ABEELOSTUUY	BEAUTEOUSLY
ABEEEIILNPZ	PLEBEIANIZE	ABEEOPRRTTU	PROTUBERATE
ABEEEIILPRV	REPLEVIABLE	ABEFFIILORT	FORTIFIABLE
ABEEEILMMPR	IMPERMEABLE	ABEFHLNSSSU	BASHFULNESS
ABEEEILMMTZ	EMBLEMATIZE	ABEFIIILRTV	VITRIFIABLE
ABEEEILRRTV	RETRIEVABLE	ABEFIIILSTY	FEASIBILITY
ABEEEIMNSST	ABSENTEEISM	ABEFIIJLSTU	JUSTIFIABLE
ABEEEELMNRRU	REMUNERABLE	ABEFILLTUUY	BEAUTIFULLY
ABEEEELNNSST	TENABLENESS	ABEFILRRTUY	IRREFUTABLY
ABEEEELNPRST	PRESENTABLE	ABEGGIILNOR	GLOBIGERINA
ABEEEELNPRTV	PREVENTABLE	ABEGHILLPPT	APPLE-BLIGHT
ABEEEELNQSSU	EQUABLENESS	ABEGHILMNOO	HAEMOGLOBIN
ABEEEELPPRTU	PERPETUABLE	ABEGIILMNTU	UNMITIGABLE
ABEEEELPRRSV	PRESERVABLE	ABEGILMNPRY	IMPREGNABLY
ABEEEENRRRTV	REVERBERANT	ABEGILNNNTY	BENIGNANTLY
ABEEFFILORT	FORFEITABLE	ABEGLLOSSTT	BOTTLE-GLASS
ABEEFGILNRR	REFRANGIBLE	ABEGMORRSTU	BURGOMASTER
ABEEFGLORTT	FORGETTABLE	ABEHIILNRTY	INHERITABLY
ABEEFIILLQU	LIQUEFIABLE	ABEHIILPRST	BLEPHARITIS
ABEEFILRRTU	IRREFUTABLE	ABEHIIMMNOS	BOHEMIANISM
ABEEFLLNSSU	BALEFULNESS	ABEHIINNORT	HIBERNATION
ABEEFLMOPRR	PERFORMABLE	ABEHIKLNNTU	UNTHINKABLE
ABEEGIINOSS	ABIOGENESIS	ABEHILNORSU	NOURISHABLE
ABEEGILMNPR	IMPREGNABLE	ABEHINOORTT	BOTHERATION
ABEEGINORRV	OVERBEARING	ABEHLMOPSSU	BLASPHEMOUS
ABEEHIILNRT	INHERITABLE	ABEHLMORTWY	BLAMEWORTHY

ABEHLNORRTY	ABHORRENTLY	ABIILMNOSTU	SUBLIMATION
ABEHLORRSSU	HARBOURLESS	ABIILMOSTUY	AMBITIOUSLY
ABEIIILLLMT	ILLIMITABLE	ABIILNORTTU	TRIBULATION
ABEIIILLNOR	BILLIONAIRE	ABIILNRSTUY	INSALUBRITY
ABEIIILLRTY	RELIABILITY	ABIILOPRTTY	PORTABILITY
ABEIIINNORT	INEBRIATION	ABIILRRTTUY	TRIBUTARILY
ABEIILLLLRY	ILLIBERALLY	ABIIMNOSTUU	UNAMBITIOUS
ABEIILLMMST	BIMETALLISM	ABIINOOPSTT	OBSTIPATION
ABEIILLMSTT	BIMETALLIST	ABIINOORSTT	ABORTIONIST
ABEIILMNSTY	INESTIMABLY	ABIINORTTTU	ATTRIBUTION
ABEIILNOPRT	PRELIBATION	ABILLOORSUY	LABORIOUSLY
ABEIILOPPRT	PROPITIABLE	ABINNOORSTU	SUBORNATION
ABEIIRTTTUV	ATTRIBUTIVE	ABLOPPRSTUY	SUPPORTABLY
ABEIILLLRSTY	TRISYLLABLE	ACCCDEEENNS	CANDESCENCE
ABEIILNORTY	INTOLERABLY	ACCCDEHILNO	CHALCEDONIC
ABEILMNNRUY	INNUMERABLY	ACCCDEILOPY	CYCLOPAEDIC
ABEILMORRVY	IRREMOVABLY	ACCCDENNOOR	CONCORDANCE
ABEILNNPRTU	UNPRINTABLE	ACCCEEELNOS	COALESCENCE
ABEILNNSTTY	ABSTINENTLY	ACCCEEELNST	LACTESCENCE
ABEILNOOSSS	OBSESSIONAL	ACCCEEHISTT	CATECHETICS
ABEILNOSTTY	OBSTINATELY	ACCCEEHOSUU	ACCOUCHEUSE
ABEILNPRSUY	INSUPERABLY	ACCCEEILNRT	ECCENTRICAL
ABEIMNNSSSU	BUSINESSMAN	ACCCEELMNOP	COMPLACENCE
ABEINNNRSTU	BURNT-SIENNA	ACCCEELNOPT	CONCEPTACLE
ABEINNORSTV	INOBSERVANT	ACCCEFFHIOO	COACH-OFFICE
ABEINOOPRRT	PROBATIONER	ACCCEHNORTY	TECHNOCRACY
	REPROBATION	ACCCEIILMRT	CLIMACTERIC
ABEINOORSTV	OBSERVATION	ACCCELMNOPY	COMPLACENCY
ABEINOOSTTT	OBTESTATION	ACCCHHIINNO	COCHIN-CHINA
ABEINSSTTUV	SUBSTANTIVE	ACCCHILOORT	OCHLOCRATIC
ABELNORSTVY	OBSERVANTLY	ACCDDEINORS	DISCORDANCE
ABELNRTTUUY	UNUTTERABLY	ACCDDINORSY	DISCORDANCY
ABELOPPRSTU	SUPPORTABLE	ACCDEEEENNT	ANTECEDENCE
ABENNORSTUV	UNOBSERVANT	ACCDEEELNOS	ADOLESCENCE
ABENOPRRTTU	PROTUBERANT	ACCDEEFNORY	CONFEDERACY
ABEOORRSTVY	OBSERVATORY	ACCDEEINPRS	DISCREPANCE
ABFIIILLLTY	FALLIBILITY	ACCDEEIORTT	DECORTICATE
ABFIIJLSTUY	JUSTIFIABLY	ACCDEELNNOU	UNCONCEALED
ABFILMNSTUU	FUNAMBULIST	ACCDEEMNSUU	SUCCEDANEUM
ABGGINOOSTT	TOBOGGANIST	ACCDEFILNSS	FLACCIDNESS
ABGHIINSTTU	BATHING-SUIT	ACCDEHHRSSU	ARCHDUCHESS
ABGHILMOOPY	AMPHIBOLOGY	ACCDEHILPRY	DIPHYCERCAL
ABGIIILNTTY	TANGIBILITY	ACCDEHLNOXY	CHALCEDONYX
ABGIJNOORTU	OBJURGATION	ACCDEIILLTY	DEICTICALLY
ABGIJNOSTUU	SUBJUGATION	ACCDEIINOST	DESICCATION
ABGILLORTUY	GLOBULARITY	ACCDEIKLNST	CANDLESTICK
ABGILMOSUUY	AMBIGUOUSLY	ACCDEILMOPT	COMPLICATED
ABGILORRSUU	BURGLARIOUS	ACCDEINOOTU	COEDUCATION
ABGIMNOSUUU	UNAMBIGUOUS	ACCDEINPRSY	DISCREPANCY
ABGJOORRTUY	OBJURGATORY	ACCDGILNORY	ACCORDINGLY
ABIIIILMTTY	IMITABILITY	ACCDHIIMORT	DICHROMATIC
ABIIILNOSTU	ANTIBILIOUS	ACCDHINORYY	HYDROCYANIC
ABIIILNRTTU	TRIBUNITIAL	ACCDIILLNRY	CYLINDRICAL
ABIIILNSTTY	INSTABILITY	ACCDIILLORY	CODICILLARY
ABIIILPRTTY	PARTIBILITY	ACCDIILNOOR	CROCODILIAN
ABIIILPSSTY	PASSIBILITY	ACCDIMOSSTU	DISACCUSTOM
ABIIILSTTUY	SUITABILITY	ACCEEEEHMRS	CREAM-CHEESE
ABIIINOPRTT	BIPARTITION	ACCEEEENNSV	EVANESCENCE
ABIIKLORTWY	WORKABILITY	ACCEEEFILMN	MALEFICENCE
ABIIILLLNRTY	BRILLIANTLY	ACCEEEELNOPS	OPALESCENCE
ABIIILLOSTVY	SOLVABILITY	ACCEEFIIRTT	CERTIFICATE

ACCEEFIKRRR	FIRE-CRACKER	ACCGILLMOOY	MYCOLOGICAL
ACCEEGHINTY	EYE-CATCHING	ACCGILNOORY	CARCINOLOGY
ACCEEGLNSTU	GLAUCESCENT	ACCGIMOPRTY	CRYPTOGAMIC
ACCEEHILNRT	CHANTICLEER	ACCHHIINSTT	CHAIN-STITCH
ACCEEHIRSTW	CESAREWITCH	ACCHHMNORUW	CHURCHWOMAN
ACCEEIILNRT	ELECTRICIAN	ACCHIILMOST	CATHOLICISM
ACCEEIMNNOPS	CINEMASCOPE	ACCHIILOSST	SCHOLIASTIC
ACCEEINNORV	CRACOVIENNE	ACCHIILOTTY	CATHOLICITY
ACCEEINQSTU	ACQUIESCENT	ACCHIIMNORT	CHIROMANTIC
ACCEEIOPRRT	RECIPROCATE	ACCHIIMOSST	MASOCHISTIC
ACCEFIIORTTX	EXCORTICATE	ACCHIIOPPRT	HIPPOCRATIC
ACCEELMNNOT	CONCEALMENT	ACCHIIPRSTY	PSYCHIATRIC
ACCEEMNNORR	NECROMANCER	ACCHINOPSTY	SYCOPHANTIC
ACCEEMNOPPU	COMEUPPANCE	ACCHIOORRSU	CHIAROSCURO
ACCEENNNOTU	COUNTENANCE	ACCHLLOORSY	CHRYSOCOLLA
ACCEENNORTT	CONCENTRATE	ACCHNOOOPSU	CACOPHONOUS
ACCEENNORVY	CONVEYANCER	ACCIIILNSTV	CALVINISTIC
ACCEEOPRSUY	CYPERACEOUS	ACCIIILRTTY	CRITICALITY
ACCEFFIIOSU	EFFICACIOUS	ACCIILNNOTU	INCULCATION
ACCEFHIINTY	CHIEFTAINCY	ACCIILNNQUU	QUINCUNCIAL
ACCEFILORSU	CALCIFEROUS	ACCIILNOORT	CONCILIATOR
ACCEHIILNST	CALISTHENIC	ACCIILNORTU	CIRCULATION
ACCEHIILOTZ	CATHOLICIZE	ACCIILNOTVY	VOLCANICITY
ACCEHIIRSTU	EUCHARISTIC	ACCIILNTUVY	VULCANICITY
ACCEHILLMNO	MELANCHOLIC	ACCIILRRTUY	CIRCULARITY
ACCEHILLNTY	TECHNICALLY	ACCIINORRSU	ROSICRUCIAN
ACCEHILPRTY	PHYLACTERIC	ACCILLNOOOT	COLLOCATION
ACCEIIINPRT	ACCIPITRINE	ACCILMOPRRU	CIRCUMPOLAR
ACCEIILLMRS	CLERICALISM	ACCILNOOTTU	OCCULTATION
ACCEIILRRSU	CIRCULARISE	ACCILOPRTTU	PLUTOCRATIC
ACCEIILRTUV	CIRCULATIVE	ACCILORRTUY	CIRCULATORY
ACCEIIMNOST	ENCOMIASTIC	ACCIMMNNOTU	COMMUNICANT
ACCEIINNOSU	INSOUCIANCE	ACCIMNNOOTT	CONCOMITANT
ACCEIIRRSTT	CRITICASTER	ACCINNNOSTY	INCONSTANCY
ACCEILLNRTY	CENTRICALLY	ACCINNOOOTV	CONVOCATION
ACCEILLPSTY	SCEPTICALLY	ACCINNOORTT	CONTRACTION
ACCEILNNOTY	ANTICYCLONE	ACCINOOPRSY	CRANIOSCOPY
ACCEILNORTT	CONTRACTILE	ACCINOORRRW	CARRION-CROW
ACCEILNORTU	CORNICULATE	ACCINOORSTU	CORUSCATION
ACCEILOPRST	CEROPLASTIC	ACCKOOPRRSW	COCK-SPARROW
ACCEILORSSY	ACCESSORILY	ACCLOPRRSUU	CORPUSCULAR
ACCEIMMNOTU	COMMUNICATE	ACDDEEFFIST	DISAFFECTED
ACCEIMNNORT	NECROMANTIC	ACDDEEHLNOS	CLOSE-HANDED
ACCEIMORRTY	MERITOCRACY	ACDDEEHLORT	COLD-HEARTED
ACCEINNNOTU	CONTINUANCE	ACDDEEHLRUY	CURLY-HEADED
ACCEINNORTV	CONTRIVANCE	ACDDEEIINTU	INDECIDUATE
ACCEINORSTU	CATER-COUSIN	ACDDEEIMSSU	SADDUCEEISM
ACCEIORSTUU	URTICACEOUS	ACDDEILLMSS	MIDDLE-CLASS
ACCEJLNORTU	CONJECTURAL	ACDDEIMNORU	ENDOCARDIUM
ACCELMMNOOP	COMMONPLACE	ACDDILOSTUY	DIDACTYLOUS
ACCELPRRSUU	CREPUSCULAR	ACDEEEEHLRR	CHEER-LEADER
ACCEMNOPSST	COMPACTNESS	ACDEEEFNORT	CONFEDERATE
ACCENNORSVY	CONSERVANCY	ACDEEEIILLPT	PEDICELLATE
ACCENOOPRTU	POCOCURANTE	ACDEEEILNRV	DELIVERANCE
ACCENOORRST	CONSECRATOR	ACDEEEIMRTV	DECEMVIRATE
ACCENOPRRTT	PRECONTRACT	ACDEEEINPRU	PREAUDIENCE
ACCENPRTUUU	ACUPUNCTURE	ACDEEEIPRTT	DECREPITATE
ACCEORSSTUU	CRUSTACEOUS	ACDEEEIPRTV	DEPRECATIVE
ACCFINOORST	CONFISCATOR	ACDEEELLRVW	CAVE-DWELLER
ACCGHIILRRU	CHIRURGICAL	ACDEEFFINOT	AFFECTIONED
ACCGIILNRTU	CIRCULATING	ACDEEFLNRUU	FRAUDULENCE

ACDEEGHNRRU	UNDERCHARGE
ACDEEGILNTU	GENICULATED
ACDEEGKLNOW	ACKNOWLEDGE
ACDEEHILNOP	ENCEPHALOID
ACDEEHILNPP	CHIPPENDALE
ACDEEHILPSY	PSYCHEDELIA
ACDEEHIMNRS	MERCHANDISE
ACDEEHINRTW	WINDCHEATER
ACDEEHLLOSU	CLOSE-HAULED
ACDEEHNPRSS	PARCHEDNESS
ACDEEIILTUV	ELUCIDATIVE
ACDEEIIPRTV	PREDICATIVE
ACDEEIJLTVY	ADJECTIVELY
ACDEEIJPRTU	PREJUDICATE
ACDEEILLMNY	ENDEMICALLY
ACDEEILMNRU	UNRECLAIMED
ACDEEILNNST	CLANDESTINE
ACDEEILNOTT	DELECTATION
ACDEEILNPST	LAPIDESCENT
ACDEEILNRTU	DECLINATURE
ACDEEILNTTU	DENTICULATE
ACDEEILPRTU	REDUPLICATE
ACDEEILRTTU	RETICULATED
ACDEEIMNPRT	PREDICAMENT
ACDEEIMORTZ	DEMOCRATIZE
ACDEEIMOSTT	DOMESTICATE
ACDEEINNRST	DISENTRANCE
ACDEEINOPRT	DEPRECATION
ACDEEINORST	CONSIDERATE
	DESECRATION
ACDEEIORRTT	DIRECTORATE
ACDEELNOPRW	CANDLE-POWER
ACDEELNPTUU	PEDUNCULATE
ACDEELSSTUY	DECUSSATELY
ACDEEMNRTTU	TRADUCEMENT
ACDEEOPRRTY	DEPRECATORY
ACDEFFIIRTV	DIFFRACTIVE
ACDEFGILRSU	DISGRACEFUL
ACDEFIIINNT	INFANTICIDE
ACDEFIIINOT	DEIFICATION
	EDIFICATION
ACDEFINNOTU	FECUNDATION
ACDEGHIIOPR	IDEOGRAPHIC
ACDEGHILLNT	CANDLELIGHT
ACDEGHIMOPR	DEMOGRAPHIC
ACDEGIILLOO	IDEOLOGICAL
ACDEGIIMNSU	MISGUIDANCE
ACDEHIIOPRT	DIAPHORETIC
ACDEHILOPSU	DICEPHALOUS
ACDEHIMOPRS	COMRADESHIP
ACDEHINOORS	ICOSAHEDRON
ACDEHIOOPRT	ORTHOPAEDIC
ACDEHLNPRTU	THUNDERCLAP
ACDEIIILMOT	DOMICILIATE
ACDEIIINTVV	VINDICATIVE
ACDEIIJLPRU	PREJUDICIAL
ACDEIIILLMNY	MEDICINALLY
ACDEIIILLNTY	IDENTICALLY
ACDEIIILLSTY	DEISTICALLY
ACDEIILMNOT	MALEDICTION
ACDEIILNNOT	DECLINATION

ACDEIILNORT	DIRECTIONAL
ACDEIILNOTU	ELUCIDATION
ACDEIILNOTV	VALEDICTION
ACDEIILNPTU	INDUPLICATE
ACDEIILORRT	DIRECTORIAL
ACDEIILPTUV	DUPLICATIVE
ACDEIIMMNOS	DEMONIACISM
ACDEIIMPRRU	PERICARDIUM
ACDEIINNRTY	TYRANNICIDE
ACDEIINOPRT	PREDICATION
ACDEIINORRT	DOCTRINAIRE
ACDEILLNOOT	DECOLLATION
ACDEILNOOST	CONSOLIDATE
ACDEILNORSY	SECONDARILY
ACDEILNORTY	DECLINATORY
ACDEILORTVY	VALEDICTORY
ACDEILPRTUU	DUPLICATURE
ACDEIMNORRS	MORRIS-DANCE
ACDEINNORST	CONSTRAINED
ACDEINNORTU	DENUNCIATOR
ACDEINOPSTT	CONSTIPATED
ACDEINOSSTU	DECUSSATION
ACDEINOSTTU	OUTDISTANCE
ACDEINPRSTU	UNPRACTISED
ACDEIOPRRTY	PREDICATORY
ACDELNOOPRS	SCOLOPENDRA
ACDELOPRTTY	PTERODACTYL
ACDEMMMNNOT	COMMANDMENT
ACDEMMNOORT	COMMENDATOR
ACDEMNNORTU	COUNTERMAND
ACDEMNORTUY	DOCUMENTARY
ACDENNNNOUU	UNANNOUNCED
ACDFFGIINNT	FACT-FINDING
ACDFFGILNOS	SCAFFOLDING
ACDFFIILMOO	OFFICIALDOM
ACDFFIINORT	DIFFRACTION
ACDFGHHIINS	CHAFING-DISH
ACDGGIILNNR	DANCING-GIRL
ACDGHIMOOSU	DICHOGAMOUS
ACDGHIOPRSY	DISCOGRAPHY
ACDGIILLOST	DIALOGISTIC
ACDGIINOSST	DIAGNOSTICS
ACDGIINRSTT	DISTRACTING
ACDGLLOOTYY	DACTYLOLOGY
ACDHHIOPRRS	HARPSICHORD
ACDHHIOPRTY	HYDROPATHIC
ACDHIORSTTY	HYDROSTATIC
ACDIIILLOTY	IDIOTICALLY
ACDIIILMORY	DOMICILIARY
ACDIIINNOTV	VINDICATION
ACDIIJLLRUY	JURIDICALLY
ACDIILNNOOT	CONDITIONAL
ACDIILNNOTU	INDUCTIONAL
ACDIILNOOST	DISLOCATION
ACDIILNOPTU	DUPLICATION
ACDIILNSSTY	SYNDICALIST
ACDIINNOSTY	SYNDICATION
ACDIINORSTT	DISTRACTION
ACDIINORTVY	VINDICATORY
ACDILLNORTY	DOCTRINALLY
ACDILLNOSYY	SYNODICALLY

ACDILLORSTY	CRYSTALLOID	ACEEIINNTUV	ENUNCIATIVE
ACDINNNOOOT	CONDONATION	ACEEIIPPRTT	PERIPATETIC
ACDLNOOORTY	CONDOLATORY		PRECIPITATE
ACEEEGILNRT	ENERGETICAL	ACEEIIRSSTT	CASSITERITE
ACEEEHIMNTV	ACHIEVEMENT	ACEEIJNNRTT	INTERJACENT
ACEEEHLLNRT	CHANTERELLE	ACEEIKNSSSS	SEASICKNESS
ACEEEHMNNNT	ENHANCEMENT	ACEEILLLSTY	CELESTIALLY
ACEEEILMNPT	MANTELPIECE	ACEEILLNNSS	CLEANLINESS
ACEEEILNQUV	EQUIVALENCE	ACEEILMNNRT	INCREMENTAL
ACEEEILNRRV	IRRELEVANCE	ACEEILMNRRY	MERCENARILY
ACEEEIMPRST	MASTERPIECE	ACEEILMORRT	CALORIMETER
ACEEEINSSTT	NECESSITATE	ACEEILMRTUV	VERMICULATE
ACEEEIPTTVX	EXPECTATIVE	ACEEILNNORT	INTOLERANCE
ACEEEJKLPST	STEEPLEJACK	ACEEILNNOTU	ENUCLEATION
ACEEELLMNOV	MALEVOLENCE	ACEEILNNTUY	LIEUTENANCY
ACEEELLSSSY	CEASELESSLY	ACEEILNOPTX	EXCEPTIONAL
ACEEELMNPRT	REPLACEMENT	ACEEILNOSST	COESSENTIAL
ACEEELMNRRT	RECREMENTAL	ACEEILNPRTT	CENTRIPETAL
ACEEEOPRTTX	EXPECTORATE	ACEEILNQUVY	EQUIVALENCY
ACEEFFILNTU	INEFFECTUAL	ACEEILNRRVY	IRRELEVANCY
ACEEFHINNRS	ENFRANCHISE	ACEEILNRSSY	NECESSARILY
ACEEFHNRRTU	FURTHERANCE	ACEEILORRTV	CORRELATIVE
ACEEFLLNRST	CRESTFALLEN	ACEEILORTUX	EXECUTORIAL
ACEEFLNRSSU	CAREFULNESS	ACEEILPSTUV	SPECULATIVE
ACEEFLORSUU	FERULACEOUS	ACEEILSTTTU	TESTICULATE
ACEEFMNOPRR	PERFORMANCE	ACEEIMMORST	COMMISERATE
ACEEGGIMMNO	EMMENAGOGIC	ACEEIMNNOTT	CEMENTATION
ACEEGHILPRT	TELEGRAPHIC	ACEEIMNORRT	CRANIOMETER
ACEEGHINNRT	INTERCHANGE	ACEEIMNORRT	ACTINOMETER
ACEEGHKRSTU	HUCKSTERAGE	ACEEIMNQRTU	ACQUIREMENT
ACEEGILLNRY	GENERICALLY	ACEEINNNSST	ANCIENTNESS
ACEEGILLNTY	GENETICALLY	ACEEINOPTTX	EXPECTATION
ACEEGILMMRT	TELEGRAMMIC	ACEEIOOPRTV	CO-OPERATIVE
ACEEGILMORT	GEOMETRICAL	ACEEIOPPRSU	PIPERACEOUS
ACEEGILSTTU	GESTICULATE	ACEEIORRTTV	RETROACTIVE
ACEEGIMMNPT	CAMP-MEETING	ACEEIRSSTTU	RESUSCITATE
ACEEGIRSTTT	STRATEGETIC	ACEEJNPRSTU	SUPERJACENT
ACEEGLLRSSY	GRACELESSLY	ACEELLNORTY	COETERNALLY
ACEEGMNORRS	SCAREMONGER	ACEELLNOSTT	CONSTELLATE
ACEEHHLMRST	CRASH-HELMET	ACEELLSSSUY	CAUSELESSLY
ACEEHHOPTTY	HYPOTHECATE	ACEELMNOPTT	CONTEMPLATE
ACEEHIINNRT	INHERITANCE	ACEELNOPSTT	PENTECOSTAL
ACEEHILLNNP	PANHELLENIC	ACEELNORSTU	COUNTERSEAL
ACEEHILLRTY	HERETICALLY	ACEELNPTTXY	EXPECTANTLY
ACEEHILORTT	THEORETICAL	ACEELOPPPRT	COPPERPLATE
ACEEHIMMNPT	IMPEACHMENT	ACEEMMMOORT	COMMEMORATE
ACEEHIMNNNT	ENCHAINMENT	ACEENNOPRTU	COUNTERPANE
ACEEHIMORTT	THEOREMATIC	ACEENNORRTV	CONTRAVENER
ACEEHIMRTTY	ERYTHEMATIC	ACEENNORSTT	CONSTERNATE
ACEEHINPRTT	PARENTHETIC	ACEENNRSSUY	UNNECESSARY
ACEEHLNOPSU	ENCEPHALOUS	ACEENOPRTTX	EXPECTORANT
ACEEHLOORRU	LEUCORRHOEA	ACEEOORSSTU	OSTREACEOUS
ACEEHMNNNTT	ENCHANTMENT	ACEEPRRSSUU	ACUPRESSURE
ACEEHNNRSST	ENCHANTRESS	ACEEPRSSSTT	SPECTATRESS
ACEEHORRSTT	ORCHESTRATE	ACEFFGHILNR	CLIFFHANGER
ACEEHORRSTU	TREACHEROUS	ACEFFGILNTY	AFFECTINGLY
ACEEIILLNRT	RECTILINEAL	ACEFFILRSST	TRAFFICLESS
ACEEIILNRRT	RECTILINEAR	ACEFFIOSTUV	SUFFOCATIVE
ACEEIILPTVX	EXPLICATIVE	ACEFGHLLNUY	CHANGEFULLY
ACEEIILRRST	RECTISERIAL	ACEFGIIMNNT	MAGNIFICENT
ACEEIIMNRRT	RECRIMINATE	ACEFGILNRTU	CENTRIFUGAL

ACEFHIINRTY	CHIEFTAINRY	ACEHIMNORSS	MARCHIONESS
ACEFHLOPRRU	REPROACHFUL	ACEHIMNOTTU	HUMECTATION
ACEFIILNNSS	FINICALNESS	ACEHIMOPRST	ATMOSPHERIC
ACEFIILPRSU	SUPERFICIAL	ACEHIMPSSTY	METAPHYSICS
ACEFIIMNORT	RIFACIMENTO	ACEHIMPSTTY	SYMPATHETIC
ACEFIINOPTT	PONTIFICATE	ACEHINRSSST	STARCHINESS
ACEFIINORTZ	FRACTIONIZE	ACEHIOPRRST	CREATORSHIP
ACEFILLORUW	CAULIFLOWER	ACEHIQRRSUY	SQUIREARCHY
ACEFILORSTU	LACTIFEROUS	ACEHLLMSSTY	MATCHLESSLY
ACEFILOSTUY	FACETIOUSLY	ACEHLMOOPTY	CEPHALOTOMY
ACEFIMNOTTU	TUMEFACTION	ACEHLNOPRTY	LYCANTHROPE
ACEFIMORRRT	CRATERIFORM	ACEHMNNOPRSY	PROSENCHYMA
ACEFINNOTTU	FUNCTIONATE	ACEHMOOPPST	COMPOST-HEAP
ACEFIPRRSTT	PRIESTCRAFT	ACEHMOORTTY	TRACHEOTOMY
ACEFLLLOSSW	CLASS-FELLOW	ACEHOPRRSSY	CHRYSOPRASE
ACEGGINNORU	ENCOURAGING	ACEIIILMPTV	IMPLICATIVE
ACEGGINRSSS	SCRAGGINESS	ACEIIILPSTT	PIETISTICAL
ACEGGLNOOYY	GYNAECOLOGY	ACEIIIMNNRT	INCRIMINATE
ACEGHHILRST	SEARCHLIGHT	ACEIIIMNNRTV	CRIMINATIVE
ACEGHHNORST	SHORTCHANGE	ACEIIIQSTUV	ACQUISITIVE
ACEGHILLOOT	THEOLOGICAL	ACEIIILLMPRY	EMPIRICALLY
ACEGHILNRSY	SEARCHINGLY	ACEIILLNOTV	VELLICATION
ACEGHILOPSY	GEOPHYSICAL	ACEIILLNRUV	CURVILINEAL
ACEGHIMNORU	ARCHEGONIUM	ACEIILLNSTT	SCINTILLATE
ACEGHLOOSTY	ESCHATOLOGY	ACEIILLOPST	EPISTOLICAL
ACEGHLOPTTY	GLYPTOTHECA	ACEIILLPRTU	PLEURITICAL
ACEGHNOPRSY	SCENOGRAPHY	ACEIILMORST	ISOMETRICAL
ACEGHOOPRSU	CREOPHAGOUS	ACEIILNNORT	RECLINATION
ACEGIILOSTT	EGOTISTICAL	ACEIILNOPRT	REPLICATION
ACEGIIMRRTV	GRAVIMETRIC	ACEIILNOPTX	EXPLICATION
ACEGIIPRRST	PERIGASTRIC	ACEIILNOQTU	EQUINOCTIAL
ACEGILLNOSS	LOGICALNESS	ACEIILNPRUY	PECUNIARILY
ACEGILNNOOT	CONGELATION	ACEIILNRRUV	CURVILINEAR
ACEGILNNPRS	SPRING-CLEAN	ACEIILNRSTU	UNREALISTIC
ACEGILNNRTU	CLEARING-NUT	ACEIILNRSTX	EXTRINSICAL
ACEGILNNSUY	UNCEASINGLY	ACEIILNRTTY	INTRICATELY
ACEGILNRSSY	CARESSINGLY	ACEIILOORVV	CAVO-RILIEVO
ACEGILNTUUU	UNGUICULATE	ACEIILPRSTT	PERISTALTIC
ACEGILOOPST	APOLOGETICS	ACEIILPRTUY	PECULIARITY
ACEGILRRTUU	AGRICULTURE	ACEIILRTTVY	VERTICALITY
ACEGINNRSTY	ASTRINGENCY	ACEIIMNNORT	INCREMATION
ACEGINOSTTV	CASTING-VOTE	ACEIIMNOPRT	IMPRECATION
ACEGLORRSSV	CLOVER-GRASS	ACEIIMNORST	ROMANTICISE
ACEGMNNORSS	CONGRESSMAN	ACEIIMNORTT	METRICATION
ACEHHIIMRRS	HIERARCHISM	ACEIIMNPRRU	PERICRANIUM
ACEHHIINNTY	HYACINTHINE	ACEIINNNOTU	ENUNCIATION
ACEHHOPRTYY	HYPOTHECARY	ACEIINNOPTT	PECTINATION
ACEHIILLMOT	HOMILETICAL	ACEIINNORTT	INTERACTION
ACEHIILMSTT	ATHLETICISM	ACEIINNPSTT	PINNATISECT
ACEHIILNOPR	NECROPHILIA	ACEIINOORTX	EXCORIATION
ACEHIILNPRT	NEPHRITICAL	ACEIINOPRTT	CREPITATION
ACEHIILPPTY	EPIPHYTICAL	ACEIINOPSTX	EXPISCATION
ACEHIINORRT	RHETORICIAN	ACEIINORSTT	REACTIONIST
ACEHIINPSTT	PANTHEISTIC	ACEIINORTTX	EXTRICATION
ACEHIKMNORS	CHAIN-SMOKER	ACEIINPPRTT	PRECIPITANT
ACEHILLOPRT	PLETHORICAL	ACEIINPRTTY	ANTIPYRETIC
ACEHILLPRSY	SPHERICALLY		PERTINACITY
ACEHILOPPRT	PROPHETICAL	ACEILLLMNOR	LAMELLICORN
ACEHILOPPRW	COAL-WHIPPER	ACEILLLMOPY	POLEMICALLY
ACEHIMMOPRT	METAMORPHIC	ACEILLLNRUU	UNICELLULAR
ACEHIMNOPSS	CHAMPIONESS	ACEILLMNRUY	NUMERICALLY

ACEILLMRRUY	MERCURIALLY	ACELLOOPRRY	CORPOREALLY
ACEILLNOPTU	CUPELLATION	ACELMNNOORT	NOMENCLATOR
ACEILLNOSTY	SECTIONALLY	ACELNNRSTTU	TRANSLUCENT
ACEILLNRSTY	CRYSTALLINE	ACELNORSUUV	CAVERNULOUS
ACEILLOPPRT	PROLEPTICAL	ACELOOPRRTT	PROTECTORAL
ACEILLOPPSY	EPISCOPALLY	ACELOOPRRTY	CORPORATELY
ACEILLOQUVY	EQUIVOCALLY	ACELOORRTUW	WATER-COLOUR
ACEILLRRTUY	RETICULARLY	ACELOPRTUXY	EXCULPATORY
ACEILLRSTYZ	CRYSTALLIZE	ACEMMNOORTT	COMMENTATOR
ACEILMMNOTY	METONYMICAL	ACEMMNOPRTT	COMPARTMENT
ACEILMMORRT	COAL-TRIMMER	ACEMNOOPR3T	COMPENSATOR
ACEILMMHSTY	SYMMETRICAL	ACEMORSSTTU	SCOUTMASTER
ACEILMNRTTU	CURTAILMENT	ACENNOORRTT	CONTRA-TENOR
ACEILMORRTY	CALORIMETRY	ACENOORRSTV	CONSERVATOR
ACEILNNNOSS	NONSENSICAL	ACENOPRRTTU	COUNTERPART
ACEILNNNOTT	CONTINENTAL	ACFFGINOSTU	SUFFOCATING
ACEILNNSSTY	INCESSANTLY	ACFFIIILMOS	OFFICIALISM
ACEILNOOPRR	INCORPOREAL	ACFFINOOSTU	SUFFOCATION
ACEILNOOPRT	NEOTROPICAL	ACFGIIINNST	SIGNIFICANT
	PERCOLATION	ACFGILNTTUU	FLUCTUATING
ACEILNOOORT	CORRELATION	ACFIIILMSST	FACSIMILIST
ACEILNOPSTU	SPECULATION	ACFIIINNOTU	UNIFICATION
ACEILNOPTUX	EXCULPATION	ACFIIMNOORT	FORMICATION
ACEILNOQUUV	UNEQUIVOCAL	ACFIINNOORT	FORNICATION
ACEILNORRTU	INTEROCULAR	ACFIINOOPRT	FORCIPATION
ACEILNORSTT	INTERCOSTAL	ACFILLMOORR	CORALLIFORM
ACEILNORTUV	COUNTERVAIL	ACFILMNNOTU	MALFUNCTION
ACEILNRRTUV	VENTRICULAR	ACFILMOPRRS	SCALPRIFORM
ACEILOOPPRS	POLARISCOPE	ACFILNOTTUU	FLUCTUATION
ACEILOPRRTT	PROTRACTILE	ACFILORSTUY	FRACTIOUSLY
ACEILOPRTXY	EXPLICATORY	ACFINNOOTTU	CONFUTATION
ACEILORSUVY	VERACIOUSLY	ACFINNORTUY	FUNCTIONARY
ACEILORTVYY	VICEROYALTY	ACGHHILOOPR	HOLOGRAPHIC
ACEIMMORRTU	CREMATORIUM	ACGHHIOPRRY	CHIROGRAPHY
ACEIMMOTTUV	COMMUTATIVE	ACGHHNOOPRR	CHRONOGRAPH
ACEIMNNNOTT	CONTAINMENT	ACGHHOOPRRY	CHOROGRAPHY
ACEIMNNOORY	ONEIROMANCY	ACGHIILMORT	LOGARITHMIC
ACEIMNORRTY	CRANIOMETRY	ACGHILLOOOR	HOROLOGICAL
ACEIMOPRRTY	IMPRECATORY	ACGHILMOOST	LOGOMACHIST
ACEINNOOTTV	CONNOTATIVE	ACGHILOPRXY	XYLOGRAPHIC
ACEINNORTUY	ENUNCIATORY	ACGHIMNOOPR	MONOGRAPHIC
ACEINNOSTTY	ENCYSTATION	ACGHIMOPRRY	MICROGRAPHY
ACEINNPTUUV	NUNCUPATIVE	ACGHINOOPRY	ICONOGRAPHY
ACEINNRRTUW	CURRANT-WINE	ACGHINOPRYZ	ZINCOGRAPHY
ACEINNRTTUY	UNCERTAINTY	ACGHIOOPPRT	TOPOGRAPHIC
ACEINOOOPRT	CO-OPERATION	ACGHIOPPRTY	TYPOGRAPHIC
ACEINOOPRRT	INCORPORATE	ACGHIOPRSTY	HYPOGASTRIC
	PROCREATION	ACGHMOOPRSY	COSMOGRAPHY
ACEINORRTTY	CONTRARIETY	ACGHOPPRRTY	CRYPTOGRAPH
ACEINORSUUV	UNVERACIOUS	ACGIILLLLOY	ILLOGICALLY
ACEINPPRSSS	SCRAPPINESS	ACGIILLNOST	OSCILLATING
ACEINRRTUUV	INCURVATURE	ACGIILLNTUV	VICTUALLING
ACEIOOPRTVV	PROVOCATIVE	ACGIIMNOSST	AGNOSTICISM
ACEIOOQRTUV	EQUIVOCATOR	ACGIJJKMNPU	JUMPING-JACK
ACEIOPRRSTT	TRICERATOPS	ACGIJLNOTUY	CONJUGALITY
ACEIOPRRTTV	PROTRACTIVE	ACGIJNNOOTU	CONJUGATION
ACEKKMORSTT	STOCK-MARKET	ACGIKKNOSTT	STOCKTAKING
ACEKLLRSSTY	TRACKLESSLY	ACGILLMOOTY	CLIMATOLOGY
ACEKMNORRTU	COUNTERMARK	ACGILLNOOOS	NOSOLOGICAL
ACELLNOSSSU	CALLOUSNESS	ACGILLNOOOT	ONTOLOGICAL
ACELLNRTTUY	RELUCTANTLY	ACGIMNOORST	GASTRONOMIC

ACGINOORRTU	CORRUGATION
ACGINOORSTY	CO-SIGNATORY
ACGMOOPRRTU	COMPURGATOR
ACGNOORSSTT	COTTON-GRASS
ACHHIILLPTY	ITHYPHALLIC
ACHHIILMOPT	PHILOMATHIC
ACHHILOPRSS	SCHOLARSHIP
ACHIILLMSWY	WHIMSICALLY
ACHIILOPSST	SOPHISTICAL
ACHIILPSTYY	PHYSICALITY
ACHIINNRSTU	UNCHRISTIAN
ACHILMOOPST	HOMOPLASTIC
ACHIMOPPPSU	HIPPOCAMPUS
ACHIMOPRSSY	SYMPOSIARCH
ACHIMORRSTY	CHRISMATORY
ACHIOOPPRST	APOSTROPHIC
ACHIOPRRSTU	CURATORSHIP
ACHLNOPRTYY	LYCANTHROPY
ACIIILMNOPT	IMPLICATION
ACIIILMNRST	CRIMINALIST
ACIIILMNRTY	CRIMINALITY
ACIIILNNNOT	INCLINATION
ACIIILNNRST	INTRINSICAL
ACIIILRSTTU	RITUALISTIC
ACIIIMNNORT	CRIMINATION
ACIIIMNNOSS	SOCINIANISM
ACIIINNOTTT	NICTITATION
ACIIINOQSTU	ACQUISITION
ACIIIOSSTTU	ASCITITIOUS
ACIILLLOPTY	POLITICALLY
ACIILLMNOOS	COLONIALISM
ACIILLMNOOT	COLLIMATION
ACIILLMOSUY	MALICIOUSLY
ACIILLNNSTT	SCINTILLANT
ACIILLNOOST	COLONIALIST
	OSCILLATION
ACIILLNOVVY	CONVIVIALLY
ACIILLNPPRY	PRINCIPALLY
ACIILLOPRTY	PICTORIALLY
ACIILMNNOTU	CULMINATION
ACIILMNOOPT	COMPILATION
ACIILMNSTUY	MASCULINITY
ACIILNNOOTU	INOCULATION
ACIILNNOPTU	INCULPATION
ACIILNOTTUV	CULTIVATION
ACIILORSUVY	VICARIOUSLY
ACIILOSUVVY	VIVACIOUSLY
ACIIMMNNOOT	COMMINATION
ACIIMMNORST	ROMANTICISM
ACIIMMNOSST	MONASTICISM
ACIIMMNSSTU	NUMISMATICS
ACIIMNOORSU	ACRIMONIOUS
ACIIMNORSTT	ROMANTICIST
ACIINNORTUV	INCURVATION
ACIINOPRTTU	UNPATRIOTIC
ACIINORSTTU	RUSTICATION
ACIINRTTTUY	TACITURNITY
ACIJNNOORTU	CONJURATION
ACILLMNOPTY	COMPLIANTLY
ACILLMOTYYZ	ZYMOTICALLY
ACILLNNOTUY	CONTINUALLY

ACILLOORSTY	OSCILLATORY
ACILMMMNOSU	COMMUNALISM
ACILMMNOSTU	COMMUNALIST
ACILMMORSSU	COMMISSURAL
ACILMNORTUY	COLUMNARITY
ACILMORSTUY	CUSTOMARILY
ACILMRSTUUY	MUSCULARITY
ACILNNOOOST	CONSOLATION
ACILNOOORTU	COLOURATION
ACILNOOPSTU	UNAPOSTOLIC
ACILNOORRST	CONIROSTRAL
ACILNOPRTUY	INCULPATORY
ACILNORSSTU	ULTRASONICS
ACILNPTTUUY	PUNCTUALITY
ACILOOPRRTY	CORPORALITY
ACILOORSTUY	ATROCIOUSLY
ACILOORSUVY	VORACIOUSLY
ACIMMNOORTY	COMMINATORY
ACIMMNOOTTU	COMMUTATION
ACIMMOPSTTY	SYMPTOMATIC
ACIMNNOOOST	ONOMASTICON
ACIMNOOPTTU	COMPUTATION
ACINNNNOOST	INCONSONANT
ACINNNOOOTT	CONNOTATION
ACINNOOPRTT	CONTRAPTION
ACINNOORTTU	CONTINUATOR
ACINNOPTTUU	PUNCTUATION
ACINOOOPRRT	CORPORATION
ACINOOOPRTV	PROVOCATION
ACINOOPRRST	CONSPIRATOR
ACINOOPRRTT	PROTRACTION
ACINOOPRRTU	PROCURATION
ACINOORRSTU	CONTRARIOUS
ACINOORRSUV	CARNIVOROUS
ACLLMOORSUY	CLAMOROUSLY
ACLLNNORTUY	NOCTURNALLY
ACLNNOOPTTT	COTTON-PLANT
ACLNOOORSTY	CONSOLATORY
ACLNOOPRRSU	PROCONSULAR
ACLOOPPRSUY	POLYCARPOUS
ACNNOPRTUUY	NUNCUPATORY
ADDEEEEHLLV	LEVEL-HEADED
ADDEEEHIKNS	HIDE-AND-SEEK
ADDEEGNRSSU	GUARDEDNESS
ADDEEHIKNRT	KIND-HEARTED
ADDEEHMNPTY	EMPTY-HANDED
ADDEEIMRSTU	DESIDERATUM
ADDEEINOPRT	DEPREDATION
ADDEEINSSSV	ADVISEDNESS
ADDEEOPRRTY	DEPREDATORY
ADDEFHINSSS	FADDISHNESS
ADDEGGHORTU	GODDAUGHTER
ADDEGGIIIRT	DIGITIGRADE
ADDEGHHINRT	RIGHT-HANDED
ADDEGHNORTU	DREADNOUGHT
ADDEGIIMNNR	MIND-READING
ADDEGLNRUUY	UNGUARDEDLY
ADDEHIILMOT	THALIDOMIDE
ADDEHINORTY	DEHYDRATION
ADDEIIINTUV	INDIVIDUATE
ADDEIINOOTX	DEOXIDATION

ADDEILNSUVY	UNADVISEDLY
ADDEIOOPPSU	PSEUDOPODIA
ADDELNNPRTUY	REDUNDANTLY
ADDELNNTUUY	UNDAUNTEDLY
ADDEMNOOORT	RODOMONTADE
ADEEEFILNRT	DEFERENTIAl
ADEEEGHLMPT	DEPHLEGMATE
ADEEEGILMNR	LEGERDEMAIN
ADEEEGIMNRR	GENDARMERIE
ADEEEGIMNTZ	DEMAGNETIZE
ADEEEGINNRT	TRAGEDIENNE
ADEEEGMNNRT	DERANGEMENT
ADEEEHLLORS	LEASEHOLDER
ADEEEHNNNOR	ENNEAHEDRON
ADEEEHRRTTU	TRUEHEARTED
ADEEEIMNRTT	DETERMINATE
ADEEEIMNSST	MEDIATENESS
ADEEEIMPRTT	PREMEDITATE
ADEEEIORRTT	DETERIORATE
ADEEEIPPRUZ	DEPAUPERIZE
ADEEEKLRRST	DEER-STALKER
ADEEELLSSTT	TESSELLATED
ADEEELNRTTU	LAUNDERETTE
ADEEELPRSTY	DESPERATELY
ADEEENRSSSV	ADVERSENESS
ADEEFFIINRT	DIFFERENTIA
ADEEFINNSST	DEFIANTNESS
ADEEFLRSSSU	SELF-ASSURED
ADEEGHNNPRW	GRANDNEPHEW
ADEEGILNNST	DISENTANGLE
ADEEGLLNOSU	EGLANDULOSE
ADEEGMNRRRY	GERRYMANDER
ADEEGMORTUY	DEUTEROGAMY
ADEEHHLORRS	SHAREHOLDER
ADEEHILNOPT	ELEPHANTOID
ADEEHILNPRR	PHILANDERER
ADEEHINRSST	THREADINESS
ADEEHIORTTV	DEHORTATIVE
ADEEHIRRRSS	HAIRDRESSER
ADEEHKORSTT	DEATH-STROKE
ADEEHLNNRST	NETHERLANDS
ADEEHNORRTT	TETRAHEDRON
ADEEHNSTUUX	UNEXHAUSTED
ADEEIILMMSV	MEDIEVALISM
ADEEIILMMTY	IMMEDIATELY
ADEEIILMNRT	INTERMEDIAL
ADEEIILMSTV	MEDIEVALIST
ADEEIILNNOT	DELINEATION
ADEEIILNRST	RESIDENTIAL
ADEEIIMNSST	DISSEMINATE
ADEEILMNRTT	DETRIMENTAL
ADEEILNRSTY	SEDENTARILY
ADEEILOPPRT	LEPIDOPTERA
ADEEILPQSSU	SESQUIPEDAL
ADEEILPRSSU	DISPLEASURE
ADEEIMMNOSU	EUDAEMONISM
ADEEIMNNPTU	ANTEPENDIUM
ADEEIMNNRTT	DETERMINANT
ADEEIMNOPRT	PREDOMINATE
ADEEIMNOSTU	EUDAEMONIST
ADEEIMNRSTY	SEDIMENTARY
ADEEINNRSSU	UNREADINESS
ADEEINNRTTV	INADVERTENT
ADEEINOPRST	DESPERATION
ADEEINOSTTT	DETESTATION
ADEEJMNRRRY	JERRYMANDER
ADEEKLOPRSU	LOUDSPEAKER
ADEELLMRSSY	DREAMLESSLY
ADEELLNRTUV	UNTRAVELLED
ADEELOQSSTU	SOLDATESQUE
ADEEMNORSTT	DEMONSTRATE
	ASSUREDNESS
ADEENRSSTUV	ADVENTURESS
ADEFFIORSST	DISAFFOREST
ADEFGLLRRUY	REGARDFULLY
ADEFIILNOOT	DEFOLIATION
ADEFIILNQUU	UNQUALIFIED
ADEFIINNOTU	INFEUDATION
ADEFIINSSTU	UNSATISFIED
ADEFILNOORT	DEFLORATION
ADEFILSSTTU	DISTASTEFUL
ADEFIMNOORT	DEFORMATION
ADEFNORRSSW	FORWARDNESS
	FROWARDNESS
ADEGHMNORRT	GRANDMOTHER
ADEGIILNPSS	DISPLEASING
ADEGIINNORT	DENIGRATION
ADEGIINNORZ	INORGANIZED
ADEGIINNOST	DESIGNATION
ADEGIINNTUV	UNDEVIATING
ADEGIINORSZ	DISORGANIZE
ADEGIINRSTV	ADVERTISING
ADEGIINRTTU	INGRATITUDE
ADEGIKNNRTU	UNDERTAKING
ADEGILNNRWY	WANDERINGLY
ADEGILNNSSU	LANGUIDNESS
ADEGIMNORRZ	GORMANDIZER
ADEGIMNORUZ	GOURMANDIZE
ADEGINNORSU	UNORGANISED
ADEGLMOORTY	DERMATOLOGY
ADEGLNORSUY	DANGEROUSLY
ADEHHIORRSS	HORSE-RADISH
ADEHHIRRTTW	THITHERWARD
ADEHIIOPRSS	DIAPHORESIS
ADEHILLNRST	DISENTHRALL
ADEHILMNOOP	MONODELPHIA
ADEHIMNPSSS	DAMPISHNESS
ADEHIMORSTU	DIATHERMOUS
ADEHINNRSTU	UNTARNISHED
ADEHINNRSUV	UNVARNISHED
ADEHINOORTT	DEHORTATION
ADEHINOSSSW	SHADOWINESS
ADEHINRSTTW	WITHSTANDER
ADEHIPRSSTW	STEWARDSHIP
ADEHLLLMORS	SMALLHOLDER
ADEHNOPRSTU	HEPTANDROUS
ADEHOORRTTY	DEHORTATORY
ADEIILLLOPS	ELLIPSOIDAL
ADEIILLORTY	EDITORIALLY
ADEIILMNNOS	DIMENSIONAL
ADEIILMOPTZ	DIPLOMATIZE
ADEIILMSSTU	DISSIMULATE

207

ADEIIMMNSTU	MEDIASTINUM
ADEIIMNOPSS	IMPASSIONED
ADEIIMNORSS	READMISSION
ADEIIMRSTTX	TAXIDERMIST
ADEIINNNOTT	INDENTATION
ADEIINNOOPT	OPINIONATED
ADEIINNOSTT	DESTINATION
ADEIINOPRTT	TREPIDATION
ADEIINOPRTU	REPUDIATION
ADEIINOPRTV	DEPRIVATION
ADEIINORSTY	SEDITIONARY
ADEIINORTTX	EXTRADITION
ADEIINPRSTY	STIPENDIARY
ADEIINQSTTU	EQUIDISTANT
ADEIIPSTTUV	DISPUTATIVE
ADEILMNTTUU	UNMUTILATED
ADEILNOOPRT	DEPLORATION
ADEILNQSSSU	SQUALIDNESS
ADEILNRSTWW	WINDLESTRAW
ADEILNRSTWZ	SWITZERLAND
ADEIMMMNNOPU	PANDEMONIUM
ADEIMMNSSTT	DISMASTMENT
ADEIMNNOORT	DENOMINATOR
ADEIMNNOPRT	PREDOMINANT
ADEIMNRRTUY	RUDIMENTARY
ADEINOOPRTT	DEPORTATION
ADEIORRSSTT	DISSERTATOR
ADEJMNNORTU	ADJOURNMENT
ADELLNSSTUY	DAUNTLESSLY
ADELMNOORTY	DEMONOLATRY
ADELMNORRTU	ULTRA-MODERN
ADELOOPPRTU	DEPOPULATOR
ADENNOPRSTU	PENTANDROUS
ADENOPRRSTT	TRANSPORTED
ADENORRSTTU	TETRANDROUS
ADENORSSSUU	ARDUOUSNESS
ADENORSTUUV	ADVENTUROUS
ADENPRSSSUU	UNSURPASSED
ADFIMNOPRRU	PANDURIFORM
ADGHHILNOPT	DIPHTHONGAL
ADGHHOPRRYY	HYDROGRAPHY
ADGHIINNRTW	HANDWRITING
ADGHIKNORRW	HARD-WORKING
ADGIIINNNOT	INDIGNATION
ADGIILNNNTY	INDIGNANTLY
ADGIILOPRTY	PRODIGALITY
ADGIINORSTY	GRANDIOSITY
ADGINNOSTTU	OUTSTANDING
ADGNNOORSUY	ANDROGYNOUS
ADHHOORRTXY	HYDROTHORAX
ADHIIOPRSTU	AUDITORSHIP
ADHIIORRSST	DIARTHROSIS
ADHLNORRTWY	NORTHWARDLY
ADIIILLSTUV	DILUVIALIST
ADIIILNOQTU	LIQUIDATION
ADIIINOPSST	DISSIPATION
ADIILLNOQRU	QUADRILLION
ADIILMOPSTT	DIPLOMATIST
ADIINOPSTTU	DISPUTATION
ADIIOOPRSUV	AVOIRDUPOIS
ADILOSSSUUY	ASSIDUOUSLY
AEEEEFGILPR	LIFE-PEERAGE
AEEEEHILRTZ	ETHEREALIZE
AEEEEHLRTTT	LEATHERETTE
AEEEFGIRRRT	REFRIGERATE
AEEEFHINRRT	HEREINAFTER
AEEEFILNRRT	REFERENTIAL
AEEEFLLNNTT	FLANNELETTE
AEEEFLRSSTU	FEATURELESS
AEEEFPRSTTU	SUPERFETATE
AEEEGGMMNOU	EMMENAGOGUE
AEEEGILMMRR	LAMMERGEIER
AEEEGIMNNST	STEAM-ENGINE
AEEEGIMNSST	METAGENESIS
AEEEGINPRRT	PEREGRINATE
AEEEGLMNNRT	ENLARGEMENT
AEEEGMNPRST	PRESAGEMENT
AEEEHILNNPT	ELEPHANTINE
AEEEHILRTTY	ETHEREALITY
AEEEHLMPPRT	PAMPHLETEER
AEEEHNPRSST	PARENTHESES
AEEEIIRRTTV	REITERATIVE
AEEEILNRRTV	REVERENTIAL
AEEEILNRTXZ	EXTERNALIZE
AEEEIMNPRTT	INTEMPERATE
AEEEIMNRTTX	EXTERMINATE
AEEEINNRRTT	ENTERTAINER
AEEEINOPRUZ	EUROPEANIZE
AEEEINORTVX	EXONERATIVE
AEEEINPRTTV	PENETRATIVE
AEEEKLLOSTX	EXOSKELETAL
AEEEKPSSSTW	SWEEPSTAKES
AEEELLLMNTY	ELEMENTALLY
AEEELLORTTT	TEETOTALLER
AEEELMNNSTV	ENSLAVEMENT
AEEELMPRTTY	TEMPERATELY
AEEELMRSSSU	MEASURELESS
AEEEMMNPRTT	TEMPERAMENT
AEEEMMNRSTU	MEASUREMENT
AEEEMNNRTTY	TENEMENTARY
AEEEMPRRTTU	TEMPERATURE
AEEENNRSSST	EARNESTNESS
AEEENRSSSTU	AUSTERENESS
AEEEQRSSTTU	SEQUESTRATE
AEEFFGRSTTU	SUFFRAGETTE
AEEFFLNRSSU	FEARFULNESS
AEEFGINRRRT	REFRIGERANT
AEEFHLNSSTU	HATEFULNESS
AEEFHMORRRT	FARTHERMORE
AEEFIILNNRT	INFERENTIAL
AEEFILOPRRT	PROLIFERATE
AEEFIMOPRRT	IMPERFORATE
AEEFIMORRTV	REFORMATIVE
AEEFIOPRRTV	PERFORATIVE
AEEFKLNSSUW	WAKEFULNESS
AEEFLLORRST	FORESTALLER
AEEFLNRSSTU	TEARFULNESS
AEEFMNOPRTY	FOREPAYMENT
AEEFMNORRSY	FREEMASONRY
AEEFNNOPRSS	PROFANENESS
AEEFNRRRRST	TRANSFERRER
AEEGGIINORS	SEIGNIORAGE

AEEGGGILNOST	GENEALOGIST
AEEGGIMNOSS	GAMOGENESIS
AEEGGINORST	SEGREGATION
AEEGGINQSTU	GIGANTESQUE
AEEGGIRRTTU	REGURGITATE
AEEGHHITVWY	HEAVYWEIGHT
AEEGHILNPRS	GENERALSHIP
AEEGHIMMRTU	MEGATHERIUM
AEEGHINNRTT	THREATENING
AEEGHLRRSTU	SLAUGHTERER
AEEGIILLSTV	LEGISLATIVE
AEEGIIMNRTV	GERMINATIVE
AEEGIINRTTV	VINAIGRETTE
AEEGIINSTTV	INVESTIGATE
AEEGILLNNTY	INELEGANTLY
AEEGILLRSTU	LEGISLATURE
AEEGILMNNRT	ENGRAILMENT
AEEGILMNNSS	MEANINGLESS
AEEGILNRSTV	EVERLASTING
AEEGIMNOTTW	WITENAGEMOT
AEEGINNPRTT	PENETRATING
AEEGINOPRRS	OPERA-SINGER
AEEGINORRTT	INTERROGATE
AEEGIOPRRTV	PREROGATIVE
AEEGLLMNNTY	GENTLEMANLY
AEEGLMNNOTW	GENTLEWOMAN
AEEGLMNOOPR	PROLEGOMENA
AEEGMNRTTUY	TEGUMENTARY
AEEGNNRSSST	STRANGENESS
AEEHHILNSST	HEALTHINESS
AEEHHILRTTW	THEREWITHAL
AEEHHILRTWW	WHEREWITHAL
AEEHHNORSTT	HEARTHSTONE
AEEHIILMOPT	EPITHELIOMA
AEEHILNPPRS	PLANISPHERE
AEEHILNPSSS	SHAPELINESS
AEEHILNRSST	EARTHLINESS
AEEHILNSSTW	WEALTHINESS
AEEHILPPRST	PRELATESHIP
AEEHILPSTTT	TELEPATHIST
AEEHIMNSTTY	AMETHYSTINE
AEEHINPRSST	PARENTHESIS
AEEHIORTTVX	EXHORTATIVE
AEEHIPPRRSS	PERIPHRASES
AEEHIPPSTUX	EXHAUST-PIPE
AEEHKMPRRTY	HYPERMARKET
AEEHLLMSSSY	SHAMELESSLY
AEEHLLRSSTY	HEARTLESSLY
AEEHLMNNRTT	ENTHRALMENT
AEEHLSSSTUX	EXHAUSTLESS
AEEHMOPRSTU	HEPTAMEROUS
AEEHMORSTTW	WEATHERMOST
AEEIIILMPRZ	IMPERIALIZE
AEEIIILMMORZ	MEMORIALIZE
AEEIILMNRRZ	MINERALIZER
AEEIILNNPTT	PENITENTIAL
AEEIILNNRRT	INTERLINEAR
AEEIILNNSST	INESSENTIAL
AEEIILNORTZ	ORIENTALIZE
AEEIILNSTTX	EXISTENTIAL
AEEIIMNNRTT	INTERMINATE
AEEIIMNRTTV	TERMINATIVE
AEEIINNTTTV	INATTENTIVE
AEEIINOPRTV	INOPERATIVE
AEEIINORRTT	REITERATION
AEEILLMMNPT	IMPLEMENTAL
AEEILLMPRXY	EXEMPLARILY
AEEILLNNPRY	PERENNIALLY
AEEILLNNSXY	SEXENNIALLY
AEEILLNRSST	LITERALNESS
AEEILLNSSTY	ESSENTIALLY
AEEILLRSTVY	VERSATILELY
AEEILMNNSTT	SENTIMENTAL
AEEILMNORST	SALINOMETER
AEEILMNPRST	SEMPITERNAL
AEEILMNPTTU	PENULTIMATE
AEEILMNRSTX	EXTERNALISM
AEEILMNSSSS	AIMLESSNESS
AEEILMNSSWY	WESLEYANISM
AEEILMOPRRT	POLARIMETER
AEEILMORSWY	WEARISOMELY
AEEILMOSTTT	TEETOTALISM
AEEILNNOPTX	EXPONENTIAL
AEEILNNPSTU	PENINSULATE
AEEILNNSSTU	UNESSENTIAL
AEEILNOPRSZ	PERSONALIZE
AEEILNOPRTT	INTERPOLATE
AEEILNPSVXY	EXPANSIVELY
AEEILNRRTUZ	NEUTRALIZER
AEEILNRTTXY	EXTERNALITY
AEEILNSSSTT	STATELINESS
AEEILNTTTVY	ATTENTIVELY
	TENTATIVELY
AEEILNTTUVY	EVENTUALITY
AEEILOPPSTU	EPIPETALOUS
AEEILOPRTVY	OPERATIVELY
AEEILPRSTUV	SUPERLATIVE
AEEILRRRSTT	TERRESTRIAL
AEEILRRTTTU	LITTÉRATEUR
AEEILRSSTVY	ASSERTIVELY
AEEIMMNNPRT	IMPERMANENT
AEEIMNNORTU	ENUMERATION
	MOUNTAINEER
AEEIMNNPRTT	INTEMPERANT
AEEIMNOPRST	IMPERSONATE
AEEIMNOPRTU	PERITONAEUM
AEEIMORRSTU	TEMERARIOUS
AEEIMSSTTYZ	SYSTEMATIZE
AEEINNOORTX	EXONERATION
AEEINNOPRTT	PENETRATION
AEEINNORSVV	VARSOVIENNE
AEEINNOTTUX	EXTENUATION
AEEINORRSST	REASSERTION
AEEINORRSTV	RESERVATION
AEEINPSSSSV	PASSIVENESS
AEEIOPPRRTX	EXPROPRIATE
AEEIORRSTTV	RESTORATIVE
AEEKMPRRSTU	SUPERMARKET
AEELLNPRTVY	PREVALENTLY
AEELLNSSSSW	LAWLESSNESS
AEELLPPRTUY	PERPETUALLY
AEELLSSSTTY	TASTELESSLY

AEELMNNPRTY	PERMANENTLY	AEGGHIINNRT	INGATHERING
AEELMOQRRSU	QUARRELSOME	AEGGHINSSSW	WAGGISHNESS
AEELMPRRTUY	PREMATURELY	AEGGIINRTTU	INGURGITATE
AEELNNPRTTY	REPENTANTLY	AEGHHILOPRY	HELIOGRAPHY
AEELNOSSSUZ	ZEALOUSNESS	AEGHHINSSTU	HAUGHTINESS
AEELNRSSSST	ARTLESSNESS	AEGHHLOPRSU	PLOUGHSHARE
AEELOPSTTUX	EXPOSTULATE	AEGHHNOPRTY	ETHNOGRAPHY
AEELPRSSSTU	PASTURELESS	AEGHHOPRTYY	HYETOGRAPHY
AEEMNORRSTT	REMONSTRATE	AEGHIKNRSTV	THANKSGIVER
AEEMOPRRTXY	EXTEMPORARY	AEGHILNSSST	GHASTLINESS
AEEMORRSTTU	TETRAMEROUS	AEGHIMNNRST	GARNISHMENT
AEENNNPRTTU	UNREPENTANT	AEGHIMOPRSS	SEISMOGRAPH
AEENOPRRSTT	PATERNOSTER	AEGHIMOPRSY	SEMIOGRAPHY
AEENORTTUXY	EXTENUATORY	AEGHINNSSTU	NAUGHTINESS
AEEOOPSTTTW	SWEET-POTATO	AEGHINOSSST	GOATISHNESS
AEEOPPRRRTT	PERPETRATOR	AEGHLOOPRSY	PHRASEOLOGY
AEEOQRRSTUU	TERRAQUEOUS	AEGHLOPRRXY	XYLOGRAPHER
AEFFGIMSTUU	SUFFUMIGATE	AEGHMNOOPRR	MONOGRAPHER
AEFFHILRSTY	SHERIFFALTY	AEGHNOPRSTY	STENOGRAPHY
AEFFIIMNORR	FORAMINIFER	AEGHNOPSTUY	HEPTAGYNOUS
AEFFKNRRRTU	FRANKFURTER	AEGHOOPRSTY	OSTEOGRAPHY
AEFGGHIRSTT	STAGE-FRIGHT	AEGHOPPRRSS	GRASSHOPPER
AEFGHORRTTW	AFTER-GROWTH	AEGHOPPRRTY	PETROGRAPHY
AEFGILLNRTY	FALTERINGLY		TYPOGRAPHER
AEFGILNNOOR	GONFALONIER	AEGIIILMNPR	PRIMIGENIAL
AEFGILNNRTU	UNFALTERING	AEGIIILNORS	SEIGNIORIAL
AEFGILNNSSU	GAINFULNESS	AEGIIINORTV	ORIGINATIVE
AEFGINNORRW	FOREWARNING	AEGIILLNOST	LEGISLATION
AEFGINORSUU	GUANIFEROUS	AEGIILMNORS	REGIONALISM
AEFGINRRSTU	TRANSFIGURE	AEGIIMMNNORT	GERMINATION
AEFHHLLLTUY	HEALTHFULLY	AEGIIMNNORRT	REMIGRATION
AEFHHLLNTUU	UNHEALTHFUL	AEGIIMPRSTU	EPIGASTRIUM
AEFHILLSSTY	FAITHLESSLY	AEGIINNOOTT	NEGOTIATION
AEFHLMNRSSU	HARMFULNESS	AEGIINNORST	RESIGNATION
AEFHMORRSTT	FARTHERMOST	AEGIINNORTT	INTEGRATION
AEFIILLNNTJ	INFLUENTIAL	AEGIKMMNRRY	MERRYMAKING
AEFIILNOOTX	EXFOLIATION	AEGILLRRRUY	IRREGULARLY
AEFIINNOSTT	INFESTATION	AEGILMNNNUY	UNMEANINGLY
AEFILLLLMMOR	LAMELLIFORM	AEGILMNOORT	GLOMERATION
AEFILMNOSTU	FILAMENTOUS	AEGILMNOPRU	PELARGONIUM
AEFILMORRUZ	FORMULARIZE	AEGILMNOSTU	LIGAMENTOUS
AEFILNNPSSU	PAINFULNESS	AEGILMOOPST	PLAGIOSTOME
AEFILNORSUY	NEFARIOUSLY	AEGILNNSSTY	ASSENTINGLY
AEFIMMMORSU	MAMMIFEROUS	AEGILOOTTUZ	TAUTOLOGIZE
AEFIMNNOOTT	FOMENTATION	AEGILPRTUVY	PURGATIVELY
AEFIMNOORRT	REFORMATION	AEGILRTTUUZ	GUTTURALIZE
AEFIMOPRRTZ	TRAPEZIFORM	AEGIMMOPRSU	GEMMIPAROUS
AEFINNNOPTU	FOUNTAIN-PEN	AEGIMNORSSU	IGNORAMUSES
AEFINOOPRRT	PERFORATION	AEGINNNORSU	UNREASONING
AEFINRSSTUV	TRANSFUSIVE	AEGINNOOTXY	OXYGENATION
AEFLLLNTTUY	FLATULENTLY	AEGINOPRTUX	EXPURGATION
AEFLLLSSTUY	FAULTLESSLY	AEGMMNOORRST	GASTRONOMER
AEFLLNPSSUY	PLAYFULNESS	AEGNNOPSTUY	PENTAGYNOUS
AEFLLORSSUV	FLAVOURLESS	AEGNORSTTUY	TETRAGYNOUS
AEFLLPRRUYY	PRAYERFULLY	AEGOORRRTUV	ROTOGRAVURE
AEFLNOOPSTU	TEASPOONFUL	AEGOPRRTUXY	EXPURGATORY
AEFLNORTTUY	FORTUNATELY	AEHHIIMPSSS	MESSIAHSHIP
AEFMNORRRST	TRANSFORMER	AEHHILLNTUY	UNHEALTHILY
AEFMOORRRTY	REFORMATORY	AEHHINNOPTY	HYPHENATION
AEFNNORTTUU	UNFORTUNATE	AEHHLLOPTTY	THALLOPHYTE
AEGGHIILNNT	NIGHTINGALE	AEHHMOOOPTY	HOMOEOPATHY

AEHHOOPPRST	PHOSPHORATE	AEIILNNSSST	SAINTLINESS
AEHIIILRSST	ISRAELITISH	AEIILNORSSS	INSESSORIAL
AEHIILLPSTT	PHILATELIST	AEIILNORSTT	ORIENTALIST
AEHIILOPSST	HOSPITALISE	AEIILNORTTU	ELUTRIATION
AEHIIMPPRST	PRIMATESHIP	AEIILNRSSTV	TRIVIALNESS
AEHIINOPRRS	PARISHIONER	AEIILORRRTT	TERRITORIAL
AEHIIPPRRSS	PERIPHRASIS	AEIILPRTTVY	PARTITIVELY
AEHIKMNSSSW	MAWKISHNESS	AEIILPRTVVY	PRIVATIVELY
AEHIKNNSSSV	KNAVISHNESS	AEIILRSTTVY	VERSATILITY
AEHILLNOSST	LOATHLINESS	AEIIMNNORTT	TERMINATION
AEHILLOPRST	HOSPITALLER	AEIIMOPPRRT	IMPROPRIATE
AEHILMNORTW	MOTHER-IN-LAW	AEIIMRRTTUV	TRIUMVIRATE
AEHILMNRSTU	LUTHERANISM	AEIINNNORTV	INNERVATION
AEHILMQSSUY	SQUEAMISHLY	AEIINNNOTTT	INATTENTION
AEHILOPPSST	APOSTLESHIP	AEIINNQSSTU	ANTIQUINESS
AEHIMNOPRST	MISANTHROPE	AEIINOPRRST	RESPIRATION
AEHIMOPSSTY	HAEMOPTYSIS	AEIINOPRTTX	EXTIRPATION
AEHIMPRSTYZ	SYMPATHIZER	AEIINOPRTTY	PETITIONARY
AEHINNPPSSU	UNHAPPINESS	AEIINORRTTY	ANTERIORITY
AEHINOORTTX	EXHORTATION	AEIIOOPPSSS	APOSIOPESIS
AEHINOPRSTT	ANTISTROPHE	AEIKKLMNORW	WORKMANLIKE
AEHINORRSST	ENARTHROSIS	AEILLMNNSTT	INSTALLMENT
AEHINPPRRST	PARTNERSHIP	AEILLMNOOTY	EMOTIONALLY
AEHINPSSSSW	WASPISHNESS	AEILLNOOTUV	EVOLUTIONAL
AEHINRSSSTW	SWARTHINESS	AEILLNOPTTY	POTENTIALLY
AEHIOPSTTYZ	HYPOSTATIZE	AEILLNRSUVY	UNIVERSALLY
AEHKLLNSSTY	THANKLESSLY	AEILMMNORTY	MOMENTARILY
AEHLLMOOSTY	LOATHSOMELY	AEILMNNNSSU	UNMANLINESS
AEHLLNOSSSW	SHALLOWNESS	AEILMNNOOTU	UNEMOTIONAL
AEHNORSTUWY	UNSEAWORTHY	AEILMNNOSSW	WOMANLINESS
AEHOORRTTXY	EXHORTATORY	AEILMNNRTTU	NUTRIMENTAL
AEIIILLMNOR	MILLIONAIRE	AEILMNOOSTT	MOLESTATION
AEIIILMMPRS	IMPERIALISM	AEILMNOPRSS	PERSONALISM
AEIIILMNNOT	ELIMINATION	AEILMOPRRTY	TEMPORARILY
AEIIILMNNRST	MINISTERIAL	AEILMOPRTTY	TEMPORALITY
AEIIILMPRST	IMPERIALIST	AEILMOPRTXY	PROXIMATELY
AEIIILMRRSV	VERISIMILAR	AEILNNNOPRSU	UNIPERSONAL
AEIIILMTTVY	IMITATIVELY	AEILNNRSTTY	TRANSIENTLY
AEIIIMNRSTU	MINIATURISE	AEILNOOPRTX	EXPLORATION
AEIIINNSTUV	INSINUATIVE	AEILNOPPTTY	PLATINOTYPE
AEIIILLLMNTU	MULTILINEAL	AEILNOPRRST	TRIPERSONAL
AEIIILLMRSTU	MULTISERIAL	AEILNOPRSTY	PERSONALITY
AEIIILLNNRTY	TRIENNIALLY	AEILNOPSSSS	PASSIONLESS
AEIIILLNOTVY	INVIOLATELY	AEILOOPRRRT	REPORTORIAL
AEIIILLNPTVY	PLAINTIVELY	AEILOPRSTTU	TRIPETALOUS
AEIIILLOORTV	ALTO-RILIEVO	AEILOSTUVXY	VEXATIOUSLY
AEIIILLRRSTT	ARTILLERIST	AEIMNNNOPPTT	APPOINTMENT
AEIIILMMORST	MEMORIALIST	AEIMNNORSTT	ORNAMENTIST
AEIIILMMORTZ	IMMORTALIZE	AEIMNNORSTU	MENSURATION
AEIIILMNOORT	MELIORATION	AEIMNOPRTTU	IMPORTUNATE
AEIIILMNORST	ORIENTALISM		PERMUTATION
AEIIILMNOSTT	TESTIMONIAL	AEIMNORSSTU	STRAMINEOUS
AEIIILMNPRRY	PRELIMINARY	AEIMNNRRSTTT	TRANSMITTER
AEIIILMNPTTY	IMPATIENTLY	AEIMOORRTTY	ARTERIOTOMY
AEIIILMPSSVY	IMPASSIVELY	AEIMPRRTTUY	PREMATURITY
AEIIILMRRSTT	TRIMESTRIAL	AEINNOOPRST	PERSONATION
AEIIILMSTTUV	STIMULATIVE	AEINNOOSTTT	OSTENTATION
AEIIILNNNOTT	INTENTIONAL	AEINNOPSTTY	SPONTANEITY
AEIIILNNORTV	INVENTORIAL	AEINNOSSSUX	ANXIOUSNESS
AEIIILNNOTTV	VENTILATION	AEINOOPRSSU	APONEUROSIS
AEIIILNNRTTY	INTERNALITY	AEINOOPRTTX	EXPORTATION

AEINOORRSTT	RESTORATION
AEINOQRSTUY	QUESTIONARY
AEINORSSSUV	SAVOURINESS
AEIOPPRRRTY	PROPRIETARY
AEIOPRRRSTY	RESPIRATORY
AEIOPRRRTTU	PORTRAITURE
AEIOPRRTTUV	VITUPERATOR
AEIOPRRTTXY	EXTIRPATORY
AEIPPRSTUUV	SUPPURATIVE
AELMMRSSTUU	SUMMERSAULT
AELMNOPRRSU	SUPERNORMAL
AELMPRSTYYY	MYSTERY-PLAY
AELNPRRSUUY	SUPERLUNARY
AELOOPRRTXY	EXPLORATORY
AELOOPSSTTY	OSTEOPLASTY
AEMNNORRSTT	REMONSTRANT
AEMNOORSSSU	AMOROUSNESS
AENNOOPSSTU	SPONTANEOUS
AENOPRRRSTT	TRANSPORTER
AFGIILLNNUY	UNFAILINGLY
AFGIILMNNTU	FULMINATING
AFGIIMNORRT	GRANITIFORM
AFGILNORTUU	FULGURATION
AFIIIILNNTV	INFINITIVAL
AFIILMNNOTU	FULMINATION
AFIILMNORTY	INFORMALITY
AFIILNORRTT	INFILTRATOR
AFIILORSTTU	FLIRTATIOUS
AFIIMNNOORT	INFORMATION
AFIIMNOORSU	OMNIFARIOUS
AFIIMORSTUV	FAVOURITISM
AFIINNORSTX	TRANSFIXION
AFIIOPRSSSU	FISSIPAROUS
AFILMNOORTU	FORMULATION
AFINNORSSTU	TRANSFUSION
AFINORRSTTU	FRUSTRATION
AGGHIILNNSU	LANGUISHING
AGGHIILOOST	HAGIOLOGIST
AGGIILNNOYZ	AGONIZINGLY
AGGILLNNOPY	LONG-PLAYING
AGGIMMNOPRR	PROGRAMMING
AGHHIIMNRST	NIGHTMARISH
AGHHILOPRTY	LITHOGRAPHY
AGHHMNOPRYY	HYMNOGRAPHY
AGHHOOPPRTY	PHOTOGRAPHY
AGHHOOPRRTY	ORTHOGRAPHY
AGHHOPPRTYY	PHYTOGRAPHY
AGHIIILMNTU	HUMILIATING
AGHIILLNOOP	PHILOLOGIAN
AGHIILNRSVY	RAVISHINGLY
AGHIINNOSST	ASTONISHING
AGHIINPRSTY	PHARYNGITIS
AGHILMNOOTY	MYTHOLOGIAN
AGHILOOPSTT	PATHOLOGIST
AGHIMNOPRST	PROGNATHISM
AGHIMOPRSTY	PYTHAGORISM
AGHINOOSSTY	SOOTHSAYING
AGHLLOOPSSY	HYPOGLOSSAL
AGHLOOPSUXY	XYLOPHAGOUS
AGHLOPRSTYY	STYLOGRAPHY
AGHNOOPPRRY	PORNOGRAPHY
AGHNOOPRSTU	PROGNATHOUS
AGIIILLNNOPT	OIL-PAINTING
AGIIILNORTV	INVIGILATOR
AGIIILNORTY	ORIGINALITY
AGIIIMMNORT	IMMIGRATION
AGIIILMNNSTU	INSINUATING
AGIIINNOORT	ORIGINATION
AGIIINNOSTT	INSTIGATION
AGIILMNSTTU	STIMULATING
AGIILNRSTUY	SINGULARITY
AGIIMNOORTW	WAITING-ROOM
AGIINNOPRTZ	PATRONIZING
AGIKLLNPRSY	SPARKLINGLY
AGILNOPPRVY	APPROVINGLY
AGILOORSSYY	ASSYRIOLOGY
AGILOOSTTTU	TAUTOLOGIST
AGINOOOPRRT	PROROGATION
AGINOOPRSTT	PROTAGONIST
AGINOORRSUV	GRANIVOROUS
AGLLORRSUUY	GARRULOUSLY
AGLMNOORTYY	LARYNGOTOMY
AGLMOOPRRTU	PROMULGATOR
AGLMOORRTYY	MARTYROLOGY
AGLOOOSTTUU	TAUTOLOGOUS
AHHIIIPRSST	PHTHIRIASIS
AHHILNOORTU	HOLOTHURIAN
AHHIMNOPSSW	SHOWMANSHIP
AHHLLNOPTXY	XANTHOPHYLL
AHIIILMNOTU	HUMILIATION
AHIILOPSTTY	HOSPITALITY
AHIIMNNRRTU	ANTIRRHINUM
AHIIMNOOOSU	HOMOIOUSIAN
AHIKMNOPRSW	WORKMANSHIP
AHILLOPSTXY	PHYLLOTAXIS
AHILOPRSTYY	PHYSIOLATRY
AHIMNOPRSTY	MISANTHROPY
AHINOOPSSTX	SAXOPHONIST
AHLOPRRSTUU	SULPHURATOR
AIIILLLNPTU	LILLIPUTIAN
AIIILLNOTTT	TITILLATION
AIIILNNOTTU	INTUITIONAL
AIIILNOSTTU	UTILISATION
AIIIMNRSTTU	MINIATURIST
AIIINNNOSTU	INSINUATION
AIIINNOPRST	INSPIRATION
AIIKNRSSSTT	SANSKRITIST
AIILLMNORTU	ILLUMINATOR
AIILLNNOOPT	POLLINATION
AIILLNRSSTY	SINISTRALLY
AIILLPRSTUY	SPIRITUALLY
AIILMMORTTY	IMMORTALITY
AIILMNOOPRT	IMPLORATION
AIILMNOOSTZ	SOLMIZATION
AIILMNOSTTU	STIMULATION
AIILNOOPRSV	PROVISIONAL
AIILNOPSTTU	STIPULATION
AIILNPRSTUU	UNSPIRITUAL
AIIMMNNOSSU	MANUMISSION
AIIMMNSSTTU	NUMISMATIST
AIIMNOOPRTT	IMPORTATION
AIINOPRRSTY	INSPIRATORY

AIINOPRRRTTU	PARTURITION	BCDEIOOPRSS	PROBOSCIDES
AIINORRTTTU	TRITURATION	BCDEKLOORSU	BLOOD-SUCKER
AIIOOPPRRTT	PROPITIATOR	BCDELOORSSU	DOUBLE-CROSS
AILLNORTUVY	VOLUNTARILY	BCDHHIOOPRY	HYDROPHOBIC
AILLNPPSTUY	SUPPLIANTLY	BCDILLNOORU	COLOUR-BLIND
AILLNRTUUXY	LUXURIANTLY	BCEEEELNNOV	BENEVOLENCE
AILLORRSTTU	ILLUSTRATOR	BCEEEFFORRY	COFFEE-BERRY
AILMMNOSTUU	MULTANIMOUS	BCEEEFILPRT	PERFECTIBLE
AILMNNOSUUY	UNANIMOUSLY	BCEEEGMNRSU	SUBMERGENCE
AILMNOPRTTY	IMPORTANTLY	BCEEEHKLTUW	BUCKET-WHEEL
AILMOOPRRTY	IMPLORATORY	DCEEEILPPRT	PERCEPTIBLE
AILNNORTUVY	INVOLUNTARY	BCEEEENNOSSS	OBSCENENESS
AILNOOPSTTU	POSTULATION	BCEEENQSSUU	SUBSEQUENCE
AILNRSSTUUU	LAURUSTINUS	BCEEFIMORRR	CEREBRIFORM
AIMMNORRTUU	MURMURATION	BCEEHIMNTTW	BEWITCHMENT
AIMNNOOSTUU	MOUNTAINOUS	BCEEHKLRRUY	HUCKLEBERRY
AIMNNOPRTTU	UNIMPORTANT	BCEEIJLOTVY	OBJECTIVELY
AINOOPRRSTT	PROSTRATION	BCEEILNORTV	CONVERTIBLE
AINOPPRSTUU	SUPPURATION	BCEEILPPRTY	PERCEPTIBLY
ALLNOPPRUUY	UNPOPULARLY	BCEEILPRSTU	PUTRESCIBLE
ALMNNOOSUYY	ANONYMOUSLY	BCEEILPSSTU	SUSCEPTIBLE
ALNNORSTUYY	TYRANNOUSLY	BCEEILRTUUZ	TUBERCULIZE
ALOOPRSTTUY	POSTULATORY	BCEEINSSSTU	SUBSISTENCE
ALOPRRSTUUY	RAPTUROUSLY	BCEEIPRRSSU	SUPERSCRIBE
AMOOPRRRTTY	PROTOMARTYR	BCEELMNRTUY	RECUMBENTLY
ANOOOPRRTTY	PROTONOTARY	BCEELNOOSST	OBSOLESCENT
BBCDEHIRRTU	BUTCHER-BIRD	BCEELORSTUU	TUBERCULOSE
BBCEELNOOST	COBBLE-STONE	BCEEMNORSTU	OBSCUREMENT
BBCEILMOSTU	COMBUSTIBLE	BCEENORSSSU	OBSCURENESS
BBCEKLORSTU	BLOCKBUSTER	BCEGIIMMNOS	MISBECOMING
BBDEEHHLOOY	HOBBLEDEHOY	BCEGILMOORY	EMBRYOLOGIC
BBDELNRSSUU	BLUNDERBUSS	BCEHIIIMNRS	HIBERNICISM
BBDGHLOOOTU	BLOOD-BOUGHT	BCEHLORRSYY	CHRYSOBERYL
BBDGIIKNNOO	BOOKBINDING	BCEIIJOTTVY	OBJECTIVITY
BBEEILNSSSU	SUBSENSIBLE	BCEIIKLLRST	BILL-STICKER
BBEHIIILLOP	BIBLIOPHILE	BCEIINOORSS	NECROBIOSIS
BBEHINRSSSU	SHRUBBINESS	BCEIJNSTUUV	SUBJUNCTIVE
BBGIILLNQUY	QUIBBLINGLY	BCEILLNOSUV	CONVULSIBLE
BBGMOORRSUY	BORBORYGMUS	BCEILMOOPSS	COMPOSSIBLE
BCCDEILNOTU	CONDUCTIBLE	BCEILNORTVY	CONVERTIBLY
BCCEEEEFINN	BENEFICENCE	BCEILOPRRTU	CORRUPTIBLE
BCCEEEEENRSU	ERUBESCENCE	BCEILPSSTUY	SUSCEPTIBLY
BCCEEINRSTY	CYBERNETICS	BCEIORSTTUV	OBSTRUCTIVE
BCCEGILNOOS	COGNOSCIBLE	BCEKKOOOORY	COOKERY-BOOK
BCCEIILNNOV	CONVINCIBLE	BCEKKOORRST	STOCKBROKER
BCDDDELLOOO	COLD-BLOODED	BCEKLMOSSTY	BLOCK-SYSTEM
BCDDEEEILNS	DESCENDIBLE	BCELORSTUUU	TUBERCULOUS
BCDDEHLOTUU	DOUBLE-DUTCH	BCEOOOPRSST	STROBOSCOPE
BCDEEEIINNT	BENEDICTINE	BCIIIILNTVY	VINCIBILITY
BCDEEEIINTV	BENEDICTIVE	BCIIILLORUU	CUIR-BOUILLI
BCDEEIIILRT	LIBERTICIDE	BCILMOSTTUU	CUSTOM-BUILT
BCDEEIILNRS	DISCERNIBLE	BCILOPRRTUY	CORRUPTIBLY
BCDEEIILRRU	IRREDUCIBLE	BCINOORRTTU	CONTRIBUTOR
BCDEEIILSST	DISSECTIBLE	BCINOORSTTU	OBSTRUCTION
BCDEEIINNOT	BENEDICTION	BDDDEEEGLOU	DOUBLE-EDGED
BCDEEIMNRSU	DISENCUMBER	BDDEEIINOST	DISOBEDIENT
BCDEELMNTUY	DECUMBENTLY	BDDEINRSTUU	UNDISTURBED
BCDEIIILRTY	CREDIBILITY	BDDELNOTUUY	UNDOUBTEDLY
BCDEIILNRSY	DISCERNIBLY	BDEEEIILRSV	DISBELIEVER
BCDEIILRRUY	IRREDUCIBLY	BDEEEIMNNTZ	BEDIZENMENT
BCDEIKLOQUU	DOUBLE-QUICK	BDEEELNSSSS	BLESSEDNESS

213

BDEEFIIINRZ	DEFIBRINIZE	BEELLNOSSUV	VOLUBLENESS
BDEEFLLNORU	BELL-FOUNDER	BEELMOORSTU	TROUBLESOME
BDEEGIILNRW	BEWILDERING	BEELPRSSTUU	SUPERSUBTLE
BDEEHILMNSU	UNBLEMISHED	BEENQRSSSUU	BRUSQUENESS
BDEEIILNSST	DISTENSIBLE	BEERRRSTTUU	SURREBUTTER
BDEEIIMRSTT	DISEMBITTER	BEFGHILLRTU	BULL-FIGHTER
BDEELLOOSSV	BLOOD-VESSEL	BEFGIINNTTU	UNBEFITTING
BDEELNOOSTT	BOTTLE-NOSED	BEFHILLOSSW	BELLOWS-FISH
BDEELNORTUY	DOUBLE-ENTRY	BEFIIILLTXY	FLEXIBILITY
BDEENORSTTU	DEOBSTRUENT	BEFIILLRSTU	FILLIBUSTER
BDEHHOOOORRT	BROTHERHOOD	BEFLLOOPRTU	BULLET-PROOF
BDEHIIINNTU	UNINHIBITED	BEGGIILLNNR	BELL-RINGING
BDEHILNPSUU	UNPUBLISHED	BEGGILNOOVX	BOXING-GLOVE
BDEHLNORTTU	THUNDERBOLT	BEGHILNORUY	NEIGHBOURLY
BDEIIIILNSV	INDIVISIBLE	BEGIIIILLTY	ELIGIBILITY
BDEIIILNTVY	VENDIBILITY	BEGIKLLNOOS	BOOK-SELLING
BDEINOSSSUU	DUBIOUSNESS	BEGILLMNRTY	TREMBLINGLY
BDELLOSSTUY	DOUBTLESSLY	BEGINNORSUV	UNOBSERVING
BDGGIIILNOS	DISOBLIGING	BEHIIIOPRTV	PROHIBITIVE
BDGILLOOTUY	BLOOD-GUILTY	BEHIIMNPRRS	BRINE-SHRIMP
BDIIIILNSVY	INDIVISIBLY	BEHIKNOOSSS	BOOKISHNESS
BDIIINOSSUV	SUBDIVISION	BEHILMOPRSY	HYPERBOLISM
BDIIORRSTTU	DISTRIBUTOR	BEHINOORSSS	BOORISHNESS
BEEEGILLNRT	BELLIGERENT	BEHINRSSSTU	BRUTISHNESS
BEEEGILMNSY	BESEEMINGLY	BEHIOORRSUV	HERBIVOROUS
BEEEGILMNTU	BEGUILEMENT	BEHKRRSTUUY	BRUSH-TURKEY
BEEEGLNORTT	BOTTLE-GREEN	BEIIILMNRST	LIBERTINISM
BEEEIILMRSV	MISBELIEVER	BEIIILMQRUU	EQUILIBRIUM
BEEEILPRRSS	REPRESSIBLE	BEIIILNSSTY	SENSIBILITY
BEEEILPRRTV	PERVERTIBLE	BEIIILQRSTU	EQUILIBRIST
BEEEILPRSSX	EXPRESSIBLE	BEIILMPRSSY	PERMISSIBLY
BEEEIRSTTTW	BITTER-SWEET	BEIILNOSSSU	BILIOUSNESS
BEEEELMMNOTW	EMBOWELMENT	BEIILNRSSST	BRISTLINESS
BEEEELMNNNOT	ENNOBLEMENT	BEIINORRTTU	RETRIBUTION
BEEENORSSSV	VERBOSENESS	BEIINORSTUV	INOBTRUSIVE
BEEFGINOORT	FREEBOOTING	BEILLLLOSUY	LIBELLOUSLY
BEEFIKNRTTU	BUTTER-KNIFE	BEILLMPSTUU	SUBMULTIPLE
BEEGGILSSTU	SUGGESTIBLE	BEILNOPRSSY	RESPONSIBLY
BEEGIILLNVY	BELIEVINGLY	BEILOPRRSTU	PROTRUSIBLE
BEEGIIOORSU	BOURGEOISIE	BEILORSTUVY	OBTRUSIVELY
BEEGIKKNOOP	BOOK-KEEPING	BEINOOSSSUV	OBVIOUSNESS
BEEGILNNOSS	IGNOBLENESS	BEINORSTUUV	UNOBTRUSIVE
BEEGIMNOSTT	MISBEGOTTEN	BEINPRRTTTU	BUTTER-PRINT
BEEGNNOORTU	BONNET-ROUGE	BEIORRRTTUY	RETRIBUTORY
BEEHILOPRYZ	HYPERBOLIZE	BELLNRTTUUY	TURBULENTLY
BEEHOPRRSTT	STEPBROTHER	BELNOOSTUUY	BOUNTEOUSLY
BEEIILMPRSS	IMPRESSIBLE	BFILLNOTUUY	BOUNTIFULLY
	PERMISSIBLE	BGHILOPRTTU	BOLT-UPRIGHT
BEEIILNSSSV	VISIBLENESS	BGIIILLLTUY	GULLIBILITY
BEEIIRRTTUV	RETRIBUTIVE	BHIIINOOPRT	PROHIBITION
BEEILLRRRTU	BULL-TERRIER	BHIIQOOPRRTY	PROHIBITORY
BEEILMMNORT	EMBROILMENT	BIIILOPSSTY	POSSIBILITY
BEEILMNSSSU	SUBLIMENESS	BIILLOOSUVY	OBLIVIOUSLY
BEEILNOPRSS	RESPONSIBLE	BILNOOOSUXY	OBNOXIOUSLY
BEEILNOQSSU	OBLIQUENESS	BIMORSSTUUU	RUMBUSTIOUS
BEEILNRSSTT	BRITTLENESS	BIOOOPPRRSU	OPPROBRIOUS
BEEILNSSSTU	SUBTILENESS	CCCCIMOORSU	MICROCOCCUS
BEEILPRRSSY	REPRESSIBLY	CCCDEEIINNO	COINCIDENCE
BEEINORSTTY	TENEBROSITY	CCCEEEENRSX	EXCRESCENCE
BEEINRSSTUV	SUBSERVIENT	CCCEEFLLNOU	FLOCCULENCE
BEELLMRSSSU	SLUMBERLESS	CCCEEIILMST	ECLECTICISM

CCCEENNORRU	CONCURRENCE	CCEFIINOPRY	PROFICIENCY
CCCEIMPRSTU	CIRCUMSPECT	CCEFIORRSUU	CRUCIFEROUS
CCCEINNOTTU	CONNECTICUT	CCEGHIKNRST	CHECK-STRING
CCCHHORRTUU	CHURCH-COURT	CCEGINNNOTY	CONTINGENCY
CCCIIMOOPRS	MICROSCOPIC	CCEGIORRSUU	CRUCIGEROUS
CCDDEEEENORS	DECRESCENDO	CCEHHIOSSTT	SCHOTTISCHE
CCDEEEEFHIKN	CHICKEN-FEED	CCEHIIPRRTY	HYPERCRITIC
CCDEEEIINRS	IRIDESCENCE	CCEHILNOPTY	POLYTECHNIC
CCDEEHILPSY	PSYCHEDELIC	CCEHINOPRTY	PYROTECHNIC
CCDEEIIINST	INSECTICIDE	CCEHKLOSTTU	SHUTTLECOCK
CCDEEIILNOTY	CONCEITEDLY	CCEHNOOOPRS	CHRONOSCOPE
CCDEEIOPPRU	PREOCCUPIED	CCEIILMNORT	CLINOMETRIC
CCDEELLLOTY	COLLECTEDLY	CCEIIMMORRT	MICROMETRIC
CCDEELNNOTY	CONNECTEDLY	CCEIJNNOTUV	CONJUNCTIVE
CCDEEENNNORU	UNCONCERNED	CCEILMORUVV	CIRCUMVOLVE
CCDEENNNOTU	UNCONNECTED	CCEILNORRTY	INCORRECTLY
CCDEENORRTU	UNCORRECTED	CCEINNOOSTU	CONSECUTION
CCDEHIOOPRS	DICHROSCOPE	CCEINNOPRRW	CROWN-PRINCE
CCDEIILOORT	CROCIDOLITE	CCEINNOSSTY	CONSISTENCY
CCDENORSSTU	CONDUCTRESS	CCEJNNORTUU	CONJUNCTURE
CCDHHILLOOS	SCHOOL-CHILD	CCELORSSSUU	SUCCOURLESS
CCEEEEINPRT	CENTRE-PIECE	CCENORRSTTU	CONSTRUCTER
CCEEEFHIKNR	NECKERCHIEF		RECONSTRUCT
CCEEEFLNORS	FLORESCENCE	CCFGIILNNOT	CONFLICTING
CCEEEGINRVY	VICEREGENCY	CCFIIINORUX	CRUCIFIXION
CCEEEGNNORV	CONVERGENCE	CCFIILNNOOT	CONFLICTION
CCEEEGNRSTU	TURGESCENCE	CCGGHHINORU	CHURCH-GOING
CCEEEHINNOR	INCOHERENCE	CCGHILNOOOR	CHRONOLOGIC
CCEEEHORRTT	CROTCHETEER	CCGHILOOPSY	PSYCHOLOGIC
CCEEEIINPPR	PERCIPIENCE	CCGHIOOPRSY	HYGROSCOPIC
CCEEEINNNOV	CONVENIENCE	CCHIIILMORT	MICROLITHIC
CCEEEINOPRV	PRECONCEIVE	CCHILMOOPRY	POLYCHROMIC
CCEEEINOSTX	COEXISTENCE	CCIIINOORRT	ONIROCRITIC
CCEEEINRSTV	VITRESCENCE	CCIIMMNOSTU	COMMUNISTIC
CCEEELORTTU	ELECTROCUTE	CCIINOPRTTY	NYCTITROPIC
CCEEEENNOQSU	CONSEQUENCE	CCIJNNNOOTU	CONJUNCTION
CCEEEENOPRST	TORPESCENCE	CCILNOOSSUY	CONSCIOUSLY
CCEEENPRSTU	PUTRESCENCE	CCILNOOSTUU	NOCTILUCOUS
CCEEFFIINOT	COEFFICIENT	CCIMNNOOPTU	COMPUNCTION
CCEEFIIMNNU	MUNIFICENCE	CCINNOOSSUU	UNCONSCIOUS
CCEEGINNNOT	CONTINGENCE	CCINOOPSSUU	CONSPICUOUS
CCEEGNOOPRS	PRECOGNOSCE	CCINOORRSTT	CONSTRICTOR
CCEEHHINOTT	THEOTECHNIC	CCKNOORRTUY	COUNTRY-ROCK
CCEEHINNORY	INCOHERENCY	CCNOORRSTTU	CONSTRUCTOR
CCEEHINORRS	CHOIR-SCREEN	CDDEEEIPRTU	DECREPITUDE
CCEEIILNNOS	CONSILIENCE	CDDEEEENNOPS	DESPONDENCE
CCEEIILRTTY	ELECTRICITY	CDDEEILTUVY	DEDUCTIVELY
CCEEIIMNNOS	OMNISCIENCE	CDDEEENNOPSY	DESPONDENCY
CCEEIIMNOSV	MISCONCEIVE	CDDEGIINPRU	RICE-PUDDING
CCEEIINPPRY	PERCIPIENCY	CDDEIIILNNS	DISINCLINED
CCEEILNNOTV	CONVENTICLE	CDDEIINNOOT	CONDITIONED
CCEEILNORST	ELECTRONICS	CDDEILNOOTY	DICOTYLEDON
CCEEILNQSUY	LIQUESCENCY	CDDEILNOSSU	UNDISCLOSED
CCEEIMNOORT	ECONOMETRIC	CDDEILOORSU	DISCOLOURED
CCEEINNNOVY	CONVENIENCY	CDEEEEFFLNS	SELF-DEFENCE
CCEEINNOSSS	CONCISENESS	CDEEEEFLNSS	DEFENCELESS
CCEEINNOSST	CONSISTENCE	CDEEEEINPRX	EXPERIENCED
CCEEINOSTUV	CONSECUTIVE	CDEEEFILTVY	DEFECTIVELY
CCEEMNNNORT	CONCERNMENT	CDEEEFLNRST	SELF-CENTRED
CCEENORRSST	CORRECTNESS	CDEEEFMNORT	DEFORCEMENT
CCEFFIINSUY	SUFFICIENCY	CDEEEGILNXY	EXCEEDINGLY

CDEEEILNSTT	DELITESCENT	CDEIILNTUVY	INDUCTIVELY
CDEEEILPTVY	DECEPTIVELY	CDEIIMNORST	MODERNISTIC
CDEEEINRSUX	UNEXERCISED	CDEIIMOSTTY	DOMESTICITY
CDEEEMMNORR	RECOMMENDER	CDEIINNOORT	RECONDITION
CDEEENNNSTU	UNSENTENCED	CDEIINNOSTU	DISCONTINUE
CDEEENNOPRS	RESPONDENCE	CDEIINOPRST	DESCRIPTION
CDEEEOPRRSS	PREDECESSOR	CDEILNNOTUY	CONTINUEDLY
CDEEFIILNTY	DEFICIENTLY	CDEILNOPSST	SPLIT-SECOND
CDEEFIINPSU	UNSPECIFIED	CDEILNORSUU	INCREDULOUS
CDEEFILLTUY	DECEITFULLY	CDEILOORRTU	TRICOLOURED
CDEEFILOSST	CLOSE-FISTED	CDEIMMNOTTU	UNCOMMITTED
CDEEFIMNORT	COMET-FINDER	CDEIMNOOPSU	COMPENDIOUS
CDEEFLNOSSY	CONFESSEDLY	CDEINNOPRST	NONDESCRIPT
CDEEGGLORSS	CROSS-LEGGED	CDEINNRTTUU	UNTINCTURED
CDEEHIOQSTU	DISCOTHÈQUE	CDEINORSTTU	DESTRUCTION
CDEEHNNORTU	TRUNCHEONED	CDEINORSTUY	COUNTRYSIDE
CDEEIIILNSS	DISSILIENCE	CDEIORSSTUY	DISCOURTESY
CDEEIIILNORT	DERELICTION	CDEKKNOOORR	DOOR-KNOCKER
CDEEIINRTTU	INCERTITUDE	CDELLNORSUY	SCOUNDRELLY
CDEEIIPRSTV	DESCRIPTIVE	CDELLORSUUY	CREDULOUSLY
CDEEIKLNNOO	NICKELODEON	CDEOPRRRUWY	CURRY-POWDER
CDEEILNNQUY	DELINQUENCY	CDFFIILLTUY	DIFFICULTLY
CDEEILSTUVY	SEDUCTIVELY	CDFGIILNNOY	CONFIDINGLY
CDEEIMNNRST	DISCERNMENT	CDGHILOOORY	ORCHIDOLOGY
CDEEIMNOPRS	ENDOSPERMIC	CDGIILOSSTY	DYSLOGISTIC
CDEEIMNORTV	DIVORCEMENT	CDGILOORTTY	TROGLODYTIC
CDEEIMOOPST	DECOMPOSITE	CDGINOOTTUW	WOODCUTTING
CDEEINORRTU	REINTRODUCE	CDHIIMOOPR	IDIOMORPHIC
CDEEINPRSUU	SUPERINDUCE	CDHIIOOPRST	CHIROPODIST
CDEEIOOOPPS	OPEIDOSCOPE	CDHIMOOOSTU	DICHOTOMOUS
CDEEIORRSVY	REDISCOVERY	CDIIIJNOSUU	INJUDICIOUS
CDEEIRSTTUV	DESTRUCTIVE	CDIIINNOSTT	DISTINCTION
CDEEKNOORSS	CROOKEDNESS	CDIIJLOSUUY	JUDICIOUSLY
CDEELMNNOOT	CONDOLEMENT	CDIIJNNOSTU	DISJUNCTION
CDEELNNOTTY	CONTENTEDLY	CDILLORSUUY	LUDICROUSLY
CDEELNRRTUY	DECURRENTLY	CEEEEHPRSSS	CHEESE-PRESS
CDEENNOPRSY	RESPONDENCY	CEEEEILNORT	ELECTIONEER
CDEENNORTUV	UNCONVERTED	CEEEEINRRRV	IRREVERENCE
CDEENNOSTTU	UNCONTESTED	CEEEEFFHOOSU	COFFEE-HOUSE
CDEENOPRTTU	UNPROTECTED	CEEEFFIINTV	INEFFECTIVE
CDEENPSSTUU	UNSUSPECTED	CEEEFFILTVY	EFFECTIVELY
CDEFIINNTUY	INFECUNDITY	CEEEFILRSSV	SELF-SERVICE
CDEFIINORTU	COUNTRIFIED	CEEEFMNNORT	ENFORCEMENT
CDEFILNNOTY	CONFIDENTLY	CEEEFNPRSST	PERFECTNESS
CDEFIMNNORU	UNCONFIRMED	CEEEGGNORRR	GREENGROCER
CDEGIINNORS	CONSIDERING	CEEEHILORTT	HETEROCLITE
CDEGILMNOOO	DEMONOLOGIC	CEEEHIMNRTU	HERMENEUTIC
CDEHIIMOSTT	METHODISTIC	CEEEIIMNNPT	IMPENITENCE
CDEHILPRTUU	PULCHRITUDE	CEEEIINNNRT	INTERNECINE
CDEHIMNORST	CHRISTENDOM	CEEEILNOPST	PLEISTOCENE
CDEHIMORRTY	HYDROMETRIC	CEEEILSSVXY	EXCESSIVELY
CDEHKLOORST	STOCKHOLDER	CEEEINNOSTV	VENESECTION
CDEIIILNUVZ	UNCIVILIZED	CEEEINORTUX	EXECUTIONER
CDEIIINSTTV	DISTINCTIVE	CEEEINOSTVX	COEXTENSIVE
CDEIIIOPRTY	PERIODICITY	CEEEINPRSSS	PRECISENESS
CDEIIISSTUV	VICISSITUDE	CEEEINPRSST	PERSISTENCE
CDEIIJNSTUV	DISJUNCTIVE	CEEEIPPRSTV	PERSPECTIVE
CDEIILLOSUY	DELICIOUSLY	CEEEJNNSTUV	JUVENESCENT
CDEIILLPTUY	PELLUCIDITY	CEEEKMNORSS	SMOKESCREEN
CDEIILNOSTU	UNSOLICITED	CEEELLLNTXY	EXCELLENTLY
CDEIILNRTUY	INCREDULITY	CEEELLNNNOP	PENNONCELLE

CEEELLORSTY	ELECTROLYSE	CEEIMOPRSTU	COMPUTERISE
CEEELLORTTY	ELECTROLYTE	CEEINNNOSTT	CONSENTIENT
CEEELMORRST	SCLEROMETER	CEEINNOORRT	RECONNOITRE
CEEELOPRTTY	ELECTROTYPE	CEEINOPRSTU	PERSECUTION
CEEEOOPRSST	STEREOSCOPE	CEEINORRSST	INTERCESSOR
CEEEPPRRSST	PRECEPTRESS	CEEINORRSTU	INTERCOURSE
CEEFFIIINNT	INEFFICIENT	CEEINOSSSTU	NECESSITOUS
CEEFFIILNTY	EFFICIENTLY	CEEINOSSSTV	COSTIVENESS
CEEFHHNORTT	THENCEFORTH	CEEINPRSSTY	PERSISTENCY
CEEFIIPRSSU	SUPERFICIES	CEEIOPPRSTV	PROSPECTIVE
CEEFILLORSU	CELLIFEROUS	CEEIOPRSTTY	STEREOTYPIC
CEEFILMPRTY	IMPERFECTLY	CEEIPQRSTUU	PICTURESQUE
CEEFIMNNNOT	CONFINEMENT	CEELMNOPTTY	COMPETENTLY
CEEFINNQRUY	INFREQUENCY	CEEMMNNOOSS	COMMONSENSE
CEEFINORTTU	COUNTERFEIT	CEEMNOORTUV	COUNTER-MOVE
CEEFLNORSTU	FLUORESCENT	CEEMNOPRRTU	PROCUREMENT
CEEFLOORRSU	FORECLOSURE	CEEMNOPRSTT	CONTRE-TEMPS
CEEFLORRSUU	RESOURCEFUL	CEEMOPRRSSU	COMPRESSURE
CEEGINOSSTY	CYTOGENESIS	CEENNOORRST	CORNER-STONE
CEEHHIIMPRS	HEMISPHERIC	CEEOOPRRSSTT	PROTECTRESS
CEEHHIORSVW	WHICHSOEVER	CEFFINRSSSU	SCRUFFINESS
CEEHIILLNST	HELLENISTIC	CEFIINORSUZ	ZINCIFEROUS
CEEHIIMPSTU	EUPHEMISTIC	CEFILMORSUU	CULMIFEROUS
CEEHIKNSSST	SKETCHINESS	CEFILNOORTU	COUNTERFOIL
CEEHILOPRST	ELECTORSHIP	CEFILOORSUY	FEROCIOUSLY
CEEHILPRSTU	LECTURESHIP	CEFIOPRRSUU	CUPRIFEROUS
CEEHKLNOSUY	HONEYSUCKLE	CEFLLNOORST	SELF-CONTROL
CEEHKOQRRUW	CHEQUER-WORK	CEFLMOORSST	COMFORTLESS
CEEHLLOORST	CHOLESTEROL	CEFNOORRTTU	COUNTERFORT
CEEHLLORSUY	LECHEROUSLY	CEFNOPRRTUY	PERFUNCTORY
CEEHLMOORRT	CHLOROMETER	CEGHIILNRTT	CHITTERLING
CEEHMNOORRT	CHRONOMETER	CEGHIINNRST	CHRISTENING
CEEHMOOPRST	THERMOSCOPE	CEGHILLNOOY	LICHENOLOGY
CEEHNNORRTU	TRUNCHEONER	CEGHIMORRTY	HYGROMETRIC
CEEHNORRSTY	CHERRY-STONE	CEGHLNOOORR	CHRONOLOGER
CEEHOOPSSTT	STETHOSCOPE	CEGIIILOPST	EPILOGISTIC
CEEIILNNRSY	INSINCERELY	CEGIIINNOORT	RECOGNITION
CEEIILNTVVY	INVECTIVELY	CEGILLNNOSU	COUNSELLING
CEEIIMNNRST	REMINISCENT	CEGILNOORST	NECROLOGIST
CEEIIMOPTTV	COMPETITIVE	CEGIMNNNOST	CONSIGNMENT
CEEIIMORSST	ESOTERICISM	CEGIMOOOORV	MICROGROOVE
CEEIIMORSTX	EXOTERICISM	CEGINNNORTU	INCONGRUENT
CEEIINORSTV	INSECTIVORE	CEGINNORSTU	COUNTERSIGN
CEEIIPRTTVY	RECEPTIVITY	CEGINOORRSU	CORNIGEROUS
CEEIIRRSTTV	RESTRICTIVE	CEGLOOPRSTY	SPECTROLOGY
CEEILLMNNTY	INCLEMENTLY	CEHHIILOTTY	ICHTHYOLITE
CEEILLMRSSY	MERCILESSLY	CEHHILMOORY	HELIOCHROMY
CEEILLSUVXY	EXCLUSIVELY	CEHHILOOSTT	CHISEL-TOOTH
CEEILMOORRT	COLORIMETER	CEHHLMOOSTT	CLOTHES-MOTH
CEEILNQSTUY	QUIESCENTLY	CEHIIINPSTZ	CITIZENSHIP
CEEILOPSSTT	TELESCOPIST	CEHIIJPSSTU	JUSTICESHIP
CEEILRRSTUU	SERICULTURE	CEHIIKKNNST	KITCHEN-SINK
CEEILRSUVXY	EXCURSIVELY	CEHIIKLLRSY	LICKERISHLY
CEEIMNNOOPT	OMNIPOTENCE	CEHIIMOSSUV	MISCHIEVOUS
CEEIMNNOPTT	INCOMPETENT	CEHIIOPRRST	PREHISTORIC
CEEIMNNORTU	COUNTERMINE	CEHIIOPRSVY	VICEROYSHIP
CEEIMNNSTTU	INTUMESCENT	CEHIMOOPTTY	MYTHOPOETIC
CEEIMNOORSU	CEREMONIOUS	CEHIMOPPRST	COPPERSMITH
CEEIMNRRTTU	RECRUITMENT	CEHIMORSTTY	STICHOMETRY
CEEIMOOPSSS	SIESMOSCOPE	CEHINNORSYZ	SYNCHRONIZE
CEEIMOPRSSV	COMPRESSIVE	CEHINOORRST	ORCHESTRION

CEHMNOORRTY	CHRONOMETRY	CENOOPRSSTT	COTTON-PRESS
CEHMOOSSTUU	CUSTOM-HOUSE	CENOORRSTVY	CONTROVERSY
CEHNNOSSTUU	UNCOUTHNESS	CENOORSTUUU	UNCOURTEOUS
CEHOOPSSTTY	STETHOSCOPY	CENOPRRSSTU	CORRUPTNESS
CEIIILLPTTY	ELLIPTICITY	CFFGINOORSU	OFFSCOURING
CEIIIMNOPRS	IMPRECISION	CFFIILOOSUY	OFFICIOUSLY
CEIIIMPSSST	PESSIMISTIC	CFGHIILNNNU	UNFLINCHING
CEIIINNRSTY	INSINCERITY	CFGHIMNOORT	FORTHCOMING
CEIIINNSTTV	INSTINCTIVE	CGHHILNOOST	NIGHT-SCHOOL
CEIIINORSTU	CINERITIOUS	CGHHILOOTYY	ICHTHYOLOGY
CEIIINOSTVV	VIVISECTION	CGHIILOOPSY	PHYSIOLOGIC
CEIIINPRSTV	INSCRIPTIVE	CGHILMOOOPR	MORPHOLOGIC
CEIIKLLPSTT	LICKSPITTLE	CGHILOORSTY	CHRISTOLOGY
CEIIKLNPRSS	PRICKLINESS	CGHIMNOORST	SHORTCOMING
CEIIKLQRSUV	QUICKSILVER	CGIIILNSSTU	LINGUISTICS
CEIIKNRSSST	TRICKSINESS	CGIILLOSSTY	SYLLOGISTIC
CEIILLNSUVY	INCLUSIVELY	CGIILMNOORY	CRIMINOLOGY
CEIILMSSUVX	EXCLUSIVISM	CGIILNNNSUU	CUNNILINGUS
CEIILORSSTT	SCLEROTITIS	CGIILOOOSST	SOCIOLOGIST
CEIILRTTUUV	VITICULTURE	CGILMOOOSST	COSMOLOGIST
CEIIMNOOPTT	COMPETITION	CGIMNOOOSST	COSMOGONIST
CEIIMNOPSUU	IMPECUNIOUS	CGINNNOOPRU	PRONOUNCING
CEIINNNNOTT	INCONTINENT	CGINNOORSUU	INCONGRUOUS
CEIINNNORTU	INTERNUNCIO	CGLNOORSUUY	CONGRUOUSLY
CEIINORRSTT	RESTRICTION	CHHIILOOPPS	PHILOSOPHIC
CEIINOSSSUV	VICIOUSNESS	CHHIINORSTY	ICHTHYORNIS
CEIINRRSTUZ	SCRUTINIZER	CHHIMMOOOPR	HOMOMORPHIC
CEIINRSTTUV	INSTRUCTIVE	CHHLLLOOPRY	CHLOROPHYLL
CEIIOPPRSTU	PRECIPITOUS	CHHMOOOPRTY	PHOTOCHROMY
CEIIPPRSTUY	PERSPICUITY	CHIIINORSST	HISTRIONICS
CEIKLNNSSUU	UNLUCKINESS	CHIIMNOORSS	ISOCHRONISM
CEIKNNORSTU	COUNTERSINK	CHIIOPPRRTY	PORPHYRITIC
CEILLLNOOOV	VIOLONCELLO	CHIIORSSTTU	TRISTICHOUS
CEILLLOSUVY	COLLUSIVELY	CHILMOOPPRY	POLYMORPHIC
CEILMORSUUV	VERMICULOUS	CHIMMNOOOPR	MONOMORPHIC
CEILNNNOTTY	CONTINENTLY	CHIMNNORSSY	SYNCHRONISM
CEILNORSSTU	COURTLINESS	CHINOOORSSU	ISOCHRONOUS
CEILOORRSTU	TERRICOLOUS	CHIOOOPRSST	HOROSCOPIST
CEILOORRSVY	CORROSIVELY	CHIOOPPRRST	PROCTORSHIP
CEIMNOOPRSS	COMPRESSION	CHNNOORSSUY	SYNCHRONOUS
CEIMNOPSTUV	CONSUMPTIVE	CIIIMNORTTU	MICTURITION
CEIMNORSSTU	MISCONSTRUE	CIIINNOPRST	INSCRIPTION
CEINNOORSSU	CONNOISSEUR	CIILNOPSTUU	PUNCTILIOUS
CEINNOOSTTU	CONTENTIOUS	CIILNORSUUY	INCURIOUSLY
CEINNORSTTU	TENNIS-COURT	CIIMMNNOOTU	COMMINUTION
CEINNOSTTTU	CONSTITUENT	CIIMNOOOPST	COMPOSITION
CEINOOPPRST	PROSPECTION	CIIMOPRSTUY	PROMISCUITY
CEINOOPRSTU	PROSECUTION	CIINNORSTTU	INSTRUCTION
CEINOOPSSSU	COPIOUSNESS	CIIOOPRSSUV	PISCIVOROUS
CEINORRSSSU	CURSORINESS	CILLMOORTUU	MULTICOLOUR
CEINOSSSTUV	VISCOUNTESS	CILNNOOOTUV	CONVOLUTION
CEIOPPRSSUU	PERSPICUOUS	CILNNOOSUUY	INNOCUOUSLY
CEIOPRRSTUX	PROSECUTRIX	CIMNNOOPSTU	CONSUMPTION
CEKNOORRTUW	COUNTERWORK	CIMOOPRSSUU	PROMISCUOUS
CELLMOOPRRT	COMPTROLLER	CIMOPRSSTUU	SCRUMPTIOUS
CELLNOPRTUY	CORPULENTLY	CLLNOOSUUVV	CONVOLVULUS
CELLNRTTUUY	TRUCULENTLY	DDDENNOORTW	DOWNTRODDEN
CELMNNOORTT	CONTROLMENT	DDEEEHMOPTU	DEEP-MOUTHED
CELNOOPRTTU	COUNTERPLOT	DDEEEILMNRT	INTERMEDDLE
CELOORSTUUY	COURTEOUSLY	DDEEEIMPRST	DISTEMPERED
CEMMNOOPRTT	COMPORTMENT	DDEEEINNNPT	INDEPENDENT

DDEEEELNNPTY	DEPENDENTLY
DDEEEELNPRTY	PRETENDEDLY
DDEEEENOSSTV	DEVOTEDNESS
DDEEEENRRSSU	UNREDRESSED
DDEEFIIIRSV	DIVERSIFIED
DDEEHINRSSS	REDDISHNESS
DDEEIIMNNOS	DIMENSIONED
DDEEIIQSTUU	DISQUIETUDE
DDEEILPRSSY	DISPERSEDLY
DDEFFIILNTY	DIFFIDENTLY
DDEFGIIINNU	UNDIGNIFIED
DDEGGIINNRW	WEDDING-RING
DDEGIILSSUY	DISGUISEDLY
DDEGIINRSSV	DIVING-DRESS
DDEGIINSSUU	UNDISGUISED
DDEGILNRSTU	DISGRUNTLED
DDEGNNORRUU	UNDERGROUND
DDGIIINNORV	DIVINING-ROD
DDGILMNPPUU	PLUM-PUDDING
DEEEEHNPRRR	REPREHENDER
DEEEEMOPRST	SPEEDOMETER
DEEEEQRSSTU	SEQUESTERED
DEEEFHLNSSU	HEEDFULNESS
DEEEFHLORUW	FOUR-WHEELED
DEEEFILNSTV	SELF-EVIDENT
DEEEFILNSVY	DEFENSIVELY
DEEEFLNNSSU	NEEDFULNESS
DEEEFMNNRTU	UNFERMENTED
DEEEGHILNNT	ENLIGHTENED
DEEEHHPRSSS	SHEPHERDESS
DEEEIINNPTX	INEXPEDIENT
DEEEILNPTXY	EXPEDIENTLY
DEEEILORSTU	DELETERIOUS
DEEEIMNPRTV	DEPRIVEMENT
DEEEINPRTUX	EXPENDITURE
DEEEINRRSST	RETIREDNESS
DEEELMNNOY	MONEY-LENDER
DEEELMNOPTV	DEVELOPMENT
DEEELMNOTVV	DEVOLVEMENT
DEEELNNPRST	RESPLENDENT
DEEELNNRSSS	SLENDERNESS
DEEELNNSSSS	ENDLESSNESS
DEEEMNNORST	ENDORSEMENT
DEEENOPSSSX	EXPOSEDNESS
DEEENPRRTUV	UNPERVERTED
DEEEOPRSTTY	STEREOTYPED
DEEFFIINNRT	INDIFFERENT
DEEFFILNRTY	DIFFERENTLY
DEEFFINSSSU	DIFFUSENESS
DEEFGIINSST	FIDGETINESS
DEEFGILNNUY	UNFEIGNEDLY
DEEFHIIKSWY	WHISKEYFIED
DEEFHLLNUUY	UNHEEDFULLY
DEEFIINOPRS	PERSONIFIED
DEEFILNRSSU	DIREFULNESS
DEEFLLNOSSU	DOLEFULNESS
DEEFMNOPRRU	UNPERFORMED
DEEGHHIOPRW	HIGH-POWERED
DEEGHILLSST	DELIGHTLESS
DEEGHILMOST	DELIGHTSOME
DEEGHINRTUW	UNDERWEIGHT
DEEGIIMNNOR	DOMINEERING
DEEGILNRSVY	DESERVINGLY
DEEGINNRSUV	UNDESERVING
DEEGINORSTU	DENTIGEROUS
DEEGJMNPRTU	PREJUDGMENT
DEEGLNOSSSS	GODLESSNESS
DEEHHIIMMRS	HEMIHEDRISM
DEEHHLOORSU	HOUSEHOLDER
DEEHIINNPSZ	DENIZENSHIP
DEEHINNORST	DISENTHRONE
DEEHINOSSSU	HIDEOUSNESS
DEEIILNOPRS	LEPIDOSIREN
DEEIIMMNRST	DETERMINISM
DEEIIMMNRTU	INTERMEDIUM
DEEIIMNPSST	DISSEPIMENT
DEEIIMNRSTT	DETERMINIST
DEEIINNNOTT	INTENTIONED
DEEIINNSSTT	DISSENTIENT
DEEIINPRSTY	SERENDIPITY
DEEIINRTTXY	INDEXTERITY
DEEIIOPSTUX	EXPEDITIOUS
DEEILNORRSS	ORDERLINESS
DEEINNOPSST	POINTEDNESS
DEEINNPRSTU	SUPERINTEND
DEEINNSSSTT	STINTEDNESS
DEEINNSSTUW	UNWITNESSED
DEEINOSSSTU	TEDIOUSNESS
DEEINOSSSUV	DEVIOUSNESS
DEEINPRRTTU	INTERRUPTED
DEEINRRRTUW	UNDERWRITER
DEEKNNNRSSU	DRUNKENNESS
DEELORSTUXY	DEXTEROUSLY
DEEMNOORTUY	DEUTERONOMY
DEENNSSSTTU	STUNTEDNESS
DEFFGINNNOU	UNOFFENDING
DEFFIILSUVY	DIFFUSIVELY
DEFFILLLNUU	UNFULFILLED
DEFHINNRSUU	UNFURNISHED
DEFHINPRSTT	SPENDTHRIFT
DEFILMNNSSU	MINDFULNESS
DEFILNSSTUU	DUTIFULNESS
DEFILRSSSTU	DISTRESSFUL
DEFIOOORRSU	ODORIFEROUS
DEFLLNORUWY	WONDERFULLY
DEGGKLRSUUY	SKULDUGGERY
DEGHINOSSTU	DOUGHTINESS
DEGHLMOOOTY	METHODOLOGY
DEGHNOORSUY	HYDROGENOUS
DEGHNOORXYY	OXYHYDROGEN
DEGHNORRTUW	UNDERGROWTH
DEGIIINNOST	INDIGESTION
DEGIIINQSTU	DISQUIETING
DEGIILNOTTU	DEGLUTITION
DEGIILNRTVY	DIVERTINGLY
DEGIINRSSST	DISTRESSING
DEGILLNNTUY	INDULGENTLY
DEGILNNORWY	WONDERINGLY
DEGILNNOSSU	UNGODLINESS
DEGILOOPRTY	PTERIDOLOGY
DEGILORTTUY	DEGLUTITORY
DEHHIILMNOT	HELMINTHOID

DEHIILOPRSS	SOLDIERSHIP	EEEHILNPRRS	REPLENISHER
DEHIIMNORTU	DINOTHERIUM	EEEHIMNRSST	SMITHEREENS
DEHIINSTTUW	WHITSUNTIDE	EEEHINPSSSV	PEEVISHNESS
DEHILNOSSTY	DISHONESTLY	EEEHLLRSSST	SHELTERLESS
DEHINPRSSSU	PRUDISHNESS	EEEHLNNOSST	NONETHELESS
DEHINPSSTTU	STUDENTSHIP	EEEHMMORRTT	THERMOMETER
DEHIOOPRSTT	ORTHOPEDIST	EEEHMOPRRST	SPHEROMETER
DEIIINPRTTY	INTREPIDITY	EEEIIKLNSST	TELEKINESIS
DEIILLORSUY	DELIRIOUSLY	EEEIINNPSVX	INEXPENSIVE
DEIILOSSTUY	SEDITIOUSLY	EEEIINRRTVW	INTERVIEWER
DEIINOSTTTU	DESTITUTION	EEEIIPRRTTV	PRETERITIVE
DEILLMOOSUY	MELODIOUSLY	EEEILMNNNTV	ENLIVENMENT
DEILLNORSSW	WORLDLINESS	EEEILMOORTT	METEOROLITE
DEILLORSTUY	DESULTORILY	EEEILNPRRTT	TELEPRINTER
DEILLOSSTUY	DISSOLUTELY	EEEILNPSVXY	EXPENSIVELY
DEILMNOOSUU	UNMELODIOUS	EEEILNRTTVY	RETENTIVELY
DEILMNPRTUY	IMPRUDENTLY	EEEILNSTVXY	EXTENSIVELY
DEILNOPRTVY	PROVIDENTLY	EEEIMMNNSSS	IMMENSENESS
DEIMOPPRTTU	PROMPTITUDE	EEEIMMORSST	SEISMOMETER
DEINOOPRSTY	PONDEROSITY	EEEIMNQRRTU	REQUIREMENT
DELMORRSUUY	MURDEROUSLY	EEEIMOPRTXZ	EXTEMPORIZE
DELNOOPRSUY	PONDEROUSLY	EEEINNNSSST	INTENSENESS
DENNNOSSSUU	UNSOUNDNESS	EEEINNPSSSV	PENSIVENESS
DENOPPRSTUU	UNSUPPORTED	EEEINORRRSV	REVERSIONER
DFILLMNNUUY	UNMINDFULLY	EEEINPRRRTT	INTERPRETER
DFILLNTUUUY	UNDUTIFULLY	EEEINPRRSST	INTERSPERSE
DFILRSSTTUU	DISTRUSTFUL	EEEINRSSSTV	RESTIVENESS
DGGIKLNOOOO	GOOD-LOOKING	EEEKLNOOSTX	EXOSKELETON
DGHIIINSSTU	DISTINGUISH	EEELLLPSSSY	SLEEPLESSLY
DGIIIINPRST	DISPIRITING	EEELLNSSSSY	SENSELESSLY
DGINNORRSUU	SURROUNDING	EEELMNNOPTV	ENVELOPMENT
DHILLNOOPPY	PODOPHYLLIN	EEELMORRSSS	REMORSELESS
DHNOOORTUXY	UNORTHODOXY	EEELNSSSSSU	USELESSNESS
DIIILLNOSSU	DISILLUSION	EEEMNORSTUV	VENTURESOME
DIIILNOSSUY	INSIDIOUSLY	EEENNPRSSST	PRESENTNESS
DIIILNOSUVY	INVIDIOUSLY	EEENOOPRSSS	OPEROSENESS
DIIINOOPSST	DISPOSITION	EEEOPRRSTTY	STEREOTYPER
DIILNOOSSTU	DISSOLUTION	EEFFGLLNTUY	EFFULGENTLY
DIINORSSTUU	INDUSTRIOUS	EEFFIINNOSV	INOFFENSIVE
EEEEGLNNSST	GENTEELNESS	EEFFILNOSVY	OFFENSIVELY
EEEEHKOPRSU	HOUSEKEEPER	EEFFIORRRSU	FERRIFEROUS
EEEEHNNSTTV	SEVENTEENTH	EEFFLNRSSTU	FRETFULNESS
EEEEHORRSVW	WHERESOEVER	EEFGGIOPRTT	PETTIFOGGER
EEEEKOPRRST	STOREKEEPER	EEFGILLNNUY	UNFEELINGLY
EEEELRRSSSV	REVERSELESS	EEFGILNNOUX	GENUFLEXION
EEEENPRRRST	REPRESENTER	EEFGINNORSS	FOREIGNNESS
EEEFFFMNNOT	ENFEOFFMENT	EEFGINORSSV	FORGIVENESS
EEEFHIKNRRT	FREE-THINKER	EEFGLLRRTUY	REGRETFULLY
EEEFHMNRRST	REFRESHMENT	EEFHILNSSSS	SELFISHNESS
EEEFILLRVXY	REFLEXIVELY	EEFHILOSUWY	HOUSEWIFELY
EEEFLLORVWY	YELLOW-FEVER	EEFHIORSUWY	HOUSEWIFERY
EEEGGIINNNR	ENGINEERING	EEFHLLNPSSU	HELPFULNESS
EEEGGMNNORT	ENGORGEMENT	EEFHLNOPSSU	HOPEFULNESS
EEEGHIKLPRT	LIGHTKEEPER	EEFHMORRRTU	FURTHERMORE
EEEGINNNSSU	GENUINENESS	EEFHNOORRST	FORESHORTEN
EEEGINNORVW	OVERWEENING	EEFILLLMNTU	MELLIFLUENT
EEEGINPRRSV	PERSEVERING	EEFILLMORSU	MELLIFEROUS
EEEGLLNNTUY	UNGENTEELLY	EEFILNNRTTU	INTERFLUENT
EEEGLMNNOTW	GENTLEWOMEN	EEFILNORSSW	FLOWERINESS
EEEHHILLLNP	PHILHELLENE	EEFILOOPRRT	PROFITEROLE
EEEHHNPRSTY	HYPERSTHENE	EEFIOPRSSTU	PESTIFEROUS

	SEPTIFEROUS
EEFLLNRSTUY	RESENTFULLY
EEFLMNOSSSU	FULSOMENESS
EEFNOPRSSSU	PROFUSENESS
EEGGHIINSST	SIGHTSEEING
EEGGILLNNTY	NEGLIGENTLY
EEGGILORSUY	EGREGIOUSLY
EEGHIINSSTW	WEIGHTINESS
EEGHIKNOPPS	SHOPKEEPING
EEGHILNNSST	LENGTHINESS
EEGHILOORGY	HERESIOLOGY
EEGHILOORTZ	THEOLOGIZER
EEGHIMNOOSS	HOMOGENESIS
EEGHIMNOOTY	HOMOGENEITY
EEGHINNPTWY	PENNYWEIGHT
EEGHINRSTTY	YESTERNIGHT
EEGHLOOPRTY	HERPETOLOGY
EEGHMNOOOSU	HOMOGENEOUS
EEGHMNOORRW	WHOREMONGER
EEGIILLNNTT	INTELLIGENT
EEGIILMNNRT	INTERMINGLE
EEGIIMNNNRS	MINNESINGER
EEGIINNORTZ	NITROGENIZE
EEGIINNRSTT	INTERESTING
EEGILLLSSUY	GUILELESSLY
EEGILMOOTYZ	ETYMOLOGIZE
EEGILNNNRTU	UNRELENTING
EEGILNOPSSY	POLYGENESIS
EEGILOPRSTT	POLTERGEIST
EEGIMNNOOSS	MONOGENESIS
EEGIMNNRRTU	INTERREGNUM
EEGINNOOSST	ONTOGENESIS
EEGINORRSTU	TERRIGENOUS
EEGINORSTVY	SOVEREIGNTY
EEGIOPRRSSV	PROGRESSIVE
EEGLMOOORTY	METEOROLOGY
EEGLOOQRSTUY	GROTESQUELY
EEGMNNORSST	ENGROSSMENT
EEGOQRRSTUY	GROTESQUERY
EEHHILLNSSS	HELLISHNESS
EEHHIMORSTW	SOMEWHITHER
EEHHIOPSTYZ	HYPOTHESIZE
EEHHNOPSTUY	HYPOTHENUSE
EEHHOOPPRST	PHOTOSPHERE
EEHIIMPPRRS	PREMIERSHIP
EEHIIORSTTT	HISTORIETTE
EEHILNOPSTT	TELEPHONIST
EEHIMMNNOPS	PHENOMENISM
EEHIMNNOPST	PHENOMENIST
EEHIMOPRSTU	HEMIPTEROUS
EEHINNOSSSU	HEINOUSNESS
EEHINORSSSW	SHOWERINESS
EEHIPRSSTTU	TRUSTEESHIP
EEHKNOORSTT	TENTERHOOKS
EEHLLMOOSWY	WHOLESOMELY
EEHLMNOOSUW	UNWHOLESOME
EEHLOPRRSTU	UPHOLSTERER
EEHNOOPRSTY	STEREOPHONY
EEHNOPSTTUY	THEOPNEUSTY
EEIIINNSSTV	INSENSITIVE
EEIILLPPRST	PIPISTRELLE
EEIILMNOSUZ	EMULSIONIZE
EEIILNNSTVY	INTENSIVELY
EEIILNNTVVY	INVENTIVELY
EEIILNSSTVY	SENSITIVELY
EEIILQSTUXY	EXQUISITELY
EEIIMNNPRTT	IMPERTINENT
EEIINNORRST	REINSERTION
EEIINOPRRTT	PRETERITION
EEIINRSTTUV	INVESTITURE
EEIIOPPRSTV	PREPOSITIVE
EEIIOPRSTTU	REPETITIOUS
EEIIORRTTXY	EXTERIORITY
EEIKMNORSSS	IRKSOMENESS
EEILLNOPQTU	EQUIPOLLENT
EEILLNOSSSY	NOISELESSLY
EEILLNPSTTY	PESTILENTLY
EEILLOPSVXY	EXPLOSIVELY
EEILLPRSUVY	REPULSIVELY
EEILMNNOTVV	INVOLVEMENT
EEILMNOSSSS	LISSOMENESS
EEILMOPRTUV	PLUVIOMETER
EEILNNOPPTT	PLENIPOTENT
EEILNNPRTTY	PERTINENTLY
EEILNNSSSSS	SINLESSNESS
EEILNORSSSU	ELUSORINESS
EEILNOSSTVY	OSTENSIVELY
EEILNSSSSTW	WITLESSNESS
EEILOPRSTYZ	PROSELYTIZE
EEIMMNOPRTV	IMPROVEMENT
EEIMMNPRSST	IMPRESSMENT
EEIMMORSSTY	SIESMOMETRY
EEIMNNNORTV	ENVIRONMENT
EEIMNNOOSSS	NOISOMENESS
EEIMNNOPRST	OMNIPRESENT
EEIMNNOSSSW	WINSOMENESS
EEIMNRSSTTW	WESTMINSTER
EEIMOPPRSSU	SUPERIMPOSE
EEIMPPRSTUV	PRESUMPTIVE
EEINNOSSTTU	SENTENTIOUS
EEINOORRTTX	EXTORTIONER
EEINOPRSTTU	PRETENTIOUS
EEINOPSSSTU	PITEOUSNESS
EEINORSSSSU	SERIOUSNESS
EEIOPRRSSSU	SUPERIORESS
EEIPPRSSSUV	SUPPRESSIVE
EEJLNOSSSSY	JOYLESSNESS
EELLNOPSTUY	PLENTEOUSLY
EELLNPRTUUV	PULVERULENT
EELLOPRSSWY	POWERLESSLY
EELMMOOOPPS	POMPELMOOSE
EELNOOPPSTW	TOWNSPEOPLE
EELNOORRSUY	ERRONEOUSLY
EELNOPRSTYY	POLYSTYRENE
EELOPPRSSSU	PURPOSELESS
EEMNORSSTTW	WESTERNMOST
EEMOPSSTTUU	TEMPESTUOUS
EFFGIORRSUU	FRUGIFEROUS
EFFHHIIPRSS	SHERIFFSHIP
EFGGHIINNRT	FRIGHTENING
EFGHHOORTTU	FORETHOUGHT
EFGHIILNSST	FLIGHTINESS

221

EFGIIILLMORU	FLORILEGIUM
EFGIINNPRRT	FINGERPRINT
EFGILLLORWY	GILLYFLOWER
EFGILMORSUU	GLUMIFEROUS
EFGILNOORVW	OVERFLOWING
EFGIMMORSUU	GUMMIFEROUS
EFGINORRSUU	FERRUGINOUS
EFGIORSTTUU	GUTTIFEROUS
EFGNNOORTTU	UNFORGOTTEN
EFHIINRSSTT	THRIFTINESS
EFHILLSSSTY	SHIFTLESSLY
EFHILNOOSSS	FOOLISHNESS
EFHILNSSSUW	WISHFULNESS
EFHIMNNRSTU	FURNISHMENT
EFHINOPPSSS	FOPPISHNESS
EFHLNRSSTUU	HURTFULNESS
EFHMORRSTTU	FURTHERMOST
EFIIILNRTTY	INFERTILITY
EFIIINORRTY	INFERIORITY
EFIILNPSSTU	PITIFULNESS
EFIINNORSTU	INTERFUSION
EFIINOPRSSU	SPINIFEROUS
EFIKLLNSSSU	SKILFULNESS
EFILLLMOSUU	MELLIFLUOUS
EFILLLNPTUY	PLENTIFULLY
EFILLNOOSUY	FELONIOUSLY
EFILLRSSTUY	FRUITLESSLY
EFILPRSTUUY	SUPERFLUITY
EFIMNNORSSU	UNIFORMNESS
EFINORSSSUU	FURIOUSNESS
EFLLNOSSSUU	SOULFULNESS
EFLLNSSSTUU	LUSTFULNESS
EFLOPRSSUUU	SUPERFLUOUS
EFNNNORRRTU	FRONT-RUNNER
EGGHHIILTTW	LIGHTWEIGHT
EGGHIINRRTW	RIGHT-WINGER
EGGIILLNNRY	LINGERINGLY
EGHHLOSSTTU	THOUGHTLESS
EGHIILNRSSS	GIRLISHNESS
EGHIILNRSVY	SHIVERINGLY
EGHIILNRTWY	WITHERINGLY
EGHIILNSSST	SIGHTLINESS
EGHILMNOORT	MOONLIGHTER
EGHILMOOTYZ	MYTHOLOGIZE
EGHILNOOSTT	ETHNOLOGIST
EGHILNOSSST	GHOSTLINESS
EGHILORSTUY	RIGHTEOUSLY
EGHINNNOSST	NOTHINGNESS
EGHINOPRSSU	SURGEONSHIP
EGHINORSTUU	UNRIGHTEOUS
EGHOORRTUVW	OVERWROUGHT
EGIIILMNORS	RELIGIONISM
EGIIILNORST	RELIGIONIST
EGIIILORRSU	IRRELIGIOUS
EGIIIMMNNRST	MINISTERING
EGIILLMNPSS	MISSPELLING
EGIILLNNSSW	WILLINGNESS
EGIILLORSUY	RELIGIOUSLY
EGIILMNPRSY	SIMPERINGLY
EGIILNNOSTU	LENTIGINOUS
EGIILNNOSUY	INGENIOUSLY

EGIIILNQRUVY	QUIVERINGLY
EGIIMMNNRTTU	UNREMITTING
EGIIMNOPRTZ	TEMPORIZING
EGIINNOQSTU	QUESTIONING
EGIINNPRSSS	SPRINGINESS
EGIINNRSSST	STRINGINESS
EGIINNRSSTU	UNRESISTING
EGIINORSTUV	VERTIGINOUS
EGIINPRTTWY	TYPEWRITING
EGILLLSSTUY	GUILTLESSLY
EGILLNNOSTW	WELLINGTONS
EGILLNORTVY	REVOLTINGLY
EGILMNOORTY	TERMINOLOGY
EGILMOOSTTY	ETYMOLOGIST
EGILNNOSUUY	INGENUOUSLY
EGILNNRSTTY	STRINGENTLY
EGILNOORSTU	NEUROLOGIST
EGILNOPRRVY	REPROVINGLY
EGILNORTTTY	TOTTERINGLY
EGILOOORSTY	SOTERIOLOGY
EGILOOOSSTT	OSTEOLOGIST
EGILOOPRSTT	PETROLOGIST
EGIMNNOORRY	IRONMONGERY
EGIMNNPRSUU	UNPRESUMING
EGINNOORSTU	NITROGENOUS
EGINOOPRRSS	PROGRESSION
EHHILOOPPRS	PHILOSOPHER
EHHIOOPPRSZ	PHOSPHORIZE
EHHIOOPRRSW	HERO-WORSHIP
EHHIOOPSSTT	THEOSOPHIST
EHHOPPRRTYY	HYPERTROPHY
EHIIILNPPPS	PHILIPPINES
EHIILMRSSTV	SILVERSMITH
EHIILNOOPST	OENOPHILIST
EHIILOOPTTX	TOXOPHILITE
EHIINNSSSSW	SWINISHNESS
EHILLOPPSUY	EPIPHYLLOUS
EHILMNPSSSU	LUMPISHNESS
EHILNSSSSTY	STYLISHNESS
EHIMMNPSSSU	MUMPISHNESS
EHIMNNORSTU	NOURISHMENT
EHIMNOOPSTY	MONOPHYSITE
EHIMNOPRSSS	ROMPISHNESS
EHIMOOPRSTU	HEMITROPOUS
EHINOSSSSTT	SOTTISHNESS
EHLLORSSTWY	WORTHLESSLY
EHLMNOPPSYY	NYMPHOLEPSY
EHLOPRSSUUU	SULPHUREOUS
EHMOORSTTYY	HYSTEROTOMY
EIIIINQSTUV	INQUISITIVE
EIIILMPRTVY	PRIMITIVELY
EIIILNTTUVY	INTUITIVELY
EIIIMNORSSV	REVISIONISM
EIIINOPRSTT	PERITONITIS
EIIINOQRSTU	REQUISITION
EIIINORRTTY	INTERIORITY
EIIINORSSTV	REVISIONIST
EIIINSSTTVY	SENSITIVITY
EIIINSTTTUV	INSTITUTIVE
EIIILMPSUVY	IMPULSIVELY
EIIILLOOQSUZ	SOLILOQUIZE

EIILMOPRSUY	IMPERIOUSLY
EIILNRSTUVY	INTRUSIVELY
EIILNRTTUVY	NUTRITIVELY
EIIMNNOOPRT	PREMONITION
EIIMNNOPSTU	PNEUMONITIS
EIIMOORRSTU	MERITORIOUS
EIIMOPPRRTY	IMPROPRIETY
EIIMOPSTTUY	IMPETUOSITY
EIINOOPPRST	PREPOSITION
EIINOPRSSUV	SUPERVISION
EIINORRSSST	SINISTRORSE
EIINORSTTTU	RESTITUTION
EIIOPPRRRTX	PROPRIETRIX
EIIOPRRSTUY	SUPERIORITY
EILLMOORSUV	MELLIVOROUS
EILMNNOPRTY	PROMINENTLY
EILMNOOOPRZ	MONOPOLIZER
EILMNOPTTTU	MULTIPOTENT
EILMOPRSSTY	PROSELYTISM
EILMOPSTUUY	IMPETUOUSLY
EILMORSTTUY	MULTISTOREY
EILNOPRSUUY	PENURIOUSLY
EILNOQRTUVY	VENTRILOQUY
EILOOPRRSTY	POSTERIORLY
EIMNNOOSSSU	OMINOUSNESS
EIMNOOPRRTY	PREMONITORY
EIMNOPPRSTU	PRESUMPTION
EIMOORRSUVV	VERMIVOROUS
EINNOOPPRTU	INOPPORTUNE
EINNOOPRSSS	RESPONSIONS
EINNOOSSSUX	NOXIOUSNESS
EINNOSSSSUU	SINUOUSNESS
EINOORSSSTU	RIOTOUSNESS
EINOPPRSSSU	SUPPRESSION
EIOPRRSSUVY	SUPERVISORY
EIOQRRSTTUU	TRIQUETROUS
EIORRSSTTUU	TROUSER-SUIT
EJMNNOORSTU	SOJOURNMENT
ELLMORSTUUY	TREMULOUSLY
ELLOQRSUUUY	QUERULOUSLY
ELMMNOOSTUY	MOMENTOUSLY
ELNOOOPRRTY	POLTROONERY
ELNOOPPRTUY	OPPORTUNELY
ELNORSSTUUY	STRENUOUSLY
ELNORSTUUVY	VENTUROUSLY
EMNOOPPSSSU	POMPOUSNESS
FFGHILLNSUY	SHUFFLINGLY
FFGHILLRTUY	FRIGHTFULLY
FGGIINNORUV	UNFORGIVING
FGHIILNORSU	FLOURISHING
GHILNORTTY	FORTNIGHTLY
GIOORRSUUV	FRUGIVOROUS
HHIINOOPST	PHOTO-FINISH
ILLOORSUVY	FRIVOLOUSLY
ILMRSSTTUU	MISTRUSTFUL
LLOORRSUWY	SORROWFULLY
GHIILLNSTY	SLIGHTINGLY
HHLOOPPTYY	PHOTOGLYPHY
HHMNNOOOPT	MONOPHTHONG
HIIKLNNRSY	SHRINKINGLY
GHIIKNNNRSU	UNSHRINKING
GHIILLLNRTY	THRILLINGLY
GHIILLOOPST	PHILOLOGIST
GHIJMNOPSUW	SHOW-JUMPING
GHILMNOOSTY	HYMNOLOGIST
GHILMOOSTTY	MYTHOLOGIST
GHILNOOORTY	ORNITHOLOGY
GHILOOPSTTY	PHYTOLOGIST
GHIMNOOPSYY	PHYSIOGNOMY
GIIILLOSTUY	LITIGIOUSLY
GIIIMNNOOSU	IGNOMINIOUS
GIILLLNNUWY	UNWILLINGLY
GIILLNNSTUY	INSULTINGLY
GIILMNOPRSY	PROMISINGLY
GIILNNTTUWY	UNWITTINGLY
GIIMMNOPRSU	UMPROMISING
GIINOPRRSUU	PRURIGINOUS
GIKLNNNOUWY	UNKNOWINGLY
GIKLNOOPRVY	PROVOKINGLY
GILMMNRRUUY	MURMURINGLY
GILNORRTTUY	TORTURINGLY
GIMMNNRRUUU	UNMURMURING
HHOOOPPRSSU	PHOSPHOROUS
HIIIMNORSST	HISTRIONISM
HIILMOOSTTT	LITHOTOMIST
HIILOORRTTT	LITHOTRITOR
HIILOPRSTTY	LITHOTRIPSY
HIIMMOOPRSS	ISOMORPHISM
HILLOPRSTUY	TRIPHYLLOUS
HILNOOPPSTY	POLYPHONIST
HILNOOPSTXY	XYLOPHONIST
HIMMOOOOPRSZ	ZOOMORPHISM
HIMNOOPSSUY	SYMPHONIOUS
HIMOOOPRSSU	ISOMORPHOUS
HINOOPPRSSS	SPONSORSHIP
HIOOPPRSSTV	PROVOSTSHIP
HORRSTTTUWY	TRUSTWORTHY
IIIIMPPSSSS	MISSISSIPPI
IIIINNOQSTU	INQUISITION
IIILLNNOQTU	QUINTILLION
IIILLNOSSTT	TONSILLITIS
IIILLNOSSTU	ILLUSIONIST
IIINNNORTTU	INNUTRITION
IIINNOSTTTU	INSTITUTION
IIJLNORSUUY	INJURIOUSLY
IILLORSSTUU	ILLUSTRIOUS
IILNNOOSUXY	INNOXIOUSLY
IIMNOPRTTUY	IMPORTUNITY
ILNOOOPSSUY	POISONOUSLY
ILNOOORSTUY	NOTORIOUSLY
IMNOOPPRSTU	OPPORTUNISM
IMNOORSSTTY	MONSTROSITY
INOOPPRSTTU	OPPORTUNIST
INOOPPRTTUY	OPPORTUNITY
IOOPRRSTTTU	PROSTITUTOR
LMNOOOPSUYY	POLYONYMOUS
LMNOORSSTUY	MONSTROUSLY
LMOPSSTUUUY	SUMPTUOUSLY
LOOOOPPRSSUY	POLYSPOROUS

Twelve Letter Words

AAAABCCHILNN	BACCHANALIAN	AAACILLMNOTY	ANATOMICALLY
AAAACDIILPRS	PARADISIACAL	AAACILMMNNOO	MONOMANIACAL
AAAACGIMMNRT	ANAGRAMMATIC	AAADDEGINSTV	DISADVANTAGE
AAAACIMNRSST	ANTI-MACASSAR	AAADDGILLMOY	AMYGDALOIDAL
AAAAEGNRTVXZ	EXTRAVAGANZA	AAADEGIMQRSU	QUADRAGESMIA
AAAAGILMMNOT	AMALGAMATION	AAADEGNOSTUV	ADVANTAGEOUS
AAAAILLPRRSS	SARSAPARILLA	AAADEHNRRTTW	DEATH-WARRANT
AAAAILNRSSTU	AUSTRALASIAN	AAADEILNNPRT	ANTEPRANDIAL
AAABCEEGILRR	CARRIAGEABLE	AAADFIINORTZ	FARADIZATION
AAABCEEHLRST	CALABASH-TREE	AAADGIILLORT	GLADIATORIAL
AAABCEHILLPT	ALPHABETICAL	AAADGLNQRRUU	QUADRANGULAR
AAABCEHLOPPR	APPROACHABLE	AAAEEHIMNTTZ	ANATHEMATIZE
AAABCELNRRTU	TABERNACULAR	AAAEGHLOPPRY	PALAEOGRAPHY
AAABCGIINNRT	CANTABRIGIAN	AAAEGILLMOTT	AGALMATOLITE
AAABCIINPSTT	ANABAPTISTIC	AAAEGINNNNOR	NONAGENARIAN
AAABDEMRSSSS	AMBASSADRESS	AAAEILMNOPPR	PARALIPOMENA
AAABDIILPTTY	ADAPTABILITY	AAAELQQRSUUV	QUAQUAVERSAL
AAABEEGILMRR	MARRIAGEABLE	AAAGGIOPPRTU	APPOGGIATURA
AAABEEGLMNNU	UNMANAGEABLE	AAAGHIPPRRST	PARAGRAPHIST
AAABEELLNPPU	UNAPPEALABLE	AAAGHIRSTTWY	STRAIGHTAWAY
AAABEELNPPSU	UNAPPEASABLE	AAAGIILNNOTV	NAVIGATIONAL
AAABEIILMNNT	MAINTAINABLE	AAAGILLLORRT	GRALLATORIAL
AAABEILLNSSU	UNASSAILABLE	AAAHIIMNNRTU	HUMANITARIAN
AAABEILNNTTU	UNATTAINABLE	AAAIILMPRRTY	PARAMILITARY
AAABELLNRSTT	TRANSLATABLE	AAAIILNOPPRT	APPARITIONAL
AAABELNOOPTY	PALAEOBOTANY	AAAIILNORTTT	TOTALITARIAN
AAABEMNORTTW	WATER-BOATMAN	AAAINORSSSST	ASSASSINATOR
AAABIIILLTVY	AVAILABILITY	AABBCEGIKKNR	BACKBREAKING
AAACCCILLSTT	CATALLACTICS	AABBCIIILMNO	BIBLIOMANIAC
AAACCDEILLMY	ACADEMICALLY	AABBEEEEHLQTU	BEQUEATHABLE
AAACCEHNOSTU	ACANTHACEOUS	AABBEEEHLNRTU	UNBREATHABLE
AAACCEIINPTT	INCAPACITATE	AABBEEELLMNSS	BLAMABLENESS
AAACCEILLNTU	CANALICULATE	AABBEIINORTV	ABBREVIATION
AAACCEINNQTU	ACQUAINTANCE	AABBEILNNOTU	UNOBTAINABLE
AAACDGIIMMRT	DIAGRAMMATIC	AABBEILRTTTU	ATTRIBUTABLE
AAACDIINNNSV	SCANDINAVIAN	AABBEIORRTVY	ABBREVIATORY
AAACDILLMRTY	DRAMATICALLY	AABCCDEIKNRR	CRACK-BRAINED
AAACEEENPPRR	REAPPEARANCE	AABCCDEILLSY	DECASYLLABIC
AAACEEGNRTVX	EXTRAVAGANCE	AABCCEEHLNRT	CARTE-BLANCHE
AAACEGGGLOTU	GALACTAGOGUE	AABCCEELNPTU	UNACCEPTABLE
AAACEGILMMNO	MEGALOMANIAC	AABCCEILLLNU	INCALCULABLE
AAACEGNRTVXY	EXTRAVAGANCY	AABCCEIRRTUU	BUREAUCRATIC
AAACEHILMMTT	MATHEMATICAL	AABCCENOORSU	CARBONACEOUS
AAACEHIPRRTT	PATRIARCHATE	AABCCKLNRRTU	BLACKCURRANT
AAACEILMOOST	OSTEOMALACIA	AABCDDIILNRR	CARDINAL-BIRD
AAACEMNRRSTY	SACRAMENTARY	AABCDEEHKLRT	BLACK-HEARTED
AAACGILLLNOY	ANALOGICALLY	AABCDEEIILNR	INERADICABLE
AAACHIMNSTTT	ANTASTHMATIC	AABCDEEILLPS	DISPLACEABLE
AAACIILLMNST	TALISMANICAL	AABCDEHIINRT	DIBRANCHIATE
AAACILLLNTYY	ANALYTICALLY	AABCDEHORRTY	CARBOHYDRATE

AABCDEIILNRY	INERADICABLY	AABEEFILMNST	MANIFESTABLE
AABCDEKNRSSW	BACKWARDNESS	AABEEFLNRRST	TRANSFERABLE
AABCDELRSTTY	ABSTRACTEDLY	AABEEGILMNTZ	MAGNETIZABLE
AABCDGINORST	BROADCASTING	AABEEHIILRTT	REHABILITATE
AABCDGKLLRUY	BLACKGUARDLY	AABEEHLRRSTY	BREATHALYSER
AABCDHINOOPR	BRANCHIOPODA	AABEEIILPRRR	IRREPAIRABLE
AABCDIILLLOY	DIABOLICALLY	AABEEILMMRSU	IMMEASURABLE
AABCEEEFFILN	INEFFACEABLE	AABEEILNRRST	RESTRAINABLE
AABCEEEGHLNX	EXCHANGEABLE	AABEEILNRSSV	VARIABLENESS
AABCEEEHLLNW	BALANCE-WHEEL	AABEEKLMNRRU	UNREMARKABLE
AABCEEEHLNST	BALANCE-SHEET	AABEEKLMNRTU	UNMARKETABLE
AABCEEGGPRRT	CARPET-BAGGER	AABEEELLNPPSS	PALPABLENESS
AABCEEGHLNNU	UNCHANGEABLE	AABEEELLNSSUV	VALUABLENESS
AABCEEHLMNRT	MERCHANTABLE	AABEELMNORUV	MANOEUVRABLE
AABCEEHLNRSU	UNSEARCHABLE	AABEELNNNTTU	UNTENANTABLE
AABCEEHLOPRR	REPROACHABLE	AABEELNNORSU	UNREASONABLE
AABCEEIKMNRT	CABINET-MAKER	AABEELNNRSUW	UNANSWERABLE
AABCEEILMNSS	AMICABLENESS	AABEEMORRRRU	ARMOUR-BEARER
AABCEEINORTX	EXACERBATION	AABEENNRRSTU	SUBTERRANEAN
AABCEEELLNPSS	PLACABLENESS	AABEFIILNOPS	SAPONIFIABLE
AABCEFIILLSS	CLASSIFIABLE	AABEFLNORUUV	UNFAVOURABLE
AABCEFIILLTY	BEATIFICALLY	AABEGHIKNRTT	BREATHTAKING
AABCEFLNRSTU	BLAST-FURNACE	AABEGHIMOPRR	IAMBOGRAPHER
AABCEHILNRTU	UNCHARITABLE	AABEGIILMNNU	UNIMAGINABLE
AABCEIILLNPP	INAPPLICABLE	AABEGIMNRRTT	BATTERING-RAM
AABCEILMNNOT	CONTAMINABLE	AABEHILNQSUV	VANQUISHABLE
AABCEILMNOPR	INCOMPARABLE	AABEIIILLNTY	ALIENABILITY
AABCENRSSSTT	ABSTRACTNESS	AABEIIILLMTY	MALLEABILITY
AABCFLNOORTU	CONFABULATOR	AABEIIILLRTY	ALTERABILITY
AABCGHHPRRYY	BRACHYGRAPHY	AABEIILPRRTY	REPARABILITY
AABCGHIILOPR	BIOGRAPHICAL	AABEIILPRSTY	SEPARABILITY
AABCGHNOPPRW	CAPPAGH-BROWN	AABEIKLMNSTU	UNMISTAKABLE
AABCHIINOOTT	COHABITATION	AABEILMMRSUY	IMMEASURABLY
AABCHILNRTUY	UNCHARITABLY	AABEINSSTTTU	SUBSTANTIATE
AABCILLLLSYY	SYLLABICALLY	AABELMMNOSTU	SOMNAMBULATE
AABCILMNOPRY	INCOMPARABLY	AABELMNRSTTU	TRANSMUTABLE
AABCLLOOORRT	COLLABORATOR	AABELMOPRRTU	PERAMBULATOR
AABCLNORSTUY	CONSTABULARY	AABELNNORSUY	UNREASONABLY
AABDDGHORRTU	DRAUGHT-BOARD	AABELNNRSUWY	UNANSWERABLY
AABDDGINORRW	DRAWING-BOARD	AABELNOPRSST	TRANSPOSABLE
AABDEEEGILRS	DISAGREEABLE	AABFHLMNOTUY	UNFATHOMABLY
AABDEEGILRSY	DISAGREEABLY	AABFIILLMMTY	FLAMMABILITY
AABDEEHHRRSY	HABERDASHERY	AABFLNORUUVY	UNFAVOURABLY
AABDEELLNSSU	LAUDABLENESS	AABGHIINNRSW	BRAINWASHING
AABDEELMNNSS	DAMNABLENESS	AABGIIILNTVY	NAVIGABILITY
AABDEELNORSS	ADORABLENESS	AABHIIILNOTT	HABILITATION
AABDEGIJMORR	BRIGADE-MAJOR	AABHIIINNOTT	INHABITATION
AABDEGLLMNOR	BALLAD-MONGER	AABIINNORSTU	URBANISATION
AABDEIILNRST	DISTRAINABLE	AABIINOORRTZ	ARBORIZATION
AABDEILLLOSW	DISALLOWABLE	AABILLMRSUXY	SUBMAXILLARY
AABDEIMRRSSS	DISEMBARRASS	AABILNSSTTUV	SUBSTANTIVAL
AABDEIOPPSTT	PAEDOBAPTIST	AABILOPRRSTU	SUPRAORBITAL
AABDELMORTUY	DEAMBULATORY	AABIMNORSTTU	MASTURBATION
AABDELNNOPRU	UNPARDONABLE	AABINOOPRRTY	PROBATIONARY
AABDIIILLTTY	DILATABILITY	AABLLMMOSUXY	XYLOBALSAMUM
AABDIIILSTVY	ADVISABILITY	AABLMNRSTTUY	TRANSMUTABLY
AABEEEILLPRR	IRREPEALABLE	AACCCEHIRSTT	CATACHRESTIC
AABEEEELLNSSS	SALEABLENESS	AACCCIOSSTTU	CATACOUSTICS
AABEEEELMNNSS	AMENABLENESS	AACCDDIILLTY	DIDACTICALLY
AABEEELNPRTU	UNREPEATABLE	AACCDEFILSTU	FASCICULATED
AABEEFGILRRR	IRREFRAGABLE	AACCDEHILMOT	MACHICOLATED

AACCDEHNORRY	ARCHDEACONRY	AACDEILNPPRU	APPENDICULAR
AACCDEIIILNT	DIALECTICIAN	AACDEIMNORSY	AERODYNAMICS
AACCDEILLNTY	ACCIDENTALLY	AACDEIMOOSTU	DIATOMACEOUS
AACCDIIOPRTT	CATADIOPTRIC	AACDEINNQTUU	UNACQUAINTED
AACCDMMOOOORT	ACCOMMODATOR	AACDELLORSTY	SACERDOTALLY
AACCEEEILRTV	ACCELERATIVE	AACDELPPRSTU	CUSTARD-APPLE
AACCEEEKLLNS	ALKALESCENCE	AACDGILLMOTY	DOGMATICALLY
AACCEEHIRRTZ	CHARACTERIZE	AACDIIINORTV	DIVARICATION
AACCEEIILPRZ	CAPERCAILZIE	AACDIILLMOPT	DIPLOMATICAL
AACCEEILNORT	ACCELERATION	AACDIILLNOTY	DIATONICALLY
AACCEELORRTY	ACCELERATORY	AACDIIMNRSTU	TRADUCIANISM
AACCEELPRRTU	RECEPTACULAR	AACDIINNORRT	DOCTRINARIAN
AACCEENRSSTU	ACCURATENESS	AACDILLOPRSY	SPORADICALLY
AACCEGHIILPR	ARCHIPELAGIC	AACDLLNOSSUY	SCANDALOUSLY
AACCEHHIILRR	HIERARCHICAL	AACEEEIRRSTT	SECRETARIATE
AACCEHILLMNY	MECHANICALLY	AACEEFFINOTT	AFFECTIONATE
AACCEHILORTT	THEOCRATICAL	AACEEGGILLNO	GENEALOGICAL
AACCEHIMPRTU	PHARMACEUTIC	AACEEGLLPTTU	CATTLE-PLAGUE
AACCEILLMSTU	MISCALCULATE	AACEEGLMORTT	GALACTOMETER
AACCEILLNNOT	CANCELLATION	AACEEHIMNTTX	EXANTHEMATIC
AACCEILLNOSS	NEOCLASSICAL	AACEEHINTTTU	AUTHENTICATE
AACCEILLSTTY	ECSTATICALLY	AACEEIINRSTZ	SECTARIANIZE
AACCEILMNOPS	COMPLAISANCE	AACEEIIPPRTV	APPRECIATIVE
AACCEILMTUUV	ACCUMULATIVE	AACEEILPRTTU	RECAPITULATE
AACCEILNORVY	CLAIRVOYANCE	AACEEINPRSST	PARACENTESIS
AACCEILNRRTT	RECALCITRANT	AACEEIOPRSTT	ECTOPARASITE
AACCEILNRTUY	INACCURATELY	AACEENNPPRTU	APPURTENANCE
AACCEINNOTTU	ACCENTUATION	AACEENNPRRST	TRANSPARENCE
AACCELLOORSU	CORALLACEOUS	AACEFMNRRTUU	MANUFACTURER
AACCFIIINOPT	PACIFICATION	AACEGGHILOPR	GEOGRAPHICAL
AACCFIIORRST	SCARIFICATOR	AACEGHILLPRR	CALLIGRAPHER
AACCGHHIPRTY	TACHYGRAPHIC	AACEGHNOOPRY	OCEANOGRAPHY
AACCGHHLOPRY	CHALCOGRAPHY	AACEGHOPRRRT	CARTOGRAPHER
AACCGHIILLPR	CALLIGRAPHIC	AACEGIILLNRT	INTERGLACIAL
AACCHIINNNOT	CACHINNATION	AACEGIILLOOT	AETIOLOGICAL
AACCHIOPRSTT	CATASTROPHIC	AACEGIIMMPRT	EPIGRAMMATIC
AACCIILPRTTY	PRACTICALITY	AACEGIIMMRTZ	GRAMMATICIZE
AACCIIORRSTT	ARISTOCRATIC	AACEGILLMNTY	MAGNETICALLY
AACCIIRRSTTU	CARICATURIST	AACEGILLNOSU	GALLINACEOUS
AACCILLNORTY	NARCOTICALLY	AACEGILLORSU	ARGILLACEOUS
AACCILLORSTY	SOCRATICALLY	AACEGINNOORT	OCTOGENARIAN
AACCILLOSTUY	ACOUSTICALLY	AACEGLNOOPSV	GALVANOSCOPE
AACCILMNNOOT	CONCLAMATION	AACEGLNORTTU	CONGRATULATE
AACCILMNOTUU	ACCUMULATION	AACEHIILLOPT	PALAEOLITHIC
AACCILNOOPTU	OCCUPATIONAL	AACEHIILMPRX	ALEXIPHARMIC
AACCINOPRSTY	PANTISOCRACY	AACEHIILMRTT	ARITHMETICAL
AACDDDEEHLOR	DODECAHEDRAL	AACEHIILOPRZ	PAROCHIALIZE
AACDDEIILORT	DEDICATORIAL	AACEHIINPTTT	ANTIPATHETIC
AACDDIIJNOTU	ADJUDICATION	AACEHILLMPTY	EMPHATICALLY
AACDEEFHLMSY	SHAMEFACEDLY	AACEHILLPRSY	SERAPHICALLY
AACDEEILMRVY	DEVIL-MAY-CARE	AACEHILLPTTY	PATHETICALLY
AACDEEIMNRTT	READMITTANCE	AACEHILLRTTY	THEATRICALLY
AACDEHIINNRT	CANTHARIDINE	AACEHILMNNOR	ENHARMONICAL
AACDEHLMOSUY	ACHLAMYDEOUS	AACEHPRRRTTY	CHARTER-PARTY
AACDEIIIPRST	PARASITICIDE	AACEIIINPTTV	ANTICIPATIVE
AACDEIILNORT	DILACERATION	AACEIILNOPPS	EPISCOPALIAN
AACDEIINOPTT	DECAPITATION	AACEIILNRTTU	INARTICULATE
AACDEIIOSSST	DISASSOCIATE	AACEIIMNNOPT	EMANCIPATION
AACDEILLMNOY	DEMONIACALLY	AACEIIMNRSST	SECTARIANISM
AACDEILLNOSW	DISALLOWANCE	AACEIINOPPRT	APPRECIATION
AACDEILMMORT	MELODRAMATIC	AACEIJLLMSTY	MAJESTICALLY

AACEIKLMNOPT	KLEPTOMANIAC	AACIILLMNOSY	SIMONIACALLY
AACEILLLPRTY	PRELATICALLY	AACIILLNOOTZ	LOCALIZATION
AACEILLMMTUY	IMMACULATELY	AACIILLPPSTY	PAPISTICALLY
AACEILLNOORT	REALLOCATION	AACIILLRSTTY	ARTISTICALLY
AACEILLRTTUY	ARTICULATELY	AACIILMMORSS	COMMISSARIAL
AACEILMMRSTY	ASYMMETRICAL	AACIILMNNOTU	CALUMNIATION
AACEILMNOSTU	EMASCULATION	AACIILNOOTVZ	VOCALIZATION
AACEILMSSTTY	SYSTEMATICAL	AACIILNOPTTU	CAPITULATION
AACEILRTTTVY	ATTRACTIVELY	AACIILNORTTU	ARTICULATION
AACEINORRTTT	RETRACTATION	AACIILNRSTTU	NATURALISTIC
AACEINRTTTUV	UNATTRACTIVE	AACIILORSUVY	AVARICIOUSLY
AACEIOPPRRTY	APPRECIATORY	AACIIMMORSST	COMMISSARIAT
AACEKNNORSTU	CANTANKEROUS	AACIIMNOSSTU	CAUSATIONISM
AACELLLLORTY	COLLATERALLY	AACIINNNNOTU	ANNUNCIATION
AACELLNRRUVY	VERNACULARLY	AACIINNNOOTZ	CANONIZATION
AACELMORSTUY	EMASCULATORY	AACIINOPRTTY	ANTICIPATORY
AACELNPRRSUU	SUPERNACULAR	AACIIOPPRRTT	PARTICIPATOR
AACEMNOORSTT	ENTOMOSTRACA	AACILLMNORTY	ROMANTICALLY
AACENNPRRSTY	TRANSPARENCY	AACILLMNOSTY	MONASTICALLY
AACENORRRTUV	AVERRUNCATOR	AACILLMOSTUY	CALAMITOUSLY
AACFGIIINOST	GASIFICATION	AACILLNNRTYY	TYRANNICALLY
AACFHIMNPRST	CRAFTMANSHIP	AACILLOORRTY	ORATORICALLY
AACFIIIILNRT	INARTIFICIAL	AACILLPRRTUY	PARTICULARLY
AACFIIILLRTY	ARTIFICIALLY	AACILMNOOPRT	PROCLAMATION
AACFIIIMNORT	RAMIFICATION	AACILMNORTUY	CALUMNIATORY
AACFIIINORTT	RATIFICATION	AACILMOPSTTY	ASYMPTOTICAL
AACFIILMNOST	FACTIONALISM	AACILMORRTTU	COURT-MARTIAL
AACFIINOSSTT	SATISFACTION	AACILNOSTTUU	AUSCULTATION
AACFILLLOSUY	FALLACIOUSLY	AACIMNOOPRST	PARONOMASTIC
AACFIORSSTTY	SATISFACTORY	AACLNNOPRTTU	CONTRAPUNTAL
AACGGHHIIOPR	HAGIOGRAPHIC	AADDEFINORTU	DEFRAUDATION
AACGHHOPRRTY	CHARTOGRAPHY	AADDIIILNOPT	DILAPIDATION
AACGHILLOOPT	PATHOLOGICAL	AADDIIILLNOTY	ADDITIONALLY
AACGHILOOPRR	OROGRAPHICAL	AADEEGGGIRST	DISAGGREGATE
AACGHLMOOPRY	PHARMACOLOGY	AADEEHQRRSTU	HEADQUARTERS
AACGHMMOORRT	CHROMATOGRAM	AADEEIIMNNRT	ANTEMERIDIAN
AACGHOOPRSSU	SARCOPHAGOUS	AADEEILNQTUY	INADEQUATELY
AACGIILNNORV	CARLOVINGIAN	AADEEILNRTUZ	DENATURALIZE
AACGIIMMRRTT	TRIGRAMMATIC	AADEEIMMNNST	MISDEMEANANT
AACGIINNOSTT	ANTAGONISTIC	AADEEIMQSTUV	DESQUAMATIVE
AACGILLOORST	ASTROLOGICAL	AADEEINOPRST	ENDOPARASITE
AACGILLOOTTU	TAUTOLOGICAL	AADEELLLNPRU	UNPARALLELED
AACGILLRRTUU	AGRICULTURAL	AADEELMNPRTT	DEPARTMENTAL
AACGINOOPRSU	ANGIOCARPOUS	AADEELNRTTUU	UNADULTERATE
AACGLMOOSTUU	GLAUCOMATOUS	AADEEMNNRTUX	EXTRAMUNDANE
AACGLNNORTTU	CONGRATULANT	AADEFGILNORT	DEFLAGRATION
AACHHIILNPPS	CHAPLAINSHIP	AADEFILMORTY	DEFAMATORILY
AACHHIIMNPRS	CHAIRMANSHIP	AADEFILNORTY	DEFLATIONARY
AACHIILMOPRS	PAROCHIALISM	AADEGIIMMNST	DIAMAGNETISM
AACHIIMPRRST	PATRIARCHISM	AADEGINOPPRS	PROPAGANDISE
AACHIINPRSTT	ANTIPHRASTIC	AADEGINPPRRW	DRAWING-PAPER
AACHIINRRTTT	ANTARTHRITIC	AADEGOPRSTTU	POSTGRADUATE
AACHILOPRRSU	SCROPHULARIA	AADEHHIILLPP	PHILADELPHIA
AACHILOPSTTY	HYPOSTATICAL	AADEIIILNOST	IDEALISATION
AACHIMMNNOPY	NYMPHOMANIAC	AADEIILNNOST	DESALINATION
AACHLLNNNOTY	NONCHALANTLY	AADEIILNNTUV	ANTEDILUVIAN
AACHLMORRTYY	LACHRYMATORY	AADEIILNORTV	DERIVATIONAL
AACHNOOPRSTU	ANTHOCARPOUS	AADEIIMNRSTT	ADMINISTRATE
AACIIINNOPTT	ANTICIPATION	AADEILNORTTU	ADULTERATION
AACIIINNOTTV	VATICINATION	AADEILNRTUVY	VALETUDINARY
AACIIINSSTTT	STATISTICIAN	AADEIMNOQSTU	DESQUAMATION

AADELMOPRRTU	ARMOUR-PLATED
AADEMNNPRSUU	SUPRAMUNDANE
AADEMOQRSTUY	DESQUAMATORY
AADGIMNOPPRS	PROPAGANDISM
AADHILNOPSUY	DIAPHANOUSLY
AADIIILNNOTV	INVALIDATION
AADIIRRSSTUV	STRADIVARIUS
AADINNORSTTU	TRANSUDATION
AADMNOQRSUUU	QUADRUMANOUS
AADNORRSTTUY	TRANSUDATORY
AAEFFGGIRTVX	EXAGGERATIVE
AAEEEHINSTTZ	ANAESTHETIZE
AAEEENPRSSST	SEPARATENESS
AAEEFHHLRRST	FATHERLASHER
AAEEGGIMNOSS	AGAMOGENESIS
AAEEGGINORTX	EXAGGERATION
AAEEGGORRTXY	EXAGGERATORY
AAEEGILMNNOT	ANTILEGOMENA
AAEEGIMNTTUV	AUGMENTATIVE
AAEEGIMPSSTU	SEPTUAGESIMA
AAEEGINPRSTX	EXASPERATING
AAEEGLMNORTV	GALVANOMETER
AAEEGNPRSTUY	SEPTUAGENARY
AAEEHHIMPRTT	AMPHITHEATRE
AAEEHILPRSTU	LAUREATESHIP
AAEEHMNORSUW	WAREHOUSEMAN
AAEEIILLMRSS	MARSEILLAISE
AAEEIILLRTTV	ALLITERATIVE
AAEEIILMORTV	AMELIORATIVE
AAEEILMNRSST	MATERIALNESS
AAEEILNPRSST	PLEASANTRIES
AAEEILOPRRTT	PROLETARIATE
AAEEIMNPPRST	APPRAISEMENT
AAEEINNNORTX	REANNEXATION
AAEEINOPRSSX	EXASPERATION
AAEEINORSSTV	ASSEVERATION
AAEELMMNRTTT	MALTREATMENT
AAEENNPRSTUU	SUPERANNUATE
AAEERRRSTTUU	RESTAURATEUR
AAEFFIIMNORR	FORAMINIFERA
AAEFGILLLNOT	FLAGELLATION
AAEFILNORRTY	REFLATIONARY
AAEGGHHIOPRR	HAGIOGRAPHER
AAEGHIILNRTX	EXHILARATING
AAEGHIMMNPSS	GAMESMANSHIP
AAEGHLMNRSTU	MANSLAUGHTER
AAEGHLOPRTTU	TELAUTOGRAPH
AAEGHMNOOPSU	PHAENOGAMOUS
AAEGIILLNOST	LEGALISATION
AAEGIILMNORT	EMIGRATIONAL
AAEGIILNNOTT	GELATINATION
AAEGIIMNNORT	EMARGINATION
AAEGILLNNTTY	TANGENTIALLY
AAEGIMNNOTTU	AUGMENTATION
AAEGIMNRRSTT	TRANSMIGRATE
AAEGLLNNOPTY	PENTAGONALLY
AAEGLMNORTVY	GALVANOMETRY
AAEGLMOOPSTU	GAMOPETALOUS
AAEHIILMMPTU	EPITHALAMIUM
AAEHIILNORTX	EXHILARATION
AAEHMOORSTTU	ATHEROMATOUS
AAEIIILMSSTV	ASSIMILATIVE
AAEIIILNORTT	ALLITERATION
AAEIILMNNOTT	ALIMENTATION
AAEIILMNOORT	AMELIORATION
AAEIILMNPTUV	MANIPULATIVE
AAEIILMOPRRT	IMPERATORIAL
AAEIILNOQTUZ	EQUALIZATION
AAEIILNORSTT	ARISTOTELIAN
AAEIINOPRRTT	REPATRIATION
AAEIINOPRTTX	EXPATRIATION
AAEIINQTTTUV	QUANTITATIVE
AAEILLLMRTTU	MULTILATERAL
AAEILLMPRRXY	PREMAXILLARY
AAEILLNORSTY	SENATORIALLY
AAEILLOQRTUY	EQUATORIALLY
AAEIILMNORSTV	MALVERSATION
AAEILMNRSSTT	MISTRANSLATE
AAEILNNNPSVY	PENNSYLVANIA
AAEILNOPSSTY	PASSIONATELY
AAEILNRSSSTU	SALUTARINESS
AAEIMNOOOOPT	ONOMATOPOEIA
AAEINNOPRSXY	EXPANSIONARY
AAELLMNNORTY	ORNAMENTALLY
AAELLNNPSTUY	UNPLEASANTLY
AAELMNNORTTU	ULTRAMONTANE
AAELNNPRRSTT	TRANSPLANTER
AAELNPRRSTUU	SUPERNATURAL
AAELNRSSSTTW	STALWARTNESS
AAFIIILNRTTU	FUTILITARIAN
AAFIILMMNNOT	INFLAMMATION
AAFIILNNORTY	INFLATIONARY
AAFILMMNOORT	MALFORMATION
AAGGHNOOPRRY	ORGANOGRAPHY
AAGGIIKLLNSS	GALLIGASKINS
AAGHOOPPRSSU	SAPROPHAGOUS
AAGIINNOORTZ	ORGANIZATION
AAGIINNORTUU	INAUGURATION
AAGILLMNTUWY	MULLIGATAWNY
AAGILLNRRTUY	TRIANGULARLY
AAHIIILNNNOT	ANNIHILATION
AAHIINOPSTXY	ASPHYXIATION
AAHIINPPRSST	PARTISANSHIP
AAHIMNOOPRSS	ANAMORPHOSIS
AAIIILMNOSST	ASSIMILATION
AAIIILMPRTTY	IMPARTIALITY
AAIIILNOTTVZ	VITALIZATION
AAIIILORSTTV	VISITATORIAL
AAIIIMMNOSTX	MAXIMISATION
AAIIIMNNRSTU	UNITARIANISM
AAIILLNNOSTT	INSTALLATION
AAIILMNNOPTU	MANIPULATION
AAIILNNORSTT	TRANSITIONAL
AAIILNOOPPST	APPOSITIONAL
AAIILNOOPRST	POLARISATION
AAIILNOSSTTV	SALVATIONIST
AAIIMNOORTTZ	AMORTIZATION
AAIINOOPRTVZ	VAPORIZATION
AAILMNOPRTUY	MANIPULATORY
AAIOOPPPRRRT	APPROPRIATOR
ABBCDEEHIMRR	BRIDE-CHAMBER
ABBDILOORRST	BRISTOL-BOARD

ABBEEEILLNUV	UNBELIEVABLE	ABCEIILMNOPT	INCOMPATIBLE
ABBGHIILOPRY	BIBLIOGRAPHY	ABCEIILPRSTY	PLEBISCITARY
ABCCDEEELPST	BESPECTACLED	ABCEIINORSTT	OBSTETRICIAN
ABCCDEEHKORR	CHECKER-BOARD	ABCEILLNNOOS	INCONSOLABLE
ABCCDILNOORU	COUNCIL-BOARD	ABCELLLNOORT	CONTROLLABLE
ABCCDKLORUZZ	BUZZARD-CLOCK	ABCEMOOPSSSW	BOW-COMPASSES
ABCCEEENORRS	ARBORESCENCE	ABCENOSSTUUU	SUBCUTANEOUS
ABCCEEGINNRU	BUCCANEERING	ABCGILNNOOOT	CONGLOBATION
ABCCEEIILNSS	INACCESSIBLE	ABCIIIILRSTY	IRASCIBILITY
ABCCEEIILNOR	RECONCILABLE	ABCIIILNRTUY	INCURABILITY
ABCCEEMNNRRU	ENCUMBRANCER	ABCIILMNOPTY	INCOMPATIBLY
ABCCEEENNOSTT	CONTABESCENT	ABCIILNNOTUY	CONNUBIALITY
ABCCEIIILRTZ	CRITICIZABLE	ABCILLLMOSYY	SYMBOLICALLY
ABCCEILMMNOU	COMMUNICABLE	ABCILLLOPSYY	POLYSYLLABIC
ABCCEILNNOOS	CONSCIONABLE	ABCILLMNOOSY	MONOSYLLABIC
ABCCEILNORTT	CONTRACTIBLE	ABCILLNNOOSY	INCONSOLABLY
ABCCIILOPSTU	SUBOCCIPITAL	ABCILMNOSTTU	NOCTAMBULIST
ABCCIIMOORST	MACROBIOTICS	ABCINORSSTTU	OBSCURANTIST
ABCCILMMNOUY	COMMUNICABLY	ABCOOOORRRRT	CORROBORATOR
ABCDDGIKLNPU	BLACK-PUDDING	ABDDEEEELLORU	DOUBLE-DEALER
ABCDEEEEHILPR	DECIPHERABLE	ABDDEEEELNNPU	UNDEPENDABLE
ABCDEEEILNUV	UNDECEIVABLE	ABDDEEIMNNST	ABSENT-MINDED
ABCDEEIILLNN	INDECLINABLE	ABDDEILNOOST	BLOOD-STAINED
ABCDEEEILNORS	CONSIDERABLE	ABDDGLNOOORS	DRAGON'S-BLOOD
ABCDEEILORSV	DISCOVERABLE	ABDEEEEILMRR	IRREDEEMABLE
ABCDEELMOOPS	DECOMPOSABLE	ABDEEEEFIILNS	INDEFEASIBLE
ABCDEELRTTUU	TUBERCULATED	ABDEEEIILMRR	IRREMEDIABLE
ABCDEGHIILNR	CHILD-BEARING	ABDEEEIILRTV	DELIBERATIVE
ABCDEGILNOTU	DOUBLE-ACTING	ABDEEEILLRTY	DELIBERATELY
ABCDEHHLOOOR	BACHELORHOOD	ABDEEEILMNRT	DETERMINABLE
ABCDEHKLMOTU	BLACK-MOUTHED	ABDEEEILMRRY	IRREDEEMABLY
ABCDEHNORSTY	BODY-SNATCHER	ABDEEEELMNTTT	BATTLEMENTED
ABCDEHNRRRYY	CHERRY-BRANDY	ABDEEFIIILNT	IDENTIFIABLE
ABCDEILNORSY	CONSIDERABLY	ABDEEIILMRRY	IRREMEDIABLY
ABCDEILNOSTU	DISCOUNTABLE	ABDEEIILNORT	DELIBERATION
ABCEEEENPRRT	CARPENTER-BEE	ABDEEILMNOPR	IMPONDERABLE
ABCEEEFNRSST	BENEFACTRESS	ABDEEILPRSTU	DISREPUTABLE
ABCEEEMMNRRR	REMEMBRANCER	ABDEELMNORST	DEMONSTRABLE
ABCEEFFIINRT	FEBRIFACIENT	ABDEENORSSTU	OBDURATENESS
ABCEEFIILLNY	BENEFICIALLY	ABDEFIIILLOS	SOLIDIFIABLE
ABCEEGILNORS	RECOGNISABLE	ABDEFNORRSSU	BRASS-FOUNDER
ABCEEHLNNQUU	UNQUENCHABLE	ABDEFORSTUUY	SUBFEUDATORY
ABCEEIILLNPX	INEXPLICABLE	ABDEGIIILNTT	DEBILITATING
ABCEEIILKNNNT	BICENTENNIAL	ABDEGIIKNOPR	BOARDING-PIKE
ABCEEIILNRTX	INEXTRICABLE	ABDEHHLMOORR	RHOMBOHEDRAL
ABCEEIILPPRT	PRECIPITABLE	ABDEHIIILMNS	DIMINISHABLE
ABCEEIILRSSTU	RESUSCITABLE	ABDEHIILSSST	DISESTABLISH
ABCEELLLNOSU	COUNSELLABLE	ABDEHILMNNST	BLANDISHMENT
ABCEELLNOOST	CONSOLE-TABLE	ABDEIIILMNSS	INADMISSIBLE
ABCEELLNPSSU	CULPABLENESS	ABDEIIILNOTT	DEBILITATION
ABCEELMMMOOR	COMMEMORABLE	ABDEIIILRSTY	DESIRABILITY
ABCEENOPRRTU	PROTUBERANCE	ABDEIILNPSTUU	INDUSPUTABLE
ABCEGILOORTY	BACTERIOLOGY	ABDEILPRSTUY	DISREPUTABLY
ABCEHHILOPRS	BACHELORSHIP	ABDEIMORSTUX	AMBIDEXTROUS
ABCEHHRTTTUY	BUTTERY-HATCH	ABDELMNORSTY	DEMONSTRABLY
ABCEHIKNRSSS	BRACKISHNESS	ABDFIILNNRUU	INFUNDIBULAR
ABCEHILLOPRY	HYPERBOLICAL	ABEEEHMNQTTU	BEQUEATHMENT
ABCEHILMNRUU	HIBERNACULUM	ABEEEEILLNRSS	RELIABLENESS
ABCEHKLRSSUW	SWASHBUCKLER	ABEEEEILMNPRT	IMPENETRABLE
ABCEHLNNQUUY	UNQUENCHABLY	ABEEEEILMNRTX	EXTERMINABLE
ABCEIIILTTXY	EXCITABILITY	ABEEEINNPRTV	BREVIPENNATE

ABEEEINRRTTV	INVERTEBRATE
ABEEEORRRRTV	REVERBERATOR
ABEEFFILNRSU	INSUFFERABLE
ABEEFIILMNST	MANIFESTIBLE
ABEEFILMOPRR	IMPERFORABLE
ABEEGIILNSTV	INVESTIGABLE
ABEEGILNNSST	TANGIBLENESS
ABEEGLNNORUV	UNGOVERNABLE
ABEEHIILMPRS	IMPERISHABLE
ABEEHLLRSSTY	BREATHLESSLY
ABEEHLNNOORR	BLENNORRHOEA
ABEEIILMNNRT	INTERMINABLE
ABEEIILMNNRT	INTERMINABLE
ABEEIILMPRTY	PERMEABILITY
ABEEIILNPSST	PITIABLENESS
ABEEIILORTTV	OBLITERATIVE
ABEEIILPRRRS	IRRESPIRABLE
ABEEILLNNRUV	INVULNERABLE
ABEEILLORRSV	IRRESOLVABLE
ABEEILLPRUVZ	PULVERIZABLE
ABEEILMMNRSU	IMMENSURABLE
ABEEILMNPRTY	IMPENETRABLY
ABEEILNOQSTU	QUESTIONABLE
ABEEILNSSSTU	SUITABLENESS
ABEEILOPRRRV	IRREPROVABLE
ABEEILPRRSTY	PRESBYTERIAL
ABEEINORSSTV	ABORTIVENESS
ABEEINPRRSTY	PRESBYTERIAN
ABEEIRRRSSTW	STRAWBERRIES
ABEEKLMORRTU	TROUBLEMAKER
ABEEKORRSSTT	BREASTSTROKE
ABEELLMNOPUY	UNEMPLOYABLE
ABEELMMNNOTZ	EMBLAZONMENT
ABEELNNSSSTU	UNSTABLENESS
ABEELNOSSSTU	ABSOLUTENESS
ABEENRSSSSTU	ABSTRUSENESS
ABEFFILNRSUY	INSUFFERABLY
ABEFILNOPRTU	UNPROFITABLE
ABEFILNRSSTU	TRANSFUSIBLE
ABEFLNOSSSTU	BOASTFULNESS
ABEGGIILLNST	BILLINGSGATE
ABEGHHKORRTU	BREAKTHROUGH
ABEGHJNNORSU	JOHANNESBURG
ABEGHLOPRSTU	BREAST-PLOUGH
ABEGIKLNNOOR	BOOK-LEARNING
ABEGILLLNOWY	BOWLING-ALLEY
ABEGILMNNPUU	UNIMPUGNABLE
ABEGLMORSUUY	UMBRAGEOUSLY
ABEGLNNORUVY	UNGOVERNABLY
ABEHIIIMNNRS	HIBERNIANISM
ABEHIILMPRSY	IMPERISHABLY
ABEHIILNOPST	INHOSPITABLE
ABEHIIORSTUV	BEHAVIOURIST
ABEHIKLNNRSU	UNSHRINKABLE
ABEHILNOPTYZ	HYPNOTIZABLE
ABEHILNORRTW	BROTHER-IN-LAW
ABEIIILLLRTY	ILLIBERALITY
ABEIILLLMPTU	MULTIPLIABLE
ABEIILLORTTY	TOLERABILITY
ABEIILMNNRTY	INTERMINABLY
ABEIILMORTVY	REMOVABILITY
ABEIILNNOSTU	SUBLINEATION
ABEIILNOORTT	OBLITERATION
ABEIILNORRTT	INTERORBITAL
ABEIILLOPRRVY	PROVERBIALLY
ABEILMNOSUUX	EXALBUMINOUS
ABEILMOSSTUY	ABSTEMIOUSLY
ABEILNOQSTUY	QUESTIONABLY
ABEILNORTTXY	EXORBITANTLY
ABEINOPRRTTU	PERTURBATION
ABELLLLOPSYY	POLYSYLLABLE
ABELMNORSTUU	SURMOUNTABLE
ABGGILNNRSSU	BURNING-GLASS
ABGIILLOORTY	OBLIGATORILY
ABIIIILRRTTY	IRRITABILITY
ABIIILLPSTUY	PLAUSIBILITY
ABIIILMMTTUY	IMMUTABILITY
ABIIILMNNOTZ	MOBILIZATION
ABIIILNOOSTT	ABOLITIONIST
ABIILNORSSUU	INSALUBRIOUS
ABIIOPRSTTVY	ABSORPTIVITY
ABILLORSSUUY	SALUBRIOUSLY
ABILMMMNOSSU	SOMNAMBULISM
ABILMMNOSSTU	SOMNAMBULIST
ABILMNORSTUY	SUBNORMALITY
ABNOORRSSTUU	BRONTOSAURUS
ACCCEEEINQSU	ACQUIESCENCE
ACCCEEEELNORS	CALORESCENCE
ACCCEEHMNOTU	ACCOUCHEMENT
ACCCEEIILSST	ECCLESIASTIC
ACCCEEILLLTY	ECLECTICALLY
ACCCEELNOSTY	NECTOCALYCES
ACCCEIJMNRTU	CIRCUMJACENT
ACCCEIMNNOOT	CONCOMITANCE
ACCCEIMNRSTU	CIRCUMSTANCE
ACCCENOPPRUY	PREOCCUPANCY
ACCCIMNNOOTY	CONCOMITANCY
ACCDEEEHLMNY	CHANCE-MEDLEY
ACCDEEENORST	DECONSECRATE
ACCDEEIIILPT	EPIDEICTICAL
ACCDEEILNOPY	ENCYCLOPEDIA
ACCDEEINNNST	INCANDESCENT
ACCDEELNOPRS	CORPSE-CANDLE
ACCDEENNORTT	CONCENTRATED
ACCDEENOSSUU	SUCCEDANEOUS
ACCDEHHNRRUW	CHURCHWARDEN
ACCDEIILLOPY	EPICYCLOIDAL
ACCDEIILNNOT	COINCIDENTAL
ACCDEIILLNOTY	OCCIDENTALLY
ACCDEIMNORTU	UNDEMOCRATIC
ACCDEINORRTT	CONTRADICTER
ACCDELNORTTY	CONTRACTEDLY
ACCDEMNOSTUU	UNACCUSTOMED
ACCDENNORTUY	COUNTRY-DANCE
ACCDFIIINOOT	CODIFICATION
ACCDLNNOORTY	CONCORDANTLY
ACCEEEILSSST	ECCLESIASTES
ACCEEENNORVY	RECONVEYANCE
ACCEEFGIIMNN	MAGNIFICENCE
ACCEEGHNNORX	CORN-EXCHANGE
ACCEEHIRRTTU	ARCHITECTURE
ACCEEHMNNORT	ENCROACHMENT
ACCEEIINNORT	INTEROCEANIC

231

ACCEEILLLRTY	ELECTRICALLY	ACCIILMNOOPT	COMPLICATION
ACCEEILNPTTU	CENTUPLICATE	ACCIILNOORTY	CONCILIATORY
ACCEELLOORTT	COLLECTORATE	ACCIILOPRSUY	CAPRICIOUSLY
ACCEELNNOSTV	CONVALESCENT	ACCIINNOOOST	CONSOCIATION
ACCEENNNORTU	COUNTENANCER	ACCILMOOPSST	COSMOPLASTIC
ACCEFGIIINNS	SIGNIFICANCE	ACCIMMNOORTU	COMMUNICATOR
ACCEFIILLPSY	SPECIFICALLY	ACCIMNOOSTUU	CONTUMACIOUS
ACCEGHILOOST	ESCHATOLOGIC	ACDDDEEHNOOR	DODECAHEDRON
ACCEGHINOPRS	SCENOGRAPHIC	ACDDDEEINSST	ADDICTEDNESS
ACCEGIILMOST	CLEISTOGAMIC	ACDDDENOORSU	DODECANDROUS
ACCEGIINRTUX	EXCRUCIATING	ACDDEEEHIMST	SEMI-DETACHED
ACCEGILLLOOY	ECOLOGICALLY	ACDDEEHLLNOR	CANDLE-HOLDER
ACCEGIMRRTUY	CIRCUMGYRATE	ACDDEEILNTTU	DENTICULATED
ACCEGINNNOVY	CONVEYANCING	ACDDEGHINRSU	UNDISCHARGED
ACCEGNOORRTY	GERONTOCRACY	ACDDEIINORST	ENDOCARDITIS
ACCEHIILLMRY	CHIMERICALLY	ACDDEILNOOST	CONSOLIDATED
ACCEHIILLNST	CALLISTHENIC	ACDDEILRSTTY	DISTRACTEDLY
ACCEHIILNOPR	NECROPHILIAC	ACDDIIIJNOTU	DIJUDICATION
ACCEHIILNSST	CALISTHENICS	ACDDILNORSTY	DISCORDANTLY
ACCEHIILNTTY	TECHNICALITY	ACDEEEFFNSST	AFFECTEDNESS
ACCEHIKMNSTY	CHIMNEY-STACK	ACDEEEIIPRTV	DEPRECIATIVE
ACCEHILMOPRS	ACCOMPLISHER	ACDEEEILNORT	DECELERATION
ACCEHINNNOPT	PANTECHNICON	ACDEEEILNRTZ	DECENTRALIZE
ACCEHINRSSST	SCRATCHINESS	ACDEEEILNSST	DELICATENESS
ACCEHLOORSSU	SCHORLACEOUS		DELICATESSEN
ACCEHMNORRTU	COUNTER-MARCH	ACDEEEINNRTV	INADVERTENCE
	COUNTERCHARM	ACDEEEINRSSV	DISSEVERANCE
ACCEIILLLNTY	ENCLITICALLY	ACDEEELNNTTY	ANTECEDENTLY
ACCEIILMOPTV	COMPLICATIVE	ACDEEEOPRRRT	TAPE-RECORDER
ACCEIILNORTV	INTERVOCALIC	ACDEEFHHIKNR	HANDKERCHIEF
ACCEIIOPRSUV	PERVICACIOUS	ACDEEFHNORRW	HENCEFORWARD
ACCEIIPPRSTY	PERSPICACITY	ACDEEGHILRST	CLEAR-SIGHTED
ACCEILLMMORY	COMMERCIALLY	ACDEEGHLLNNU	UNCHALLENGED
ACCEILLMNOOY	ECONOMICALLY	ACDEEGILNRSY	DECREASINGLY
ACCEILLOPRRY	RECIPROCALLY	ACDEEGINRSSS	DRESSING-CASE
ACCEILMMNORU	UNCOMMERCIAL	ACDEEGKLNORW	ACKNOWLEDGER
ACCEILMNNOOU	UNECONOMICAL	ACDEEHINNRST	DISENCHANTER
ACCEILNOORRT	CORRECTIONAL	ACDEEIILLTTY	DIETETICALLY
ACCEILNOSSSU	SUCCESSIONAL	ACDEEIIMNRTY	INTERMEDIACY
ACCEILOPRSST	CEROPLASTICS	ACDEEIINOPRT	DEPRECIATION
ACCEIMNNOORT	CONCREMATION	ACDEEIINTTUX	INEXACTITUDE
ACCEIMNRTTUU	CIRCUMNUTATE	ACDEEIKLOOPS	KALEIDOSCOPE
ACCEINNOORST	CONSECRATION	ACDEEILMNPST	DISPLACEMENT
ACCELLMNOPTY	COMPLACENTLY	ACDEEILNNOSS	DESCENSIONAL
ACCELLOOORSU	COROLLACEOUS	ACDEEILORTUV	EDULCORATIVE
ACCELNNRSTUY	TRANSLUCENCY	ACDEEIMMNOPR	PREDOMINANCE
ACCENOPRRSTU	COUNTERSCARP	ACDEEINNRTVY	INADVERTENCY
ACCFIIMNNOSU	CONFUCIANISM	ACDEEIOPRRTY	DEPRECIATORY
ACCFIINNOOST	CONFISCATION	ACDEELOPRTTY	PTERODACTYLE
ACCFINOORSTY	CONFISCATORY	ACDEEMNOPPTY	APPENDECTOMY
ACCGHIINOPRZ	ZINCOGRAPHIC	ACDEENNNOTUV	UNCOVENANTED
ACCGHIMOOPRS	COSMOGRAPHIC	ACDEFFIINOST	DISAFFECTION
ACCGIILLOOOS	SOCIOLOGICAL	ACDEFHIINRSS	DISFRANCHISE
ACCGILLMOOOS	COSMOLOGICAL	ACDEFHINNRSU	UNFRANCHISED
ACCHHINOPRSY	CHRYSOPHANIC	ACDEFIILNNOT	CONFIDENTIAL
ACCHHIOPPSTY	PSYCHOPATHIC	ACDEFIILNSSU	UNCLASSIFIED
ACCHIIINSTUV	CHAUVINISTIC	ACDEFIINNSTT	DISINFECTANT
ACCHIILOPRTY	HYPOCRITICAL	ACDEFIINNSTU	UNSANCTIFIED
ACCHIIOPRSTY	PHYSIOCRATIC	ACDEFIINOORT	DEFORCIATION
ACCHILLNNOOO	NON-ALCOHOLIC	ACDEGILLOOTY	DIALECTOLOGY
ACCIIILNNOOT	CONCILIATION	ACDEGINORRSS	CROSS-GRAINED

ACDEHIIILSTT	DITHEISTICAL	ACEEEFNNRRST	TRANSFERENCE
ACDEHIILMMOT	IMMETHODICAL	ACEEEGHINPRS	CHEESE-PARING
ACDEHILLMOTY	METHODICALLY	ACEEEGNNRRUY	UNREGENERACY
ACDEHIOOPRST	ORTHOPAEDICS	ACEEEHLNNOPP	EPENCEPHALON
ACDEIIILNTVY	INDICATIVELY	ACEEEIMNNPRT	INTEMPERANCE
ACDEIIIMNNRS	INCENDIARISM	ACEEEIPRRTUV	RECUPERATIVE
ACDEIIIMNRST	DISCRIMINATE	ACEEELLOPRTT	ELECTROPLATE
ACDEIIINPPST	APPENDICITIS	ACEEELNNSTVY	EVANESCENTLY
ACDEIIIPRRST	PERICARDITIS	ACEEELNRSSSS	CARELESSNESS
ACDEIILLNNTY	INCIDENTALLY	ACEEEMNNNRTT	ENTRANCEMENT
ACDEIILLOPRY	PERIODICALLY	ACEEENNRRTTY	TERCENTENARY
ACDEIILLOPSY	EPISODICALLY	ACEEFFINOTTU	EFFECTUATION
ACDEIILNORST	DISCRETIONAL	ACEEFGLNRSSU	GRACEFULNESS
ACDEIINNNOTU	DENUNCIATION	ACEEFHIINSST	CHIEFTAINESS
ACDEIINNORTT	INDOCTRINATE	ACEEFIILNQTU	LIQUEFACIENT
ACDEIINOORTV	CO-ORDINATIVE	ACEEFIIPRTTV	PETRIFACTIVE
ACDEIINOSTTU	EDUCATIONIST	ACEEFIKNNNRS	FRANKINCENSE
ACDEIJLNTUVY	ADJUNCTIVELY	ACEEFILNNORT	CONFERENTIAL
ACDEIILLMOSTY	DOMESTICALLY	ACEEFINPSTTU	STUPEFACIENT
ACDEILLOPSTY	DESPOTICALLY	ACEEFIPSTTUV	STUPEFACTIVE
ACDEILNOOORT	DECOLORATION	ACEEGHIRRSST	CASH-REGISTER
ACDEILNOORTU	EDULCORATION	ACEEGHLNOORT	COLOGNE-EARTH
ACDEILNOORTY	CO-ORDINATELY	ACEEGIILMNSV	EVANGELICISM
ACDEILNOOSST	DISCONSOLATE	ACEEGIIMNORT	GEOMETRICIAN
ACDEILNORSSW	COWARDLINESS	ACEEGILLLOOT	TELEOLOGICAL
ACDEILNTTUUV	UNCULTIVATED	ACEEGLMNOORT	CONGLOMERATE
ACDEIMMMNNOOT	COMMENDATION	ACEEGNNORTTU	COUNTER-AGENT
ACDEIMNNNOOT	CONDEMNATION	ACEEHHIPRRSU	HIRE-PURCHASE
ACDEINNNOOST	CONDENSATION	ACEEHHLNORSU	CHARNEL-HOUSE
ACDEINNORTTU	DETRUNCATION	ACEEHHOPRSTU	CHAPTER-HOUSE
ACDEINNORTUY	DENUNCIATORY	ACEEHHORRSTU	CHARTERHOUSE
ACDEINORSTTU	DECRUSTATION	ACEEHIILNPST	ENCEPHALITIS
ACDELNOORTYY	COTYLEDONARY	ACEEHIILPPRR	PERIPHERICAL
ACDELOPRRTTY	PROTRACTEDLY	ACEEHIIMSSTT	AESTHETICISM
ACDEMMMNNOORTY	COMMENDATORY	ACEEHILLMRTY	HERMETICALLY
ACDEMMNNOORTY	CONDEMNATORY	ACEEHIMNSSTT	CHASTISEMENT
ACDFIIIINNOT	NIDIFICATION	ACEEHIPRSTTU	THERAPEUTICS
ACDFIIIMNOOT	MODIFICATION	ACEEHLLRRRUY	CHERRY-LAUREL
ACDFIIMOORTY	MODIFICATORY	ACEEIILLRTTV	VERTICILLATE
ACDGGIINORSU	DISCOURAGING	ACEEIILMRRUZ	MERCURIALIZE
ACDGILLOOTYY	DACTYLIOLOGY	ACEEIIMNPRSU	EPICUREANISM
ACDGILMNOORR	CORN-MARIGOLD	ACEEIINORSTV	EVISCERATION
ACDHHIIOPSTY	ICHTHYOPSIDA	ACEEIINORTTX	EXERCITATION
ACDHHINOOPRY	HYPOCHONDRIA	ACEEIILLNTTU	INTELLECTUAL
ACDHIIOPRSTT	DICTATORSHIP	ACEEIILLMNORY	CEREMONIALLY
ACDHIORSSTTY	HYDROSTATICS	ACEEIILLNNORT	CRENELLATION
ACDIIILNPRSY	DISCIPLINARY	ACEEIILLNRSUV	SURVEILLANCE
ACDIIINOOSST	DISSOCIATION	ACEEIILLORSTY	ESOTERICALLY
ACDIIIOSSTTU	ADSCITITIOUS	ACEEIILLORTXY	EXOTERICALLY
ACDIIILLMNPTU	MULTIPLICAND	ACEEILMMNNPST	MISPLACEMENT
ACDIILNOOQTU	COLOQUINTIDA	ACEEILOPPRRT	PRECEPTORIAL
ACDIINNOOORT	CO-ORDINATION	ACEEIMMPRTUY	EMPYREUMATIC
ACDIINORSSYY	IDIOSYNCRASY	ACEEIMNORSSX	CROSS-EXAMINE
ACDILNOOORST	CONSOLIDATOR	ACEEINOPPPRT	APPERCEPTION
ACDILORSTTUY	TRIDACTYLOUS	ACEEINOPRRTU	RECUPERATION
ACDINOOQRSTU	CONQUISTADOR	ACEEINOPRSTT	INSPECTORATE
ACEEEEGILPTX	EPEXEGETICAL	ACEEINOPRSTU	PERTINACEOUS
ACEEEEHLPSST	STEEPLECHASE	ACEEINORSTVV	CONSERVATIVE
ACEEEELNORTT	COELENTERATE	ACEELLMMNOPT	COMPLEMENTAL
ACEEEENPRRSV	PERSEVERANCE	ACEELMNNORTU	NOMENCLATURE
ACEEEFLNPSSU	PEACEFULNESS	ACEELNSSSSTT	TACTLESSNESS

ACEEMMNORSTU	COMMENSURATE
ACEEMNNNNOTU	ANNOUNCEMENT
ACEEMNNNORRST	REMONSTRANCE
ACEEOOPRRTTT	PROTECTORATE
ACEEOPRRRTUY	RECUPERATORY
ACEFFILNNSSU	FANCIFULNESS
ACEFFORRSUUU	FURFURACEOUS
ACEFGLLNRUUY	UNGRACEFULLY
ACEFHHIMNSTY	CHIMNEY-SHAFT
ACEFHLNSSTUW	WATCHFULNESS
ACEFIIILNOTT	FELICITATION
ACEFIIINORTV	VERIFICATION
ACEFIILLNNOT	INFLECTIONAL
ACEFIILLRRTY	TERRIFICALLY
ACEFIILNOQTU	LIQUEFACTION
ACEFIILORSTU	LATICIFEROUS
ACEFIIMNORTV	CONFIRMATIVE
ACEFIINOORTV	VOCIFERATION
ACEFIINOPRTT	PETRIFICATION
ACEFIIORRSTV	VERSIFICATOR
ACEFIIRRTTUV	VITRIFACTURE
ACEFILNNOOSS	CONFESSIONAL
ACEFILORRRTY	REFRACTORILY
ACEFINOORRTT	TORREFACTION
ACEFINOPRTTU	PUTREFACTION
ACEFINOPSTTU	STUPEFACTION
ACEFINORRSST	FORNICATRESS
ACEFINOSSSTU	FACTIOUSNESS
ACEFLLMOOPRW	CAMP-FOLLOWER
ACEGGILLLOOY	GEOLOGICALLY
ACEGGINNOORT	CONGREGATION
ACEGHHIOPRRR	CHIROGRAPHER
ACEGHHOOPRRY	CHOREOGRAPHY
ACEGHIILLNYY	HYGIENICALLY
ACEGHIKNPRTT	CARPET-KNIGHT
ACEGHILLNOOT	ETHNOLOGICAL
ACEGHILNNNTY	ENCHANTINGLY
ACEGHILOOPRS	PHRASEOLOGIC
ACEGHILOPRXY	LEXICOGRAPHY
ACEGHINOPRST	STENOGRAPHIC
ACEGHMOOPRRS	COSMOGRAPHER
ACEGIIILLMTY	ILLEGITIMACY
ACEGIILNNOTU	GENICULATION
ACEGIILNNOTY	CONGENIALITY
ACEGIILNNRSY	INCREASINGLY
ACEGIILORSSU	SACRILEGIOUS
ACEGIINOOTTX	EXCOGITATION
ACEGILLLNOOY	NEOLOGICALLY
ACEGILLMOOTY	ETYMOLOGICAL
ACEGILNNOTTU	CONGLUTINATE
ACEGILORSTTU	GESTICULATOR
ACEGIMNNORSU	COUSIN-GERMAN
ACEGINORSSSU	GRACIOUSNESS
ACEGLNOOPRSY	LARYNGOSCOPE
ACEGLOORSUUY	COURAGEOUSLY
ACEHHILOOPST	THEOSOPHICAL
ACEHHILOPTTY	HYPOTHETICAL
ACEHHIMOOOPT	HOMOEOPATHIC
ACEHHMORSTTY	CHRESTOMATHY
ACEHHOOPRTTY	HYPOTHECATOR
ACEHIIINRSTZ	CHRISTIANIZE
ACEHIIINSTTT	ANTITHEISTIC
ACEHIILMNNTT	ANTHELMINTIC
ACEHIILNPPRS	PLANISPHERIC
ACEHIINSSTTU	ENTHUSIASTIC
ACEHIINTTTUY	AUTHENTICITY
ACEHIIOPSSTT	SOPHISTICATE
ACEHIKLMNSTY	CHIMNEY-STALK
ACEHILLNOPTY	PHONETICALLY
ACEHILLRSTYY	HYSTERICALLY
ACEHILNNNSSS	CLANNISHNESS
ACEHINOPPRTU	HIPPOCENTAUR
ACEHLMMNOOTW	COMMONWEALTH
ACEHLMOORSST	SCHOOLMASTER
ACEIIILMNPUZ	MUNICIPALIZE
ACEIIILNSTTY	INELASTICITY
ACEIIIMNPRSS	PRECISIANISM
ACEIIINNNORT	INCINERATION
ACEIILLLLPTY	ELLIPTICALLY
ACEIILLNORRT	TORRICELLIAN
ACEIILNNNRTU	INTERNUNCIAL
ACEIILNNORSS	IRONICALNESS
ACEIILNORTTU	RETICULATION
ACEIILPRRSUY	SUPERCILIARY
ACEIILRRSSTU	SURREALISTIC
ACEIIMNORSTT	CREMATIONIST
ACEIINNNORTU	RENUNCIATION
ACEIINOOQTUV	EQUIVOCATION
ACEIINOPRRTT	PRACTITIONER
ACEIINORRSTW	CONTRARIWISE
ACEILLLNRTUY	LENTICULARLY
ACEILLMMNOOT	MONOMETALLIC
ACEILLMNOOPT	COMPELLATION
ACEILLMNOOPX	COMPLEXIONAL
ACEILLNOPTUY	UNPOETICALLY
ACEILMMMNOSS	COMMENSALISM
ACEILMOOPRRS	CORPOREALISM
ACEILMOPRRTY	PYROMETRICAL
ACEILMOSTTTU	MULTICOSTATE
ACEILNNNOOTV	CONVENTIONAL
ACEILNOSTTUV	CONSULTATIVE
ACEILOOPRRST	CORPOREALIST
ACEILOOPRRTY	CORPOREALITY
ACEIMMNNOOTT	COMMENTATION
ACEIMMNNOSTUV	CONSUMMATIVE
ACEIMMOORRST	COMMISERATOR
ACEIMNNOOPST	COMPENSATION
ACEIMNNOPRTU	UNIMPORTANCE
ACEIMNOOOOPT	ONOMATOPOEIC
ACEIMNORSSTV	CONSERVATISM
ACEIMNSSTTUY	UNSYSTEMATIC
ACEINNOORSTV	CONSERVATION
	CONVERSATION
ACEINNOOSTTT	CONTESTATION
ACEINNORRSST	CONTRARINESS
ACEINOPSSSSU	SPACIOUSNESS
ACEINOPSSSTU	CAPTIOUSNESS
ACEINOSSSTUU	CAUTIOUSNESS
ACEIOOQRTUVY	EQUIVOCATORY
ACEIORRSSTTU	RESUSCITATOR
ACEJLLNRRTUY	CURRANT-JELLY
ACELMMNOSTUY	CONSUMMATELY

234

ACELMNOOPRTT	CONTEMPLATOR	ACHILLORSUVY	CHIVALROUSLY
ACELMNPRSUUU	SUPERNACULUM	ACHILOOPPRRS	CORPORALSHIP
ACELOOOPSTTU	OCTOPETALOUS	ACHIMNNOORTY	ORNITHOMANCY
ACELOPRRSTTU	COURT-PLASTER	ACIIIILMRSTT	MILITARISTIC
ACEMMMOOORRT	COMMEMORATOR	ACIIIILNOTVZ	CIVILIZATION
ACEMNOOPRRTY	CONTEMPORARY	ACIIILMNPTUV	MUNICIPALITY
ACEMNOOPRSTY	COMPENSATORY	ACIIILNOOSTT	COALITIONIST
ACEMOOPRRSTU	MACROPTEROUS	ACIIILNOPRTT	TRIPLICATION
ACENOORRSTVY	CONSERVATORY	ACIIILNOSTVV	CONVIVIALIST
ACFGIIINORST	SIGNIFICATOR	ACIIILNOTVVY	CONVIVIALITY
ACFIIIILNOTV	VILIFICATION	ACIIILNPPRTY	PRINCIPALITY
ACFIIINNOOTT	NOTIFICATION	ACIIINNOOTTX	INTOXICATION
ACFIIINNORTT	ANTIFRICTION	ACIIINOPSSUU	INAUSPICIOUS
ACFIIINOOSST	OSSIFICATION	ACIIJLNORSTU	JOURNALISTIC
ACFIIINOPRTU	PURIFICATION	ACIILLOSSUVY	LASCIVIOUSLY
ACFIIINORTTV	VITRIFICATION	ACIILNNOOOTZ	COLONIZATION
ACFIILOSTTUY	FACTITIOUSLY	ACIILNNOOSTU	INOSCULATION
ACFIIMNNOORT	CONFIRMATION	ACIILNOORSST	CONSISTORIAL
ACFILLNNOTUY	FUNCTIONALLY	ACIILNOPPSTU	SUPPLICATION
ACFIMNNOOORT	CONFORMATION	ACIILNOSTUUY	INCAUTIOUSLY
ACFIMNOORRTY	CONFIRMATORY	ACIILOPSSUUY	AUSPICIOUSLY
ACGGILNPPSSU	CUPPING-GLASS	ACIINNNOOTTU	CONTINUATION
ACGHHIILOPRT	LITHOGRAPHIC	ACIINNOOPSTT	CONSTIPATION
ACGHHINOORTT	ORTHOGNATHIC	ACILLLLOOQUY	COLLOQUIALLY
ACGHHIOOPPRT	PHOTOGRAPHIC	ACILLLOPRRUU	PLURILOCULAR
ACGHHIOOPRRT	ORTHOGRAPHIC	ACILLMNOSUUY	CALUMNIOUSLY
ACGHHNOOPRRY	CHRONOGRAPHY	ACILLMORSUUY	MIRACULOUSLY
ACGHIILLLOOT	LITHOLOGICAL	ACILLNNOOSUV	CONVULSIONAL
ACGHIIPRSSST	SPHRAGISTICS	ACILLNOPSTYY	SYNOPTICALLY
ACGHILLMOOTY	MYTHOLOGICAL	ACILLOOQSUUY	LOQUACIOUSLY
ACGHILOPRSTY	STYLOGRAPHIC	ACILLPRRSTUY	SCRIPTURALLY
ACGHINOOPPRR	PORNOGRAPHIC	ACILMNOOOPST	COSMOPOLITAN
ACGHOOOPPRSU	COPROPHAGOUS	ACILMOOPPRST	PROTOPLASMIC
ACGHOPPRRTYY	CRYPTOGRAPHY	ACILNNNOSTTY	INCONSTANTLY
ACGIIINNOTTX	INTOXICATING	ACILNNOOSTTU	CONSULTATION
ACGIILMNOSUU	MUCILAGINOUS	ACILNPRRSTUU	UNSCRIPTURAL
ACGIILNOORST	CRANIOLOGIST	ACILOPPRRSTY	SUPPLICATORY
ACGIINNNOOST	CONSIGNATION	ACILORRRSTUV	CURVIROSTRAL
ACGILLOOOPRT	TROPOLOGICAL	ACIMMMNNOOSTU	CONSUMMATION
ACGILNOOSTUY	CONTAGIOUSLY	ACLLLPRSTUUY	SCULPTURALLY
ACGILNOPSUUY	PUGNACIOUSLY	ACMNNOORTUWY	COUNTRYWOMAN
ACGILNORSUUY	UNGRACIOUSLY	ADDDDEEEEHLMU	MUDDLEHEADED
ACGIMNOOPRTU	COMPURGATION	ADDDIILLMNOR	DIAMOND-DRILL
ACGMOOPRSTUY	CRYPTOGAMOUS	ADDEEEIIRSTV	DESIDERATIVE
ACHHIILMNOPR	PHILHARMONIC	ADDEEEINSSSS	DISEASEDNESS
ACHHIIMNOPPS	CHAMPIONSHIP	ADDEEEKLNOOY	YANKEE-DOODLE
ACHHILLMRTYY	RHYTHMICALLY	ADDEEENPRSSV	DEPRAVEDNESS
ACHHILORTTYY	ICHTHYOLATRY	ADDEEFLNRSSU	DREADFULNESS
ACHHINOPSSTY	SYCOPHANTISH	ADDEEGHILNNS	SINGLE-HANDED
ACHIIIINRSST	TRICHINIASIS	ADDEEGNORSTU	ADDER'S-TONGUE
ACHIIILMSTWY	WHIMSICALITY	ADDEEILLPSSY	DISPLEASEDLY
ACHIIILNORST	HISTRIONICAL	ADDEFGILRRSU	DISREGARDFUL
ACHIIIMNPSSU	MUSICIANSHIP	ADDEFHILNOOS	OLD-FASHIONED
ACHIIINRSTTY	CHRISTIANITY	ADDEFIIISSST	DISSATISFIED
ACHIILLORSTY	HISTORICALLY	ADDEHMNOOORT	RHODOMONTADE
ACHIILNNOORT	CHLORINATION	ADDEIINOPPST	DISAPPOINTED
ACHIILNOPRST	RHINOPLASTIC	ADDEIMNNORRW	NARROW-MINDED
ACHIILNORSTU	UNHISTORICAL	ADDFIILLNSUY	DISDAINFULLY
ACHIIMNOPRST	MISANTHROPIC	ADEEEEGLNRTY	DEGENERATELY
ACHIINOPRSTT	ANTISTROPHIC	ADEEEGHLMMRS	SLEDGE-HAMMER
ACHIIPRSSTTY	PSYCHIATRIST	ADEEEGIMNRST	DISAGREEMENT

Letters	Word	Letters	Word
ADEEEGINNORT	DEGENERATION	ADEGIILMNORZ	DEMORALIZING
ADEEEGINRRTT	REDINTEGRATE	ADEGIILNORSS	DIGRESSIONAL
ADEEEHHLORTW	WHOLE-HEARTED	ADEGIILNPRSY	DESPAIRINGLY
ADEEEHIIMNPR	EPHEMERIDIAN	ADEHHIRRSTTW	THITHERWARDS
ADEEEHINSSSV	ADHESIVENESS	ADEHHLMORRTY	HYDROTHERMAL
ADEEEIIMNRTT	INTERMEDIATE	ADEHIIMOPRST	MEDIATORSHIP
ADEEEIIORRST	AEROSIDERITE	ADEHILMNNOOP	MONODELPHIAN
ADEEEILLMMOS	MADEMOISELLE	ADEHILOPRSTU	TRIADELPHOUS
ADEEEILNPRRT	INTERPLEADER	ADEHIMMNNNOST	ADMONISHMENT
ADEEEINPRSTT	PREDESTINATE	ADEHINQRRSTU	HINDQUARTERS
ADEEELNOSSST	DESOLATENESS	ADEHLMNNOSUY	UNHANDSOMELY
ADEEENOPPRRT	PREPONDERATE	ADEIIILMNOTT	DELIMITATION
ADEEEOPPRRSV	EAVESDROPPER	ADEIIINTTTUZ	ATTITUDINIZE
ADEEFFIILNRT	DIFFERENTIAL	ADEIIILLMNORY	MERIDIONALLY
ADEEGHHILRTT	LIGHT-HEARTED	ADEIILMNSTTT	DILETTANTISM
ADEEGHINNRRT	HEART-RENDING	ADEIILNNORTY	INORDINATELY
ADEEGHPRSTTU	STEPDAUGHTER	ADEIILNOOPST	DESPOLIATION
ADEEGIINRSTT	DISINTEGRATE	ADEIILNOPRTV	PROVIDENTIAL
ADEEGIKLNRST	DEER-STALKING	ADEIILNORSST	DILATORINESS
ADEEGIKNNRRT	KINDERGARTEN	ADEIILSSSUVY	DISSUASIVELY
ADEEGLLRRSSY	REGARDLESSLY	ADEIIMMNOORT	IMMODERATION
ADEEGNPRTUUX	UNEXPURGATED	ADEIIMNNNOOT	DENOMINATION
ADEEGORRTTXY	DEXTRO-GYRATE	ADEIIMNNOSTU	MOUNTAIN-SIDE
ADEEHHIKNRRS	HEADSHRINKER	ADEIIMNORSST	DISSEMINATOR
ADEEHIMNPPRS	MISAPPREHEND	ADEIINNOPSST	DISPENSATION
ADEEHIMRSSST	HEADMISTRESS	ADEIINORSSTT	DISSERTATION
ADEEHINNOOST	HINDOOSTANEE	ADEIINOSTTUV	ADVENTITIOUS
ADEEHLPRSTUU	DESULPHURATE	ADEIILLNOOTVY	DEVOTIONALLY
ADEEHMOPRTTY	DERMATOPHYTE	ADEILLNPRTUY	PRUDENTIALLY
ADEEIIILLNTVY	EVIDENTIALLY	ADEILMNNNSTU	DISANNULMENT
ADEEIILMNNSS	MAIDENLINESS	ADEILNOOPPTU	DEPOPULATION
ADEEIILMTTVY	MEDITATIVELY	ADEILNORRSTT	DENTIROSTRAL
ADEEIILNPRST	PRESIDENTIAL	ADEINNOPRTUZ	UNPATRONIZED
ADEEIILRTVVY	DERIVATIVELY	ADEINOPRSSTY	DISPENSATORY
ADEEIIMNNOTV	DENOMINATIVE	ADELLNORSSUY	SLANDEROUSLY
ADEEIIMNRRTY	INTERMEDIARY	ADELLORSTUUY	ADULTEROUSLY
ADEEIINORSTT	DISORIENTATE	ADEMNOORRSTT	DEMONSTRATOR
ADEEIINRRSTY	RESIDENTIARY	ADEMNRRSTTUU	UNDERSTRATUM
ADEEIIPPRSUZ	DISPAUPERIZE	ADENNORSSTUW	UNTOWARDNESS
ADEEILMMORTY	IMMODERATELY	ADFGHIINRSTV	DRIVING-SHAFT
ADEEIMMNORSU	MISDEMEANOUR	ADFIILNOORTU	FLUORIDATION
ADEEIMNNNRTU	INTERMUNDANE	ADFIILOSSTUY	FASTIDIOUSLY
ADEEIMNRSTUV	MISADVENTURE	ADGHILLLMNOS	SMALLHOLDING
ADEEINNOPRST	RESPONDENTIA	ADGIILLNNOTU	LONGITUDINAL
ADEEINNRRSTU	UNRESTRAINED	ADGIMNNOORST	STANDING-ROOM
ADEEINNSSSTU	UNSTEADINESS	ADHHIOPRSTTY	HYDROPATHIST
ADEEJMNRSTTU	READJUSTMENT	ADIIIIMMNNOTT	INTIMIDATION
ADEELLMMNRTU	UNTRAMMELLED	ADIIIILLMRSSY	DISSIMILARLY
ADEELNPPRRUY	UNPREPAREDLY	ADIIILLNOSTT	DISTILLATION
ADEEMNNPRSUU	SUPERMUNDANE	ADIIINORSTTT	TRADITIONIST
ADEFGILNORSU	GLANDIFEROUS	ADIIILLORSTTY	DISTILLATORY
ADEFHINRSSSW	DWARFISHNESS	ADIILMORSSTU	DISSIMULATOR
ADEFIIILNNOT	DEFINITIONAL	ADIILNORSTTU	STRIDULATION
ADEFIINRSTTU	UNSTRATIFIED	ADIIOPSSTTUU	DISPUTATIOUS
ADEFINNOORTU	FOUNDATIONER	ADILLOORSTUY	IDOLATROUSLY
ADEFLLNRTUUY	FRAUDULENTLY	ADILORSSSTUY	DISASTROUSLY
ADEGHHOPRRRY	HYDROGRAPHER	AEEEEGINRRTV	REGENERATIVE
ADEGHIINRRSS	HAIRDRESSING	AEEEEFFILMNTY	EFFEMINATELY
ADEGHINRSSTU	DRAUGHTINESS	AEEEFILNPRRT	PREFERENTIAL
ADEGHLLNORST	STRANGLEHOLD	AEEEFIMNRTTV	FERMENTATIVE
ADEGIIILNRTT	INTERDIGITAL	AEEEFLNRSSSS	FEARLESSNESS

AEEEGIMNNSTV	ENVISAGEMENT
AEEEGINNORRT	REGENERATION
AEEEGIRRSTTV	TERGIVERSATE
AEEEGLMNNNTT	ENTANGLEMENT
AEEEGMNNRSTT	ESTRANGEMENT
AEEEGMNOPRSU	PERGAMENEOUS
AEEEGNORRRTY	REGENERATORY
AEEEHILMPRTY	EPHEMERALITY
AEEEHINPPRSV	APPREHENSIVE
AEEEHINPRSST	PARENTHESISE
AEEEHLORSTUX	HETEROSEXUAL
AEEEIILNPRIX	EXPERIENTIAL
AEEEIILNPRTT	INTERPELLATE
AEEEILMNPRTX	EXPERIMENTAL
AEEEILNRSSTV	RELATIVENESS
AEEEIMNRRTUV	REMUNERATIVE
AEEEIMORSTTV	OVERESTIMATE
AEEEINPRTTVV	PREVENTATIVE
AEEEIPRRSTVV	PRESERVATIVE
AEEEKLRRSTTW	STREETWALKER
AEEEELMNNSSSS	NAMELESSNESS
AEEEELMNORSYY	ELEEMOSYNARY
AEEEELMNSSSST	TAMELESSNESS
AEEEEMNNORSTY	EARNEST-MONEY
AEEFFHORRSTT	FOSTER-FATHER
AEEFGIORRRRT	REFRIGERATOR
AEEFGLNRSSTU	GRATEFULNESS
AEEFHLMNSSSU	SHAMEFULNESS
AEEFHOOPRRTW	WEATHERPROOF
AEEFIKNNNRST	FRANKENSTEIN
AEEFILMNORRT	INTERFEMORAL
AEEFIMNNORTT	FERMENTATION
AEEFINNORSTT	FENESTRATION
AEEFLNSSSTTU	TASTEFULNESS
AEEFLNSSSTUW	WASTEFULNESS
AEEFNOPRRSST	FOSTER-PARENT
AEEFOOPRRSST	PROFESSORATE
AEEGHHNOPRRT	ETHNOGRAPHER
AEEGHILPRSTT	TELEGRAPHIST
AEEGHINRRSTT	STRAIGHTENER
AEEGHLNOPRSY	SELENOGRAPHY
AEEGHMOOPRRT	METEOROGRAPH
AEEGHNORSSTU	ANOTHER-GUESS
AEEGHOPPRRRT	PETROGRAPHER
AEEGHOPRRSTY	STEREOGRAPHY
AEEGIIILLMTT	ILLEGITIMATE
AEEGIILLMTTY	LEGITIMATELY
AEEGIILNNPSS	PALINGENESIS
AEEGIINNNRTT	ENTERTAINING
AEEGIINORRTV	REINVIGORATE
AEEGILNNRTTY	ENTREATINGLY
AEEGIMNNOSTT	SEGMENTATION
AEEGINNNSSSU	SANGUINENESS
AEEGINOPRRRT	PEREGRINATOR
AEEGLMNNORTV	GOVERNMENTAL
AEEHIINORTTZ	ETHERIZATION
AEEHILLMNNPS	PANHELLENISM
AEEHILNSSSTT	STEALTHINESS
AEEHIMMORRTT	ARITHMOMETER
AEEHIMORSTTT	THEOREMATIST
AEEHINNOPPRS	APPREHENSION
AEEHIPRSTTTU	THERAPEUTIST
AEEHLLMMORWY	YELLOW-HAMMER
AEEHLMNRSSSS	HARMLESSNESS
AEEHLNOPRTUY	POLYURETHANE
AEEHMMOOPRST	METAMORPHOSE
AEEHMORSTTUY	ERYTHEMATOUS
AEEHOPRRSSTT	STRATOSPHERE
AEEIIKLMNPRS	MARLINESPIKE
AEEIILLMRSTU	MITRAILLEUSE
AEEIILLNPSTT	PESTILENTIAL
AEEIIIMPRTVY	IMPERATIVELY
AEEIILNNRRTY	INTERLINEARY
AEEIILNSSTTY	ESSENTIALITY
AEEIIINNPRTTY	PENITENTIARY
AEEIIPRTTUVV	VITUPERATIVE
AEEIJNNORTUV	REJUVENATION
AEEIILLNNPSTY	SEPTENNIALLY
AEEIILLNOSSTT	TESSELLATION
AEEIILLNQTUVY	EQUIVALENTLY
AEEIILLNSSSUV	ALLUSIVENESS
AEEIILMNNRSTT	REINSTALMENT
AEEILMNRSSST	MASTERLINESS
AEEILNNPSSSS	PAINLESSNESS
AEEIILNOPRSSX	EXPRESSIONAL
AEEILPRSSUVY	PERSUASIVELY
AEEIMMNRSSTU	IMMATURENESS
AEEIMMNRSTTT	MISTREATMENT
AEEIMMNSSTTT	MISSTATEMENT
AEEIMNNORRTU	REMUNERATION
AEEIMNORRTTX	EXTERMINATOR
AEEINNOPRSTT	PRESENTATION
AEEINOORTTTX	EXTORTIONATE
AEEINOPPRRTT	PERPETRATION
AEEINOPPRTTU	PERPETUATION
AEEINOPRRSTV	PRESERVATION
AEEINRSSTTTV	TRANSVESTITE
AEEINRSTTTUV	STERNUTATIVE
AEEKLMNRSSUW	LUKEWARMNESS
AEEKMORRSSTT	MASTER-STROKE
AEELLLMNOTVY	MALEVOLENTLY
AEELLMNPPSTU	SUPPLEMENTAL
AEELNORSTUXY	EXTRANEOUSLY
AEELNRRSSTVY	TRANSVERSELY
AEEMNOOPRSTU	TEMPORANEOUS
AEEMNOORTUUV	OUTMANOEUVRE
AEEOPRRSTTTU	TETRAPTEROUS
AEEOQRRSSTTU	SEQUESTRATOR
AEFFHILNSSTU	FAITHFULNESS
AEFGHHOORRTU	THOROUGHFARE
AEFGHHOORTTU	AFORETHOUGHT
AEFGHHORTTTU	AFTER-THOUGHT
AEFGIILRTUVY	FIGURATIVELY
AEFGILLNRTTY	FLATTERINGLY
AEFGILNNRTTU	UNFLATTERING
AEFGINORSSUU	SANGUIFEROUS
AEFGLLNRTUUY	UNGRATEFULLY
AEFHKLNNSSTU	THANKFULNESS
AEFHLNRSSTUW	WRATHFULNESS
AEFIINORSTTU	TITANIFEROUS
AEFILNOOPRSS	PROFESSIONAL
AEFILOPRRSTT	SELF-PORTRAIT

AEFINNORSSTU	STANNIFEROUS	AEIILLLPRRTU	PLURILITERAL
AEFLLNNSSUUW	UNLAWFULNESS	AEIILLMMMORY	IMMEMORIALLY
AEGGILORRSUY	GREGARIOUSLY	AEIILLNQRTUZ	TRANQUILLIZE
AEGHHILOPRRT	LITHOGRAPHER	AEIILLRSTTUV	ILLUSTRATIVE
AEGHHMNOPRRY	HYMNOGRAPHER	AEIILMMNOOST	EMOTIONALISM
AEGHHMOPRRTY	MYTHOGRAPHER	AEIILMNNOTVY	NOMINATIVELY
AEGHHOOPPRRT	PHOTOGRAPHER	AEIILMNRSSUV	UNIVERSALISM
AEGHHOOPRRRT	ORTHOGRAPHER	AEIILMNSTTUY	SIMULTANEITY
AEGHIILMNSST	ALMIGHTINESS	AEIILNOOPTTX	EXPLOITATION
AEGHIILNSTTY	HESITATINGLY	AEIILNOPPSTY	INAPPOSITELY
AEGHIINNSTTU	UNHESITATING	AEIILNORSSST	SOLITARINESS
AEGHILMNNSTU	LANGUISHMENT	AEIILNRSSTUV	UNIVERSALIST
AEGHILNPRRSW	WRANGLERSHIP	AEIILNRSTTVY	TRANSITIVELY
AEGHINRSSSTT	STRAIGHTNESS	AEIIMNNOOTTZ	MONETIZATION
AEGHLORSSTUU	SLAUGHTEROUS	AEIINNOPSSTX	EXPANSIONIST
AEGHNNOOPRTY	ANTHROPOGENY	AEIINOPPRRST	PERSPIRATION
AEGHOOPRRTUV	PHOTOGRAVURE	AEIINOPRTTUV	VITUPERATION
AEGIIILMNOTT	LEGITIMATION	AEIKMNOQRSTU	QUESTION-MARK
AEGIILLNNOTW	WELLINGTONIA	AEILLMNOPRSY	IMPERSONALLY
AEGIILLNPRVY	PREVAILINGLY	AEILLNNORTTY	INTOLERANTLY
AEGIILNORSTY	SEIGNIORALTY	AEILMNNRSTTU	INSTRUMENTAL
AEGIILRRRTUY	IRREGULARITY	AEILMNOOPRTT	METROPOLITAN
AEGIIMNNNOPRT	IMPREGNATION	AEILMNOQSUUY	EQUANIMOUSLY
AEGIIMNNNOPTT	PIGMENTATION	AEILMNOSSTUU	SIMULTANEOUS
AEGIINNNRSTT	INTRANSIGENT	AEILNOORTVUY	EVOLUTIONARY
AEGIINNPPSTU	UNAPPETISING	AEILNORRSTTU	TENUIROSTRAL
AEGIINORRSTT	REGISTRATION	AEIMNNORSTTU	MENSTRUATION
AEGIINORSTTV	INVESTIGATOR	AEIMNOOPRRST	IMPERSONATOR
AEGILLMRSTTU	METALLURGIST	AEIMNOPRSSTU	REASSUMPTION
AEGILLNNPSUY	UNPLEASINGLY	AEIMNPRSTTUV	TRANSUMPTIVE
AEGILMNNOQTU	MAGNILOQUENT	AEINNNOPRSTT	TRANSPONTINE
AEGILNNNOSTU	SANGUINOLENT	AEINNORSTTTU	STERNUTATION
AEGILNNRSTTY	ASTRINGENTLY	AEINNOSSTTTU	SUSTENTATION
AEGINNOSSUUX	EXSANGUINOUS	AEINOOPRSTTT	PROTESTATION
AEGINOORRRTT	INTERROGATOR	AEINOORRTTXY	EXTORTIONARY
AEGINOPRSTWY	STAYING-POWER	AEINOOSSTTTU	OSTENTATIOUS
AEGLMNOOPTUY	PNEUMATOLOGY	AEIOOOOPPPRS	PROSOPOPOEIA
AEGLOORSTUUY	OUTRAGEOUSLY	AEIOPPRRRSTY	PERSPIRATORY
AEGNORRRSSST	TRANSGRESSOR	AELLLMORSUVY	MARVELLOUSLY
AEGOOPSSTTUY	STEATOPYGOUS	AELLMMMNNOTUY	MONUMENTALLY
AEHHOOPRRSST	SHARPSHOOTER	AELMNOOOPSTU	MONOPETALOUS
AEHIILNOPRST	RELATIONSHIP	AELOOPRSTTUX	EXPOSTULATOR
AEHIKKMNRRSS	SKRIMSHANKER	AEMNOOOOPRSTZ	SPERMATOZOON
AEHILMNOOPSU	ANEMOPHILOUS	AENORRSTTTUY	STERNUTATORY
AEHILMNOQSSU	QUALMISHNESS	AFFHILLNTUUY	UNFAITHFULLY
AEHIMMOPSTTU	IMPOSTHUMATE	AFFIILNNOSTU	INSUFFLATION
AEHIMNNOPPSU	ONE-UPMANSHIP	AFGIILLNSSU	FISSILINGUAL
AEHIMNNOSSSW	WOMANISHNESS	AFGIILLMNORU	ANGUILLIFORM
AEHIMNNOSSTT	ASTONISHMENT	AFGIILLOSTUY	FLAGITIOUSLY
AEHINNPPSSSS	SNAPPISHNESS	AFGIINNSSTUY	UNSATISFYING
AEHINOPRSTTY	ATTORNEYSHIP	AFIIILLNNORTT	INFILTRATION
AEHIOOPPRSTZ	APOSTROPHIZE	AFIILMORSTUU	MULTIFARIOUS
AEHIOPRRSTWY	PRAISEWORTHY	AFIILORRSSST	FISSIROSTRAL
AEHLNOPSSTUY	POLYANTHUSES	AGGHHLOPPRYY	GLYPHOGRAPHY
AEHNNORSSTUY	SYNANTHEROUS	AGGHHMOPPRSY	SPHYGMOGRAPH
AEIILLNRSTTT	INTERSTITIAL	AGGHIIKNNSTV	THANKSGIVING
AEIIILPRSTUZ	SPIRITUALIZE	AGGHLOOPRSSY	GLOSSOGRAPHY
AEIIIMNNNOST	INSEMINATION	AGGIKLLNOOSS	LOOKING-GLASS
AEIIIMNRSTTV	MINISTRATIVE	AGHHIIOPPPST	HIPPOPHAGIST
AEIIINNOOPTV	OPINIONATIVE	AGHHILOOPSTU	LITHOPHAGOUS
AEIIINNRSTTV	INTRANSITIVE	AGHHIOOOPPSU	OPHIOPHAGOUS

238

AGHHIOOPRSUZ	RHIZOPHAGOUS	BCCEHORSTTTU	BUTTER-SCOTCH
AGHHIOPPRSYY	PHYSIOGRAPHY	BCCINOOSSSUU	SUBCONSCIOUS
AGHHOOPPSTUY	PHYTOPHAGOUS	BCDDEEEIINOS	DISOBEDIENCE
AGHILMNOOOOT	HOMOLOGATION	BCDDEIIILTUY	DEDUCIBILITY
AGHIMNOOPRST	MONOGRAPHIST	BCDEEEILNRSS	CREDIBLENESS
AGHLNOOOPRTY	ANTHROPOLOGY	BCDEEILRSTTU	DESTRUCTIBLE
AGHMNOOPRTYY	PHARYNGOTOMY	BCDEIILNOORR	INCORRODIBLE
AGIILLLMNTUU	MULTILINGUAL	BCDENORSTTUU	UNOBSTRUCTED
AGIILNNPRSUY	UNASPIRINGLY	BCEEEEGILLNR	BELLIGERENCE
AGIILNOORSUV	VAINGLORIOUS	BCEEEFILNNTY	BENEFICENTLY
AGII MNOOPRTU	PROMULGATION	BCEEEGHILNSY	BESEECHINGLY
AGILNNOOOPRT	PROLONGATION	BCEEEINRSSUV	SUBSERVIENCE
AGILORSTTUUY	GRATUITOUSLY	BCEEFILNORSS	FORCIBLENESS
AGINNOPRRSTT	TRANSPORTING	BCEEIJLSTUVY	SUBJECTIVELY
AHHILNOPPRTY	PHILANTHROPY	BCEEILMNOPTT	CONTEMPTIBLE
AHILLNOORTYZ	HORIZONTALLY	BCEEILMOPRSS	COMPRESSIBLE
AHILMNOORSUY	HARMONIOUSLY	BCEEIMMOSTTU	SUBCOMMITTEE
AHILMNPRTTUY	TRIUMPHANTLY	BCEEINRSSUVY	SUBSERVIENCY
AHILNOPRSTUU	SULPHURATION	BCEGHIILNTWY	BEWITCHINGLY
AHIMMOOPSSTU	AMPHISTOMOUS	BCEGIIILNORR	INCORRIGIBLE
AHIMOOPPPSTU	HIPPOPOTAMUS	BCEGIKLNOSTU	BLUE-STOCKING
AHINORRSSSTY	SYNARTHROSIS	BCEGILMNNOUY	UNBECOMINGLY
AHMNOOOOPRTTY	ANTHROPOTOMY	BCEHIIMORSTY	BIOCHEMISTRY
AHNOOOOPRRTTY	PROTHONOTARY	BCEIIJSTTUVY	SUBJECTIVITY
AIIIMMMNNOST	MINIMISATION	BCEIIKLLNRTU	CLINKER-BUILT
AIIILLMNNOTU	ILLUMINATION	BCEIINORTTUV	CONTRIBUTIVE
AIIILMPRSSTU	SPIRITUALISM	BCEILMNOPTTY	CONTEMPTIBLY
AIIILNOORTTV	VITRIOLATION	BCEILORSSTUU	TUBERCULOSIS
AIIILNOOSSTT	ISOLATIONIST	BCEINNNOSTTU	SUBCONTINENT
AIIILPRSSTTU	SPIRITUALIST	BCERRSSTTUUU	SUBSTRUCTURE
AIIILPRSTTUY	SPIRITUALITY	BCGIILMOOORY	MICROBIOLOGY
AIIIMMMNNOSTU	IMMUNISATION	BCGIKKNOORST	STOCKBROKING
AIIIMNNORSTT	MINISTRATION	BCIINNOORTTU	CONTRIBUTION
AIIIMNOOPSTT	OPTIMISATION	BCIINOPRSSTU	SUBSCRIPTION
AIIINNOPSSST	INSPISSATION	BCIKNOOOOPRS	BOOK-SCORPION
AIIINOOPPRTT	PROPITIATION	BCINOORRTTUY	CONTRIBUTORY
AIIILLLNOSUVY	VILLAINOUSLY	BCINORSSTTUU	SUBSTRUCTION
AIIILLNORSTTU	ILLUSTRATION	BDDEEEEFILMN	FEEBLE-MINDED
AIIILLNQRTTUY	TRANQUILLITY	BDDEEEINNSST	INDEBTEDNESS
AIIILMNNORTTU	MALNUTRITION	BDDFGIILNORY	FORBIDDINGLY
AIIILMNOPRSTT	TRAMPOLINIST	BDEEEFIILNNS	INDEFENSIBLE
AIIILMORSTUUV	MULTIVARIOUS	BDEEEFMNOORT	FOREBODEMENT
AIIILNORRSTTY	TRANSITORILY	BDEEEILMNRTW	BEWILDERMENT
AIIILOPRSUVVY	VIVIPAROUSLY	BDEEEILNNSSV	VENDIBLENESS
AIIIMNNORSSST	TRANSMISSION	BDEEEENOSSSTT	BESOTTEDNESS
AIIIMNOOORSTT	MOTORISATION	BDEEGIIILNST	INDIGESTIBLE
AIIIMNOOPRSSU	PARSIMONIOUS	BDEEHIILLMSS	DISEMBELLISH
AIIIMOOPPRRRT	IMPROPRIATOR	BDEEHLLOORTT	BOTTLE-HOLDER
AILNOOOOPPRRT	PROPORTIONAL	BDEEIIRRSTTU	REDISTRIBUTE
AILNOPPRTUUY	UNPOPULARITY	BDEEIMNRSSTU	DISBURSEMENT
AILOOPRRSUUY	UPROARIOUSLY	BDEELNORSUVY	UNOBSERVEDLY
AILOORRSTTUY	TRAITOROUSLY	BDEFLNOSSTUU	DOUBTFULNESS
BBCIIKLORRST	BRISTOL-BRICK	BDEGHHOORRTU	THOROUGHBRED
BBDEEEELORTW	BEETLE-BROWED	BDEGILLNOOTT	BLOOD-LETTING
BBDEEGGKLOOO	GOBBLEDEGOOK	BDEHHMNOOORR	RHOMBOHEDRON
BBDEIIILSSUV	SUBDIVISIBLE	BDEIIIILLNTY	INDELIBILITY
BBEHINNOSSSS	SNOBBISHNESS	BDEIIIRSTTUV	DISTRIBUTIVE
BBENNORSSSTU	STUBBORNNESS	BDEIILLNOSSU	INDISSOLUBLE
BBIIILLOOPST	BIBLIOPOLIST	BDEILNNPRSSU	PURBLINDNESS
BCCCEIIMRRSU	CIRCUMSCRIBE	BDHILOORSTTY	BLOODTHIRSTY
BCCEEELNOOSS	OBSOLESCENCE	BDIIIIILSTVY	DIVISIBILITY

BDIIIILNOSTY	LIBIDINOSITY	CCDEEIORRTTU	CORRECTITUDE
BDIIILLNOSUY	LIBIDINOUSLY	CCDEIILNNOTY	COINCIDENTLY
BDIIINORSTTU	DISTRIBUTION	CCDHHILOORRY	HYDROCHLORIC
BEEEEEFLMNNT	ENFEEBLEMENT	CCDIINOTTUVY	CONDUCTIVITY
BEEEELMMNTZZ	EMBEZZLEMENT	CCEEEEEJNNSUV	JUVENESCENCE
BEEEFILLNSSX	FLEXIBLENESS	CCEEEELLMNOS	EMOLLESCENCE
BEEEHIINNRTT	TEREBINTHINE	CCEEEEFLNORSU	FLUORESCENCE
BEEEIILRRRSV	IRREVERSIBLE	CCEEEHIIMNPY	CHIMNEY-PIECE
BEEEIILRSSTT	BLISTER-STEEL	CCEEEIIMNNRS	REMINISCENCE
BEEEILNNSSSS	SENSIBLENESS	CCEEEIMNNOPT	INCOMPETENCE
BEEEILNRRSST	TERRIBLENESS	CCEEEIINNNOST	CONSENTIENCE
BEEEIMMNRTTT	EMBITTERMENT	CCEEELOOPRST	ELECTROSCOPE
BEEELLNNOTVY	BENEVOLENTLY	CCEEEMMMMNNOT	COMMENCEMENT
BEEELNOOSSST	OBSOLETENESS	CCEEENNORSST	CONCRETENESS
BEEGGILNNORW	BOWLING-GREEN	CCEEFFIIINNY	INEFFICIENCY
BEEGIIILLLNT	INTELLIGIBLE	CCEEFHIIJSTU	CHIEF-JUSTICE
BEEGIIILMNSV	MISBELIEVING	CCEEFINNOORT	CONFECTIONER
BEEHIIINORTX	EXHIBITIONER	CCEEFNOORRTU	COUNTER-FORCE
BEEHLORRRTWY	WHORTLEBERRY	CCEEGILLOOSY	ECCLESIOLOGY
BEEIIILMRRSS	IRREMISSIBLE	CCEEHIILNORT	HELIOCENTRIC
BEEIIILRRSST	IRRESISTIBLE	CCEEIINNNNOT	INCONTINENCE
BEEIILRRRSVY	IRREVERSIBLY	CCEEIILLOTVY	COLLECTIVELY
BEEIILLLORSUY	REBELLIOUSLY	CCEEILLNOORT	RECOLLECTION
BEEILPPRSSSU	SUPPRESSIBLE	CCEEILLORTTY	ELECTROLYTIC
BEELNOOSSSST	BOOTLESSNESS	CCEEILNNORTV	CONVENTICLER
BEELNQSSTUUY	SUBSEQUENTLY	CCEEILOPRTTY	ELECTROTYPIC
BEEOOPRRSSTU	OBSTREPEROUS	CCEEILSSSUVY	SUCCESSIVELY
BEFILLNSSSSU	BLISSFULNESS	CCEEIMNNOPTY	INCOMPETENCY
BEGGHIINNORU	NEIGHBOURING	CCEEIMNOORST	ECONOMETRICS
BEGGIILNNOSS	OBLIGINGNESS	CCEEIINNNORTT	INTERCONNECT
BEGIIIILLLTY	ILLEGIBILITY	CCEEOOPPRSST	SPECTROSCOPE
BEHILMOOPSTT	PHLEBOTOMIST	CCEFHINOORSU	CONCHIFEROUS
BEHINOSSSSUW	SHOW-BUSINESS	CCEFILMNRTUU	CIRCUMFLUENT
BEIIILRRSSTY	IRRESISTIBLY	CCEFLLSSSUUY	SUCCESSFULLY
BEIILLLLLORU	LILLIBULLERO	CCEFLNSSSUUU	UNSUCCESSFUL
BEIILMSSSUVY	SUBMISSIVELY	CCEHILNOORTU	TECHNICOLOUR
BEILOOQSSUUY	OBSEQUIOUSLY	CCEHILNOOSUU	COUNCIL-HOUSE
BEILOORSSTUY	BOISTEROUSLY	CCEHIMNOORRT	CHRONOMETRIC
BFGGHIILLNTU	BULLFIGHTING	CCEIILLMOSTV	COLLECTIVISM
BGILLORSUUUY	LUGUBRIOUSLY	CCEIILLOSTTV	COLLECTIVIST
BGILNOORRUWW	BURROWING-OWL	CCEIILNNOSUV	INCONCLUSIVE
BIIIILNSTVY	INVISIBILITY	CCEIILPRSTUU	PISCICULTURE
BIIILLNOSTUY	INSOLUBILITY	CCEIINORSTTV	CONSTRICTIVE
BIILOQSTUUUY	UBIQUITOUSLY	CCEILLNOSUVY	CONCLUSIVELY
BIINOSSTTTUU	SUBSTITUTION	CCEILLOOOPSS	OSCILLOSCOPE
CCCCEEENNORS	CONCRESCENCE	CCEILOOPRSUY	PRECOCIOUSLY
CCCDHIIOOPRS	DICHROSCOPIC	CCEINNOSTTUY	CONSTITUENCY
CCCEEHKNORTU	COUNTERCHECK	CCEINOORSSST	CROSS-SECTION
CCCEEIINRTTY	ECCENTRICITY	CCEINORSTTUV	CONSTRUCTIVE
CCCEEILMORTUU	CIRCUMLOCUTE	CCELNNORRTUY	CONCURRENTLY
CCCEEINNOPSTU	CONCUPISCENT	CCEOOPPRSSTY	SPECTROSCOPY
CCCEEINNSSTU	SUCCINCTNESS	CCFGGHIIKNOT	COCKFIGHTING
CCCHHHIRRSTU	CHRISTCHURCH	CCFIIMNORSUU	CIRCUMFUSION
CCCIIIMNORSU	CIRCUMCISION	CCGHILNOOOST	CONCHOLOGIST
CCCIIIMORRTU	MICROCIRCUIT	CCGIILNNNOVY	CONVINCINGLY
CCDEEEEILNST	DELITESCENCE	CCGIINNNOVU	UNCONVINCING
CCDEEEEFNNORS	FRONDESCENCE	CCGIKLNOOSTU	CUCKING-STOOL
CCDEEEHNOSTU	ESCUTCHEONED	CCIILORSTUUY	CIRCUITOUSLY
CCDEEENRRSTU	RECRUDESCENT	CCIIMOOPRSST	MICROSCOPIST
CCDEEILMORRS	SCLERODERMIC	CCIINNOOPRST	CONSCRIPTION
CCDEEILNNORU	UNRECONCILED	CCIINNOORSTT	CONSTRICTION

CCIMNOOPSTUU	COMPUNCTIOUS
CCINNOORSTTU	CONSTRUCTION
CCLMOOOSSTUY	CYCLOSTOMOUS
CDDEEEEINNNP	INDEPENDENCE
CDDEEEEJNSST	DEJECTEDNESS
CDDEEIJNPRUU	UNPREJUDICED
CDDEEINNOSTT	DISCONTENTED
CDDEEINORSUV	UNDISCOVERED
CDDEFIIKLSST	FIDDLESTICKS
CDDEFLNNOOUY	CONFOUNDEDLY
CDDIIMMOOSTY	DISCOMMODITY
CDFFFFIINNPX	INEXPEDIENCE
CDEEEELNNPRS	RESPLENDENCE
CDEEEFFIINNR	INDIFFERENCE
CDEEEHIMNPRT	DECIPHERMENT
CDEEEHNRSSTW	WRETCHEDNESS
CDEEEIINNPXY	INEXPEDIENCY
CDEEEIINSSSV	DECISIVENESS
CDEEEILMNORT	DECLINOMETER
CDEEEILNQSTU	DELIQUESCENT
CDEEEINPRSST	DECREPITNESS
CDEEEINRSSST	DISCREETNESS
CDEEELNNPRSY	RESPLENDENCY
CDEEELNPTUXY	UNEXPECTEDLY
CDEEEMMNNNOTU	DENOUNCEMENT
CDEEFHLNOOOV	CLOVEN-HOOFED
CDEEFLNOOOTV	CLOVEN-FOOTED
CDEEHIOPRRRS	RECORDERSHIP
CDEEHLNORSTU	UNDERCLOTHES
CDEEIIILNSVY	INDECISIVELY
CDEEIILNRSTY	INDISCREETLY
CDEEIILOPSTV	VELOCIPEDIST
CDEEIILRSTVY	DISCRETIVELY
CDEEIIMNOPRV	IMPROVIDENCE
CDEEIINNRSST	INDIRECTNESS
CDEEIILNPSSU	PELLUCIDNESS
CDEEILMNOOPX	COMPLEXIONED
CDEEINRRSTTU	UNRESTRICTED
CDEEIOPRRTUV	REPRODUCTIVE
CDEEMNOOPSSS	COMPOSEDNESS
CDEENNOOPRST	CO-RESPONDENT
CDEENNRRRTUU	UNDERCURRENT
CDEEOOPRSTUY	DEUTEROSCOPY
CDEFIIINNOST	DISINFECTION
CDEFIIMORSTU	DISCOMFITURE
CDEGIIINNNRSU	UNDISCERNING
CDEHHIIIPRTT	DIPHTHERITIC
CDEHHIILNSSS	CHILDISHNESS
CDEHIIILPPSS	DISCIPLESHIP
CDEHIIKKNNST	THICKSKINNED
CDEHIIOPRRST	DIRECTORSHIP
CDEIIILNTVVY	VINDICTIVELY
CDEIIIMNORST	MISDIRECTION
CDEIIINNORST	INDISCRETION
CDEIIINNORTT	INTERDICTION
CDEIILNNPPRU	UNPRINCIPLED
CDEIILRSSUVY	DISCURSIVELY
CDEIIMMNOOSS	COMMISSIONED
CDEIINNOOPRT	PRECONDITION
CDEIINNSSSTT	DISTINCTNESS
CDEIINORRTTY	INTERDICTORY
CDEIINORTTUV	INTRODUCTIVE
CDEILMNORSSU	SCOUNDRELISM
CDEILNOORSUY	INDECOROUSLY
CDEIMOOPRSSU	DISCOMPOSURE
CDEINNRSTTUU	UNINSTRUCTED
CDEINOOPRRTU	REPRODUCTION
CDEINOPRTUUV	UNPRODUCTIVE
CDEIOORSSTUU	DISCOURTEOUS
CDELNOOOSTUY	COTYLEDONOUS
CDFHILOORRUY	HYDROFLUORIC
CDFIILMNORRY	CYLINDRIFORM
CDGIIKLNOSSU	CLOUD-KISSING
CDGIKLNOOSTU	DUCKING-STOOL
CDHIMNOOPRUY	HYPOCONDRIUM
CDIIIJNORSTU	JURISDICTION
CDIILLORSUUY	RIDICULOUSLY
CDIIMMNOOOSU	INCOMMODIOUS
CDIINNOORTTU	INTRODUCTION
CDIIOPRTTUVY	PRODUCTIVITY
CDILMMOOOSUY	COMMODIOUSLY
CDINOORRTTUY	INTRODUCTORY
CEEEEFFNRSTV	EFFERVESCENT
CEEEEFINNRRT	INTERFERENCE
CEEEEHNORSVW	WHENCESOEVER
CEEEEIINNPRX	INEXPERIENCE
CEEEEELMORRTT	ELECTROMETER
CEEEFFLNORST	EFFLORESCENT
CEEEFHLNRSSU	CHEERFULNESS
CEEEFIILRRTV	IRREFLECTIVE
CEEEFILLRTVY	REFLECTIVELY
CEEEGIILLNNT	INTELLIGENCE
CEEEHIMNPSWY	CHIMNEY-SWEEP
CEEEHIMNRSTU	HERMENEUTICS
CEEEHINOSSSV	COHESIVENESS
CEEEHMNNNRTT	ENTRENCHMENT
CEEEHMNNRRTT	RETRENCHMENT
CEEEHPPPRRRY	CHERRY-PEPPER
CEEEIILLNTTV	INTELLECTIVE
CEEEIIMNNPRT	IMPERTINENCE
CEEEIINRRSST	IRRESISTENCE
CEEEIIPRRSTV	IRRESPECTIVE
CEEEILLNOPQU	EQUIPOLLENCE
CEEEILNNOPPT	PLENIPOTENCE
CEEEILNOPRST	PRESELECTION
CEEEIILPRSTVY	RESPECTIVELY
CEEEIMMNNOPRS	OMNIPRESENCE
CEEEINNNOSTX	NON-EXISTENCE
CEEEIPRRSSUV	REPERCUSSIVE
CEEEKLNRSSSS	RECKLESSNESS
CEEEELMNOPSST	COMPLETENESS
CEEEELMORRTTY	ELECTROMETRY
CEEEELORRSSUU	RESOURCELESS
CEEEMNNNNORTU	RENOUNCEMENT
CEEEMOPRRSTT	SPECTROMETER
CEEFGILNNOTU	GENUFLECTION
CEEFGLLLNTUY	NEGLECTFULLY
CEEFIIMNOPRT	IMPERFECTION
CEEFIINOPRST	FRONTISPIECE
CEEFILMNRSSU	MERCIFULNESS
CEEFLLPRSTUY	RESPECTFULLY

Code	Word	Code	Word
CEEGHILNOPTY	PHYLOGENETIC	CEGHHIILOPRY	HIEROGLYPHIC
CEEGHILOOPRT	HERPETOLOGIC	CEGHIIOPSSTY	GEOPHYSICIST
CEEGHINORTUW	COUNTERWEIGH	CEGHILNOOSTT	TECHNOLOGIST
CEEGMNOORRST	COSTERMONGER	CEGIILLOOSTX	LEXICOLOGIST
CEEHHIILLLNP	PHILHELLENIC	CEGIINNOOPRT	PRECOGNITION
CEEHHLOORSST	CLOTHES-HORSE	CEGILNNNOTTY	CONTINGENTLY
CEEHHMOOPRRS	CHROMOSPHERE	CEGILNNORSTU	CURLING-STONE
CEEHHOOPPRSS	PHOSPHORESCE	CEGINNNORSTT	CONSTRINGENT
CEEHIKMNOSSS	HOMESICKNESS	CEGINNPSSTUU	UNSUSPECTING
CEEHINOOPRST	STEREOPHONIC	CEGINOPPRSSY	COPYING-PRESS
CEEHIOPRSTUX	EXECUTORSHIP	CEHHILNRSSSU	CHURLISHNESS
CEEHMOPRRSTY	PSYCHROMETER	CEHIIKLNSSST	TICKLISHNESS
CEEIIJNNORTT	INTERJECTION	CEHIILOORSTU	LEIOTRICHOUS
CEEIIILLNNOTT	INTELLECTION	CEHILNNOSSSW	CLOWNISHNESS
CEEIILNPSSTX	EXPLICITNESS	CEHILOQSSTTU	COQUETTISHLY
CEEIIMNOSSSS	SECESSIONISM	CEHILORRTTUU	HORTICULTURE
CEEIIMNOSTTU	CEMENTITIOUS	CEHIMOORSTYZ	ZOOCHEMISTRY
CEEIIMORRSTU	MERETRICIOUS	CEHINOPRSTTY	PYROTECHNIST
CEEIINNNNOTV	INCONVENIENT	CEIILLNOSTUY	LICENTIOUSLY
CEEIINNOPRST	REINSPECTION	CEIILMNNOSTY	OMNISCIENTLY
CEEIINNORSST	INTERCESSION	CEIILNOOSTTU	ELOCUTIONIST
CEEIINOPRSTT	RECEPTIONIST	CEIILNOSSTUX	EXCLUSIONIST
CEEIINOSSSST	SECESSIONIST	CEIILOPRSSUU	SUPERCILIOUS
CEEIIPPRRSTV	PRESCRIPTIVE	CEIIMMNOORSS	COMMISSIONER
CEEIIPPRTTVY	PERCEPTIVITY	CEIINNNOSSTT	INCONSISTENT
CEEIILLMNOPTY	INCOMPLETELY	CEIINNORRSTU	INSURRECTION
CEEIILLNOPQUY	EQUIPOLLENCY	CEIINOOPRRTY	INCORPOREITY
CEEILLORSSTY	ELECTROLYSIS	CEIINOPPRRST	PRESCRIPTION
CEEILMMNOPRT	COMPLIMENTER	CEIINORSSTUX	EXCURSIONIST
CEEILNNNOTVY	CONVENIENTLY	CEIINOSTTTUV	CONSTITUTIVE
CEEILNNOPPTY	PLENIPOTENCY	CEIIOPPRRSTV	PROSCRIPTIVE
CEEIMMMNORTT	RECOMMITMENT	CEIIPSSTTUVY	SUSCEPTIVITY
CEEINNNOQSTU	INCONSEQUENT	CEILLMOPSUVY	COMPULSIVELY
CEEINNORSSTT	CONTRITENESS	CEILLNOSUVVY	CONVULSIVELY
CEEINNRRRTTU	INTERCURRENT	CEILMNOOSTUU	CONTUMELIOUS
CEEINOOPRSTT	STEREOPTICON	CEILNNOSSTTY	CONSISTENTLY
CEEINOOPRSTU	COUNTERPOISE	CEILNOORRTTU	INTERLOCUTOR
CEEINOORRSST	RETROCESSION	CEILNOORSSUY	CENSORIOUSLY
CEEINOPRRSSU	REPERCUSSION	CEIMNNOOPRSU	MISPRONOUNCE
CEEINOPRSSSU	PRECIOUSNESS	CEIMNNOORSTU	CONTERMINOUS
CEEINORRRSTU	RESURRECTION	CEINNOOPRTTU	COUNTERPOINT
CEEINORSTTTU	RECONSTITUTE	CEINPSSSTTUU	INTUSSUSCEPT
CEELMOOORRTT	ELECTROMOTOR	CEINRRSSSTTU	INSTRUCTRESS
CEELNNOQSTUY	CONSEQUENTLY	CELMNOPRTUUU	MUCOPURULENT
CEELOOOPRSTU	COLEOPTEROUS	CEMNOOPSTTUU	CONTEMPTUOUS
CEENNOORRTTU	COUNTER-TENOR	CENNOSSSTUUU	UNCTUOUSNESS
CEENOOSSSTUV	COVETOUSNESS	CEOOPPRRSSSU	CROSS-PURPOSE
CEFFIIINNSTU	INSUFFICIENT	CFIIILOSTTUY	FICTITIOUSLY
CEFFIILNSTUY	SUFFICIENTLY	CGGILNNORSTU	CURLING-TONGS
CEFFIORSSTUU	SUFFRUTICOSE	CGHILNOOORST	CHRONOLOGIST
CEFIIILNOSTU	INFELICITOUS	CGHILOOPSSTY	PSYCHOLOGIST
CEFIIILLOSTUY	FELICITOUSLY	CGIILMOOSSTU	MUSICOLOGIST
CEFIILNOPRSS	PROLIFICNESS	CGIILNNORRSU	CURLING-IRONS
CEFIILNOSTUY	INFECTIOUSLY	CGIILOOOSTTX	TOXICOLOGIST
CEFILLMNRUUY	UNMERCIFULLY	CGILNOOSTUUY	CONTIGUOUSLY
CEFILLMOORSY	FROLICSOMELY	CHHINORRSSTT	CHRIST'S-THORN
CEFILLORRTUU	FLORICULTURE	CHIINOPSSTUV	VISCOUNTSHIP
CEFILOORSUVY	VOCIFEROUSLY	CHINOOOPRSTY	ORNITHOSCOPY
CEFILOPRSUUU	CUPULIFEROUS	CIIILLMPTTUY	MULTIPLICITY
CEFLNNORSSSU	SCORNFULNESS	CIILMNOOOPST	MONOPOLISTIC
CEFNOOOPRRTU	COUNTER-PROOF	CIILOORSTUVY	VICTORIOUSLY

TWELVE-LETTER WORDS

EEE

CIILOPSSSUUY	SUSPICIOUSLY	DEEIINPRSSST	SPIRITEDNESS
CIINNOOPPRRTU	INCORRUPTION	DEEIJNORRRSU	SURREJOINDER
CIINNOOSTTTU	CONSTITUTION	DEEILMNNSSSS	MINDLESSNESS
CIINOOPPRRST	PROSCRIPTION	DEEINNOQSTUU	UNQUESTIONED
CIINOPSSSUUU	UNSUSPICIOUS	DEELLNOPSSTU	POLLUTEDNESS
CIJLNORSSTUU	JURISCONSULT	DEELNOSSSSUU	SEDULOUSNESS
CILLORRSSUUY	SCURRILOUSLY	DEENNNOSSTUW	UNWONTEDNESS
CILNNOOSTUUY	CONTINUOUSLY	DEENOOPRSSST	DESSERT-SPOON
CILOPRSSTUUY	SCRUPULOSITY	DEENORSSSTUX	DEXTROUSNESS
CLLOPRSSUUUY	SCRUPULOUSLY	DEENPPRSSSUU	UNSUPPRESSED
CLNOPRSSUUUU	UNSCRUPULOUS	DEFFINOORRSU	FRONDIFEROUS
DDDEEGINRSSW	WEDDING-DRESS	DEFGHHIIILTY	HIGH-FIDELITY
DDDEHNNOOORR	RHODODENDRON	DEFGHILLLTUY	DELIGHTFULLY
DDEEEFMNORSS	DEFORMEDNESS	DEFIILOPRSUY	PERFIDIOUSLY
DDEEEILMNRRT	INTERMEDDLER	DEFILOORSTUY	DO-IT-YOURSELF
DDEEIILMNRTY	DETERMINEDLY	DEFIOORRSSUU	SUDORIFEROUS
DDEEEIMNNRTU	UNDETERMINED	DEFNNOOPRSSU	PROFOUNDNESS
DDEEEELNRSUVY	UNDESERVEDLY	DEGGINNORSSW	DRESSING-GOWN
DDEEFIIINNTU	UNIDENTIFIED	DEGHHIINOPTZ	DIPHTHONGIZE
DDEEGHIILMTW	MIDDLEWEIGHT	DEGHHIORSSTT	SHORT-SIGHTED
DDEEGILMNOST	DISLODGEMENT	DEGHINORSSTU	DROUGHTINESS
DDEEIILMMNPS	SIMPLE-MINDED	DEGIILNOPRSU	LIGNIPERDOUS
DDEEEIMNNOSTW	DISENDOWMENT	DEGIINNOSSUU	DISINGENUOUS
DDEEELNNOPSTY	DESPONDENTLY	DEGIINNRRTUW	UNDERWRITING
DDEEGHILNRSUY	SHUDDERINGLY	DEGILMNOOOST	DEMONOLOGIST
DDEGILNOORST	DENDROLOGIST	DEGILNOOOSTT	DEONTOLOGIST
DDEIIILPRSTY	DISPIRITEDLY	DEGIMNOORRSS	DRESSING-ROOM
DEEEEIMNPRRT	PREDETERMINE	DEGLLNORSSUY	GROUNDLESSLY
DEEEEELNNSSSS	NEEDLESSNESS	DEHIIKLLNOOU	UNLIKELIHOOD
DEEEEFIINNSST	DEFINITENESS	DEHLLNOOPSUY	ENDOPHYLLOUS
DEEEEFLLMOPSY	SELF-EMPLOYED	DEHMNORRSTTU	THUNDERSTORM
DEEEFNNQRTUU	UNFREQUENTED	DEIIILMNTUVY	DIMINUTIVELY
DEEEGIINNRRV	ENGINE-DRIVER	DEIIKLNNNSSU	UNKINDLINESS
DEEEGIKNNNOY	DONKEY-ENGINE	DEIJNPRRSTUU	JURISPRUDENT
DEEEGINRRSTU	UNREGISTERED	DEINOSSSSTUU	STUDIOUSNESS
DEEEHMNNORTT	DETHRONEMENT	DELNNOOPSTYY	POLYSYNDETON
DEEEILNSSSUV	DELUSIVENESS	DELNOPSSTUUY	STUPENDOUSLY
DEEEINNRSTTU	UNINTERESTED	DEMNOOPSSUUY	PSEUDONYMOUS
DEEEKLNNOOST	ENDOSKELETON	DGGIILNSSTUY	DISGUSTINGLY
DEEEELMNOPRTY	REDEPLOYMENT	DGIILOOPRSUY	PRODIGIOUSLY
DEEELNORSSSV	RESOLVEDNESS	DHINOOORSTTT	ORTHODONTIST
DEEEELNRRSUVY	UNRESERVEDLY	DIIIINOQSSTU	DISQUISITION
DEEEMMNOORST	ENDOSMOMETER	DIIIOQRSSTUY	DISQUISITORY
DEEFIIILNNTY	INDEFINITELY	EEEEHLNRSSTV	NEVERTHELESS
DEEFIIILNTVY	DEFINITIVELY	EEEEIMNPRRTX	EXPERIMENTER
DEEFIILNNRSS	FRIENDLINESS	EEEEIMNRRTTV	RETRIEVEMENT
DEEFILLMNORW	WELL-INFORMED	EEEEINNQRSTU	EQUESTRIENNE
DEEFILLPSTUY	DESPITEFULLY	EEEEMMNPRSST	EMPRESSEMENT
DEEGGIMNORST	DISGORGEMENT	EEEENNPRRRTU	ENTREPRENEUR
DEEGHIILNRVW	DRIVING-WHEEL	EEEFFINSSSUV	EFFUSIVENESS
DEEGIILMOOPY	EPIDEMIOLOGY	EEEFGLLNRUVY	REVENGEFULLY
DEEGIILNPRUV	UNPRIVILEGED	EEEFGLNNSSUV	VENGEFULNESS
DEEGIILRSSVY	DIGRESSIVELY	EEEFHINRSSSV	FEVERISHNESS
DEEGIIMNSSTU	DISGUISEMENT	EEEFIIMNNNSS	FEMININENESS
DEEGILNPRSSY	DEPRESSINGLY	EEEFILLNSSSS	LIFELESSNESS
DEEGINNNPRTU	UNPRETENDING	EEEFLLNSSSSS	SELFLESSNESS
DEEHILPRSUUZ	DESULPHURIZE	EEEFNNORSSTU	FREQUENTNESS
DEEHLPRSTTUU	SULPHURETTED	EEEGHIKNOPSU	HOUSEKEEPING
DEEIILNNSSUW	UNWIELDINESS	EEEGHINNRSSS	GREENISHNESS
DEEIIMNNRSTT	DISINTERMENT	EEEGHNNRRSTT	STRENGTHENER
DEEIIMNRSSST	DISSENTERISM	EEEGHNORSSTT	TOGETHERNESS

243

EEEGIILMNNNTV	INVEIGLEMENT	EEIILNPPRSSS	SLIPPERINESS
EEEGIINNORRT	ORIENTEERING	EEIILNPRSSST	PRIESTLINESS
EEEHHINPSSSS	SHEEPISHNESS	EEIILNPSSSST	PITILESSNESS
EEEHINNOPRRS	REPREHENSION	EEIIMNNRTTTT	INTERMITTENT
EEEHLLNPSSSS	HELPLESSNESS	EEIIMNPRRSTT	MISINTERPRET
EEEHLMNOSSSS	HOMELESSNESS	EEIIMNPRSSUV	UNIMPRESSIVE
EEEHLNOPSSSS	HOPELESSNESS	EEIIMNRRTTUX	INTERMIXTURE
EEEHMNNNORTT	ENTHRONEMENT	EEIINNNORTTV	INTERVENTION
EEEIIPQRRSTU	PREREQUISITE	EEIINOPRRSSV	IRRESPONSIVE
EEEILMNNSSSU	UNSEEMLINESS	EEIINOPSSSTV	POSITIVENESS
EEEILMNSSSST	TIMELESSNESS	EEIINPRRTTUV	INTERRUPTIVE
EEEILNRRRTVY	IRREVERENTLY	EEIILLNNOSSSV	SLOVENLINESS
EEEILPRRSSVY	REPRESSIVELY	EEILLNSSSSST	LISTLESSNESS
EEEIMNNPRSTU	SUPEREMINENT	EEILLRSSSSTY	RESISTLESSLY
EEEIMNNRSTTV	REINVESTMENT	EEILMOPPRRTY	PEREMPTORILY
EEEIMNPRRSST	MISREPRESENT	EEILNOORRSTU	RESOLUTIONER
EEEINNPRSSTX	INEXPERTNESS	EEILNOPRSSVY	RESPONSIVELY
EEEINRRTTTUX	INTERTEXTURE	EEILNPRSSTTY	PERSISTENTLY
EEELLLNRSSTY	RELENTLESSLY	EEILOPPRSSVY	OPPRESSIVELY
EEELMNNOOSSS	LONESOMENESS	EEILOPRRSTYZ	PROSELYTIZER
EEELNORSSSTU	RESOLUTENESS	EEILOPSSSSVY	POSSESSIVELY
EEELNRSSSSST	RESTLESSNESS	EEINNOPRSSUV	UNRESPONSIVE
EEENNOPPRSSS	PROPENSENESS	EEINOORRSTVX	EXTROVERSION
EEEOOPRRSUVX	OVEREXPOSURE	EEINORSSSTUV	VITREOUSNESS
EEFGGIOPRTTY	PETTIFOGGERY	EEIOPRSSTTTY	STEREOTYPIST
EEFGHILNRRSY	REFRESHINGLY	EELMMNNOPTUY	UNEMPLOYMENT
EEFGIIMNNNRT	INFRINGEMENT	EELNOPSSSSST	SPOTLESSNESS
EEFGIINOPRRT	PROFITEERING	EEMNNOOPPSTT	POSTPONEMENT
EEFGIINSSTUV	FUGITIVENESS	EENNOSSSSSUU	SENSUOUSNESS
EEFHMOORRSTT	FOSTER-MOTHER	EEOOPPRRSSTU	PREPOSTEROUS
EEFIIMNORSSU	SEMINIFEROUS	EFFILNRSSTUU	FRUITFULNESS
EEFIINORRSSU	RESINIFEROUS	EFHILLRSSTTY	THRIFTLESSLY
EEFILMORSTTU	FLITTERMOUSE	EFHILMNRSSTU	MIRTHFULNESS
EEFILNNQRTUY	INFREQUENTLY	EFHLNOSSTUUY	YOUTHFULNESS
EEFILNPSSSTU	SPITEFULNESS	EFHLNRSSTTUU	TRUTHFULNESS
EEFIMNOPRRST	SERPENTIFORM	EFIIIILNNTVY	INFINITIVELY
EEFLLMORRSUY	REMORSEFULLY	EFIILMNORSUU	LUMINIFEROUS
EEFLMNORSSSS	FORMLESSNESS	EFIILMOPRSVY	OVERSIMPLIFY
EEFLNOPRSSUW	POWERFULNESS	EFIOOOPRRSSU	SOPORIFEROUS
EEGGILSSTUVY	SUGGESTIVELY	EFLMNNORSSUU	MOURNFULNESS
EEGHHHORRTUW	WHERETHROUGH	EGGHILNSSSSU	SLUGGISHNESS
EEGHIINRSTUX	EXTINGUISHER	EGGILOOPSTTY	EGYPTOLOGIST
EEGHILNOPSSY	PHYLOGENESIS	EGHHNOORSSTU	THOROUGHNESS
EEGHINOPSSTY	PHYTOGENESIS	EGHIILNPRSWY	WHISPERINGLY
EEGHLOOORSTU	HETEROLOGOUS	EGHILNOOPRST	PHRENOLOGIST
EEGIILLNORSS	RELIGIONLESS	EGHINOOPRRSV	GOVERNORSHIP
EEGIINNPRRST	ENTERPRISING	EGIIILNOSTTU	GENTILITIOUS
EEGILLNPPRXY	PERPLEXINGLY	EGIIIMNOPSTU	IMPETIGINOUS
EEGILMOOPSTY	EPISTEMOLOGY	EGIILMOOSSST	SEISMOLOGIST
EEGINORSSSUV	GRIEVOUSNESS	EGIIMNOOPRRT	PRIMOGENITOR
EEGLMNNOOOPR	PROLEGOMENON	EGILMNOOOSTT	ENTOMOLOGIST
EEGLNNORSUUY	UNGENEROUSLY	EGIMNOORRTTY	TRIGONOMETRY
EEHHIINSSSTV	THIEVISHNESS	EGINOORSSSUV	VIGOROUSNESS
EEHHINRSSSSW	SHREWISHNESS	EHHIILOOPPSZ	PHILOSOPHIZE
EEHLNRSSSSTU	RUTHLESSNESS	EHIILMOOPRST	HELIOTROPISM
EEHMNRRRSUYY	NURSERY-RHYME	EHILNOOPSUUY	EUPHONIOUSLY
EEIIKLLNNSSU	UNLIKELINESS	EHILNSSSSTTU	SLUTTISHNESS
EEIILLMPQTUU	EQUIMULTIPLE	EHINNORSSTUW	UNWORTHINESS
EEIILMNNPTTY	IMPENITENTLY	EHIOPRRSSUVY	SURVEYORSHIP
EEIILMOORVZZ	MEZZORILIEVO	EHMNNOORRSTT	NORTHERNMOST
EEIILMPRSSVY	IMPRESSIVELY	EHMNOORSSSUU	HUMOROUSNESS

EHMNOORSSTTU	SOUTHERNMOST
EIIIILMRSTVY	VERISIMILITY
EIIIMMNORSST	IMMERSIONIST
EIIIMNNORSST	INTERMISSION
EIIIMNOOPRST	REIMPOSITION
EIIINOPQRSTU	PERQUISITION
EIILLPRSSSTY	SPIRITLESSLY
EIILMOPRSUVY	IMPERVIOUSLY
EIILNOORRSTU	IRRESOLUTION
EIILNOOSTTUV	EVOLUTIONIST
EIIMMNNOPRST	IMPRISONMENT
EIIMNNNQQUUU	QUINQUENNIUM
EIIMNOOQRSUU	QUERIMONIOUS
EIINNOORRSTV	INTROVERSION
EIINNOPRRTTU	INTERRUPTION
EIINOPRSSTTU	SUPERSTITION
EILMNNOOPTTY	OMNIPOTENTLY
EILMNNOSSSUU	LUMINOUSNESS
EILMOPPRSTUU	MULTIPURPOSE
EILMORSSTUYY	MYSTERIOUSLY
EINOPRSSSSUU	SPURIOUSNESS
ELNOOPPSSSUU	POPULOUSNESS
ELNOOPRSTTUY	PORTENTOUSLY
ELOOPPRRSSUY	PROSPEROUSLY
EMOPPRSSTUUU	PRESUMPTUOUS
ENNOOORSSSSU	SONOROUSNESS
ENOOPPRRSSUU	UNPROSPEROUS
ENOORSSSTTUU	TORTUOUSNESS
FFILLNRTUUUY	UNFRUITFULLY
FGHHLLOTTUUY	THOUGHTFULLY
FHILLOPRSUWY	WORSHIPFULLY

FHLLNRTTUUUY	UNTRUTHFULLY
FIILMMORTTUY	MULTIFORMITY
FILOORSTTUUY	FORTUITOUSLY
GGHHILOPRTUW	PLOUGHWRIGHT
GGIILLOORTUY	LITURGIOLOGY
GGILLOOOSSST	GLOSSOLOGIST
GHIIKLNNNTUY	UNTHINKINGLY
GHILMOOOPRST	MORPHOLOGIST
GHIMNOOPSSTY	GYMNOSOPHIST
GHLOOOOPTYYZ	ZOOPHYTOLOGY
GIILMMNOOPEW	SWIMMING-POOL
GIILNPRRSSUY	SURPRISINGLY
GIINNNOPRTTU	TURNING-POINT
GLLNOOSTTUUY	GLUTTONOUSLY
HHIILMOOPPSS	PHILOSOPHISM
HHIMMMOOOPRS	HOMOMORPHISM
HIIIILMNPSST	PHILISTINISM
HIIOPRRSSUVV	SURVIVORSHIP
HILMMOOPPRSY	POLYMORPHISM
HLLLOOPPSUYY	POLYPHYLLOUS
HMMNOOOOPRSU	MONOMORPHOUS
IIIMNNOORSST	INTROMISSION
IIINNORSTTUU	INNUTRITIOUS
IILNORSTTUUY	NUTRITIOUSLY
IILOOPPRSTUY	PROPITIOUSLY
IINOOPPRSTUU	UNPROPITIOUS
IINOOPRSTTTU	PROSTITUTION
ILLMNOOSUUVY	VOLUMINOUSLY
LLMOSTTUUUVY	TUMULTUOUSLY
LLOOPSTUUUVY	VOLUPTUOUSLY
LMNNOOSSUYYY	SYNONYMOUSLY

Thirteen Letter Words

AAAADCCEELRTU	BACCALAUREATE	AAAEEHIKNPRSS	SHAKESPEARIAN
AAAABDILMORSS	AMBASSADORIAL	AAAEFIILMMRST	MATERFAMILIAS
AAAACCDIIKLLS	LACKADAISICAL	AAAEFIILMPRST	PATERFAMILIAS
AAAACCLMNORST	MALACOSTRACAN	AAAEGLLLMOPRR	PARALLELOGRAM
AAAACGHILPPRR	PARAGRAPHICAL	AAAEGLNRTTVXY	EXTRAVAGANTLY
AAAAEGIMMNRST	ANAGRAMMATISE	AAAEIILNPRRTT	INTRAPARIETAL
AAAAEHILNPPRR	PARAPHERNALIA	AAAEILMNPRRTY	PARLIAMENTARY
AAAAGIMMNRSTT	ANAGRAMMATIST	AAAEINORSTTVX	EXTRAVASATION
AAABCDIKNORTW	BACKWARDATION	AAAFHILLLMORT	THALAMIFLORAL
AAABCEEILNRST	ASCERTAINABLE	AAAGGGILNRTVY	AGGRAVATINGLY
AAABCILLLOPRY	PARABOLICALLY	AAAGIILNNOTVZ	GALVANIZATION
AAABEEHLLRSTV	BALLAST-HEAVER	AAAGIILNORTTV	GRAVITATIONAL
AAABEEILLNSSV	AVAILABLENESS	AAAGLLNOPSTVY	GALVANOPLASTY
AAABEELLNPSST	PALATABLENESS	AAAHIINORRTTU	AUTHORITARIAN
AAABEGIILMNTY	MANAGEABILITY	AAAIIILMNNOTZ	ANIMALIZATION
AAABELNNRRTUW	UNWARRANTABLE	AAAIILNNOTTTZ	TANTALIZATION
AAABIIILNTTTY	ATTAINABILITY	AAAIINNOSSSST	ASSASSINATION
AAABLNNRRTUWY	UNWARRANTABLY	AABBBIILORSTY	ABSORBABILITY
AAACCDHIILNOR	ARCHIDIACONAL	AABBCILLMOSTY	BOMBASTICALLY
AAACCIILLSTTT	STALACTITICAL	AABBDEIILLLRT	BILLIARD-TABLE
AAACCIILMNOTT	ACCLIMATATION	AABBEHIILNNTU	UNINHABITABLE
AAACCILLRSSTY	SARCASTICALLY	AABCCEEIILMPRT	IMPRACTICABLE
AAACDEEINPPRS	DISAPPEARANCE	AABCCEIILPTTY	ACCEPTABILITY
AAACDEIIINPRT	PAEDIATRICIAN	AABCCELNNOTUU	UNACCOUNTABLE
AAACDGHIIMPRT	DIAPHRAGMATIC	AABCCIILMPRTY	IMPRACTICABLY
AAACDHIINOPRS	ANAPHRODISIAC	AABCDEEEFNRSS	BAREFACEDNESS
AAACDILLOPRXY	PARADOXICALLY	AABCDEEFIPRRT	PREFABRICATED
AAACEEOPPRSUV	PAPAVERACEOUS	AABCDEENNORUV	OVERABUNDANCE
AAACEGHILOPPR	PALAEOGRAPHIC	AABCDEGILLRRT	BALL-CARTRIDGE
AAACEGILMNNOR	ANGLO-AMERICAN	AABCDGIKLMRSU	BLACKGUARDISM
AAACEHIILLMNV	MACHIAVELLIAN	AABCDIMNNORST	CONTRABANDISM
AAACEHIIMMNTT	MATHEMATICIAN	AABCDINNORSTT	CONTRABANDIST
AAACEHIMOOPPR	PHARMACOPOEIA	AABCEEEELNPSS	PEACEABLENESS
AAACEHNRRRSTW	SEARCH-WARRANT	AABCEEEGHLLLN	CHALLENGEABLE
AAACEIILMNNRT	LATIN-AMERICAN	AABCEEEHLNSST	TEACHABLENESS
AAACELLMNRSTY	SACRAMENTALLY	AABCEEEILLPRR	IRREPLACEABLE
AAACFILLNSTTY	FANTASTICALLY	AABCEEHILMNPU	UNIMPEACHABLE
AAACGIILLMSTT	STALAGMITICAL	AABCEEIILLMRR	IRRECLAIMABLE
AAACGILLMMRTY	GRAMMATICALLY	AABCEEIILNPPR	INAPPRECIABLE
AAACGILLMPRTY	PRAGMATICALLY	AABCEEMMNORSU	MEMBRANACEOUS
AAACGILMMNRTU	UNGRAMMATICAL	AABCEFIIINOTT	BEATIFICATION
AAACHIILLPRSY	PHARISAICALLY	AABCEGHIILNTY	CHANGEABILITY
AAACHILLMSTTY	ASTHMATICALLY	AABCEILLMOPRT	PROBLEMATICAL
AAACIILLMOTXY	AXIOMATICALLY	AABCEILMNNOOP	COMPANIONABLE
AAACIILLPRSTY	PARASITICALLY	AABCEILNNORST	CONSTRAINABLE
AAACILLMOTTUY	AUTOMATICALLY	AABCFILNNOOTU	CONFABULATION
AAACILNNRSTTT	TRANSATLANTIC	AABCFLNOORTUY	CONFABULATORY
AAADEGILMQRSU	QUADRAGESIMAL	AABCHIMNOPRRS	MARSIPOBRANCH
AAADEILLQRRTU	QUADRILATERAL	AABCIIILLMPTY	IMPLACABILITY
AAADIIMNORSTT	DRAMATISATION	AABCIIILLPPTY	APPLICABILITY

AABCIINNOORTZ	CARBONIZATION
AABCILLNOOOORT	COLLABORATION
AABCILMNNOOPY	COMPANIONABLY
AABDEEFGIILNT	INDEFATIGABLE
AABDEEILMNRSS	ADMIRABLENESS
AABDEEILNSSSV	ADVISABLENESS
AABDEEMNRRSSU	UNEMBARRASSED
AABDEFGIILNTY	INDEFATIGABLY
AABDENNPRSTUU	SUPERABUNDANT
AABEEEEGLNRSS	AGREEABLENESS
AABEEEEHNRTTW	WEATHER-BEATEN
AABEEELLLMNSS	MALLEABLENESS
AABEEELNORSST	ELABORATENESS
AABEEEELNPRSSS	SEPARABLENESS
AABEEGHIKNRRT	HEARTBREAKING
AABEEGHLLNSSU	LAUGHABLENESS
AABEELLLNOSSW	ALLOWABLENESS
AABEELLLRSTTY	TETRASYLLABLE
AABEEMMNRRSST	EMBARRASSMENT
AABEFHILNNOSU	UNFASHIONABLE
AABEFILMORSSU	BALSAMIFEROUS
AABEGILNORRTU	GUBERNATORIAL
AABEHMORRRSTU	HARBOURMASTER
AABEIILLLOTVZ	VOLATILIZABLE
AABEIILNORSTV	VERBALISATION
AABEIILNRSTWY	ANSWERABILITY
AABEIINRRRSST	ARBITRARINESS
AABEILMNOPRTU	PERAMBULATION
AABEILMNRSTTT	TRANSMITTABLE
AABEILNOORSTV	OBSERVATIONAL
AABELNOPRRSTT	TRANSPORTABLE
AABELNPRSSSUU	UNSURPASSABLE
AABFHILNNOSUY	UNFASHIONABLY
AABFILMNNOTUU	FUNAMBULATION
AABGHIOOPRTUY	AUTOBIOGRAPHY
AABHIIILNPRRS	LIBRARIANSHIP
AABIIIILNSTTY	INSATIABILITY
AABIIILNOSSTT	STABILISATION
AABIILNNNRTTU	TINTINNABULAR
AABILLNSSTTUY	SUBSTANTIALLY
AABILNNSSTTUU	UNSUBSTANTIAL
AABLMMNOORSTU	SOMNAMBULATOR
AACCCEHIILSTT	CATECHISTICAL
AACCCFIIILNOT	CALCIFICATION
AACCDEEILNOPY	ENCYCLOPAEDIA
AACCDEHMOOPWY	CAMPEACHY-WOOD
AACCDEIILLLTY	DIALECTICALLY
AACCDEIILMNST	ACCIDENTALISM
AACCDEILNOOTU	COEDUCATIONAL
AACCDEIMMOOTV	ACCOMMODATIVE
AACCDEIMNNOPU	UNACCOMPANIED
AACCDFIIILNOT	ACIDIFICATION
AACCDGIMMNOOT	ACCOMMODATING
AACCDIMMNOOOT	ACCOMMODATION
AACCEEGIMORTT	CATEGOREMATIC
AACCEEHIMRRST	SACCHARIMETER
AACCEEHLRRSST	CHARACTERLESS
AACCEEHMORRST	SACCHAROMETER
AACCEELMNRUUV	VACUUM-CLEANER
AACCEFIIINOTT	ACETIFICATION
AACCEGHHLOPRR	CHALCOGRAPHER
AACCEGILLORTY	CATEGORICALLY
AACCEHIILMORT	IATROCHEMICAL
AACCEHIILRSTU	EUCHARISTICAL
AACCEHILLPPTY	PLATYCEPHALIC
AACCEHILLPRTY	PHYLACTERICAL
AACCEHILRRTTU	ARCHITECTURAL
AACCEHIMPRSTU	PHARMACEUTICS
AACCEHMOOPRSU	CAMPHORACEOUS
AACCEIILMNOST	ENCOMIASTICAL
AACCEIINNORRT	INCARCERATION
AACCEILLMRTUV	CIRCUMVALLATE
AACCEILNPRSST	PRACTICALNESS
AACCEILOPRSTY	PALAEOCRYSTIC
AACCEIMMNNOPT	ACCOMPANIMENT
AACCEINNNOOTT	CONCATENATION
AACCEINOPSSSU	CAPACIOUSNESS
AACCEKNORTTTU	COUNTER-ATTACK
AACCFIIILNORT	CLARIFICATION
AACCFIIINORST	SCARIFICATION
AACCFINORSSTY	SACROSANCTIFY
AACCGHILLNOOT	ANGLO-CATHOLIC
AACCHIILMNOOT	MACHICOLATION
AACCHIILPRSTY	PSYCHIATRICAL
AACCHIINNORST	ANACHRONISTIC
AACCIIINORTTZ	CICATRIZATION
AACCILLNSTTYY	SYNTACTICALLY
AACCILNNOOOTV	CONVOCATIONAL
AACDDEHIINPST	CANDIDATESHIP
AACDEEGINORRS	COARSE-GRAINED
AACDEEHIMNORT	ECHINODERMATA
AACDEEHINTTTU	AUTHENTICATED
AACDEEILMNPRT	PREDICAMENTAL
AACDEEILNPPTU	APPENDICULATE
AACDEEIMNNOTT	DECONTAMINATE
AACDEEINPPRTU	UNAPPRECIATED
AACDEGHIILOPR	IDEOGRAPHICAL
AACDEGIMNNRST	DANCING-MASTER
AACDEGLMNNORS	SCANDALMONGER
AACDEHIIMNRRT	ARCHIMANDRITE
AACDEIIJLRTUX	EXTRAJUDICIAL
AACDEIILLMRTY	DIAMETRICALLY
AACDEILLNOTUY	EDUCATIONALLY
AACDEILMORSST	SACERDOTALISM
AACDEILPQRTUU	QUADRUPLICATE
AACDEINNORSUU	ARUNDINACEOUS
AACDEINOSSSUU	AUDACIOUSNESS
AACDGIIILLOST	DIALOGISTICAL
AACDHILLOPRSY	RHAPSODICALLY
AACDHIMMOOSSS	SADO-MASOCHISM
AACDHIMOOSSST	SADO-MASOCHIST
AACDIIILLMOTY	IDIOMATICALLY
AACDIIIORTTVY	RADIOACTIVITY
AACDIILLORTTY	DICTATORIALLY
AACDIILNNOPTU	PANDICULATION
AACDIIMNOPSST	ANTISPASMODIC
AACDILMOPSSYY	SPASMODICALLY
AACDILLOQRRUU	QUADRILOCULAR
AACEEGHLMOPSU	MEGACEPHALOUS
AACEEGHNOOPRR	OCEANOGRAPHER
AACEEGILLLNVY	EVANGELICALLY
AACEEGILRSTTT	STRATEGETICAL

248

AACEEHILLSTTY	AESTHETICALLY	AACGHILLOPRXY	XYLOGRAPHICAL
AACEEHILNPRTT	PARENTHETICAL	AACGHILMNOOPR	MONOGRAPHICAL
AACEEHOPRRTXY	ARCHAEOPTERYX	AACGHILMOPRTY	CLIMATOGRAPHY
AACEEIILPPRTT	PERIPATETICAL	AACGHILOOPPRT	TOPOGRAPHICAL
AACEEIINNRSST	NECESSITARIAN	AACGHILOPPRTY	TYPOGRAPHICAL
AACEEIMNNRSTT	ASCERTAINMENT	AACGHIMRSTTUU	THAUMATURGICS
AACEFIIILQTUV	QUALIFICATIVE	AACGIILMMOPRT	LIPOGRAMMATIC
AACEGHILLLRTY	LETHARGICALLY	AACGIILNORSTU	CARTILAGINOUS
AACEGHILOORST	ARCHAEOLOGIST	AACGIILNORTTU	GRATICULATION
AACEGHIMNOPRT	CINEMATOGRAPH	AACGIJLNNOOTU	CONJUGATIONAL
AACEGIILLMNOR	MINERALOGICAL	AACGILLMNSTYY	GYMNASTICALLY
AACEGIILLMNTY	ENIGMATICALLY	AACGILMNOOPST	CAMPANOLOGIST
AACEGIILLLORY	ALLEGORICALLY	AACGIMMMNOORT	MONOGRAMMATIC
AACEGILLNPRYY	PANEGYRICALLY	AACGLNOORRTTU	CONGRATULATOR
AACEGILLRSTTY	STRATEGICALLY	AACHHIILLMOPT	PHILOMATHICAL
AACEGINOSSSSU	SAGACIOUSNESS	AACHHIMNPSSTY	YACHTSMANSHIP
AACEGLLNRRTUY	RECTANGULARLY	AACHIIINNRSTT	ANTICHRISTIAN
AACEHHLOOPRTX	CEPHALO-THORAX	AACHIILLNNOTU	HALLUCINATION
AACEHIIIMNRTT	ARITHMETICIAN	AACHILLNORTUY	HALLUCINATORY
AACEHIILLSTTY	ATHEISTICALLY	AACHIMOPRSSTT	CATASTROPHISM
AACEHIILNPSTT	PANTHEISTICAL	AACHLNOPSSTYY	PSYCHOANALYST
AACEHIILRTTTY	THEATRICALITY	AACIIIILNOSTT	ITALICISATION
AACEHIIMNNOST	MECHANISATION	AACIIILLPPRTY	PARTICIPIALLY
AACEHIIMNPSTY	METAPHYSICIAN	AACIIILNNOSTT	NATIONALISTIC
AACEHIIOPSSST	ASSOCIATESHIP	AACIIILNOOSST	SOCIALISATION
AACEHILLNTTUY	AUTHENTICALLY	AACIIILNORSTT	RATIONALISTIC
AACEHILMPSTTY	SYMPATHETICAL	AACIIINNOORTT	RATIOCINATION
AACEHIMPRSTTU	PHARMACEUTIST	AACIIINOPPRTT	PARTICIPATION
AACEHLNOPSSYY	PSYCHOANALYSE	AACIIIOSSTTVY	ASSOCIATIVITY
AACEHMSSSSTTU	MASSACHUSETTS	AACIILLMPRSTY	PRISMATICALLY
AACEIIILMRSTT	MATERIALISTIC	AACIILLNPRTUY	PURITANICALLY
AACEIIINORTTV	RATIOCINATIVE	AACIILLOPRTTY	PATRIOTICALLY
AACEIIILLLRSTY	REALISTICALLY	AACIILLSSTTTY	STATISTICALLY
AACEIILNNORTT	INTERCALATION	AACIILMNORTTU	MATRICULATION
AACEIILPRRTUZ	PARTICULARIZE	AACIILMPRRSTU	PARTICULARISM
AACEIIMNNOTTV	CONTAMINATIVE	AACIILNNOTUVZ	VULCANIZATION
AACEIINNNORRT	REINCARNATION	AACIILNOPRRTT	INTRATROPICAL
AACEIINOPRRTV	PREVARICATION	AACIILPRRSTTU	PARTICULARIST
AACEIINORTTUZ	CAUTERIZATION	AACIILPRRTTUY	PARTICULARITY
AACEILLMNPTUY	PNEUMATICALLY	AACIIMNNNOOTT	CONTAMINATION
AACEILMNRRSUV	VERNACULARISM	AACIINOORRTTY	RATIOCINATORY
AACEILMOPRTVY	COMPARATIVELY	AACILLMNOPSTY	COMPLAISANTLY
AACEILNNOPSTU	ENCAPSULATION	AACILLNOOPSTU	UNAPOSTOLICAL
AACEILNOSSSSU	SALACIOUSNESS	AACILMMOPSTTY	SYMPTOMATICAL
AACEILOPRRTTX	EXTRATROPICAL	AACILMNOOPTTU	COMPUTATIONAL
AACEIMNOOPSST	COMPASSIONATE	AADDEEEELMPRST	PADDLE-STEAMER
AACEINOPRRSTT	PROCRASTINATE	AADDEEGGILLRT	DRAGGLE-TAILED
AACEINOPRRTUY	PRECAUTIONARY	AADDEEGNRRTUU	UNDERGRADUATE
AACEINOPRSSSU	RAPACIOUSNESS	AADDEGGHNRRTU	GRANDDAUGHTER
AACFFIIILNOST	FALSIFICATION	AADDEGHNORRUY	ROUGH-AND-READY
AACFGIIIMNNOT	MAGNIFICATION	AADDEILNRSSST	DASTARDLINESS
AACFGIIINORTT	GRATIFICATION	AADEEEIMNNRRT	MEDITERRANEAN
AACFGILNNOORT	CONFLAGRATION	AADEEEMMNRSTU	ADMEASUREMENT
AACFGIMNNRTUU	MANUFACTURING	AADEEFNSSSSTT	STEADFASTNESS
AACFHIMNPRSST	CRAFTSMANSHIP	AADEEGIMNPRST	DISPARAGEMENT
AACFIIIILRTTY	ARTIFICIALITY	AADEEHIMMMNOZ	MOHAMMEDANIZE
AACFIIILMNOPT	AMPLIFICATION	AADEEIILNNOTZ	DENATIONALIZE
AACFIIILNOQTU	QUALIFICATION	AADEENNPRSTUU	SUPERANNUATED
AACGHHIMNNTTW	NIGHT-WATCHMAN	AADEFIILOQRTU	QUADRIFOLIATE
AACGHIILLMORT	LOGARITHMICAL	AADEFLLMNNTUY	FUNDAMENTALLY
AACGHIIPRRSTT	STRATIGRAPHIC	AADEGHILNRTUW	DAUGHTER-IN-LAW

AADEGIMNRRSTW	DRAWING-MASTER	AAEIIILMMRSTT	IMMATERIALIST
AADEHIMMMMNOS	MOHAMMEDANISM	AAEIIILNORSST	SERIALISATION
AADEHIMNORSTU	DIATHERMANOUS	AAEIIIMNNPPRT	IMPARIPINNATE
AADEIIILLMORTY	MEDIATORIALLY	AAEIILLQTTUVY	QUALITATIVELY
AADEIIILLQRRTU	QUADRILITERAL	AAEIILMNNORTT	TERMINATIONAL
AADEIILMNSSTU	UNASSIMILATED	AAEIILNNNORTT	INTERNATIONAL
AADEIILNRSTUZ	DISNATURALIZE	AAEIILNOPRRST	RESPIRATIONAL
AADEIIMNNORSV	ANIMADVERSION	AAEIIMOPPRTVX	APPROXIMATIVE
AADEIINOPSSST	DISPASSIONATE	AAEIINNNOSTTX	ANNEXATIONIST
AADEIIPQRRTTU	QUADRIPARTITE	AAEIINOPPPRRT	INAPPROPRIATE
AADEILMMORSTT	MELODRAMATIST	AAEILLNNOSSTY	SENSATIONALLY
AADEINORRRTXY	EXTRAORDINARY	AAEILMOPPRTXY	APPROXIMATELY
AADEJLMMNSTTU	MALADJUSTMENT	AAEILNNOPRSTU	SUPERNATIONAL
AADFHIMNPRSST	DRAFTSMANSHIP	AAEILNOOPRTTX	EXTRAPOLATION
AADGGIILNPRSY	DISPARAGINGLY	AAEILNOORTUVV	OVERVALUATION
AADGIIILNNTWY	LADY-IN-WAITING	AAEILOPPPRRTY	APPROPRIATELY
AADIILLNORTTY	TRADITIONALLY	AAEIMMNNPPRSST	PANSPERMATISM
AADIILNNOPSTT	DISPLANTATION	AAEIMNNNOORTT	ORNAMENTATION
AADIIMNORRSTT	ADMINISTRATOR	AAEIMNNORSSTTT	STATION-MASTER
AAEEEGMNNRRRT	REARRANGEMENT	AAEINNNOSSTTU	INSTANTANEOUS
AAEEELMMNPRTT	TEMPERAMENTAL	AAELLNRRSSTVY	TRANSVERSALLY
AAEEGIIMMPRTZ	EPIGRAMMATIZE	AAELNNPRRSTTY	TRANSPARENTLY
AAEEGIIMNRRRT	INTERMARRIAGE	AAFFGHINPRSSU	SUFFRAGANSHIP
AAEEGIIMNRSTV	VEGETARIANISM	AAFIIILMNRTUY	UNFAMILIARITY
AAEEGIMMMNNST	MISMANAGEMENT	AAGGIILNNOTTU	AGGLUTINATION
AAEEGIMNRTTUV	ARGUMENTATIVE	AAGHHINOOPPRT	ANTHROPOPHAGI
AAEEGJMNORRST	SERGEANT-MAJOR	AAGHHNOOPPRTU	PHONAUTOGRAPH
AAEEHIILNPSST	ELEPHANTIASIS	AAGHHNOOPPRTY	ANTHROPOPHAGY
AAEEHILMOPRTU	PALAEOTHERIUM	AAGHIILMNORTT	ANTILOGARITHM
AAEEHMNOSTTUX	EXANTHEMATOUS	AAGHIMRSTTTUU	THAUMATURGIST
AAEEIKLMNSSTT	STATESMANLIKE	AAGIILMNOORST	GLAMORISATION
AAEEIKLNSSTTV	TALKATIVENESS	AAGIILNNORTTU	TRIANGULATION
AAEEIILLLPPTVY	APPELLATIVELY	AAGIILNORSTUV	VULGARISATION
AAEEIILLNRTTVY	ALTERNATIVELY	AAGIILNRRTTUY	TRIANGULARITY
AAEEIILPPRRTVY	PREPARATIVELY	AAGILMMNNNOSUY	MAGNANIMOUSLY
AAEEIMNPRRSTV	PRIVATEERSMAN	AAGILNNORSTTU	STRANGULATION
AAEELNPRRRTTU	PRETERNATURAL	AAGIMNORRRSTT	TRANSMIGRATOR
AAEEMQRRRSTTU	QUARTERMASTER	AAHHNOOPPRTTY	ANTHROPOPATHY
AAEEPRRSSTTUU	SUPERSATURATE	AAHIIMMNNOOPR	MORPHINOMANIA
AAEFFIILMNORR	FORAMINIFERAL	AAHIIMNNOORTZ	HARMONIZATION
AAEFFIILMRTVY	AFFIRMATIVELY	AAHIINOORSTTU	AUTHORISATION
AAEFFINOORSTT	AFFORESTATION	AAHLLMOOPSTUY	POLYTHALAMOUS
AAEFGIMNNORTT	FRAGMENTATION	AAHLMMNOOOSTU	MONOTHALAMOUS
AAEFIIMNNOSTT	MANIFESTATION	AAHLNOOPRRTTY	ANTHROPOLATRY
AAEGGHNOPRSTY	STEGANOGRAPHY	AAIIILLNNOPRST	INSPIRATIONAL
AAEGGIILNTTUV	AGGLUTINATIVE	AAIIILNORRTTY	IRRATIONALITY
AAEGGILMNOORT	AGGLOMERATION	AAIILLMMNORTY	MATRIMONIALLY
AAEGHMNOOPRSU	PHANEROGAMOUS	AAIILLMNNOTTU	MULTINATIONAL
AAEGIILLMRSTY	MAGISTERIALLY	AAIILLMNOPRTY	PATRIMONIALLY
AAEGIIMMPRSTT	EPIGRAMMATIST	AAIILLNOPRTUZ	PLURALIZATION
AAEGIIMNNOTTZ	MAGNETIZATION	AAIIMNOOPPRTX	APPROXIMATION
AAEGIIMNQQSUU	QUINQUAGESIMA	AAIINNOPRRSTT	TRANSPIRATION
AAEGIMNNORTTU	ARGUMENTATION	AAIINNORRSTTY	TRANSITIONARY
AAEGLLNOOOPTY	PALAEONTOLOGY	AAIINOOPPPRRT	APPROPRIATION
AAEGLLOOOOPYZ	PALAEOZOOLOGY	AAILLNNOPPSTTU	SUPPLANTATION
AAEHHILMOPRTX	XEROPHTHALMIA	AAIMNNORSTTTU	TRANSMUTATION
AAEHIIIMNNSTT	ANTIHISTAMINE	ABBCDEEIILNRS	INDESCRIBABLE
AAEHIIORTTTUV	AUTHORITATIVE	ABBCEEIJLNOOT	OBJECTIONABLE
AAEHIMNPSSSTT	STATESMANSHIP	ABBCEHIILORTY	BIBLIOTHECARY
AAEHINOPPRSTU	APHANIPTEROUS	ABBCEHKOORRSS	SHOCK-ABSORBER
AAEIIILMMMRST	IMMATERIALISM	ABBCEIJLNOOTY	OBJECTIONABLY

ABBCEILNORTTU	CONTRIBUTABLE	ABCFLMNOORTUY	UNCOMFORTABLY
ABBDEIILRSTTU	DISTRIBUTABLE	ABCIIILMOPTTY	COMPATIBILITY
ABBDFFILMNNSU	BLINDMAN'S-BUFF	ABCIILMMOTTUY	COMMUTABILITY
ABBEEILMPRRTU	IMPERTURBABLE	ABCINOOOORRRT	CORROBORATION
ABBEGHIILOPRR	BIBLIOGRAPHER	ABCOOOORRRRTY	CORROBORATORY
ABBEIIILOPRST	PROBABILITIES	ABDDEEEHLORTU	DOUBLE-HEARTED
ABBIIILMOPRTY	IMPROBABILITY	ABDDEEGILLNOU	DOUBLE-DEALING
ABCCCEEENNOST	CONTABESCENCE	ABDEEEGKLLNOW	KNOWLEDGEABLE
ABCCCILLMOOXY	COXCOMBICALLY	ABDEEEHKNORRT	BROKEN-HEARTED
ABCCEEIILNNOV	INCONCEIVABLE	ABDEEEILNRSSS	DESIRABLENESS
ABCCEEJLNORTU	CONJECTURABLE	ABDEEELNNRSSU	ENDURABLENESS
ABCCFIIILMPTY	IMPECCABILITY	ABDEEFIIILRSV	DIVERSIFIABLE
ABCCEIIILSSTY	ACCESSIBILITY	ABDEEGIILNRST	DISINTEGRABLE
ABCCEIILNNOVY	INCONCEIVABLY	ABDEEGILNRSST	DRESSING-TABLE
ABCCEIIMMNRTU	CIRCUMAMBIENT	ABDEEIILNNPSS	INDISPENSABLE
ABCCHHIIOPRRS	ARCHBISHOPRIC	ABDEEIIMRTTXY	AMBIDEXTERITY
ABCCIINORSTTU	ANTISCORBUTIC	ABDEEIKMMNRST	DISEMBARKMENT
ABCCNOORRSTTU	SUBCONTRACTOR	ABDEFIIINNORT	DEFIBRINATION
ABCDDEEGINPRT	CARPET-BEDDING	ABDEFIILNNTUU	INFUNDIBULATE
ABCDDEEIILRST	DISCREDITABLE	ABDEGHINOORSU	BOARDING-HOUSE
ABCDDEEIILRSTY	DISCREDITABLY	ABDEHILNOORSU	DISHONOURABLE
ABCDEEELMMNOR	RECOMMENDABLE	ABDEIILLNOSSV	INDISSOLVABLE
ABCDEEGHILNOR	BREECH-LOADING	ABDEIILNNPSSY	INDISPENSABLY
ABCDEEILNNNOS	INCONDENSABLE	ABDEIILNOPRTY	PONDERABILITY
ABCDEEILNPRTU	UNPREDICTABLE	ABDEIINNORSTU	INSUBORDINATE
ABCDEHINOPSSU	SUBDEACONSHIP	ABDEIINORSTUV	SUBORDINATIVE
ABCDEIIILLNPS	DISCIPLINABLE	ABDEILLNOOORT	BLOOD-RELATION
ABCDEIIILNOSS	INDISSOCIABLE	ABDEILNORSTUY	SUBORDINATELY
ABCDEIIILPRTY	PREDICABILITY	ABDHILNOORSUY	DISHONOURABLY
ABCEEEFIILLRT	ELECTRIFIABLE	ABDIIIILMSSTY	ADMISSIBILITY
ABCEEEEILNOPTX	EXCEPTIONABLE	ABDIINNOORSTU	SUBORDINATION
ABCEEEILNPRUV	UNPERCEIVABLE	ABEEEELNNRSSV	VENERABLENESS
ABCEEEILNRSUV	UNSERVICEABLE	ABEEEELNPRRST	REPRESENTABLE
ABCEEEILNSSTX	EXCITABLENESS	ABEEEEHILNPPRS	APPREHENSIBLE
ABCEEEILORRRV	IRRECOVERABLE	ABEEEIILRRRTV	IRRETRIEVABLE
ABCEEELNSSSUX	EXCUSABLENESS	ABEEEEILMNRSSS	MISERABLENESS
ABCEEIIILRTVY	RECEIVABILITY	ABEEEEILNPRRTT	INTERPRETABLE
ABCEEILNNOSTT	INCONTESTABLE	ABEEEEILNQSTTU	EQUITABLENESS
ABCEEIILNNRSSU	INCURABLENESS	ABEEEINORRRTV	REVERBERATION
ABCEEIILNOPRRS	CEREBRO-SPINAL	ABEEEELLMNSSSS	BLAMELESSNESS
ABCEEILORRRVY	IRRECOVERABLY	ABEEELNNPRSTU	UNPRESENTABLE
ABCEEIMNOSSTV	COMBATIVENESS	ABEEEORRRRTVY	REVERBERATORY
ABCEELMMNORSU	COMMENSURABLE	ABEEFGLNORTTU	UNFORGETTABLE
ABCEELNNOOPRU	PRONOUNCEABLE	ABEEFIILPRRTY	PREFERABILITY
ABCEELNNOQRUU	UNCONQUERABLE	ABEEGHIKNORSU	HOUSEBREAKING
ABCEFINOORRSU	CARBONIFEROUS	ABEEHIILNSTUX	INEXHAUSTIBLE
ABCEFLMNNOORU	UNCONFORMABLE	ABEEHILMNSSTT	ESTABLISHMENT
ABCEFLMNOORTU	UNCOMFORTABLE	ABEEIILNPRTTY	PENETRABILITY
ABCEGILLMOORY	EMBRYOLOGICAL	ABEEIILQSTUYZ	SQUEEZABILITY
ABCEHILLMOOOT	HOLOMETABOLIC	ABEEIILRRRTVY	IRRETRIEVABLY
ABCEHILNOPSST	CONSTABLESHIP	ABEEILLNPSSSU	PLAUSIBLENESS
ABCEIIILLLMPTU	MULTIPLICABLE	ABEEILMMNOSSV	IMMOVABLENESS
ABCEIILMNPRSU	REPUBLICANISM	ABEEILMMNSSTU	IMMUTABLENESS
ABCEIILNOPRTU	REPUBLICATION	ABEEILMNNNOTU	UNMENTIONABLE
ABCEILNNOSTTY	INCONTESTABLY	ABEEINNOSSSTT	OBSTINATENESS
ABCEILORRRTUU	ARBORICULTURE	ABEFIIJLNSTUU	UNJUSTIFIABLE
ABCEIOOORRRTV	CORROBORATIVE	ABEFLLNOOPSTU	TABLESPOONFUL
ABCELMMNORSUY	COMMENSURABLY	ABEGIIILNOTTY	NEGOTIABILITY
ABCELNNOQRUUY	UNCONQUERABLY	ABEGILNOPPRTT	BLOTTING-PAPER
ABCFILMMORRUU	UMBRACULIFORM	ABEHHINNOORST	HEATH-ROBINSON
ABCFLMNNOORUY	UNCONFORMABLY	ABEHIIILPRSTY	PERISHABILITY

251

ABEHIILNSTUXY INEXHAUSTIBLY
ABEHLLMOPSSUY BLASPHEMOUSLY
ABEIIILLNRTUY UNRELIABILITY
ABEIIILNOQRTU EQUILIBRATION
ABEIIILNPSTXY EXPANSIBILITY
ABEIILLNRTUVY VULNERABILITY
ABEIILLORSTVY RESOLVABILITY
ABEIILMNRSSST TRANSMISSIBLE
ABEIILMNRSTUY MENSURABILITY
ABEIILOPRRSTV PROVERBIALIST
ABEIILRTTTUVY ATTRIBUTIVELY
ABEILNOORSSSU LABORIOUSNESS
ABEILNOPPRSTU INSUPPORTABLE
ABEILNSSTTUVY SUBSTANTIVELY
ABEINOOPRRTTU PROTUBERATION
ABFIIIILLLMNS INFALLIBILISM
ABFIIIILLLNST INFALLIBILIST
ABFIIIILLLNTY INFALLIBILITY
ABFIIILOPRTTY PROFITABILITY
ABFIIJLNSTUUY UNJUSTIFIABLY
ABGIIIILNNTTY INTANGIBILITY
ABGILLORRSUUY BURGLARIOUSLY
ABIIIIILNOTVY INVIOLABILITY
ABIIIILMPRTTY IMPARTIBILITY
ABIIIILMPSSTY IMPASSIBILITY
ABIIILMOPRTVY IMPROVABILITY
ABIIILNOSTTUZ SUBTILIZATION
ABIIILNSTTUUY UNSUITABILITY
ABILNOPPRSTUY INSUPPORTABLY
ACCCCEIJMNRUY CIRCUMJACENCY
ACCCDEEEINNNS INCANDESCENCE
ACCCDEEILNOPY ENCYCLOPAEDIC
ACCCDEHILNOSY SYNECDOCHICAL
ACCCEEEELNNOSV CONVALESCENCE
ACCCEEILLNRTY ECCENTRICALLY
ACCCEEELNNOSVY CONVALESCENCY
ACCCEHINNOOSU CINCHONACEOUS
ACCCENNOOOVVX CONCAVO-CONVEX
ACCCIILMOOPRS MICROSCOPICAL
ACCDEEEENNNRST TRANSCENDENCE
ACCDEEIILNOTZ OCCIDENTALIZE
ACCDEEENNNRSTY TRANSCENDENCY
ACCDEIIKLOOPS KALEIDOSCOPIC
ACCDEIINOORTT DECORTICATION
ACCDEIINORTTV CONTRADICTIVE
ACCDHHINOOPRY HYPOCHONDRIAC
ACCDIIINORSTY IDIOSYNCRATIC
ACCDIIMMNNOOU INCOMMUNICADO
ACCDIINNOORTT CONTRADICTION
ACCDINOORRTTY CONTRADICTORY
ACCEEGHNNORTU COUNTERCHANGE
ACCEEGHNORRTU COUNTERCHARGE
ACCEEHHLOORST SCHOOL-TEACHER
ACCEEHILMOPRT PETROCHEMICAL
ACCEEIILMMORS COMMERCIALISE
ACCEEIMMNOTUX EXCOMMUNICATE
ACCEEINNORTTV CONCENTRATIVE
ACCEEINOPRTTV CONTRACEPTIVE
ACCEEINORTTUV COUNTERACTIVE
ACCEEOORRSSTU STERCORACEOUS
ACCEFFIIINOSU INEFFICACIOUS

ACCEFFIILOSUY EFFICACIOUSLY
ACCEFHILMOORR COCHLEARIFORM
ACCEFIIINOPST SPECIFICATION
ACCEFIIINORTT CERTIFICATION
              RECTIFICATION
ACCEFINNOORTY CONFECTIONARY
ACCEGHIILOPRX LEXICOGRAPHIC
ACCEGHILLNOOT TECHNOLOGICAL
ACCEGHILNOPTT PLECTOGNATHIC
ACCEHIILLNSST CALLISTHENICS
ACCEHIILPRRTY HYPERCRITICAL
ACCEHIIMRSSTT CHREMATISTICS
ACCEHILNOPRTY PYROTECHNICAL
ACCEHILOOPPRS CHOREPISCOPAL
ACCEIIKNNPRST PANIC-STRICKEN
ACCEIILMMMORS COMMERCIALISM
ACCEIILMMORRT MICROMETRICAL
ACCEIILNOPRRT CALICO-PRINTER
ACCEIIMMNOTUV COMMUNICATIVE
ACCEIINOOPRRT RECIPROCATION
ACCEIINOORTTX EXCORTICATION
ACCEIIOPPRSSU PERSPICACIOUS
ACCEILMNOPSTU CONCEPTUALISM
ACCEILNOPSTTU CONCEPTUALIST
ACCEINNNOORTT CONCENTRATION
ACCEINNOOPRTT CONTRACEPTION
ACCEINNOORRTY CONCRETIONARY
ACCEINNOORSSY CONCESSIONARY
ACCEINNOORTTU COUNTERACTION
ACCEINOOPPRTU PREOCCUPATION
ACCEJLLNORTUY CONJECTURALLY
ACCFGHHIKNRTU CHUCK-FARTHING
ACCFHIIIMNOTY CHYMIFICATION
ACCFIILLLNOOT FLOCCILLATION
ACCGHHINORSST CROSS-HATCHING
ACCGHILLNOOOR CHRONOLOGICAL
ACCGHILLOOPSY PSYCHOLOGICAL
ACCGHIOPPRRTY CRYPTOGRAPHIC
ACCGIILLOOOTX TOXICOLOGICAL
ACCGILNOOPRSY LARYNGOSCOPIC
ACCHIILMOSSST SCHOLASTICISM
ACCHILMOOPRTY POLYCHROMATIC
ACCHIMMNOOORT MONOCHROMATIC
ACCHIMOOPSSTY PSYCHOSOMATIC
ACCIILLPRSTUU PISCICULTURAL
ACCIILNORTTTY CONTRACTILITY
ACCIIMMNNOOTU COMMUNICATION
ACCIINOOPRSST CRANIOSCOPIST
ACCIJLNNNOOTU CONJUNCTIONAL
ACCILMNNOOTTY CONCOMITANTLY
ACCIMNNOOPRSTU POCOCURANTISM
ACDDEEGIKNNOR DEAD-RECKONING
ACDDEHILMOSUY DICHLAMYDEOUS
ACDDHIMNORSYY HYDRODYNAMICS
ACDEEEFHILRSV CHEVAL-DE-FRISE
ACDEEEFINORTV CONFEDERATIVE
ACDEEEIIRSTTV CARTE-DE-VISITE
ACDEEEIMNRSTV MISADVERTENCE
ACDEEENNOPPRR PREPONDERANCE
ACDEEFIIILNRT DELIRIFACIENT
ACDEEFINNOORT CONFEDERATION

ACDEEFNORRRTW	CENTRE-FORWARD	ACEEGILLMORTY	GEOMETRICALLY
ACDEEGILNPRTY	DEPRECATINGLY	ACEEGILMNNOQU	MAGNILOQUENCE
ACDEEGORRRSST	CROSS-GARTERED	ACEEHHIILMPRS	HEMISPHERICAL
ACDEEIILLMPRY	EPIDERMICALLY	ACEEHHILNPSSS	SENESCHALSHIP
ACDEEIIILPRTVY	PREDICATIVELY	ACEEHILLORTTY	THEORETICALLY
ACDEEIINNORST	INCONSIDERATE	ACEEHILOPRSTT	HETEROPLASTIC
ACDEEIINOPRTT	DECREPITATION	ACEEHIMRRSSTT	CHRISTMAS-TREE
ACDEEIILLNNSTY	CLANDESTINELY	ACEEHINOPRRST	TERPSICHOREAN
ACDEEILNORSTY	CONSIDERATELY	ACEEHIPRRSSTY	SECRETARYSHIP
ACDEEILNPPRRU	PERPENDICULAR	ACEEHLLMOOOORT	ALCOHOLOMETER
ACDEEINNORSSS	SECONDARINESS	ACEEHLMNORRTU	THERMONUCLEAR
ACDEEFGILLRSUY	DISGRACEFULLY	ACEEHLMOOPSSU	MESOCEPHALOUS
ACDEGILLNOOOT	DEONTOLOGICAL	ACEEHOOPRRSTU	HETEROCARPOUS
ACDEHHLOPRSUY	HYDROCEPHALUS	ACEEIIIMNRRTV	RECRIMINATIVE
ACDEHIILMOSTT	METHODISTICAL	ACEEIILPPRTTY	PRECIPITATELY
ACDEHIIOPSSTT	SOPHISTICATED	ACEEIIMMORSTV	COMMISERATIVE
ACDEHILMORRTY	HYDROMETRICAL	ACEEIIMNNRTTT	INTERMITTANCE
ACDEHIMMNOPRS	COMMANDERSHIP	ACEEILLLNPSTY	SPLENETICALLY
ACDEIIJLLPRUY	PREJUDICIALLY	ACEEILLLNRRTU	INTERCELLULAR
ACDEIIJNOPRTU	PREJUDICATION	ACEEILLMNOSSU	MISCELLANEOUS
ACDEIILNNOTTU	DENTICULATION	ACEEILLNOPTXY	EXCEPTIONALLY
ACDEIILNORPTU	REDUPLICATION	ACEEILLORRTVY	CORRELATIVELY
ACDEIIMNOOSTT	DOMESTICATION	ACEEILLPSTUVY	SPECULATIVELY
ACDEIINNOORST	CONSIDERATION	ACEEILMNNSSSU	MASCULINENESS
ACDEIINORRSTY	DISCRETIONARY	ACEEILMNOPTTV	CONTEMPLATIVE
ACDEILNNORSTY	CONSTRAINEDLY	ACEEILNNOQSTU	CONSEQUENTIAL
ACDEILOOPRRTU	PARTICOLOURED	ACEEILNNRSSUY	UNNECESSARILY
ACDEIMNNOOTTU	DOCUMENTATION	ACEEILNOQSSUV	EQUIVOCALNESS
ACDELNOOOSTUY	ACOTYLEDONOUS	ACEEILNORSTTU	INTEROSCULATE
ACDGLOOSTUYYZ	ZYGODACTYLOUS	ACEEIMMMOORTV	COMMEMORATIVE
ACDHIJOOPRSTU	COADJUTORSHIP	ACEEINNNQRTUY	QUINCENTENARY
ACDIIIILMNOOT	DOMICILIATION	ACEEINNOORSVZ	CONVERSAZIONE
ACDIIIMNORRST	DISCRIMINATOR	ACEEINNOSSSTU	TENACIOUSNESS
ACDIILLNNOOTY	CONDITIONALLY	ACEEINOOPRTTX	EXPECTORATION
ACDIILNNNOOTU	UNCONDITIONAL	ACEEINOOPRTUV	UNCOOPERATIVE
ACDIILNNOOOST	CONSOLIDATION	ACEEINOORRSTV	CONSERVATOIRE
ACDIILNOOOORST	DISCOLORATION	ACEEKLNRSSSST	TRACKLESSNESS
ACDILLMOPSTYY	POLYDACTYLISM	ACEELLNOOPRSU	PORCELLANEOUS
ACEEEGILLNRTY	ENERGETICALLY	ACEELLOORRRST	ROLLER-COASTER
ACEEEGLMNORTT	ELECTRO-MAGNET	ACEELMMNOPRTY	COMPLEMENTARY
ACEEEGLNRSSSS	GRACELESSNESS	ACEEMMNNOPSST	ENCOMPASSMENT
ACEEEGMNNORTU	ENCOURAGEMENT	ACEEENNNOOSSTU	CONSENTANEOUS
ACEEEHILMNRTU	HERMENEUTICAL	ACEFGIIIINSTV	SIGNIFICATIVE
ACEEEHLMNNOPS	MESENCEPHALON	ACEFGIILMNNTY	MAGNIFICENTLY
ACEEEHRRSSTTU	TREASURE-CHEST	ACEFHLLOPRRUY	REPROACHFULLY
ACEEEILMNNRTT	INTERLACEMENT	ACEFIIIJSTTUV	JUSTIFICATIVE
ACEEEIOPRTTVX	EXPECTORATIVE	ACEFIIINOPRTT	PETRIFICATION
ACEEEIOQSSTUU	EQUISETACEOUS	ACEFIIINORSTV	VERSIFICATION
ACEEEELNSSSSSU	CAUSELESSNESS	ACEFIILLPRSUY	SUPERFICIALLY
ACEEFFILLNTUY	INEFFECTUALLY	ACEFILLOORRSU	CORALLIFEROUS
ACEEFGHLNNSSU	CHANGEFULNESS	ACEFINNOORSSY	CONFESSIONARY
ACEEFHIMNNRST	FRANCHISEMENT	ACEFINNORRTTY	CONFRATERNITY
ACEEFINOSSSTU	FACETIOUSNESS	ACEFINORSSSTU	FRACTIOUSNESS
ACEEFMNORSTUU	FRUMENTACEOUS	ACEGGILNNORUY	ENCOURAGINGLY
ACEEGHHOOPRRR	CHOREOGRAPHER	ACEGGILNOOSTY	GYNAECOLOGIST
ACEEGHILNORSU	CLEARING-HOUSE	ACEGHHNOOPRRR	CHRONOGRAPHER
ACEEGHILOPRRX	LEXICOGRAPHER	ACEGHIIMOPRSS	SEISMOGRAPHIC
ACEEGHIOPRRST	STEREOGRAPHIC	ACEGHILLLOOTY	THEOLOGICALLY
ACEEGIIMNNOST	MISCEGENATION	ACEGHILLNOOPR	PHRENOLOGICAL
ACEEGIINNNRST	INTRANSIGENCE	ACEGHILORRSTT	CLOISTER-GARTH
ACEEGIINOPRRR	CARRIER-PIGEON	ACEGHOPPRRRTY	CRYPTOGRAPHER

ACEGIILLOSTTY	EGOTISTICALLY
ACEGIILNOSTTU	GESTICULATION
ACEGILLMNOOOT	ENTOMOLOGICAL
ACEGILMOOSSTU	CLEISTOGAMOUS
ACEGILNNOORSS	CONGRESSIONAL
ACEGILNNORSTU	COUNTER-SIGNAL
ACEGILORSTTUY	GESTICULATORY
ACEGIMNOPRSTU	PNEUMOGASTRIC
ACEGIMNORSSTU	GASTROCNEMIUS
ACEGINOOPRSTT	PROGNOSTICATE
ACEHHINOOPTTY	HYPOTHECATION
ACEHHMMNNRSTUY	CHRYSANTHEMUM
ACEHHMOOOPRRT	CHROMATOPHORE
ACEHIIINNPRTT	ANTINEPHRITIC
ACEHILLLOPRTY	PLETHORICALLY
ACEHILLNSTTYY	SYNTHETICALLY
ACEHILLOPPRTY	PROPHETICALLY
ACEHIMNPSTTUY	UNSYMPATHETIC
ACEHINOORRSTT	ORCHESTRATION
ACEHINOPPRRST	COPARTNERSHIP
ACEHINOPSSTTU	PENTASTICHOUS
ACEHIOPRRSSTT	STRATOSPHERIC
ACEHLOOOPRRSU	RHOPALOCEROUS
ACEIIIMNNORRT	RECRIMINATION
ACEIIINOPPRTT	PRECIPITATION
ACEIILLNNOORT	INTERCOLONIAL
ACEIILLNRSTXY	EXTRINSICALLY
ACEIILMNORTUV	VERMICULATION
ACEIILMNOSSSU	MALICIOUSNESS
ACEIILNOOPSTT	POLICE-STATION
ACEIILNOPRRTT	INTERTROPICAL
ACEIILNPPRTTY	PRECIPITANTLY
ACEIIMMNOORST	COMMISERATION
ACEIIMNNOOOTZ	ECONOMIZATION
ACEIIMNORRRTY	RECRIMINATORY
ACEIINORSSTTU	RESUSCITATION
ACEIINOSSSUVV	VIVACIOUSNESS
ACEIINPRRSTTV	TRANSCRIPTIVE
ACEILLLOPPRTY	PROLEPTICALLY
ACEILLMMNOTYY	METONYMICALLY
ACEILLMMRSTYY	SYMMETRICALLY
ACEILLNNNOSSY	NONSENSICALLY
ACEILLNNOOSTT	CONSTELLATION
ACEILLNOOPRRY	INCORPOREALLY
ACEILMMNOPRTY	COMPLIMENTARY
ACEILMMNRSTUY	UNSYMMETRICAL
ACEILMMOTTUVY	COMMUTATIVELY
ACEILMNNOOPSS	COMPANIONLESS
ACEILMNNOOPTT	CONTEMPLATION
ACEILNOORRSTV	CONTROVERSIAL
ACEILOOPRTVVY	PROVOCATIVELY
ACEIMMMNOOORT	COMMEMORATION
ACEIMNNNNOOST	CINNAMON-STONE
ACEIMNORSSSTU	CUSTOMARINESS
ACEINNNOORSTT	CONSTERNATION
ACEINNNOORTTV	CONTRAVENTION
ACEINNNOORTVY	CONVENTIONARY
ACEINOORSSSTU	ATROCIOUSNESS
ACEINOORSSSUV	VORACIOUSNESS
ACEINOPRRSSST	CONSPIRATRESS
ACEINOPRRSTTU	PERSCRUTATION
ACELLNNRSTTUY	TRANSLUCENTLY
ACELMNOORSSSU	CLAMOROUSNESS
ACFFIIINOORTT	FORTIFICATION
ACFGIIIILNNOT	LIGNIFICATION
ACFGIIIINNNST	INSIGNIFICANT
ACFGIIIINNOST	SIGNIFICATION
ACFGIIIILNNSTY	SIGNIFICANTLY
ACFGIIILNOORT	GLORIFICATION
ACFGIIINORSTY	SIGNIFICATORY
ACFGIINNOORTU	CONFIGURATION
ACFIIINORTTV	VITRIFICATION
ACFIIIJLLNOOT	JOLLIFICATION
ACFIIIJNOSTTU	JUSTIFICATION
ACFIIILLMNOOT	MOLLIFICATION
ACFIIILLNNOTU	NULLIFICATION
ACFIIIMMMNOTU	MUMMIFICATION
ACFIIIMNOORTT	MORTIFICATION
ACFIIIMNOSTTY	MYSTIFICATION
ACFIIJORSTTUY	JUSTIFICATORY
ACFILLLLOOORR	COROLLIFLORAL
ACFILLLORRTUU	FLORICULTURAL
ACFINNNOOORTT	CONFRONTATION
ACGGILLLOOOSS	GLOSSOLOGICAL
ACGHIILLOOPSY	PHYSIOLOGICAL
ACGHIMNNOOOPT	PATHOGNOMONIC
ACGIILLLOSSTY	SYLLOGISTICAL
ACGIILLMNNOPY	COMPLAININGLY
ACGIILMNNNOPU	UNCOMPLAINING
ACGIILRRSTTUU	AGRICULTURIST
ACGIINNNOSTUY	CONSANGUINITY
ACHHIILLOOPPS	PHILOSOPHICAL
ACHHIILNOPPRT	PHILANTHROPIC
ACHHNOOOSTTUU	AUTOCHTHONOUS
ACHIILLOPSSTY	SOPHISTICALLY
ACHIIMNNOOPPS	COMPANIONSHIP
ACHIIOOPRSSTT	SOPHISTICATOR
ACHILLORRTTUU	HORTICULTURAL
ACIIIIMNOSTTV	VICTIMISATION
ACIIILLNNOSTT	SCINTILLATION
ACIIILLNNRSTY	INTRINSICALLY
ACIIILMNOPRSV	PROVINCIALISM
ACIIILLMOOQSU	COLLOQUIALISM
ACIIILLLOOQSTU	COLLOQUIALIST
ACIIILLMOPRTTU	MULTIPLICATOR
ACIILMNOORSUY	ACRIMONIOUSLY
ACIILMPRRSSTU	SCRIPTURALISM
ACIILNNORSTTU	INSTRUCTIONAL
ACIILPRRSSTTU	SCRIPTURALIST
ACIIMNNOOSSTU	SANCTIMONIOUS
ACIINNNOOPRTU	PRONUNCIATION
ACIINNOOOPRRT	INCORPORATION
ACIINNOPRRSTT	TRANSCRIPTION
ACILNNOORSUVY	CONVULSIONARY
ACINNOPRSTTTU	CONTRAPUNTIST
ADDDEGGLLNOSY	DADDY-LONG-LEGS
ADDEEGNNRSSUU	UNGUARDEDNESS
ADDEEHILMNRTY	EARTHLY-MINDED
ADDEGINNNRSTU	UNDERSTANDING
ADDEGLNOORTUY	GOODNATUREDLY
ADDEIIIILNUVZ	INDIVIDUALIZE
ADDEIINOOORTZ	DEODORIZATION

ADDEIINOPRSTU	SUPERADDITION
ADDEIMNNRSSTU	MISUNDERSTAND
ADDIIIILMNSUV	INDIVIDUALISM
ADDIIIILNSTUV	INDIVIDUALIST
ADDIIIILNTUVY	INDIVIDUALITY
ADDIIIINNOTUV	INDIVIDUATION
ADEEEFFGILNST	SELF-DEFEATING
ADEEEFFIINRTT	DIFFERENTIATE
ADEEEFILLNRTY	DEFERENTIALLY
ADEEEGGIMNNST	DISENGAGEMENT
ADEEEGOPRRTUY	DAGUERREOTYPE
ADEEEIILNRRST	INTERSIDEREAL
ADEEEIIMNNRTT	INDETERMINATE
ADEEEIIMNRTTV	DETERMINATIVE
ADEEEILMNRTTY	DETERMINATELY
ADEEEILNOPRSS	DEPERSONALISE
ADEEEIMNRSTTU	UNDERESTIMATE
ADEEEIMNRSTTV	ADVERTISEMENT
ADEEEINNRSSST	SEDENTARINESS
ADEEEINOPQRTU	EQUIPONDERATE
ADEEEELLMNOPTV	DEVELOPMENTAL
ADEEFFIILSSST	SELF-SATISFIED
ADEEGIIINRTTT	INTERDIGITATE
ADEEGILLNRRST	DRILL-SERGEANT
ADEEGIMORSTTU	DEUTEROGAMIST
ADEEGINOPPRSV	EAVESDROPPING
ADEEGNNORSSSU	DANGEROUSNESS
ADEEHHIMOPRRT	HERMAPHRODITE
ADEEHLNOPPSTU	PENTADELPHOUS
ADEEHMNOORRSY	DYSMENORRHOEA
ADEEIIMNNORTT	DETERMINATION
ADEEIIMNNOSTT	SEDIMENTATION
ADEEIIMNOPRTT	PREMEDITATION
ADEEIIMNORRTT	INTERMEDIATOR
ADEEIIMNPRSST	PEDESTRIANISM
ADEEIINOORRTT	DETERIORATION
ADEEIINOPRTXY	EXPEDITIONARY
ADEEILNNRTTVY	INADVERTENTLY
ADEEIMNORSTTV	DEMONSTRATIVE
ADEEINNOPQRTU	EQUIPONDERANT
ADEEINOPRRSTT	PREDESTINATOR
ADEELNNSSSSTU	DAUNTLESSNESS
ADEENPPRRRSTU	UNDERSTRAPPER
ADEFHILNOORSS	FOOLHARDINESS
ADEFILLSSTTUY	DISTASTEFULLY
ADEGGIILNNRSS	NIGGARDLINESS
ADEGHLMNORRTY	GRANDMOTHERLY
ADEGILLNOSTUU	SOLIDUNGULATE
ADEGILMOORSTT	DERMATOLOGIST
ADEGILNNOQRTU	GRANDILOQUENT
ADEGOOOPRSSTU	GASTEROPODOUS
ADEHIMOOPRRST	MODERATORSHIP
ADEIIIMNNOSST	DISSEMINATION
ADEIIIMNOSSTT	DISESTIMATION
ADEIILNQSTTUY	EQUIDISTANTLY
ADEIIMNNOOPRT	PREDOMINATION
ADEIIMNNOORST	MODERNISATION
ADEIIMNNOPSSU	UNIMPASSIONED
ADEIINNOOPRRT	PREORDINATION
ADEILMNNOPRTY	PREDOMINANTLY
ADEIMNNOORSTT	DEMONSTRATION
ADEIMNNOPRSTU	SUPERDOMINANT
ADEINOSSSSSUU	ASSIDUOUSNESS
ADELNORSTUUVY	ADVENTUROUSLY
ADENNORSTUUUV	UNADVENTUROUS
ADENOOPRRRSTU	PROTERANDROUS
ADFGIINORSTU	DISFIGURATION
ADGHHILLNOPTY	DIPHTHONGALLY
ADGIIINNOPPST	DISAPPOINTING
ADHIMNOPRSSSW	SWORDSMANSHIP
ADIIIILMNOSST	DISSIMILATION
ADIIIILMRSSTY	DISSIMILARITY
ADIIILMNOSSTU	DISSIMULATION
ADIIILMNRSSTU	INDUSTRIALISM
ADIIILNRSSTTU	INDUSTRIALIST
ADIILNOPSTTUU	PLATITUDINOUS
AEEEEMNPRSSTT	TEMPERATENESS
AEEEFGHHIRTTW	FEATHERWEIGHT
AEEEFGIIRRRTV	REFRIGERATIVE
AEEEFINQRTTUV	FREQUENTATIVE
AEEEGIKLLMNNT	GENTLEMANLIKE
AEEEGINORRRTT	REINTERROGATE
AEEEHLMNSSSSS	SHAMELESSNESS
AEEEHLNPSSSSS	SHAPELESSNESS
AEEEHLNRSSSST	HEARTLESSNESS
AEEEEILLNRRTVY	REVERENTIALLY
AEEEILMNPRTY	INTEMPERATELY
AEEEIMNNNRTTT	ENTERTAINMENT
AEEEIMNNRSTTT	REINSTATEMENT
AEEEIMNOSSSW	WEARISOMENESS
AEEEINNPSSSVX	EXPANSIVENESS
AEEEINNSSTTTV	ATTENTIVENESS
AEEEINPRSSSVV	PERVASIVENESS
AEEEINRSSSSTV	ASSERTIVENESS
AEEEELNSSSSSTT	TASTELESSNESS
AEEEMMNOPRTTU	PNEUMATOMETER
AEEEMNORSTTTV	OVERSTATEMENT
AEEEMNPRRSSTU	PREMATURENESS
AEEFGIINORRRT	REFRIGERATION
AEEFGINORRSTU	ARGENTIFEROUS
AEEFGIORRRRTY	REFRIGERATORY
AEEFHHLLNSSTU	HEALTHFULNESS
AEEFIILLNNRTY	INFERENTIALLY
AEEFILLMORSTU	METALLIFEROUS
AEEFINOPRSTTU	SUPERFETATION
AEEFIOOPRRSST	PROFESSORIATE
AEEFLLNSSSSTU	FAULTLESSNESS
AEEFLMNRSSSTU	MASTERFULNESS
AEEFLNPRRSSUY	PRAYERFULNESS
AEEGGINNOORSS	ORGANOGENESIS
AEEGHILNNRTTY	THREATENINGLY
AEEGIIINSTTVV	INVESTIGATIVE
AEEGIILMNORSS	GENERALISSIMO
AEEGIIMNNORTT	REGIMENTATION
AEEGIINNOPRRT	PEREGRINATION
AEEGIINORRTTV	INTERROGATIVE
AEEGILLNRSTVY	EVERLASTINGLY
AEEGILNNPRTTY	PENETRATINGLY
AEEGIMNNRTTUY	INTEGUMENTARY
AEEGINNOSSUUX	EXSANGUINEOUS
AEEGIORRRSTTV	TERGIVERSATOR
AEEHILMMNNOPS	PHENOMENALISM

AEEHIMNQSSSSU	SQUEAMISHNESS
AEEHIMOPPRRTY	HYPERMETROPIA
AEEHLMNOOSSST	LOATHSOMENESS
AEEIILLNNPTTY	PENITENTIALLY
AEEIILNNORRTT	INTERRELATION
AEEIILNNPSSTV	PLAINTIVENESS
AEEIILNNTTTVY	INATTENTIVELY
AEEIILNOPRRTT	INTERPETIOLAR
AEEIILORRRTTX	EXTERRITORIAL
AEEIIMMNNORSST	MESMERISATION
AEEIIMNNORTTX	EXTERMINATION
AEEIIMNPSSSSV	IMPASSIVENESS
AEEIIMNQRSSTU	EQUESTRIANISM
AEEIINNOORRTT	REORIENTATION
AEEIINNOQRSTU	QUESTIONNAIRE
AEEIILLMNNSTTY	SENTIMENTALLY
AEEIILLNNOPTXY	EXPONENTIALLY
AEEIILNRRSTTY	INTERSTELLARY
AEEIILPRSTUVY	SUPERLATIVELY
AEEIILRRRSTTY	TERRESTRIALLY
AEEILMNNNORTV	ENVIRONMENTAL
AEEILMOPRRTXY	EXTEMPORARILY
AEEILOPRSSTUY	ERYSIPELATOUS
AEEIMMNNORSST	MOMENTARINESS
AEEIMNNOPPRTT	REAPPOINTMENT
AEEIMNORRSTTV	REMONSTRATIVE
AEEIMNORRTTXY	EXTERMINATORY
AEEINNNRSSSTT	TRANSIENTNESS
AEEINOPRSTTTZ	PROTESTANTIZE
AEEINOQRSSTTU	SEQUESTRATION
AEEINOSSSTUVX	VEXATIOUSNESS
AEELMNPPRSTUY	SUPPLEMENTARY
AEFGHINNNPRTY	PENNY-FARTHING
AEFGIINOPRRTU	PREFIGURATION
AEFIIILMNNST	INFINITESIMAL
AEFIIILNORTTZ	FERTILIZATION
AEFIIILLNNTUY	INFLUENTIALLY
AEFIILMNORSUU	ALUMINIFEROUS
AEFIILNOOPRRT	PROLIFERATION
AEFIIMNORSSTU	STAMINIFEROUS
AEFIINRRSTTTY	INTERSTRATIFY
AEFLNNORTTUUY	UNFORTUNATELY
AEGGHLOOPRRSS	GLOSSOGRAPHER
AEGGIINORRTTU	REGURGITATION
AEGGINNNOORSS	NON-AGGRESSION
AEGHHILMNOSTU	LIGHTHOUSEMAN
AEGHIIPRRRSST	REGISTRARSHIP
AEGHILOOPRSST	PHRASEOLOGIST
AEGHINOPRSSTT	STENOGRAPHIST
AEGHMNOOOPSTU	ENTOMOPHAGOUS
AEGIIIIMNNTUV	UNIMAGINITIVE
AEGIIIMNORSTT	EMIGRATIONIST
AEGIIMNNOSTTV	INVESTIGATION
AEGIINNOORRTT	INTERROGATION
AEGIKLLNORRST	ROLLER-SKATING
AEGILNOOPRRSS	PROGRESSIONAL
AEGIMNOOPRSSU	ANGIOSPERMOUS
AEGIMOOOPPRST	APOGEOTROPISM
AEGINNORRSSST	TRANSGRESSION
AEGINOORRRTTY	INTERROGATORY
AEHHIMNOPRSTT	THEANTHROPISM
AEHHIMOOOPSTT	HOMOEOPATHIST
AEHHIOPPRSTYY	PHYSIOTHERAPY
AEHHNORSSTTUY	HYSTERANTHOUS
AEHILMOOSTUXY	HOMOSEXUALITY
AEHIMMOOPRSST	METAMORPHOSIS
AEHMNOOPRRTTY	ANTHROPOMETRY
AEIIILLMNORSS	MILLIONAIRESS
AEIIILLMNPRRY	PRELIMINARILY
AEIIILLMNRSTY	MINISTERIALLY
AEIIILNORSSTT	STERILISATION
AEIIINNORSSSV	VISIONARINESS
AEIIINNOSSSTT	SENSITISATION
AEIIILLNNNOTTY	INTENTIONALLY
AEIIILLNNORTVY	INVENTORIALLY
AEIIILLNOQRTUV	VENTRILOQUIAL
AEIIILLNQRRTUZ	TRANQUILLIZER
AEIIILLORRRTTY	TERRITORIALLY
AEIIILMNNOOSTZ	SOLEMNIZATION
AEIIILMNOPRSTY	IMPERSONALITY
AEIIILNNNNOTTU	UNINTENTIONAL
AEIIILNNOOPRTT	INTERPOLATION
AEIIILNOOPPRST	PREPOSITIONAL
AEIIILNOPRTUVZ	PULVERIZATION
AEIIILOOPPRRRT	PROPRIETORIAL
AEIIMNNOOPRST	IMPERSONATION
AEIIMNOOPRTTZ	TEMPORIZATION
AEIIMNOSSSTTY	SYSTEMISATION
AEIINOOPPRRTX	EXPROPRIATION
AEIINOORRRSTT	TERRORISATION
AEIINOPRSSTTV	TRANSPOSITIVE
AEIINORRSSSTT	TRANSISTORISE
AEIKKLMNNORUW	UNWORKMANLIKE
AEILLMMMNOOST	MONOMETALLISM
AEILLMMNOOSTT	MONOMETALLIST
AEILMNOPRTTUY	IMPORTUNATELY
AEILNNORSSTUV	VOLUNTARINESS
AEILNOOPSTTUX	EXPOSTULATION
AEILNOORRTUVY	REVOLUTIONARY
AEIMNNOOPPRTT	APPORTIONMENT
AEIMNNOORRSTT	REMONSTRATION
AEIMNOPRSSTTT	PROTESTANTISM
AEINNORSSSUUV	UNSAVOURINESS
AEINOOOPPRRTT	PROPORTIONATE
AEINOOPRSSSSY	POSSESSIONARY
AELNNOOPSSTUY	SPONTANEOUSLY
AELOOPRSTTUXY	EXPOSTULATORY
AEMMNOOORSTTU	MONOTREMATOUS
AEMNOORRRSTTY	REMONSTRATORY
AFFGIIMNOSTUU	SUFFUMIGATION
AFIIILNOOSSTZ	FOSSILIZATION
AGGHIILLNNSUY	LANGUISHINGLY
AGGIILNNOPPRR	GRAPPLING-IRON
AGHHINOOPPRST	PHONOGRAPHIST
AGHHLLMOOOPTY	OPHTHALMOLOGY
AGHHLLOOPPSUY	PHYLLOPHAGOUS
AGHHNOOORSTTU	ORTHOGNATHOUS
AGHIIILNPRSTT	HAIRSPLITTING
AGHIILNNOSSTY	ASTONISHINGLY
AGIIILNNNSTUY	INSINUATINGLY
AGIILNNOPRTYZ	PATRONIZINGLY
AGIILOORSSSTY	ASSYRIOLOGIST

AGIIMNOORRSUV	GRAMINIVOROUS
AGILMOORRSTTY	MARTYROLOGIST
AHIIILNOOPRRT	HORRIPILATION
AHIIILNOPSTTY	INHOSPITALITY
AHIIILNOPSTYZ	SYPHILIZATION
AHIILNOORTTYZ	HORIZONTALITY
AHIIMNOPRSSTT	MISANTHROPIST
AHIMNOPPRSSST	SPORTSMANSHIP
AIIIILNNOQSTU	INQUISITIONAL
AIIIILNNOQRSTU	INQUISITORIAL
AIIILLMNPSTUY	PUSILLANIMITY
AIIILNNOSTTTU	INSTITUTIONAL
AIIIMNOOPPRRT	IMPROPRIATION
AIIIMNOOPRSTV	IMPROVISATION
AIIJNOOPSTTUX	JUXTAPOSITION
AIILLMNOPSSUU	PUSILLANIMOUS
AIILLNNORTUVY	INVOLUNTARILY
AIILLNOOPRSVY	PROVISIONALLY
AIILNOOOPPRST	PROPOSITIONAL
AIILNOOPPSSTU	SUPPOSITIONAL
AIIMOOPRRSTVY	IMPROVISATORY
AIINNOOPRSSTT	TRANSPOSITION
AIIOOOPRSUVVV	OVOVIVIPAROUS
BBCEHMOORRSTU	BUTCHER'S-BROOM
BBCEIILMNOSTU	INCOMBUSTIBLE
BBEEEEILLRSTT	BLISTER-BEETLE
BCCEGIILNNOOS	INCOGNOSCIBLE
BCCEHIILLNRTU	CLINCHER-BUILT
BCCEIIILNNNOV	INCONVINCIBLE
BCDDGILLNOORU	BLOOD-CURDLING
BCDEEGINORRSS	CROSS-BREEDING
BCDEEIILNNRSU	UNDISCERNIBLE
BCDEELOORRSSU	DOUBLE-CROSSER
BCDEIIIILNRTY	INCREDIBILITY
BCEEEEFFILRSV	EFFERVESCIBLE
BCEEEGILLNORT	CO-BELLIGERENT
BCEEEIILMPPRT	IMPERCEPTIBLE
BCEEEIJNOSSTV	OBJECTIVENESS
BCEEIILNNORTV	INCONVERTIBLE
BCEEIILNPSSTU	INSUSCEPTIBLE
BCEEIILPPRRST	PRESCRIPTIBLE
BCEEILNPSSTUU	UNSUSCEPTIBLE
BCEFFGIIKNOOO	BOOKING-OFFICE
BCEIILNOPRRTU	INCORRUPTIBLE
BCEILORSTTUVY	OBSTRUCTIVELY
BCGIIIILORRTY	CORRIGIBILITY
BCIIIIILNNTVY	INVINCIBILITY
BCIILNOPRRTUY	INCORRUPTIBLY
BDDEEGLNOOTUU	DOUBLE-TONGUED
BDDEEIILNOSTY	DISOBEDIENTLY
BDDEILNRSTUUY	UNDISTURBEDLY
BDEEEIMMMNRST	DISMEMBERMENT
BDEEFIIILNSTY	DEFENSIBILITY
BDEEGIILMNOST	DISOBLIGEMENT
BDEELNNOSSSSU	BOUNDLESSNESS
BDEGHHINOOORU	NEIGHBOURHOOD
BDEGIIIILSTTY	DIGESTIBILITY
BDFFIIIILSTUY	DIFFUSIBILITY
BDGGIIIILLNOSY	DISOBLIGINGLY
BDIIILLOSSTUY	DISSOLUBILITY
BEEEEHILNPRRS	REPREHENSIBLE
BEEEELLLRSSTT	BELLES-LETTRES
BEEEGIILLLNSS	ILLEGIBLENESS
BEEEHILLMMNST	EMBELLISHMENT
BEEEHILNPRRSY	REPREHENSIBLY
BEEEIILNPRSSX	INEXPRESSIBLE
BEEEIILPRRRSS	IRREPRESSIBLE
BEEEILNPRSSSU	SUPERSENSIBLE
BEEEIMMNRRSTU	REIMBURSEMENT
BEEFGINRRSTTU	BUTTER-FINGERS
BEEFIIILLRTXY	REFLEXIBILITY
BEEFILLMORSUU	UMBELLIFEROUS
BEEGGIILNNNSS	BEGINNINGLESS
BEEHILNORRSST	BROTHERLINESS
BEEHIPPRRSSTY	PRESBYTERSHIP
BEEIIILNNSSSV	INVISIBLENESS
BEEIIILNSTTXY	EXTENSIBILITY
BEEIIILRRSTVY	REVERSIBILITY
BEEIILMNPRSSU	UNIMPRESSIBLE
BEEIILNOPRRSS	IRRESPONSIBLE
BEEIILNPRSSXY	INEXPRESSIBLY
BEEIILPRRRSSY	IRREPRESSIBLY
BEEINORSSSTUV	OBTRUSIVENESS
BEELLMOORSTUY	TROUBLESOMELY
BEFFGINNORRTU	BURNT-OFFERING
BEFIIIILLNTXY	INFLEXIBILITY
BEFIIILMRSSTU	FILIBUSTERISM
BEFILNNOSSTUU	BOUNTIFULNESS
BEGHILNNORUUY	UNNEIGHBOURLY
BEGIIIIILLNTY	INELIGIBILITY
BEHIIIIMNOSTX	EXHIBITIONISM
BEHIIIINOSTTX	EXHIBITIONIST
BEIIILMRSSTY	REMISSIBILITY
BEIIIILNNSSTY	INSENSIBILITY
BEIIIILRSSTTY	RESISTIBILITY
BEIIILNOSSTTY	OSTENSIBILITY
BEIILNOOSSSUV	OBLIVIOUSNESS
BEIILNOPRRSSY	IRRESPONSIBLY
BEILNORSTUUVY	UNOBTRUSIVELY
BEIMNOPSSSTUU	BUMPTIOUSNESS
BEINNOOOSSSUX	OBNOXIOUSNESS
BGIIMNNORRRRU	BURNING-MIRROR
BIIILMOPPSSTY	IMPOSSIBILITY
BILOOOPPRRSUY	OPPROBRIOUSLY
CCCCEEINNOPSU	CONCUPISCENCE
CCCDEEEENRRSU	RECRUDESCENCE
CCCDEEEENRRSUY	RECRUDESCENCY
CCCDIIMNORTUU	CIRCUMDUCTION
CCCEEEFIMNRRU	CIRCUMFERENCE
CCCEEFILMNRUU	CIRCUMFLUENCE
CCCEEHHIRRSUV	CHURCH-SERVICE
CCCEILMPRSTUY	CIRCUMSPECTLY
CCCEIOOPPRSST	SPECTROSCOPIC
CCDDEEGINNNOS	CONDESCENDING
CCDEEEEEFNRSV	DEFERVESCENCE
CCDEEEEFNRSVY	DEFERVESCENCY
CCDEEEEILNQSU	DELIQUESCENCE
CCDEEEINNOSST	CONCEITEDNESS
CCDEEELLNOSST	COLLECTEDNESS
CCDEEINNNOOSS	CONDESCENSION
CCDEIINNNOOST	DISCONNECTION
CCDEIMNOORSTU	SEMICONDUCTOR

CCEEEEEFFNRSV	EFFERVESCENCE
CCEEEEFFLNORS	EFFLORESCENCE
CCEEEFILNNORS	INFLORESCENCE
CCEEEIINNNNOV	INCONVENIENCE
CCEEEIILMNNORT	RECONCILEMENT
CCEEEILMORRTT	ELECTROMETRIC
CCEEEINNNOQSU	INCONSEQUENCE
CCEEFIIINPRST	PRESCIENTIFIC
CCEEFINNOORTY	CONFECTIONERY
CCEEHILOOPRTT	PHOTOELECTRIC
CCEEHIMNNORRY	CHIMNEY-CORNER
CCEEHIMOSSTYZ	SCHIZOMYCETES
CCEEIIMNRTUVV	CIRCUMVENTIVE
CCEEIINNNOSST	INCONSISTENCE
CCEEILNOORTTU	ELECTROCUTION
CCEEILNOSTUVY	CONSECUTIVELY
CCEEINNOOPPRT	PRECONCEPTION
CCEEINNORRSST	INCORRECTNESS
CCEEINOOPRRUW	OWNER-OCCUPIER
CCEENNOOOVVXX	CONVEXO-CONVEX
CCEFFIIINNSUY	INSUFFICIENCY
CCEIIMNNOOPST	MISCONCEPTION
CCEIIMNNORTUV	CIRCUMVENTION
CCEIINNNOSSTY	INCONSISTENCY
CCEIINNOOSSTU	CONSCIENTIOUS
CCEIINOSSSSTU	SUCCESSIONIST
CCEIJLNNOTUVY	CONJUNCTIVELY
CCEINNOOSSSSU	CONSCIOUSNESS
CCIINNOOPSSUU	INCONSPICUOUS
CCILNOOPSSUUY	CONSPICUOUSLY
CDDEEEEENNPRTU	UNPRECEDENTED
CDDEIIILNNPSU	UNDISCIPLINED
CDDEIINNNOOTU	UNCONDITIONED
CDEEEEFINSSTV	DEFECTIVENESS
CDEEEEFLLNSSY	DEFENCELESSLY
CDEEEEIINNPRX	INEXPERIENCED
CDEEEEINPSSTV	DECEPTIVENESS
CDEEEEELLPRSTW	WELL-RESPECTED
CDEEEEFILNSSTU	DECEITFULNESS
CDEEEIINPRSTV	VICE-PRESIDENT
CDEEEMNNOPRSU	UNRECOMPENSED
CDEEEENNOSSTT	CONTENTEDNESS
CDEEFFILNNOST	SELF-CONFIDENT
CDEEFILPRSSTU	DISRESPECTFUL
CDEEFINNOORTV	OVER-CONFIDENT
CDEEIIIMNRSTT	DETERMINISTIC
CDEEIILNOSSSU	DELICIOUSNESS
CDEEIILPRSTVY	DESCRIPTIVELY
CDEEIJNPRRSUU	JURISPRUDENCE
CDEEILOORRSUV	VERSICOLOURED
CDEEILRSTTUVY	DESTRUCTIVELY
CDEEIMNOOPRSS	DECOMPRESSION
CDEELNORSSSUU	CREDULOUSNESS
CDEENNOOPRRST	CORRESPONDENT
CDEFGIINNNOSS	CONFIDINGNESS
CDEGHILNNORTU	UNDERCLOTHING
CDEGINNOOPRRS	CORRESPONDING
CDEHIIKNORSTY	HYDROKINETICS
CDEHIIMNOPRRU	PERICHONDRIUM
CDEHKNRRSTTUU	THUNDER-STRUCK
CDEIIIINNSTTV	INDISTINCTIVE
CDEIIILNSTTVY	DISTINCTIVELY
CDEIIJLNSTUVY	DISJUNCTIVELY
CDEIIJNOSSSUU	JUDICIOUSNESS
CDEIIMNOOOPST	DECOMPOSITION
CDEILLMOORTUU	MULTICOLOURED
CDEILLNORSUUY	INCREDULOUSLY
CDEILMNOOPSUY	COMPENDIOUSLY
CDEILNORSSSUU	LUDICROUSNESS
CDELMNNOOOOTY	MONOCOTYLEDON
CDGLNNOOOORRTU	GROUND-CONTROL
CDHILMOOOSTUY	DICHOTOMOUSLY
CDIIIJLNOSUUY	INJUDICIOUSLY
CDIIINNOSTTUY	DISCONTINUITY
CDIINNOOSSTUU	DISCONTINUOUS
CEEEEFFINSSTV	EFFECTIVENESS
CEEEEFFPPRRRTT	PRETERPERFECT
CEEEEIMNNPRSU	SUPEREMINENCE
CEEEEINPRSSTV	RECEPTIVENESS
CEEEEINRSSSTV	SECRETIVENESS
CEEEEJNNRSTUV	REJUVENESCENT
CEEEFFIILNTVY	INEFFECTIVELY
CEEEFIMNNORRT	REINFORCEMENT
CEEEFIMNPRSST	IMPERFECTNESS
CEEEFINORRTTU	COUNTERFEITER
CEEEGHIKNNOTU	TONGUE-IN-CHEEK
CEEEGIILLNNRT	INTELLIGENCER
CEEEHIMNOPRSV	COMPREHENSIVE
CEEEHLNORSSSU	LECHEROUSNESS
CEEEILMNPRSTU	MULTIPRESENCE
CEEEILMNRSSSS	MERCILESSNESS
CEEEILMOORTTV	ELECTROMOTIVE
CEEEILNSSSUVX	EXCLUSIVENESS
CEEEILPPRSTVY	PERSPECTIVELY
CEEEIOPRRSTTV	RETROSPECTIVE
CEEFFIIILNNTY	INEFFICIENTLY
CEEFIIKLNORSU	NICKELIFEROUS
CEEFIIMNOPRST	PERFECTIONISM
CEEFIINOPRSTT	PERFECTIONIST
CEEFINOORSSSU	FEROCIOUSNESS
CEEGHINORTTUW	COUNTERWEIGHT
CEEGILLNORSSV	LEVEL-CROSSING
CEEHHIMOOPRRT	HETEROMORPHIC
CEEHHNORSSTTU	HORSE-CHESTNUT
CEEHIIKLNRSSS	LICKERISHNESS
CEEHIMNNOOPRS	COMPREHENSION
CEEHINNOPSSSY	SYNECPHONESIS
CEEHINOPPRRST	PRECENTORSHIP
CEEHIOOPRRSTU	CHEIROPTEROUS
CEEHLOOPRRSTU	ELECTROPHORUS
CEEIIMMMPRST	METEMPIRICISM
CEEIILRRSTTVY	RESTRICTIVELY
CEEIINOPRSTTV	INTROSPECTIVE
CEEILMNNOOQSU	SOMNILOQUENCE
CEEILMNNOPTTY	INCOMPETENTLY
CEEILMNOORSUY	CEREMONIOUSLY
CEEILNOSSSTUY	NECESSITOUSLY
CEEILOPPRSTVY	PROSPECTIVELY
CEEILPQRSTUUY	PICTURESQUELY
CEEINOOPRRSSV	CORRESPONSIVE
CEEINOOPRRSTT	RETROSPECTION
CEEINOORRSSSV	CORROSIVENESS

CEEKNOORRSTTU	COUNTER-STROKE	DDEEGGHHINRTUW	HUNDREDWEIGHT
CEELPQRSSTUUU	SCULPTURESQUE	DDEGHIIINNSSTU	DISTINGUISHED
CEELRRSSSTTUU	STRUCTURELESS	DDEIIILLMSSTU	DISSIMILITUDE
CEEMNNNOOPRTU	PRONOUNCEMENT	DDEIIILLNOSSU	DISILLUSIONED
CEENOORSSSTUU	COURTEOUSNESS	DEEEEELMNOPRTV	REDEVELOPMENT
CEFFIINOOSSSU	OFFICIOUSNESS	DEEEENNPRRSTU	UNREPRESENTED
CEFGHIIKNNOPP	CHOPPING-KNIFE	DEEEFFIINQRTU	EQUIDIFFERENT
CEFHINOOPRSSS	CONFESSORSHIP	DEEEFGKLNOORW	FOREKNOWLEDGE
CEFILNOPRRTUY	PERFUNCTORILY	DEEEFIMNNOORT	FOREMENTIONED
CEGHIIILLNNPS	SPINE-CHILLING	DEEEGHILNNNTU	UNENLIGHTENED
CEGIIMNOORRTT	TRIGONOMETRIC	DEEEIILNNPTXY	INEXPEDIENTLY
CEHHIIINNORTT	ORNITHICHNITE	DEEEELLNNPRSTY	RESPLENDENTLY
CEHHIIMOOPRRT	THERIOMORPHIC	DEEEENORSSSTUX	DEXTEROUSNESS
CEHIILMOSSUVY	MISCHIEVOUSLY	DEEFFIILNNRTY	INDIFFERENTLY
CEHIINOPPRSST	INSPECTORSHIP	DEEFFIINSSSUV	DIFFUSIVENESS
CEHILNOOSTTTT	COTTON-THISTLE	DEEFGIIMNRSTU	DISFIGUREMENT
CEHILNOPSTTYY	POLYSYNTHETIC	DEEFGILLNNSTU	SELF-INDULGENT
CEHIOOPPRRSTT	PROTECTORSHIP	DEEFLNNORSSUW	WONDERFULNESS
CEHIOOPSSSTTT	STETHOSCOPIST	DEEGHILLNOSUW	DWELLING-HOUSE
CEHMNOORRTTUY	MOTHER-COUNTRY	DEEHHOPPRSTTU	PHOSPHURETTED
CEIIILNNSTTVY	INSTINCTIVELY	DEEHIIINPPRSST	PRESIDENTSHIP
CEIIIMNNOPSTUY	IMPECUNIOSITY	DEEIILNORSSSU	DELIRIOUSNESS
CEIIJNOOPRSTT	PROJECTIONIST	DEEIILOPSTUXY	EXPEDITIOUSLY
CEIILLLNOOSTV	VIOLONCELLIST	DEEIIMNNRTTTU	UNINTERMITTED
CEIILNNNNOTTY	INCONTINENTLY	DEEIINOSSSSTU	SEDITIOUSNESS
CEIILNNOORTTU	INTERLOCUTION	DEEILMNOOSSSU	MELODIOUSNESS
CEIILNRSTTUVY	INSTRUCTIVELY	DEEILNORSSSTU	DESULTORINESS
CEIILOPPRSTUY	PRECIPITOUSLY	DEEILNOSSSSTU	DISSOLUTENESS
CEIIMNOOPRSTT	PROTECTIONISM	DEEILNPRRTTUY	INTERRUPTEDLY
CEIINNNOOSTTV	CONVENTIONIST	DEEILOOPPRSTU	LEPIDOPTEROUS
CEIINNNOOPRSTT	INTROSPECTION	DEEINNPRRTTUU	UNINTERRUPTED
CEIINNRSTTUUV	UNINSTRUCTIVE	DEELNNOPSSSUU	PENDULOUSNESS
CEIINOOPRSTTT	PROTECTIONIST	DEENNOOPRSSSU	PONDEROUSNESS
CEIINOORSSTUV	INSECTIVOROUS	DEFFGIIKNNORR	DRINK-OFFERING
CEILMNOPSTUVY	CONSUMPTIVELY	DEFILLRSSSTUY	DISTRESSFULLY
CEILNNOOSTTUY	CONTENTIOUSLY	DEFILMNNNSSUU	UNMINDFULNESS
CEILNOOORRTTUY	INTERLOCUTORY	DEFILOOORRSUY	ODORIFEROUSLY
CEILOPPRSSUUY	PERSPICUOUSLY	DEGIILNRSSSTY	DISTRESSINGLY
CEIMNNOOORTTU	COUNTER-MOTION	DEIIINNOSSSSU	INSIDIOUSNESS
CEINNNOOPRSTT	COTTON-SPINNER	DEIIINNOSSSUV	INVIDIOUSNESS
CEINNOOOPRSTU	COUNTER-POISON	DEIILMNOPRTVY	IMPROVIDENTLY
CEINOOQRSSSTU	CROSS-QUESTION	DEIINOOPSSSSS	DISPOSSESSION
CEINOORRSTTTV	CONTROVERTIST	DEILLNNORSSUW	UNWORLDLINESS
CFGIMNNNNOOOR	NONCONFORMING	DFGGHIILLNOOT	FLOODLIGHTING
CFIMNNNOOOORST	NONCONFORMIST	DFILLRSSTTUUY	DISTRUSTFULLY
CFIMNNNOOOORTY	NONCONFORMITY	DGLMNOOOOSSTU	ODONTOGLOSSUM
CGHHIILLOOSTTY	ICHTHYOLOGIST	DIIIINNOOPSST	INDISPOSITION
CGIIILMNOORST	CRIMINOLOGIST	DIILMNOSTTUUU	MULTITUDINOUS
CGILNNOORSUUY	INCONGRUOUSLY	DIILNORSSTUUY	INDUSTRIOUSLY
CHHIILNOOPPSU	UNPHILOSOPHIC	DIINOOOPPRRST	DISPROPORTION
CHILNOOPPRSSU	PROCONSULSHIP	EEEEGHINORSST	HETEROGENESIS
CHLNNOORSSUYY	SYNCHRONOUSLY	EEEEGHINORTTY	HETEROGENEITY
CIILLNOPSTUUY	PUNCTILIOUSLY	EEEEGHNOORSTU	HETEROGENEOUS
CIILMMOOOPSST	COSMOPOLITISM	EEEEHKLLRRSTT	HELTER-SKELTER
CIINNOOORSTTT	CONTORTIONIST	EEEEIINNPSSSVX	EXPENSIVENESS
CIINOOPRRSTTU	CORRUPTIONIST	EEEEINNRSSTTV	RETENTIVENESS
CILMOOPRSSUUY	PROMISCUOUSLY	EEEEINNSSSTVX	EXTENSIVENESS
DDDEEILNNOOPR	LEPIDODENDRON	EEEELNNSSSSSS	SENSELESSNESS
DDEEEIINRSSTT	DISINTERESTED	EEEFFINNOSSSV	OFFENSIVENESS
DDEEEILNNNPTY	INDEPENDENTLY	EEEFGIMNPRRTU	PREFIGUREMENT
DDEEFIIINRSUV	UNDIVERSIFIED	EEEFLLNORRTTU	FORTUNE-TELLER

EEEGHILMNNNTT	ENLIGHTENMENT
EEEGILNPRRSVY	PERSEVERINGLY
EEEGIORRRSSTV	RETROGRESSIVE
EEEGNOQRSSSTU	GROTESQUENESS
EEEHHIORRRSTVW	WHITHERSOEVER
EEEHILMNNPRST	REPLENISHMENT
EEEHILMOPRRTY	PYRHELIOMETER
EEEHLMNOOSSSW	WHOLESOMENESS
EEEHOOPRRSTTU	HETEROPTEROUS
EEEIILNNPSVXY	INEXPENSIVELY
EEEIIMNPRSTTX	EXPERIMENTIST
EEEIINNNSSSTV	INTENSIVENESS
EEEIINNNSSTVV	INVENTIVENESS
EEEIINNSSSSTV	SENSITIVENESS
EEEIINQSSSTUX	EXQUISITENESS
EEEILNNNPSSSS	PENNILESSNESS
EEEILNNOSSSSS	NOISELESSNESS
EEEILNPRSSSUV	REPULSIVENESS
EEEIMMOPRSSTY	SYMPIESOMETER
EEELLMORRSSSY	REMORSELESSLY
EEELMMNOORTUV	VOLUMENOMETER
EEELMNOSTTTTU	OUTSETTLEMENT
EEELNNOPSSSTU	PLENTEOUSNESS
EEELNOPRSSSSW	POWERLESSNESS
EEFFGLNORSSTU	FORGETFULNESS
EEFFIILNNOSVY	INOFFENSIVELY
EEFILLLLMNTUY	MELLIFLUENTLY
EEFILLNNPSSTU	PLENTIFULNESS
EEFILOPRSSTUY	PESTIFEROUSLY
EEGGHINNNRSTT	STRENGTHENING
EEGGINOORSSUU	EGREGIOUSNOUS
EEGHILMNOSSST	LIGHTSOMENESS
EEGHILNSSSSST	SIGHTLESSNESS
EEGHILOOPRSTT	HERPETOLOGIST
EEGHINORSSSTU	RIGHTEOUSNESS
EEGIILLLNNTTY	INTELLIGENTLY
EEGIILNNRSTTY	INTERESTINGLY
EEGIILNORSSSU	RELIGIOUSNESS
EEGIIMNOPRRTU	PRIMOGENITURE
EEGIINNNOPRSSU	INGENIOUSNESS
EEGIINNNRSTTU	UNINTERESTING
EEGILLNSSSSTU	GUILTLESSNESS
EEGILMOOORSTT	METEOROLOGIST
EEGILOPRRSSVY	PROGRESSIVELY
EEGIMMNNORSTV	MISGOVERNMENT
EEGINOORRRSST	RETROGRESSION
EEGINOPPRSSSS	PREPOSSESSING
EEGINORSTTTUW	TONGUE-TWISTER
EEHHIILLLMNPS	PHILHELLENISM
EEHILLNOSSSWY	YELLOWISHNESS
EEHLNORSSSSTW	WORTHLESSNESS
EEHMNOOPRSTUY	HYMENOPTEROUS
EEIIIMNPRSSTV	PRIMITIVENESS
EEIILMNNPRTTY	IMPERTINENTLY
EEIILNOORSTUV	REVOLUTIONISE
EEIILNOQRTUVZ	VENTRILOQUIZE
EEIIMNOPRRSST	PRETERMISSION
EEIIMNOPRSSSU	IMPERIOUSNESS
EEIINNOPRRSST	INTERSPERSION
EEIINNRSSSTUV	INTRUSIVENESS
EEILMPPRSTUVY	PRESUMPTIVELY
EEILNNOPSSSST	POINTLESSNESS
EEILNNOSSTTUY	SENTENTIOUSLY
EEILNOPRSTTUY	PRETENTIOUSLY
EEIMNOPSSSTUU	IMPETUOUSNESS
EEINNOPRSSSUU	PENURIOUSNESS
EEINOOPPRSSSS	PREPOSSESSION
EELMNORSSSTUU	TREMULOUSNESS
EELMOPSSTTUUY	TEMPESTUOUSLY
EELNOQRSSSUUU	QUERULOUSNESS
EEMMNNOOSSSTU	MOMENTOUSNESS
EENNOOPPRSSTU	OPPORTUNENESS
EFFGGILNNORSU	LONG-SUFFERING
EFFGHILNRSSTU	FRIGHTFULNESS
EFFIILOORSSSU	FOSSILIFEROUS
EFGILLNOORVWY	OVERFLOWINGLY
EFHIINNRSSTTU	UNTHRIFTINESS
EFIILLNOOPRSU	POLLINIFEROUS
EFIKLLNNSSSUU	UNSKILFULNESS
EFILLLLMOSUUY	MELLIFLUOUSLY
EFILNOOORSSTU	STOLONIFEROUS
EFILNOORSSSUV	FRIVOLOUSNESS
EFLLOPRSSUUUY	SUPERFLUOUSLY
EFLNOORRSSSUW	SORROWFULNESS
EGHHIILOPRSTY	HIEROGLYPHIST
EGHHILLMNOOTY	HELMINTHOLOGY
EGHHLLOSSTTUY	THOUGHTLESSLY
EGHIILNNSSSTU	UNSIGHTLINESS
EGHIILNPRSSST	SPRIGHTLINESS
EGHIILNORSTUY	UNRIGHTEOUSLY
EGIIILLORRSUY	IRRELIGIOUSLY
EGIIILNOSSSTU	LITIGIOUSNESS
EGIILLNNNSSUW	UNWILLINGNESS
EGMMNOOPRSSUY	GYMNOSPERMOUS
EGNOOOPRRSTUY	PROTEROGYNOUS
EHHHIIOOPPPSTY	HYPOPHOSPHITE
EHHIILOOPPRSZ	PHILOSOPHIZER
EHILMNOOOPSTU	ENTOMOPHILOUS
EHLLOPRSSUUUY	SULPHUREOUSLY
EIIIILNQSTUVY	INQUISITIVELY
EIIIMMNOPRSSS	IMPRESSIONISM
EIIIMNOPRSSST	IMPRESSIONIST
EIIINNOOPRSTT	INTERPOSITION
EIILMNOORSTUV	REVOLUTIONISM
EIILMNOQRSTUV	VENTRILOQUISM
EIILMOORRSTUY	MERITORIOUSLY
EIILNOORSTTUV	REVOLUTIONIST
EIILNOQRSTTUV	VENTRILOQUIST
EIINOOPPRSSTU	SUPERPOSITION
EIIOPRRSSTTUU	SURREPTITIOUS
EIIOPRSSSTTUU	SUPERSTITIOUS
EILNNOOPPRTUY	INOPPORTUNELY
EILNOOQRSTUUV	VENTRILOQUOUS
EILNORSSSUUUX	LUXURIOUSNESS
EINNOOOPSSSSU	POISONOUSNESS
EINNOOORSSSTU	NOTORIOUSNESS
EMNNOORSSSSTU	MONSTROUSNESS
GHIILNOOORSTT	ORNITHOLOGIST
GHIIMNOOPSSTY	PHYSIOGNOMIST
GIIILMNNOOSUY	IGNOMINIOUSLY
HHIMOOOOPPRSU	OPHIOMORPHOUS
HNORRSTTTUUWY	UNTRUSTWORTHY

IIINOOOPPSSTT   OPPOSITIONIST
IILLLORSSTUUY   ILLUSTRIOUSLY

Fourteen Letter Words

AAAAACGILMMNRT	ANAGRAMMATICAL	AABCDEENRSSSTT	ABSTRACTEDNESS
AAAABBIIMNRSST	SABBATARIANISM	AABCDEGIKLNRRT	BLANK-CARTRIDGE
AAAACDIIMMNOTZ	MACADAMIZATION	AABCEEEGHLNNSS	CHANGEABLENESS
AAAACEIMNNRRST	SACRAMENTARIAN	AABCEEEGHLNRSS	CHARGEABLENESS
AAAACHILPPRRST	PARAPHRASTICAL	AABCEEHILNRSST	CHARITABLENESS
AAAADEGINNQRRU	QUADRAGENARIAN	AABCEEHILOPRRR	IRREPROACHABLE
AAAAGHIMNOPRST	PHANTASMAGORIA	AABCEEILLMMTY	EMBLEMATICALLY
AAAAGIMMPRRSTT	PARAGRAMMATIST	AABCEEILLMNPSS	IMPLACABLENESS
AAABCEHILLLPTY	ALPHABETICALLY	AABCEFGIILORRT	FIBROCARTILAGE
AAABCEHILNOPPR	INAPPROACHABLE	AABCEFIIINOTTU	BEAUTIFICATION
AAABDIINORSSTT	BASTARDISATION	AABCEFIINOPRRT	PREFABRICATION
AAABEEILNNSSTT	ATTAINABLENESS	AABCEGHHIIMNNT	BATHING-MACHINE
AAABELLNNRSTTU	UNTRANSLATABLE	AABCEHILOPRRRY	IRREPROACHABLY
AAABIILNORTTUZ	TABULARIZATION	AABCEILLLRSTYZ	CRYSTALLIZABLE
AAACCDIILOPRTT	CATADIOPTRICAL	AABCEILLMORRTY	BAROMETRICALLY
AAACCEGHILLOOR	ARCHAEOLOGICAL	AABCGHIILLMOOP	AMPHIBOLOGICAL
AAACCEHILMPRTU	PHARMACEUTICAL	AABCGHIILLOPRY	BIOGRAPHICALLY
AAACCIIINNOPTT	INCAPACITATION	AABCGHIIOOPRTU	AUTOBIOGRAPHIC
AAACDDEGGKLNOR	CLOAK-AND-DAGGER	AABCHILOOPRSTU	CLAUSTROPHOBIA
AAACDHIINOPRST	ANTAPHRODISIAC	AABCIIILNRTTTY	INTRACTABILITY
AAACEEGILNNPRT	CAPTAIN-GENERAL	AABCILLLLOPSYY	POLYSYLLABICAL
AAACEGIILMMPRT	EPIGRAMMATICAL	AABCILLORRRTUU	ARBORICULTURAL
AAACEHILLMMTTY	MATHEMATICALLY	AABCILNNOSSTTU	CONSUBSTANTIAL
AAACEHILOPRRTX	EXTRAPAROCHIAL	AABDDEELNNRSTU	UNDERSTANDABLE
AAACEIMNORSTTT	CASTRAMETATION	AABDDEFIIOPRRS	BIRD-OF-PARADISE
AAACGHIMNOPRST	PHANTASMAGORIC	AABDEIIKLLMRRR	BILLIARD-MARKER
AAACIIILNOPTTZ	CAPITALIZATION	AABDEIIKMNORST	DISEMBARKATION
AAADEGLNOSTUVY	ADVANTAGEOUSLY	AABDEILLLQRSUY	QUADRISYLLABLE
AAADEIILNNRTUV	VALETUDINARIAN	AABEEELNNORSSS	REASONABLENESS
AAADIIILNNRTTU	LATITUDINARIAN	AABEEELNNOSSSS	SEASONABLENESS
AAAEGHILOPPRST	PALAEOGRAPHIST	AABEEFLNORSSUV	FAVOURABLENESS
AAAEGIIILMNRST	EGALITARIANISM	AABEEIILNNRSSV	INVARIABLENESS
AAAGIILNNOORST	ORGANISATIONAL	AABEEIILNNSSST	INSATIABLENESS
AAAGIINNNOOSTT	ANTAGONISATION	AABEEILMNPSSSS	IMPASSABLENESS
AAAIIIMNNQRSTU	ANTIQUARIANISM	AABEGHIOOPRRTU	AUTOBIOGRAPHER
AAAIILNNORTTUZ	NATURALIZATION	AABEHIIILNORTT	REHABILITATION
AABBDDEENRRTTU	BREAD-AND-BUTTER	AABEIIIILLNNTY	INALIENABILITY
AABBDGGIINNNOR	BROBDINGNAGIAN	AABEIIILLNORST	LIBERALISATION
AABBEEILMNNOSS	ABOMINABLENESS	AABEIIILMNRRST	LIBERTARIANISM
AABCCCEHHILPRY	BRACHYCEPHALIC	AABEIIILNPRSTY	INSEPARABILITY
AABCCDEILNORTT	CONTRADICTABLE	AABEIIILPRRRTY	IRREPARABILITY
AABCCEEELNPSST	ACCEPTABLENESS	AABEIILNSSTTUZ	SUBSTANTIALIZE
AABCCEELNNORTU	COUNTERBALANCE	AABEILMNNRSTTU	INTRANSMUTABLE
AABCCEHILLMOPS	ACCOMPLISHABLE	AABFIIILLMMNTY	INFLAMMABILITY
AABCCEILMMRTUU	CIRCUMAMBULATE	AABIILNNNRTTUY	TINTINNABULARY
AABCCIIILPRTTY	PRACTICABILITY	AABIILNSSTTTUY	SUBSTANTIALITY
AABCCIILNOTTUY	ACCOUNTABILITY	AABIINNOSSTTTU	SUBSTANTIATION
AABCDDEELLLOSY	DODECASYLLABLE	AABILMMNNOOSTU	SOMNAMBULATION
AABCDEEINRRSTT	SCATTER-BRAINED	AACCCCENNOOOVV	CONCAVO-CONCAVE
AABCDEENNPRSUU	SUPERABUNDANCE	AACCCEEHILLTTY	CATECHETICALLY

AACCCEEIILLSST	ECCLESIASTICAL	AACEHILLMNNNORY	ENHARMONICALLY
AACCCEHIIRRSTT	CHARACTERISTIC	AACEHILLMOPRTY	METAPHORICALLY
AACCDEIINNORTT	CONTRAINDICATE	AACEHILLMPSTYY	METAPHYSICALLY
AACCDEILLMORTY	DEMOCRATICALLY	AACEHMNOPRSTUY	PARENCHYMATOUS
AACCEEHILMOTUY	LEUCOCYTHAEMIA	AACEIIILNOPSTZ	SPECIALIZATION
AACCEEEINNNORSS	RECONNAISSANCE	AACEIIILLNRTTUY	INARTICULATELY
AACCEFHIORRSSU	SACCHARIFEROUS	AACEIILNNORTTZ	CENTRALIZATION
AACCEGIIMNRTUV	CIRCUMNAVIGATE	AACEIILNOOPPSU	PAPILIONACEOUS
AACCEHIILOPPRS	ARCHIEPISCOPAL	AACEIILNOPRTTU	RECAPITULATION
AACCEHIKLOOSVZ	CZECHOSLOVAKIA	AACEIILNORSTUZ	SECULARIZATION
AACCEHLMOOPRSU	MACROCEPHALOUS	AACEILLLNOPSTY	PLEONASTICALLY
AACCEIILNORRTT	RECALCITRATION	AACEILLMSSTTYY	SYSTEMATICALLY
AACCELNNORSUUU	RANUNCULACEOUS	AACEILMMNNOORTT	COMMENTATORIAL
AACCFIIILNOORT	CALORIFICATION	AACEILNNOORSTV	CONVERSATIONAL
AACCFIIILNOSST	CLASSIFICATION	AACEILOPRRTTUY	RECAPITULATORY
AACCFIIINNOSTT	SANCTIFICATION	AACFIIIILLNRTY	INARTIFICIALLY
AACCGHHILOOPRR	CHOROGRAPHICAL	AACFIIINNOQTTU	QUANTIFICATION
AACCGHHILOPRST	CHALCOGRAPHIST	AACFIIINORSTTT	STRATIFICATION
AACCGHIILNOPRZ	ZINCOGRAPHICAL	AACFIILORSSTTY	SATISFACTORILY
AACCHILLLOSSTY	SCHOLASTICALLY	AACFINORSSTTUY	UNSATISFACTORY
AACCHINNOPSTTU	ACCOUNTANTSHIP	AACGHHILOOPPRT	PHOTOGRAPHICAL
AACCIILLMNOSTU	MISCALCULATION	AACGHHILOOPRRT	ORTHOGRAPHICAL
AACCIILMNRSTTU	CIRCUMSTANTIAL	AACGHHMOOPRRTY	CHROMATOGRAPHY
AACCLLMNORSTYY	CRYSTALLOMANCY	AACGHILLLOOPTY	PATHOLOGICALLY
AACDEEGIPPRRRT	CARTRIDGE-PAPER	AACGHILMOOPRST	PHARMACOLOGIST
AACDEEILOPPRTU	PROPAEDEUTICAL	AACGILLLOORSTY	ASTROLOGICALLY
AACDEELNNNRSTT	TRANSCENDENTAL	AACGILLLOOTTUY	TAUTOLOGICALLY
AACDEFHIMNNRST	HANDICRAFTSMEN	AACGILNNOORTTU	CONGRATULATION
AACDEFILLNORRW	CARDINAL-FLOWER	AACGLNOORRTTUY	CONGRATULATORY
AACDEHMOPRSTUY	PACHYDERMATOUS	AACHIILLOPRSTY	APHORISTICALLY
AACDEIIILMNOST	DECIMALISATION	AACHIILMNOPRST	MISANTHROPICAL
AACDEIILNOSTTU	EDUCATIONALIST	AACHILLOPSTTYY	HYPOSTATICALLY
AACDELNNOSSSSU	SCANDALOUSNESS	AACHILMOOPPRST	PHARMACOPOLIST
AACDELNOPSTTUY	PENTADACTYLOUS	AACHILNOPSSSYY	PSYCHOANALYSIS
AACDELORSTTTUY	TETRADACTYLOUS	AACIIILMNOPPST	MISAPPLICATION
AACDFIIIILNOPT	LAPIDIFICATION	AACIILNOOPRRST	CONSPIRATORIAL
AACDGHHILOPRRY	HYDROGRAPHICAL	AACIILNPRRSTTU	ANTISCRIPTURAL
AACDHIIILLOPTY	IDIOPATHICALLY	AACILLMNNOORSTY	ASTRONOMICALLY
AACDIIIILNNPRS	DISCIPLINARIAN	AACINOOPRRRSTT	PROCRASTINATOR
AACDIILLLMOPTY	DIPLOMATICALLY	AADEEEEHLRRRSSS	DRESS-REHEARSAL
AACEEFFILNOTTY	AFFECTIONATELY	AADEEEIILLPPPR	PARALLELEPIPED
AACEEGGILLLNOY	GENEALOGICALLY	AADEEFHILNRTTY	FAINTHEARTEDLY
AACEEGHHLNOPPR	ENCEPHALOGRAPH	AADEEGGIMMNNRTZ	AGGRANDIZEMENT
AACEEGIILLMNSV	EVANGELICALISM	AADEEGIMNNRRTZ	DISARRANGEMENT
AACEEIINPPRTUV	UNAPPRECIATIVE	AADEEIILNPQSSU	SESQUIPEDALIAN
AACEEILMMPRTUY	EMPYREUMATICAL	AADEEIINNPRRST	PREDESTINARIAN
AACEEINRSSTTTV	ATTRACTIVENESS	AADEEIILLOPPPR	PARALLELOPIPED
AACEFILLNOSSSU	FALLACIOUSNESS	AADEEILMNORTTT	TATTERDEMALION
AACEGGHILLOPRY	GEOGRAPHICALLY	AADEGGGIINORST	DISAGGREGATION
AACEGGILNNOORT	CONGREGATIONAL	AADEGINOORRRTT	RETROGRADATION
AACEGHHIIMNNSW	WASHING-MACHINE	AADEIIIMNRSTTV	ADMINISTRATIVE
AACEGHHIMOPPTT	APOPHTHEGMATIC	AADEIILMNNNOOT	DENOMINATIONAL
AACEGHILLOOPRS	PHRASEOLOGICAL	AADEIILMNOORTZ	DEMORALIZATION
AACEGHILNOPRST	STENOGRAPHICAL	AADEIILNOOPRTZ	DEPOLARIZATION
AACEGHIMNOPRTY	CINEMATOGRAPHY	AADEIILNORSSTT	DISSERTATIONAL
AACEGILLLOOPTY	APOLOGETICALLY	AADEIIOPPPRRST	DISAPPROPRIATE
AACEHIILLMRTTY	ARITHMETICALLY	AADEINOPPPRRTU	UNAPPROPRIATED
AACEHIILLNTTTY	ANTITHETICALLY	AADIIILMNORSTT	TRADITIONALISM
AACEHIILNSSTTU	ENTHUSIASTICAL	AADIIIMNNORSTT	ADMINISTRATION
AACEHIILPPRRST	PERIPHRASTICAL	AAEEEHHIPRSSTY	HYPERAESTHESIA
AACEHIINNOTTTU	AUTHENTICATION	AAEEGIILNNORTZ	GENERALIZATION

AAEEGIILNNOTVZ	EVANGELIZATION	ABCDEIILNNOSTY	CONDENSABILITY
AAEEILNNPRRTTY	INTERPLANETARY	ABCDGHILNOOORS	BOARDING-SCHOOL
AAEEINNOPSSSST	PASSIONATENESS	ABCEEEEILNRSSV	RECEIVABLENESS
AAEELNNNPSSSTU	UNPLEASANTNESS	ABCEEELNNRSSSU	CENSURABLENESS
AAEFFIIILMORST	FORISFAMILIATE	ABCEEGIILNORRZ	IRRECOGNIZABLE
AAEFIINNORRTTZ	FRATERNIZATION	ABCEEGIINORSUZ	ZINGIBERACEOUS
AAEGIINNOORRST	REORGANISATION	ABCEEGILNNORUZ	UNRECOGNIZABLE
AAEIIILMNNORTZ	MINERALIZATION	ABCEEIILPRSTTY	RESPECTABILITY
AAEIILLMNNRRTXY	INTERMAXILLARY	ABCEEIINORSUZZ	ZINZIBERACEOUS
AAEIILMNNOSSSTU	SENSATIONALISM	ABCEEILNNNOSSSU	UNSOCIABLENESS
AAEIILMNOPRRST	PROLETARIANISM	ABCEGIILOORSTT	BACTERIOLOGIST
AAEIILNNORTTUZ	NEUTRALIZATION	ABCEHILLLOPRYY	HYPERBOLICALLY
AAEIILNNOSSSTT	SENSATIONALIST	ABCELLLNNOORTU	UNCONTROLLABLE
AAEIILNQTTTUVY	QUANTITATIVELY	ABCIILMMNOSSTU	SOMNAMBULISTIC
AAEIIMOPPPRRST	MISAPPROPRIATE	ABCLLLNNOORTUY	UNCONTROLLABLY
AAEIINNORSSSTT	STATIONARINESS	ABDDIILMNOORST	BRISTOL-DIAMOND
AAEIINOPRSSTTU	PASTEURISATION	ABDEEEEILNRSST	DELIBERATENESS
AAEILLLLMORRST	LAMELLIROSTRAL	ABDEEEELNSSSTT	DETESTABLENESS
AAEINNNOPRSTUU	SUPERANNUATION	ABDEEEIILMNNRT	INDETERMINABLE
AAELLNPRRSTUUY	SUPERNATURALLY	ABDEEELLNOPRSS	DEPLORABLENESS
AAFIMNNOORRSTT	TRANSFORMATION	ABDEEFILMNORSS	FORMIDABLENESS
AAGHHNOOPPRRTY	ANTHROPOGRAPHY	ABDEFIINNOSTUU	SUBINFEUDATION
AAGIIMNOSTTTZ	STIGMATIZATION	ABDEIILMNOOST	DEMOBILISATION
AAGIMNORRRSTTY	TRANSMIGRATORY	ABDEIILNOORSTW	BOWDLERISATION
AAIIIILMNORSTT	MILITARISATION	ABEEEFFLNRSSSU	SUFFERABLENESS
AAIIIILMNRSTTU	UTILITARIANISM	ABEEEHILNPRSSS	PERISHABLENESS
AAIIIILNORSTTV	TRIVIALISATION	ABEEEHLNRSSSST	BREATHLESSNESS
AAIIIILNOOTTVZ	VOLATILIZATION	ABEEEIILLNNRSSU	UNRELIABLENESS
AAIIILMNOOPSTT	OPTIMALISATION	ABEEELLNNRSSUV	VULNERABLENESS
AAIIILNOOPPRTUZ	POPULARIZATION	ABEEGHIILNSTUX	EXTINGUISHABLE
AAIIMNOORRSSTZ	ZOROASTRIANISM	ABEEGIILNNNSST	INTANGIBLENESS
AAILMMNNORSTTU	ULTRAMONTANISM	ABEEHLNNOORSSU	HONOURABLENESS
AAILMNNORSTTTU	ULTRAMONTANIST	ABEEIILLNNOSSV	INVIOLABLENESS
AAINNOOPRRSTTT	TRANSPORTATION	ABEEIILMNOPRSS	IMPRESSIONABLE
ABBCEENORRSSTU	SUBARBORESCENT	ABEEIILMNRRTUY	REMUNERABILITY
ABBDDEEEELORSTU	DOUBLEBREASTED	ABEEILMNOPRSSV	IMPROVABLENESS
ABBEEHINNOOPRT	PHENOBARBITONE	ABEEILNNOQSTUU	UNQUESTIONABLE
ABCCCEIIMMNRUY	CIRCUMAMBIENCY	ABEEILNNSSSTUU	UNSUITABLENESS
ABCCCEIORSTUUU	CUCURBITACEOUS	ABEEIMNOSSSSTU	ABSTEMIOUSNESS
ABCCDEEIMNNRSU	DISENCUMBRANCE	ABEGIILNOORSST	OBLIGATORINESS
ABCCEEHLMNORSU	CHAMBER-COUNSEL	ABEIIILMORRTVY	IRREMOVABILITY
ABCCEEIILLNORR	IRRECONCILABLE	ABEIIILNPRSTUY	INSUPERABILITY
ABCCEEILMMNOUX	EXCOMMUNICABLE	ABEILMNNORSTUU	INSURMOUNTABLE
ABCCEIIILNOTVY	CONCEIVABILITY	ABEILNNOQSTUUY	UNQUESTIONABLY
ABCCEIILLNORRY	IRRECONCILABLY	ABEILNOOOPPRRT	PROPORTIONABLE
ABCCEIILMMNNOU	INCOMMUNICABLE	ABIIIILMPPSTUY	IMPLAUSIBILITY
ABCCEILNNNOOSU	UNCONSCIONABLE	ABIIIILMMNOOST	IMMOBILISATION
ABCCILNNNOOSUY	UNCONSCIONABLY	ABILNOOOPPRRTY	PROPORTIONABLY
ABCCINOOOORRSTT	BOA-CONSTRICTOR	ACCCEENNOOOVVX	CONVEXO-CONCAVE
ABCDEEEEILNSSV	DECEIVABLENESS	ACCCEILLNNORTY	CONCENTRICALLY
ABCDEEEHIILNPR	INDECIPHERABLE	ACCDEEEHHIKNRT	CHICKEN-HEARTED
ABCDEEEEILNPSSS	DESPICABLENESS	ACCDEEILNOPSTY	ENCYCLOPAEDIST
ABCDEEEILNRSST	CREDITABLENESS	ACCDEEINNNOSTU	DISCOUNTENANCE
ABCDEEEILPRSST	DISRESPECTABLE	ACCDEEINNNOORST	DECONSECRATION
ABCDEEIILNNORS	INCONSIDERABLE	ACCDEENNORSSTT	CONTRACTEDNESS
ABCDEEILMNOOPS	INDECOMPOSABLE	ACCDEIINNNOSTU	DISCONTINUANCE
ABCDEEILNORSUV	UNDISCOVERABLE	ACCDIINOORSTTJ	CONTRADICTIOUS
ABCDEELMNOOPSU	UNDECOMPOSABLE	ACCEEGILLNORTY	GEOCENTRICALLY
ABCDEGIILLNSTU	CASTLE-BUILDING	ACCEEIINNOORSS	CONCESSIONAIRE
ABCDEIIILPRTTY	PREDICTABILITY	ACCEEIILLLOPSTY	TELESCOPICALLY
ABCDEIILNNORSY	INCONSIDERABLY	ACCEEILORSSTTT	ELECTROSTATICS

ACCEFGIIIINNNS	INSIGNIFICANCE	ACDIIINNNOORTT	INDOCTRINATION
ACCEFIIILLNSTY	SCIENTIFICALLY	ACDIMNOOPRSSTU	MASS-PRODUCTION
ACCEGIILNRTUXY	EXCRUCIATINGLY	ACEEEEHHILNRTW	CATHERINE-WHEEL
ACCEHHILLNOPRS	CHANCELLORSHIP	ACEEEFLLORRTUW	FELLOW-CREATURE
ACCEHILMMNOPST	ACCOMPLISHMENT	ACEEEIILMNRTTX	EXCREMENTITIAL
ACCEHILMOOPRSU	MICROCEPHALOUS	ACEEEIILPRSSTU	SUPERCELESTIAL
ACCEIIILNNOORT	RECONCILIATION	ACEEEMNOOPRSTV	OVERCOMPENSATE
ACCEIINOPRSSSU	CAPRICIOUSNESS	ACEEEMNORRSTUU	COUNTER-MEASURE
ACCFFIIINORTTU	FRUCTIFICATION	ACEEFGLNNRSSUU	UNGRACEFULNESS
ACCFGIIIINNNSY	INSIGNIFICANCY	ACEEFINORRRSST	REFRACTORINESS
ACCGHHIILLOOTY	ICHTHYOLOGICAL	ACEEGILLLLOOTY	TELEOLOGICALLY
ACCGIIMNORRTUY	CIRCUMGYRATION	ACEEGILLMOOORT	METEOROLOGICAL
ACCHIILLOPRTYY	HYPOCRITICALLY	ACEEGILLNOPRTT	ELECTROPLATING
ACCHILLNNORSYY	SYNCHRONICALLY	ACEEGLNOORRSTU	COLOUR-SERGEANT
ACCIIIMNORRSSU	ROSICRUCIANISM	ACEEGNOORSSSUU	COURAGEOUSNESS
ACCIILLMOOOPST	COSMOPOLITICAL	ACEEHIINPPPRST	APPRENTICESHIP
ACCIILLMORRTTU	CIRCUMLITTORAL	ACEEIIILMNNRST	REMINISCENTIAL
ACCIILNNOOPRST	CONSCRIPTIONAL	ACEEIIILNRRTTY	RECTILINEARITY
ACCIIMNNORTTUU	CIRCUMNUTATION	ACEEIIIMPPRSTT	PERIPATETICISM
ACCILMNOOSTUUY	CONTUMACIOUSLY	ACEEIIJLNNORTT	INTERJECTIONAL
ACCILNNOORSTTU	CONSTRUCTIONAL	ACEEIIILNNORSST	INTERCESSIONAL
ACDDEEGKLNNOUW	UNACKNOWLEDGED	ACEEIILNOSSTTY	COESSENTIALITY
ACDDEEINRSSSTT	DISTRACTEDNESS	ACEEILLLLNTTUY	INTELLECTUALLY
ACDEEEFNOPPRST	COPPER-FASTENED	ACEEIMMNNORSTU	INCOMMENSURATE
ACDEEEINNOPQRU	EQUIPONDERANCE	ACEEINOPRRSSSU	PRECARIOUSNESS
ACDEEEINORSSTV	DECORATIVENESS	ACEELMMNORSTUY	COMMENSURATELY
ACDEEENRRRSTUY	UNDER-SECRETARY	ACEEMNOOOPRSTU	COTEMPORANEOUS
ACDEEFHIINNRSS	DISENFRANCHISE	ACEFGIILLNORSU	FRINGILLACEOUS
ACDEEGILNNOQRU	GRANDILOQUENCE	ACEFIIIINORTVV	REVIVIFICATION
ACDEEGIMNORSTU	DISCOURAGEMENT	ACEFIIILPRSTUY	SUPERFICIALITY
ACDEEGKLMNNOTW	ACKNOWLEDGMENT	ACEGGIILNNNPRS	SPRING-CLEANING
ACDEEHIIINNRST	DISINHERITANCE	ACEGHHIILLOPRY	HIEROGLYPHICAL
ACDEEHIIINRSTZ	DECHRISTIANIZE	ACEGHLNOOPSTTU	PLECTOGNATHOUS
ACDEEHIMNNNSTT	DISENCHANTMENT	ACEGIIILLLOSTUY	EULOGISTICALLY
ACDEEHINNRSSST	DISENCHANTRESS	ACEGIILLMNNOORT	TERMINOLOGICAL
ACDEEIMMNNOORT	RECOMMENDATION	ACEGIILLORSSUY	SACRILEGIOUSLY
ACDEEINNOORSST	CO-ORDINATENESS	ACEGIILNNOTTUV	CONGLUTINATIVE
ACDEEMMNOORRTY	RECOMMENDATORY	ACEGIILLLMOOTYY	ETYMOLOGICALLY
ACDEFIIIINNOTT	IDENTIFICATION	ACEGILMNNOOORT	CONGLOMERATION
ACDEFIIILLNNOTY	CONFIDENTIALLY	ACEGINNNOOSSUU	CONSANGUINEOUS
ACDEHHIIMOPRRT	HERMAPHRODITIC	ACEGINNOOSSSTU	CONTAGIOUSNESS
ACDEHIIILOOPRT	DIAHELIOTROPIC	ACEHHIILLOPTTYY	HYPOTHETICALLY
ACDEHIMMNORSTY	THERMODYNAMICS	ACEHHLMOOOPPST	OPHTHALMOSCOPE
ACDEIIIIMNNRST	INDISCRIMINATE	ACEHIILLOPSTTY	POLYTHEISTICAL
ACDEIIIIMNRSTV	DISCRIMINATIVE	ACEHILLLOPPSST	PHELLOPLASTICS
ACDEIIIILMNRSTY	DISCRIMINATELY	ACEHILLMNOSWWY	CHIMNEY-SWALLOW
ACDEIIILNORSTY	DISCRETIONALLY	ACEIIILLMPTTUV	MULTIPLICATIVE
ACDEIILNOOORTZ	DECOLORIZATION	ACEIIILNRSTTXY	EXTRINSICALITY
ACDEIINOOPRRST	DISINCORPORATE	ACEIIIMMNOORSS	COMMISSIONAIRE
ACDEILLNOOSSTY	DISCONSOLATELY	ACEIILLMOOPRTT	METROPOLITICAL
ACDEINNOOPRRTU	UNINCORPORATED	ACEIILMNNNOSTT	CONTINENTALISM
ACDEINNORSTUUY	CONSUETUDINARY	ACEIILNNNOSTTT	CONTINENTALIST
ACDFIIIILNOOST	SOLIDIFICATION	ACEIILNNORRSTU	INSURRECTIONAL
ACDGGIILNORSUY	DISCOURAGINGLY	ACEIILNOOPRRTY	INCORPOREALITY
ACDGHILLOPTYYY	DACTYLIOGLYPHY	ACEIILNOPRSTUY	PERTINACIOUSLY
ACDGIIIIMNNRST	DISCRIMINATING	ACEIINNOSSSTUU	INCAUTIOUSNESS
ACDIIILLNNNOST	DISINCLINATION	ACEIINOPSSSSUU	AUSPICIOUSNESS
ACDIIIIMNNORST	DISCRIMINATION	ACEILLNNNOOTVY	CONVENTIONALLY
ACDIIIJLNORSTU	JURISDICTIONAL	ACEILMNORSSSUU	MIRACULOUSNESS
ACDIIILLNNOOTTY	CONDITIONALITY	ACEILNNNNOOTUV	UNCONVENTIONAL
ACDIIIMNORRSTY	DISCRIMINATORY	ACEILNOOQSSSUU	LOQUACIOUSNESS

ACEILORRRRSTUV	RECURVIROSTRAL
ACEIMMNNOORSTU	COMMENSURATION
ACEINNOOPRSSTT	CORNET-À-PISTONS
ACFIIIILMNOPST	SIMPLIFICATION
ACFIIILNOSTTTU	STULTIFICATION
ACGHHHIIOPSTTY	ICHTHYOPHAGIST
ACGHHIIOOPSTUY	ICHTHYOPHAGOUS
ACGHHIIOOPPRST	OPISTHOGRAPHIC
ACGHIIILNOPSTT	ANTIPHLOGISTIC
ACGHIILLNOOORT	ORNITHOLOGICAL
ACGHIILMNOOPSY	PHYSIOGNOMICAL
ACGHILLLMOOTYY	MYTHOLOGICALLY
ACGIILNNNOOTTU	CONGLUTINATION
ACGINOOOPRRSTT	PROGNOSTICATOR
ACHHLMOOOOPPSTY	OPHTHALMOSCOPY
ACHIIILLNORSTY	HISTRIONICALLY
ACHIIINOOPSSTT	SOPHISTICATION
ACHIIMMOPRSSSY	COMMISSARYSHIP
ACHIOOPPRRRSTU	PROCURATORSHIP
ACIIILLMNOPTTU	MULTIPLICATION
ACIIILLMOPSTTY	OPTIMISTICALLY
ACIIILNOPSSUUY	INAUSPICIOUSLY
ACIILNNOOSTTTU	CONSTITUTIONAL
ACIINNOOOPRSTT	CONTRAPOSITION
ACILLNPRRSTUUY	UNSCRIPTURALLY
ADDEEEGGINNSSS	DISENGAGEDNESS
ADDEEEIMMPRTTU	UMPREMEDITATED
ADDEFIILNNSSSU	DISDAINFULNESS
ADEEEEEGNNRSST	DEGENERATENESS
ADEEEEIMNPRRTT	PREDETERMINATE
ADEEEFIMNNOORT	AFOREMENTIONED
ADEEEGLNRRSSSS	REGARDLESSNESS
ADEEEHILNOOPRT	RADIOTELEPHONE
ADEEEIILMNRTTY	INTERMEDIATELY
ADEEEIMPRRSTTU	DISTEMPERATURE
ADEEEMNNRSTTTU	UNDERSTATEMENT
ADEEGIINNORRTT	REDINTEGRATION
ADEEGINOORRSST	DEROGATORINESS
ADEEHHIILMOPRS	HEMISPHEROIDAL
ADEEHILMNNRSTT	DISENTHRALMENT
ADEEIIIMNNRTTN	INTERMEDIATION
ADEEIILMNNOTVY	DENOMINATIVELY
ADEEIIMNNOOTTZ	DEMONETIZATION
ADEEIINNNORSST	INORDINATENESS
ADEEIINNOPRSTT	PREDESTINATION
ADEEILNNRRSTUY	UNRESTRAINEDLY
ADEFGHIMOORRTY	FAIRY-GODMOTHER
ADEFIINNOOORRT	FOREORDINATION
ADEFIINOSSSSTU	FASTIDIOUSNESS
ADEGIIINNORSTT	DISINTEGRATION
ADEGIIMNOQRSUU	QUADRIGEMINOUS
ADEHHIILNOOPRT	ORNITHODELPHIA
ADEIIILMNNORST	TRIDIMENSIONAL
ADEIIINNOORSTT	DISORIENTATION
ADEIILLNOPRTVY	PROVIDENTIALLY
ADEIILNOSTTUVY	ADVENTITIOUSLY
ADEIIMNNOPPSTT	DISAPPOINTMENT
ADGIIILLNNOTUY	LONGITUDINALLY
ADGIILNOPPRSVY	DISAPPROVINGLY
ADIIIILNOQSSTU	DISQUISITIONAL
AEEEEEKLPRRSSU	PLEASURE-SEEKER

AEEEEEFFIMNNSST	EFFEMINATENESS
AEEEEEINNPRRTTT	INTERPENETRATE
AEEEEINPRRSTTV	REPRESENTATIVE
AEEEFILLNPRRTY	PREFERENTIALLY
AEEEEGGINRSSSSV	AGGRESSIVENESS
AEEEGHHIOPRRRS	HERESIOGRAPHER
AEEEIILMNNSTTZ	SENTIMENTALIZE
AEEEIINPRRTTTV	INTERPRETATIVE
AEEEILLMNPRTXY	EXPERIMENTALLY
AEEEIMMMNRSSTU	MISMEASUREMENT
AEEEINNOPRRSTT	REPRESENTATION
AEEEINPRSSSSUV	PERSUASIVENESS
AEEEMNOOPRSTUX	EXTEMPORANEOUS
AEEFGIINRSSTUV	FIGURATIVENESS
AEEFGLNNRSSTUU	UNGRATEFULNESS
AEEFHHLNNOPSVY	SHOVE-HALFPENNY
AEEGGINORRSSSU	GREGARIOUSNESS
AEEGIIILLLMTTY	ILLEGITIMATELY
AEEGIIILLNNSTT	INTELLIGENTSIA
AEEGIIMNNNNORTU	MOUNTAINEERING
AEEGNOORSSSTUU	OUTRAGEOUSNESS
AEEGOOPRRRSTUY	SUPEREROGATORY
AEEHHOPPPRSSTU	SUPERPHOSPHATE
AEEHIILNNPSTTU	LIEUTENANTSHIP
AEEHIINNNOPPRS	INAPPREHENSION
AEEIIIILNNNORTT	INTERLINEATION
AEEIIILNSSTTTX	EXISTENTIALIST
AEEIILLLNPSTTY	PESTILENTIALLY
AEEIILLNNOPRTT	INTERPELLATION
AEEIILMMNNOPTT	IMPLEMENTATION
AEEIILMMNNSSTT	SENTIMENTALISM
AEEIILMNNSSTTT	SENTIMENTALIST
AEEIILMNNSTTTY	SENTIMENTALITY
AEEIILNNQSSTTU	QUINTESSENTIAL
AEEIIILPRTTUVVY	VITUPERATIVELY
AEEIIMNNOORTTZ	REMONETIZATION
AEEIINNOPRRTTT	INTERPRETATION
AEEIILLNNRSSSTT	SLATTERNLINESS
AEEFFHILNNSSTUU	UNFAITHFULNESS
AEEFFIIMNOORRSU	FORAMINIFEROUS
AEFGIILNOSSSTU	FLAGITIOUSNESS
AEFILLNOOPRSSY	PROFESSIONALLY
AEGGHHOOPPRTYY	PHYTOGEOGRAPHY
AEGGINOOSSTTUU	AUTO-SUGGESTION
AEGHIIMNNOOOST	HOMOGENISATION
AEGHLNOOOPRTUY	NEUROPATHOLOGY
AEGIIMNNORRTT	INTERMIGRATION
AEGILLMNNOQTUY	MAGNILOQUENTLY
AEGILMNOOPSTTU	PNEUMATOLOGIST
AEHIILMOOPPRST	APHELIOTROPISM
AEHIINNNOORTTZ	ENTHRONIZATION
AEHILOPPPRSSUY	PLEURAPOPHYSIS
AEHIMNNOORSSSU	HARMONIOUSNESS
AEHIMOOPPPSSTU	HIPPOPOTAMUSES
AEIIIILMNRSSTT	MINISTERIALIST
AEIIILNNOOPTVY	OPINIONATIVELY
AEIIILNNRSTTVY	INTRANSITIVELY
AEIILLLLRSTTUVY	ILLUSTRATIVELY
AEIIILNNOPRSSTU	UNIPERSONALIST
AEIILNOPRRSSTT	TRIPERSONALIST
AEIINNORRSSSTT	TRANSITORINESS

Letters	Word	Letters	Word
AEIINOPRSSSUVV	VIVIPAROUSNESS	BEIIILNOPRSSTY	RESPONSIBILITY
AEILLMNNRSTTUY	INSTRUMENTALLY	BHIIIINOOPRSTT	PROHIBITIONIST
AEILLMNOSSTUUY	SIMULTANEOUSLY	CCCEIIMNOPRSTU	CIRCUMSPECTION
AEILNOOOPPRTUV	OVERPOPULATION	CCCIILMNOORTUU	CIRCUMLOCUTION
AEILNOOSSTTTUY	OSTENTATIOUSLY	CCCILMOORRTUUY	CIRCUMLOCUTORY
AEINNOOSSTTTUU	UNOSTENTATIOUS	CCDEEEFFILNNOS	SELF-CONFIDENCE
AFIIIMMNNOORST	MISINFORMATION	CCDEEELNOPRRTY	PRECONCERTEDLY
AFIIILLMORSTUUY	MULTIFARIOUSLY	CCDEEENNOOPRRS	CORRESPONDENCE
AGHHLOOOPPTTYY	PHYTOPATHOLOGY	CCDEENNOOPRRSY	CORRESPONDENCY
AGHILNOOOOPRSTT	ANTHROPOLOGIST	CCDENOOPRRSTUU	SUPERCONDUCTOR
AGIINNOORSSUUV	SANGUINIVOROUS	CCEEEEEJNNRSUV	REJUVENESCENCE
AHHIILNOPPRSTT	PHILANTHROPIST	CCEEEEFNORRRSS	CROSS-REFERENCE
AHIILMNNOORSUY	INHARMONIOUSLY	CCEEEHILMORSTT	ELECTROCHEMIST
AIIILOOPPRRTTY	PROPITIATORILY	CCEEFIMNORRRTU	CIRCUMFERENTOR
AIIINNORSTTTUY	INSTITUTIONARY	CCEEGIILLOOSST	ECCLESIOLOGIST
AIILMNOOPRSSUY	PARSIMONIOUSLY	CCEEILNNOSSUVY	CONCLUSIVENESS
AILLNOOOPPRRTY	PROPORTIONALLY	CCEEINOOPRSSSU	PRECOCIOUSNESS
BBCIIILMOSTTUY	COMBUSTIBILITY	CCEFLLNSSSUUUY	UNSUCCESSFULLY
BBEILNOORRSTUU	RUBBER-SOLUTION	CCEHIIIMPRRSTY	HYPERCRITICISM
BCCEEIKKKNORRS	KNICKERBOCKERS	CCEIILLNNOSUVY	INCONCLUSIVELY
BCCILNOOSSSUUY	SUBCONSCIOUSLY	CCEIINORSSSTUU	CIRCUITOUSNESS
BCDEEIILNRSTTU	INDESTRUCTIBLE	CCEILNORSTTUVY	CONSTRUCTIVELY
BCDEEMOOOPPRTT	COPPER-BOTTOMED	CCEINNOORRSTTU	RECONSTRUCTION
BCDEIIILPPRSTU	PUBLIC-SPIRITED	CCEIOOPPRSSSTT	SPECTROSCOPIST
BCDEIILNRSTTUY	INDESTRUCTIBLY	CCGIIKMNOOPSST	COMPOSING-STICK
BCEEEHILMNOPRS	COMPREHENSIBLE	CCIIILPRSSTTUU	PISCICULTURIST
BCEEFIIILPRTTY	PERFECTIBILITY	CCIILMNOORTUUV	CIRCUMVOLUTION
BCEEGILLOOORTY	ELECTROBIOLOGY	CDDEEILNNOSTTY	DISCONTENTEDLY
BCEEHILMNOPRSY	COMPREHENSIBLY	CDDEILNOOOSTUY	DICOTYLEDONOUS
BCEEIIILNNNSSV	INVINCIBLENESS	CDEEEIINNRSSST	INDISCREETNESS
BCEEIIILPPRTTY	PERCEPTIBILITY	CDEEFIIILLNPSS	SELF-DISCIPLINE
BCEEIILMNOPRSS	INCOMPRESSIBLE	CDEEIIINNSSTVV	VINDICTIVENESS
BCEEILNOORRTTV	CONTROVERTIBLE	CDEEIINRSSSSUV	DISCURSIVENESS
BCEEIMNNPRSTUU	SUPERINCUMBENT	CDEEIKNNORRSTW	WONDERSTRICKEN
BCEIIILNORTTVY	CONVERTIBILITY	CDEEIMNNNOSTTT	DISCONTENTMENT
BCEIIILPSSTTUY	SUSCEPTIBILITY	CDEEINNOORSSSU	INDECOROUSNESS
BCEILNOORRTTVY	CONTROVERTIBLY	CDEEINOPRSSTUV	PRODUCTIVENESS
BCIIILOPRRTTUY	CORRUPTIBILITY	CDEHHIILNOOPRT	ORNITHODELPHIC
BCIINOORSSTTTU	OBSTRUCTIONIST	CDEIIINNNSSSTT	INDISTINCTNESS
BDEEEGIMMNOSTU	DISEMBOGUEMENT	CDEIINNOORRTTU	REINTRODUCTION
BDEEEILMMNOSTW	DISEMBOWELMENT	CDEIINORSSTTTU	DESTRUCTIONIST
BDEIIIILNSSTTY	DISTENSIBILITY	CDEILOORSSTUUY	DISCOURTEOUSLY
BDEIIILNNOSSSU	LIBIDINOUSNESS	CDEIMMNOOOSSSU	COMMODIOUSNESS
BDEIIILRSTTUVY	DISTRIBUTIVELY	CEEEEFILNRSSTV	REFLECTIVENESS
BDEIIINORRSTTU	REDISTRIBUTION	CEEEEGIILNNORT	ELECTIONEERING
BDIIIIILNSTVY	INDIVISIBILITY	CEEEEHLNPSSSSS	SPEECHLESSNESS
BEEEELMNORSTUV	BOULEVERSEMENT	CEEEIILPRRSTVY	IRRESPECTIVELY
BEEEFIILLNNSSX	INFLEXIBLENESS	CEEFFFIILNSSTU	SELF-SUFFICIENT
BEEEHILMNOSSST	BLITHESOMENESS	CEEFIINNOSSSTU	INFECTIOUSNESS
BEEEIILNPRSSSX	INEXPRESSIBLES	CEEFILMNNRSSUU	UNMERCIFULNESS
BEEGIIIILLLNNTU	UNINTELLIGIBLE	CEEFILMNOORSSS	FROLICSOMENESS
BEEHLOOOORRSTTU	TROUBLESHOOTER	CEEFLLMMNOOORW	FELLOW-COMMONER
BEEIILNPPRSSSU	INSUPPRESSIBLE	CEEGIILNNORRTY	NITROGLYCERINE
BEEIIMNSSSSSUV	SUBMISSIVENESS	CEEHIMMOPSSSTY	METEMPSYCHOSIS
BEEINOOQSSSSUU	OBSEQUIOUSNESS	CEEIILMORRSTUY	MERETRICIOUSLY
BEEINOORSSSSTU	BOISTEROUSNESS	CEEIILNNNNOTVY	INCONVENIENTLY
BEELOOPRRSSTUY	OBSTREPEROUSLY	CEEIILNNOSSSTU	LICENTIOUSNESS
BEGGHHILNOORSU	BOROUGH-ENGLISH	CEEIINNOPRSSSU	PERNICIOUSNESS
BEGIIILLLNNTUY	UNINTELLIGIBLY	CEEINNOORSSSSU	CENSORIOUSNESS
BEIIIILMPRSSTY	IMPRESSIBILITY	CEEINNOSSSSTUU	INCESTUOUSNESS
	PERMISSIBILITY	CEEPRRRSSTTUUU	SUPERSTRUCTURE

CEFFIIILNNSTUY	INSUFFICIENTLY	EEEEFGLNNRSSUV	REVENGEFULNESS
CEGINNOOSSSTUU	CONTIGUOUSNESS	EEEEFKNNOPRSSS	FREESPOKENNESS
CEHILLNOOPRRST	CONTROLLERSHIP	EEEEHILNPRRSVY	REPREHENSIVELY
CEHILLNOOPRSSU	COUNSELLORSHIP	EEEEIINPRSSTTV	REPETITIVENESS
CEHILMOORSSSST	SCHOOLMISTRESS	EEEEINPRSSSSVX	EXPRESSIVENESS
CEHILOOOOPSSTU	OPISTHOCOELOUS	EEEELLNNRSSSST	RELENTLESSNESS
CEIIIINOSSTTVV	VIVISECTIONIST	EEEELMMNOSSSTT	METTLESOMENESS
CEIILLOPRSSUUY	SUPERCILIOUSLY	EEEFGLMNNORSTV	SELF-GOVERNMENT
CEIILNNNOSSTTY	INCONSISTENTLY	EEEFLMNORRSSSU	REMORSEFULNESS
CEIIMMNNNOORTU	INTERCOMMUNION	EEEGHILNSSSSTW	WEIGHTLESSNESS
CEIIMMNNORTTUY	INTERCOMMUNITY	FFFHHILMOPPSST	MCΓIII3TOPHELES
CEIINNOORSTTTU	RECONSTITUTION	EEEHIINPRSSTVY	HYPERSENSITIVE
CEIINOPPRRSSTU	SUPERSCRIPTION	EEEIIMNPRSSSSV	IMPRESSIVENESS
CEIINOPSSSSSUU	SUSPICIOUSNESS		PERMISSIVENESS
CEILLMNOOSTUUY	CONTUMELIOUSLY	EEEIINPRSSSTUV	SUPERSENSITIVE
CEILNORRSSSSUU	SCURRILOUSNESS	EEEILMNNPRSTUY	SUPEREMINENTLY
CEINNNOOSSSTUU	CONTINUOUSNESS	EEEILNOPRSSSSX	EXPRESSIONLESS
CELMNOOPSTTUUY	CONTEMPTUOUSLY	EEEILNORRSSSTU	IRRESOLUTENESS
CELNOPRSSSSUUU	SCRUPULOUSNESS	EEEINNOPRSSSSV	RESPONSIVENESS
CFIILLORRSTTUU	FLORICULTURIST	EEEINOPPRSSSSV	OPPRESSIVENESS
CFILLLOOOORRSU	COROLLIFLOROUS	EEEINOPSSSSSSV	POSSESSIVENESS
CGIIMMNNOOPRSU	UNCOMPROMISING	EEFHILNRSSSSTT	THRIFTLESSNESS
CHIILORRSTTTUU	HORTICULTURIST	EEGHIIMNNSTTUX	EXTINGUISHMENT
CLLNOPRSSUUUUY	UNSCRUPULOUSLY	EEGHILLMNORVWY	OVERWHELMINGLY
DDEEEEINNNPRTT	INTERDEPENDENT	EEGIILNNPRRSTY	ENTERPRISINGLY
DDEEIIJNNOSSST	DISJOINTEDNESS	EEGILNOOPRRVWY	OVERPOWERINGLY
DDEEIILNORRSSS	DISORDERLINESS	EEHHLLOOPRSTUY	HETEROPHYLLOUS
DDEEIINNOPSSSS	INDISPOSEDNESS	EEHHMOOOPRRSTU	HETEROMORPHOUS
DDEGHLMOOORUUY	GOODHUMOUREDLY	EEHIILMNNQRSTU	RELINQUISHMENT
DEEEFIIINNNSST	INDEFINITENESS	EEHIIMMNOPRSTV	IMPOVERISHMENT
DEEEFIIINNSSTV	DEFINITIVENESS	EEIILMNNRTTTTY	INTERMITTENTLY
DEEEFILNNRSSSS	FRIENDLESSNESS	EEIIMNOPRSSSSV	IMPERVIOUSNESS
DEEEFILNPSSSTU	DESPITEFULNESS	EEIMNORSSSSTUY	MYSTERIOUSNESS
DEEEGIIKLNNNTT	KNITTING-NEEDLE	EELOOPPRRSSTUY	PREPOSTEROUSLY
DEEEIIMNRSSTTV	DIVERTISSEMENT	EENOOPPRRSSSSU	PROSPEROUSNESS
DEEEIINNPRSTTU	SUPERINTENDENT	EFFILNNRSSTUUU	UNFRUITFULNESS
DEEENOPPRSSSSU	UNPREPOSSESSED	EFGHHLNOSSTTUU	THOUGHTFULNESS
DEEFFIIIMNNRST	INDIFFERENTISM	EFHLNNRSSTTUUU	UNTRUTHFULNESS
DEEFGHILLNSSTU	DELIGHTFULNESS	EFINOORSSSTTUU	FORTUITOUSNESS
DEEFIILNNNRSSU	UNFRIENDLINESS	EGHLNNOOOPRUYY	NEUROHYPNOLOGY
DEEFIINOPRSSSU	PERFIDIOUSNESS	EGIIMNNNRTTTU	UNINTERMITTING
DEEGLNNORSSSSU	GROUNDLESSNESS	EHIIOOPPPRRRST	PROPRIETORSHIP
DEEIIIILMRSTUV	VERISIMILITUDE	EIIIINOQRSSTTU	REQUISITIONIST
DEEIIIMNNSSTUV	DIMINUTIVENESS	EIILMNOOQRSUUY	QUERIMONIOUSLY
DEEIIINRSSTTUV	DISINVESTITURE	EIINOOPPRSSSTU	PROPITIOUSNESS
DEENNOPSSSSTUU	STUPENDOUSNESS	ELMNOSSSTTUUUU	TUMULTUOUSNESS
DEFGILNSSSSTUU	DISGUSTFULNESS	ELMOPPRSSTUUUY	PRESUMPTUOUSLY
DEGIILNNOSSUUY	DISINGENUOUSLY	ELNOOPPRRSSUUY	UNPROSPEROUSLY
DEIIIILLNOSSUZ	DISILLUSIONIZE	EMNOPPRSSTUUUU	UNPRESUMPTUOUS
DGHIIIINNQSSTU	DISTINQUISHING	IIIOOPPSSSTTUU	SUPPOSITITIOUS
DGHIINNOOPPSWW	WINDOW-SHOPPING		

Fifteen Letter Words

AAAAACEGHILLOPPR	PALAEOGRAPHICAL	AACCDHHILNOOPRY	HYPOCHONDRIACAL
AAAAEIILMNNPRRT	PARLIAMENTARIAN	AACCEGHIILLOPRX	LEXICOGRAPHICAL
AAAAGHILMNOPRST	PHANTASMAGORIAL	AACCEHNOOPPRRTU	COUNTER-APPROACH
AAABBBEGHIKNRST	SABBATH-BREAKING	AACCEIILLMNOSTY	ENCOMIASTICALLY
AAABCEILLLRSTTY	TETRASYLLABICAL	AACCEIIMNRSTTU	CIRCUMSTANTIATE
AAABCHIILOPPRTY	APPROACHABILITY	AACCGIIMNORRTUV	CIRCUMNAVIGATOR
AAAACCHIILMNNORT	ANTIMONARCHICAL	AACCIILLMNORTUV	CIRCUMVALLATION
AAACCIIILMNOTTZ	ACCLIMATIZATION	AACDEEHINNTTTUU	UNAUTHENTICATED
AAAACEFILNNSSSTT	FANTASTICALNESS	AACDEGHIILLOPRY	IDEOGRAPHICALLY
AAAACEHHIILMPRTT	AMPHITHEATRICAL	AACDEHHIILNPRST	CHRISTADELPHIAN
AAACGHIILPRRSTT	STRATIGRAPHICAL	AACDEIIJLLRTUXY	EXTRAJUDICIALLY
AAACGILLMMNNRTUY	UNGRAMMATICALLY	AACDEIIMNNNOOTT	DECONTAMINATION
AAACIIORSSTTTTW	STRAIT-WAISTCOAT	AACDFIIINOSSSTT	DISSATISFACTION
AAACILLNNOORTTV	CONTRAVALLATION	AACDFIIORSSSTTY	DISSATISFACTORY
AAADDEGINOSSTUV	DISADVANTAGEOUS	AACDHILLORSTTYY	HYDROSTATICALLY
AAADDIINNORSSTT	STANDARDISATION	AACEEEGMNOPRSTU	PERGAMENTACEOUS
AAADGHIIIMPRSTT	DIAPHRAGMATITIS	AACEEEHILLLMNUW	WHEEL-ANIMALCULE
AAAEIIILMNORSTT	MATERIALISATION	AACEEENNQRRTTUY	QUATERCENTENARY
AAAEILMNNPRRTUY	UNPARLIAMENTARY	AACEEFFHIMNNRST	AFFRANCHISEMENT
AAAHIIIMMNNRSTU	HUMANITARIANISM	AACEEGILLRSTTTY	STRATEGETICALLY
AAAIIINNNRRTTT	ANTITRINITARIAN	AACEEHILLNPRTTY	PARENTHETICALLY
AAAIIILMNORSTTT	TOTALITARIANISM	AACEEHILLPRTTUY	THERAPEUTICALLY
AAAIIILNNNOOTTZ	NATIONALIZATION	AACEEHILLMPSTTYY	SYMPATHETICALLY
AAAIIILNNOORSTT	RATIONALISATION	AACEIIILMNOPPSS	EPISCOPALIANISM
AAAILNNNOPRSTTT	TRANSPLANTATION	AACEIIIMNNOPSTT	EMANCIPATIONIST
AABBCGHIIILLOPR	BIBLIOGRAPHICAL	AACEIIINNORSSTT	CANISTERISATION
AABCCCEEHIMPRRT	CHAMBER-PRACTICE	AACEILMNOOPSSTY	COMPASSIONATELY
AABCCEEILNPRSST	PRACTICABLENESS	AACGHHIILOPPRSY	PHYSIOGRAPHICAL
AABCCEELNNOSSTU	ACCOUNTABLENESS	AACGHIIILLMORTY	LOGARITHMICALLY
AABCCEGIILMNRUV	CIRCUMNAVIGABLE	AACGHILLNOOOPRT	ANTHROPOLOGICAL
AABCCEHHLOPRSUY	BRACHYCEPHALOUS	AACGHILLOOPPRTY	TOPOGRAPHICALLY
AABCDEEEHLLLNSY	HENDECASYLLABLE	AACGHLLOPRRSTYY	CRYSTALLOGRAPHY
AABCDEIINNOORTZ	DECARBONIZATION	AACGIIILLRRSTTU	AGRICULTURALIST
AABCDEIINORRTUZ	DECARBURIZATION	AACIIIMNNOORSTT	ROMANTICISATION
AABCEEEGHILNNRT	INTERCHANGEABLE	AACIILLNORSTTYZ	CRYSTALLIZATION
AABCEEGHIILNTXY	EXCHANGEABILITY	AACIINNOOPRRSTT	PROCRASTINATION
AABCEEGHILNNRTY	INTERCHANGEABLY	AACILLMMOPSTTYY	SYMPTOMATICALLY
AABCEEILNNRSSTT	INTRACTABLENESS	AADDDEEIINOSSSS	ADDISONS-DISEASE
AABCEHHIILMNPRS	CHAMBERLAINSHIP	AADEEEILMNPRSTT	DEPARTMENTALISE
AABCEHILMNOPRTU	PULMOBRANCHIATE	AADEEGIIMNNOTTZ	DEMAGNETIZATION
AABCEINNOSSTTTU	CONSUBSTANTIATE	AADEIILNOPSSSTY	DISPASSIONATELY
AABCIIIILLNPPTY	INAPPLICABILITY	AADEIILNORRRTXY	EXTRAORDINARILY
AABDEEGIIILRSTY	DISAGREEABILITY	AADFGHIORRRSTTW	STRAIGHTFORWARD
AABEEEILNNPRSSS	INSEPARABLENESS	AADGHHIMNPRSSTU	DRAUGHTSMANSHIP
AABEEEELNNORSSST	TREASONABLENESS	AADGIIINNOORSTZ	DISORGANIZATION
AABEEFILLMMNNSS	INFLAMMABLENESS	AAEEEHIILNORTTZ	ETHEREALIZATION
AABEIILMNORTUVY	MANOEUVRABILITY	AAEEEILMNNPTTTU	ANTEPENULTIMATE
AABIILMNRSTTTUY	TRANSMUTABILITY	AAEEELLMMNPRTTY	TEMPERAMENTALLY
AACCCDEFIIILNOT	DECALCIFICATION	AAEEFGIMNNRRSST	FRAGMENTARINESS
AACCCEHIIOPPRSY	ARCHIEPISCOPACY	AAEEFIILMNNOSIX	SELF-EXAMINATION

AAEEFLLNOPRSTXY	SELF-EXPLANATORY
AAEEGILMNRTTUVY	ARGUMENTATIVELY
AAEEIILNNORTTXZ	EXTERNALIZATION
AAEEIKLMNNSSTTU	UNSTATESMANLIKE
AAEEILMNOOPRTTT	METROPOLITANATE
AAEEINOPPPRRSST	APPROPRIATENESS
AAEELLNPRRRTTUY	PRETERNATURALLY
AAEEENNNPRRSSSTT	TRANSPARENTNESS
AAEGHHILLMOOPPT	OPHTHALMOPLEGIA
AAEGHLLOOOPPTYY	PALAEOPHYTOLOGY
AAEGILLNOOOPSTT	PALAEONTOLOGIST
AAEHIILORTTTUVY	AUTHORITATIVELY
AAEIILLNNNORTTY	INTERNATIONALLY
AAEIILNNORRSTTT	TRANSLITERATION
AAEIILNOPPPRRTY	INAPPROPRIATELY
AAEILMNPRRSSTUU	SUPERNATURALISM
AAEILNNNOSSTTUY	INSTANTANEOUSLY
AAEILNPRRSSTTUU	SUPERNATURALIST
AAFGIINNORRSTTU	TRANSFIGURATION
AAFIILMNOORRTUZ	FORMULARIZATION
AAGHHNOOOPPRSTU	ANTHROPOPHAGOUS
AAHIIILNOOPSSTT	HOSPITALISATION
AAIIIIMNNORSTTU	MINIATURISATION
AAIIILMMNOORSTT	IMMORTALISATION
AAIILNNOOPRSSTT	TRANSPOSITIONAL
ABBCCCEIILMRRSU	CIRCUMSCRIBABLE
ABBDDEEEELLLORRU	DOUBLE-BARRELLED
ABCCEEEILNNOSSV	CONCEIVABLENESS
ABCCEIIIILNSSTY	INACCESSIBILITY
ABCCIIILMMNOTUY	COMMUNICABILITY
ABCCIIILNORTTTY	CONTRACTIBILITY
ABCEEEILNNOPTUX	UNEXCEPTIONABLE
ABCEEEILNNSSSUX	INEXCUSABLENESS
ABCEEILMMNNORSU	INCOMMENSURABLE
ABCEEILNNRSSSTU	INSCRUTABLENESS
ABCEELNNNOOPRUU	UNPRONOUNCEABLE
ABCEIIIILLNPTXY	INEXPLICABILITY
ABCIIIIILMNOPTTY	INCOMPATIBILITY
ABCIILORRRSTTUU	ARBORICULTURIST
ABDEEEEILMNPRRT	PREDETERMINABLE
ABDEEIIILMNRTTY	DETERMINABILITY
ABDEGHIIILNSSTU	DISTINGUISHABLE
ABDEIILMNORSTTY	DEMONSTRABILITY
ABDGHIIILNSSTUY	DISTINGUISHABLY
ABDIIINNNOORSTU	INSUBORDINATION
ABEEEHILMNRSSTT	REESTABLISHMENT
ABEEEILLNNORSST	INTOLERABLENESS
ABEEIIILMNPRTTY	IMPENETRABILITY
ABEEIIMNPRRSSTY	PRESBYTERIANISM
ABEIIILLNNRTUVY	INVULNERABILITY
ABEIIILMNNRSSST	INTRANSMISSIBLE
ACCCDEHHIILLOOP	DOLICHOCEPHALIC
ACCCIILLMOOPRSY	MICROSCOPICALLY
ACCDEEILMNORSTY	ELECTRO-DYNAMICS
ACCDIILNOORRTTY	CONTRADICTORILY
ACCEEEGILMNORTT	ELECTRO-MAGNETIC
ACCEEEIILMNRSST	ÉCLAIRCISSEMENT
ACCEEFFIINOSSSU	EFFICACIOUSNESS
ACCEEFIIILNORTT	ELECTRIFICATION
ACCEFFIIILNOSUY	INEFFICACIOUSLY
ACCEFIMNOORRSUU	CIRCUMFORANEOUS
ACCEGHILLLNOOTY	TECHNOLOGICALLY
ACCEHIILLPRRTYY	HYPERCRITICALLY
ACCEIIIMMNNOTUV	INCOMMUNICATIVE
ACCEIILMMNOTUVY	COMMUNICATIVELY
ACCEIILOPPRSSUY	PERSPICACIOUSLY
ACCEIIMMNNOOTUX	EXCOMMUNICATION
ACCEIIMMNNOTUUV	UNCOMMUNICATIVE
ACCGHILLLNOOORY	CHRONOLOGICALLY
ACCIJLLNNNOOTUY	CONJUNCTIONALLY
ACDDIIIIILNSTUV	INDIVIDUALISTIC
ACDEEEGKLMNNOTW	ACKNOWLEDGEMENT
ACDEEEIIMNPRSSV	MANIC-DEPRESSIVE
ACDEEEINNNORSSST	CONSIDERATENESS
ACDEEFGILNRSSSU	DISGRACEFULNESS
ACDEEGHIILOPSTT	DEPHLOGISTICATE
ACDEEHIMNOORSTU	ECHINODERMATOUS
ACDEEHLOORSTTUY	HETERODACTYLOUS
ACDEEIILNNORSTY	INCONSIDERATELY
ACDEEIINNOORRST	RECONSIDERATION
ACDEEIILLNPPRRUY	PERPENDICULARLY
ACDEFIIIIMMNNOT	INDEMNIFICATION
ACDEFIIIIINORSTV	DIVERSIFICATION
ACDEFIIIINORTTV	DEVITRIFICATION
ACDEHIINOPSSTTU	UNSOPHISTICATED
ACDEHLMMNOOOSUY	MONOCHLAMYDEOUS
ACDEIIILMNNOORT	OMNIDIRECTIONAL
ACDEIIILNORRSTY	DISCRETIONARILY
ACDEILNNNORSTUY	UNCONSTRAINEDLY
ACDIIINNNOOSTTU	DISCONTINUATION
ACDIILLNNNOOTUY	UNCONDITIONALLY
ACEEEEEGILNORTTV	ELECTRO-NEGATIVE
ACEEEFHIMMNNRST	ENFRANCHISEMENT
ACEEEGHINNOPRTT	PARTHENOGENETIC
ACEEEGIIILLNORTT	INTERCOLLEGIATE
ACEEEHIILMNRTUY	HERMENEUTICALLY
ACEEEHNORRSSSTU	TREACHEROUSNESS
ACEEEIIILLLNTTUZ	INTELLECTUALIZE
ACEEEILNORRSSTV	CORRELATIVENESS
ACEEFHLNOPRRSSU	REPROACHFULNESS
ACEEFIIILMNOPTX	EXEMPLIFICATION
ACEEFIILNPRSSSU	SUPERFICIALNESS
ACEEHIILLMPSTUY	EUPHEMISTICALLY
ACEEHIKNOOPPSST	PHENAKISTOSCOPE
ACEEIIILMOPRRST	ISOPERIMETRICAL
ACEEIIINQSSSTUV	ACQUISITIVENESS
ACEEIIJNNORRTTY	INTERJECTIONARY
ACEEIIILLMNSTTU	INTELLECTUALISM
ACEEIIILLLNSTTTU	INTELLECTUALIST
ACEEIIILLLNTTTUY	INTELLECTUALITY
ACEEIIILLNNNOOTVZ	CONVENTIONALIZE
ACEEIILNNNOQSTU	INCONSEQUENTIAL
ACEEIILLMNOPTTVY	CONTEMPLATIVELY
ACEEIILLNNOQSTUY	CONSEQUENTIALLY
ACEEIMMNNOOPRTY	CONTEMPORANEITY
ACEELNNNOOSSTUY	CONSENTANEOUSLY
ACEEMNNOOOPRSTU	CONTEMPORANEOUS
ACEFIIIINNNOSTT	INTENSIFICATION
ACEFIIINNOOPRST	PERSONIFICATION
ACEFIILNNOOSSST	CONFESSIONALIST
ACEGHILLLNOOPRY	PHRENOLOGICALLY
ACEGIILMNOORRTT	TRIGONOMETRICAL

272

ACEGILLLMNOOOTY	ENTOMOLOGICALLY
ACEHHILMOORSSST	SCHOOLMASTERISH
ACEHHIOPPRSSTTY	PSYCHOTHERAPIST
ACEIILLLNNOORTY	INTERCOLONIALLY
ACEIILMNNNOOSTV	CONVENTIONALISM
ACEIILNNNOOSTTV	CONVENTIONALIST
ACEIILNNNOOTTVY	CONVENTIONALITY
ACEIIMNNOORSSTV	CONSERVATIONISM
ACEIIMNOOPRSTTU	COMPUTERISATION
ACEIINNOORSSTTV	CONSERVATIONIST
	CONVERSATIONIST
ACEIINNORRRSTUY	INSURRECTIONARY
ACEIINNORRRTTTU	COUNTER-IRRITANT
ACEILLNOORRSTVY	CONTROVERSIALLY
ACEILMMNNOPRTUY	UNCOMPLIMENTARY
ACFGIIIILNNNSTY	INSIGNIFICANTLY
ACGHHIIIOOPRRST	HISTORIOGRAPHIC
ACGHIILLLOOPSYY	PHYSIOLOGICALLY
ACGIINNOOOPRSTT	PROGNOSTICATION
ACHHIILLLOOPPSY	PHILOSOPHICALLY
ACHHIILLNOOPPSU	UNPHILOSOPHICAL
ACHHIMNOOOPPRRT	ANTHROPOMORPHIC
ACHIINNNOORSSTY	SYNCHRONISATION
ACIILMMNOOOOPSST	COSMOPOLITANISM
ACIILMNNOOSSTUY	SANCTIMONIOUSLY
ADDEGHHINOOSTWY	WOODY-NIGHTSHADE
ADDEGILNNNRSTUY	UNDERSTANDINGLY
ADEEEGILMNNNSTT	DISENTANGLEMENT
ADEEEIILMNNRTTY	INDETERMINATELY
ADEEFFIIINNORTT	DIFFERENTIATION
ADEEFILNSSSSTTU	DISTASTEFULNESS
ADEEIIIMNNNORTT	INDETERMINATION
ADEEILMNORSTTVY	DEMONSTRATIVELY
ADEEIMNNORSTTUV	UNDEMONSTRATIVE
ADEENNORSSSTUUV	ADVENTUROUSNESS
ADEFINNNOOOSTTU	FOUNDATION-STONE
ADEGIIIINNORTTT	INTERDIGITATION
ADEGIIIOPRRSTTT	PRESTIDIGITATOR
ADEHIIILMIOTOPRST	DIAHELIOTROPISM
ADEIIJLNPRRSTUU	JURISPRUDENTIAL
ADGHIINNNOSTTTW	NOTWITHSTANDING
ADIILNOOOPPRRST	DISPROPORTIONAL
AEEEEIILMNPRTXZ	EXPERIMENTALIZE
AEEEEIILNNPRRRTU	ENTREPRENEURIAL
AEEEEIMNNPRSSTT	INTEMPERATENESS
AEEEGGLNNOORRRV	GOVERNOR-GENERAL
AEEEGHINNOPRSST	PARTHENOGENESIS
AEEEGIKLLMNNNTU	UNGENTLEMANLIKE
AEEEGILLMNNNSST	GENTLEMANLINESS
AEEEHIIMNPPRSSV	MISAPPREHENSIVE
AEEEHILORSTTUXY	HETEROSEXUALITY
AEEEIIILMNPRSTX	EXPERIENTIALISM
AEEEIIILNPRSTTX	EXPERIENTIALIST
AEEEIILMNPRSTTX	EXPERIMENTALIST
AEEEIIMNNOPRTTX	EXPERIMENTATION
AEEEIINNNSSTTTV	INATTENTIVENESS
AEEFIILNOOPRSSS	PROFESSIONALISE
AEEGHHLOOPPRTTY	TELEPHOTOGRAPHY
AEEGIIIIMNNSSTV	IMAGINITIVENESS
AEEGIILNORRTTVY	INTERROGATIVELY
AEEGIINORRSSTTT	GASTROENTERITIS
AEEEGIKMNNPPRSTTU	SPEAKING-TRUMPET
AEEHIIMNNOPPRSS	MISAPPREHENSION
AEEIIMNOOPRSTTX	EXTEMPORISATION
AEEILMNNOOPPRUU	PLEURO-PNEUMONIA
AEEILMNNOPPSTTU	SUPPLEMENTATION
AEFIILMNOOPRSSS	PROFESSIONALISM
AEGGHILLNOORSTY	SHOOTING-GALLERY
AEGHHIIOOPRRRST	HISTORIOGRAPHER
AEHHIIOPPRSSTTY	PHYSIOTHERAPIST
AEIILLNNNNOTTUY	UNINTENTIONALLY
AEIILLNOOPPRSTY	PREPOSITIONALLY
AEIILMNNRSSTTTU	INSTRUMENTALIST
AEIILMNNRSTTTUY	INSTRUMENTALITY
AEIIMNNNORSTTTU	INSTRUMENTATION
AEIKLMNNOPRSSTU	UNSPORTSMANLIKE
AEILNOOOPPRRTTY	PROPORTIONATELY
AIIIILLNOQRSTUY	INQUISITORIALLY
AIILNOOOPPRRTTY	PROPORTIONALITY
BBCEEILMNOSSSTU	COMBUSTIBLENESS
BCDEIIILRSTTTUY	DESTRUCTIBILITY
BCEEIIILMPPPRRST	IMPRESCRIPTIBLE
BCEEILNOPRRSSTU	CORRUPTIBLENESS
BCEIILMNOPTTTY	CONTEMPTIBILITY
BCEIIILMOPRSSTY	COMPRESSIBILITY
BCGIIIIILNORRTY	INCORRIGIBILITY
BDEGIILLNOOSSTU	BLOOD-GUILTINESS
BDFFIIILMNNORUU	INFUNDIBULIFORM
BEEEEHIILNPRRRS	IRREPREHENSIBLE
BEEELMNOORSSSTU	TROUBLESOMENESS
BEGIIIIILLLNTTY	INTELLIGIBILITY
BEIIIIILRRSSTTY	IRRESISTIBILITY
CCCEEIMNPRSSSTU	CIRCUMSPECTNESS
CCCEIIIMPRRSTUV	CIRCUMSCRIPTIVE
CCCIIIMNOPRRSTU	CIRCUMSCRIPTION
CCDDEEGILNNNOSY	CONDESCENDINGLY
CCDEEEEINNORTUV	COUNTER-EVIDENCE
CCDEEINOPRSTUUV	SUPERCONDUCTIVE
CCEEEEELLNPRSUX	SUPEREXCELLENCE
CCEEEHHNOOPPRSS	PHOSPHORESCENCE
CCEEEIIKLNORSTT	ELECTRO-KINETICS
CCEEFFFIILNSSUY	SELF-SUFFICIENCY
CCEEIINNNNOORTT	INTERCONNECTION
CCEFILNNOOSSSUU	UNSELFCONSCIOUS
CCEIILNNOOSSTUY	CONSCIENTIOUSLY
CCEINNNOOSSSSUU	UNCONSCIOUSNESS
CCEINNOOPSSSSUU	CONSPICUOUSNESS
CCIILNNOOPSSUUY	INCONSPICUOUSLY
CCIIMNNOORSSTTU	MISCONSTRUCTION
CDDEEEEEINNNPRT	INTERDEPENDENCE
CDDEEHKLOOORRSU	CROOK-SHOULDERED
CDEEEEEFLNNSSSS	DEFENCELESSNESS
CDEEEEINNNPRSTU	SUPERINTENDENCE
CDEEEFILRSSTTUV	SELF-DESTRUCTIVE
CDEEEIINPRSSSTV	DESCRIPTIVENESS
CDEEEINRSSSTTUV	DESTRUCTIVENESS
CDEEFILLPRSSTUY	DISRESPECTFULLY
CDEEIIINNSSSTTV	DISTINCTIVENESS
CDEELNNOOPRRSTY	CORRESPONDENTLY
CDEGILNNOOPRRSY	CORRESPONDINGLY
CDEIIIJNNOSSSUU	INJUDICIOUSNESS
CDHIILNOPRSTUUU	PULCHRITUDINOUS

CDIIIINOSSSTUUV	VICISSITUDINOUS	DDEEEIILNRSSTTY	DISINTERESTEDLY
CEEEFLNORRSSSUU	RESOURCEFULNESS	DEEEELMNOOPRTVV	OVERDEVELOPMENT
CEEEHIIMNNOPRSV	INCOMPREHENSIVE	DEFILNRSSSSTTUU	DISTRUSTFULNESS
CEEEHILMNNOPRSVY	COMPREHENSIVELY	DEIIILLMNNOSSTU	DISILLUSIONMENT
CEEEIILOOPRSTTV	ELECTRO-POSITIVE	EEEELMNORRSSSSS	REMORSELESSNESS
CEEEIIMNORSTTUX	EXCREMENTITIOUS	EEEFFIINNNOSSSV	INOFFENSIVENESS
CEEEIMNNOORSSSU	CEREMONIOUSNESS	EEEGHMNNOOOSSSU	HOMOGENEOUSNESS
CEEEINPQRSSSTUU	PICTURESQUENESS	EEEGILORRRSSTVY	RETROGRESSIVELY
CEEEMMNNOORTTUV	COUNTER-MOVEMENT	EEEINNNOSSSSTTU	SENTENTIOUSNESS
CEEEENOPRRRSSTUU	COUNTER-PRESSURE	EEEINNOPRSSSTTU	PRETENTIOUSNESS
CEEHIIMNNNOOPRS	INCOMPREHENSION	EEGHHLNOSSSSTTU	THOUGHTLESSNESS
CEEHIIMNOSSSSUV	MISCHIEVOUSNESS	EEGHINNORSSSTUU	UNRIGHTEOUSNESS
CEEILMNNOORSUUY	UNCEREMONIOUSLY	EEGIIILNORRSSSU	IRRELIGIOUSNESS
CEEINNNOOSSSTTU	CONTENTIOUSNESS	EEGINNOPPRSSSSU	UNPREPOSSESSING
CEEINOPPRSSSSUU	PERSPICUOUSNESS	EEIIIINNQSSSTUV	INQUISITIVENESS
CEHIINNOOPRSSSU	CONNOISSEURSHIP	EEIIINNNORSTTTV	INTERVENTIONIST
CEIIIIMNOPRSSST	IMPRESSIONISTIC	EEIILNNOORRTTTU	TRINITROTOLUENE
CEIIINNORRSSTTU	INSURRECTIONIST	EHINORRSSSTTTUW	TRUSTWORTHINESS
CEIINNOOPRSSTTU	INTROSUSCEPTION	EIILLNORSSSSTUU	ILLUSTRIOUSNESS
CHHHINNOORRSTUY	ORNITHORHYNCHUS	EIILOPRRSSTTUUY	SURREPTITIOUSLY